AF207883

IMPRESSIONISM

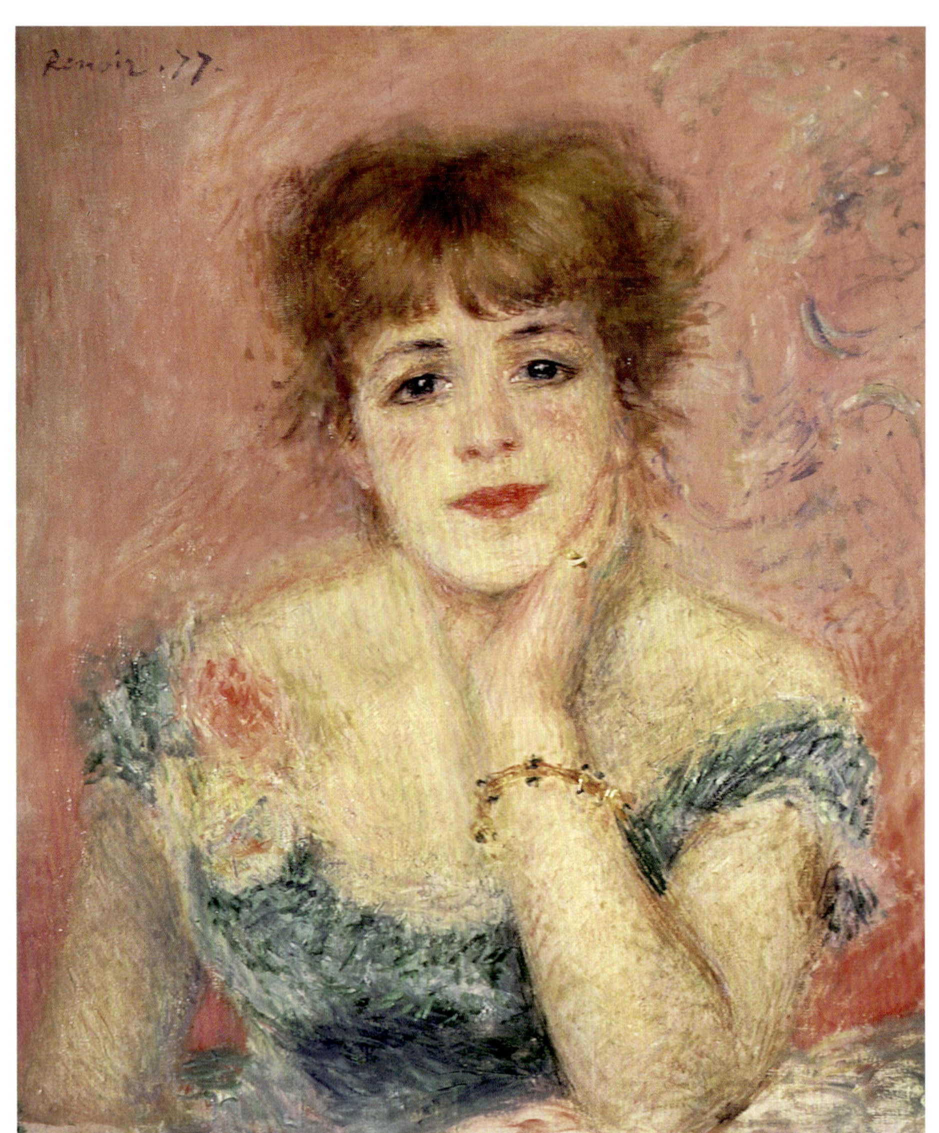

HAJO DÜCHTING

IMPRESSIONISM
IMPRESSIONNISME
IMPRESSIONISMUS
IMPRESIONISMO
IMPRESSIONISMO
IMPRESSIONISME

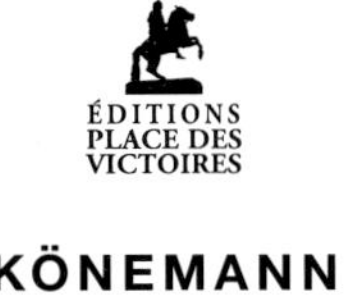

KÖNEMANN

p. 2

Pierre-Auguste Renoir (1841–1919)

Portrait of the actress Jeanne Samary

Portrait de l'actrice Jeanne Samary

Porträt der Schauspielerin Jeanne Samary

Retrato de la actriz Jeanne Samary

Ritratto dell'attrice Jeanne Samary

Portret van de actrice Jeanne Samary

1877, Oil on canvas/Huile sur toile, 56 × 46 cm, Pushkin State Museum of Fine Arts, Moscow

KÖNEMANN

© 2016 koenemann.com GmbH
www.koenemann.com

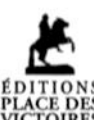

© Éditions Place des Victoires
6, rue du Mail – 75002 Paris
www.victoires.com
ISBN : 978-2-8099-1680-5
Dépôt légal : 2ᵉ trimestre 2019

Concept, Project Management: koenemann.com GmbH
Text: Hajo Düchting
Editing: Petra Böttcher

Translation into French: Denis-Armand Canal

Translations into English, Spanish, Italian, Dutch:
TEXTCASE Translation Agency
info@textcase.nl
textcase.de   textcase.eu

Layout: Christoph Eiden
Picture credits: Bridgeman Images, akg-images gmbh (p. 302)

ISBN: 978-3-7419-2418-7

Printed in China by Shenzen Hua Xin Colour-printing & Platemaking Co., Ltd

Contents   Sommaire   Inhalt   Índice   Indice   Inhoud

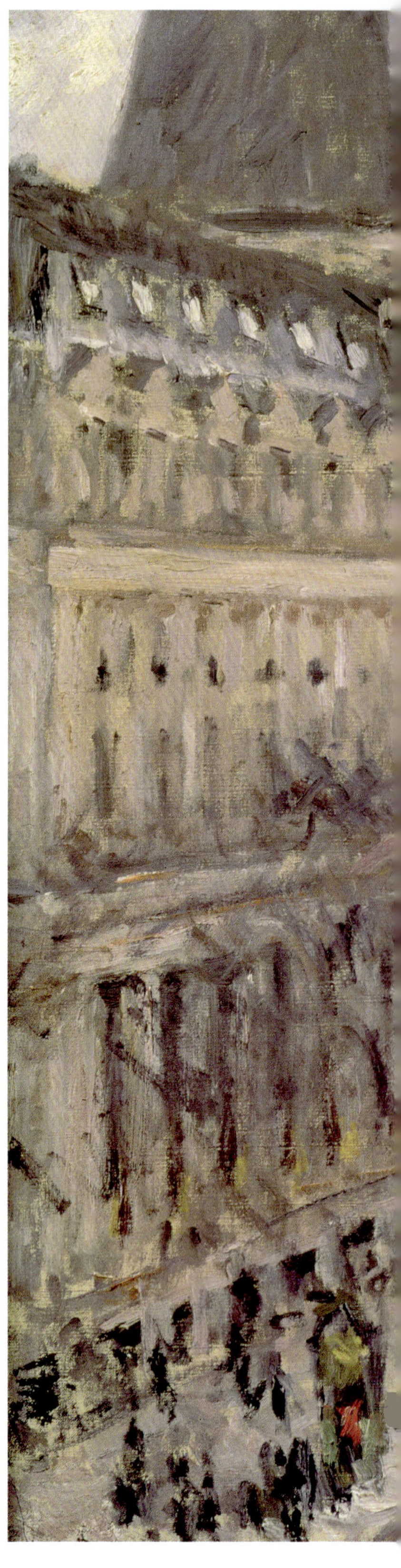

Gustave Caillebotte (1848–94)

Boulevard des Italiens

c. 1880, Oil on canvas/Huile sur toile, 54 × 56 cm, Private collection

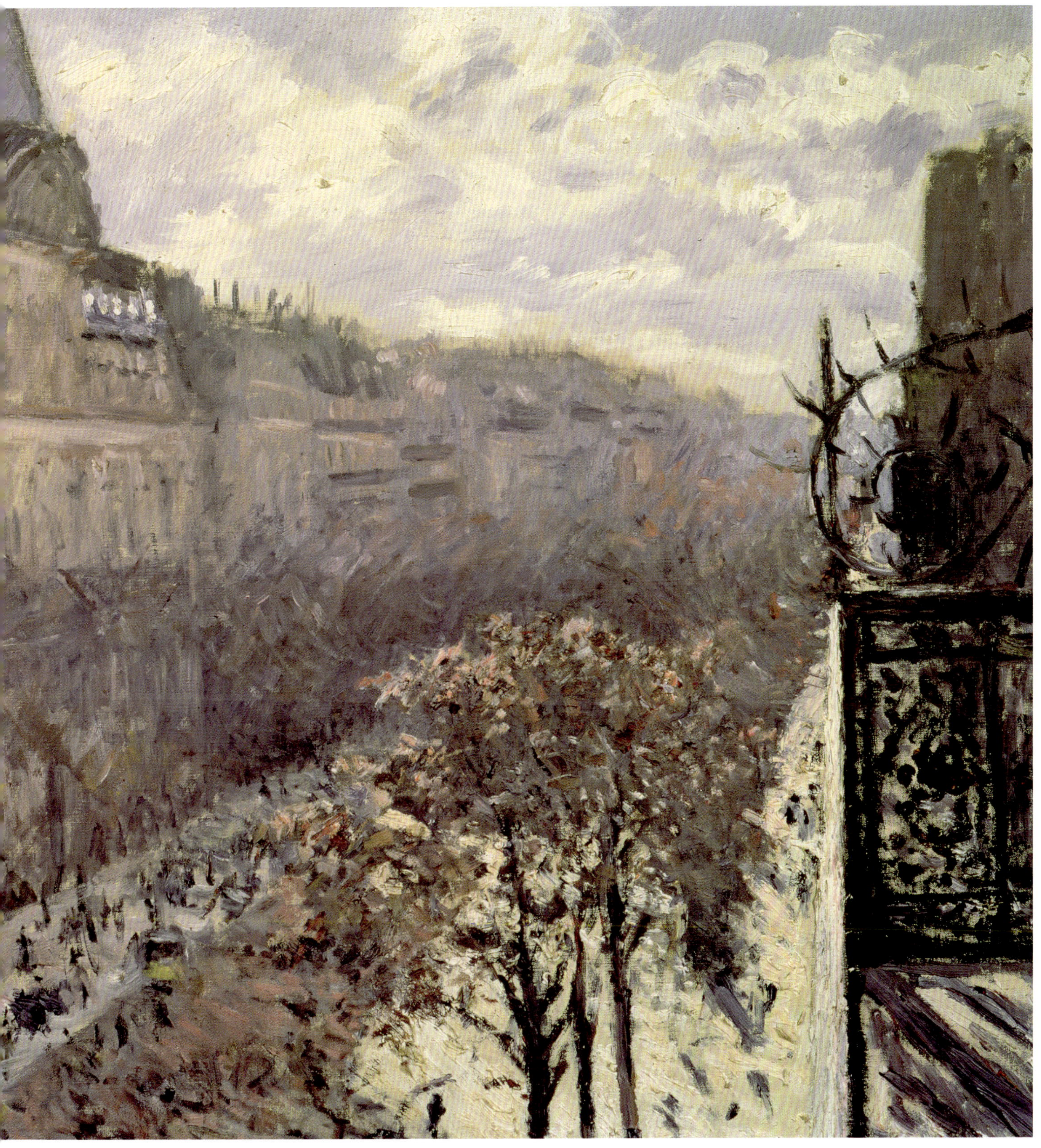

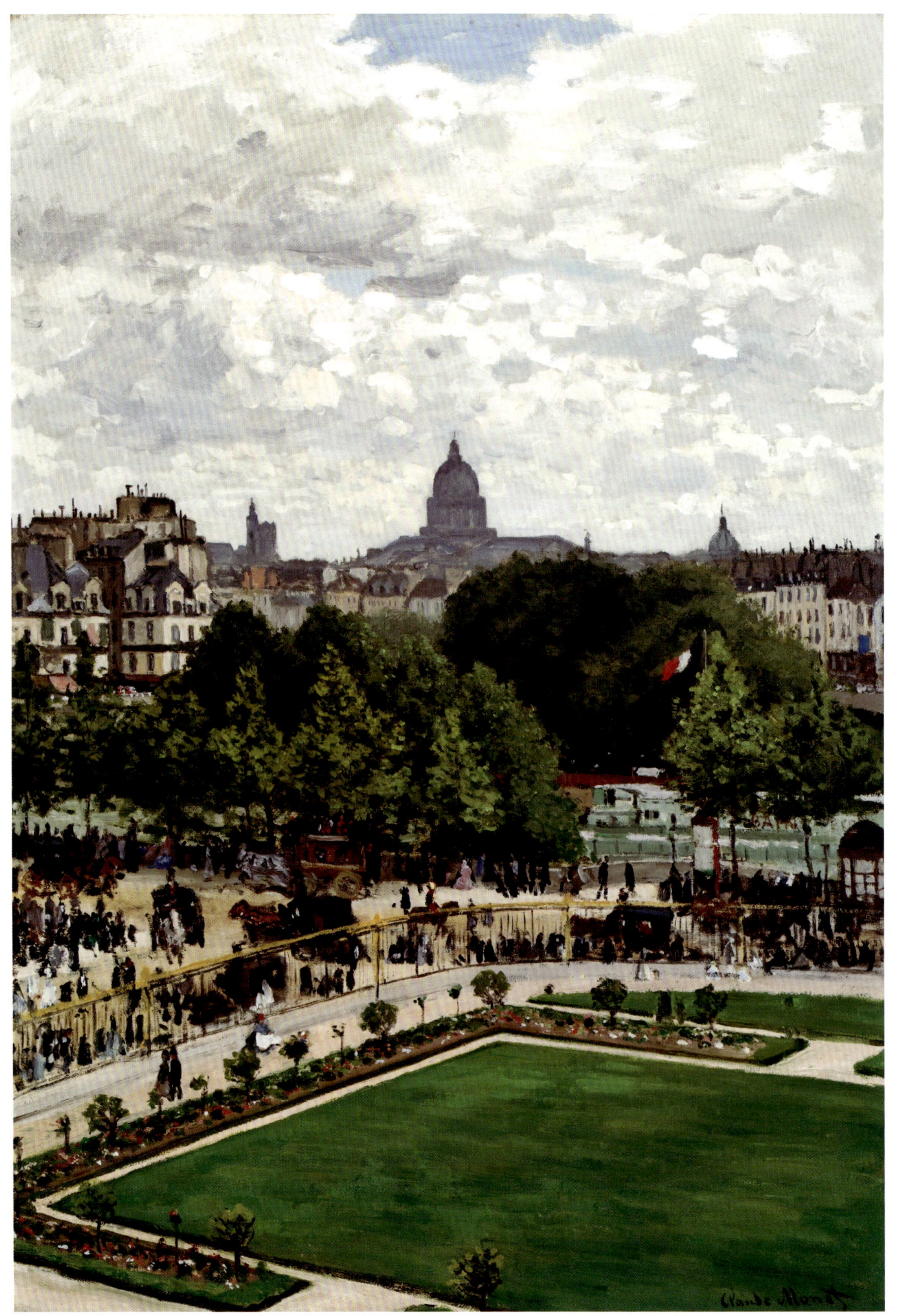

Claude Monet (1840–1926)

Garden of the Princess

Le jardin de l'infante, Louvre

Prinzessinnengarten, Louvre

El jardín de la princesa con el Louvre

Giardino della principessa, Louvre

Le Jardin de l'Infante met het Louvre

1867, Oil on canvas/Huile sur toile,
91,8 × 61,9 cm, Allen Memorial
Art Museum, Oberlin

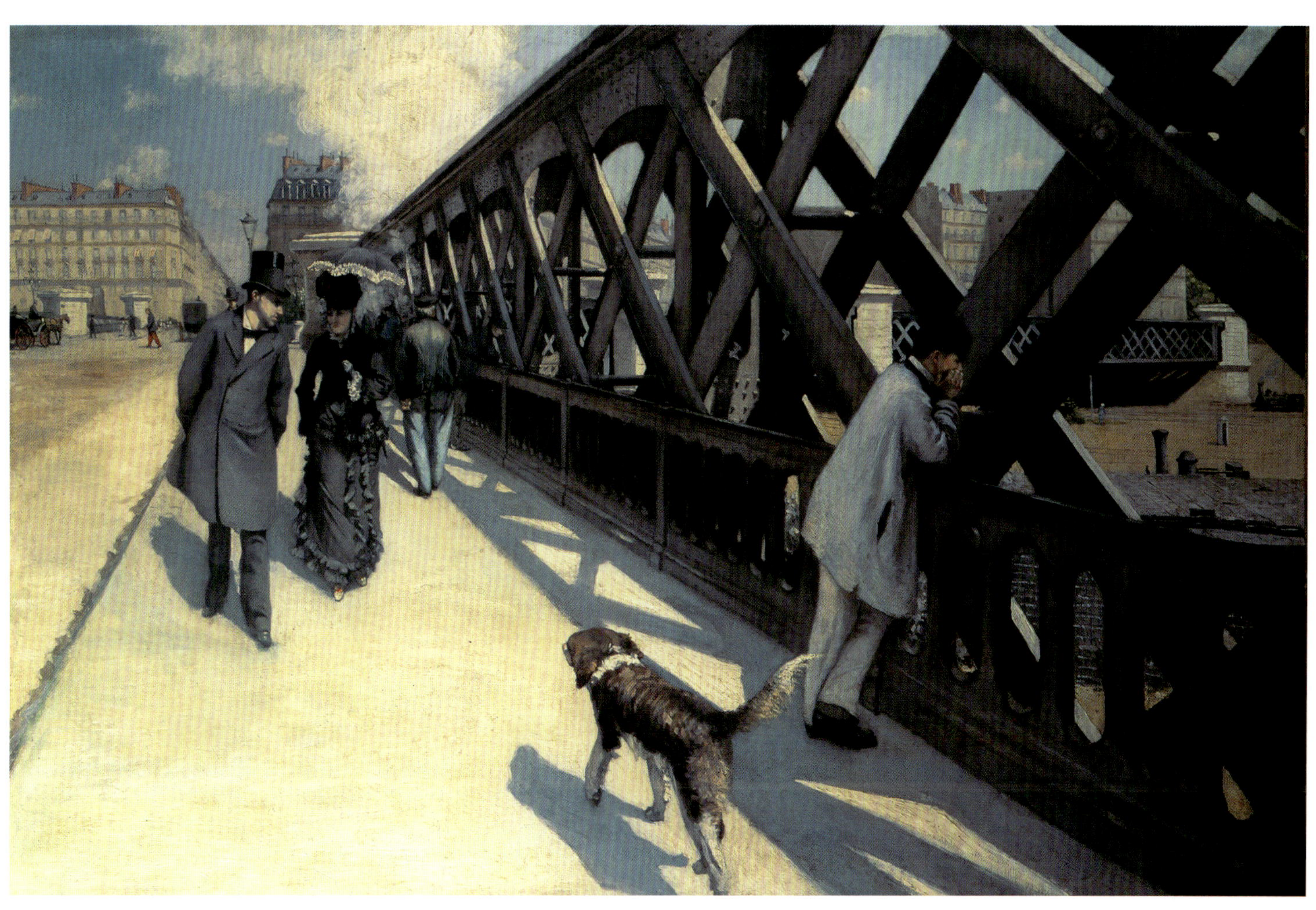

Gustave Caillebotte (1848–94)

Pont de L'Europe

1876, Oil on canvas/Huile sur toile, 125 × 180 cm, Private collection

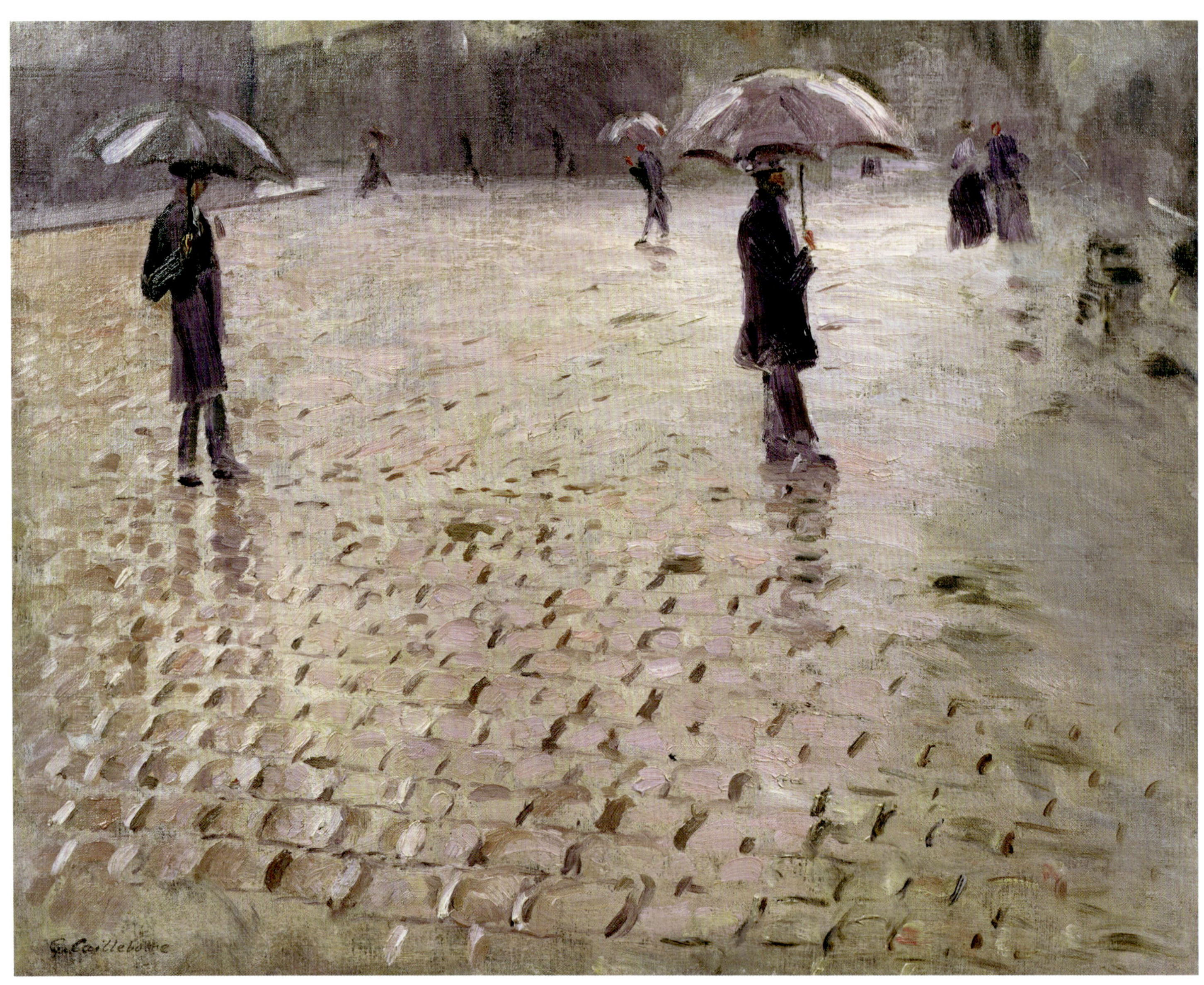

Gustave Caillebotte (1848–94)

Study for a Paris Street, Rainy Day

Étude pour Rue de Paris, temps de pluie

Studie für Regentag in Paris

Estudio para día de lluvia en París

Studio per Giorno di pioggia a Parigi

Studie voor Parijs, Place de l'Europe, een regenachtige dag

1877, Oil on canvas/Huile sur toile, 54 × 65 cm, Private collection

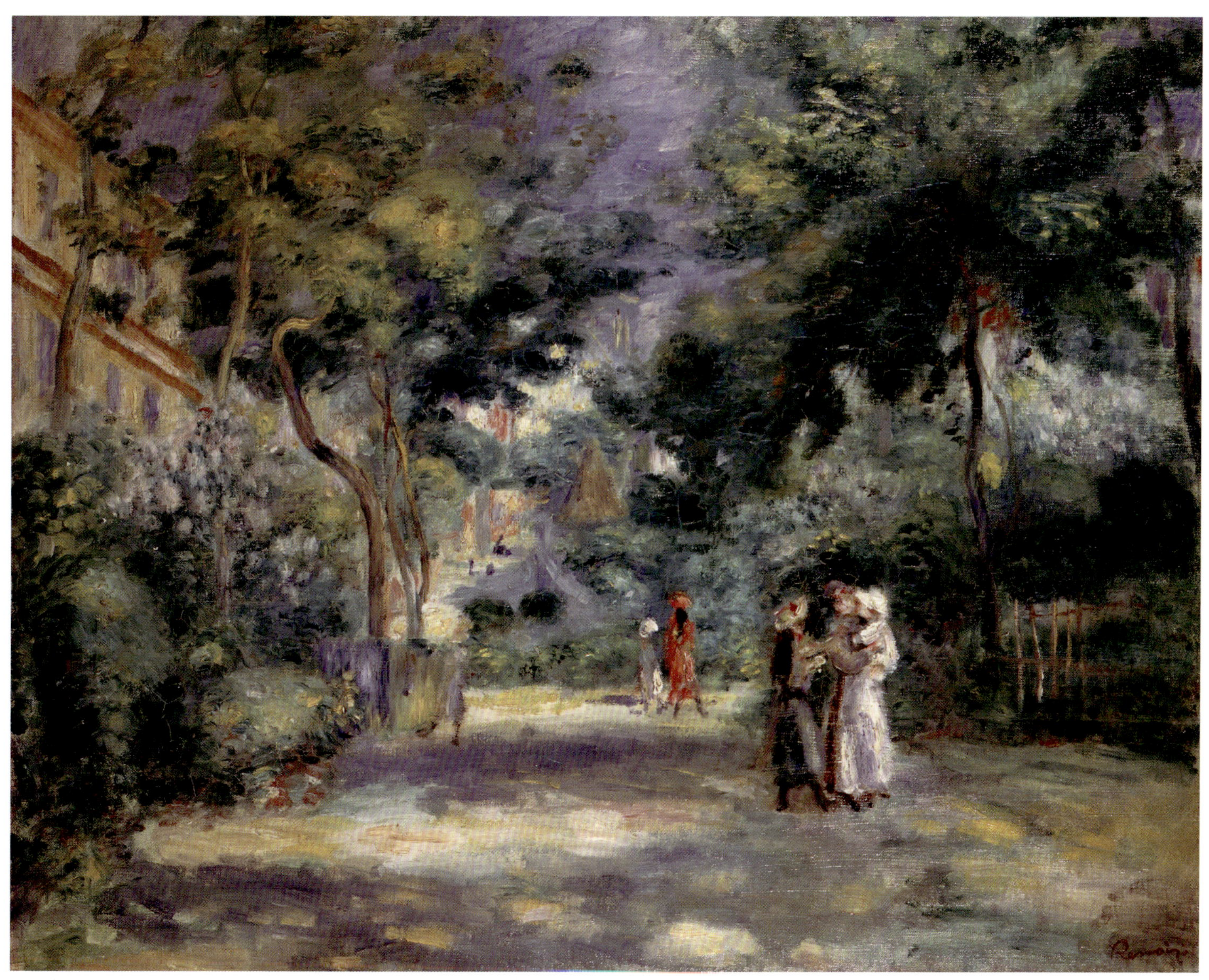

Pierre-Auguste Renoir (1841–1919)

The Gardens in Montmartre

Les jardins de Montmartre

Ein Garten auf dem Montmartre

Los jardines de Montmartre

I giardini di Montmartre

Tuin op de Montmartre

c. 1890, Oil on canvas/Huile sur toile, 46 × 55 cm, Ashmolean Museum, Oxford

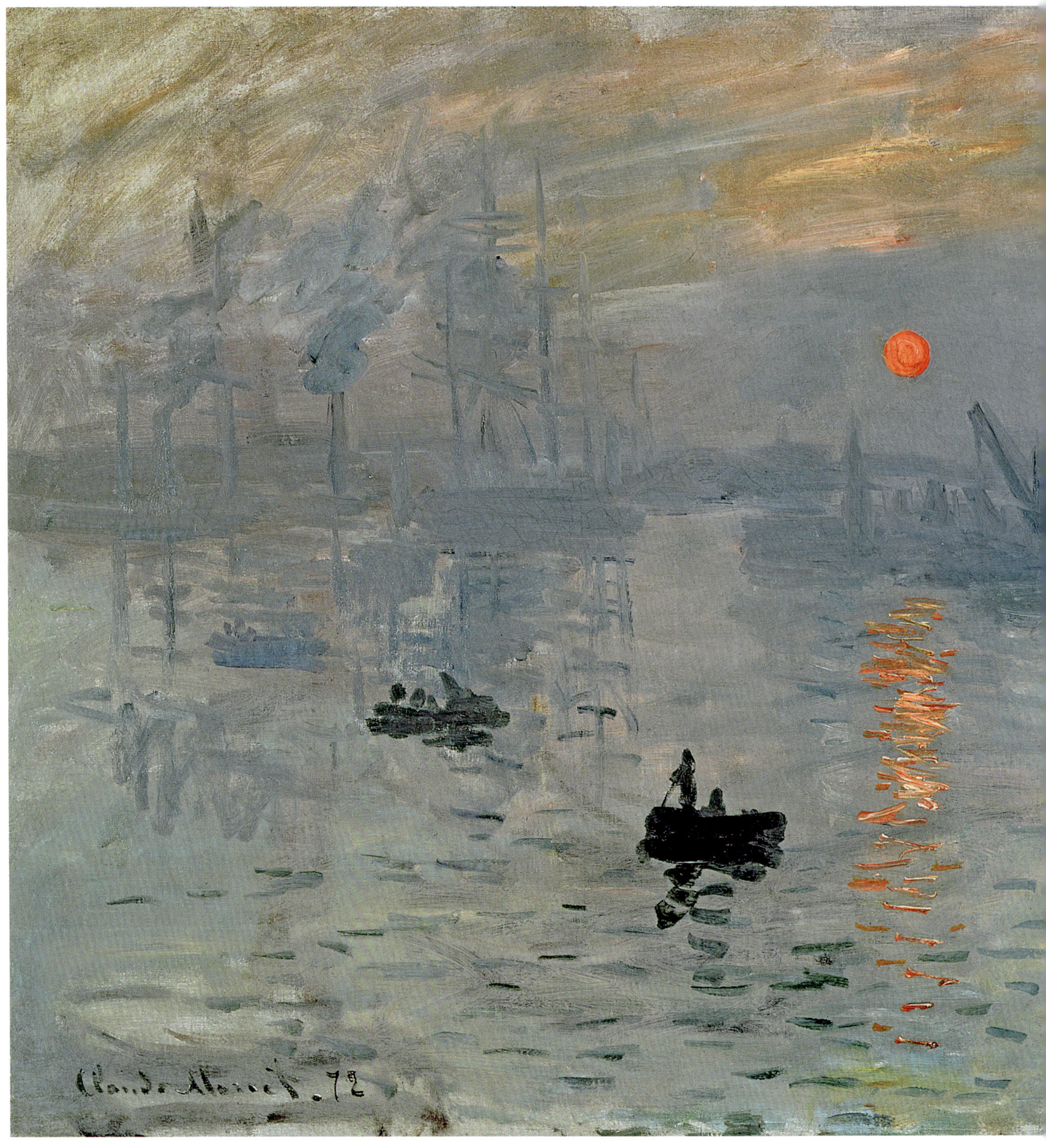

Claude Monet (1840–1926)

Impression: Sunrise

Impression soleil levant

Impression, Sonnenaufgang

Impresión, sol naciente

Impressione, levar del sole

Impressie, zonsopgang

1872, Oil on canvas/Huile sur toile, 48 × 63 cm, Musée Marmottan Monet, Paris

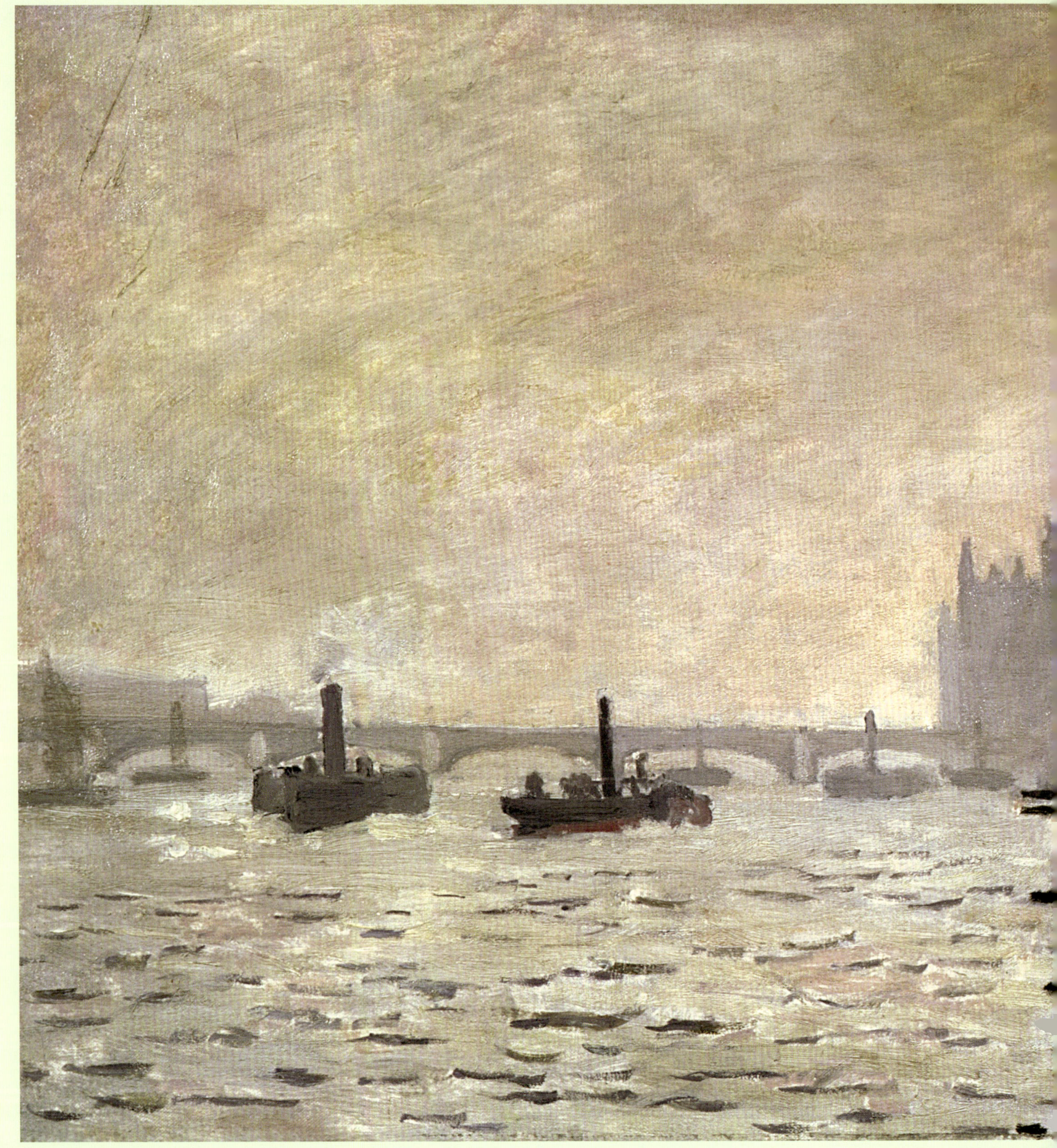

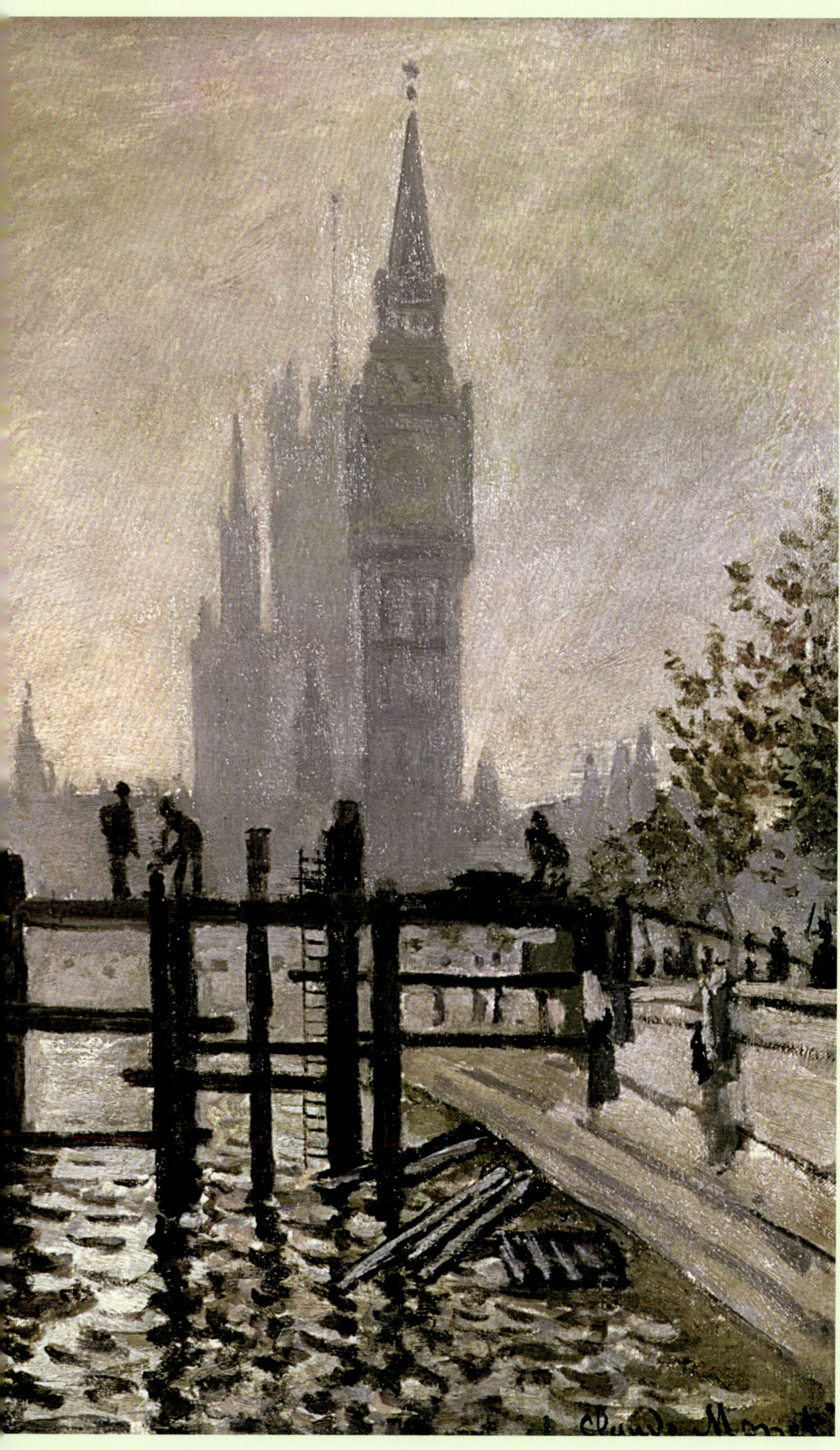

THE NEW IMPRESSIONIST PAINTING
LA NOUVELLE PEINTURE IMPRESSIONNISTE
DIE NEUE MALEREI DES IMPRESSIONISMUS
LA NUEVA PINTURA: EL IMPRESIONISMO
LA NUOVA PITTURA IMPRESSIONISTA
DE NIEUWE SCHILDERKUNST

Claude Monet (1840–1926)

The Thames below Westminster

La Tamise en bas de Westminster

Die Themse unterhalb Westminster

El Támesis bajo Westminster

Il Tamigi nei pressi di Westminster

De Theems onder Westminster

c. 1871, Oil on canvas/Huile sur toile, 47 × 73 cm, National Gallery, London

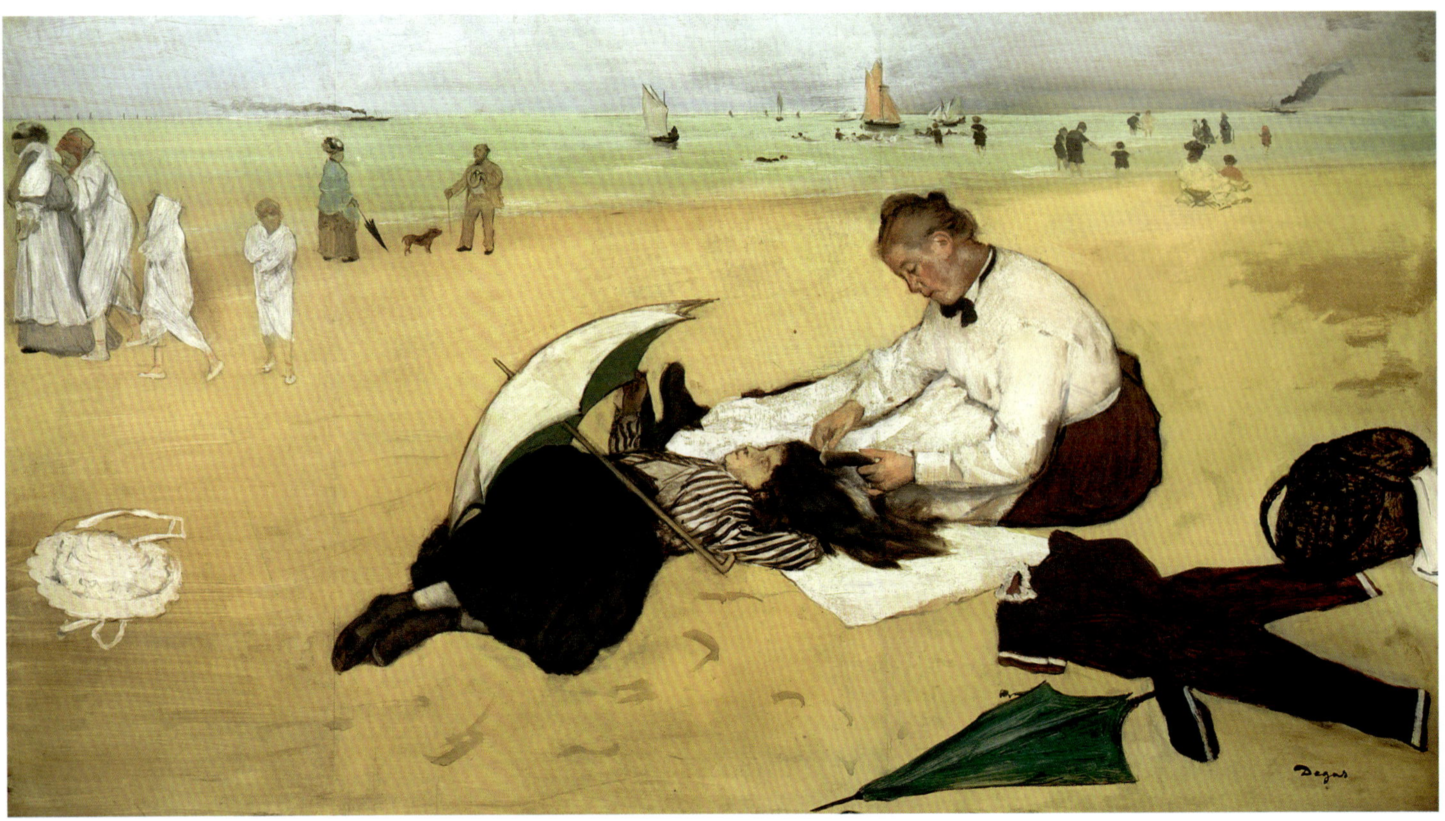

The new impressionist painting

In contrast to the classically oriented painting, which was supported by the official art exhibitions, impressionism was interested in moving the atmospheric interplay of light and color to the foreground. The impressionist painters set themselves the goal of painting simple motifs and scenes from daily life, with particular regard to the appearance of color. Light and color consequently gained a whole new meaning. The endeavour to capture the fleeting glimpses of the ever-changing light and weather conditions in the outdoors required very swift work. The old masters' method of layering down many coats of paint was no longer suitable for this faster way of painting. Instead, the artists produced paintings which were sketchy in appearance, with the often unmixed colors being applied to the canvas with rapid brushstrokes in flowing transitions. Preparatory sketches were omitted not only for limitations of time, but also because they didn't conform to the new understanding of painting as "catching the moment".

Typical of the new style of painting was the lightening of the color tones through the emphasis of light. The strict geometrically derived perspectives gave way to a perspective produced with gradations of color, as applied quite extremely by Monet, for example, in the

La nouvelle peinture impressionniste

Contrairement à la peinture de style classique, soutenue par les expositions d'art officielles, l'impressionnisme voulait déplacer le jeu atmosphérique de la lumière et de la couleur au premier plan. L'objectif des peintres impressionnistes était de peindre des motifs simples et des scènes de la vie quotidienne, en mettant particulièrement l'accent sur l'apparence de la couleur. Lumière et couleur acquièrent par conséquent une signification totalement nouvelle. Tenter de saisir la fugacité des conditions changeantes de la lumière et de la météo en extérieur impliquait de travailler très rapidement. La technique des anciens maîtres, qui consistait à superposer plusieurs couches de peinture, n'était plus adaptée à cette façon de peindre plus rapide. Au lieu de cela, les artistes réalisèrent des tableaux d'apparence lacunaire dont les couleurs, souvent non mélangées, étaient appliquées sur la toile dans des transitions fluides par touches rapides. Il n'y avait plus de croquis préparatoires, non seulement pour des raisons de contraintes de temps, mais aussi parce qu'ils n'étaient pas conformes à cette nouvelle vision de la peinture consistant à « capter l'instant ».

L'éclaircissement des tons par l'accent mis sur la lumière était typique de cette nouvelle façon de peindre. Les perspectives strictement basées sur la géométrie

Die neue Malerei des Impressionismus

Im Gegensatz zu der klassizistisch orientierten Malerei, die von den offiziellen Kunstausstellungen gefördert wurde, rückte beim Impressionismus das Interesse am atmosphärisch bedingten Spiel von Licht und Farbe in den Vordergrund. Die impressionistischen Maler setzten sich zum Ziel, einfache Motive und Szenen aus dem täglichen Leben unter dem besonderen Aspekt ihrer farbigen Erscheinung zu malen. Licht und Farbe gewannen somit eine ganz neue Bedeutung. Das Bemühen, in der freien Natur die flüchtigen Eindrücke des ständig wechselnden Lichts und der Wetterphänomene einzufangen, erforderte jedoch ein sehr rasches Arbeiten. Die altmeisterliche Schichtenmalerei war für diese schnelle Malweise nicht mehr geeignet. Man bediente sich stattdessen einer skizzenhaft erscheinenden Malerei, bei der die Farben mit zügigen Pinselstrichen oft unvermischt und in fließenden Übergängen auf die Leinwand gebracht wurden. Eine Vorzeichnung musste nicht nur aus Zeitgründen entfallen, sondern entsprach auch nicht dem neuen Verständnis von Malerei als „Festhalten des Augenblicks".

Das Typische der neuen Malweise war die Aufhellung der Farbpalette durch die Betonung des Lichts. Die strenge, geometrisch abgeleitete

La nueva pintura: el impresionismo

Al contrario que en el caso de la pintura más clásica que se exigía desde las exposiciones de arte, los impresionistas centraron su interés en el juego atmosférico de la luz y el color. Los pintores impresionistas se marcaron como objetivo pintar escenas simples y temas cotidianos subrayando el aspecto particular de su apariencia cromática. La luz y el color adquirieron entonces un significado totalmente nuevo. Sin embargo, el deseo de capturar las impresiones fugaces de la luz, constantemente cambiante, y otros fenómenos atmosféricos necesitaba de un método de trabajo muy rápido. La forma clásica de pintura en capas ya no era adecuada para esta nueva técnica pictórica, más ágil. En su lugar se tendía ahora hacia una pintura con apariencia de boceto, en la que los colores a menudo se aplicaban en el lienzo con rápidos trazos, sin mezclar y con transiciones fluidas entre ellos. No era necesario tampoco el clásico dibujo previo, no tanto por cuestiones de economía de tiempo, sino porque no se adecuaba al nuevo concepto de esta pintura de "capturar el momento".

La paleta de colores se fue volviendo además más clara por el énfasis que recibió la luz. La perspectiva estricta resultante de la geometría perdió importancia a favor de una perspectiva atmosférica conseguida con

La nuova pittura impressionista

A differenza della pittura di orientamento classico sostenuta dalle mostre d'arte ufficiali, l'Impressionismo metteva in primo piano i giochi atmosferici di luce e colore. I pittori impressionisti si erano posti l'obiettivo di dipingere motivi semplici e scene di vita quotidiana risaltandone il carattere cromatico. Luce e colore acquistarono così un nuovo significato. Per poter catturare le fuggevoli impressioni dei mutevoli fenomeni luminosi e meteorologici presenti in natura occorreva lavorare molto velocemente. Pertanto, il vecchio stile di pittura accademico non era più adatto. Nacque dunque al suo posto uno stile di pittura basato su schizzi, in cui i colori venivano applicati sulla tela con pennellate rapide e fluide, spesso senza essere mescolati. La fase di disegno previo veniva omessa non solo per ragioni di tempo, ma anche in virtù della nuova concezione della pittura come "cattura dell'istante".

Tipica di questo nuovo stile era una tavolozza più chiara in virtù dell'enfasi posta sulla luce. La rigorosa prospettiva geometrica lasciò spazio ad una prospettiva aerea ottenuta mediante gradazioni cromatiche, come ad esempio quella utilizzata da Monet nella serie *Il ponte di Waterloo*, così estrema che le forme quasi svaniscono nella nebbia.

De nieuwe schilderkunst

In tegenstelling tot de classicistische schilderkunst die in de officiële Salons werd gepresenteerd, stond in het impressionisme het spel van licht en kleur als gevolg van weersomstandigheden op de voorgrond. De impressionisten stelden zich ten doel alledaagse onderwerpen en scènes in het licht van hun bijzonder kleurstelling te verbeelden. Licht en kleur kregen daarmee een geheel nieuwe betekenis. Maar deze poging om in de vrije natuur de vluchtige indrukken van lichtval en weersomstandigheden vast te leggen, vereiste een snelle manier van werken. De traditionele schilderkunst, met haar zorgvuldige opbouw van verflagen, was voor deze snelle momentopnamen niet langer geschikt. In plaats daarvan gebruikten de impressionisten een schetsmatig overkomende stijl, waarin kleuren met snelle penseelstreken en vaak met ongemengde verf en in vloeiende overgangen werden opgebracht. De ondertekening verviel niet alleen vanwege tijdsgebrek, maar werd bewust weggelaten omdat deze nieuwe schilderkunst gericht was op het 'vastleggen van het moment'.

Typerend voor de nieuwe stijl was een veel helderder kleurenpalet en de nadruk op lichtval. Het geometrische perspectief maakte plaats voor het atmosferisch perspectief, waarin diepte wordt bereikt

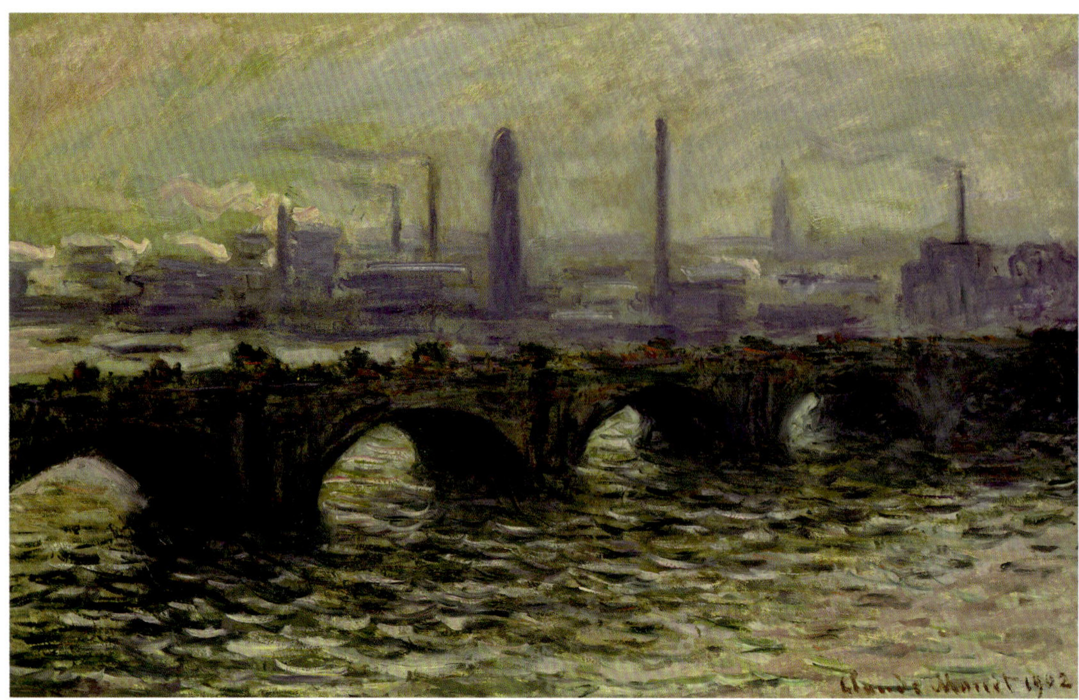

series of *Waterloo Bridge* where the forms dissolve in the haze.

Impressionism also broke with the traditional principles of composition, which had previously been placed at the service of conceptual or narrative elements. In place of the classical composition methods came the painting style of *alla prima* ('wet-on-wet'), which captured the subject *en plein air* (in the outdoors) in an atmospheric whole. Impressionism meant, above all, a revolution of seeing and the reproduction of the seen, thereby heralding the beginning of modern painting.

The term traces back to the critic Louis Leroy who, at the time of the first Impressionist exhibition in 1874, published an article in the journal *Charivari* under the title "The Exhibition of the Impressionists". The word was coined after Claude Monet's painting *Impression, Sunrise* dating from 1873 and which portrayed the port of Le Havre in the morning mist.

This neologism united the critics in their contention that the artistic cooperative holding the exhibition, which in addition to some conventional artists numbered among others Frédéric Bazille (1841–1870), Paul Cézanne (1839–1906), Edgar Degas (1834–1917), Claude Monet (1840–1926), Berthe Morisot (1841–1895), Camille Pissarro (1830–1903), Pierre-Auguste Renoir (1841–1919) and Alfred Sisley (1839–1899), were renouncing the traditional methods of painting and reproducing only their first impressions. They were criticized not only for their poor technique, as judged

firent place à une perspective obtenue par des dégradés de couleur, comme celle vraiment extrême de Monet, dans la série *Le pont de Waterloo,* où les formes se dissolvent dans la brume.

L'impressionnisme rompit également avec les principes traditionnels de la composition au service d'éléments conceptuels ou narratifs. Les méthodes de composition classiques furent remplacées par une technique de peinture *alla prima* (« humide sur humide »), qui capturait le sujet *en plein air* dans un tout atmosphérique. L'impressionnisme fut surtout une révolution quant à la vision et à la reproduction des sujets, annonçant ainsi le début de la peinture moderne.

Le terme fut employé pour la première fois par le critique Louis Leroy qui, lors de la première exposition impressionniste de 1874, publia un article intitulé « L'exposition des impressionnistes » dans la revue *Charivari*. Il inventa ce qualificatif en référence à la peinture de Claude Monet *Impression, soleil levant* datant de 1873 et représentant le port du Havre dans la brume du matin.

Ce néologisme unit les critiques dans leur affirmation selon laquelle les membres de la coopérative artistique organisant l'exposition – qui, en plus de quelques artistes classiques, comptait entre autres Frédéric Bazille (1841–1870), Paul Cézanne (1839–1906), Edgar Degas (1834–1917), Claude Monet (1840–1926), Berthe Morisot (1841–1895), Camille Pissarro (1830–1903), Pierre-Auguste Renoir (1841–1919) et Alfred Sisley (1839–1899) –, renonçaient aux méthodes de la peinture traditionnelle

Perspektive wich einer aus Farbstufungen gewonnenen Luftperspektive, wie sie Monet zum Beispiel in der Serie der *Waterloo Bridge* sehr extrem bis zur Auflösung der Formen im Dunst anwandte.

Der Impressionismus brach auch mit den überlieferten Kompositionsprinzipien, die bisher der Darstellung gedanklicher oder erzählender Elemente gedient hatten. Anstelle der klassischen Komposition trat die Malweise *alla prima* (in einem Sitz), die das Motiv *en plein air* (in freier Natur) als stimmungsvolles Ganzes erfasste. Der Impressionismus bedeutete also vor allem eine Revolution des Sehens und der Wiedergabe des Gesehenen. Damit leitete er auch den Beginn der modernen Malerei ein.

Der Begriff geht auf den Kritiker Louis Leroy zurück, der anlässlich der ersten Impressionistenausstellung 1874 einen Artikel in der Zeitschrift *Charivari* mit dem Titel „L'exposition des Impressionistes" veröffentlichte. Das Wort war durch Claude Monets Bild *Impression, Sonnenaufgang* von 1873 geprägt, das den Hafen von Le Havre im Morgennebel darstellt.

Mit dieser Wortschöpfung war die Kritik verbunden, dass die Künstlerkooperative dieser Ausstellung, neben einigen konventionellen Künstlern unter anderem Frédéric Bazille (1841–1870), Paul Cézanne (1839–1906), Edgar Degas (1834–1917), Claude Monet (1840–1926), Berthe Morisot (1841–1895), Camille Pissarro (1830–1903), Pierre-Auguste Renoir (1841–1919), Alfred Sisley (1839–1899), unter Verzicht auf die herkömmlichen Mittel der Malerei nur ihre ersten Eindrücke (frz.

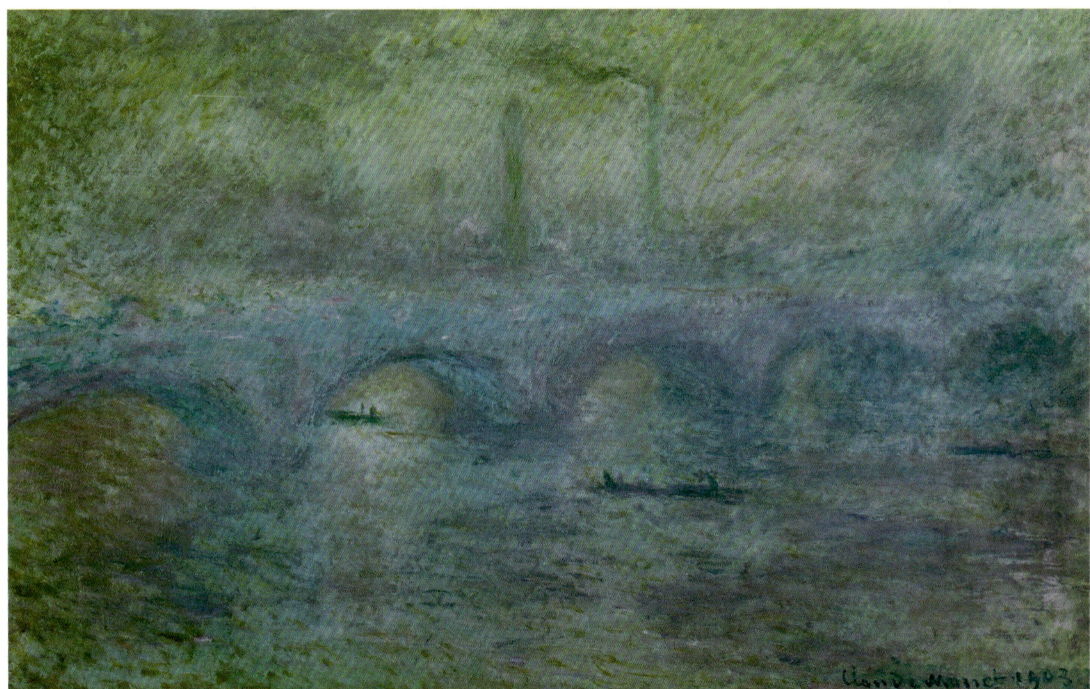

gradaciones de color, como la que p. ej. Monet llevó al extremo, hasta diluir las formas, en su serie del *puente de Waterloo.*

El impresionismo también rompió con los principios compositivos heredados, que habían servido hasta ahora a la representación de elementos narrativos o simbólicos. El lugar de la composición clásica lo ocupó la técnica *alla prima* (de una vez), que capturaba el motivo *en plein air* como un sugerente total. El impresionismo supuso por tanto una revolución de la mirada y de la reproducción de lo visto, abriendo con ello el camino a la pintura moderna.

El nombre proviene del crítico Louis Leroy, quien con motivo de la primera exposición impresionista en 1874 publicó un artículo en la revista *Charivari* con el título "L'exposition des Impressionistes". La palabra había sido "acuñada" por el cuadro de Claude Monet *Impresión, sol naciente* de 1873, que representa el puerto de Le Havre en la niebla matutina.

Con esta denominación se expresaba también la crítica aplicada a los artistas de esta exposición y otros artistas convencionales, entre otros Frédéric Bazille (1841–1870), Paul Cézanne (1839–1906), Edgar Degas (1834–1917), Claude Monet (1840–1926), Berthe Morisot (1841–1895), Camille Pissarro (1830–1903), Pierre-Auguste Renoir (1841–1919) y Alfred Sisley (1839–1899), que decía que al renunciar a los medios tradicionales de la pintura solo representaban primeras impresiones. Desde el campo académico se criticó además no solo la deficiente técnica sino también

L'Impressionismo rompeva anche con i principi tradizionali della composizione usati in precedenza per raffigurare elementi concettuali o narrativi. Alla composizione classica subentrarono la pittura alla prima e il suggestivo motivo *en plein air* (all'aperto). L'Impressionismo era dunque in primo luogo una rivoluzione nel modo di osservare e riprodurre il soggetto, e segnò l'inizio della pittura moderna.

Il termine fu coniato dal critico Louis Leroy, il quale, in occasione della prima mostra impressionista nel 1874, pubblicò sulla rivista *Charivari*. un articolo dal titolo "L'exposition des Impressionistes". La parola fu tratta dal titolo del quadro Impressione, levar del sole di Claude Monet del 1873, in cui l'artista francese raffigurò il porto di Le Havre avvolto dalla nebbia mattutina.

Con questo neologismo la critica indicava che la cooperativa di artisti partecipanti alla mostra, oltre ad alcuni artisti convenzionali, tra cui Frédéric Bazille (1841–1870), Paul Cézanne (1839–1906), Edgar Degas (1834–1917), Claude Monet (1840–1926), Berthe Morisot (1841–1895), Camille Pissarro (1830–1903), Pierre-Auguste Renoir (1841–1919) e Alfred Sisley (1839–1899), rinunciavano ai mezzi tradizionali della pittura per riprodurre solo le loro prime impressioni (*impression* in francese). Oltre alla tecnica carente e antiaccademica della corrente, ne veniva criticata anche la nuova tematica, in cui il motivo protagonista era il paesaggio. Gli impressionisti potevano contare su una serie di predecessori: la luce nel paesaggio e

door kleurschakeringen; een schoolvoorbeeld daarvan is Monets serie *Waterloo Bridge,* waarin de vormen bijna in de mist oplossen.

Het impressionisme brak ook met de klassieke compositie, die tot dan toe in dienst had gestaan van welomschreven ideeën en vertellingen. In plaats daarvan kwam nu het schilderen *alla prima* (in één sessie) en werden onderwerpen *en plein air* (in de openlucht) in een sfeervol geheel vastgelegd. Het impressionisme betekende dus vooral een revolutie in het kijken en in het weergeven van wat werd waargenomen. En daarmee stond de stroming aan het begin van de moderne schilderkunst.

Het begrip 'impressionisme' werd bedacht door de kunstcriticus Louis Leroy, die in 1874 in een artikel in het tijdschrift *Charivari* de eerste expositie van impressionisten besprak, onder de titel 'L'exposition des Impressionistes'. Het woord was ontleend aan Monets schilderij Impressie, zonsopgang uit 1873, waarop de Le Havre in de ochtendnevel is uitgebeeld.

Maar het woord was een kritische noot: deze kunstenaarsgroep – waartoe behalve enkele conventionele schilders ook Frédéric Bazille (1841–1870), Paul Cézanne (1839–1906), Edgar Degas (1834–1917), Claude Monet (1840–1926), Berthe Morisot (1841–1895), Camille Pissarro (1830–1903), Pierre-Auguste Renoir (1841–1919) en Alfred Sisley (1839–1899) behoorden – hield zich niet aan de traditionele schilderstijl en zou daardoor slechts eerste indrukken (impressions) vastleggen. Naast

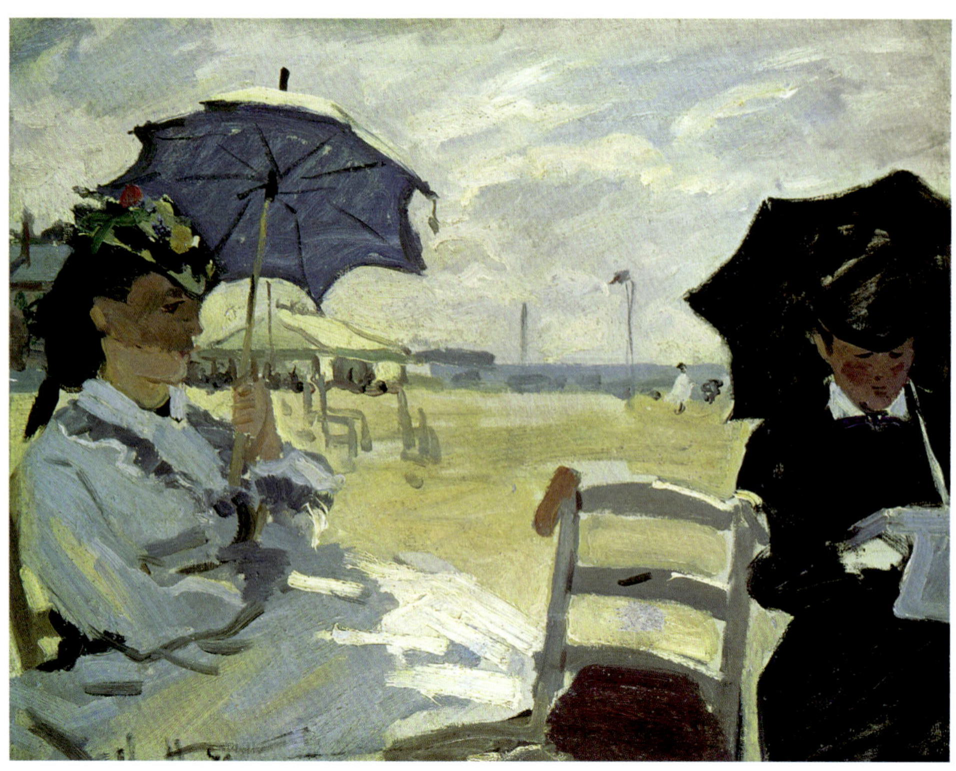

from an academic point of view, but also for their choices of themes in which the landscape dominated. Here, however, the impressionist painters were able to refer back to a number of antecedents. The light and the landscape, natural scenes free from mythological and historical themes, were the subjects which had fascinated the artists of the Barbizon school (including Camille Corot, Théodore Rousseau and Jean-François Millet), whereby the painting process, however, was mostly completed in the studio. Other important landscape painters were Eugène Boudin (1824–1898) and Johan Barthold Jongkind (1819–1891), who had devoted themselves to creating atmospheric landscape paintings of Normandy, around the estuary of the Seine and on the English Channel coast between Deauville, Trouville, Honfleur and Le Havre. This was the cradle of impressionism, as it was here, for the first time, that a group of artists had decided to paint directly and exclusively under the open skies. An equally important forerunner had been the realist painter Gustave Courbet (1819–1877), who had renounced the traditional motifs and painting techniques in favor of "realistically" (unvarnished, in impasto painting) reproduced subjects of everyday life, including landscapes of the coast of Étretat. The influence of Courbet can be seen most clearly in Édouard Manet (1832–1883), who also realistically portrayed motifs from modern life in powerful chiaroscuro colors,

et ne reproduisaient que leurs premières impressions. Ils furent critiqués non seulement pour leur technique jugée médiocre d'un point de vue académique, mais aussi pour leurs choix de thèmes parmi lesquels dominait le paysage. Les peintres impressionnistes se référaient pourtant à un certain nombre de prédécesseurs. La lumière et le paysage, des scènes naturelles sans thèmes mythologiques ou historiques, étaient des sujets qui avaient fasciné les artistes de l'école de Barbizon (dont Camille Corot, Théodore Rousseau et Jean-François Millet), avec cependant un processus de peinture finalisé la plupart du temps à l'atelier. Eugène Boudin (1824–1898) et Johan Barthold Jongkind (1819–1891) furent d'autres peintres paysagistes importants qui consacrèrent leur vie à peindre les paysages atmosphériques de Normandie, autour de l'estuaire de la Seine et sur la côte de la Manche entre Deauville, Trouville, Honfleur et Le Havre. Cette région fut le berceau de l'impressionnisme, car c'est là que la pour la première fois, un groupe d'artistes décidait de peindre directement et exclusivement à ciel ouvert. Un précurseur tout aussi important fut le peintre réaliste Gustave Courbet (1819–1877), qui avait renoncé aux motifs et aux techniques de peinture traditionnels en faveur de la reproduction « réaliste » (brute, par empâtement) de sujets de la vie quotidienne, dont les paysages de la côte d'Étretat. L'influence de Courbet se retrouve clairement chez Édouard Manet (1832–1883),

impression) wiedergebe. Kritisiert wurde neben der aus akademischer Sicht mangelhaften Technik auch die neue Thematik, bei der das Landschaftsmotiv dominierte. Dabei konnten sich die impressionistischen Maler auf eine Reihe von Vorgänger stützen. Das Licht in der Landschaft, das von mythologischen und historischen Themen freie Naturmotiv hatte bereits die Maler von Barbizon (unter anderem Camille Corot, Théodore Rousseau und Jean-François Millet) fasziniert, wobei der Bildprozess jedoch meist im Atelier abgeschlossen wurde. Andere wichtige Landschaftsmaler waren Eugène Boudin (1824–1898) und Johan Barthold Jongkind (1819–1891), die sich in der Normandie, im Mündungsgebiet der Seine, an der Kanalküste zwischen Deauville, Trouville, Honfleur und Le Havre einer stimmungsbetonten Landschaftsmalerei zugewandt hatten. Hier stand die Wiege des Impressionismus, da sich hier zum ersten Mal eine Gruppe von Künstlern entschloss, direkt und ausschließlich unter freiem Himmel zu malen. Eine ebenso wichtige Vorläuferrolle hatte der realistische Maler Gustave Courbet (1819–1877), der die tradierten Motive und Maltechniken zugunsten „wahrhaftig" (das heißt ungeschönt, in pastoser Malweise) wiedergegebener Themen des Alltagslebens, darunter auch Landschaften an der Küste von Étretat, aufgab. Der Einfluss Courbets ist am meisten bei Édouard Manet (1832–1883) zu spüren, der ebenfalls

la nueva temática, dominada por los paisajes. En este caso los impresionistas podían apoyarse en una serie de predecesores. La luz en los paisajes de temas históricos y mitológicos presentados en la naturaleza había fascinado a los pintores de Barbizon (entre otros Camille Corot, Théodore Rousseau y Jean-François Millet), si bien el proceso de pintura se acababa por lo general en el taller. Otros importantes paisajistas como Eugène Boudin (1824–1898) y Johan Barthold Jongkind (1819–1891) también se habían dedicado a pintar sugerentes paisajes en Normandía, en la desembocadura del Sena a lo largo de la costa, entre Deauville, Trouville, Honfleur y Le Havre. Aquí se dieron los inicios del impresionismo, puesto que por primera vez un grupo de artistas decidió pintar de forma única y directa a cielo abierto. Otro importante precursor fue el realista Gustave Courbet (1819–1877), que abandonó los tradicionales temas y técnicas en favor de motivos cotidianos más "veraces" (sin refinar y con una pintura más pastosa), entre los cuales también se contaban paisajes de la costa de Étretat. La influencia de Courbet es más claramente perceptible en Édouard Manet (1832–1883) que pintaba temas modernos, también en estilo realista, pero con unas pinceladas vivas y unos colores potentes determinados por el claroscuro reminiscentes ambas de los pintores españoles y holandeses del XVII. Su famoso desayuno sobre la hierba (1863) se mostró ese mismo año en

il motivo dei soggetti mitologici e storici all'aperto avevano infatti già affascinato i pittori di Barbizon (tra cui Camille Corot, Théodore Rousseau e Jean-François Millet), sebbene nel loro caso il lavoro pittorico fosse in gran parte eseguito all'interno dello studio. Tra gli altri importanti paesaggisti si annoverano Eugène Boudin (1824–1898) e Johan Barthold Jongkind (1819–1891), che si erano dedicati alla pittura paesaggistica raffigurando scorci della Normandia, alla foce della Senna, sulla costa della Manica tra Deauville, Trouville, Honfleur e Le Havre. Fu qui che nacque l'Impressionismo, perché in questo luogo, per la prima volta, un gruppo di artisti decise di dipingere direttamente ed esclusivamente all'aria aperta. Un ruolo di precursore altrettanto importante fu svolto dal pittore realista Gustave Courbet (1819–1877), il quale rinunciò ai motivi e alle tecniche pittoriche tradizionali per rappresentare in modo veritiero (ossia raffigurando la realtà nuda e cruda) soggetti della vita quotidiana, quali i paesaggi della costa di Étretat. L'influenza di Courbet si avverte più spiccatamente in Édouard Manet (1832–1883), che dipinse motivi realistici tratti dalla vita moderna usando pennellate forti, vivaci, dai colori chiaroscurali e ispirate alla pittura spagnola e olandese del XVII secolo. Il suo famoso quadro *Colazione sull'erba* del 1863 fu esposto nello stesso anno nel "Salon des Refusés", la piattaforma espositiva riservata ai pittori esclusi dal Salon ufficiale, e attrasse l'attenzione dei

de kritiek op de vanuit academisch oogpunt gebrekkige techniek van de schilders, stond ook hun onderwerpkeuze – vooral landschappen – de critici niet aan. Eerder al waren de schilders van Barbizon (onder wie Camille Corot, Théodore Rousseau en Jean-François Millet) gefascineerd geraakt door het licht in het natuurlandschap, los van mythologische en historische thematiek; zij schilderden in de vrije natuur, maar voltooiden hun doeken meestal in het atelier. Andere voorlopers waren in dat opzicht Eugène Boudin (1824–1898) en Johan Barthold Jongkind (1819–1891), die zich aan de Kanaalkust van Deauville, Trouville, Honfleur en Le Havre wijdden aan het vastleggen van sfeervolle landschappen. Hier stond de wieg van het impressionisme, want het was hier, rond de Seinemonding, dat een groep kunstenaars voor het eerst besloot direct en uitsluitend in de vrije natuur te schilderen. Een niet minder belangrijke voorloper was de realist Gustave Courbet (1819–1877), die traditionele onderwerpen en technieken meed ten gunste van thema's uit het dagelijks leven en landschappen van de kust bij Étretat, die hij op 'waarachtige' wijze wilde uitbeelden: ongepolijst en in robuuste verfstroken. Courbets invloed is het duidelijkst te bespeuren bij Édouard Manet (1832–1883), die zijn eveneens realistische, aan het dagelijks leven ontleende onderwerpen in krachtige kleuren en sterke contrasten van licht en donker verbeeldde, waarbij

using the trained brushwork style of the 17th century Spanish and Dutch painters. His famous painting *Le Déjeuner sur l'herbe (Luncheon on the Grass)* (1863) was shown in that same year in the "Salon des Refusés", the exhibiting platform for those painters rejected by the official Salon. This attracted the attention of the young artists who met between 1868 and 1870 in the Café Guérbois to discuss the future of painting, amongst whom were Edgar Degas, Auguste Renoir, Claude Monet, Alfred Sisley, Camille Pissarro and, as occasional guest, Paul Cézanne. These were the core of the later "impressionists". These painters had, in some cases, no academic training but studied in independent art schools and studios, augmented by copying sessions in the Louvre and, of course, working outdoors. Manet, however, decided somewhat later, after 1871, to paint in the outdoors.

At the centre of discussion was the concept of modernity, which Charles Baudelaire had so emphasized his 1868 text *Curiosités esthétiques*. Modern was the "fugitive beauté", the fleeting beauty

qui a également représenté des motifs réalistes de la vie moderne dans des clairs-obscurs puissants, utilisant le style de travail au pinceau élaboré par les peintres espagnols et hollandais du XVIIème siècle. Son célèbre tableau, *le Déjeuner sur l'herbe* (1863) fut présenté la même année au « Salon des refusés », qui exposait les peintres rejetés par le Salon officiel. Ce salon attira l'attention de jeunes artistes qui se réunirent de 1868 et 1870 au café Guerbois pour discuter de l'avenir de la peinture. Parmi ces artistes figuraient Edgar Degas, Auguste Renoir, Claude Monet, Alfred Sisley, Camille Pissarro et, comme invité occasionnel, Paul Cézanne. Ils furent le noyau dur des futurs « Impressionnistes ». Ces peintres n'avaient, pour certains d'entre eux, aucune formation académique, mais avaient étudié dans les écoles et ateliers d'art indépendants, formation doublée par des sessions de copie au Louvre et bien sûr par un travail en plein air. Manet, pourtant, décida plutôt tardivement (après 1871) de peindre en extérieur.

Au cœur du débat se trouvait le concept de modernité, souligné avec force par Charles Baudelaire

realistische, dem modernen Leben entnommene Motive in kräftigen, auf Helldunkel abgestimmten Farben und lebhaftem, an den spanischen und niederländischen Malern des 17. Jahrhunderts geschulten Pinselduktus malte. Sein berühmtes Bild *Frühstück im Grünen* (1863) wurde im gleichen Jahr im „Salon des Refusés" gezeigt, der Ausstellungsplattform für die vom offiziellen Salon abgewiesenen Maler, und erregte die Aufmerksamkeit der jungen Künstler, die sich im Café Guérbois in den Jahren 1868 bis 1870 zu Diskussionen um die Zukunft der Malerei trafen, darunter Edgar Degas, Auguste Renoir, Claude Monet, Alfred Sisley, Camille Pissarro und als seltener Gast auch Paul Cézanne, der Kern der späteren „Impressionisten". Diese Maler hatten zum Teil keine akademische Ausbildung, sondern bildeten sich in freien Kunstschulen und Ateliers aus, ergänzt durch Kopien im Louvre und natürlich der Arbeit im Freien. Manet entschied sich allerdings erst später (nach 1871) in der freien Natur zu malen.

Im Mittelpunkt der Diskussionen stand der Begriff der Modernität, den Charles Baudelaire in seinen

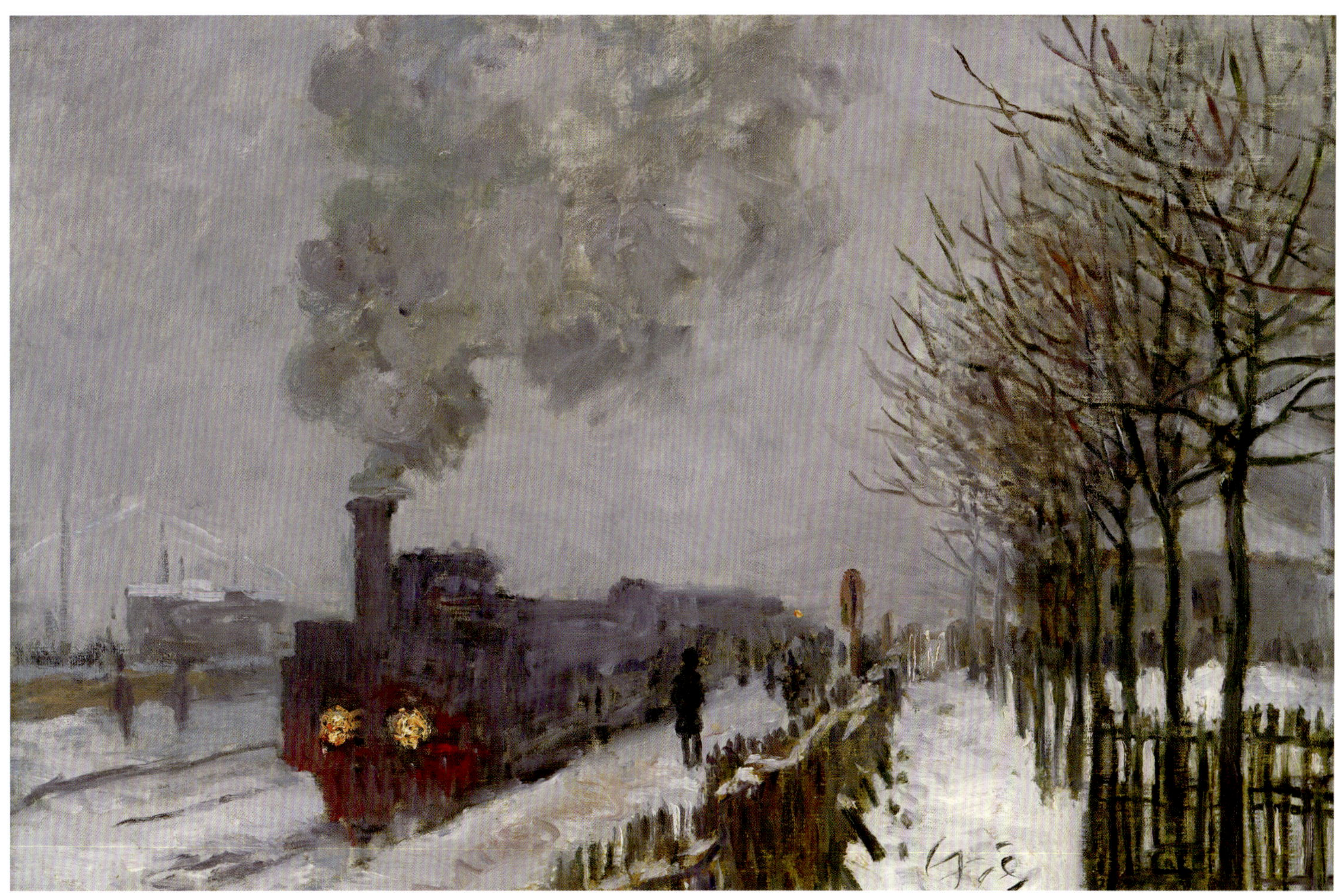

el "Salon des Refusés", el espacio para los pintores que habían sido rechazados por el salón oficial, y allí capturó la atención de jóvenes pintores que se reunieron en el Café Guérbois entre 1868 y 1870 a discutir sobre el futuro de la pintura; entre ellos estaban Edgar Degas, Auguste Renoir, Claude Monet, Alfred Sisley, Camille Pissarro y también Paul Cézanne como invitado ocasional: el núcleo de lo que después serían "los impresionistas". Algunos de estos pintores no contaban con formación académica, sino que se formaban en escuelas no oficiales y en talleres, complementados con copias realizadas en el Louvre y por supuesto trabajo al aire libre. Manet sin embargo decidió pintar al aire libre relativamente tarde (a partir de 1871).

En el centro de las discusiones se situaba el concepto de modernidad, que tanto había enfatizado Charles Baudelaire en sus escritos (*Curiosités esthétiques*, 1868). Lo moderno era la "fugitive beauté", la belleza fugitiva de la vida moderna, que había que tratar de capturar en sus momentos más llenos de vida. Los impresionistas habían desarrollado de forma paralela

giovani artisti che negli anni 1868–1870 si riunirono nel Sichim Café Guérbois per discutere sul futuro della pittura, tra cui Edgar Degas, Auguste Renoir, Claude Monet, Alfred Sisley, Camille Pissarro e, talvolta, Paul Cézanne: il nucleo dei futuri "impressionisti". Questi pittori avevano ricevuto in parte una formazione accademica, tuttavia si erano formati in studi e scuole d'arte liberi, oltre che attraverso copie di opere del Louvre e, naturalmente, al lavoro all'aperto. Manet, tuttavia, decise solo più tardi (dopo il 1871) di dipingere in mezzo alla natura.

Al centro delle discussioni stava la definizione di modernità, su cui Charles Baudelaire aveva posto fortemente l'accetto nei suoi scritti (*Curiosités esthétiques*, 1868). La modernità era la "fugitive beauté", la bellezza fugace della vita contemporanea, che doveva essere catturata nei suoi momenti più vivi. I mezzi per farlo, ovvero la pennellata veloce, i contrasti di colore e la fine luminosità della luce nel quadro, erano stati ulteriormente sviluppati dagli impressionisti parallelamente all'osservazione della natura. Un

zijn penseelvoering herinnerde aan de techniek van Spaanse en Nederlandse meesters uit de 17e eeuw. Manets beroemde *Déjeuner sur l'herbe ('Ontbijt op het gras';* 1863) werd in dat jaar getoond op de 'Salon des Refusés', de tentoonstelling voor schilders wier werken voor de officiële Salon waren afgewezen. Het doek wekte grote belangstelling bij een groep jonge schilders die tussen 1868 en 1870 in het Café Guerbois over een nieuwe schilderkunst discussieerden. Tot de groep behoorden Edgar Degas, Auguste Renoir, Claude Monet, Alfred Sisley, Camille Pissarro en ook Paul Cézanne – de kern van wat later als 'de impressionisten' zou worden omschreven. Sommigen hadden geen academische kunstopleiding gevolgd, maar leerden het vak in private schilderscholen, door het kopiëren van oude meesters in het Louvre en natuurlijk door het schilderen in de vrije natuur. Alleen Manet besloot pas na 1871 in de openlucht te gaan werken.

Centraal in de discussies stond het begrip 'moderniteit', dat in de geschriften van Charles

of contemporary life which was to be captured in its most vivid moments. The means to convey this, using rapid brushstrokes, color contrasts and a finely balanced treatment of light in the paintings, had been developed by the impressionists parallel to their observations of nature. Another catalyst for the impressionist movement was the recently invented process of photography, which opened up to the artists new and previously unknown aspects of the world. Novel viewpoints, close-ups, overlaps, snapshots, sharp reflections and finally, with Étienne-Jules Marey (1830–1904) and Eadweard Muybridge (1830–1904), the analysis of movement; these were all innovations that molded and stimulated the perceptions of the impressionists, as well as the impetus of modern society (the dynamics of metropolitan life, the excitement of movement through railways, automobiles and bicycles, as well as sports activities in the outdoors).

dans son texte de 1868 *Curiosités esthétiques*. Était moderne la « beauté fugitive », la beauté éphémère de la vie contemporaine, qui devait être capturée dans ses moments les plus extraordinaires. Les moyens de cette transmission – l'utilisation de coups de pinceau rapides, de contrastes de couleurs et un traitement bien équilibré de la lumière dans les peintures – avaient été mis au point par les impressionnistes parallèlement à leurs observations de la nature. Un autre catalyseur du mouvement impressionniste fut l'invention récente du processus de la photographie, qui ouvrit aux artistes des aspects du monde nouveaux et jusqu'alors inconnus. Points de vue nouveaux, gros plans, superpositions, instantanés, reflets prononcés et, enfin, avec Étienne-Jules Marey (1830–1904) et Eadweard Muybridge (1830–1904), l'analyse du mouvement. Telles sont toutes les innovations qui formèrent et stimulèrent les perceptions des impressionnistes, autant que l'impulsion de la société moderne (la dynamique de la vie métropolitaine,

Schriften (*Curiosités esthétiques*, 1868) so betont hatte. Modern war die „fugitive beauté", die flüchtige Schönheit des zeitgenössischen Lebens, die es in ihren lebhaftesten Augenblicken festzuhalten galt. Die Mittel dazu, der schnell erfassende Pinselstrich, die Farbkontraste wie auch die fein abgestimmte Helligkeit des Lichts im Bild hatten die Impressionisten parallel zur Naturbeobachtung weiterentwickelt. Ein anderer Katalysator für die impressionistische Bewegung war die erst vor kurzem erfundene Fotografie, die den Künstlern neue, bisher unbekannte Aspekte der Welt erschloss. Neuartige Blickwinkel, Nahaufnahmen, Überschneidungen, Schnappschüsse, scharfe Lichtreflexe, schließlich bei Étienne-Jules Marey (1830–1904) und Eadweard Muybridge (1830–1904) die Zerlegung der Bewegung – all dies waren Neuerungen, die die Wahrnehmung der Impressionisten – neben den Anregungen der modernen Gesellschaft (Dynamik des großstädtischen Lebens, Bewegungsreize durch

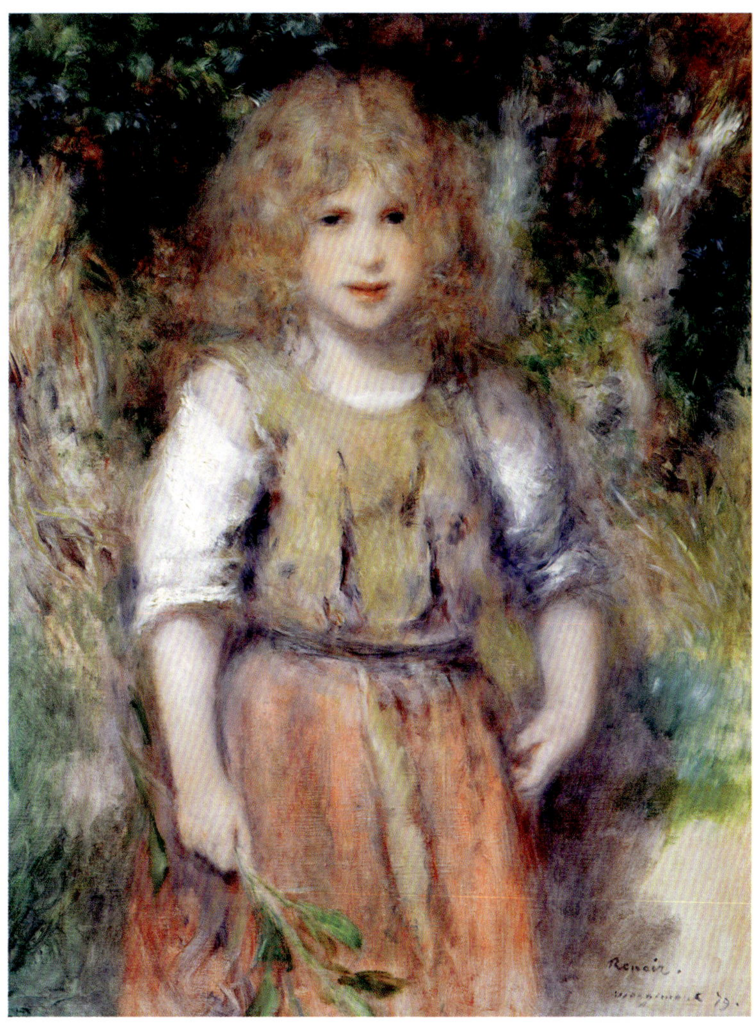

los medios necesarios a tal efecto con su observación de la naturaleza, los trazos ágiles y los contrastes cromáticos, así como la refinada composición de la luz en la imagen. Otro catalizador para el impresionismo fue la recientemente inventada fotografía, que abría a los artistas nuevos y hasta entonces desconocidos aspectos del mundo. Nuevas perspectivas, primeros planos, solapamientos, instantáneas, nítidos reflejos de luz, hasta llegar a la descomposición del movimiento en Étienne-Jules Marey (1830–1904) y Eadweard Muybridge (1830–1904); todas estas constituían innovaciones que, junto a los estímulos de la sociedad moderna (la dinámica de la gran ciudad, el nuevo movimiento generado por el ferrocarril, auto y bicicleta, las actividades deportivas en la naturaleza) inspiraban y formaban a los impresionistas.

Otro tipo de influencia, no menos significativa, vino dada por el arte japonés, en concreto las imágenes de los grandes Utamaro (1753–1806), Hokusai (1760–1849)

altro catalizzatore del movimento impressionista fu la recente invenzione della fotografia, che permise agli artisti di esplorare aspetti del mondo nuovi e precedentemente sconosciuti. Nuove angolature, primi piani, accavallamenti, istantanee, riflessi taglienti e, infine, la decomposizione del movimento di Étienne-Jules Marey (1830–1904) ed Eadweard Muybridge (1830–1904) erano tutte innovazioni create e promosse dalla percezione degli impressionisti, oltre che dagli stimoli della società moderna (dinamica della vita metropolitana, spostamenti in treno, automobile e bicicletta, attività sportive all'aperto ecc.).

D'altro lato, non meno importante fu l'influenza dell'arte giapponese, in particolar modo dei grandi artisti grafici Utamaro (1753–1806), Hokusai (1760–1849) e Hiroshige (1797–1858), le cui xilografie colorate furono collezionate da molti pittori impressionisti, tra cui Monet, Degas e Renoir, per la loro audace composizione e le luminose superfici colorate.

Baudelaire (*Curiosités esthétiques*, 1868) was benadrukt. Modern was de "fugitive beauté", de "vluchtige schoonheid" van het eigentijdse leven, die in al haar levendigheid op het doek gevangen moest worden. De methoden om dat te bereiken – de snelle penseelstrook, scherpe kleurcontrasten en subtiele lichtnuances – hadden de impressionisten parallel aan hun observatie van de natuur ontwikkeld. Een andere katalysator voor de impressionistische stroming was de nog maar pas uitgevonden fotografie, die de kunstenaars een nieuwe, tot dan toe ongekende blik op de wereld bood. Nieuwe invalshoeken, 'close-ups', overlappingen, momentopnamen, felle lichtreflecties en uiteindelijk, bij Étienne-Jules Marey (1830–1904) en Eadweard Muybridge (1830–1904), de ontleding van beweging – dat alles waren innovaties die samen met andere aspecten van de moderne samenleving, zoals de nieuwe dynamiek van de grote stad, de spoorwegen, het automobiel, het rijwiel en het sporten in de vrije

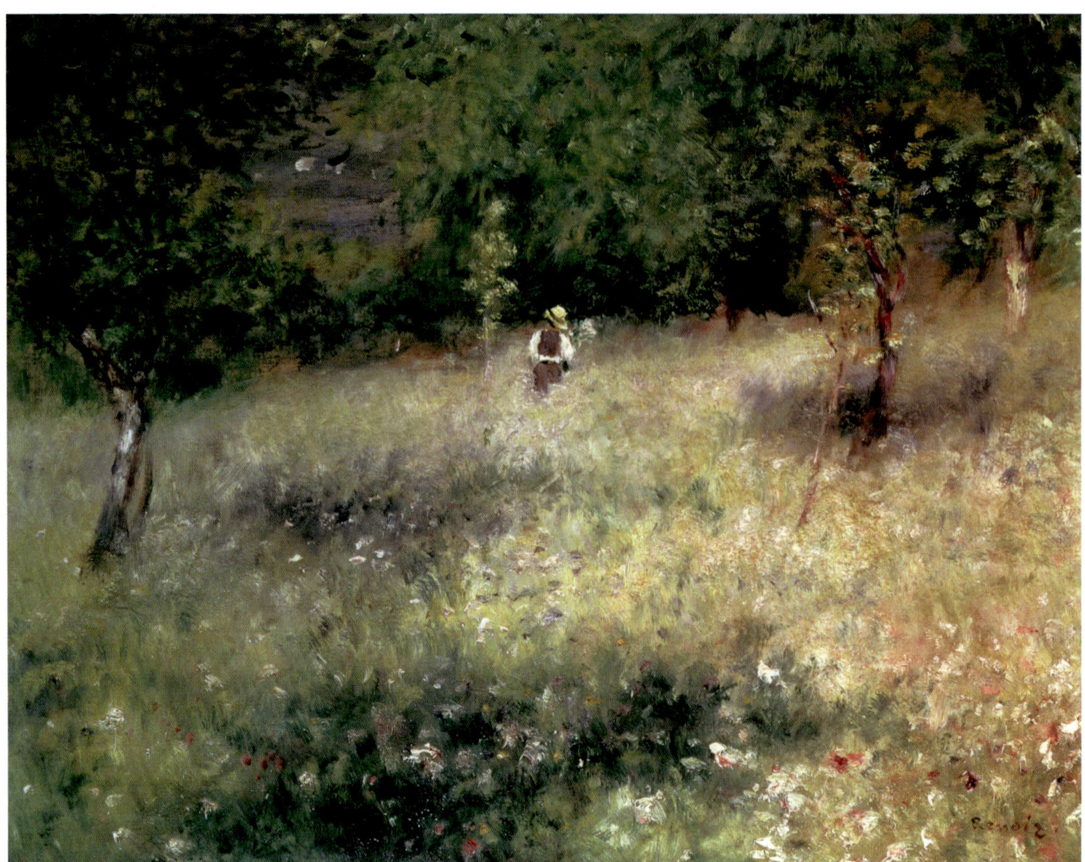

Another significant, but not less important influence was that of Japanese art, particularly the great graphic artists Utamaro (1753–1806), Hokusai (1760–1849) and Hiroshige (1797–1858), whose colored woodcuts were collected by many of the impressionist painters, such as Monet, Degas and Renoir, for their bold compositional style and use of clear luminous colors.

While Monet, Sisley and Pissarro mainly studied and reproduced their impressions of the landscape, Degas and Renoir in particular devoted themselves to the human image which, in addition to "classical" topics such as bathers, also included unconventional motifs such as ballerinas, singers of café-concerts, ironing women and washerwomen. The subject of the hard world of work as experienced by the poorer layers of society was left, however, untouched, as was also history, mythology and allegory which would have marked them as "salon art". These were not included in their renewal of form and color.

l'enthousiasme pour le mouvement avec les chemins de fer, les automobiles et les bicyclettes, ainsi que des activités sportives de plein air).

Une autre influence notable, mais non moins importante, fut celle de l'art japonais, en particulier les grands artistes graphiques Utamaro (1753–1806), Hokusai (1760–1849) et Hiroshige (1797–1858), dont les estampes colorées furent collectionnées par un grand nombre de peintres impressionnistes comme Monet, Degas et Renoir, pour l'audace de leurs compositions et l'utilisation de couleurs claires lumineuses.

Alors que Monet, Sisley et Pissarro étudiaient et reproduisaient essentiellement leurs impressions du paysage, Degas et Renoir, en particulier, se consacraient à la représentation humaine qui, en plus de sujets « classiques » comme les baigneurs, comprenait également des motifs non conventionnels tels que ballerines, chanteurs de cafés-concerts, repasseuses et lavandières. Le sujet du difficile monde du travail, tel que vécu par les couches les plus pauvres de la société, ne fut cependant pas abordé, pas plus que l'histoire, la mythologie et l'allégorie qui auraient été étiquetées « art de salon ». Ces sujets ne faisaient pas partie de leur volonté de renouvellement de la forme et la couleur.

Eisenbahn, Automobil und Fahrrad, sportliche Aktivitäten in der freien Natur) schulte und anregte.

Von anderer, nicht weniger wichtigen Bedeutung war der Einfluss der japanischen Kunst, namentlich der großen Grafiker Utamaro (1753–1806), Hokusai (1760–1849) und Hiroshige (1797–1858), deren farbige Holzschnitte von vielen impressionistischen Malern, wie zum Beispiel Monet, Degas und Renoir, wegen ihrer kühnen Kompositionsweise und den klaren leuchtenden Farbflächen gesammelt wurde.

Während Monet, Sisley und Pissarro vorwiegend das Landschaftserlebnis suchten und wiedergaben, widmete sich vor allem Degas und Renoir dem Figurenbild, das neben „klassischen" Themen (Badende) auch ganz unkonventionelle Motive, wie Ballettänzerinnen, Sängerinnen der Café-Konzerte, Büglerinnen und Wäscherinnen, einschloss. Die harte Arbeitswelt sozial armer Schichten blieb jedoch ausgespart, ebenso wie Zeitereignisse, Historie, Mythologie und Allegorie, die als „Salonkunst" abgestempelt, nicht in die formale und farbige Erneuerung übernommen wurden.

y Hiroshige (1797–1858). Sus xilografías a color fueron coleccionadas por muchos pintores impresionistas como por ejemplo Monet, Degas y Renoir, por sus audaces composiciones y sus superficies de colores claros y luminosos.

Mientras que Monet, Sisley y Pissarro buscaron y cultivaron principalmente el paisaje, Degas y Renoir se concentraron sobre todo en escenas que, junto a los temas más clásicos (bañistas), incluían motivos más originales como bailarinas de ballet, cantantes o conciertos de café, lavanderas o planchadoras. Se omitieron sin embargo las duras condiciones del mundo de trabajo de las clases bajas, así como eventos históricos, mitológicos y alegorías, que se consideraban "arte de salón" y no formaban parte de las innovaciones formales y cromáticas.

Mentre Monet, Sisley e Pissarro studiarono e riprodussero soprattutto paesaggi, Degas e Renoir si dedicarono alla riproduzione di figure umane, da soggetti "classici" (i bagnanti) a motivi non convenzionali, come ballerine, cantanti di caffè-concerto, stiratrici e lavandaie. Il duro mondo del lavoro dei ceti sociali più poveri fu invece messo da parte, così come gli eventi contemporanei, la storia, la mitologia e l'allegoria, che furono etichettati come "arte da salone" e non furono inclusi nel rinnovamento formale e cromatico.

natuur, de waarneming van de impressionisten vormden en inspireerden.

Van niet minder belang was ook de invloed van de Japanse kunst, met name die van de grote prentkunstenaars Utamaro (1753–1806), Hokusai (1760–1849) en Hiroshige (1797–1858), wier kleurige houtsneden vanwege hun gedurfde composities en heldere en lichte kleurvlakken door veel impressionisten werden verzameld, bijvoorbeeld door Monet, Degas en Renoir.

Terwijl Monet, Sisley en Pissarro de ervaring van het landschap wilden vastleggen, wijdden Degas en Renoir zich aan het figurenschilderij, waarin ze naast 'klassieke' thema's (zoals baders) ook minder gebruikelijke onderwerpen schilderden, zoals ballerina's en mensen in de cafés-dansants. De harde wereld van de arbeider bleef buiten beschouwing, evenals gebeurtenissen en historische en mythologische voorstellingen, die door de impressionisten als 'Salonkunst' waren bestempeld en niet in hun formele en coloristische vernieuwing werden opgenomen.

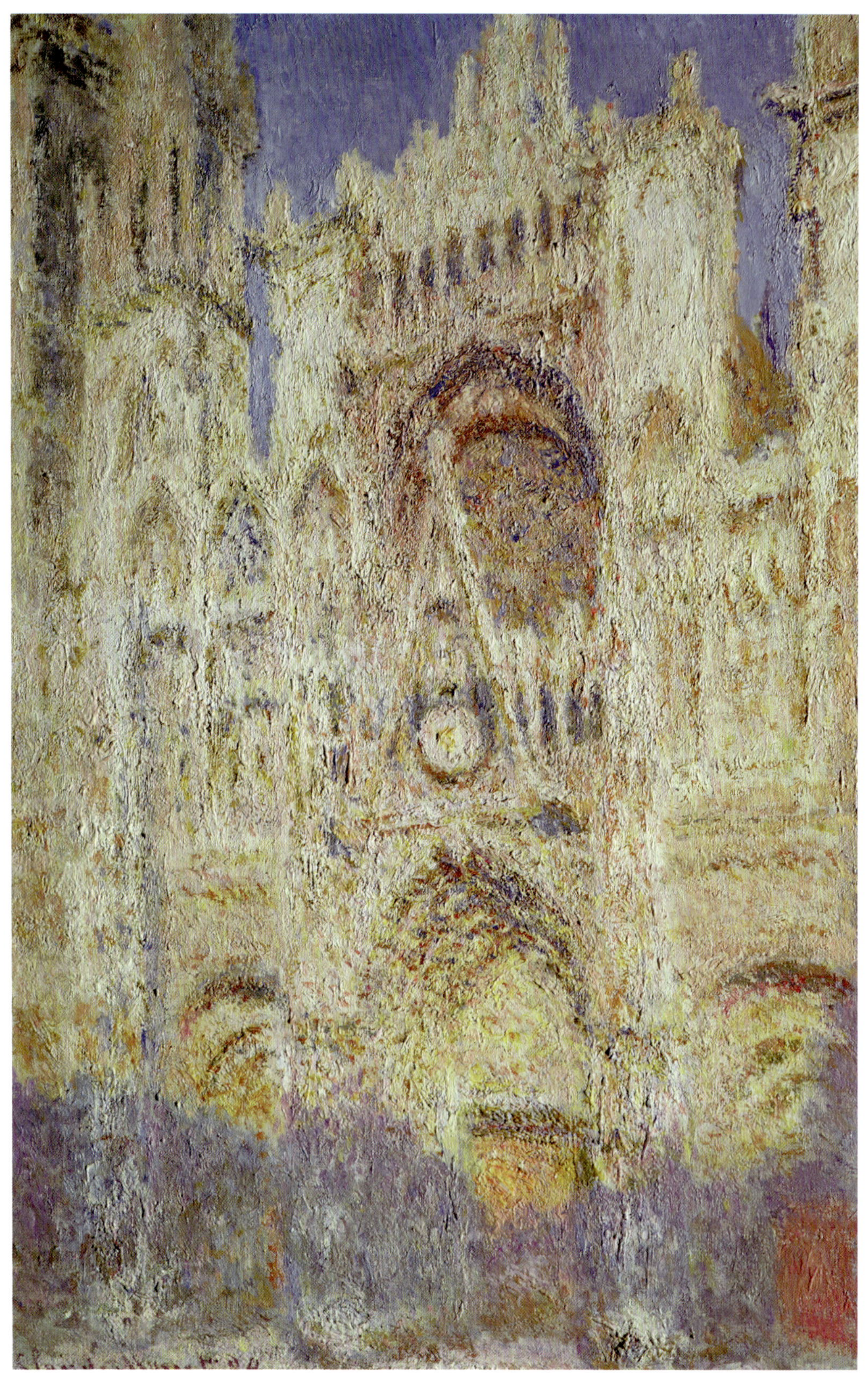

Claude Monet (1840–1926)

Rouen Cathedral at Sunset

La cathédrale de Rouen, effet du matin

Die Kathedrale von Rouen am Morgen

La catedral de Rouen por la mañana

La Cattedrale di Rouen, effetti di luce mattutina

De kathedraal van Rouen in de ochtend

1894, Oil on canvas/Huile sur toile, 100 × 65 cm,
Pushkin State Museum of Fine Arts, Moscow

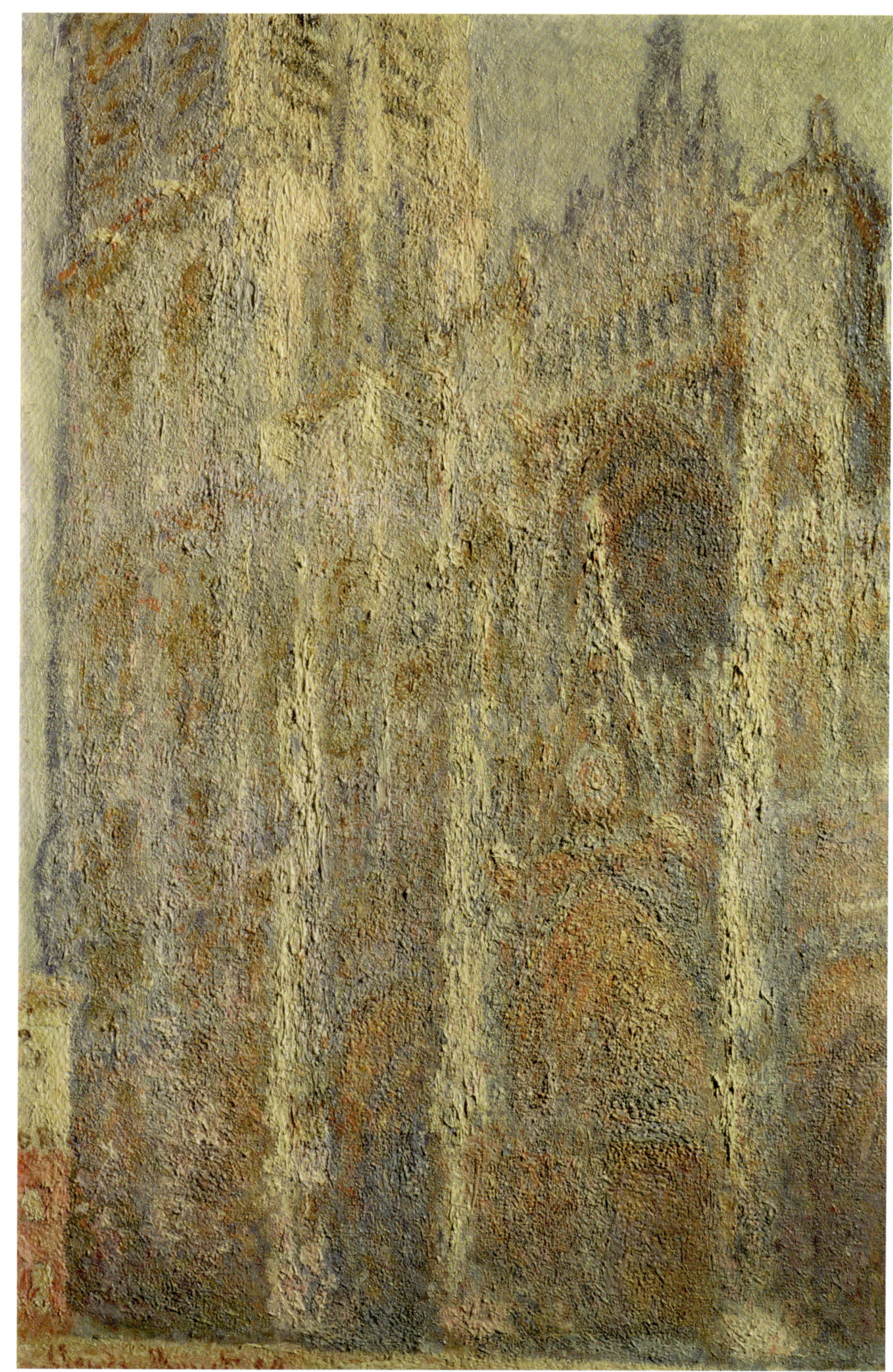

Claude Monet (1840–1926)
Rouen Cathedral, Midday
La cathédrale de Rouen à midi
Die Kathedrale von Rouen am Mittag
La catedral de Rouen al mediodía
La Cattedrale di Rouen a mezzogiorno
De kathedraal van Rouen in de middag
1894, Oil on canvas/Huile sur toile, 101 × 65 cm,
Pushkin State Museum of Fine Arts, Moscow

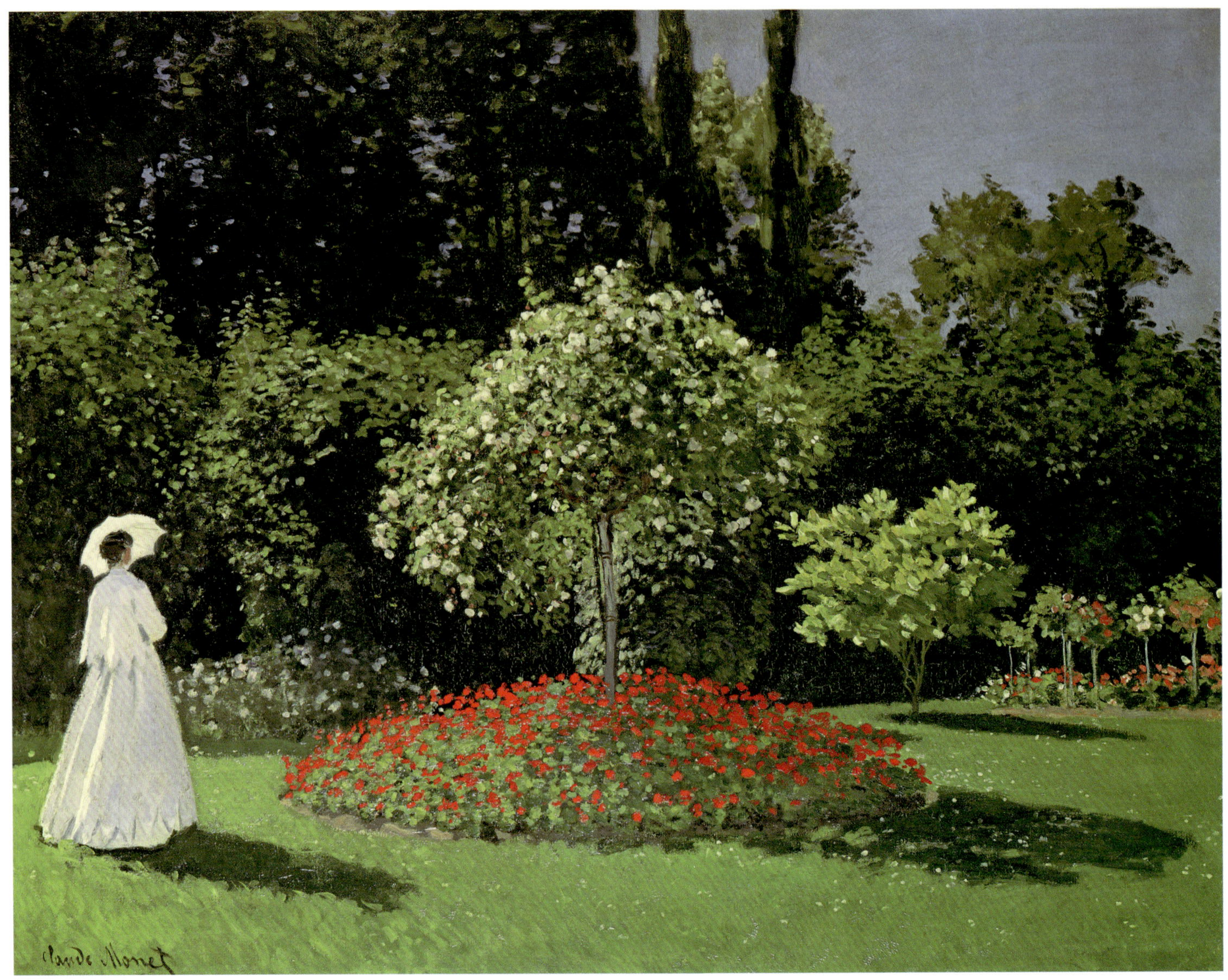

Claude Monet (1840–1926)

Jeanne Marie Lecadre in the Garden

Jeanne Marie Lecadre au jardin

Jeanne Marie Lecadre im Garten

Jeanne Marie Lecadre en el jardín

Jeanne Marie Lecadre in giardino

Jeanne Marie Lecadre in de tuin

1866, Oil on canvas/Huile sur toile, 80 × 99 cm, State Hermitage Museum, St. Petersburg

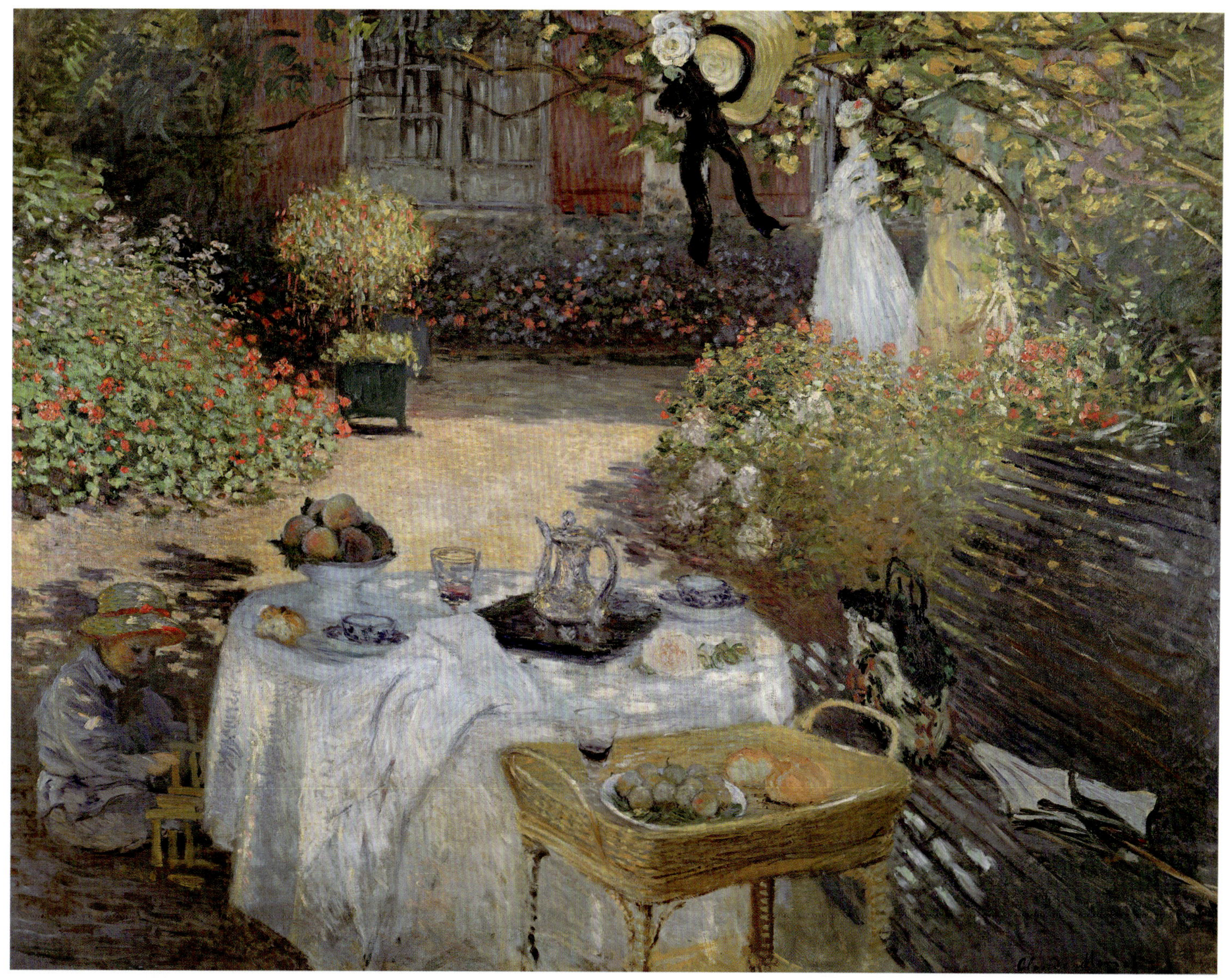

Claude Monet (1840–1926)

The Luncheon: Monet's garden at Argenteuil

Le déjeuner (dans le jardin de Claude Monet à Argenteuil)

Das Mittagsmahl. Monets Garten in Argenteuil

El almuerzo. El jardín de Monet en Argenteuil

Il pranzo: giardino di Monet ad Argenteuil

Het middagmaal. Monets tuin in Argenteuil

c. 1873, Oil on canvas/Huile sur toile, 160 × 201 cm, Musée d'Orsay, Paris

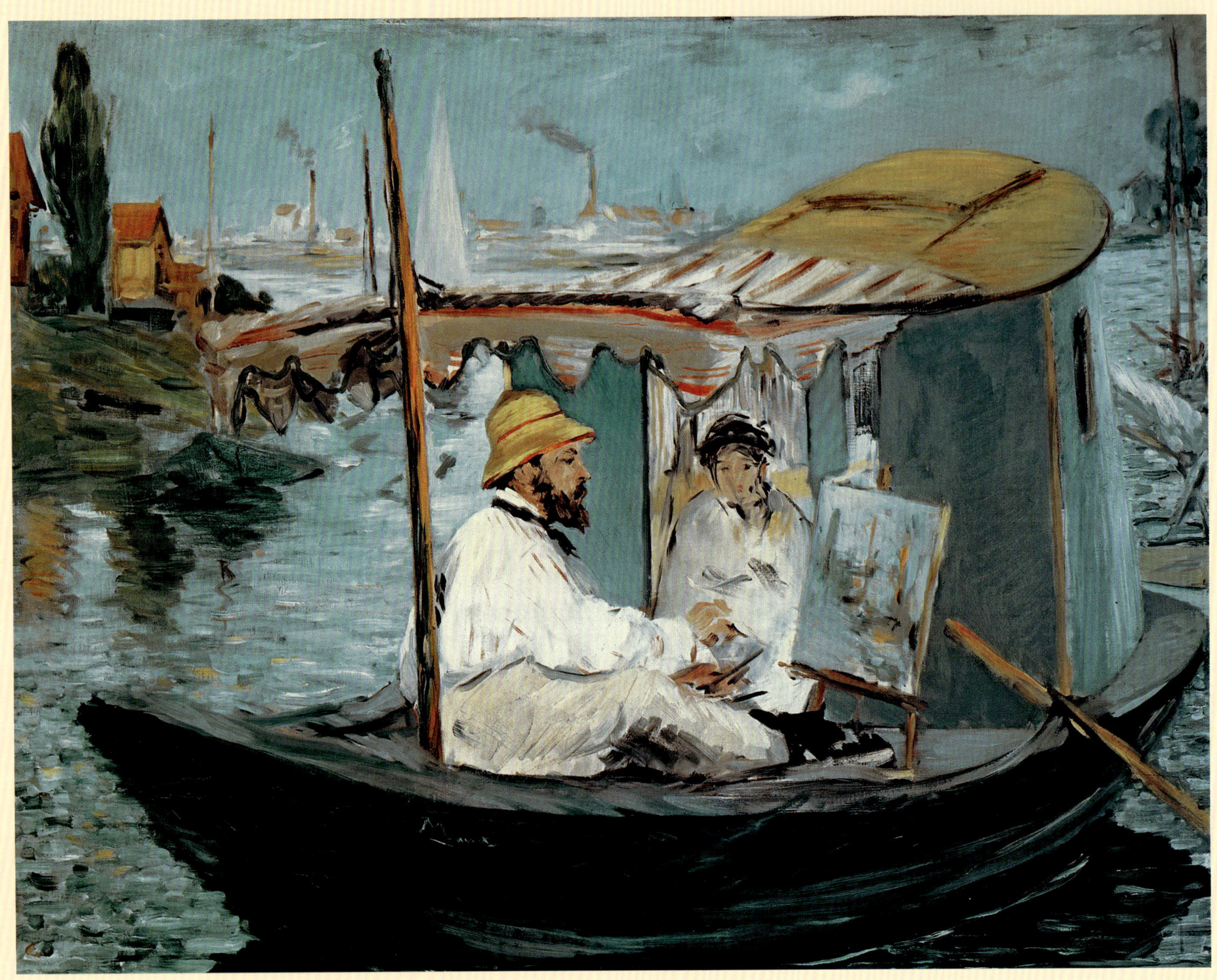

Édouard Manet (1832–83)

Monet in his Floating Studio

La barque

Die Barke

Monet en su estudio flotante

La barca

Claude Monet schilderend in zijn atelier

1874, Oil on canvas/Huile sur toile, 82,5 × 105 cm, Neue Pinakothek, München

This famous picture impressively demonstrates the open-air painting of the impressionists. Here we see Monet working with loose brush strokes to portray an image of the banks of the Seine, whilst his wife Camille follows the progress of his work. Monet liked to use his houseboat for his painting excursions, where he could observe his subject undisturbed. Manet has again reproduced this scene with shimmering light reflections on the water.

Ce tableau célèbre est une impressionnante démonstration de la peinture de plein air telle que pratiquée par les impressionnistes. Nous voyons là Monet en train de représenter les bords de Seine par d'amples coups de pinceau, alors que son épouse Camille suit l'avancement de son travail. Monet aimait utiliser son bateau-atelier pour ses excursions de peinture, afin de pouvoir observer son sujet sans être dérangé. Manet a également reproduit cette scène avec les reflets chatoyants de la lumière sur l'eau.

Das bekannte Bild zeigt eindrucksvoll die *Plein-air*-Malerei der Impressionisten. Hier sucht Monet mit lockerer Pinselführung ein Bild des Seineufers wiederzugeben, während seine Frau Camille dem Fortgang der Arbeit zuschaut. Monet benutzte für seine Malausflüge gerne sein Hausboot, auf dem er ungestört das Motiv beobachten konnte. Manet hat diese Szene wiederum mit flimmernden Lichtreflexen auf dem Wasser festgehalten.

Esta famosa imagen muestra de manera imponente la pintura al aire libre de los impresionistas. En ella Monet trata de pintar la orilla del Sena con trazos relajados de su pincel, bajo la atenta mirada de su esposa Camille. Monet utilizaba a menudo esta casa bote para sus sesiones de pintura al aire libre, desde donde podía observar tranquilamente su tema. Manet captura esta escena con reflejos centelleantes de luz sobre el agua.

Questo famoso quadro è un chiaro esempio di pittura impressionistica *en plein air*. Nel dipinto viene raffigurato Monet nell'atto di cercare di riprodurre con pennellate più fluide le rive della Senna, mentre sua moglie Camille osserva lo stato di avanzamento dei lavori. Monet utilizzava volentieri per le sue escursioni pittoriche la sua casa galleggiante, da dove poteva osservare indisturbato il soggetto. Manet catturò a sua volta questa scena con tremolanti riflessi di luce sull'acqua.

Dit beroemde doek toont overduidelijk de *plein air*-schildermethode van de impressionisten. Het laat Claude Monet zien, die met losse penseelstreken de Seine-oever uitbeeldt terwijl zijn vrouw Camille toekijkt. Monet gebruikte voor zijn uitstapjes vaak zijn eigen boot, vanwaaruit hij zijn onderwerp ongestoord kon bestuderen. Op zijn beurt heeft Manet het tafereel met glinsterende lichteffecten op het water weergegeven.

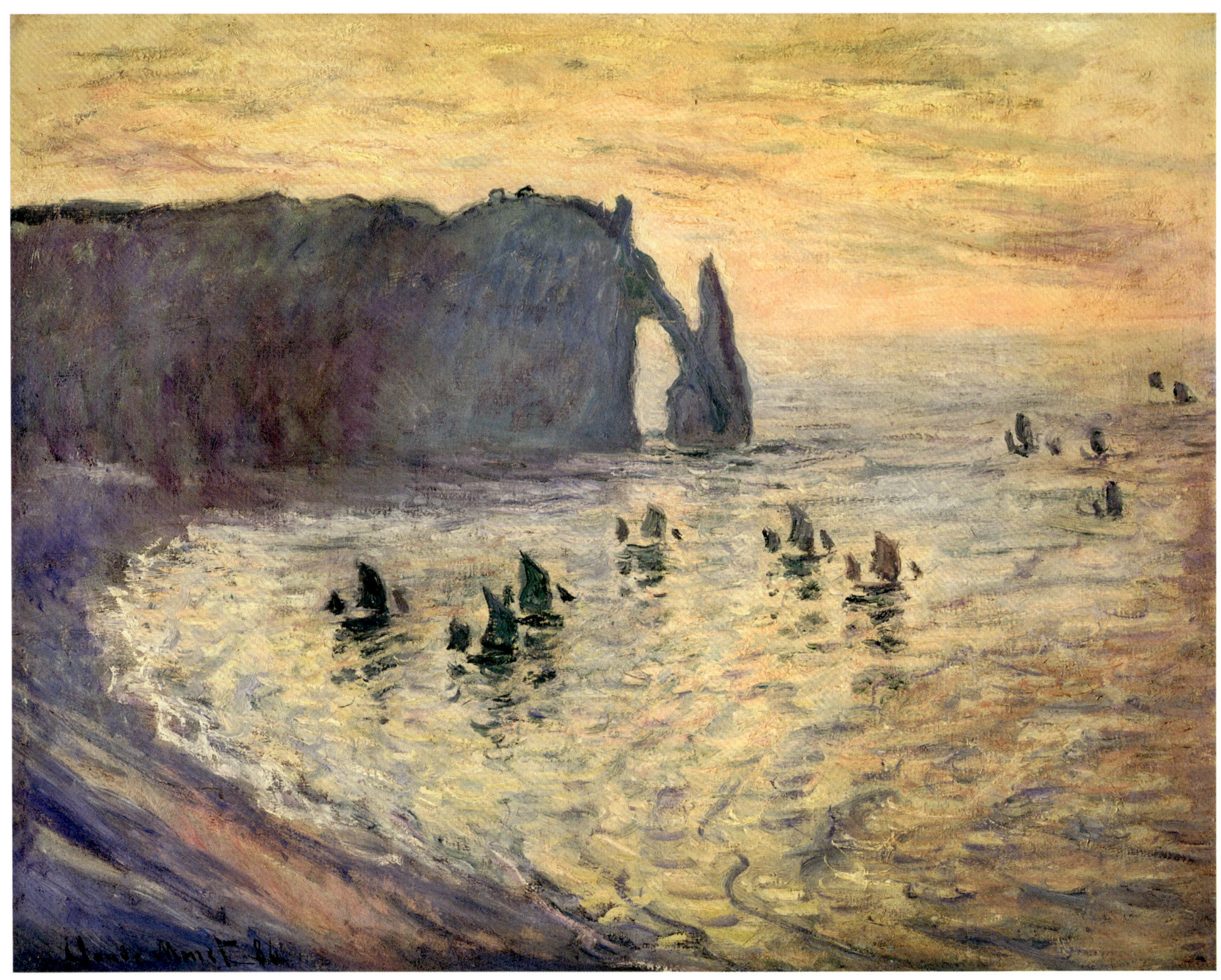

Claude Monet (1840–1926)

The Cliffs at Étretat

Les falaises d'Étretat

Die Klippen von Étretat

Los acantilados de Étretat

Le scogliere di Étretat

De klippen van Étretat

1886, Oil on canvas/Huile sur toile, 66 × 81 cm, Pushkin State Museum of Fine Arts, Moscow

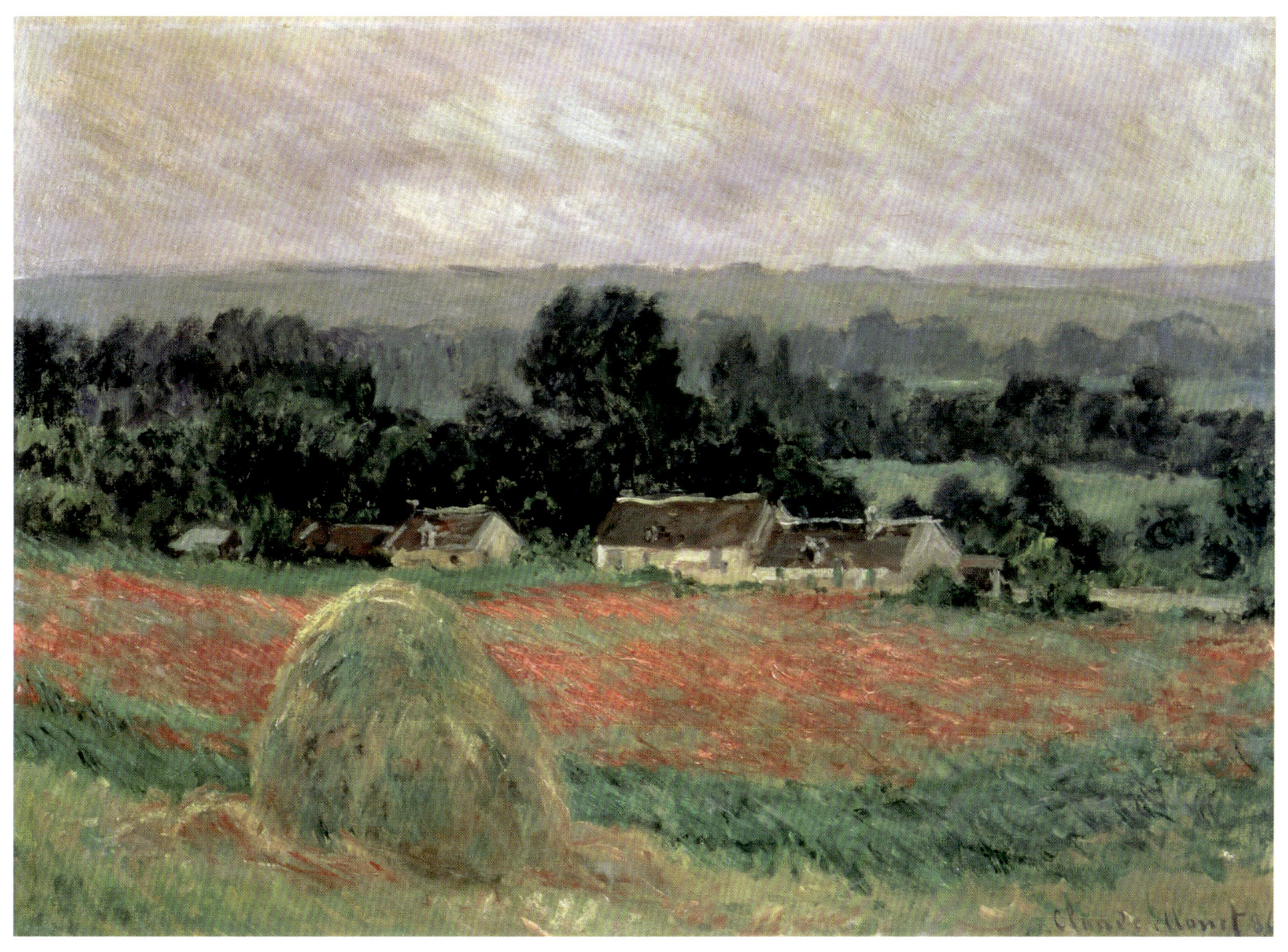

Claude Monet (1840–1926)

Haystack at Giverny

La meule de foin

Heuschober in Giverny

Montones de heno en Giverny

Covoni a Giverny

Hooiberg bij Giverny

1886, Oil on canvas/Huile sur toile, 61 × 81 cm, State Hermitage Museum, St. Petersburg

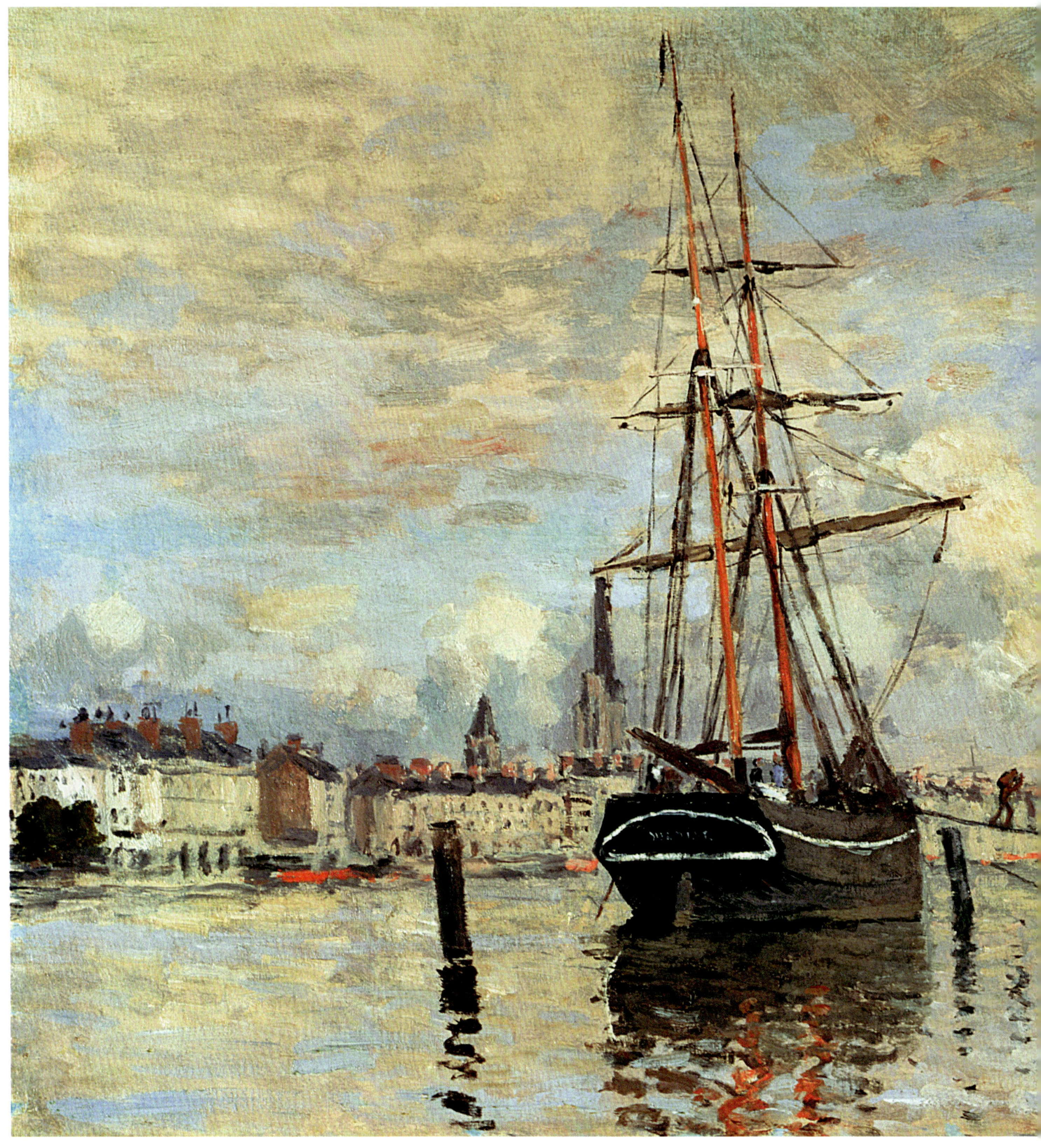

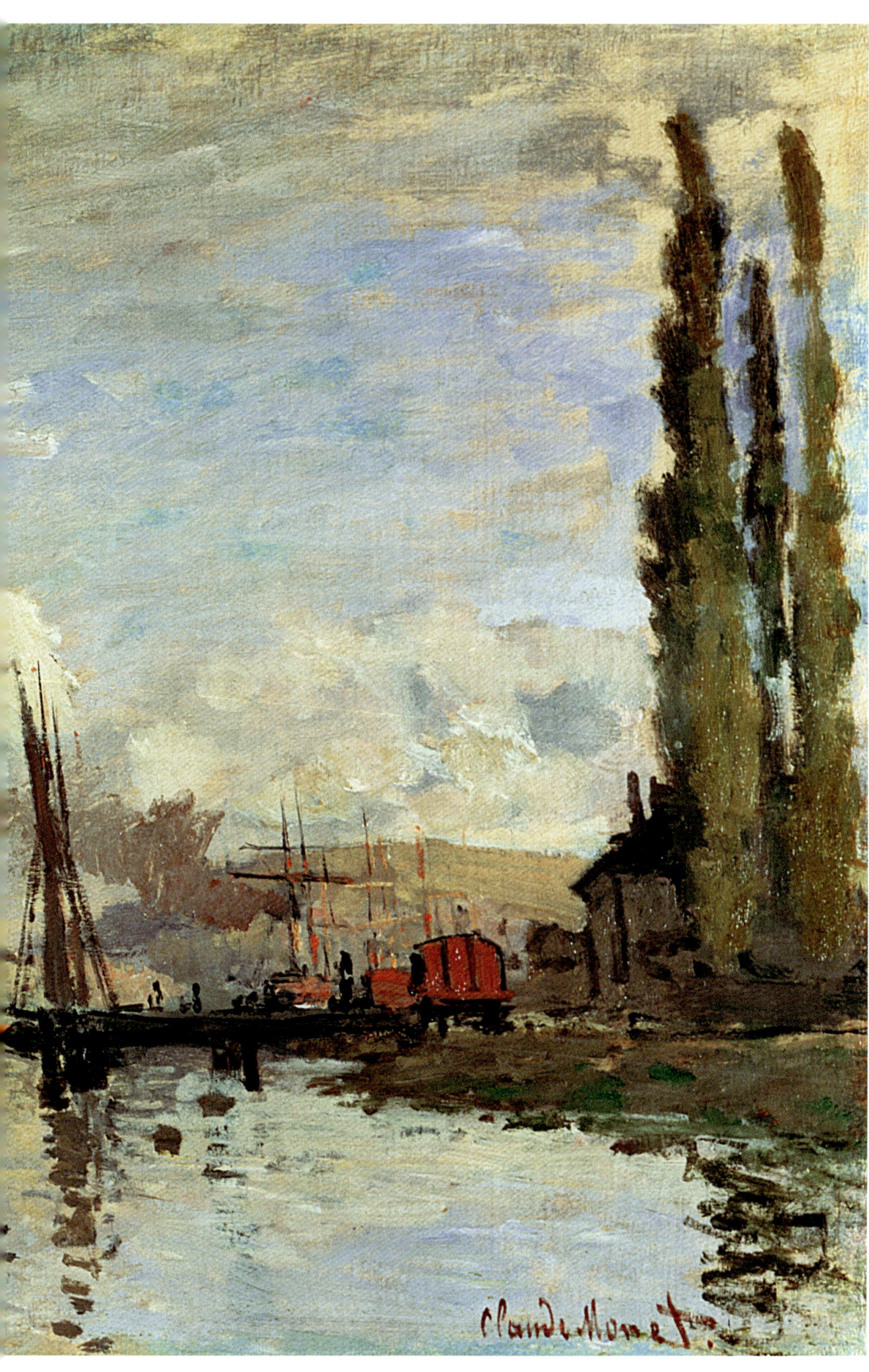

Claude Monet (1840–1926)

The Seine at Rouen

La Seine à Rouen

Die Seine bei Rouen

El Sena a su paso por Rouen

La Senna a Rouen

De Seine bij Rouen

1872, Oil on canvas/Huile sur toile,
49,5 × 77,5 cm, Private collection

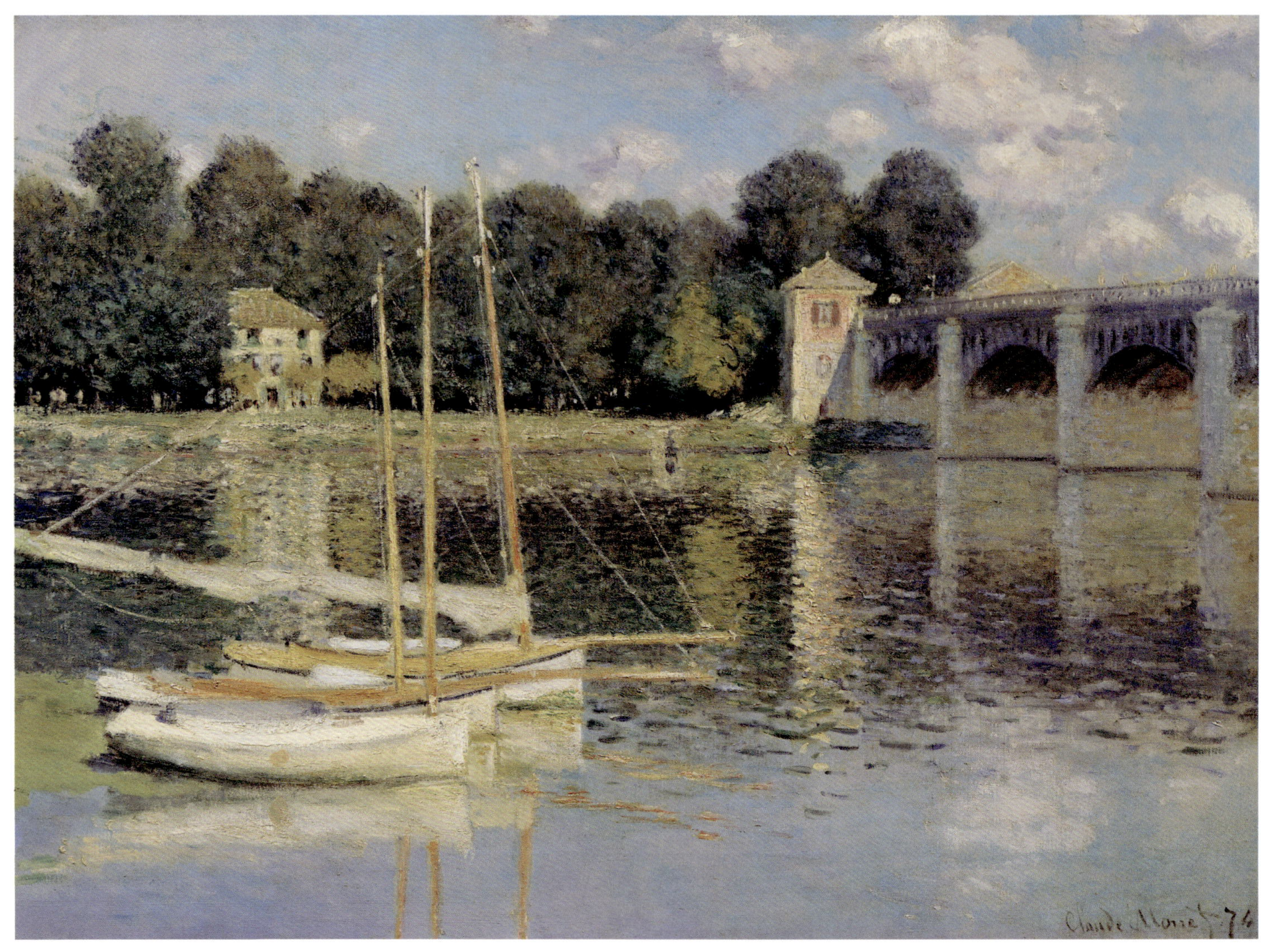

Claude Monet (1840–1926)

The Bridge at Argenteuil

Le pont d'Argenteuil

Die Brücke in Argenteuil

El puente en Argenteuil

Il ponte di Argenteuil

De brug van Argenteuil

1874, Oil on canvas/Huile sur toile, 60,3 × 80 cm, Musée d'Orsay, Paris

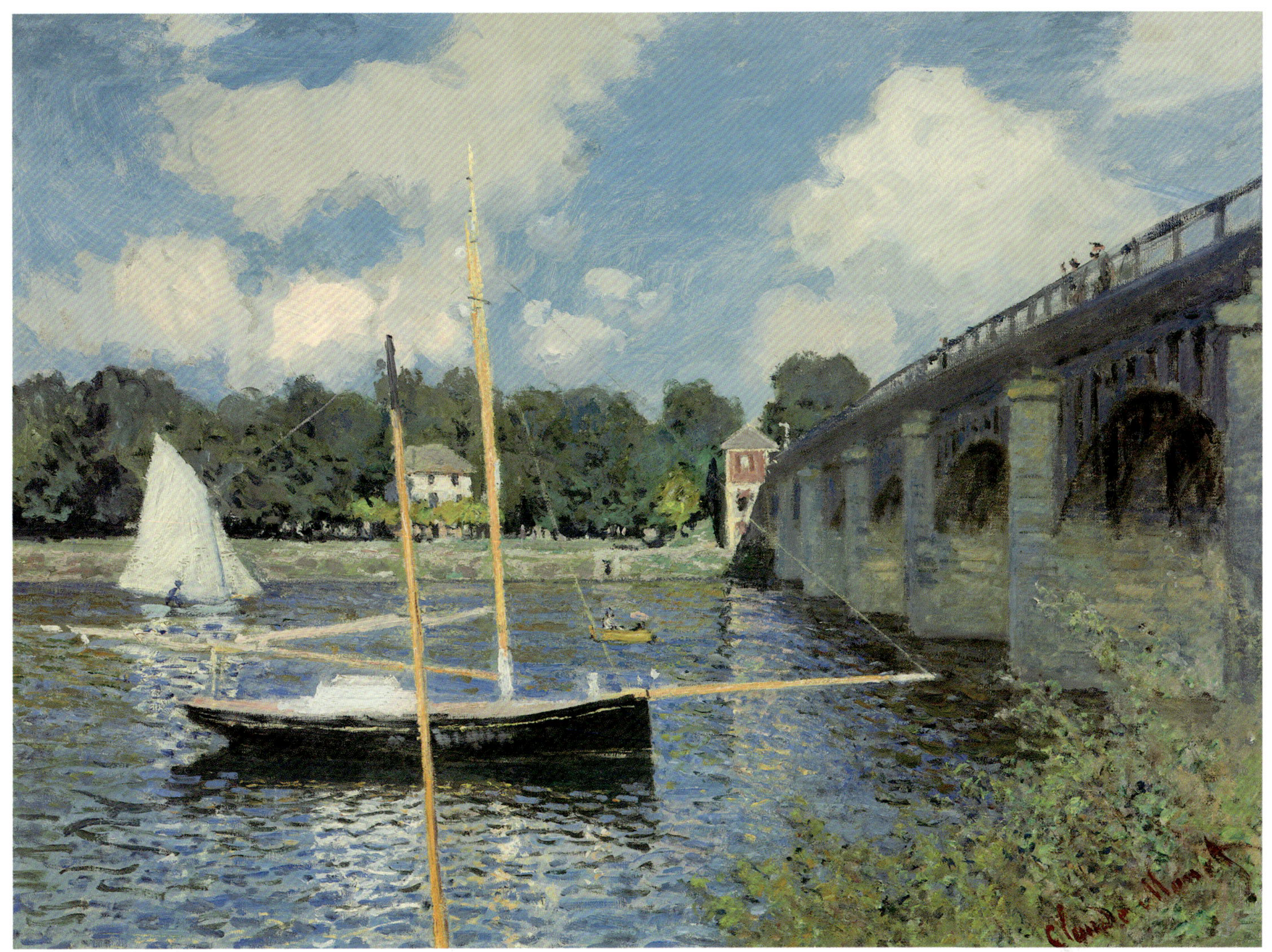

Claude Monet (1840–1926)

The Bridge at Argenteuil

Le pont d'Argenteuil

Die Brücke von Argenteuil

El puente en Argenteuil

Il ponte ad Argenteuil

De brug van Argenteuil

1874, Oil on canvas/Huile sur toile, 60 × 79,7 cm, National Gallery of Art, Washington

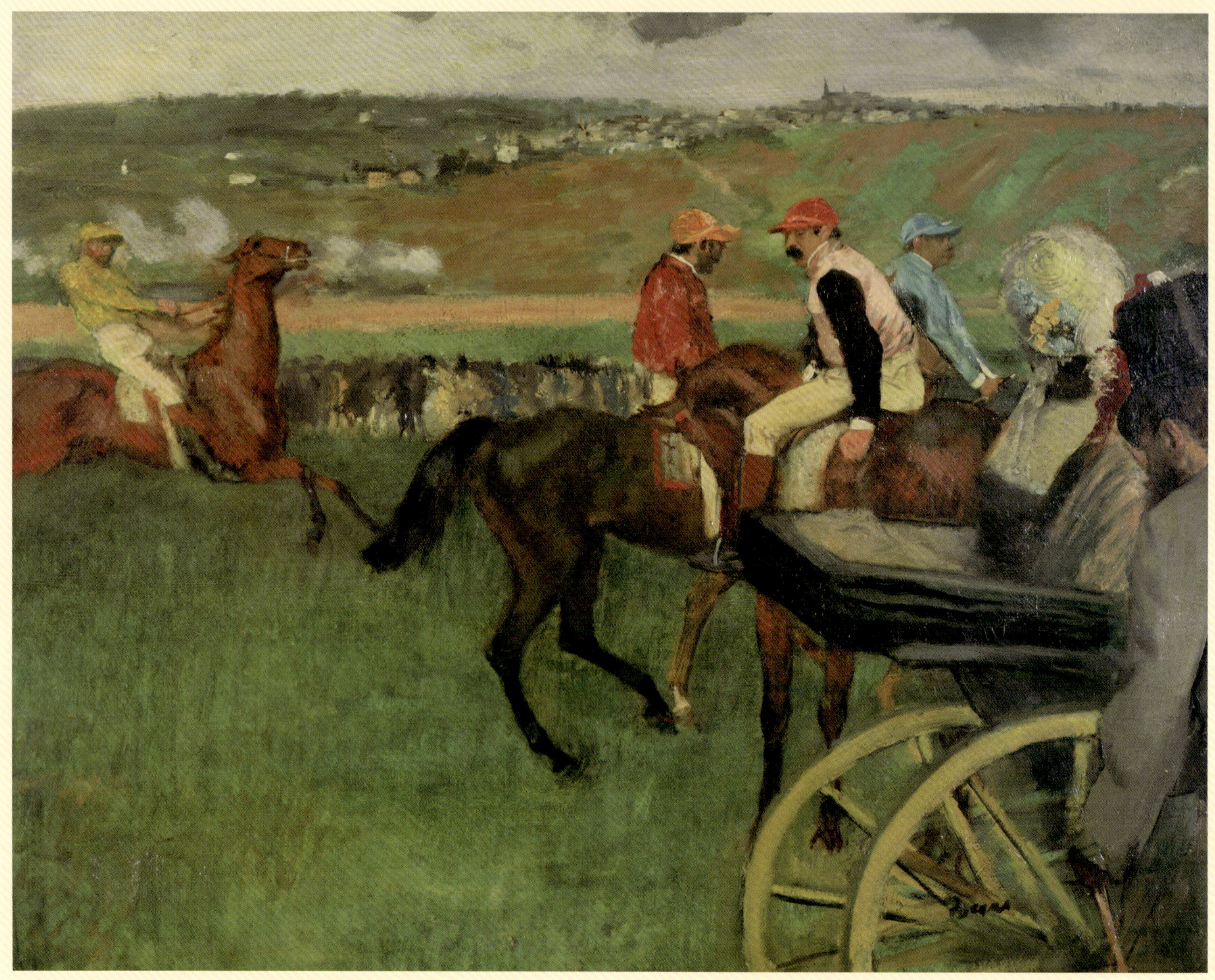

Edgar Degas (1834–1917)

The Race Course – Amateur Jockeys near a Carriage

Le champ de courses. Jockeys amateurs près d'une voiture

Das Pferderennen – Jockeys bei einer Kutsche

La carrera de caballos – Jockeys junto a un carruaje

Il campo di gara: fantini amatoriali vicino a una carrozza

De paardenrennen – Amateurjockeys bij een rijtuig

c. 1876–87, Oil on canvas/Huile sur toile, 65,2 × 81,2 cm, Musée d'Orsay, Paris

Degas always chose unusual perspectives for his paintings of Parisian life. In this scene the steeply aligned viewpoint, a method of photography, leads the eye through the row of waiting jockeys and horses to the bolting horse in the background.

Degas choisissait toujours des perspectives inhabituelles pour ses peintures de la vie parisienne. Dans cette scène, le point de vue fortement aligné, selon une méthode photographique, conduit l'œil à travers la rangée des jockeys qui attendent et les chevaux jusqu'au cheval qui se cabre à l'arrière.

Degas wählte immer ungewöhnliche Perspektiven für seine Bilder des Pariser Lebens. Auch bei dieser Szene fällt der steil fluchtende Blickwinkel auf, ein Mittel aus der Fotografie, der den Blick durch die Reihe der wartende Jockeys und Pferde auf das schreckhaft „durchgehende" Pferd im Hintergrund führt.

Degas escogía siempre perspectivas inusuales para sus imágenes de la vida parisina. En esta escena llama además la atención la perspectiva de fuga inclinada, un medio sacado de la fotografía, que lleva la mirada desde los jockeys y caballos que esperan hacia el caballo que irrumpe, asustado, en la escena.

Degas sceglieva sempre prospettive insolite per i suoi dipinti sulla vita parigina. In questa scena colpisce la prospettiva a fuga, un mezzo tratto dalla fotografia che conduce lo sguardo attraverso la fila di fantini e cavalli in attesa per farlo ricadere sul cavallo "in azione" sullo sfondo.

Voor zijn doeken over het dagelijks leven in Parijs koos Degas ongebruikelijke gezichtspunten. Ook in deze scène valt de scherpe invalshoek op, een methode uit de fotografie, die de blik van de beschouwer langs de wachtende jockeys en paarden naar het 'op hol geslagen' renpaard op de achtergrond voert.

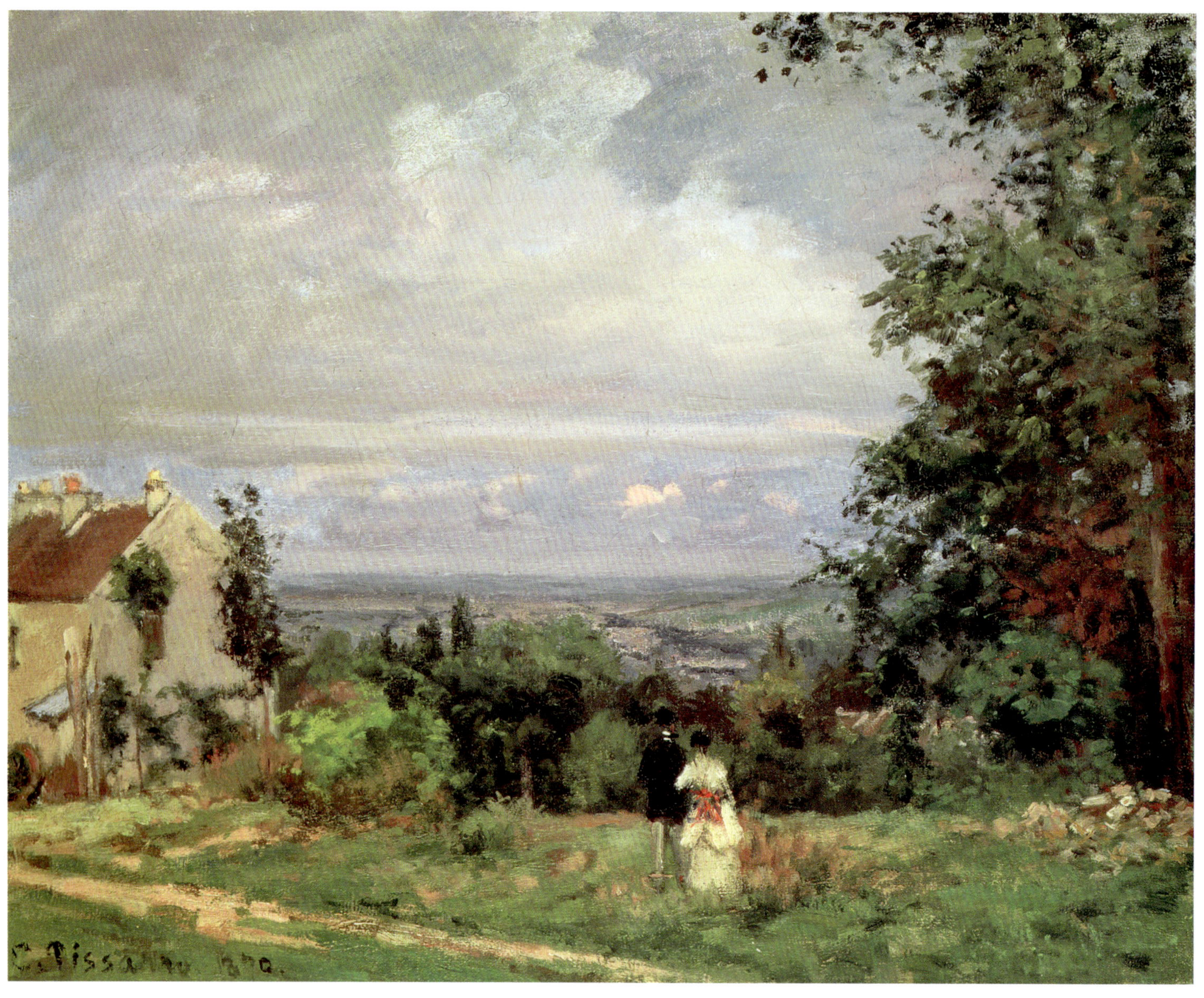

Camille Pissarro (1840–1926)

Louveciennes

Paysage près de Louveciennes

Ansicht von Louveciennes

Vista de Louveciennes

Louveciennes

Gezicht op Louveciennes

1870, Oil on canvas/Huile sur toile, 45,8 × 55,7 cm, Southampton City Art Gallery, Southampton

Claude Monet (1840–1926)

Woman with a Parasol – Madame Monet and Her Son

La promenade, La femme à l'ombrelle

Der Spaziergang – Frau mit Sonnenschirm

El paseo – mujer con sombrilla

La passeggiata – Donna con parasole

De wandeling – vrouw met parasol

1875, Oil on canvas/Huile sur toile, 100 × 81 cm, National Gallery of Art, Washington

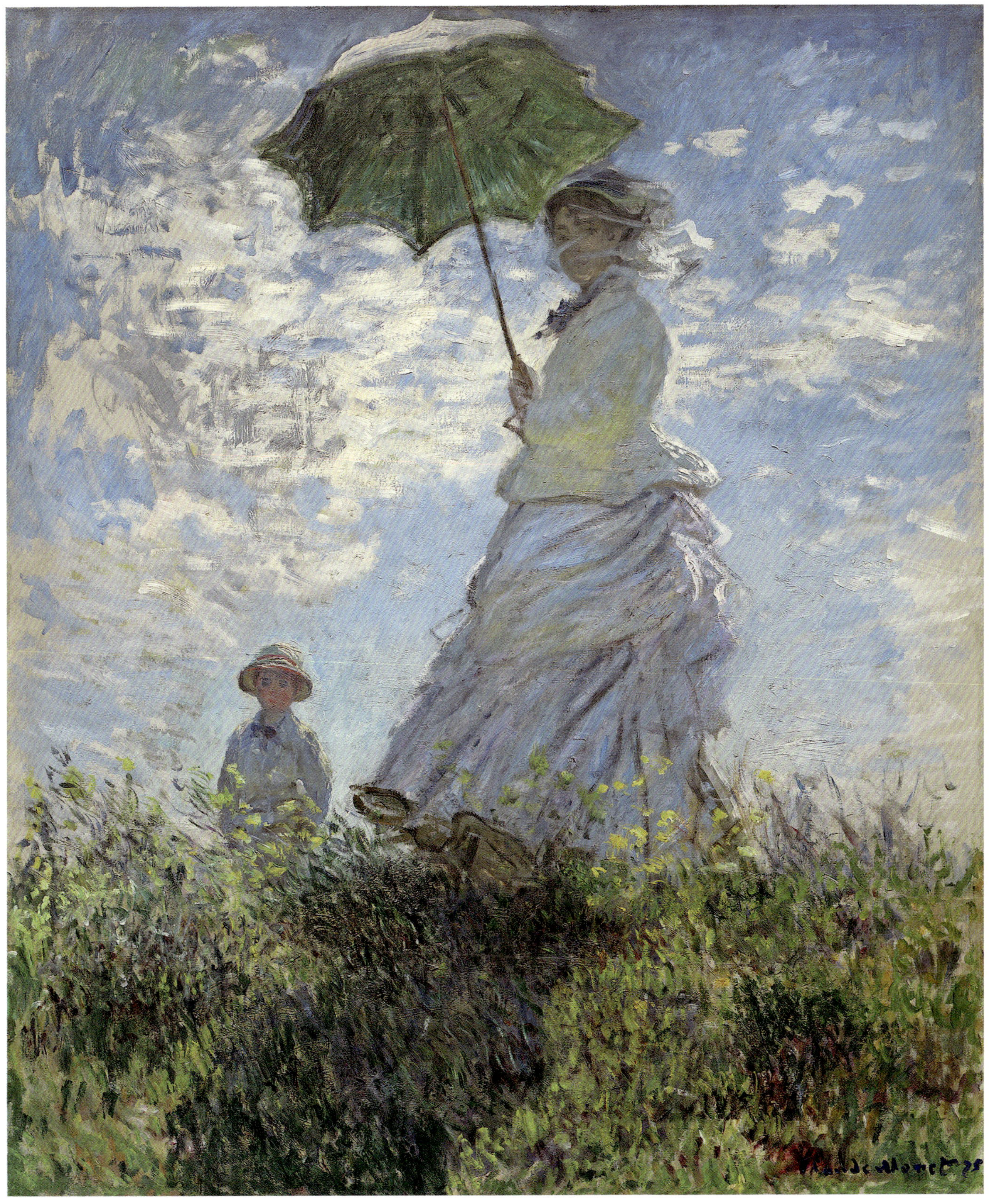

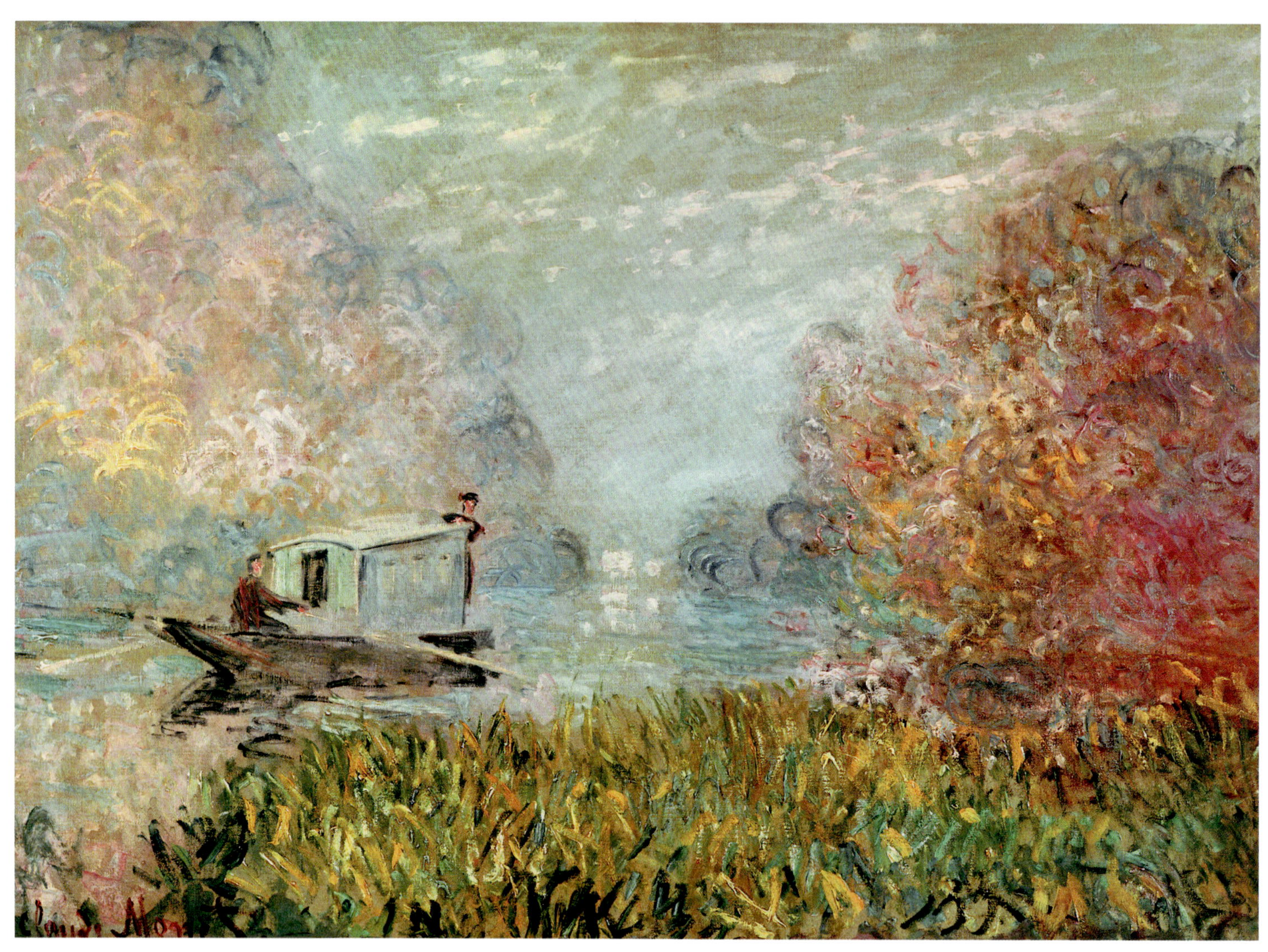

Claude Monet (1840–1926)

The Boat Studio on the Seine

Le bateau-atelier sur la Seine

Das Atelierboot auf der Seine

El bote-estudio en el Sena

La barca-studio sulla Senna

De atelierboot op de Seine

1875, Oil on canvas/Huile sur toile, Private collection

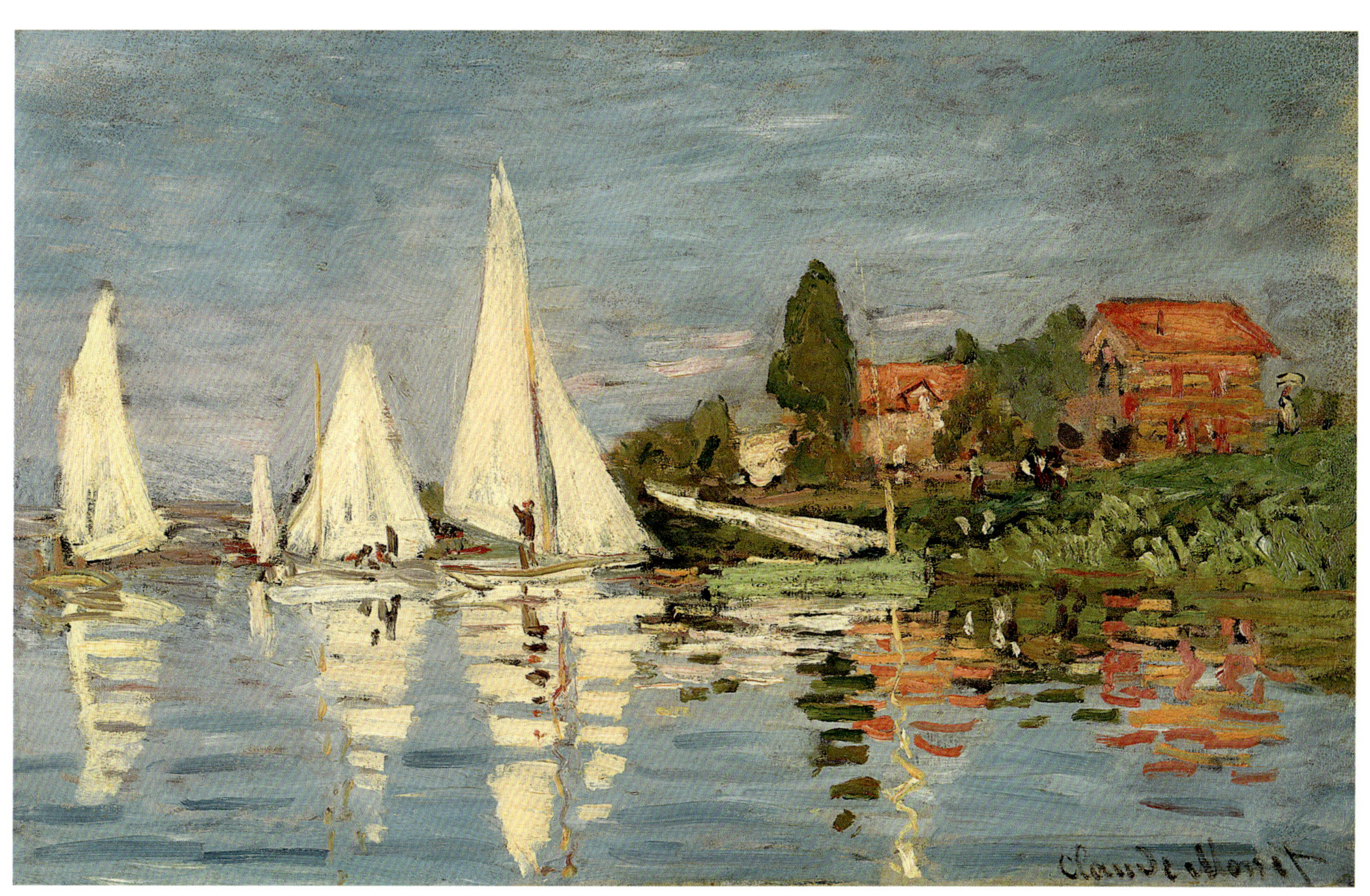

Claude Monet (1840–1926)

Regatta at Argenteuil

Régates à Argenteuil

Regatta in Argenteuil

Regata en Argenteuil

Regata ad Argenteuil

Regatta in Argenteuil

c. 1872, Oil on canvas/Huile sur toile, 48 × 75 cm, Musée d'Orsay, Paris

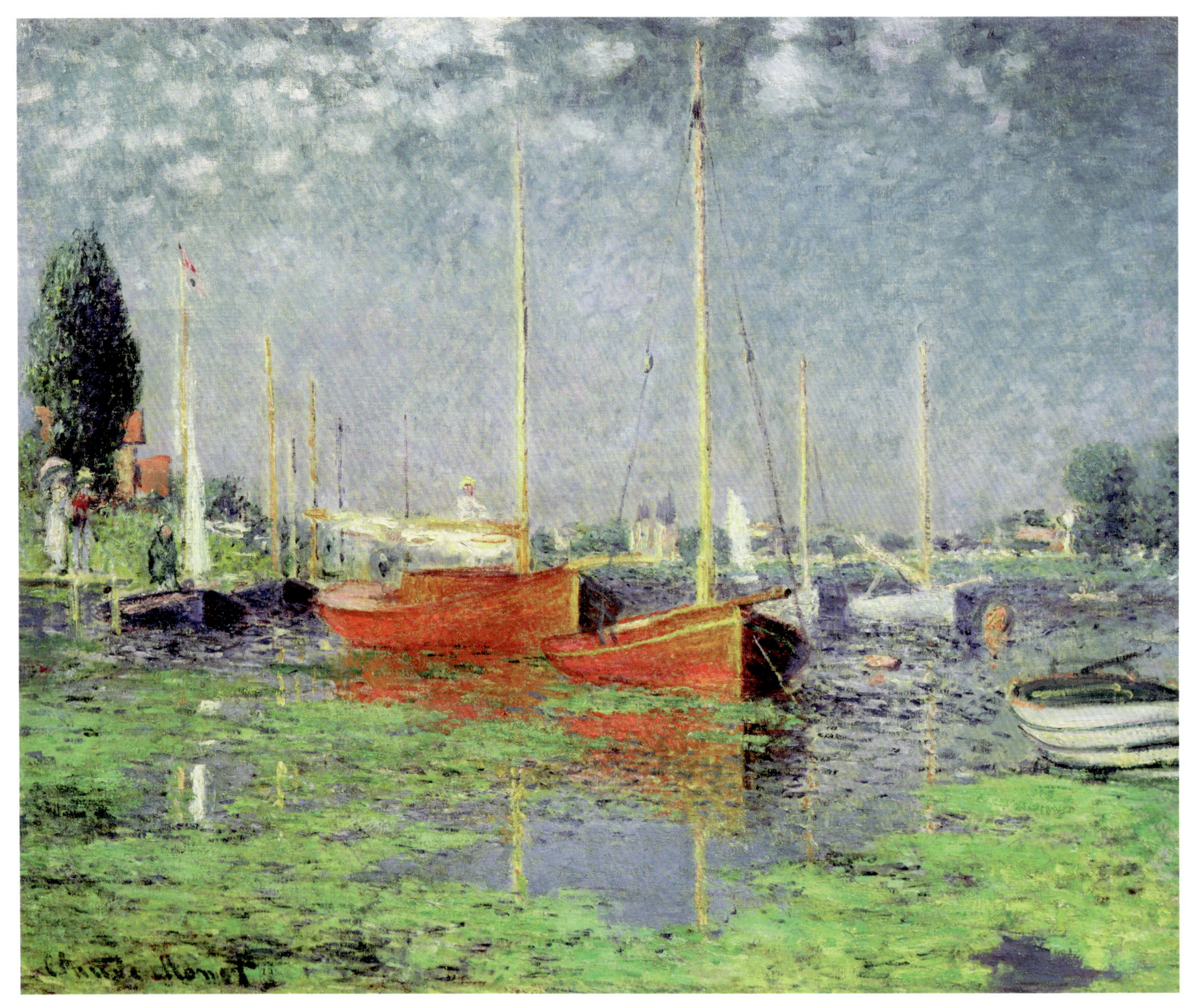

Claude Monet (1840–1926)

Argenteuil

1875, Oil on canvas/Huile sur toile, 56 × 67 cm, Musée de l'Orangerie, Paris

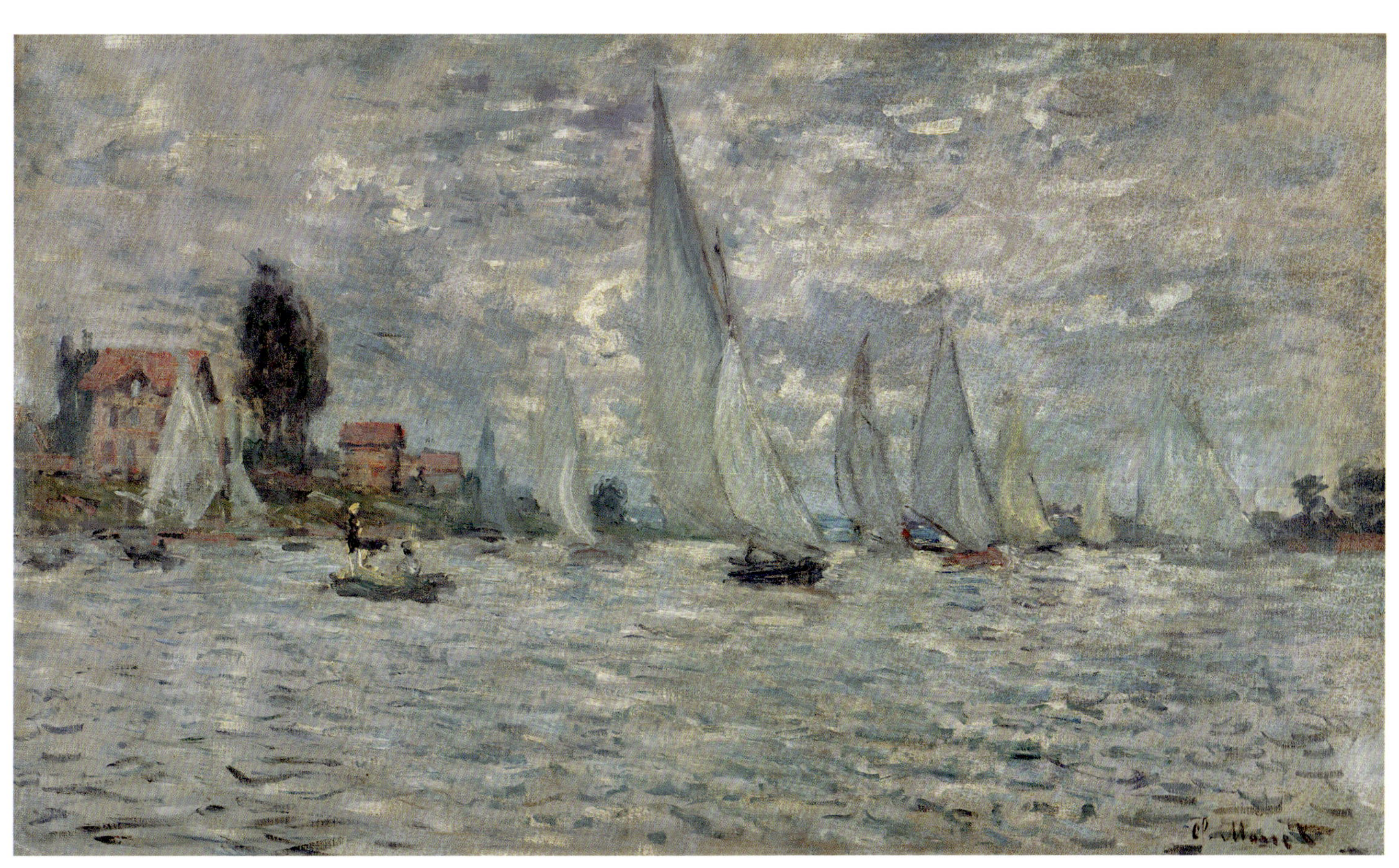# Claude Monet (1840–1926)

The Boats *or* Regatta at Argenteuil

Régates à Argenteuil

Regatta in Argenteuil

Regata en Argenteuil

Regata ad Argenteuil

Regatta in Argenteuil

c. 1874, Oil on canvas/Huile sur toile, 60,5 × 105 cm, Musée d'Orsay, Paris

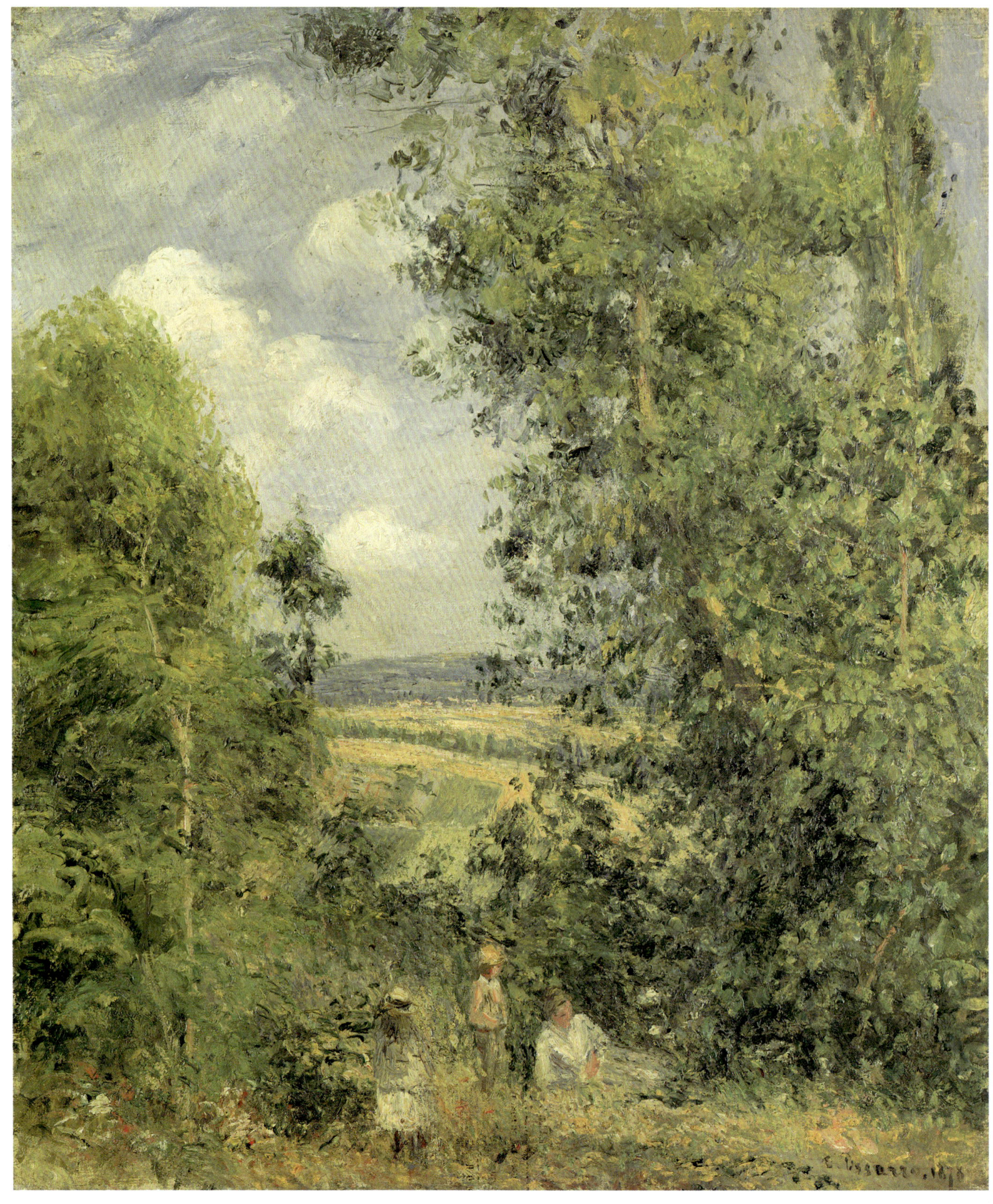

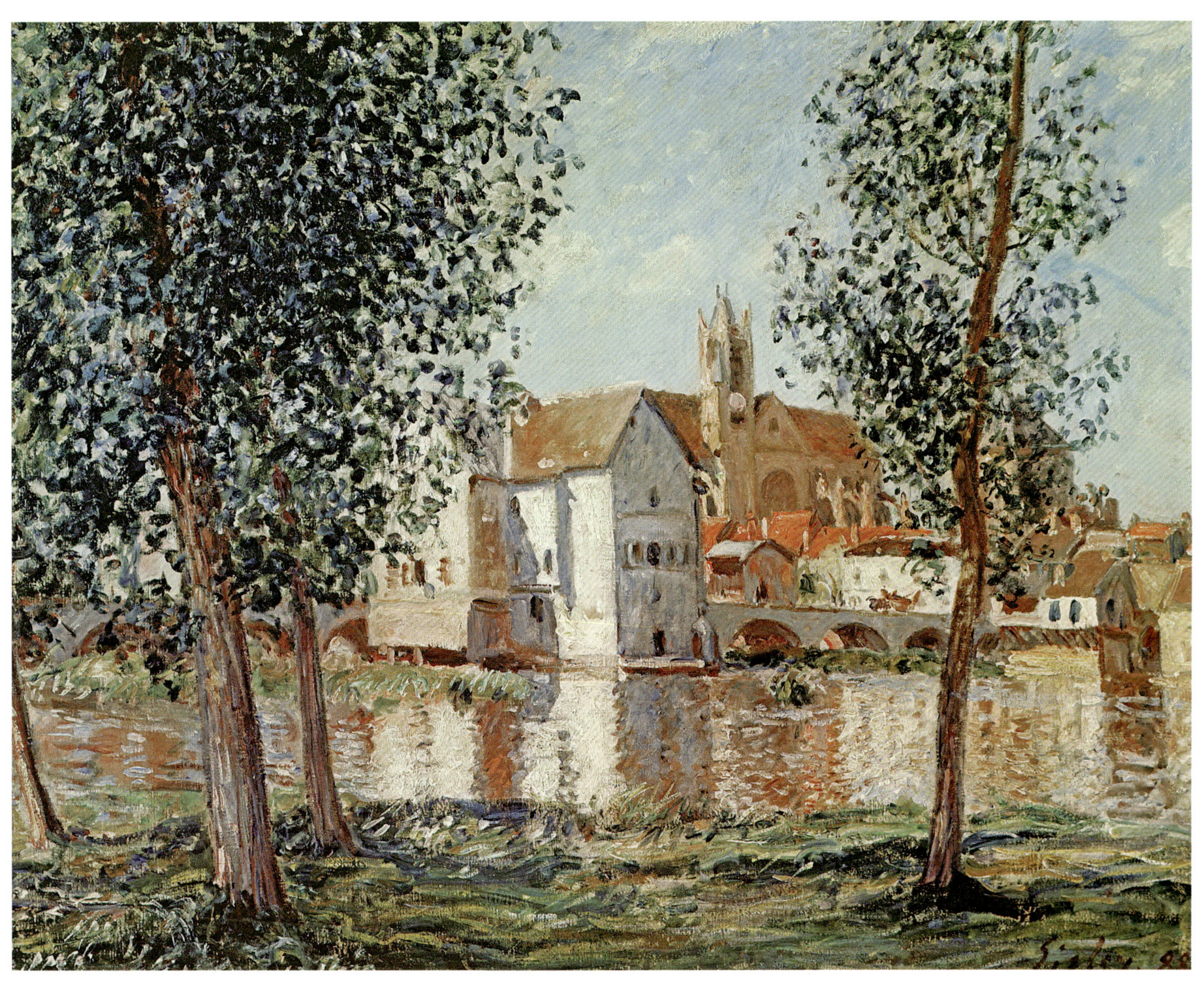

Camille Pissarro (1830–1903)

A Rest in the Meadow

Un repos dans la prairie

Rast unter Bäumen bei Pontoise

Una pausa en la pradera

Riposo sul prato

Rust in de bossen bij Pontoise

1878, Oil on canvas/Huile sur toile, 65 × 54 cm, Kunsthalle, Hamburg

Alfred Sisley (1839–99)

The Loing at Moret

Moret-sur-Loing au soleil levant

Moret am Ufer des Loing

Moret a orillas del Loing

Moret sulle rive della Loing

Moret aan de oever van de Loing

1888, Oil on canvas/Huile sur toile, 73 × 60 cm, Private collection

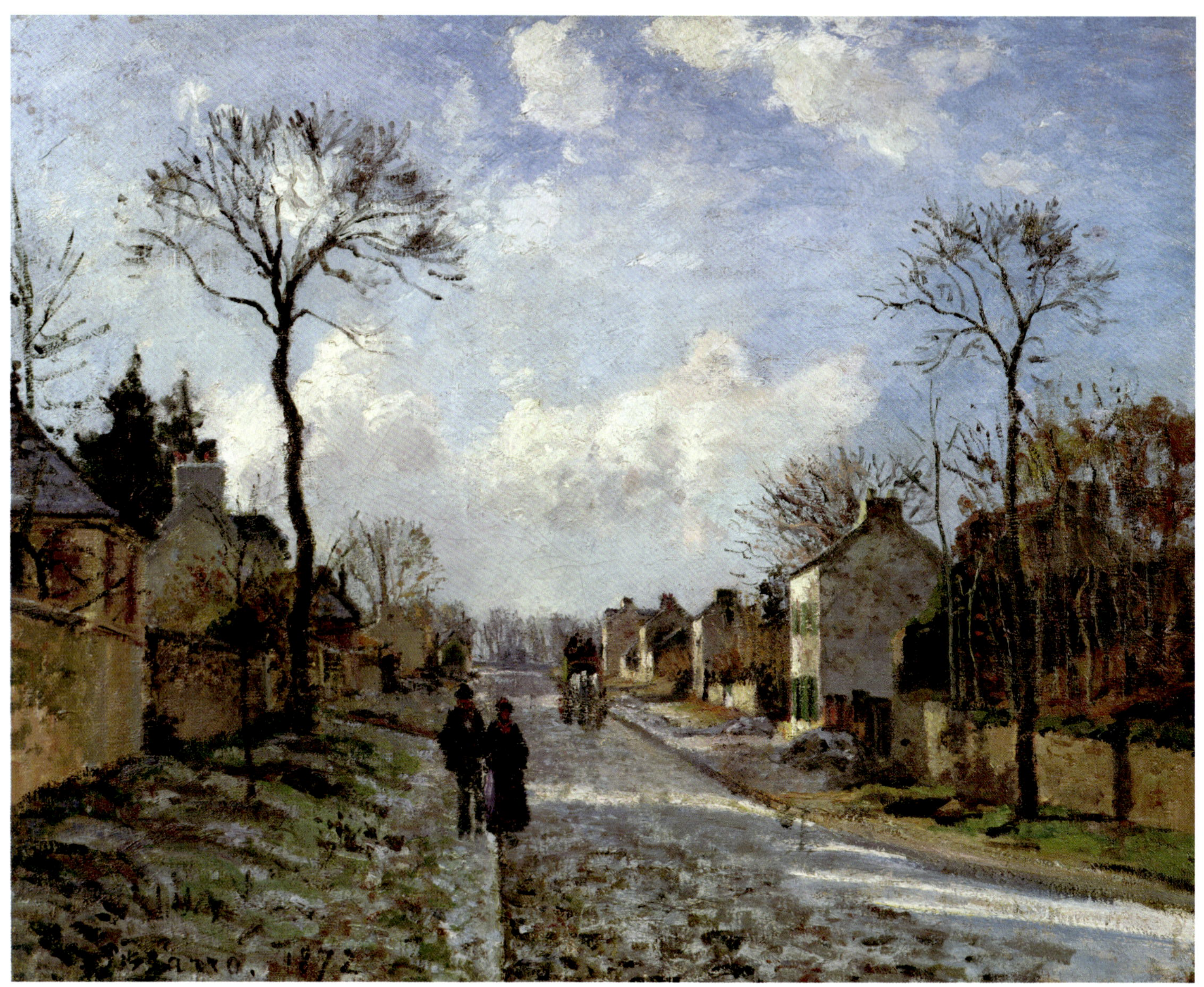

Camille Pissarro (1830–1903)

The Road to Louveciennes
La route de Louveciennes
Die Straße nach Louveciennes
La carretera hacia Louveciennes
La strada per Louveciennes
De weg naar Louveciennes

1872, Oil on canvas/Huile sur toile, 59,8 × 73,5 cm, Musée d'Orsay, Paris

Claude Monet (1840–1926)

The Artist's Garden at Vetheuil
Le jardin de l'artiste à Vetheuil
Der Garten des Künstlers in Vetheuil
El jardín del artista en Vetheuil
Il giardino di Monet a Vetheuil
De tuin van de kunstenaar in Vetheuil

1880, Oil on canvas/Huile sur toile, 151,5 × 121 cm, National Gallery of Art, Washington

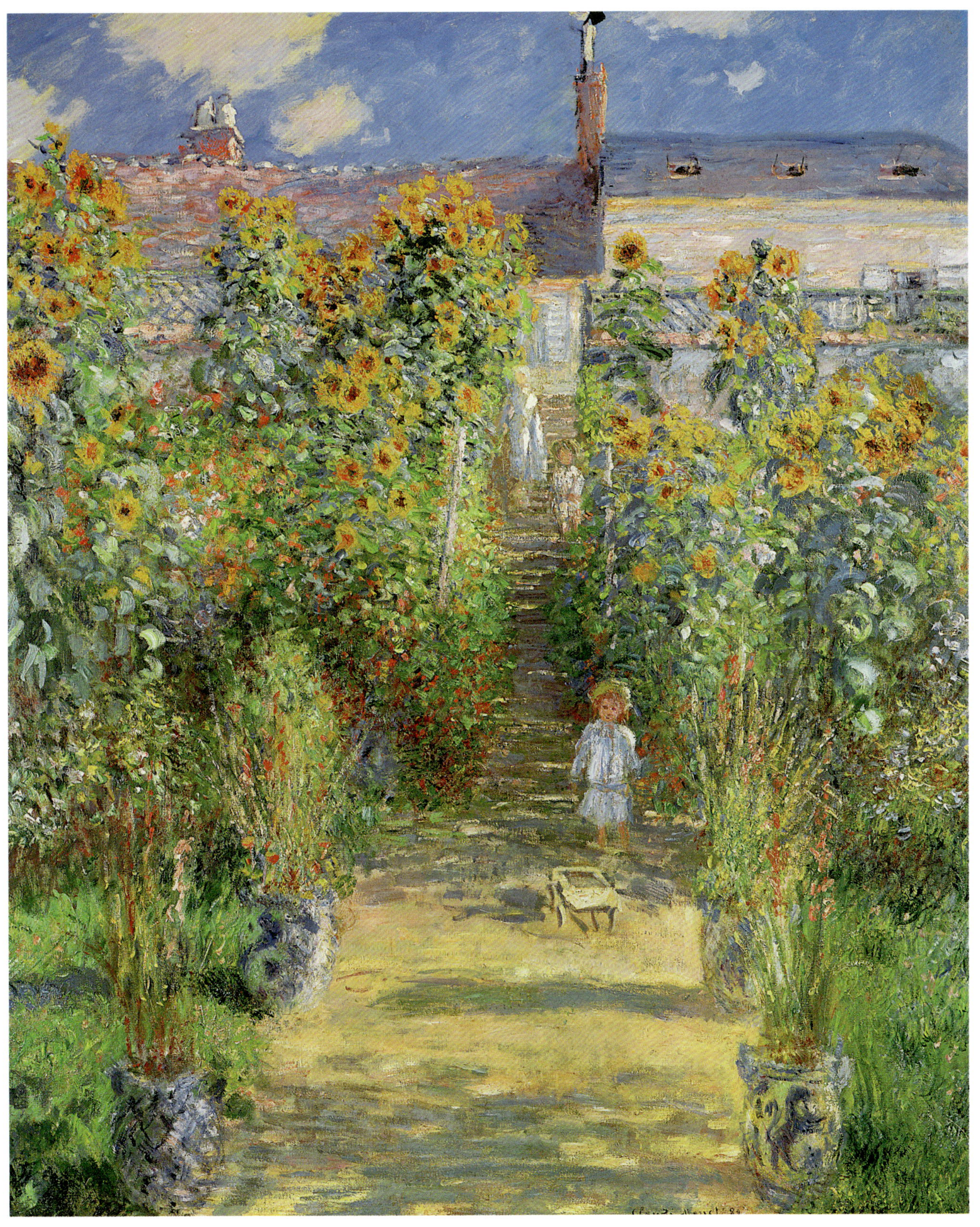

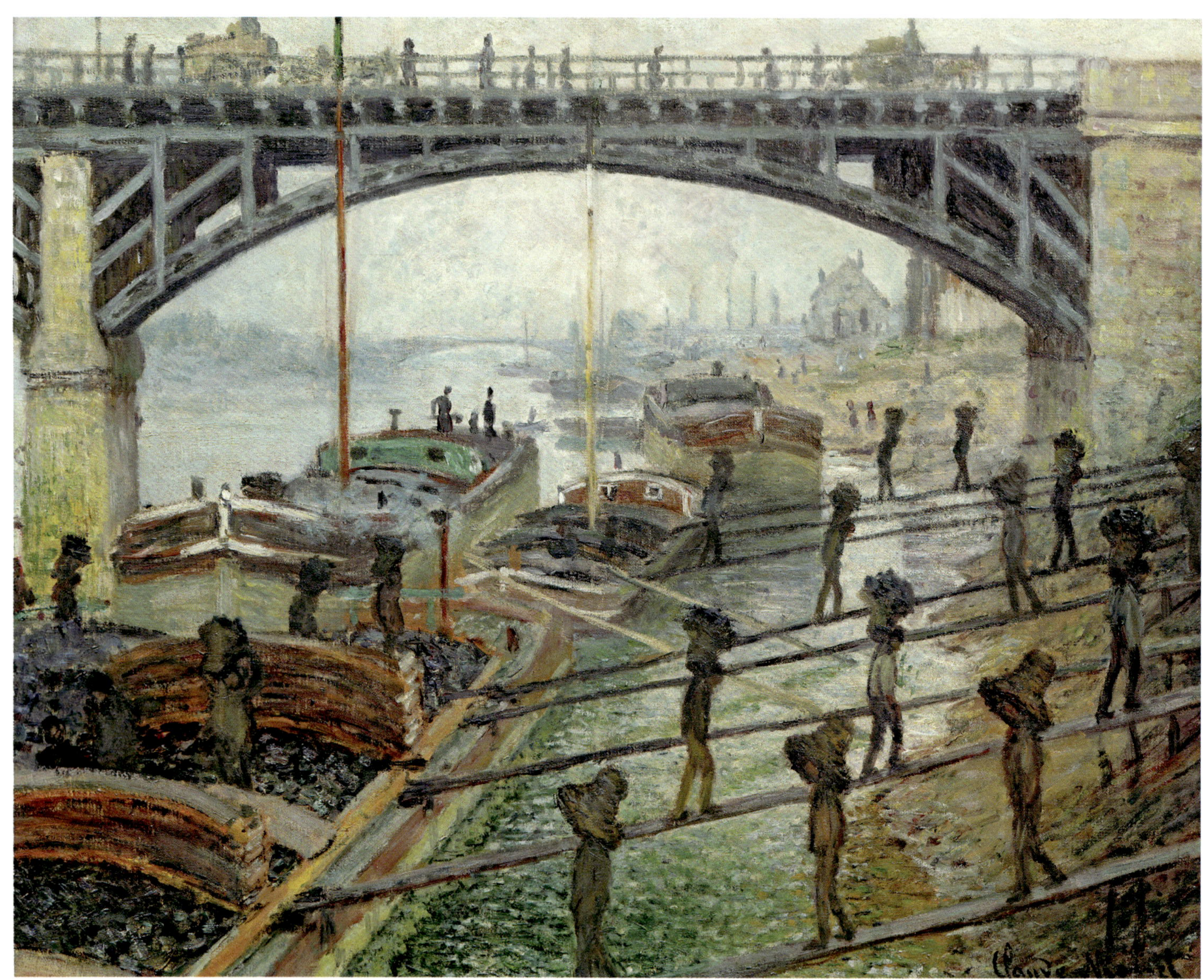

Claude Monet (1840–1926)

The Coal Workers

Les charbonniers

Die Kohlenträger

Los carboneros

I carbonai o Gli Scaricatori di carbone

De kolensjouwers

c. 1875, Oil on canvas/Huile sur toile, 54 × 65,5 cm, Musée d'Orsay, Paris

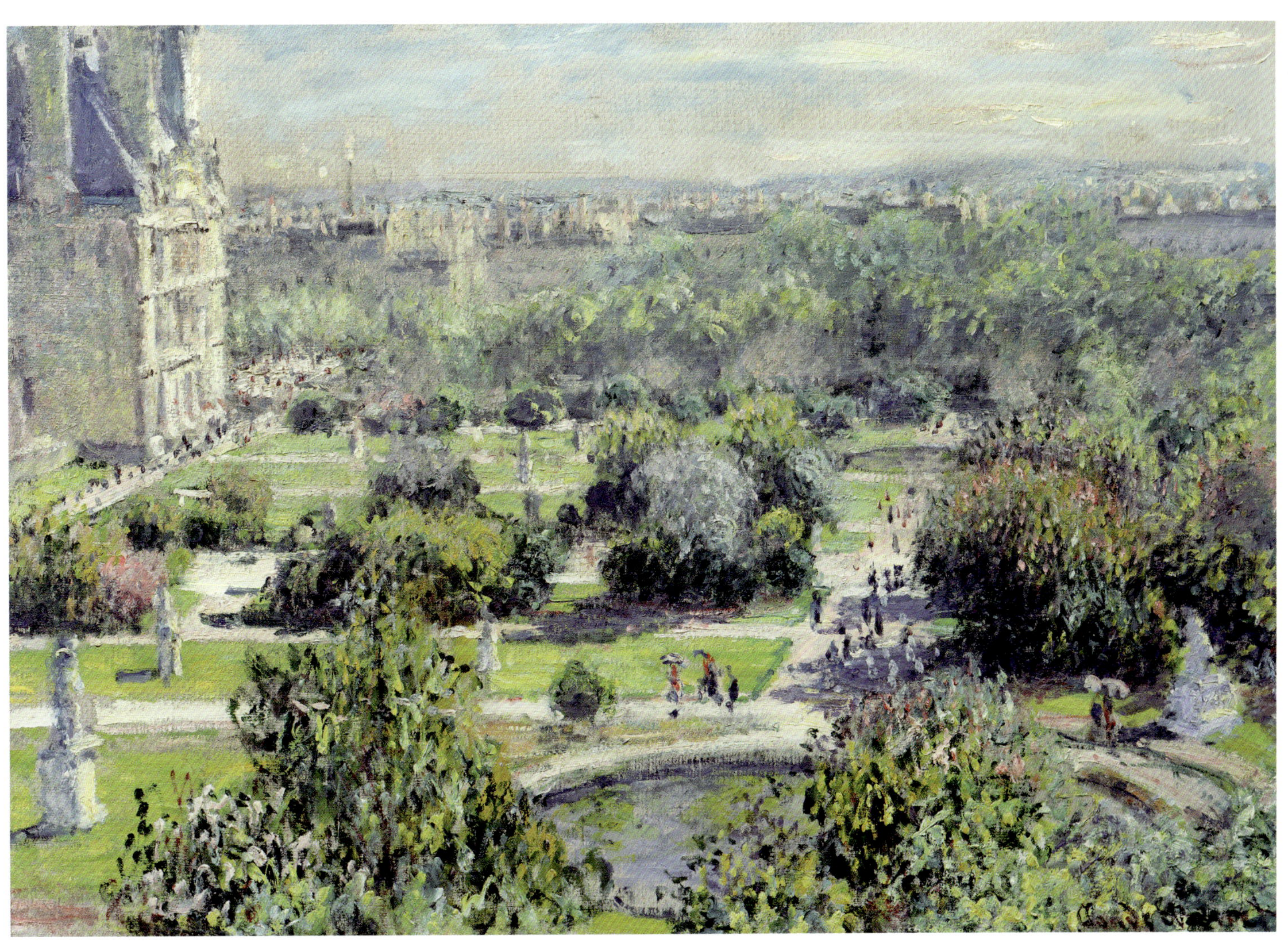

Claude Monet (1840–1926)

View of the Tuileries Gardens, Paris

Vue des Tuileries

Blick auf die Tuilerien

Vista del Jardín de las Tullerías

Paama dei giardini delle Tuileries

Gezicht op de Tuilerieën

1876, Oil on canvas/Huile sur toile, 54 × 73 cm, Musée Marmottan Monet, Paris

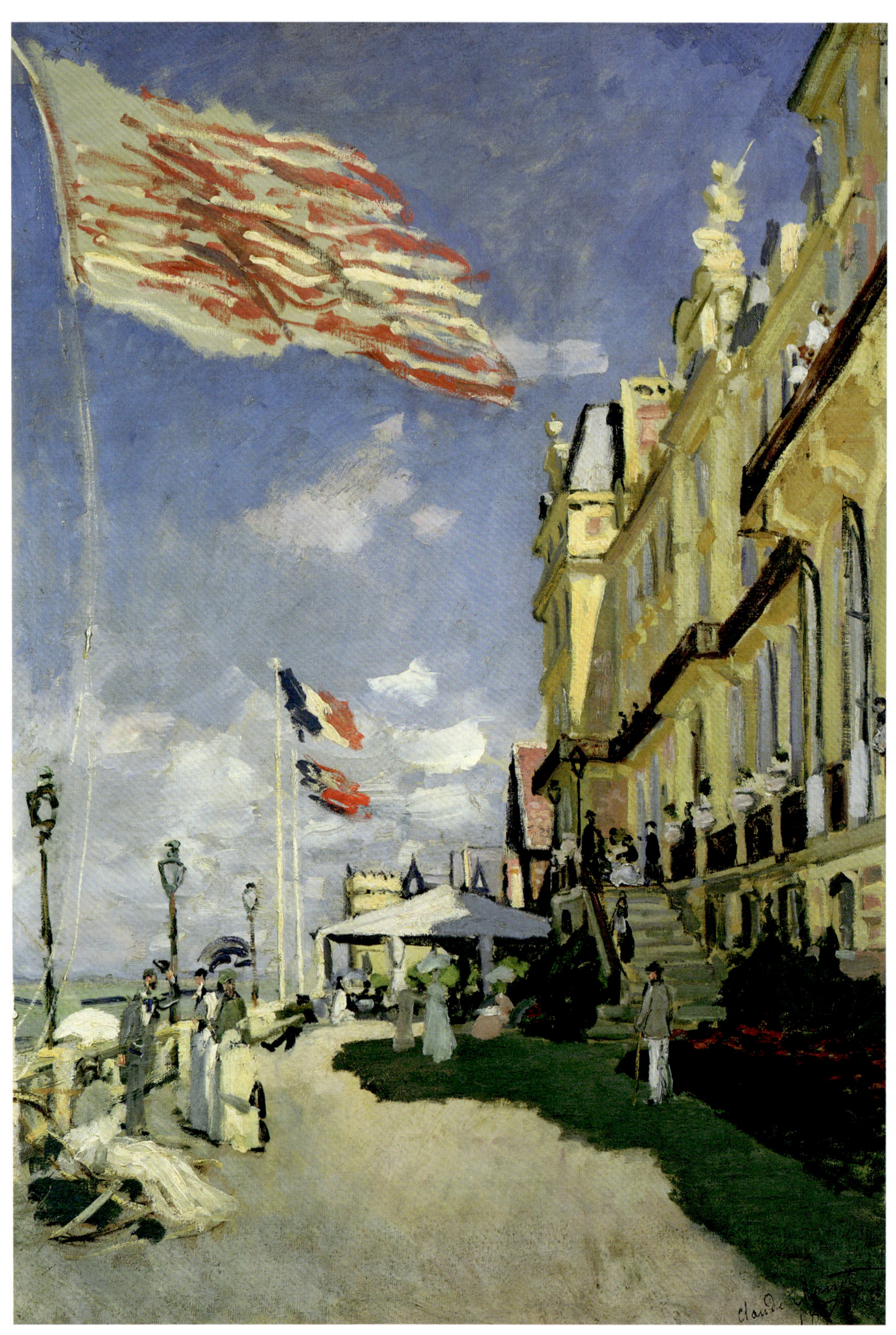

Claude Monet (1840–1926)

The Hôtel des Roches
Noires at Trouville

Hôtel des roches Noires, Trouville

Das Hôtel des Roches
Noires in Trouville

El Hôtel de Roches Noires en Trouville

Hôtel des Roches Noires a Trouville

Het Hôtel des Roches
Noires in Trouville

1870, Oil on canvas/Huile sur toile,
81 × 58 cm, Musée d'Orsay, Paris

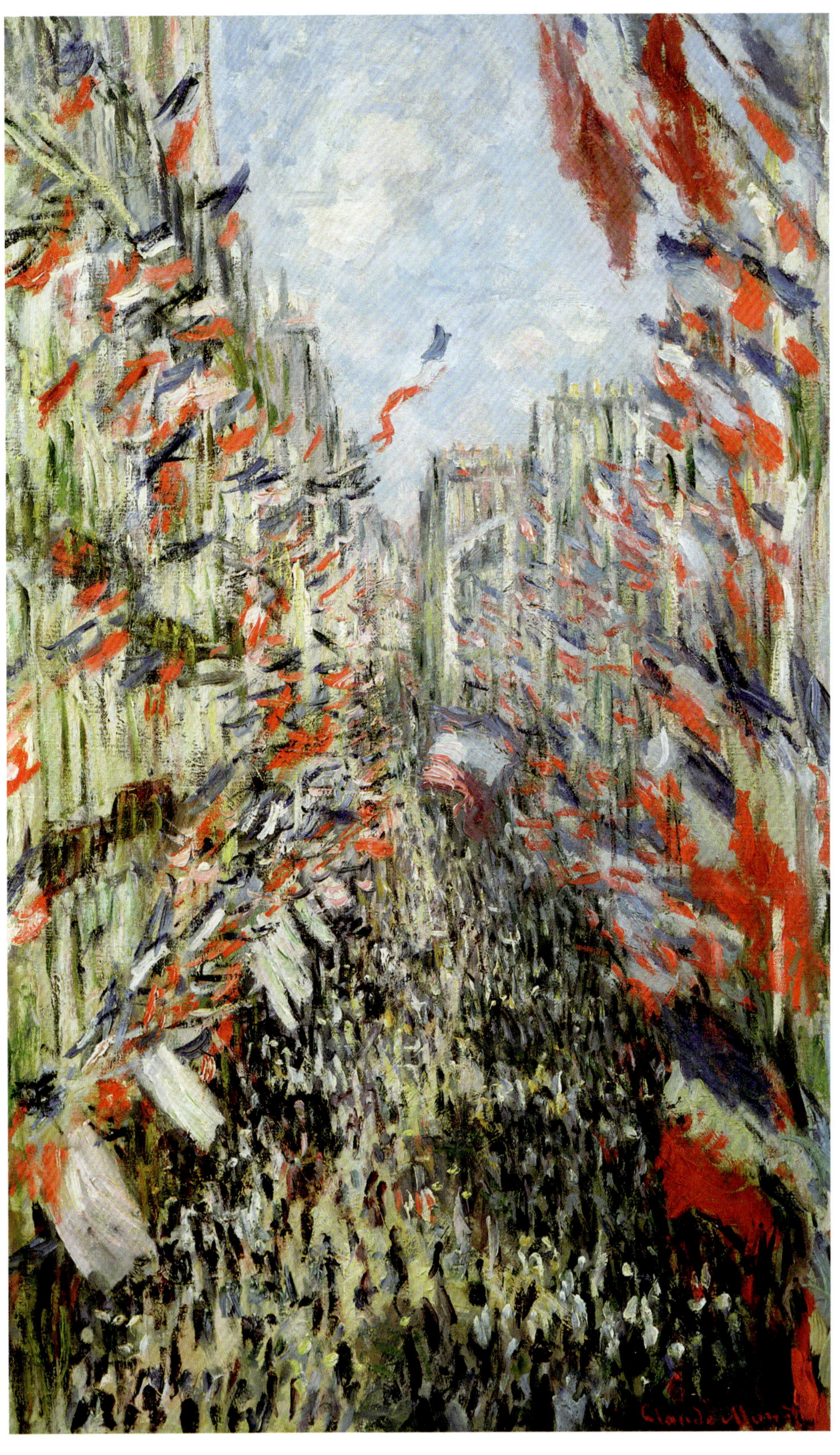

Claude Monet (1840–1926)

The Rue Montorgueil, Paris, Celebration of June 30 1878

La rue Montorgueil, à Paris. Fête du 30 juin 1878

Die Rue Montorgueil in Paris am 30. Juni 1878

La calle Montorgueil en París el 30 de junio

La Rue Montorgueil a Parigi (Festa del 30 giugno 1878)

De Rue Montorgueil in Paris op de 30ste juli 1878

1878, Oil on canvas/Huile sur toile, 81 × 50 cm,
Musée d'Orsay, Paris

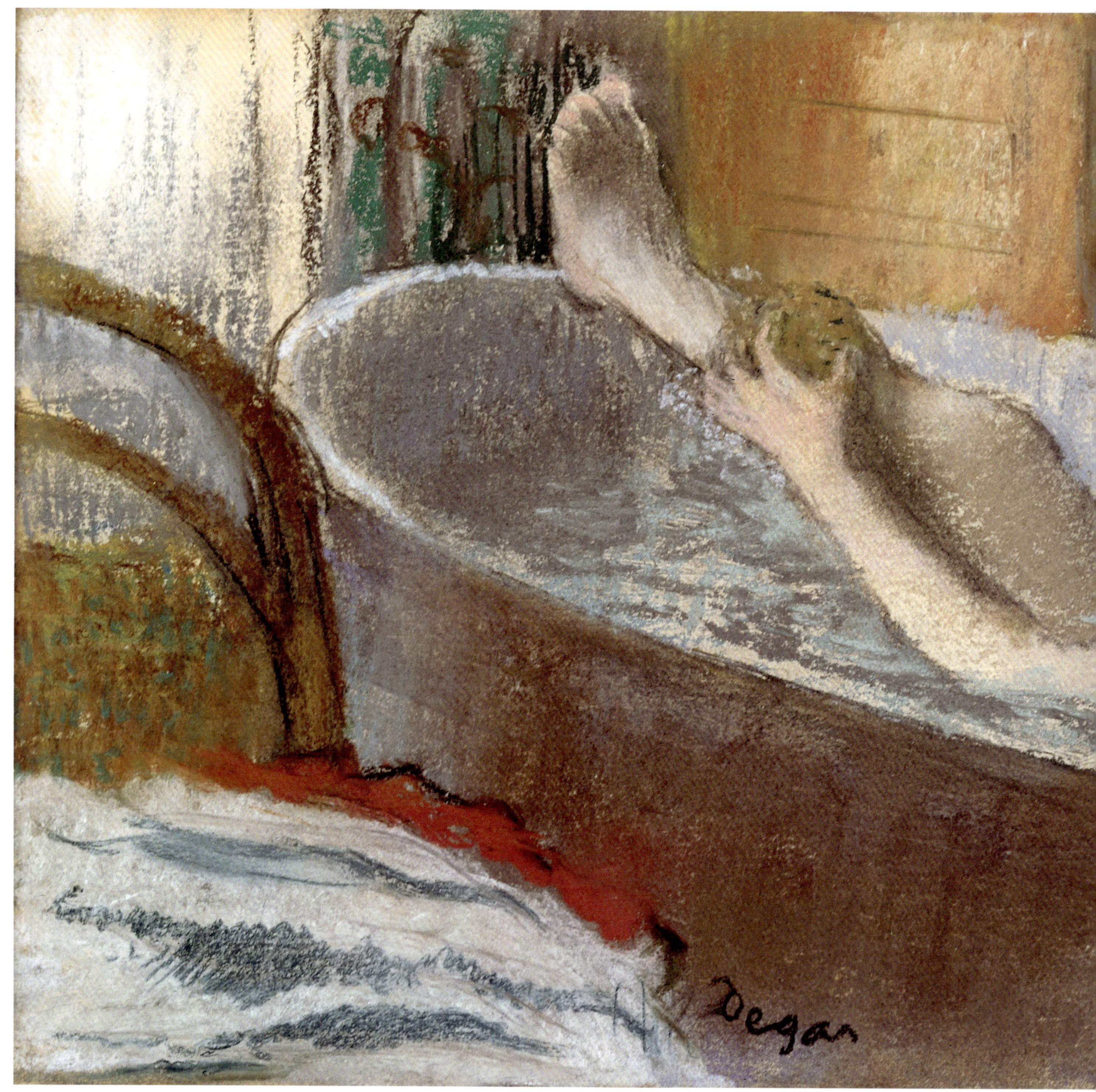

Edgar Degas (1834–1917)

Woman in her Bath, Sponging her Leg

Femme dans son bain s'épongeant la jambe

Frau im Bad, sich das Bein waschend

Mujer en baño lavándose la pierna

Donna nel suo bo che si lava la gamba

Vrouw die in bad haar been wast

c. 1883, Pastel on monotype/Pastel sur monotype, 19,7 × 41 cm, Musée d'Orsay, Paris

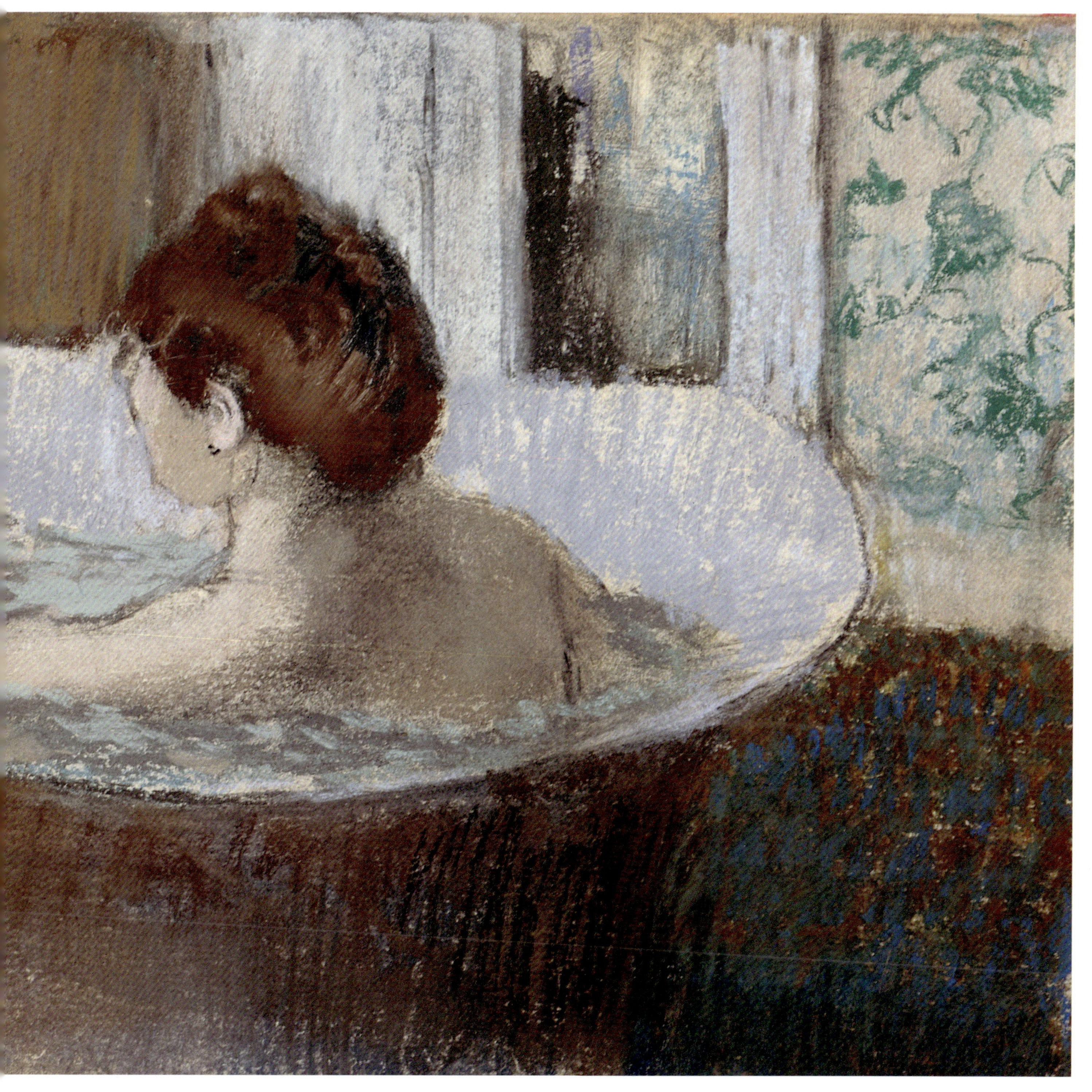

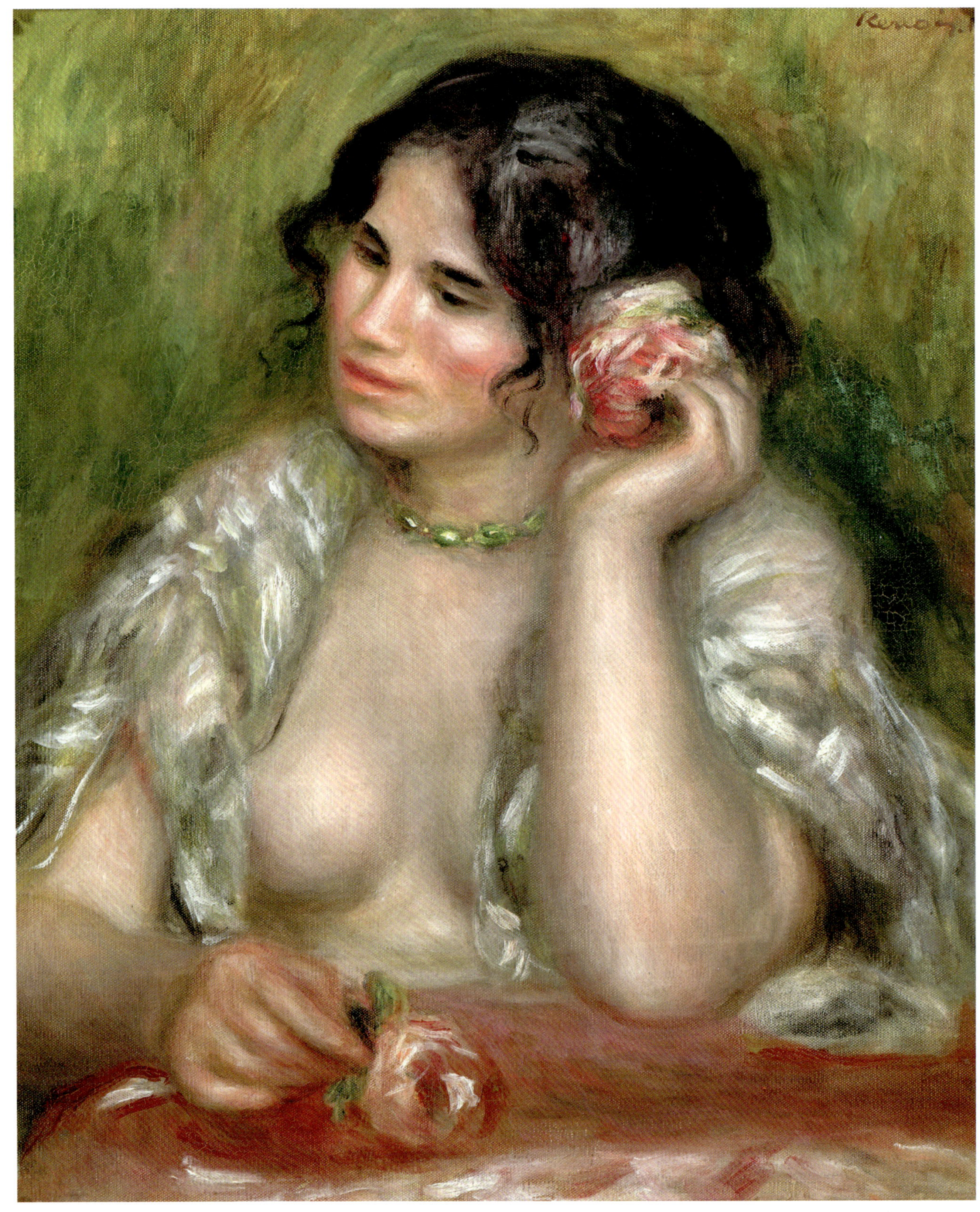

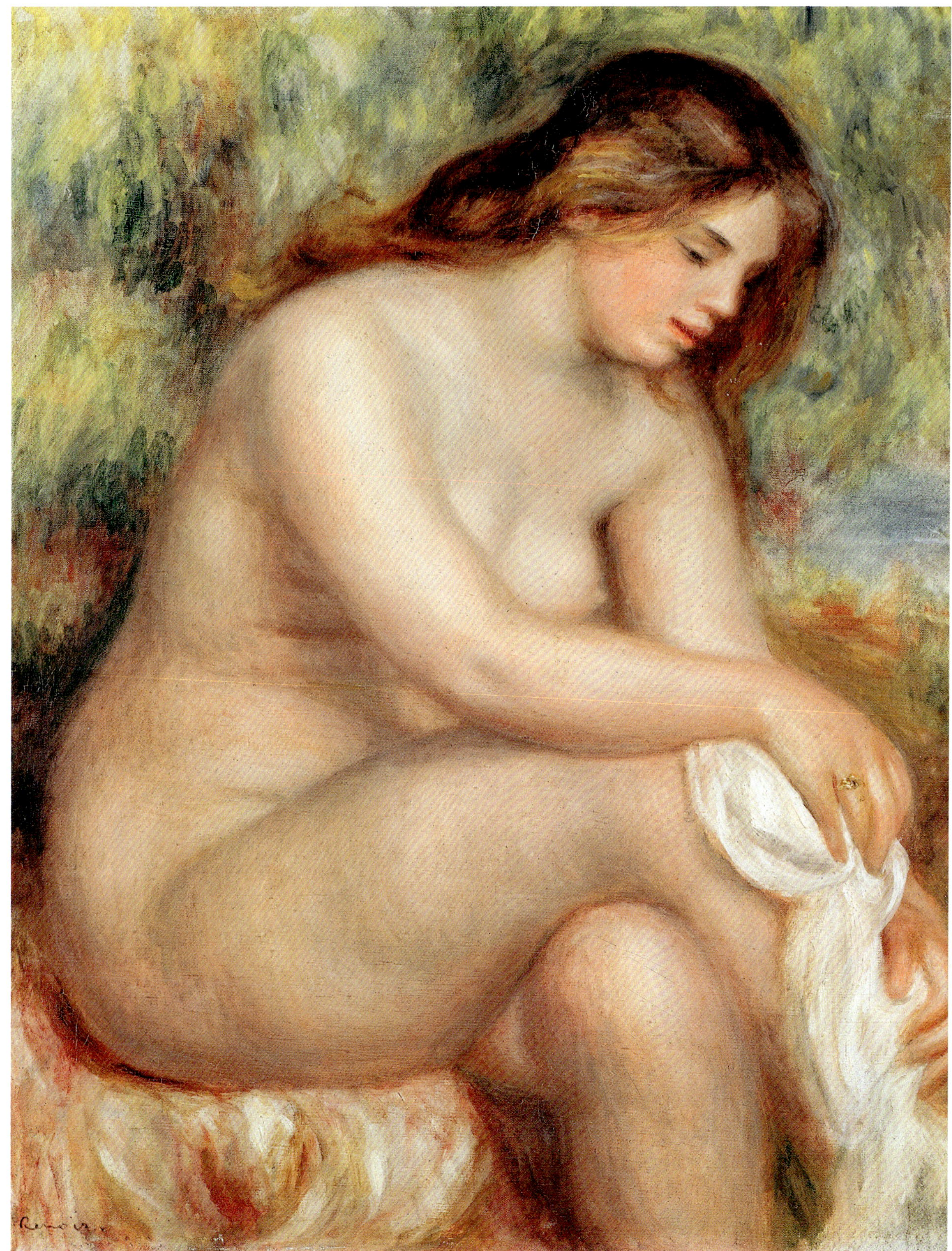

Pierre-Auguste Renoir
(1841–1919)

Gabrielle with a Rose

Gabrielle à la rose

Gabrielle mit Rose

Gabrielle con una rosa

Gabrielle con la rosa
o La donna siciliana

Gabrielle met roos

1911, Oil on canvas/Huile
sur toile, 55,5 × 47 cm,
Musée d'Orsay, Paris

Pierre-Auguste Renoir
(1841–1919)

Bather Drying Herself

Baigneuse assise
s'essuyant une jambe

Badende, sich
abtrocknend

Bañista secándose

Bante che si asciuga
una gamba

Baadster die
zich afdroogt

c. 1910, Oil on
canvas/Huile sur
toile, 84 × 65 cm,
Museu de Arte de São
Paulo, São Paulo

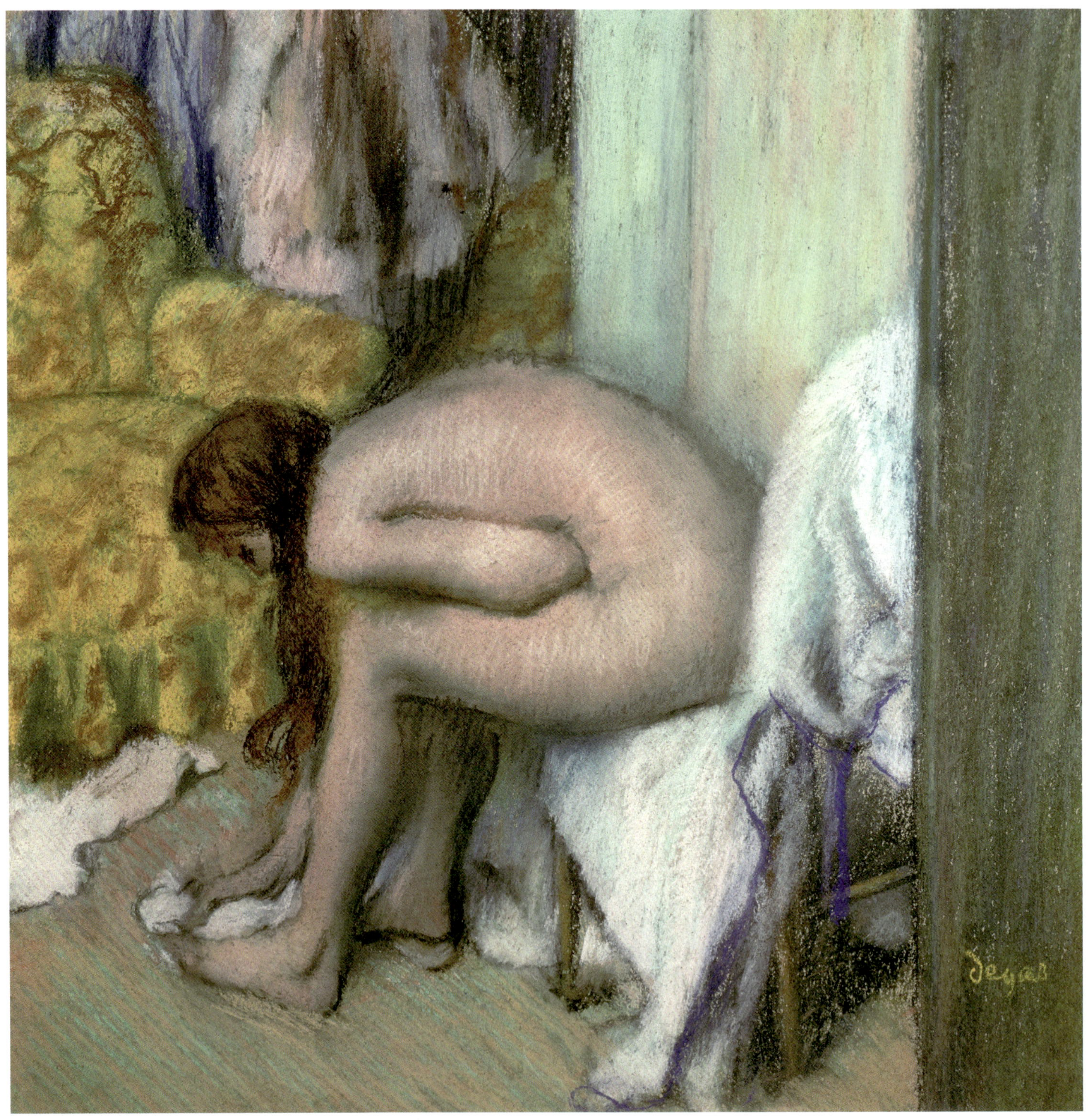

Edgar Degas (1834–1917)

After the Bath, Woman Drying her Left Foot

Femme à sa toilette essuyant son pied gauche

Nach dem Bad. Frau, sich den linken Fuß abtrocknend

Tras el baño. Mujer secándose el pie izquierdo

Dopo il bo, donna che si asciuga il piede sinistro

Na het bad. Vrouw die haar linkervoet afdroogt

1886, Pastel on cardboard/Pastel sur carton, 54,3 × 52,4 cm, Musée d'Orsay, Paris

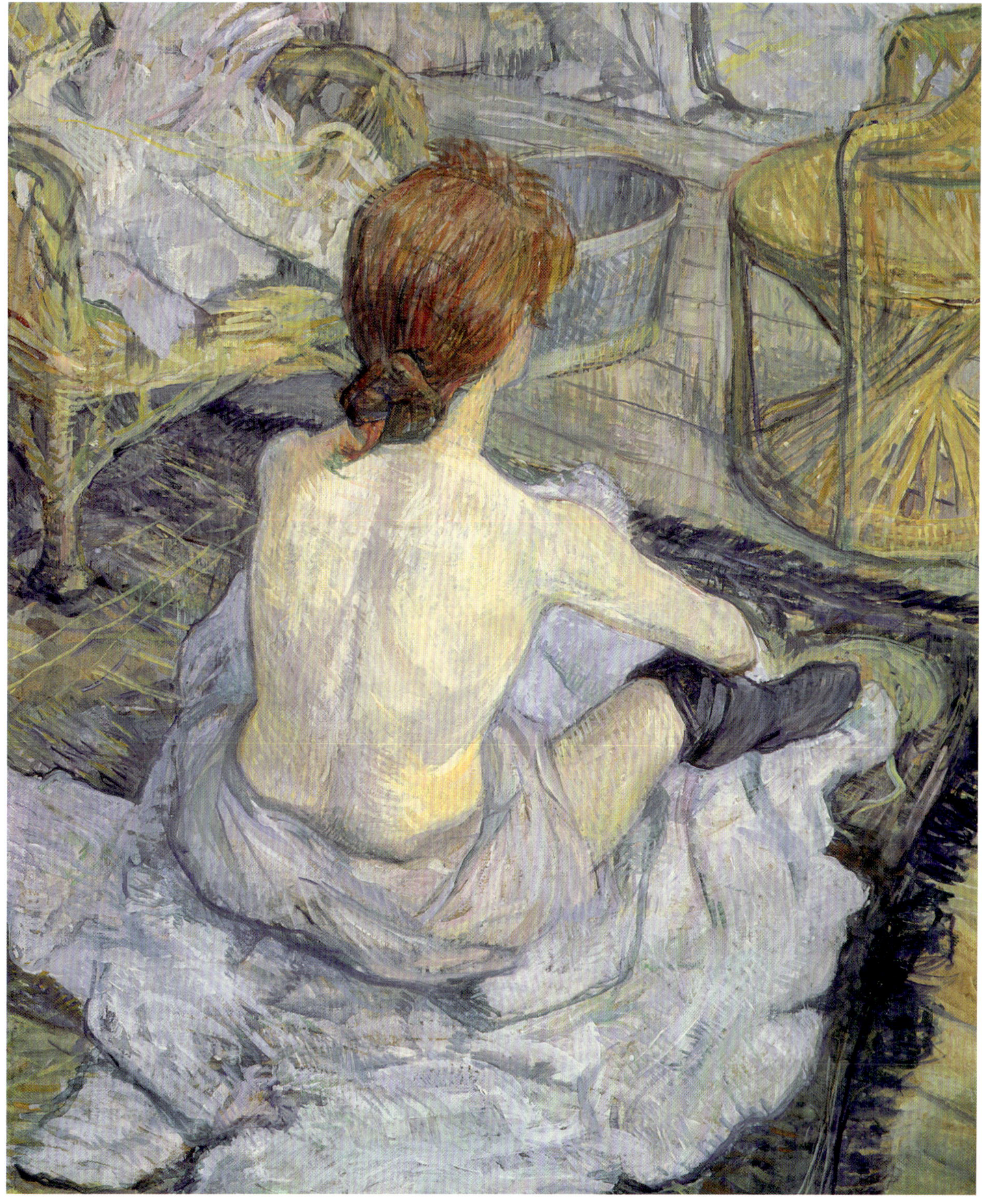

Henri de Toulouse-Lautrec (1864–1901)

Woman at her Toilet   Frau bei der Toilette   Donna alla sua toilette

Femme à sa toilette   Mujer en el baño   Vrouw bij het toilet

1898, Oil on cardboard/Huile sur carton, 67 × 54 cm, Musée d'Orsay, Paris

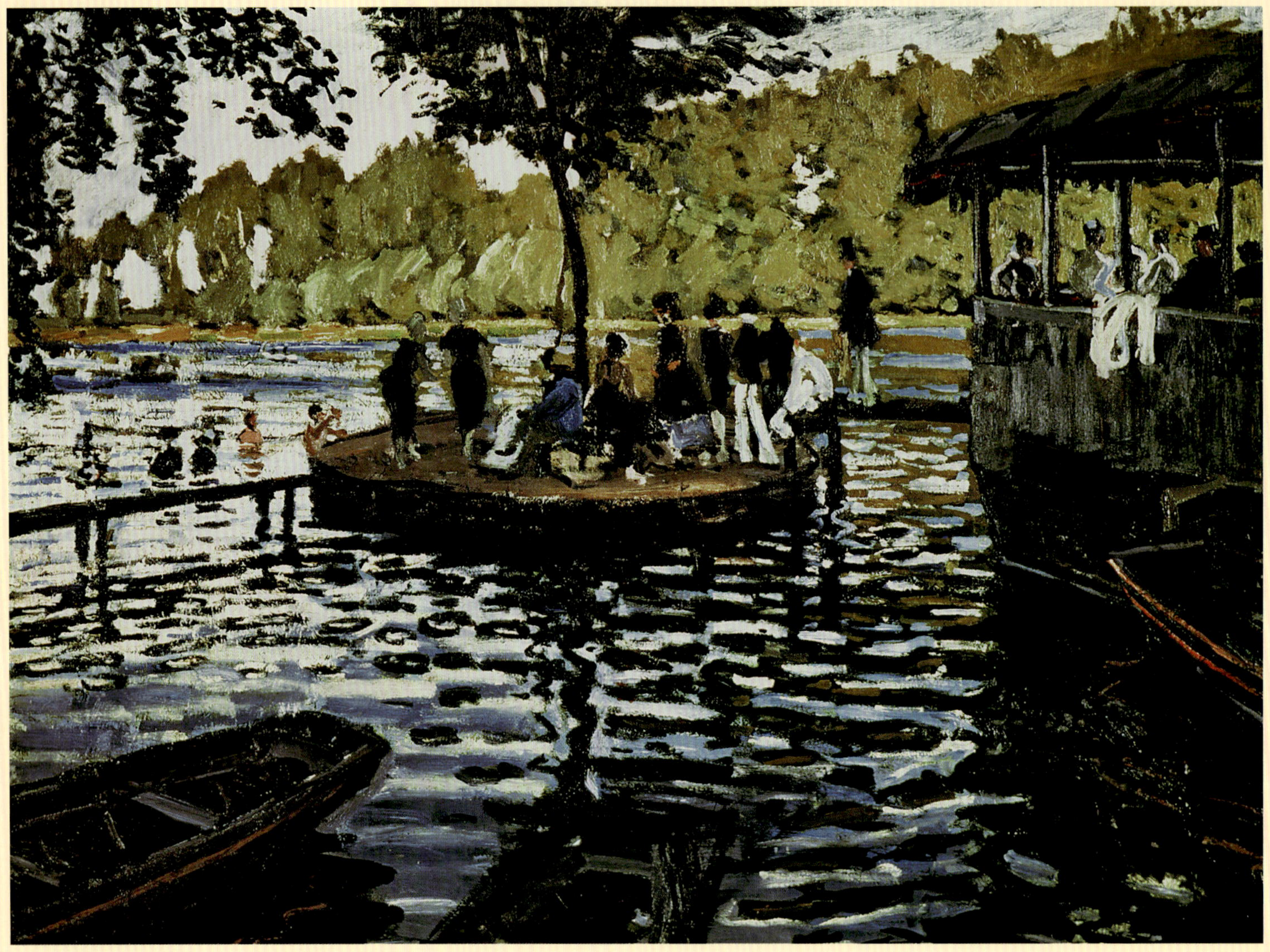

Claude Monet (1840–1926)

La Grenouillère

1869, Oil on canvas/Huile sur toile, 74,6 × 99,7 cm, Metropolitan Museum of Art, New York

This image shows the breakthrough to impressionism. In August 1869, Monet and Renoir simultaneously painted the same scene at La Grenouillère, which was a boating and bathing resort located on the Seine not far from Paris, a favorite haunt of artists and a destination for the city-weary citizens of Paris. Monet has here focused entirely on the reproduction of the reflections in the water, with the bathers being reproduced only as spots of color.

Cette image montre la percée de l'impressionnisme. En août 1869, Monet et Renoir peignirent simultanément la même scène à La Grenouillère, une station de navigation de plaisance et de baignade située sur la Seine, non loin de Paris, lieu de prédilection des artistes et destination appréciée des Parisiens fatigués de la ville. Ici, Monet s'est uniquement concentré sur la reproduction des reflets dans l'eau, représentant les baigneurs par de simples taches de couleur.

Dieses Bild zeigt den Durchbruch zum impressionistischen Stil. Monet und Renoir malten im August 1869 gemeinsam die Badeinsel La Grenouillère, am oberen Seinelauf gelegen, ein beliebter Treffpunkt von Künstlern und Ausflugsziel der stadtmüden Bürger aus Paris. Monet hat sich hier ganz auf die Wiedergabe der Lichtreflexe im Wasser konzentriert und die Badegäste nur als Farbtupfen wiedergegeben.

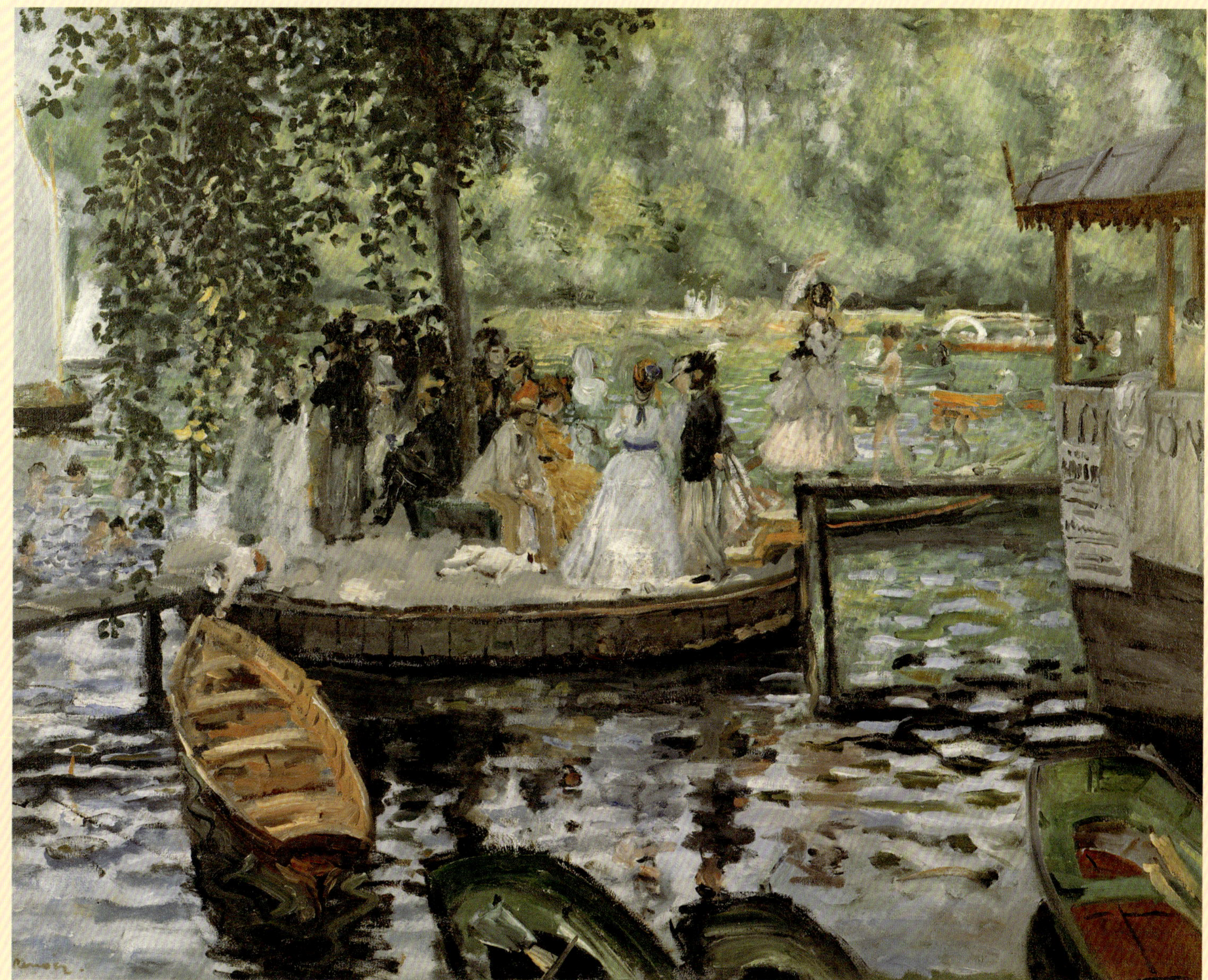

Pierre-Auguste Renoir (1841–1919)

La Grenouillère

1869, Oil on canvas/Huile sur toile, 66,5 × 81 cm, Nationalmuseum, Stockholm

Esta imagen muestra el paso decisivo hacia el estilo impresionista. Monet y Renoir pintaron en agosto de 1869 juntos la isla de recreo La Grenouillère, en la parte norte del Sena, un popular punto de encuentro de artistas y lugar de excursión para los parisinos cansados de la ciudad. Monet se ha concentrado aquí exclusivamente en la reproducción de los reflejos del agua, reduciendo a los bañistas a manchas de color.

Questo quadro segna il passaggio all'Impressionismo. Monet e Renoir dipinsero congiuntamente, nell'agosto 1869, lo stagno La Grenouillère situato nel tratto superiore della Senna, uno dei luoghi di incontro preferiti degli artisti e uno dei più celebri ritrovi dei parigini. Monet concentra tutta l'attenzione sulla riproduzione dei riflessi nell'acqua e raffigura i bagnanti esclusivamente come macchie di colore.

Dit schilderij toont de doorbraak naar de impressionistische stijl. In augustus 1869 schilderden Monet en Renoir samen La Grenouillère, een geliefd ontspanningsoord voor gestreste Parijzenaren, badgasten en ook kunstenaars aan de bovenloop van de Seine. Monet verbeeldt hier vooral de weerkaatsing van het licht op het water – de badgasten worden slechts in losse verfvlekjes weergegeven.

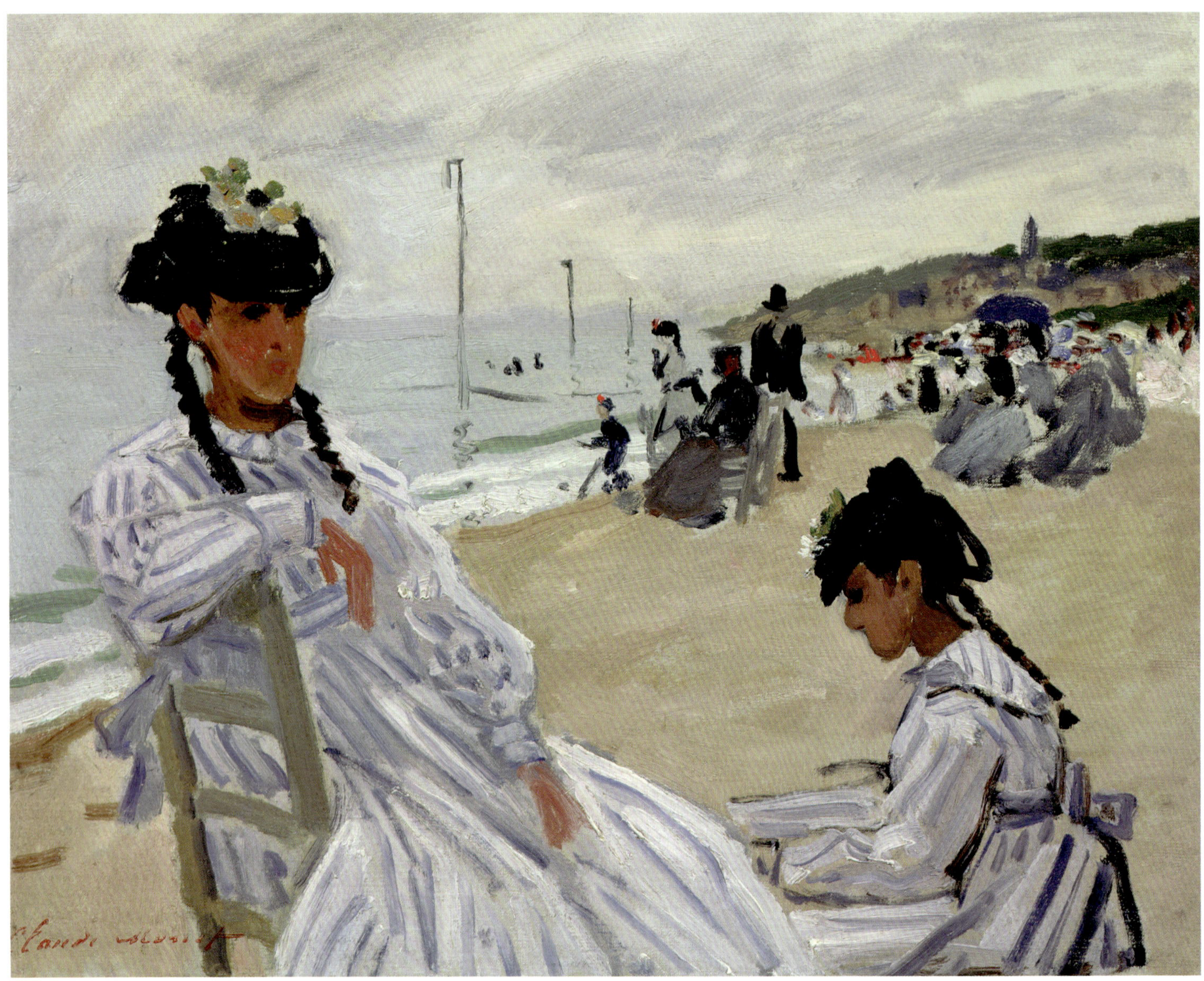

Claude Monet (1840–1926)

On the Beach at Trouville

La plage de Trouville

Am Strand von Trouville

En la playa de Trouville

In spiaggia a Trouville

Op het strand van Trouville

1870/71, Oil on canvas/Huile sur toile, 38 × 46 cm, Musée Marmottan Monet, Paris

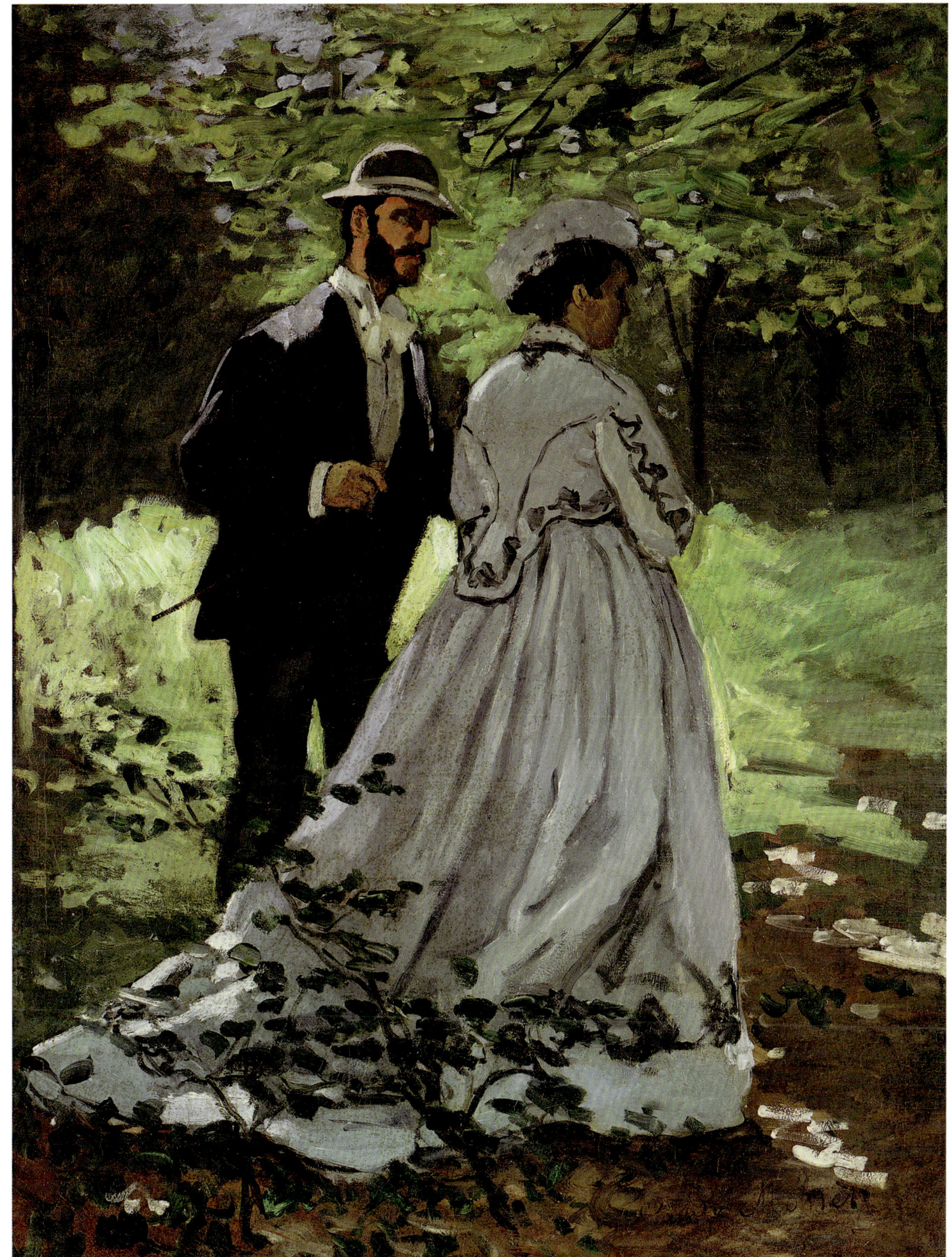

Claude Monet
(1840–1926)

The Promenaders
(Bazille and Camille)

Les Promeneurs
(Bazille et Camille)

Die Spaziergänger
(Bazille und Camille)

El paseo (Bazille
y Camille)

La passeggiata
(Bazille e Camille)

Wandelaars (Bazille
en Camille)

1865, Oil on canvas/Huile
sur toile, 93 × 68,9 cm,
National Gallery of
Art, Washington

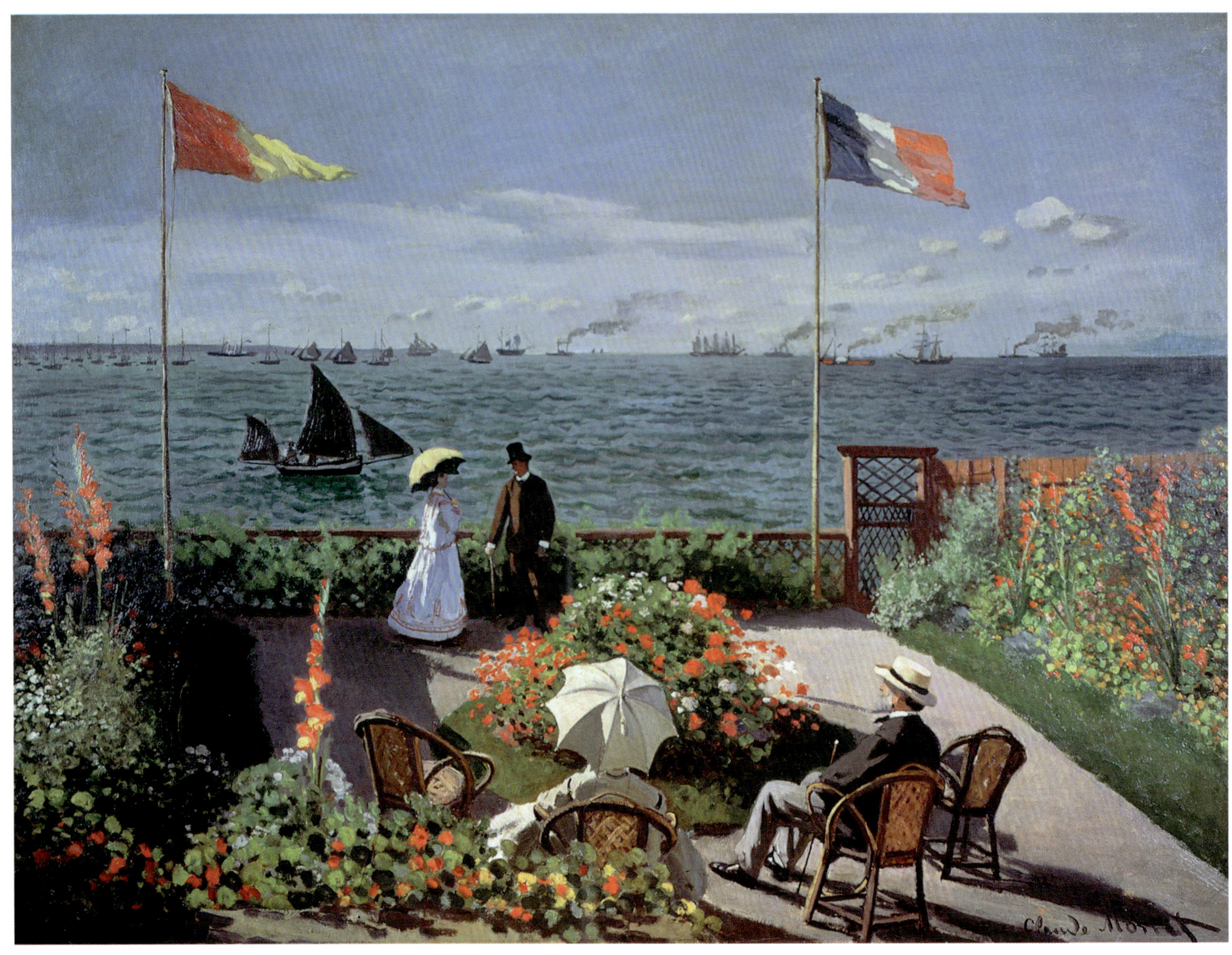

Claude Monet (1840−1926)

The Terrace at Sainte–Adresse

Terrasse à Sainte-Adresse

Die Terrasse am Meeresufer, Sainte-Adresse

La terraza a la orilla del mar, Sainte-Adresse

La terrazza a Sainte-Adresse

Het terras aan zee in Sainte-Adresse

1867, Oil on canvas/Huile sur toile, 98,1 × 129,9 cm, Metropolitan Museum of Art, New York

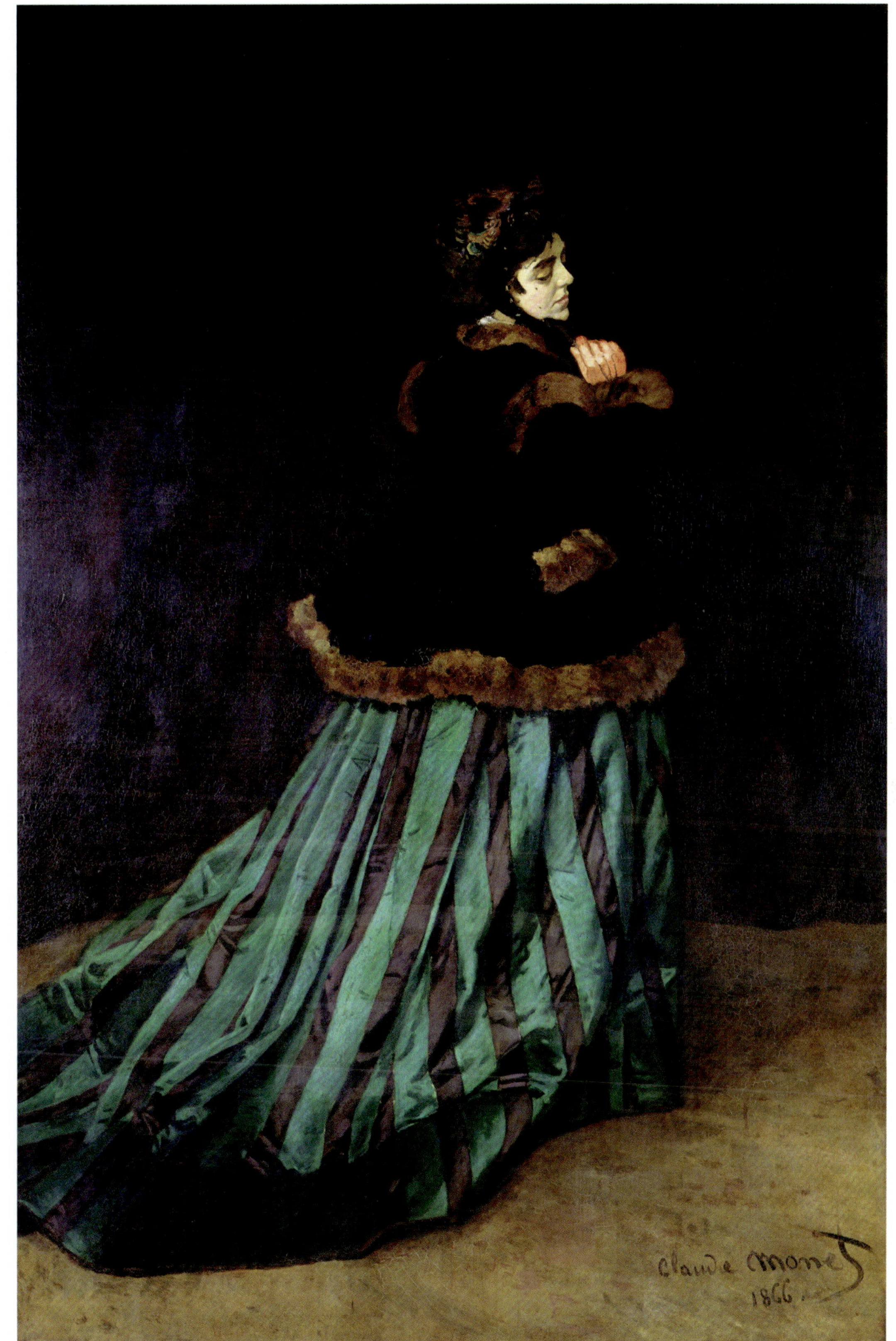

Claude Monet (1840–1926)

Camille *or* The Woman in the Green Dress
Camille, femme à la robe verte
Camille im grünen Kleid
Camille vestida de verde
Camille in abito verde
Camille in groene jurk

1866, Oil on canvas/Huile sur toile,
231 × 151 cm, Kunsthalle, Bremen

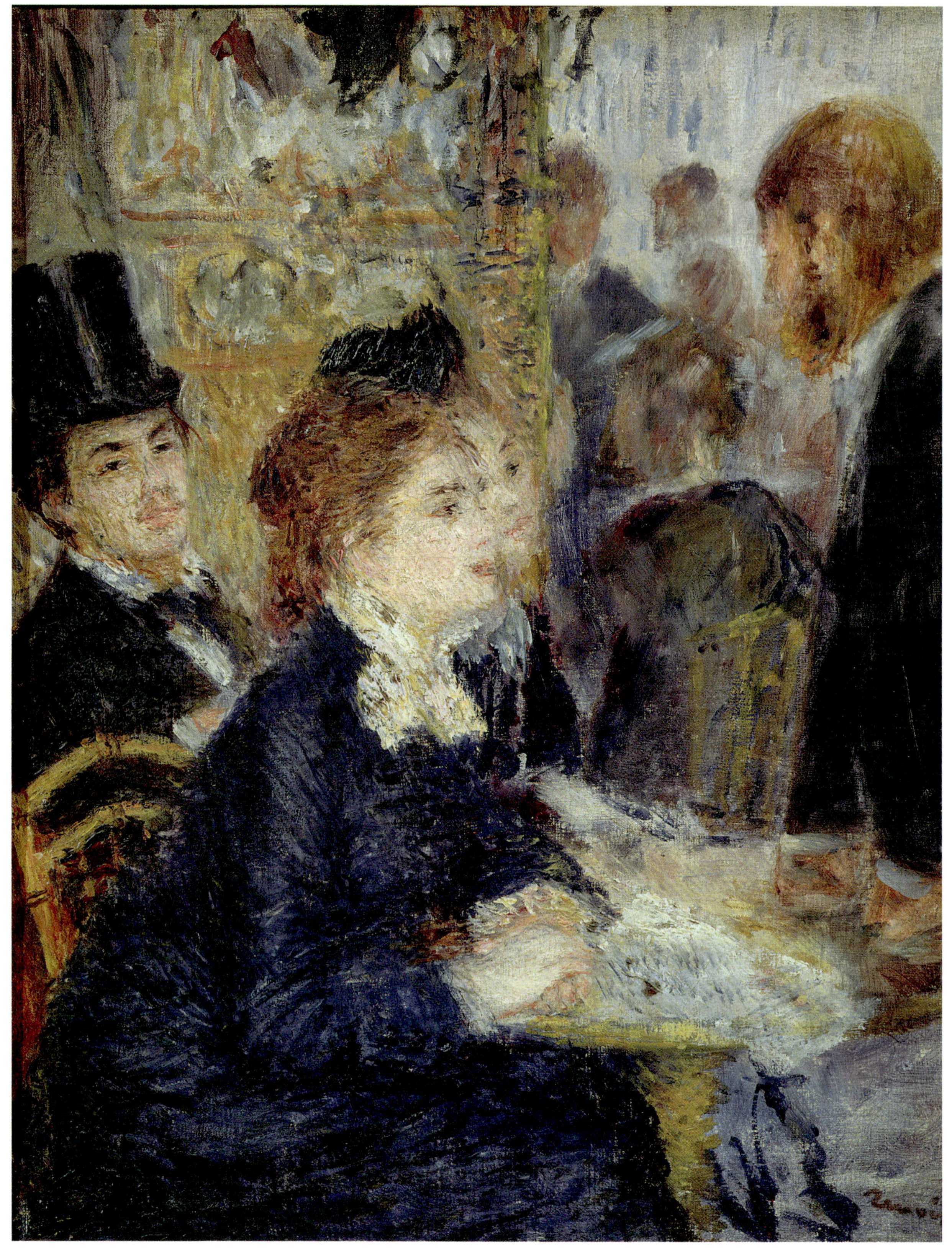

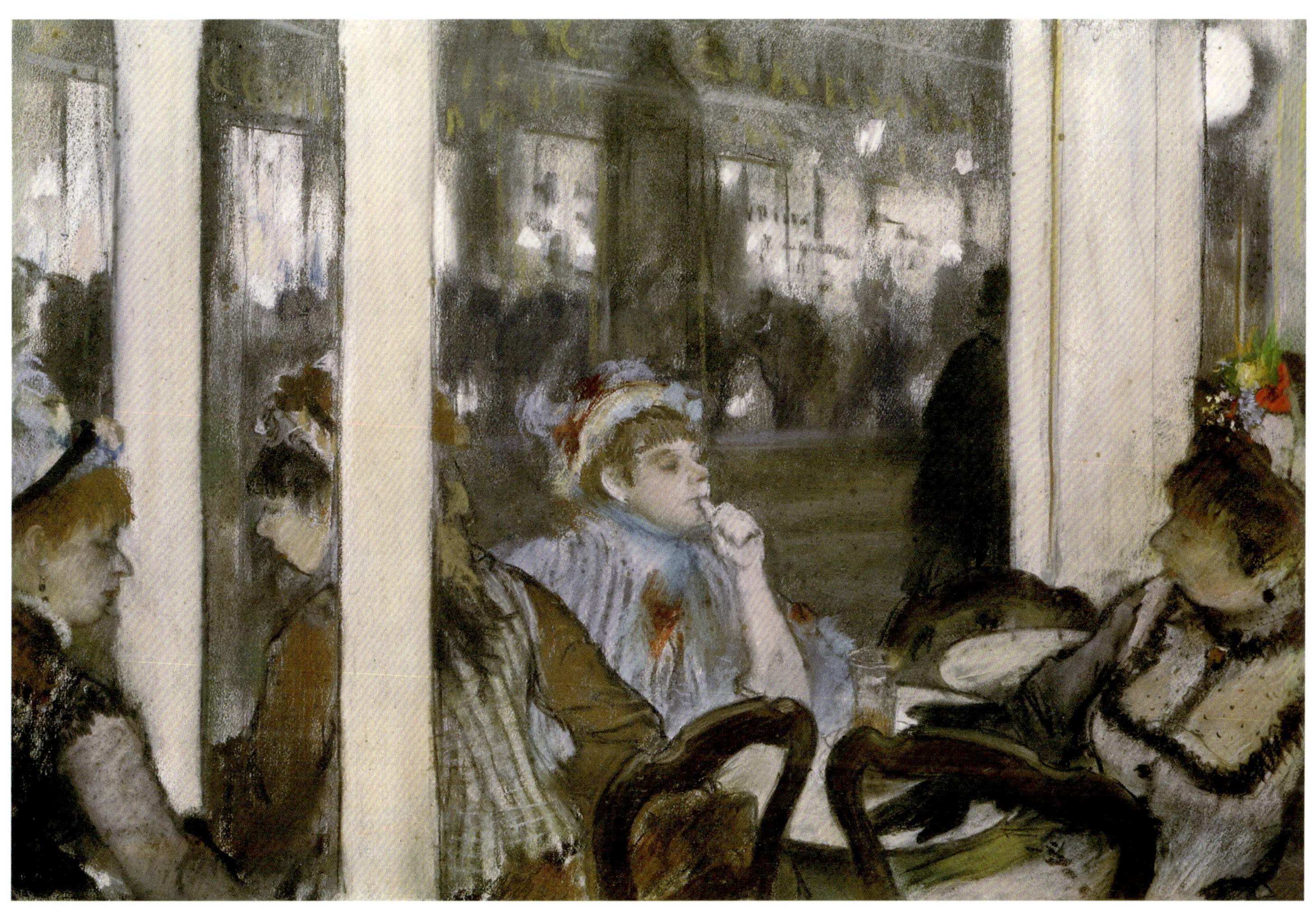

Pierre-Auguste Renoir (1841–1919)

At the Cafe

Au café

Im Café

En el café

Al caffè

In het café

c. 1874–77, Oil on canvas/Huile sur toile, 35,7 × 27,5 cm, Kröller-Müller Museum, Otterlo

Edgar Degas (1834–1917)

Women on a Cafe Terrace

Femmes à la terrasse d'un café le soir

Frauen auf einer Café-Terrasse

Mujeres en la terraza del café

Donne fuori da un caffè la sera

Vrouwen op een caféterras

1877, Pastel on monotype/Pastel sur monotype, 41 × 60 cm, Musée d'Orsay, Paris

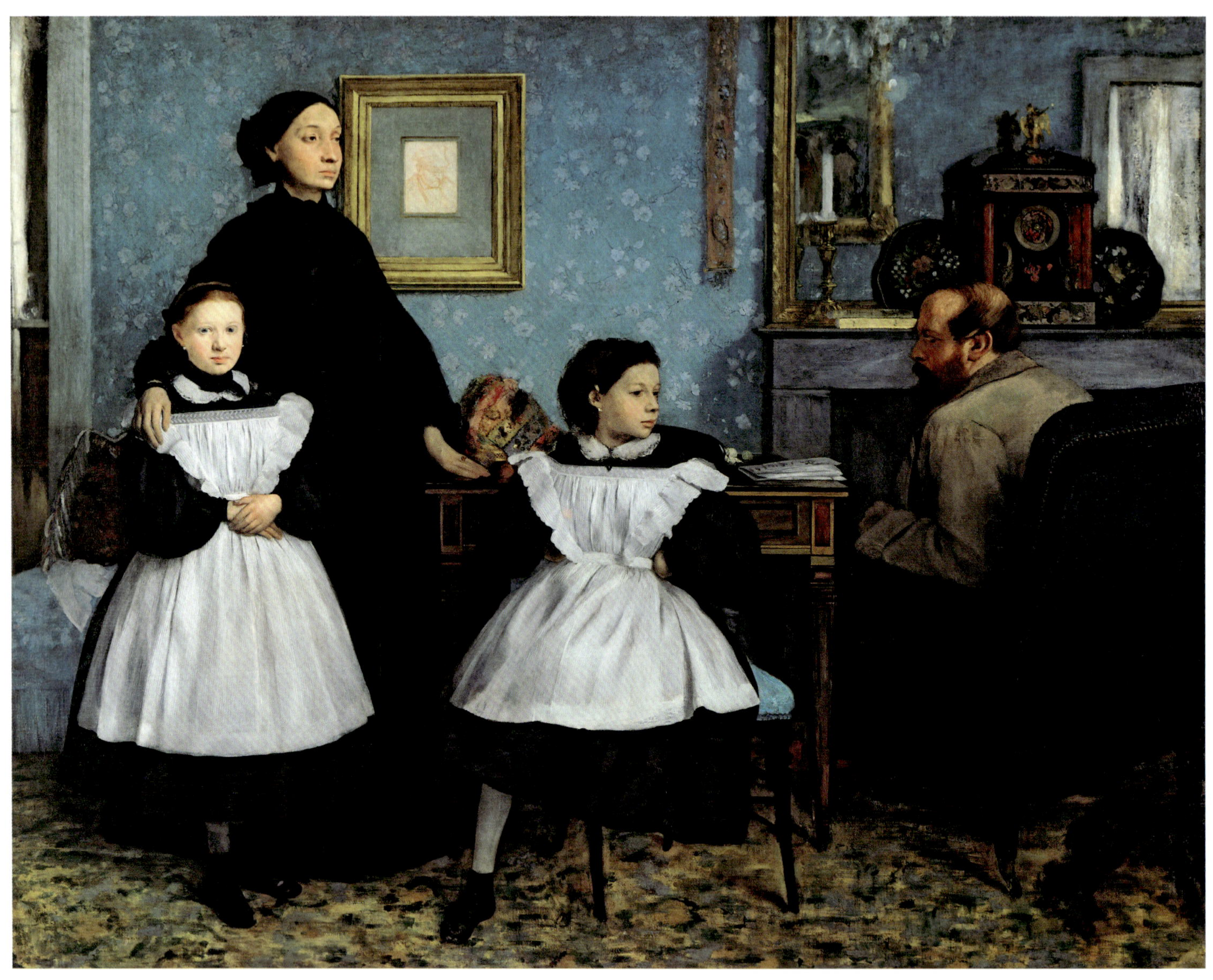

Edgar Degas (1834–1917)

The Bellelli Family
La famille Bellelli
Die Famiie Bellelli
La familia Bellelli
La famiglia Bellelli
De familie Bellelli

1858–69, Oil on canvas/Huile sur toile, 201 × 249,5 cm, Musée d'Orsay, Paris

Edgar Degas (1834–1917)

In a Cafe *or* The Absinthe
Absinthe
Der Absinth
La absenta
L'assenzio
Absint

c. 1875/76, Oil on canvas/Huile sur toile, 92 × 68,5 cm, Musée d'Orsay, Paris

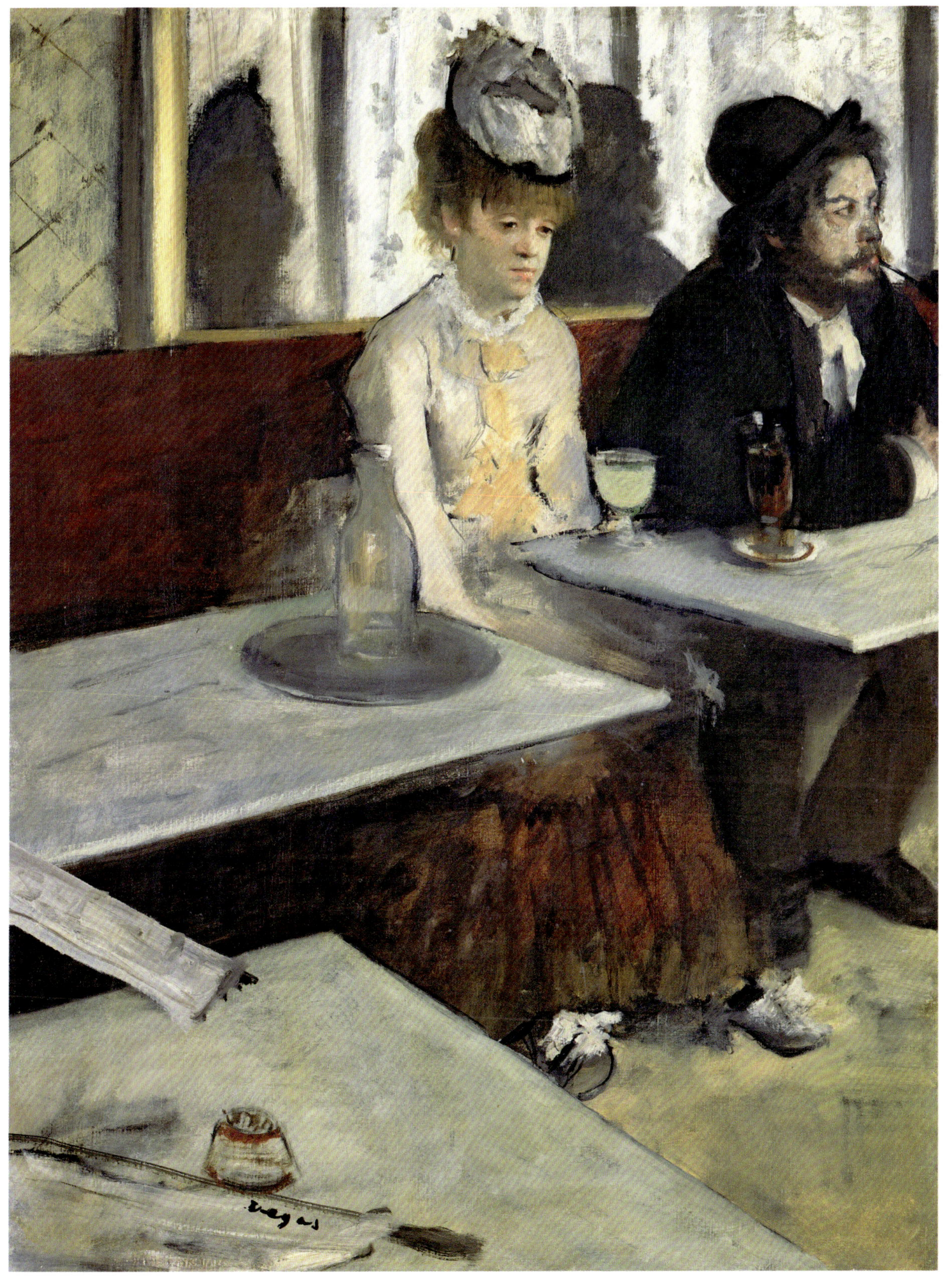

Degas

Degas enjoyed spending his time in the Café des Ambassadeurs, located on the Champs-Elysées, where famous singers like Emilie Bécat would perform, capturing the atmosphere of the place in his brilliantly colored pastels.

Degas aimait passer son temps au Café des Ambassadeurs, situé sur les Champs-Élysées – où se produisaient des chanteurs célèbres comme Émile Bécat –, pour y capturer l'atmosphère de l'endroit dans ses pastels aux couleurs éclatantes.

Degas hielt sich gerne in dem an den Champs-Élysées gelegenen Café des Ambassadeurs auf und fing in seinen farbig brillanten Pastellen die Atmosphäre dieses Ortes, an dem berühmte Sängerinnen wie Emilie Bécat auftraten, ein.

Degas acudía a menudo a este café de los embajadores, situado en los Campos Elíseos, y capturó la atmósfera del lugar, en el que actuaban famosas cantantes como Emilie Bécat, con su paleta de brillantes colores pastel.

Degas frequentava volentieri il Café des Ambassadeurs sugli Champs-Elysées, e catturò con i suoi brillanti pastelli colorati l'atmosfera di questo luogo, in cui si esibivano cantanti famose come Emilie Bécat.

Degas vertoefde graag in het Café des Ambassadeurs aan de Champs-Élysées en legde in zeer kleurrijke pastels de sfeer van deze plek vast, waar beroemde zangeressen als Emilie Bécat optraden.

Edgar Degas (1834–1917)
Cafe Concert at Les Ambassadeurs
Le Café-concert aux Ambassadeurs
Café-Konzert im Les Ambassadeurs
El café-concierto de Les Ambassadeurs
Il caffè-concerto agli Ambassadeurs
Café chantant in Les Ambassadeurs
1876/77, Pastel on paper/Pastel sur papier, 37 × 26 cm, Musée des Beaux-Arts, Lyon

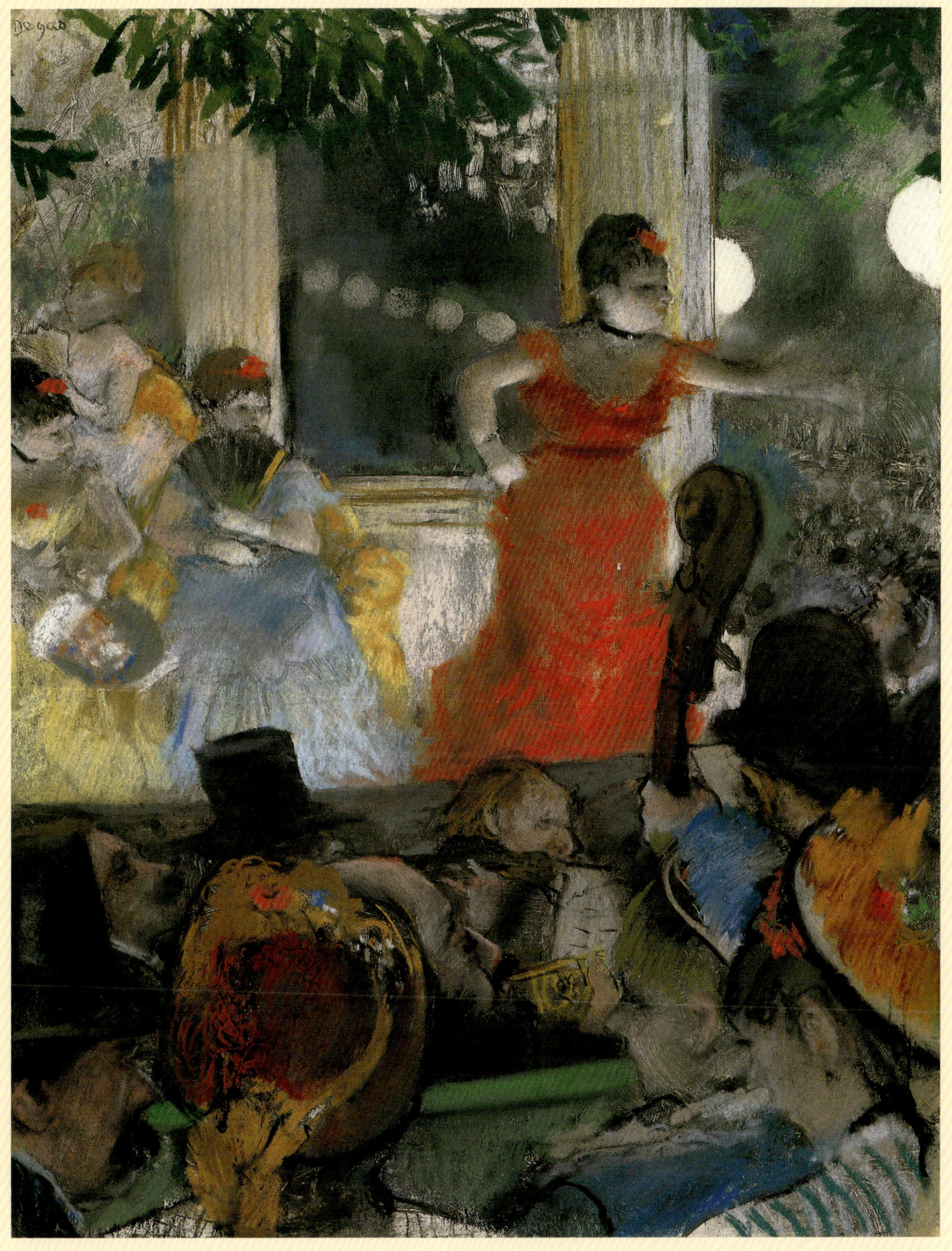

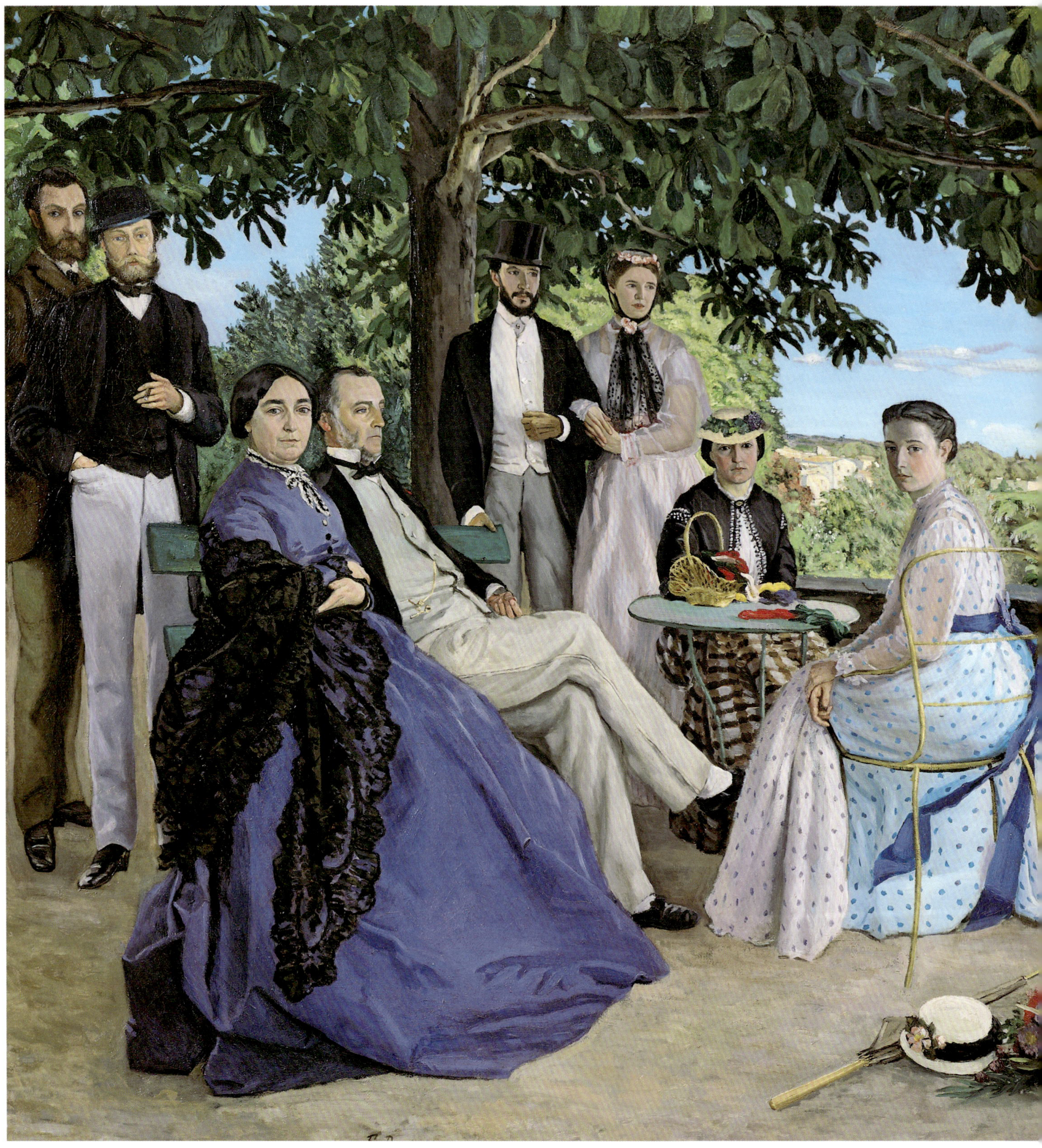

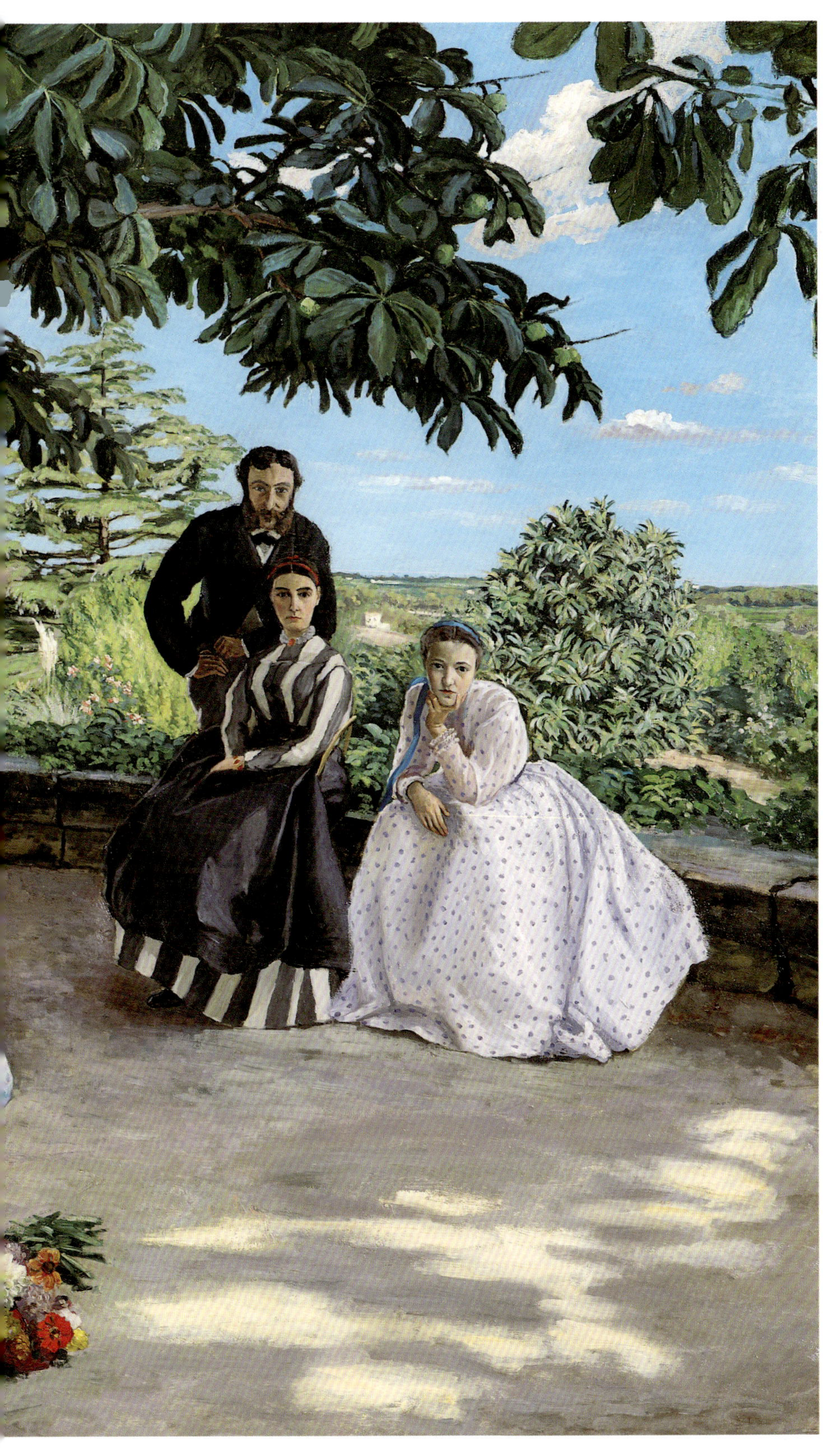

Jean-Frédéric Bazille (1841–70)

Family reunion

Réunion de famille

Familientreffen

Encuentro familiar

Riunione familiare

Familiebijeenkomst

1867, Oil on canvas/Huile sur toile, 152 × 230 cm, Musée d'Orsay, Paris

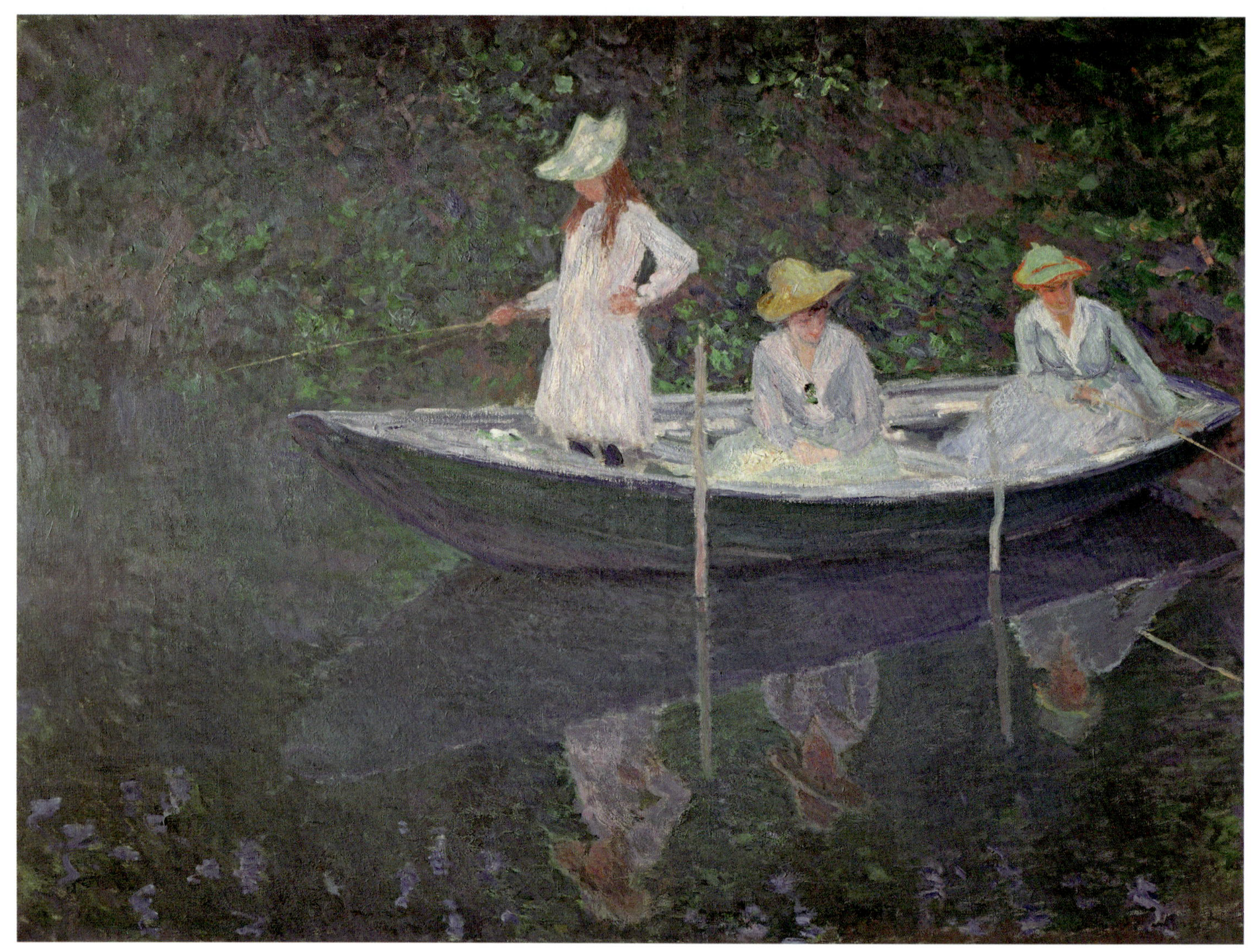

Claude Monet (1840–1926)

In Norway

En norvégienne

In Norwegen

En Noruega

In Norvegia

In Noorwegen

c. 1887, Oil on canvas/Huile sur toile, 98 × 131 cm, Musée d'Orsay, Paris

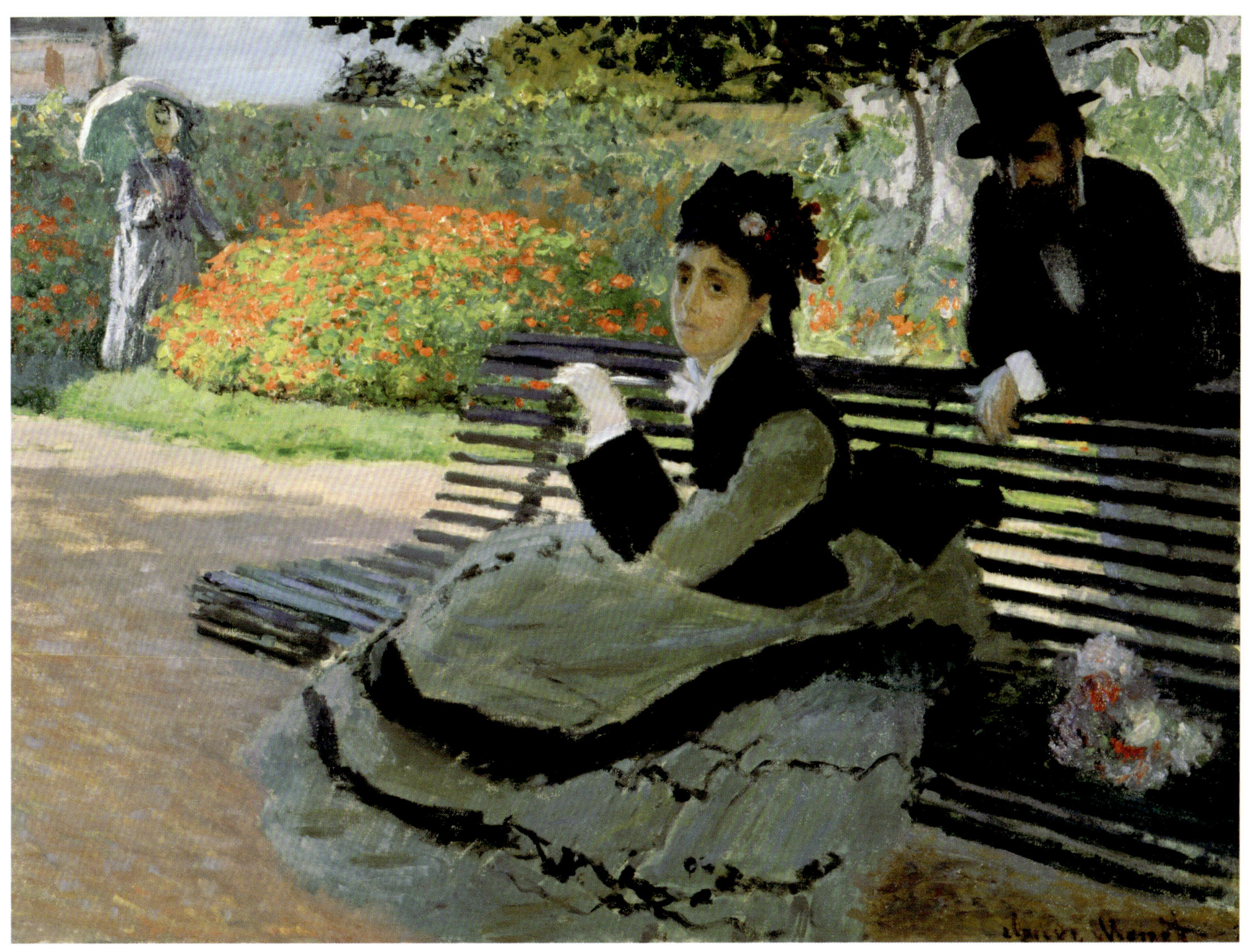

Claude Monet (1840–1926)

Madame Monet on a Garden Bench

Madame Monet sur un banc de jardin

Madame Monet auf einer Gartenbank

Madame Monet en un banco en el parque

Camille Monet su una panchina da giardino

Madame Monet op een tuinbankje

1873, Oil on canvas/Huile sur toile, 60,6 × 80,3 cm, Metropolitan Museum of Art, New York

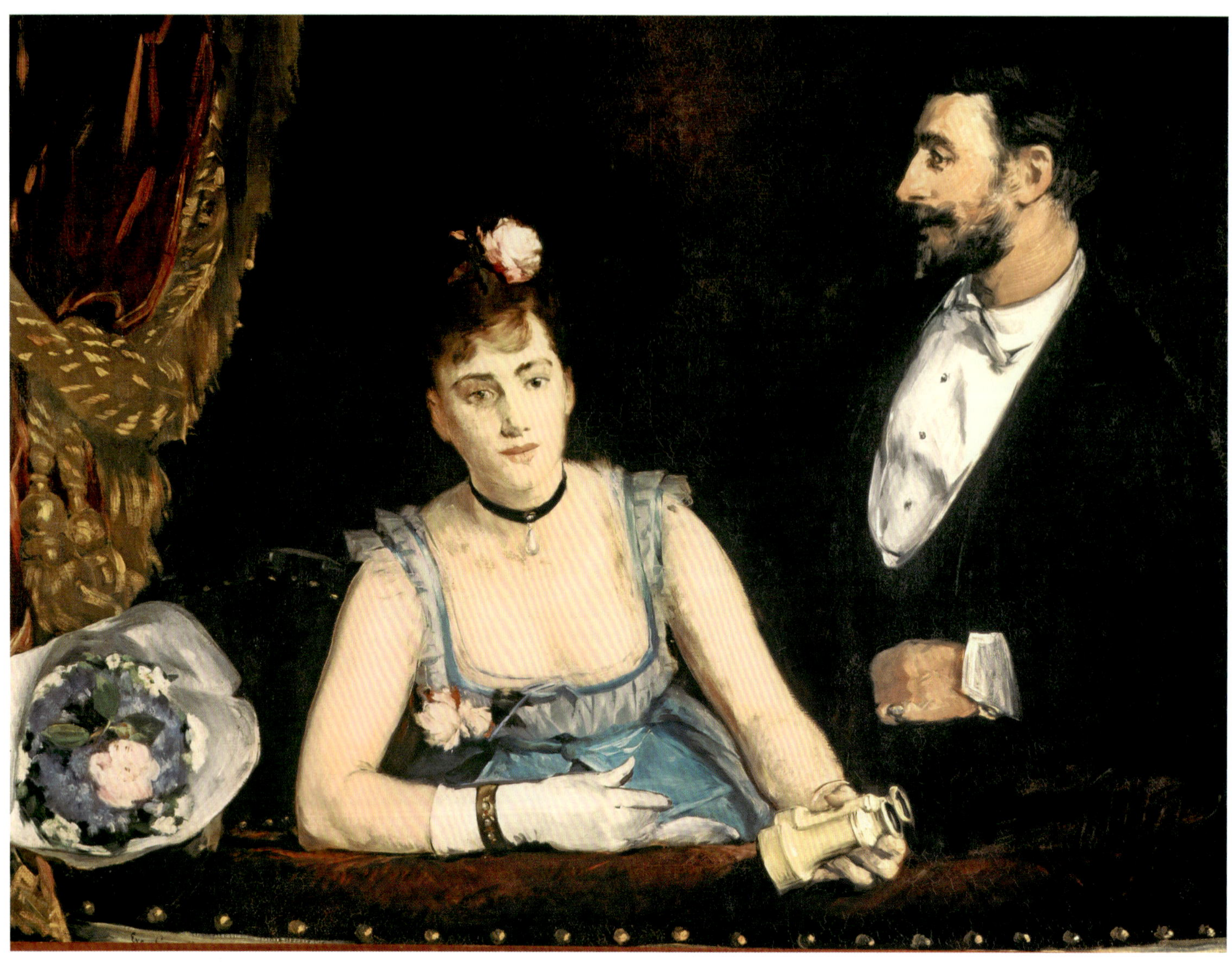

Eva Gonzalès (1849–83)

A Box at the Italians' Theatre

Une loge aux Italiens

Eine Loge im Théâtre des Italiens

Un palco en los italianos

Un palco al Théâtre des Italiens

Loge in het Théâtre des Italiens

c. 1874, Oil on canvas/Huile sur toile, 97,7 × 130 cm, Musée d'Orsay, Paris

Edgar Degas (1834–1917)

The Opera Orchestra

L'orchestre

Das Orchester der Oper

La orquesta

L'orchestra dell'Opéra

Het orkest

c. 1870, Oil on canvas/Huile sur toile, 56,5 × 46 cm, Musée d'Orsay, Paris

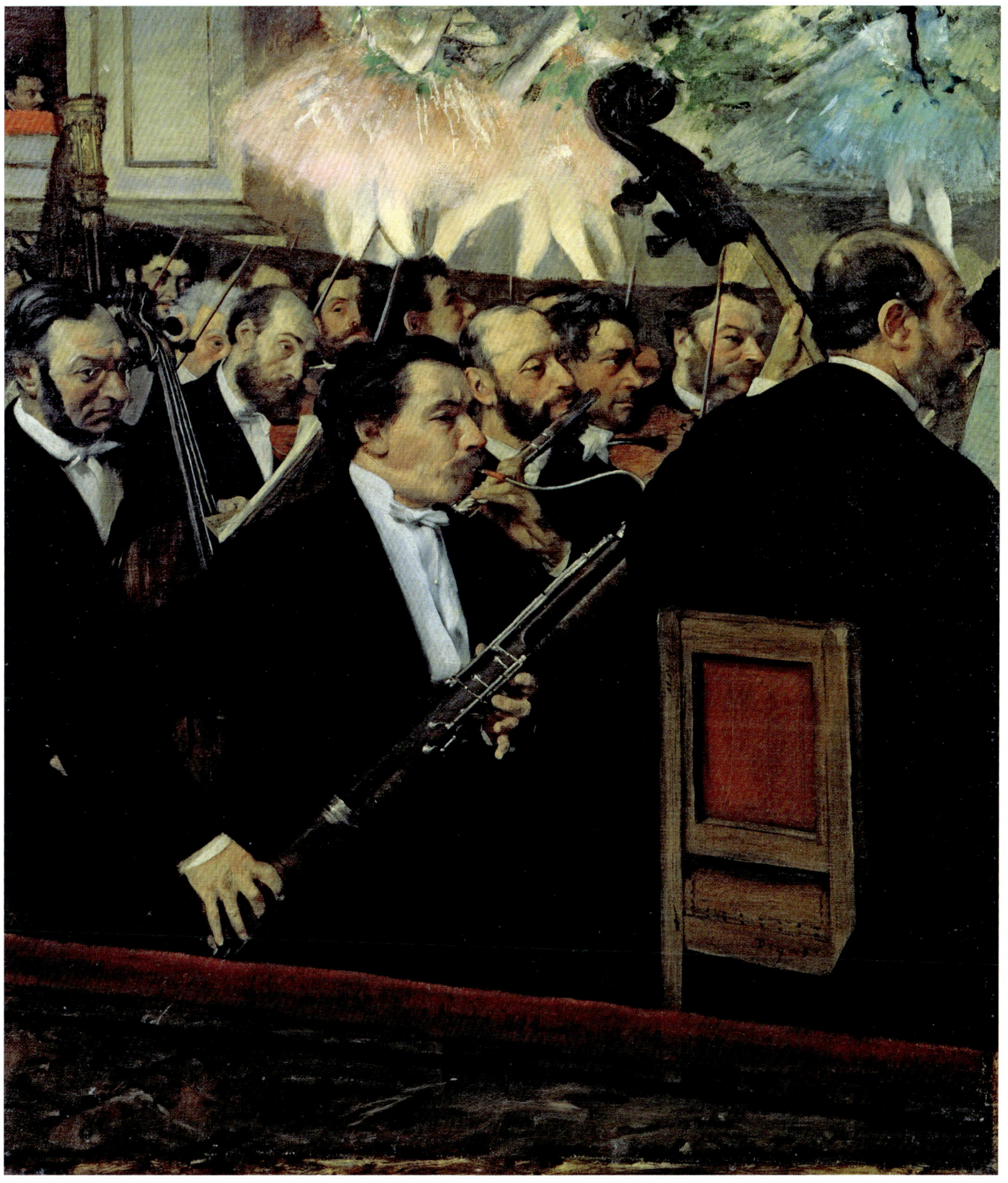

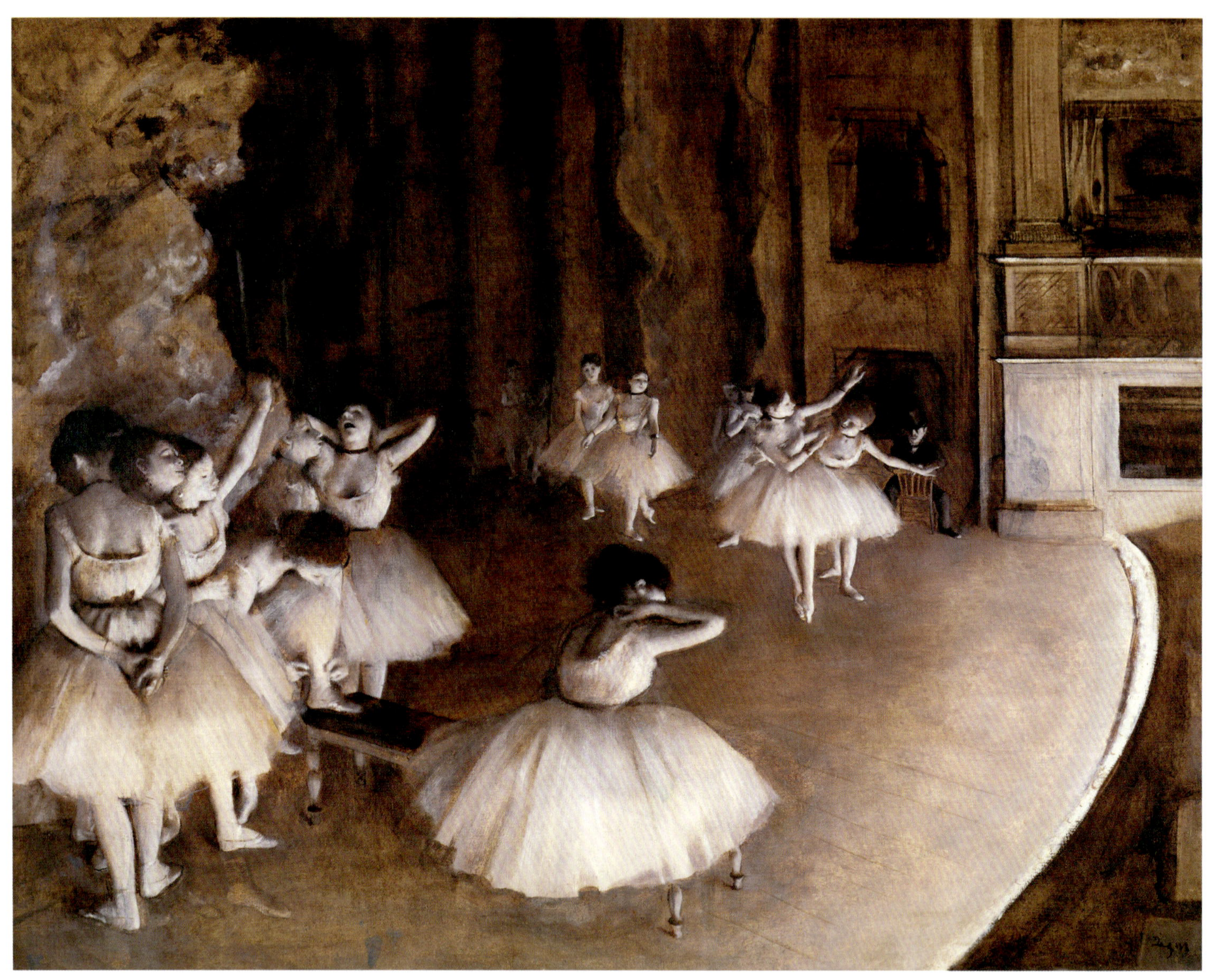

Edgar Degas (1834–1917)

Ballet Rehearsal on the Stage

Répétition d'un ballet sur la scène

Ballettprobe auf der Bühne

Ensayo de ballet en el escenario

La prova del balletto sul palco

Balletrepetitie op het podium

1874, Oil on canvas/Huile sur toile, 65 × 81,5 cm, Musée d'Orsay, Paris

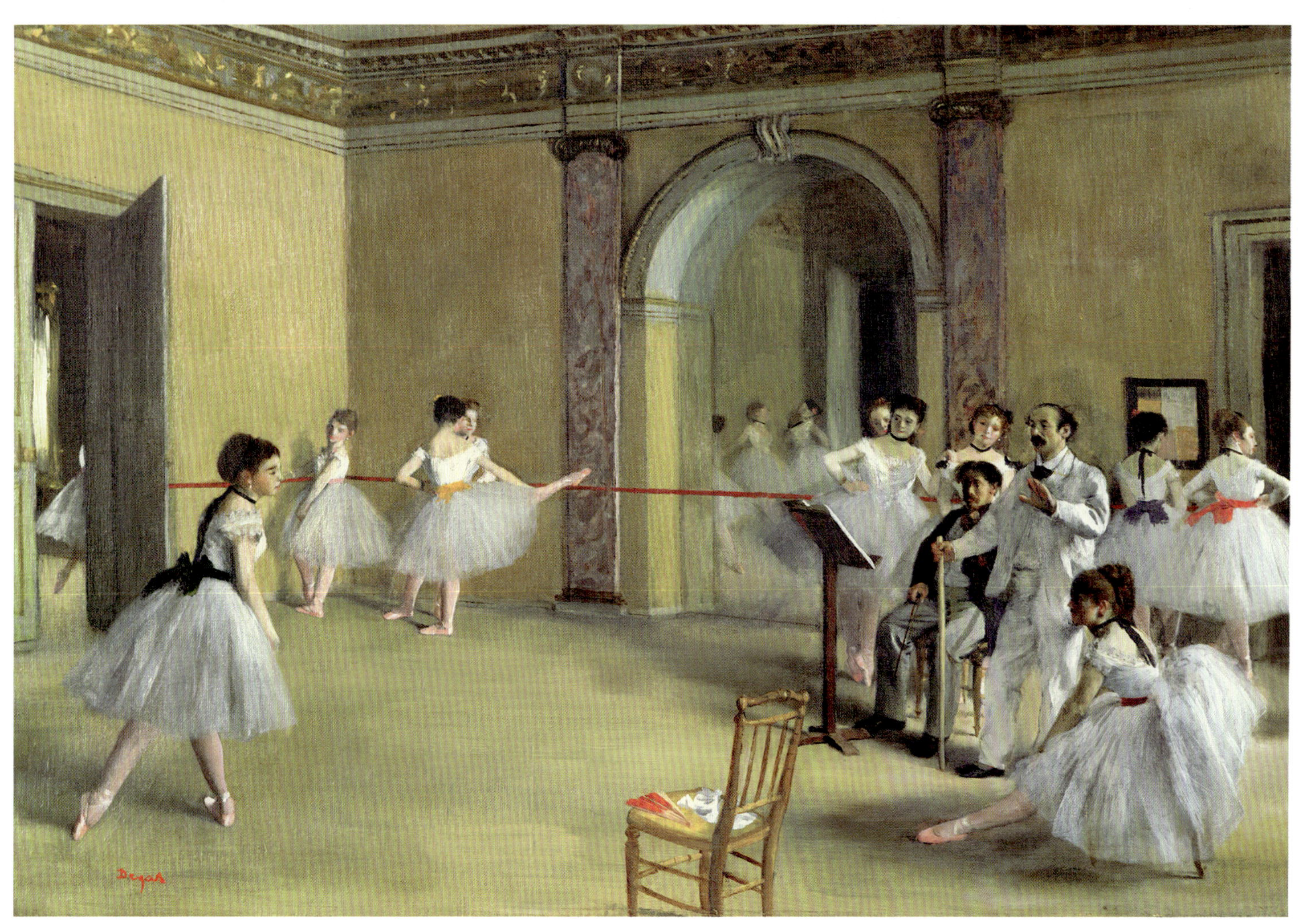

Edgar Degas (1834–1917)

The Dance Foyer at the Opera on the rue Le Peletier

Le foyer de la danse à l'Opéra de la rue Le Peletier

Der Proberaum in der Oper an der Rue Le Peletier

El local de ensayos en la Ópera de la calle Le Peletier

La sala prove nell'Opera in rue Le Peletier

De repetitieruimte van de Opéra in de Rue le Peletier

1872, Oil on canvas/Huile sur toile, 32,7 × 46 cm, Musée d'Orsay, Paris

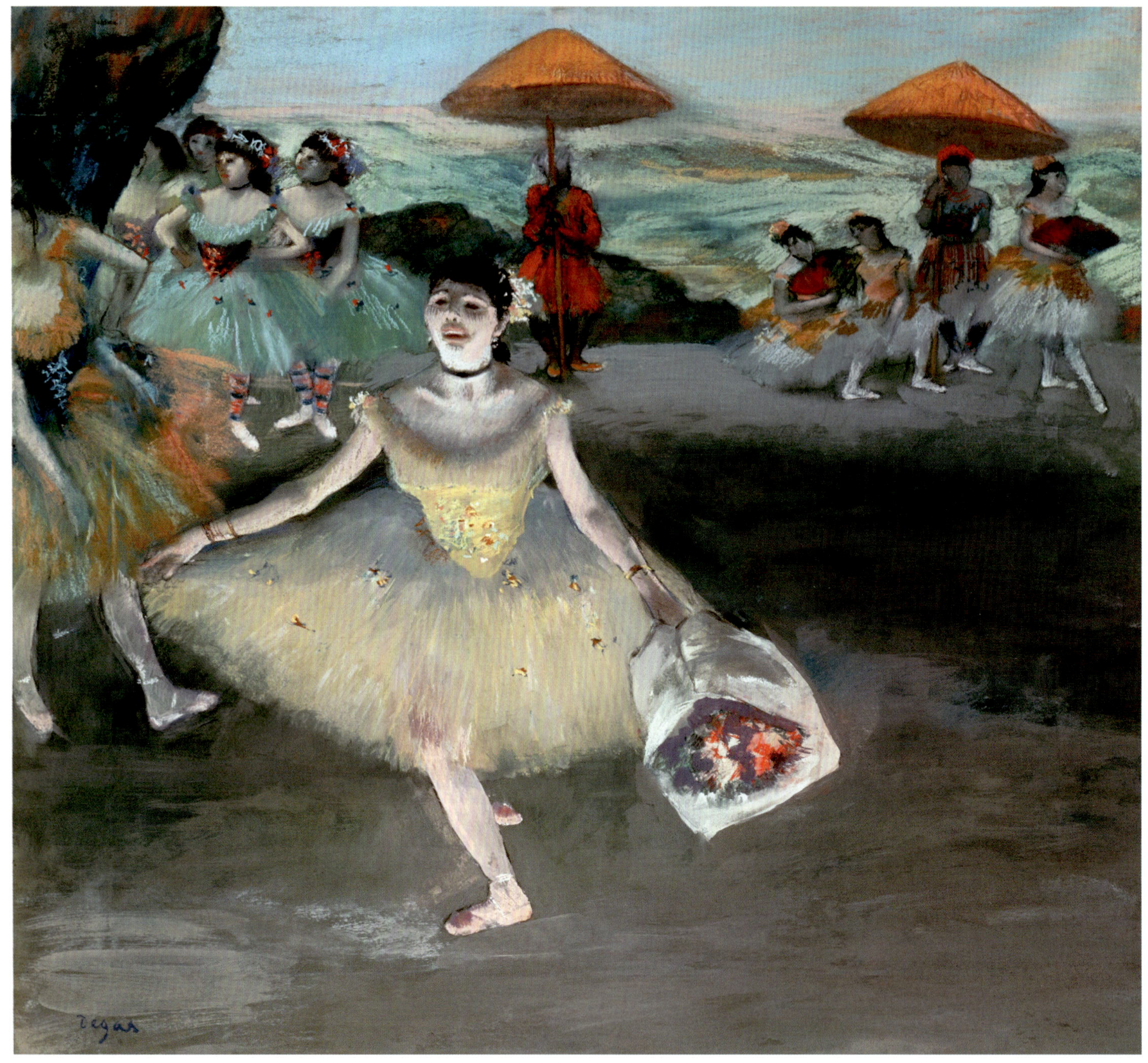

Edgar Degas (1834–1917)

Dancer with bouquet, curtseying

Danseuse au bouquet

Tänzerin mit Blumenstrauß

Bailarina con ramo de flores

Ballerina con bouquet sulla scena

Danseres met boeket bloemen

1878, Pastel on paper mounted on canvas/Pastel sur papier marouflé sur toile, 72 × 77,5 cm, Musée d'Orsay, Paris

Edgar Degas (1834–1917)

The Dancing Class

La classe de danse

Die Ballettprobe

El ensayo de ballet

La classe di danza

De balletrepetitie

c. 1873–76, Oil on canvas/Huile sur toile, 85,5 × 75 cm, Musée d'Orsay, Paris

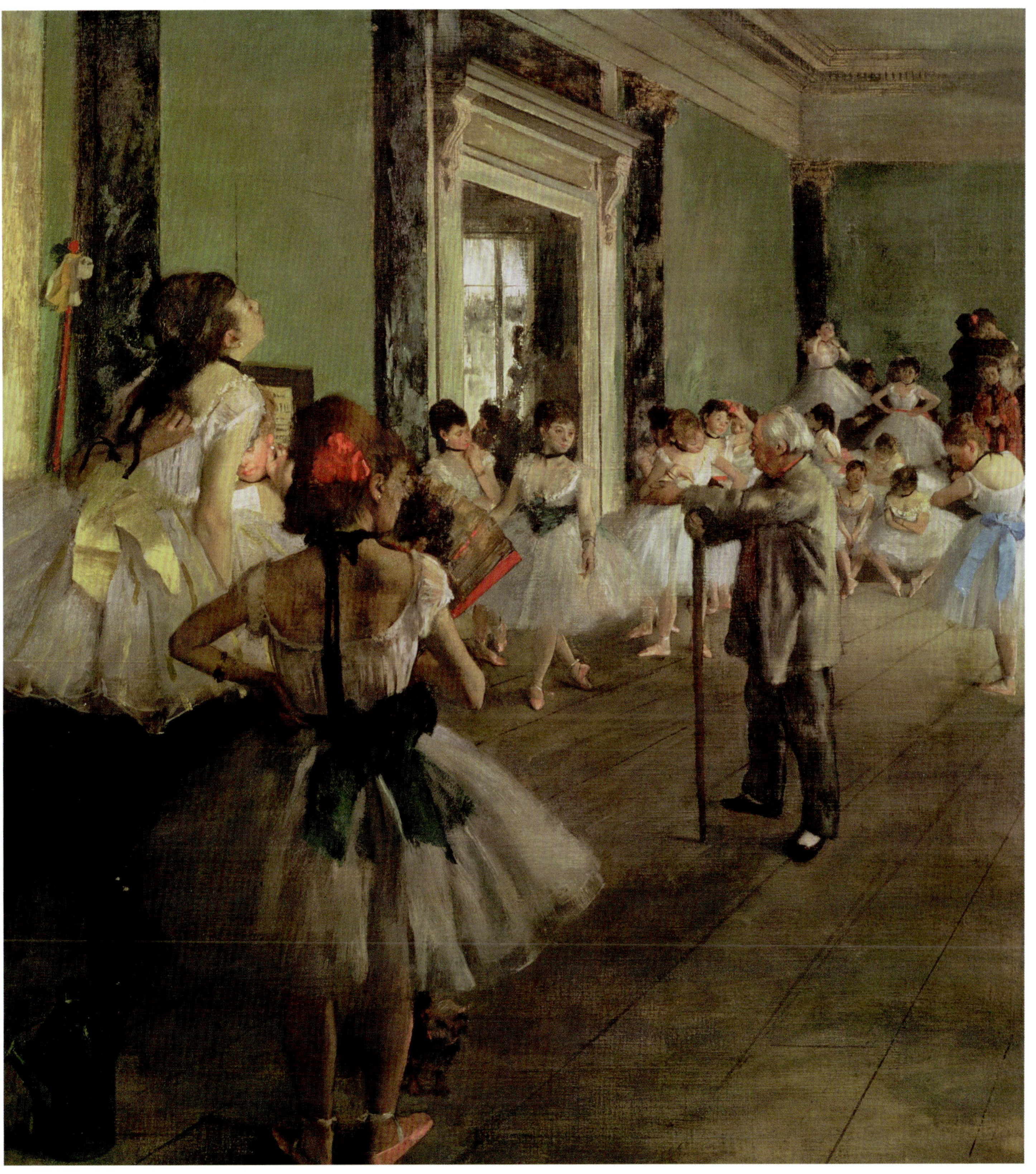

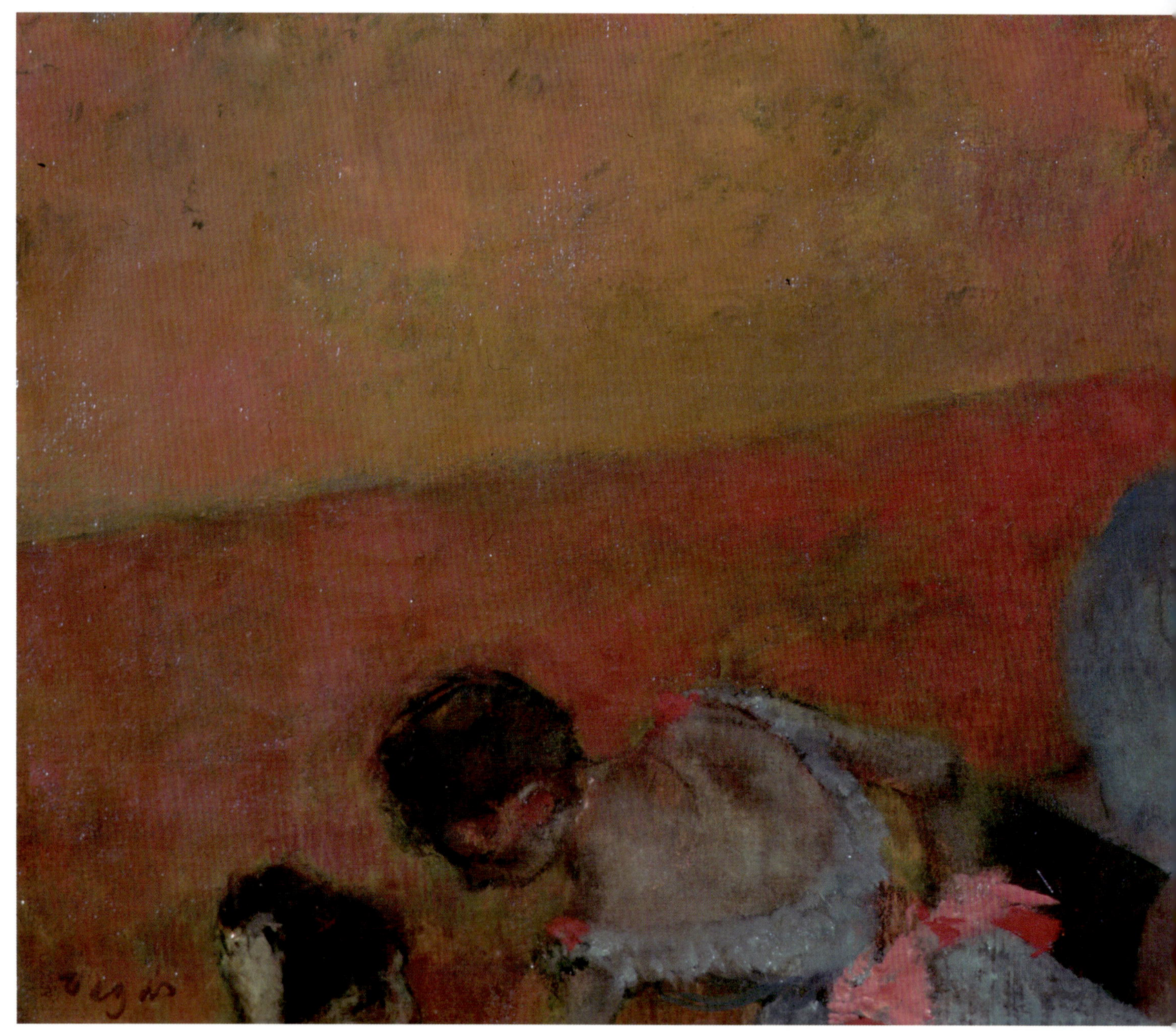

Edgar Degas (1834–1917)

Dancers Ascending a Staircase

Danseuses montant un escalier

Tänzerinnen auf einer Treppe

Bailarinas subiendo una escalera

Ballerine che salgono una scala

Danseressen op een trap

c. 1886–90, Oil on canvas/Huile sur toile, 39 × 89,5 cm, Musée d'Orsay, Paris

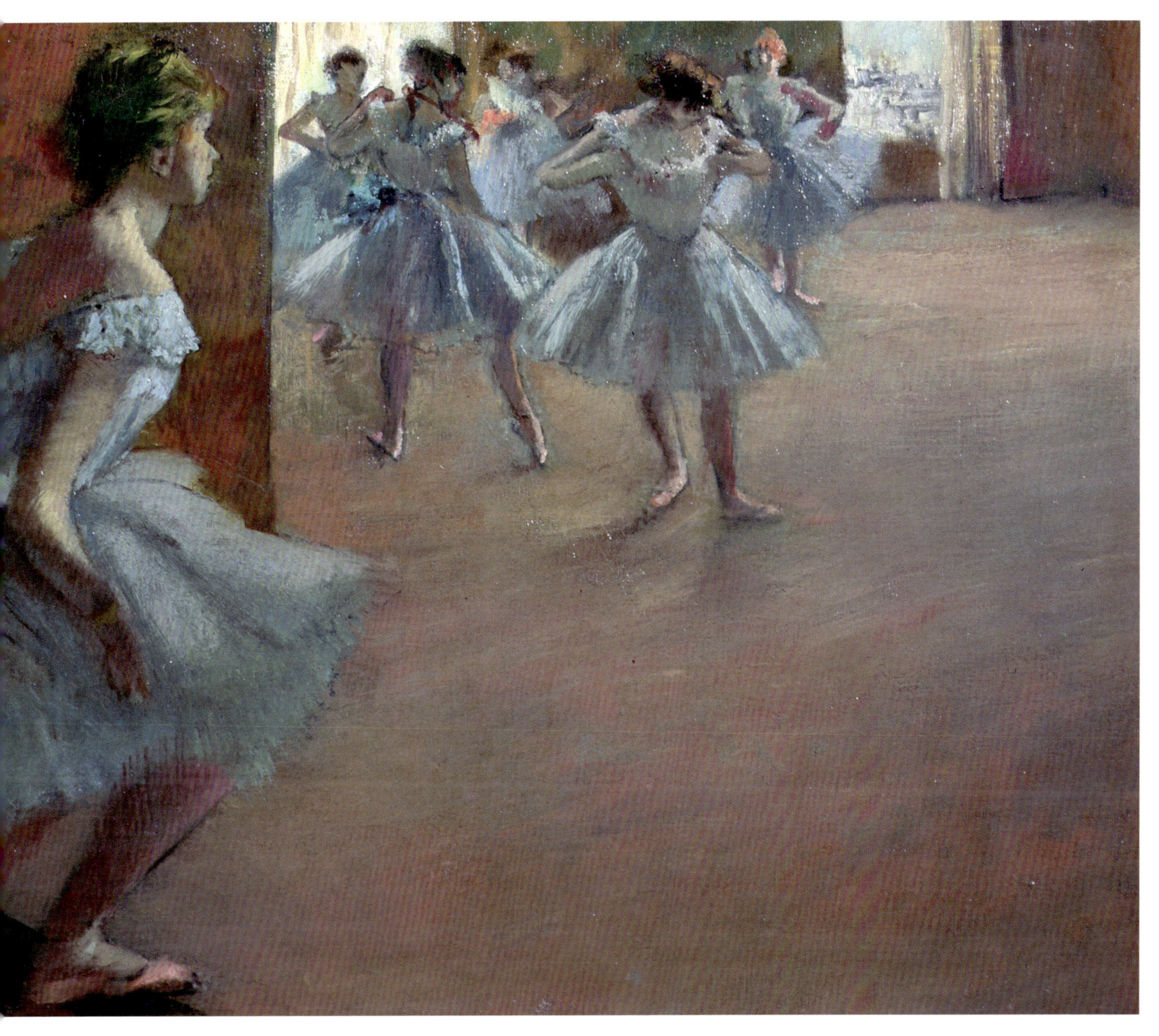

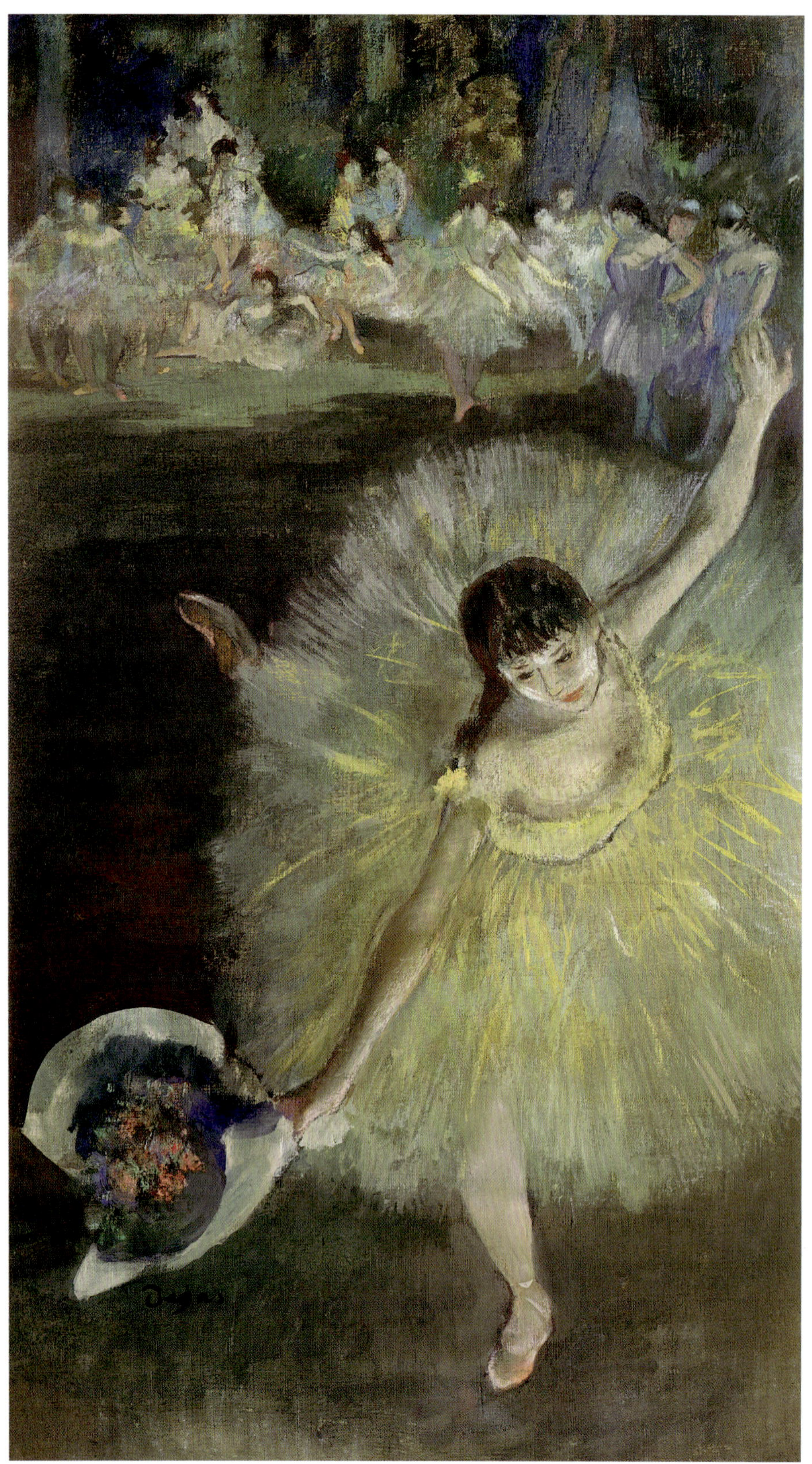

Edgar Degas (1834–1917)

End of an Arabesque

Fin d'arabesque

Ende einer Vorstellung

Final de un arabesco

Fin d'arabesque (Ballerina con bouquet)

Einde van een voorstelling

1877, Oil and pastel on canvas/Huile et pastel sur toile, 67,4 × 38 cm, Musée d'Orsay, Paris

Edgar Degas (1834–1917)

Dancers in blue

Danseuses en bleu

Tänzerinnen in Blau

Bailarinas de azul

Ballerine in blu

Danseressen in het blauw

c. 1890, Oil on canvas/Huile sur toile, 85,3 × 75,3 cm, Musée d'Orsay, Paris

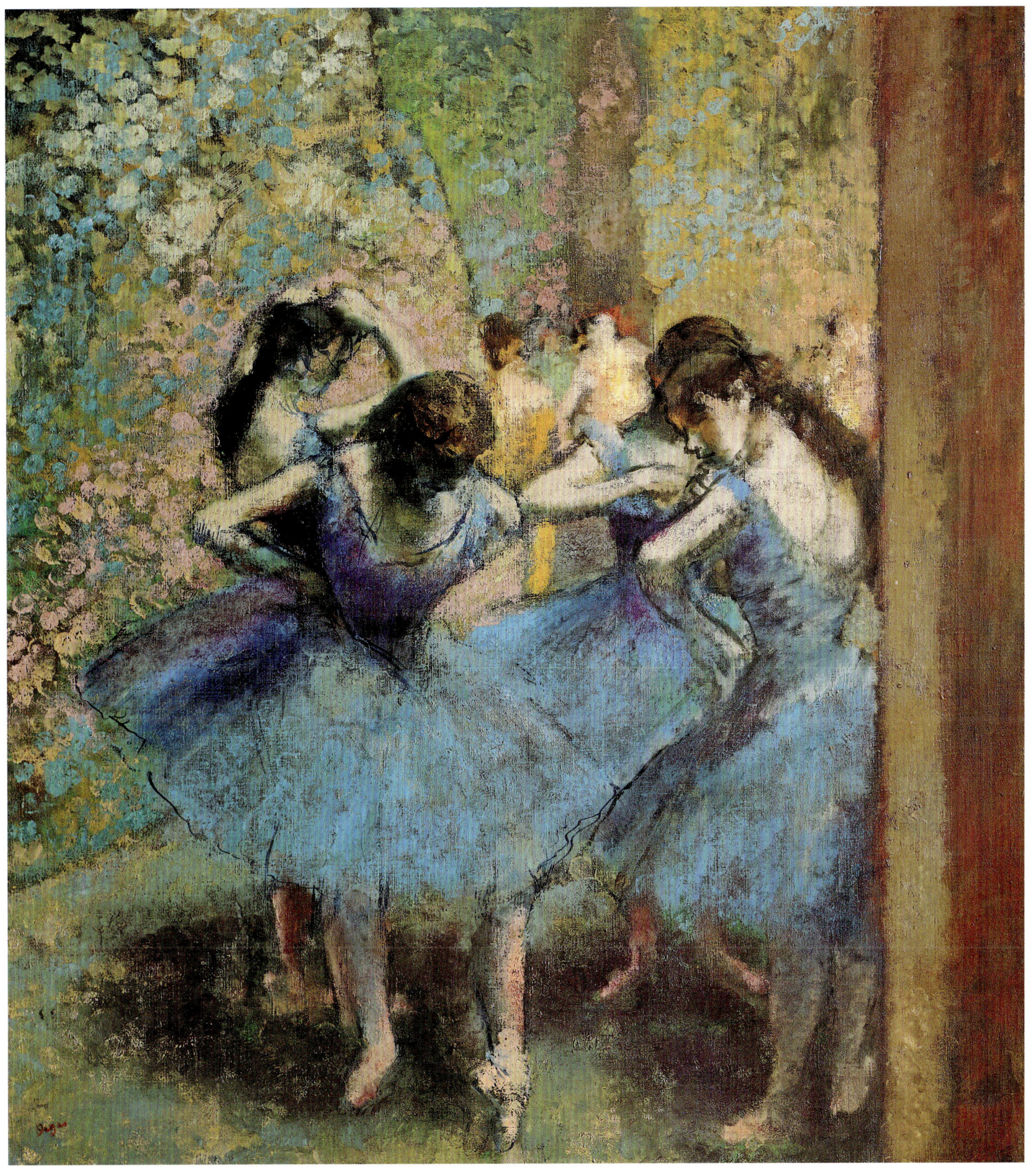

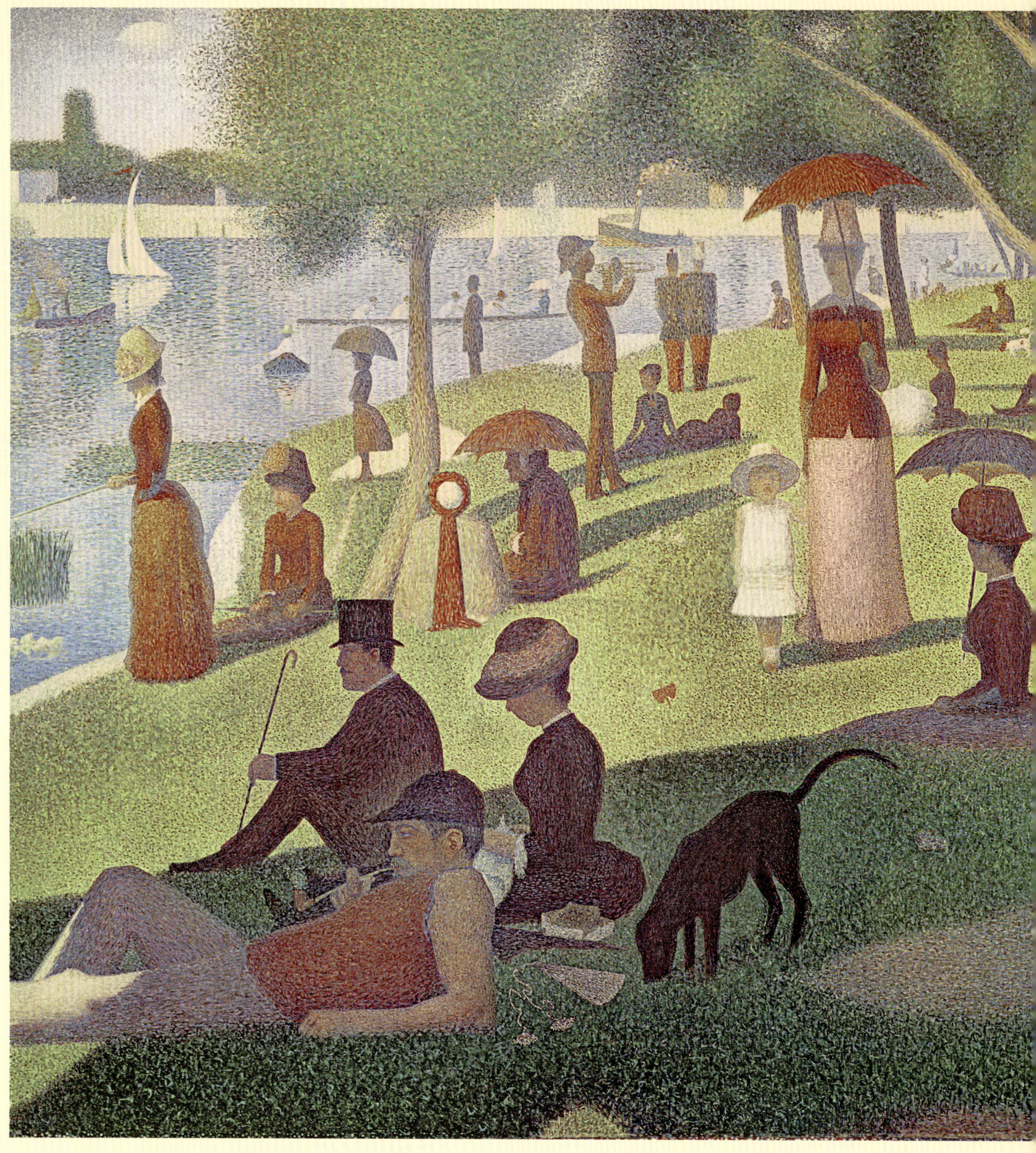

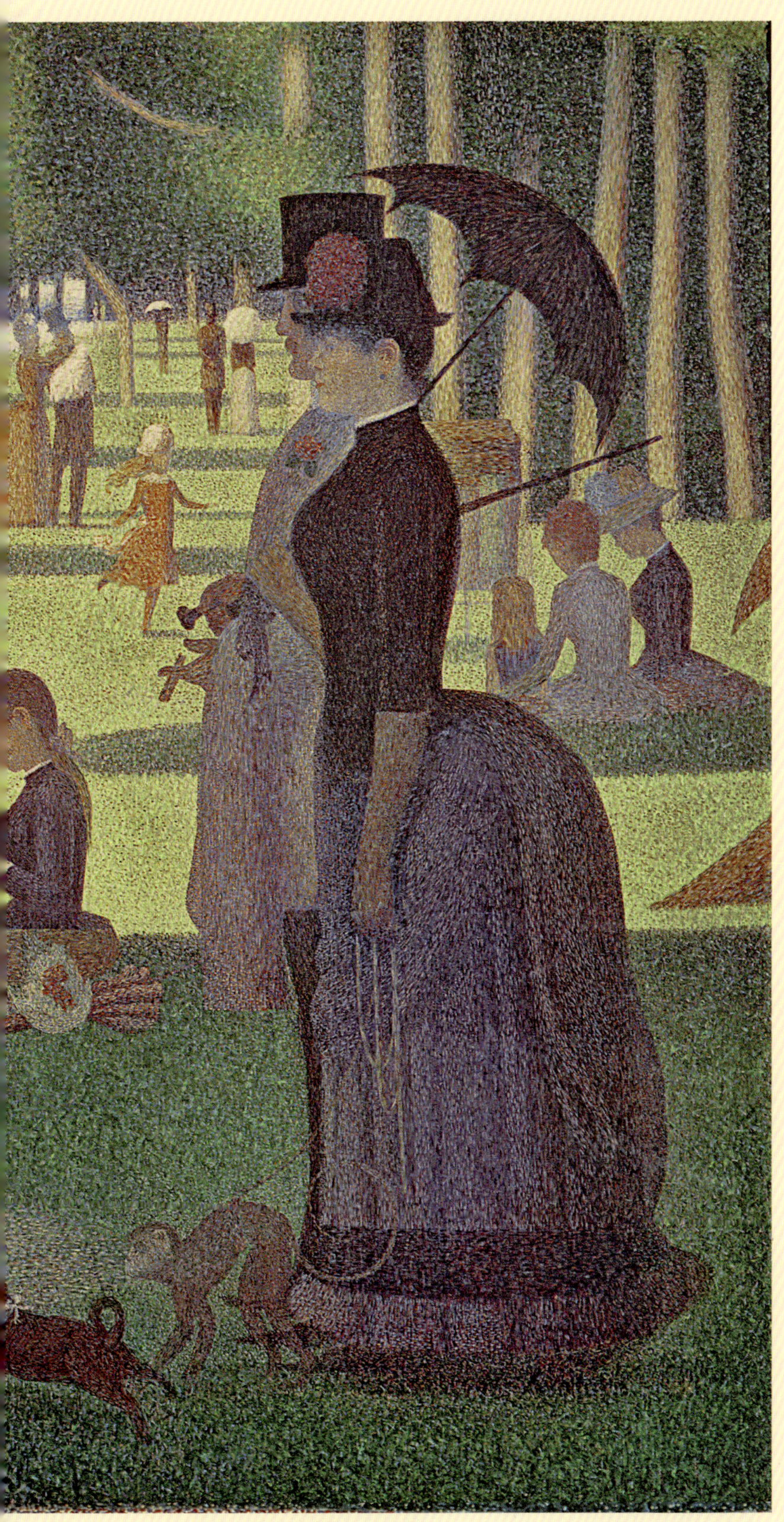

Georges-Pierre Seurat (1859–91)
Sunday Afternoon on the Island of La Grande Jatte
Un dimanche après-midi à l'île de la Grande Jatte
Ein Sonntachmittag auf der Insel La Grande Jatte
Un Domingo por la tarde en la isla de La Grande Jatte
Una domenica pomeriggio sull'isola della Grande-Jatte
Een zondagmidddag op het eiland La Grande Jatte
1884–86, Oil on canvas/Huile sur toile, 207,5 × 308,1 cm, Art Institute of Chicago, Chicago

Seurat's masterpiece, shown at the eighth and final group exhibition demonstrates the continuation of impressionism by other means. With a familiar theme, a scene from contemporary Parisian life, Seurat had used a new technique to discipline the "random" impressionist brush strokes in order to draw more luminosity from the colors.

Le chef-d'œuvre de Seurat, présenté à la huitième et dernière exposition du groupe, montre la continuité de l'impressionnisme par d'autres moyens. Avec un thème familier, une scène de la vie parisienne contemporaine, Seurat a utilisé une technique nouvelle pour discipliner les coups de pinceau impressionnistes «aléatoires», afin d'obtenir plus de luminosité des couleurs.

Seurats Meisterwerk zeigt auf der achten und letzten Gruppenausstellung die Fortführung des Impressionismus mit anderen Mitteln. Bei gleichbleibender Thematik, einer Szene aus dem zeitgenössischen Pariser Leben, hatte Seurat mithilfe einer neuen Technik versucht, den „zufälligen" impressionistischen Pinselstrich zu disziplinieren und dadurch mehr Leuchtkraft aus den Farben zu ziehen.

Esta obra maestra de Seurat mostró, en la octava y última exposición grupal de los impresionistas, la continuación del impresionismo con otros medios. Manteniendo la temática de una escena de la vida moderna parisina, Seurat intenta, por medio de una nueva técnica, disciplinar los trazos "casuales" de los impresionistas, extrayendo más luminosidad de los colores.

Il capolavoro di Seurat presentò, in occasione dell'ottava e ultima mostra collettiva, la continuazione dell'Impressionismo con altri mezzi. Rappresentando un tema consueto, una scena di vita parigina contemporanea, Seurat aveva provato ad utilizzare una nuova tecnica per disciplinare le pennellate "casuali" dell'Impressionismo, facendo così risaltare maggiormente la luminosità dei colori.

In Seurats meesterwerk, dat op de achtste en laatste groepsexpositie van de impressionisten werd getoond, zette hij hun benadering tot het uiterste door. Seurat koos een bekend thema uit het dagelijks leven in Parijs, maar probeerde met behulp van een nieuwe techniek de "toevallige" impressionistische penseelvoering te disciplineren en zo meer helderheid in het kleurpalet te scheppen.

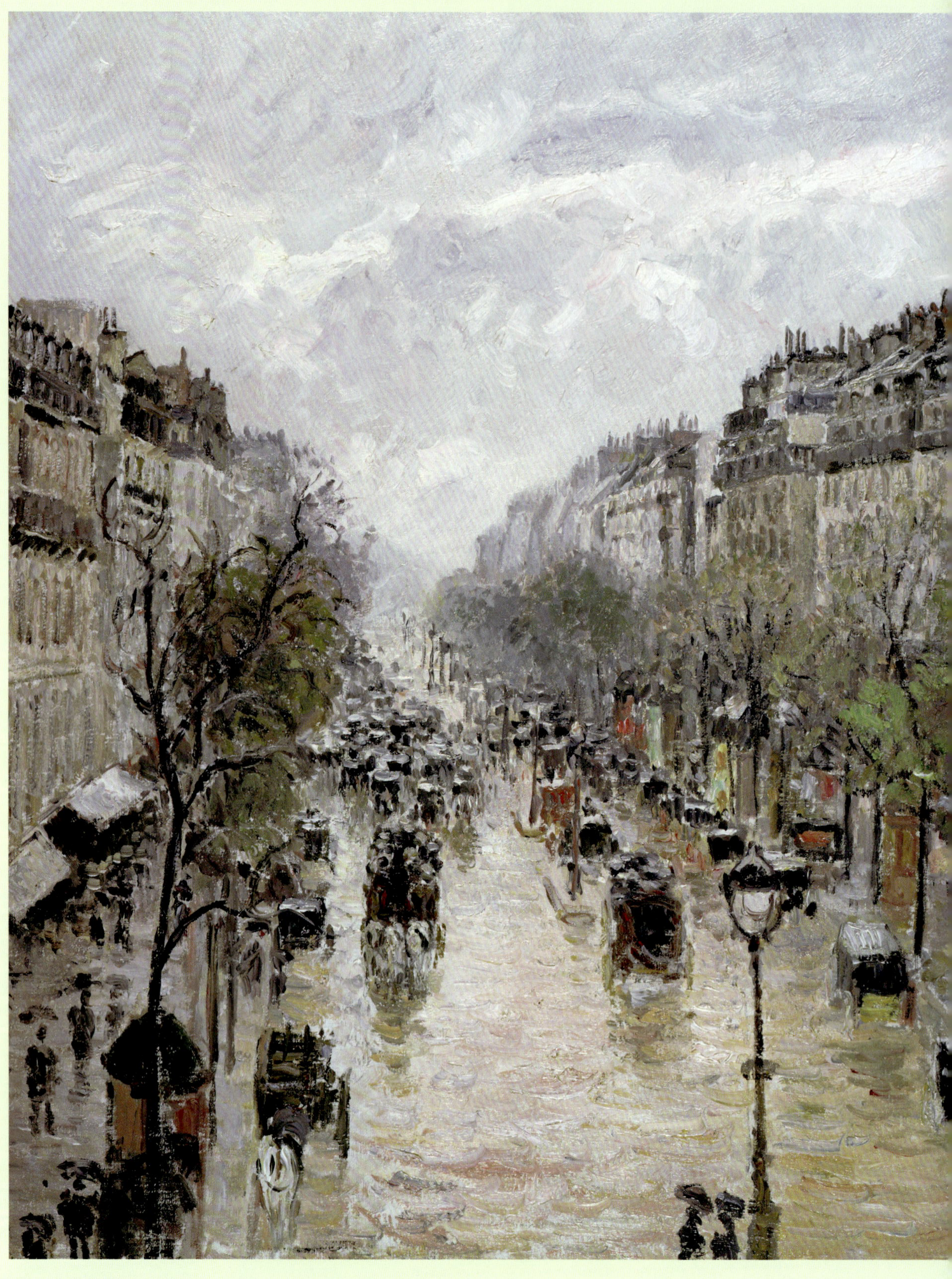

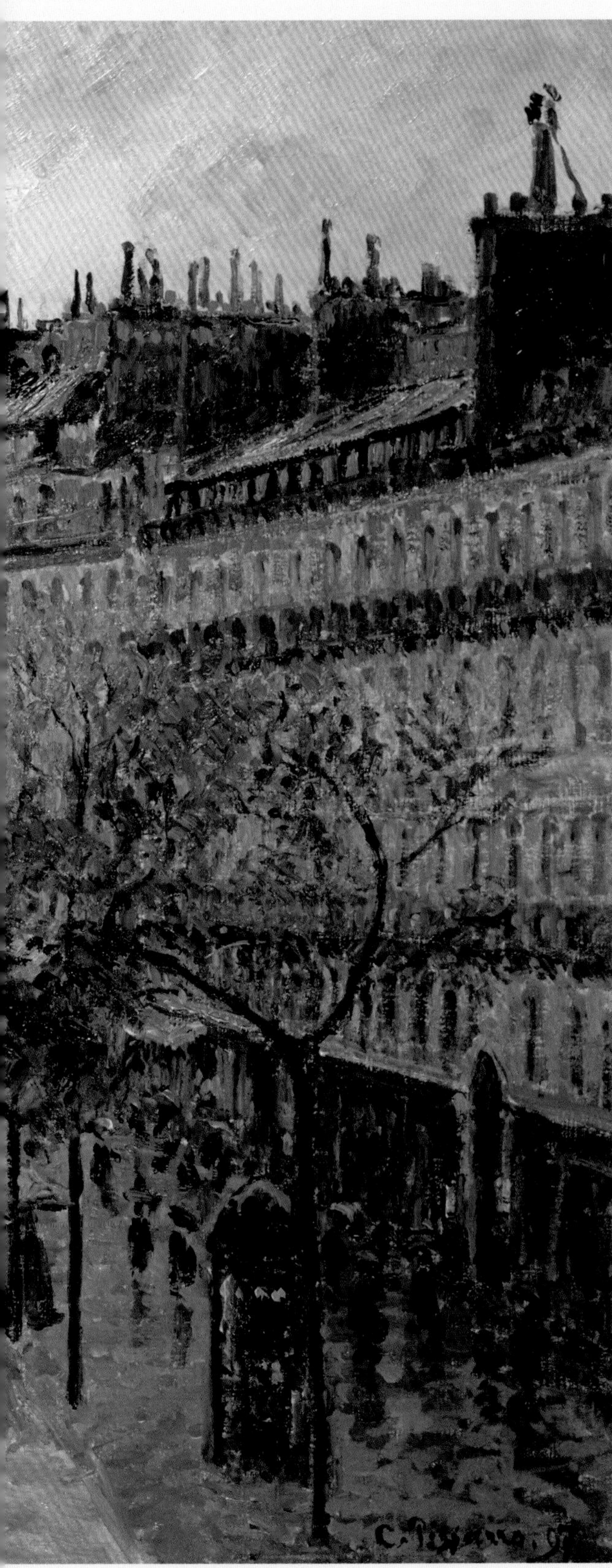

NEW SUBJECTS: THE CITY AND SCENES OF COUNTRY LIFE

NOUVEAUX SUJETS : LA VILLE ET LES SCÈNES DE LA VIE RURALE

NEUE THEMEN: GROSSSTADT UND SZENEN VOM LANDLEBEN

NUEVOS TEMAS: LA GRAN CIUDAD Y ESCENAS CAMPESTRES

LA NUOVA PITTURA IMPRESSIONISTA

NIEUWE THEMA'S: DE GROTE STAD EN DE NATUUR

Camille Pissarro (1830–1903)
Boulevard Montmartre
Boulevard Montmartre
Boulevard Montmartre
Boulevard Montmartre
Boulevard Montmartre
De Boulevard Montmartre

1897, Oil on canvas/Huile sur toile, 54,1 × 65,1 cm, Private collection

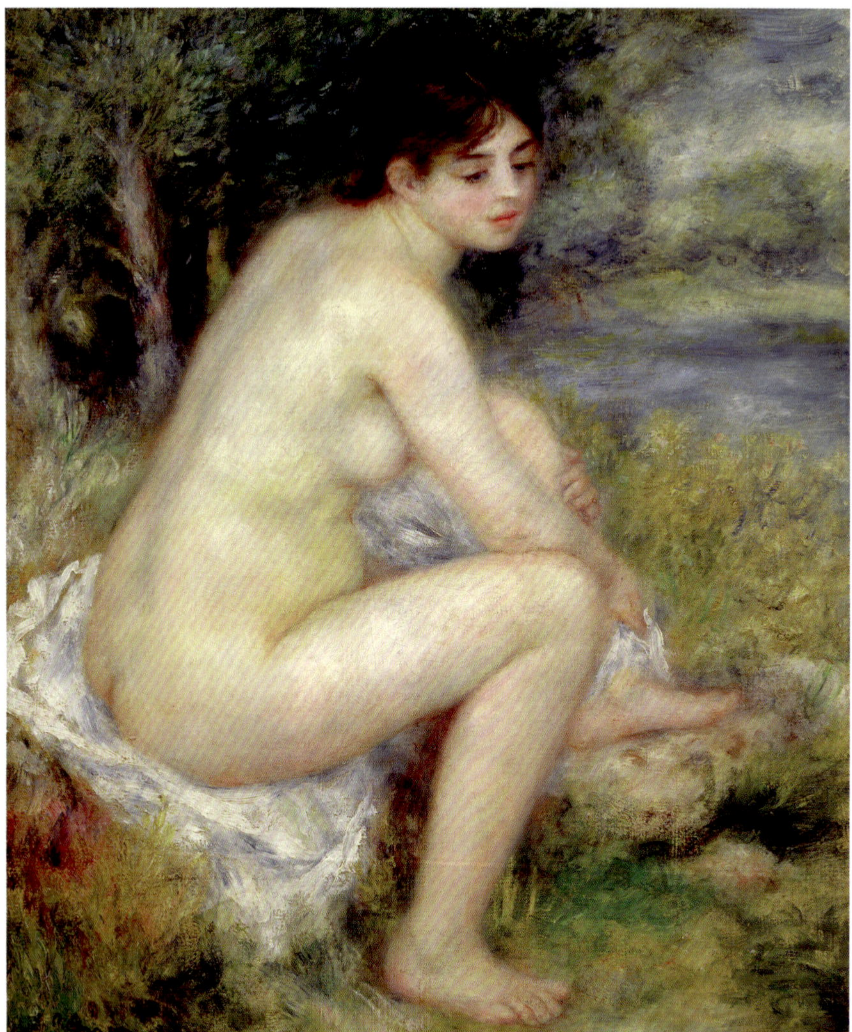

Pierre-Auguste Renoir (1841–1919)

Nude in a Landscape

Femme nue dans un paysage

Akt in Landschaft

Desnudo en un paisaje

Donna nuda in un paesaggio

Naakt in landschap

1883, Oil on canvas/Huile sur toile, 65 × 54 cm, Musée de l'Orangerie, Paris

New subjects: the city and scenes of country life

Impressionism originated in the then most modern and beautiful city in Europe, Paris, at a time when the face of the old city had begun to change completely. From 1853, the city prefect Baron Haussmann (1809-1891), under the instructions of Napoleon III, undertook a profound transformation of Paris. The tight, winding streets of the medieval city center gave way to a wide-ranging redevelopment. Driving through the middle of the centuries-old neighborhoods, huge thoroughfares were created which would become the future boulevards of Paris. Not only did the impressionists take their urban motifs from these new neighborhoods but, being aware of their importance, consciously organized six of their eight group exhibitions on these 'Grands Boulevards'. Renoir in particular, painted during this time some remarkable

Nouveaux sujets : la ville et les scènes de la vie rurale

L'impressionnisme est né dans la ville alors la plus moderne et la plus belle d'Europe, Paris, à un moment où le visage de la vieille ville commença à changer complètement. À partir de 1853, le préfet de la ville, le baron Haussmann (1809–1891), entreprit sous les ordres de Napoléon III une transformation profonde de Paris. Les rues étroites et sinueuses du centre-ville médiéval laissèrent place à un réaménagement de grande envergure. Traversant des quartiers vieux de plusieurs siècles, d'immenses artères furent ouvertes qui deviendraient les futurs boulevards de Paris. Les impressionnistes tirèrent non seulement leurs motifs urbains de ces nouveaux quartiers, mais, conscients de leur importance, ils organisèrent volontairement six des huit expositions du groupe sur ces « Grands Boulevards ». Renoir, en particulier, peignit durant

Neue Themen: Großstadt und Szenen vom Landleben

Der Impressionismus entstand in der damals modernsten und schönsten Stadt Europas, in Paris, und zwar zu einem Zeitpunkt, als sich das Gesicht der alten Stadt vollkommen zu verändern begann. Ab 1853 übernahm der Stadtpräfekt Baron Haussmann (1809–1891) nach Anweisungen von Napoleon III. die tiefgreifende Umgestaltung von Paris. Die zum Teil sehr verwinkelte, noch mittelalterliche Innenstadt musste einer breit angelegten Sanierungsmaßnahme weichen. Mitten in die alten, seit Jahrhunderten gewachsenen Stadtviertel wurden riesige Schneisen geschlagen, die zukünftigen Prachtstraßen von Paris, die Boulevards. Die Impressionisten bezogen in diesen neuen Vierteln nicht nur ihre städtischen Motive, sondern veranstalteten im Bewusstsein ihrer Bedeutung auch sechs ihrer acht Gruppenausstellungen

Nuevos temas: La gran ciudad y escenas campestres

El impresionismo nació en la ciudad más moderna y hermosa de la Europa de la época, París, y en un momento en el que la larga historia de la ciudad había empezado a cambiar completamente. A partir de 1853 el Barón Haussmann (1809–1891), prefecto de la ciudad, puso en marcha bajo órdenes de Napoleón III una profunda transformación de la ciudad. El antiguo centro urbano medieval, en partes todavía de calles tortuosas, fue objeto de unas medidas de rehabilitación exhaustivas. En medio de este antiguo barrio, formado a los largo de siglos, se abrieron enormes arterias, las futuras calles comerciales de París, los *Boulevards.* Los impresionistas utilizaron estos nuevos barrios no solo para su búsqueda de motivos, sino que, conscientes del significado, presentaron seis de sus ocho exposiciones grupales en los *Grands Boulevards.* Especialmente

Nuovi soggetti: la grande città e le scene di vita di campagna

L'Impressionismo ebbe origine a Parigi, nella città allora più moderna e più bella d'Europa, in un momento in cui il volto della città vecchia stava iniziando a cambiare completamente. Nel 1853, l'incarico di prefetto di Parigi fu affidato a Barone Haussmann (1809–1891) secondo le istruzioni di Napoleone III, il quale avviò una profonda trasformazione. La città in parte molto tortuosa ma medievale fu sottoposta a lavori di risanamento ad ampio raggio. Nei vecchi e secolari quartieri furono aperti enormi corridoi, che più tardi diventarono i viali della città, i famosi *boulevards.* Gli impressionisti non solo trassero da questi nuovi quartieri i loro motivi urbani ma, consapevoli della loro importanza, organizzarono presso i *Grands Boulevards* sei delle loro otto mostre collettive. Soprattutto Renoir dipinse

Nieuwe thema's: de grote stad en de natuur

Het impressionisme ontstond in de destijds modernste en mooiste stad van Europa, Parijs, en wel in een tijd waarin de aanblik van de oude metropool een enorme gedaanteverandering onderging. Vanaf 1853 nam stadsprefect baron Haussmann (1809–1891) op aanwijzingen van Napoleon III de ingrijpende herinrichting van Parijs ter hand. De middeleeuwse binnenstad, deels nog een doolhof van straatjes en steegjes, moest wijken voor een groots opgezet stadsherstel. Het oude centrum, dat in de loop der eeuwen op organische wijze was gegroeid, werd nu doorsneden door indrukwekkende boulevards. De impressionisten ontleenden aan dit nieuwe stedelijke landschap niet alleen hun stadsmotieven, maar hielden hun acht groepsexposities ook bewust in gebouwen aan deze Grands Boulevards, om hun betekenis te

Pierre-Auguste Renoir (1841–1919)

Young Girl in a White Hat

Jeune Fille au Chapeau Blanc

Mädchen mit weißem Hut

Niña con sombrero blanco

Ragazza con il cappello bianco

Meisje met witte hoed

c. 1870, Oil on canvas/Huile sur toile, 98 × 76 cm, Private collection

cityscapes, which give a vivid impression of the urban atmosphere with its throng of pedestrians, carriages and so on.

The boulevards themselves already served as a public stage for the promenaders of the city, but even more popular were the many venues dotted along the main avenues; the multitude of cafes, theaters, opera houses, music halls, restaurants and dance halls. The impressionists were not only the amused observers of this bustle, but were obviously only too happy to participate. Larger and more fashionable were the newly built 'variétés', such as the Folies-Bergère, which were a wonderful mix of restaurant, music hall and nightclub. If one wanted to venture out onto the dancefloor, then there were opportunities to do so at the numerous public dances, whether they were in theaters, parks or open-air public places, such as the famous Moulin de la Galette, a former mill located in Montmartre, which was then still a village and where every weekend dance music was played, and waffles (fr. 'galette') were served. Renoir captured the unadulterated 'joie de vivre' of one such event in one of his most famous paintings.

cette période de remarquables paysages urbains qui donnent une vive impression de l'atmosphère, avec sa foule de piétons, voitures, etc.

Les boulevards eux-mêmes servaient déjà de scène publique aux promeneurs citadins, mais plus populaires encore étaient les nombreux lieux qui jalonnaient les principales avenues : une multitude de cafés, théâtres, opéras, salles de concert, restaurants et salles de bal. Les impressionnistes furent non seulement des observateurs amusés de cette agitation, mais ils furent visiblement très heureux d'y prendre part. La mode était aux théâtres de variétés, comme celui des Folies-Bergère récemment construit, qui était un merveilleux mélange de restaurant, music-hall et salle de bal. Pour qui voulait s'aventurer sur une piste de danse, les possibilités ne manquaient pas, avec les nombreux bals publics donnés dans des théâtres, des parcs ou des lieux publics en plein air, comme au célèbre Moulin de la Galette, un ancien moulin situé à Montmartre – qui était alors encore un village –, où il y avait de la musique chaque week-end et où l'on servait des « galettes ». Renoir a capturé la véritable joie de vivre d'un tel événement dans l'un de ses tableaux les plus célèbres.

an den Grands Boulevards. Besonders Renoir malte in dieser Zeit einige bemerkenswerte Stadtansichten, die einen lebendigen Eindruck der städtischen Atmosphäre mit ihrem Gedränge von Passanten, Kutschen und Spaziergängern vermitteln.

Die Boulevards dienten zwar selbst schon als öffentliche Bühne für die Flaneure der Großstadt, doch noch beliebter waren die vielen Treffpunkte entlang der großen Prachtstraßen, die vielen Cafés, Theater, die Oper, Musikhallen, Restaurants und Ballhäuser. Die Impressionisten waren nicht nur amüsierte Beobachter dieses Treibens, sondern nahmen offensichtlich auch gerne daran teil. Größer und mondäner waren die neu errichteten Variétés, wie das Folies-Bergère, eine wunderbare Mischung aus Restaurant, Musikhalle und Nachtbar. Wollte man sich selbst auf das Parkett der Eitelkeiten wagen, so gab es dazu Gelegenheit auf den zahlreichen öffentlichen Tanzveranstaltungen, sei es in Sälen, Parks oder Freilichtlokalen, wie dem bekannten Moulin de la Galette, einer ehemaligen Mühle auf dem noch dörflichen Montmartre gelegen, in der jedes Wochenende zum Tanz aufgespielt wurde und Waffeln (frz. *galette*) serviert wurden. Renoir hat in einem seiner berühmtesten Bilder eine solche Tanzveranstaltung in unverfälschter Lebensfreude festgehalten.

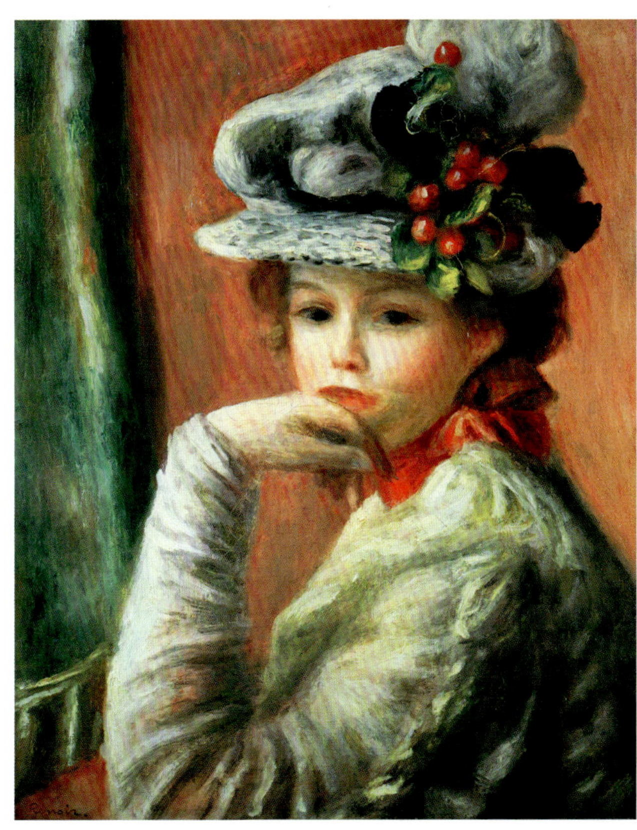

Renoir pintó durante esta época sus admirables vistas de la ciudad, que transmiten una atmósfera cosmopolita con el ir y venir de transeúntes, carruajes y paseantes.

Si bien los *boulevards* servían como decorado para los *flâneurs* de la ciudad, los diversos puntos de encuentro alrededor de estas calles (muchos cafés, teatros, óperas, salas de conciertos y bailes o restaurantes) eran incluso más populares. Los impresionistas no eran tan solo observadores de esta actividad, sino que aparentemente disfrutaban de tomar una parte activa en la misma. Más grandes y mundanos eran los teatros de variedades como el Folies-Bergère, una increíble mezcla de restaurante, sala de conciertos y local nocturno. Si se buscaba dar rienda suelta a la vanidad, había múltiples ocasiones para ello en los diversos eventos de baile públicos, en salas, parques o ocales al aire libre, como el conocido Moulin de la Galette, un antiguo molino en el todavía pintoresco Montmartre, en el que cada fin de semana se invitaba a bailar mientras se servían gofres (en francés *galette*). Renoir capturó en una de sus imágenes más famosas uno de estos eventos, transmitiendo una honesta alegría de vivir.

in questo periodo alcuni notevoli paesaggi urbani che danno una vivida impressione dell'atmosfera urbana con la sua folla di passanti, carrozze e persone a passeggio.

I *boulevards* stessi servivano da palcoscenico pubblico per i *flâneurs* della città, tuttavia ancora più popolari erano i numerosi luoghi di ritrovo che sorgevano lungo i viali principali: caffè, teatri, opera, music hall, ristoranti e sale da ballo. Gli impressionisti erano non solo osservatori divertiti di questo viavai, ma vi partecipavamo anche volentieri e apertamente. Più grandi e mondani erano poi i nuovi *variétés,* come il Folies-Bergère, un meraviglioso locale a mezza strada tra ristorante, music hall e discoteca. Coloro che volevano dare sfogo alla propria vanità avevano l'opportunità di partecipare ai numerosi balli pubblici allestiti nei teatri, nei parchi o in luoghi pubblici all'aperto, come il famoso Moulin de la Galette, un antico mulino di Montmartre, allora ancora villaggio, che ogni fine settimana apriva le sue porte per i ballerini e serviva cialde (*galette* in francese). Renoir catturò la gioia pura di questa danza in uno dei suoi dipinti più famosi.

benadrukken. Het was vooral Renoir die in deze tijd enkele opmerkelijke stadsgezichten schilderde, waarin hij het drukke straatleven met zijn voetgangers, koetsen en wandelaars op levendige wijze verbeeldde.

De boulevards dienden weliswaar als schouwtoneel voor de Parijse flaneurs, maar nog geliefder waren de vele ontmoetingsplekken aan deze nieuwe doorgansroutes: de talloze cafés, theaters, de opera, muziekhallen, restaurants en balzalen. De impressionisten waren niet alleen geamuseerde waarnemers van dit vertier, maar namen er ook graag aan deel. Groter en mondainer waren de nieuwe variététheaters, zoals de Folies-Bergère, een prachtige combinatie van restaurant, muziekhal en nachtkroeg. Wie zich op de dansvloer wilde wagen, had daartoe de kans op talrijke openbare plekken, van zalen en parken tot openluchtgelegenheden als de befaamde Moulin de la Galette, een voormalige molen in het destijds nog dorpse Montmartre, waar elke week werd gedanst en wafels (galettes) werden geserveerd. In een van zijn beroemdste doeken heeft Renoir zo'n dansgelegenheid met onverbloemd levensplezier vastgelegd.

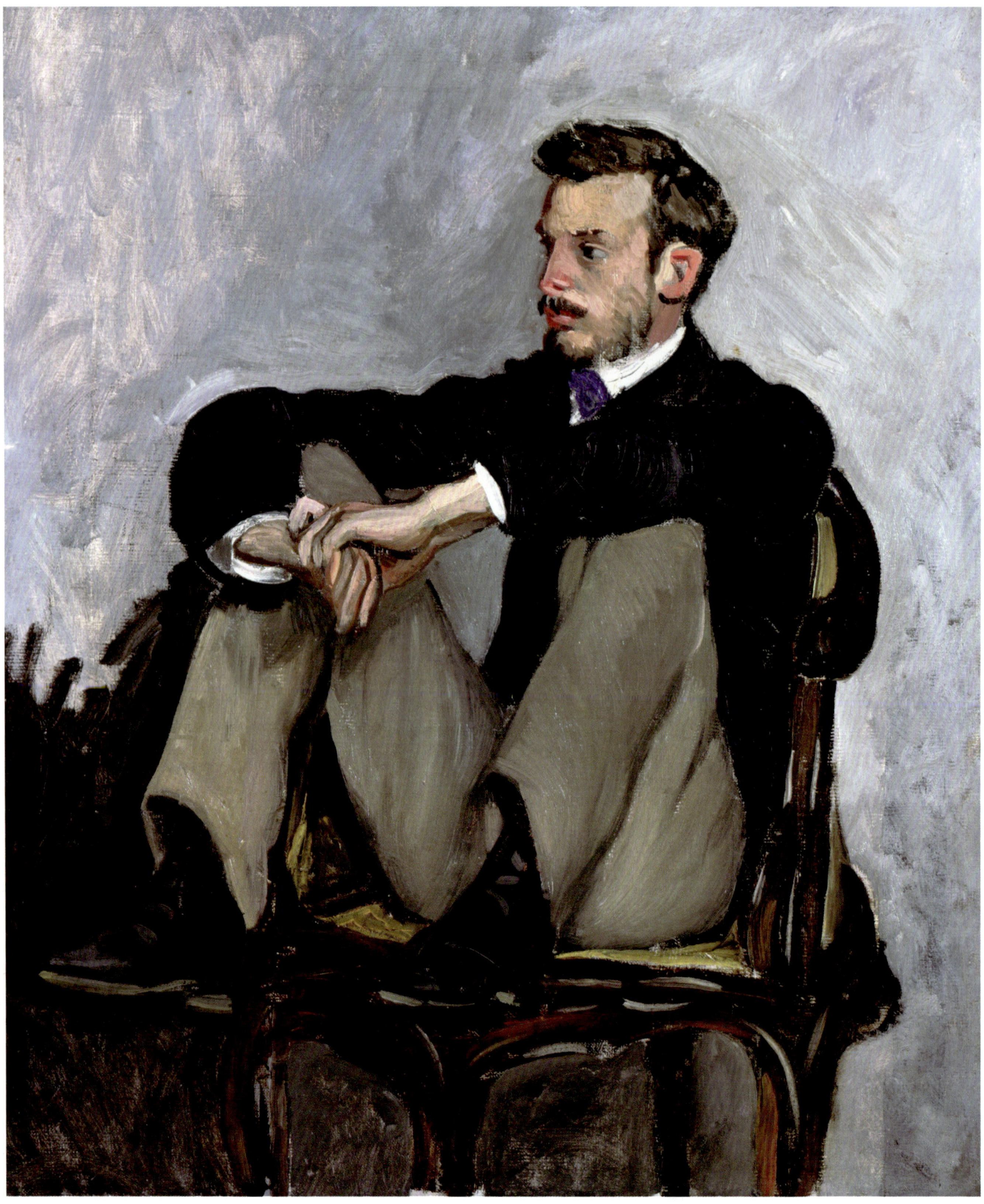

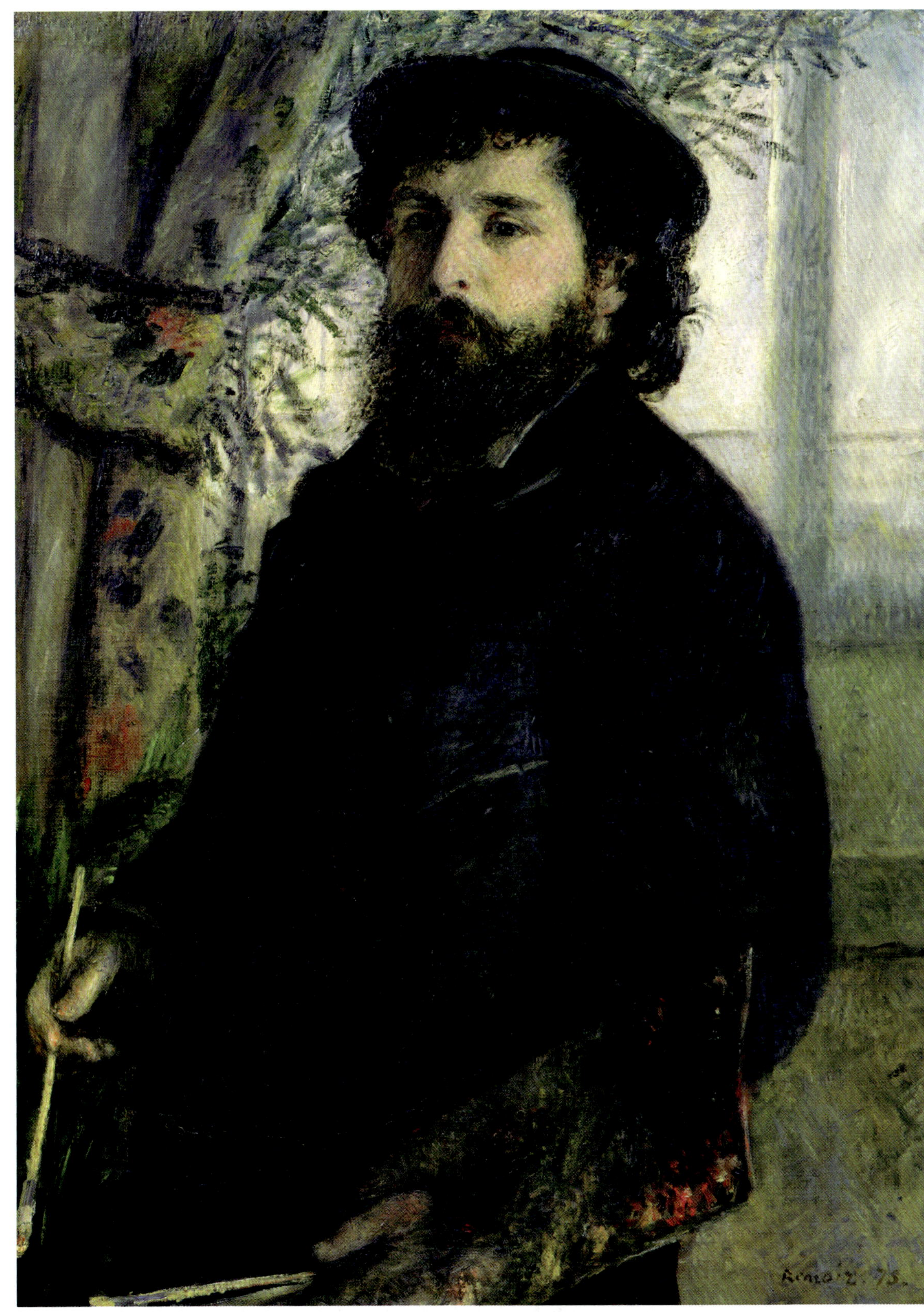

Jean-Frédéric Bazille (1841–70)

Portrait of Auguste
Renoir (1841–1919)

Portrait d'Auguste Renoir

Bildnis Auguste Renoir

Retrato de Auguste Renoir

Ritratto di Auguste Renoir

Portret van Auguste Renoir

1867, Oil on canvas/Huile sur toile,
61,2 × 51 cm, Musée d'Orsay, Paris

**Pierre-Auguste Renoir
(1841–1919)**

Portrait of Claude
Monet (1840–1926)

Portrait de Claude Monet

Porträt von Claude Monet

Retrato de Claude Monet

Ritratto di Claude Monet

Portret van Claude Monet

1875, Oil on canvas/Huile sur toile,
84 × 60,5 cm, Musée d'Orsay, Paris

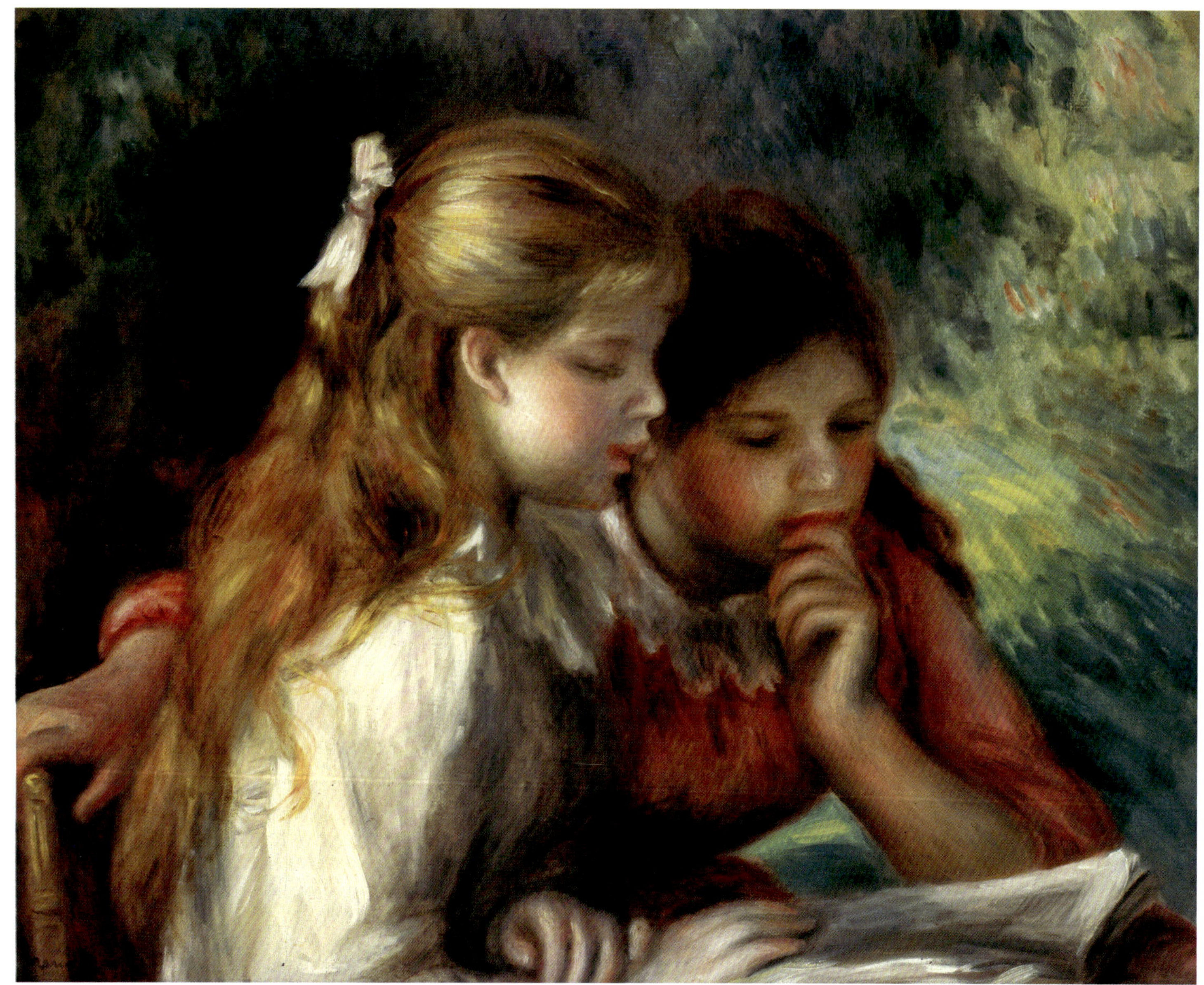

Pierre-Auguste Renoir (1841–1919)

The Reading

La lecture

Die Lektüre

La lectura

La lettura

La lecture

c. 1890–95, Oil on canvas/Huile sur toile, 55 × 65 cm, Musée du Louvre, Paris

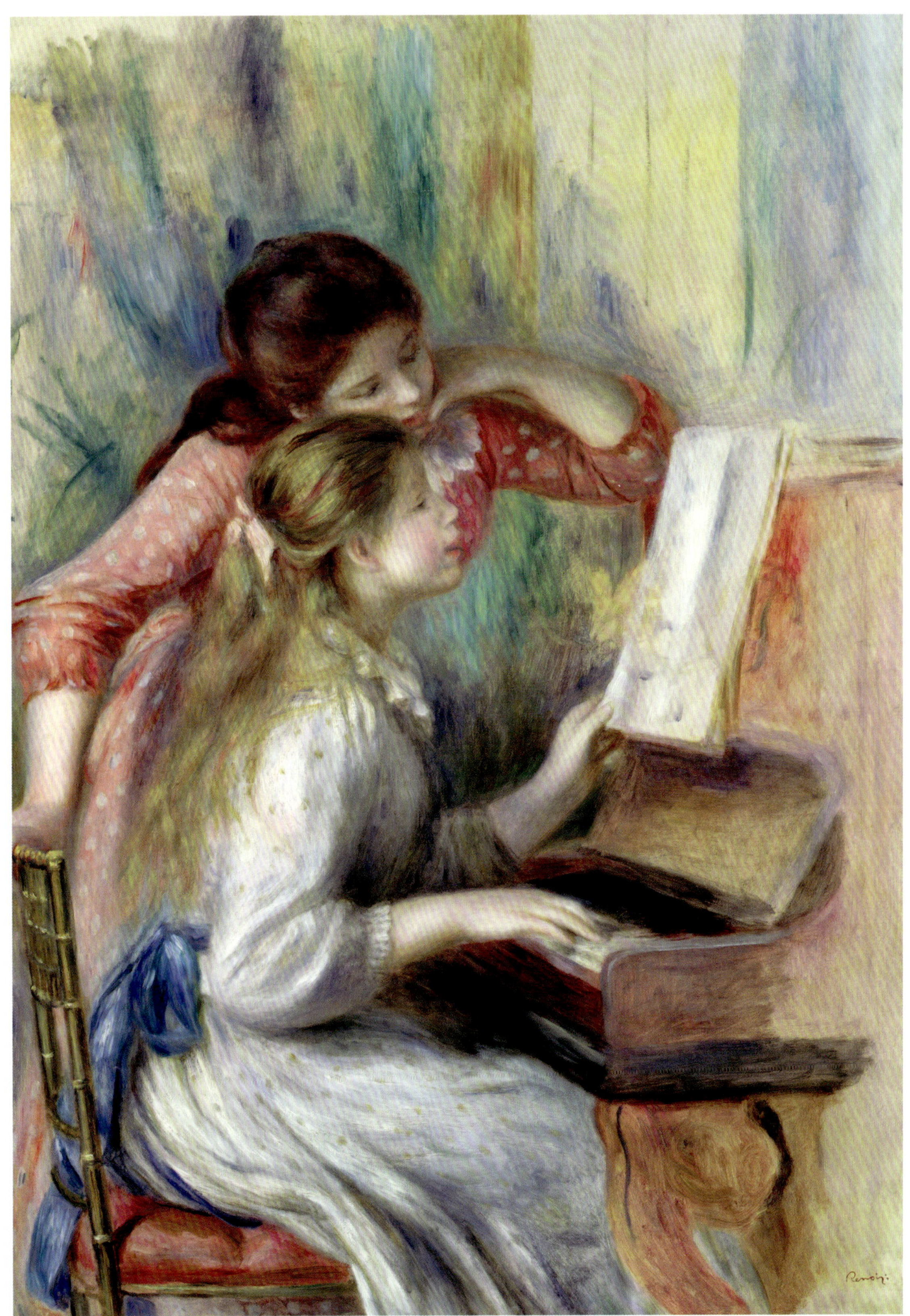

Pierre-Auguste Renoir (1841–1919)

Young Girls at the Piano

Jeunes filles au piano

Mädchen am Klavier

Jovencitas al piano

Ragazze al pianoforte

Meisjes aan de piano

c. 1892, Oil on canvas/Huile sur toile,
116 × 81 cm, Musée de l'Orangerie, Paris

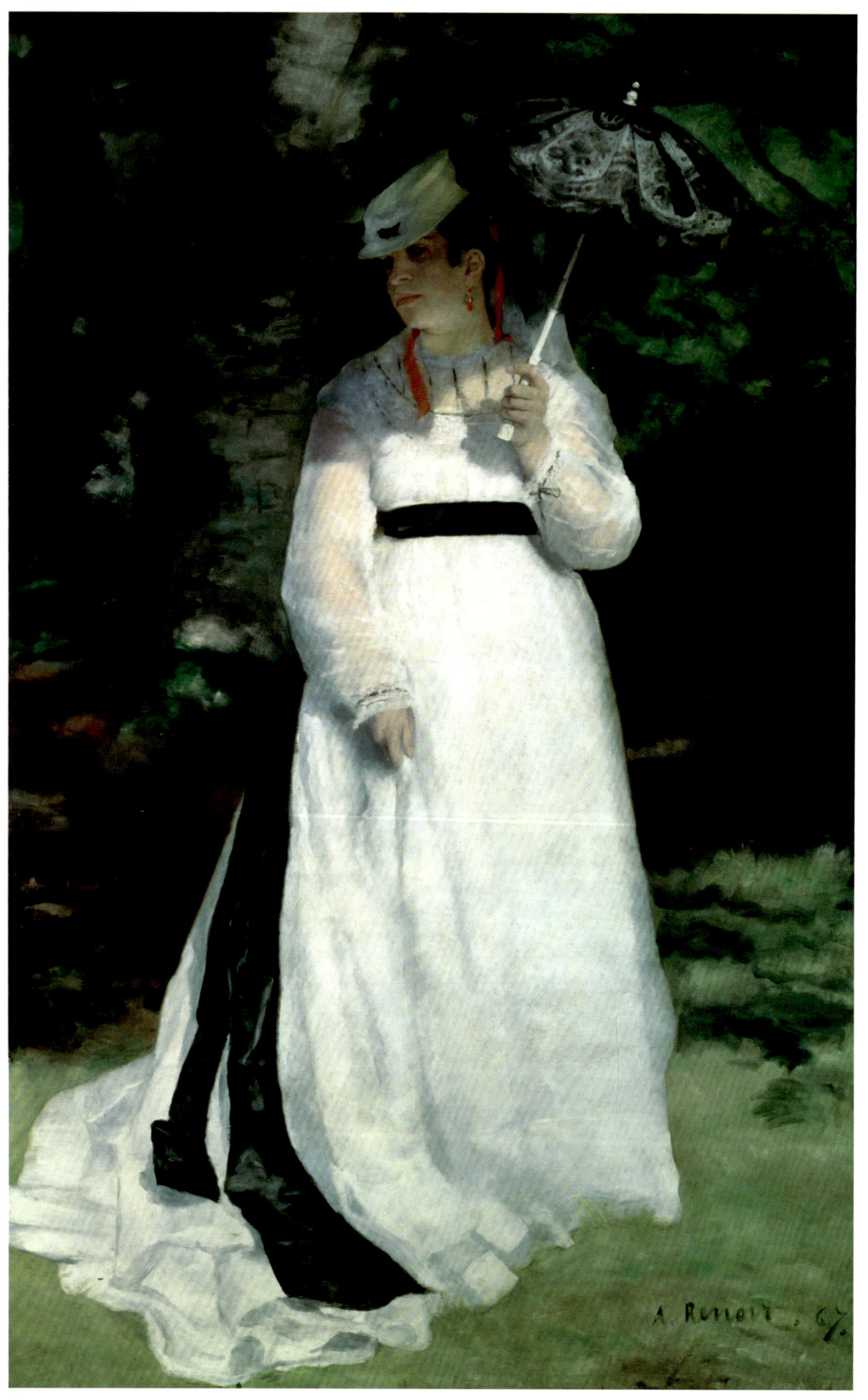

Pierre-Auguste Renoir (1841–1919)

Portrait of Lise

Portrait de Lise

Porträt von Lise

Retrato de Lise

Ritratto di Lise

Portret van Lise

1867, Oil on canvas/Huile sur toile, 184 × 115,5 cm,
Museum Folkwang, Essen

Pierre-Auguste Renoir (1841–1919)

The Swing

La balançoire

Die Schaukel

El columpio

L'altalena

De schommel

1876, Oil on canvas/Huile sur toile,
92 × 73 cm, Musée d'Orsay, Paris

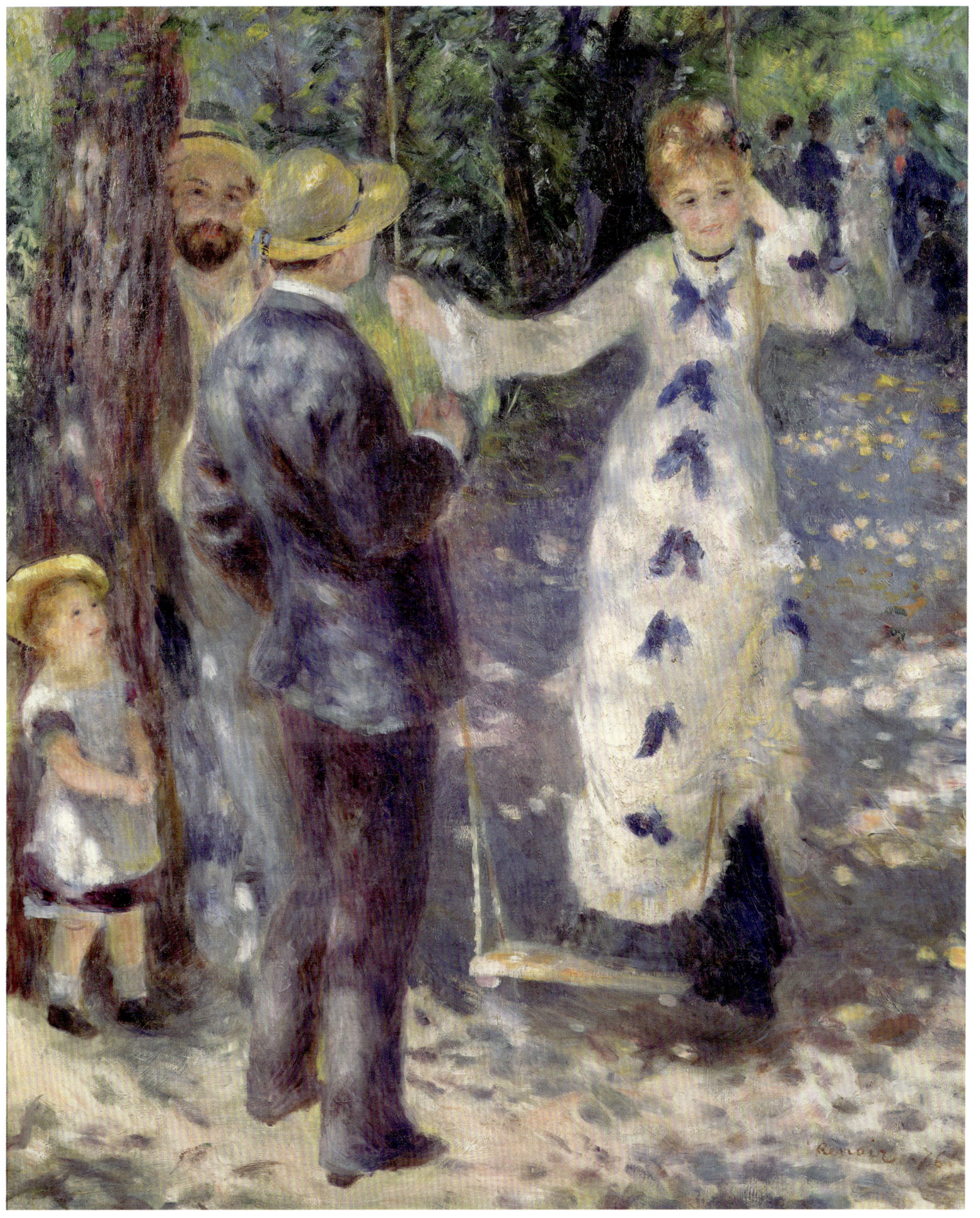

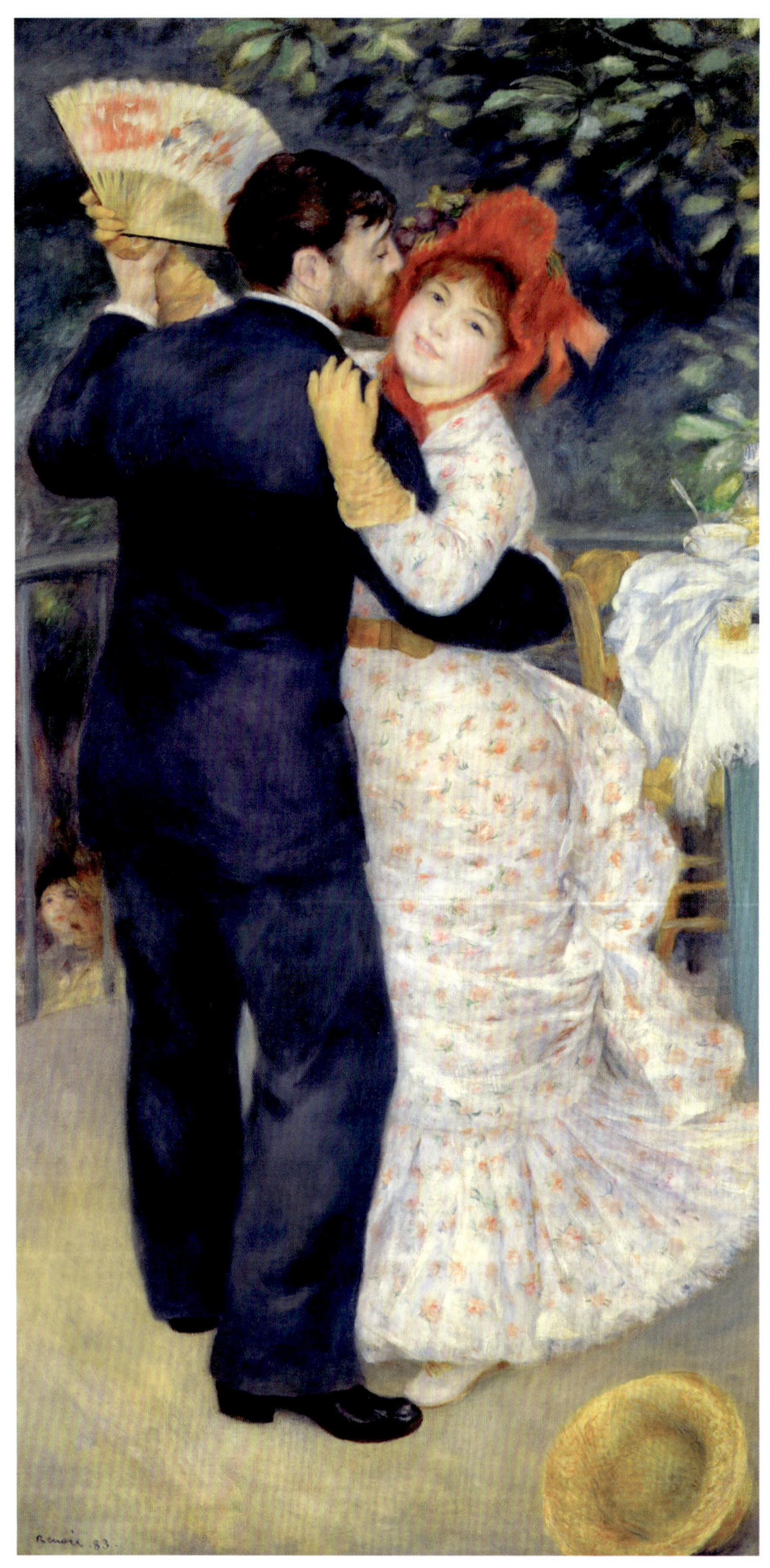

Pierre-Auguste Renoir (1841–1919)

A Dance in the Country

Danse à la campe

Ein Tanz auf dem Lande

Baile en el campo

Ballo in campa

Dans op het land

1883, Oil on canvas/Huile sur toile,
180,3 × 90 cm, Musée d'Orsay, Paris

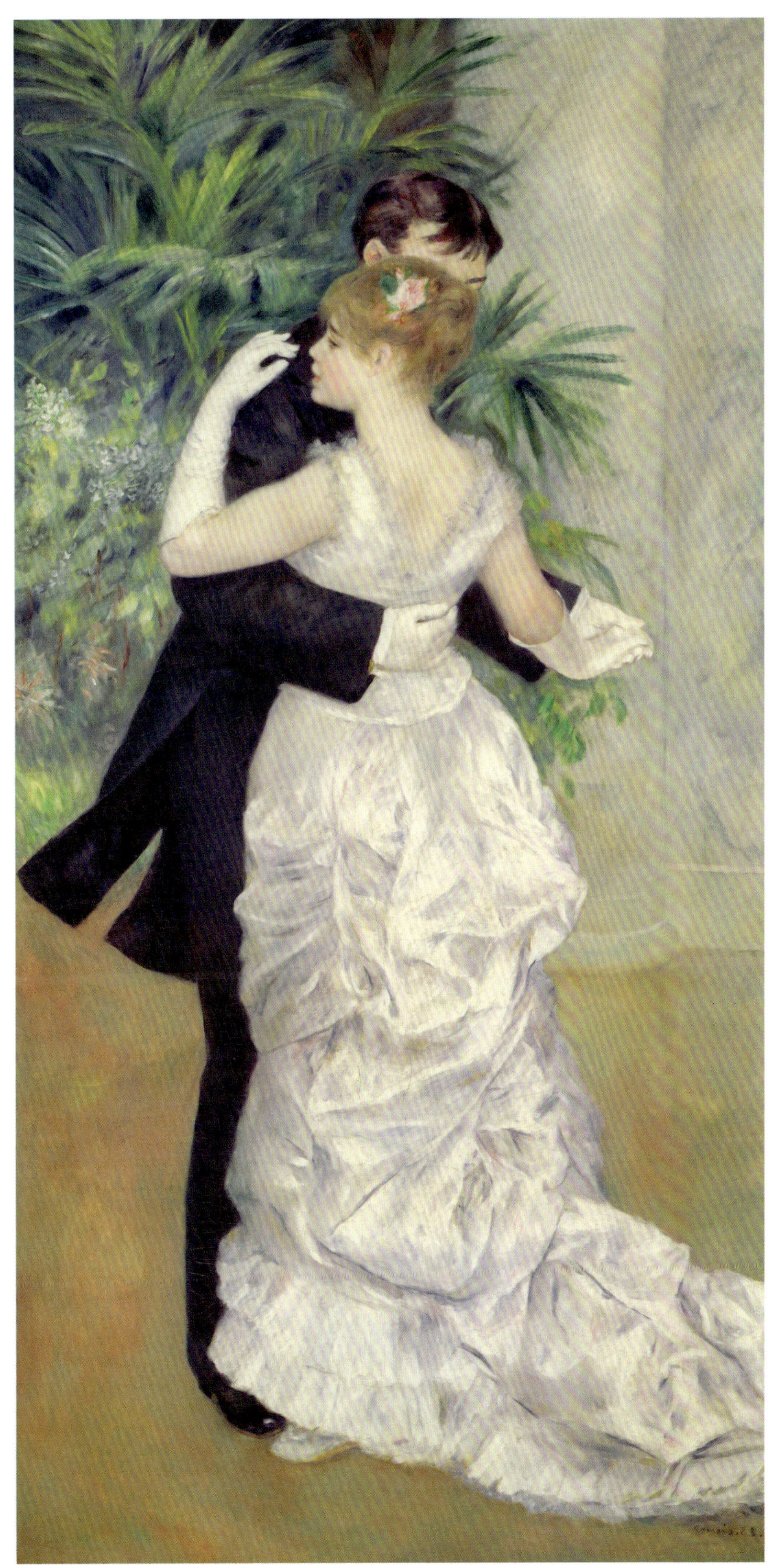

Pierre-Auguste Renoir (1841−1919)

Dance in the City

Danse à la ville

Tanz in der Stadt

Baile en la ciudad

Ballo in città

Dans in de stad

1883, Oil on canvas/Huile sur toile,
179,7 × 89,1 cm, Musée d'Orsay, Paris

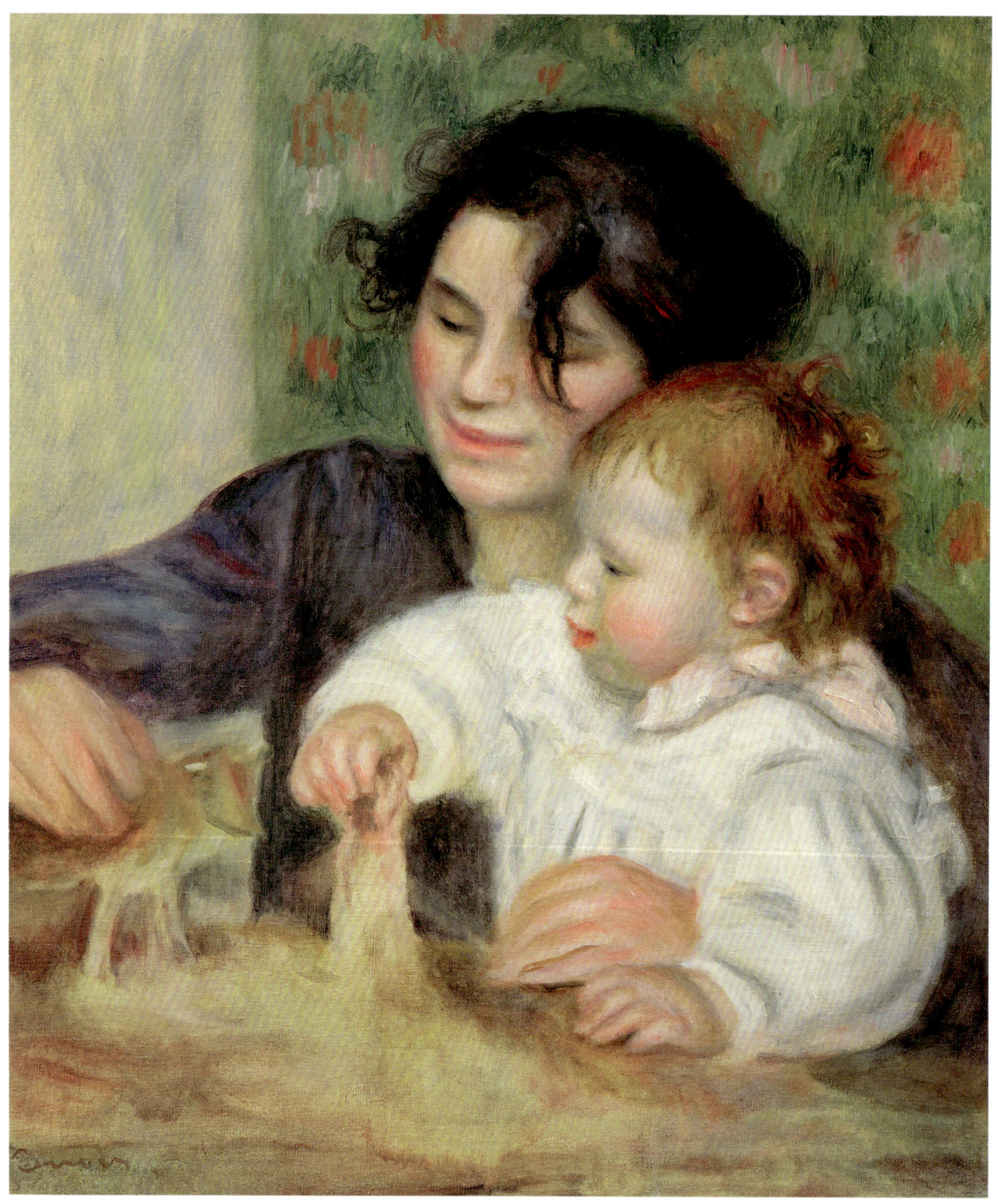

Pierre-Auguste Renoir (1841–1919)

Gabrielle and Jean

Gabrielle et Jean

Gabrielle und Jean

Gabrielle y Jean

Gabrielle e Jean

Gabrielle en Jean

c. 1895/96, Oil on canvas/Huile sur toile, 65 × 54 cm, Musée de l'Orangerie, Paris

Berthe Morisot (1841–95)

The Cradle

Le Berceau

Die Wiege

La cuna

La culla

De wieg

1872, Oil on canvas/Huile sur toile, 56 × 46 cm, Musée d'Orsay, Paris

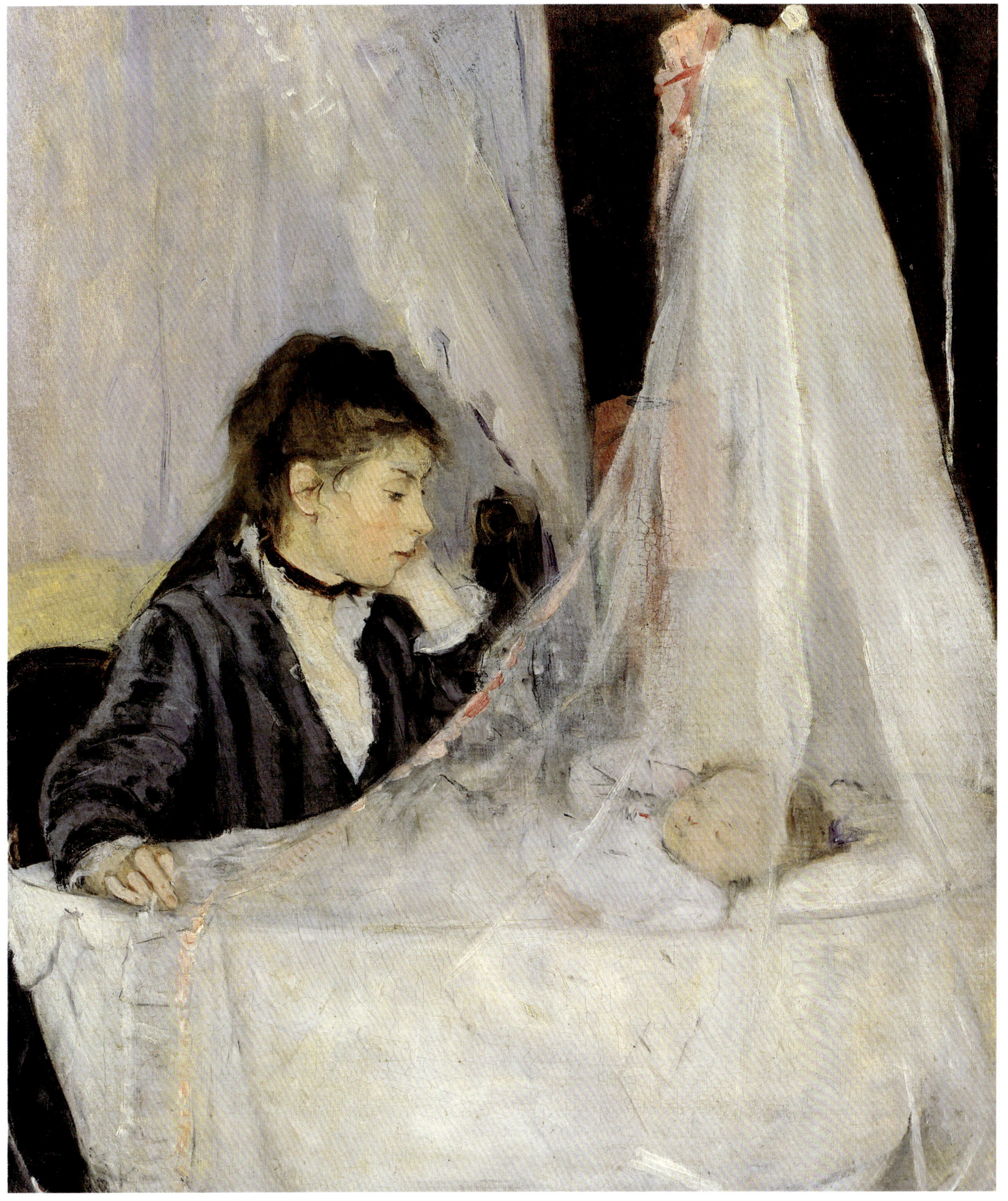

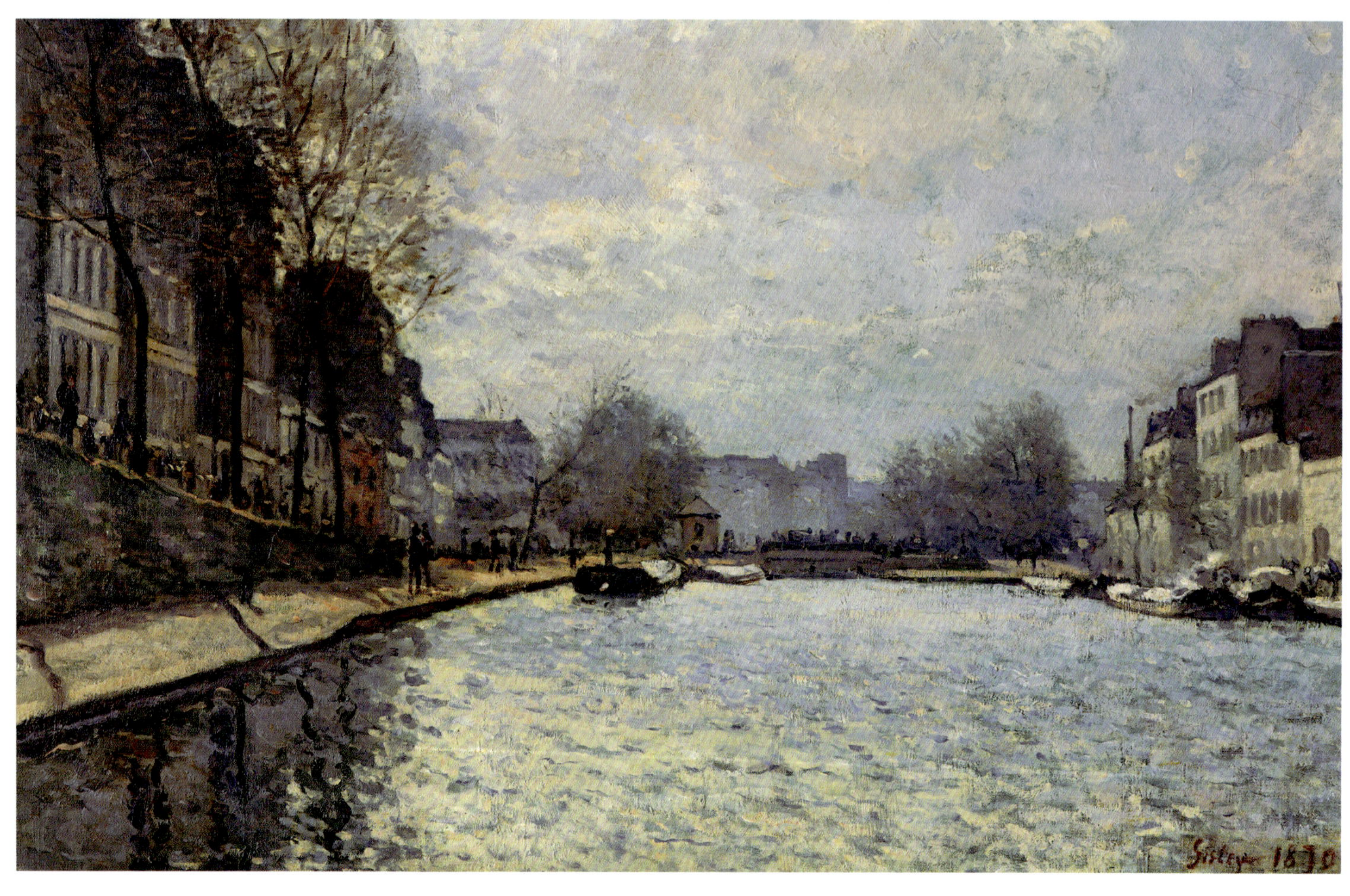

Alfred Sisley (1839–99)

View of the Canal Saint–Martin

Vue du canal Saint-Martin

Ansicht des Kanals Saint-Martin

Vista del canal de Saint-Martin

Veduta del Canale San-Martino

Gezicht op het kanaal Saint-Martin

1870, Oil on canvas/Huile sur toile, 50 × 65 cm, Musée d'Orsay, Paris

Alfred Sisley (1839–99)

Snow at Louveciennes

La neige à Louveciennes

Schnee in Louveciennes

Louveciennes bajo la nieve

La neve a Louveciennes

Sneeuw in Louveciennes

1878, Oil on canvas/Huile sur toile, 61 × 50 cm, Musée d'Orsay, Paris

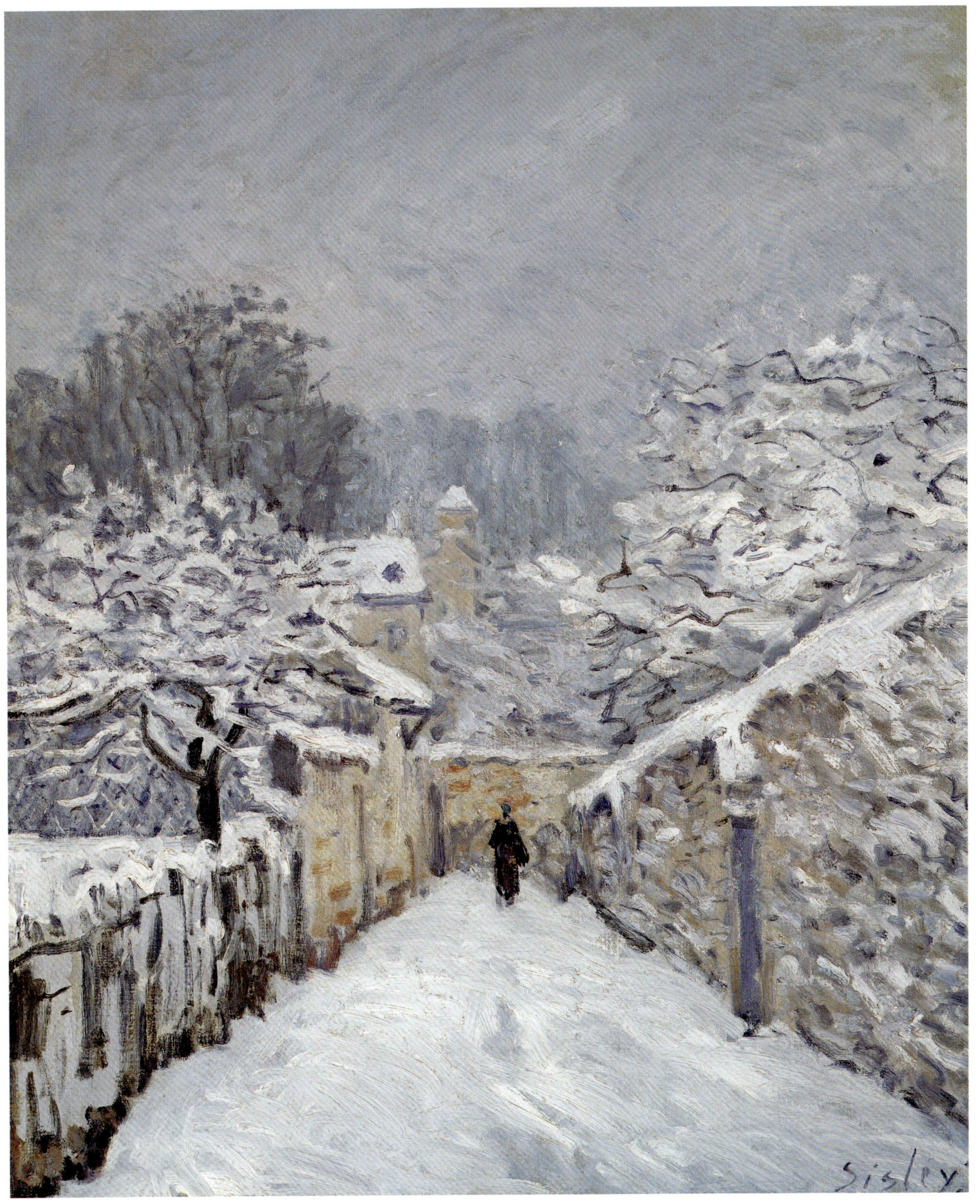

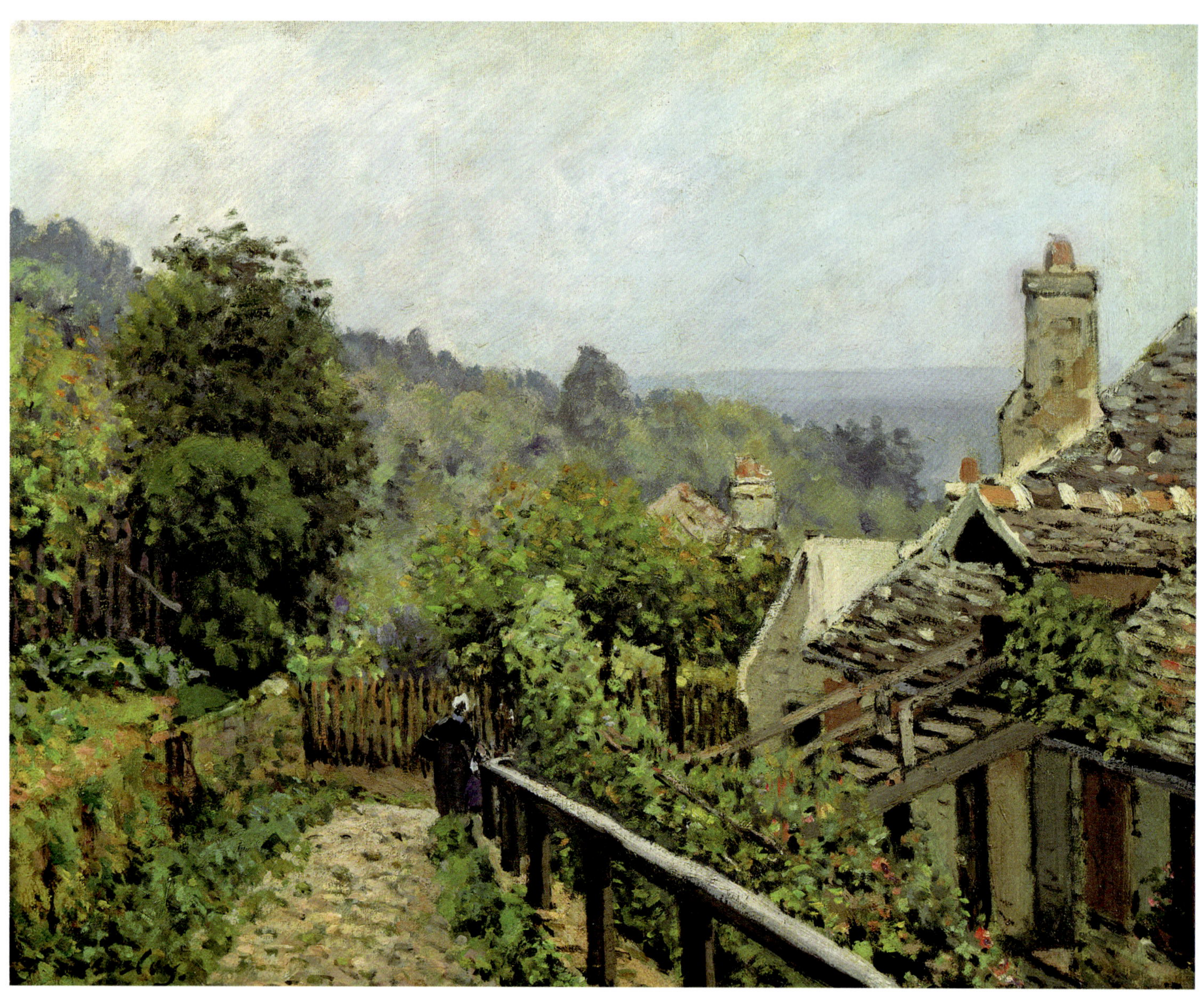

Alfred Sisley (1839–99)

Louveciennes *or* The Heights at Marly

Louveciennes. Sentier de la Mi-Côte, *dit autrefois* Hauteurs de Marly

Louveciennes auf den Höhen von Marly

Louveciennes sobre los altos de Marly

Louveciennes *o* Le cime di Marly

Louveciennes. Het pad halfweg de heuvel

c. 1873, Oil on canvas/Huile sur toile, 38 × 46,5 cm, Musée d'Orsay, Paris

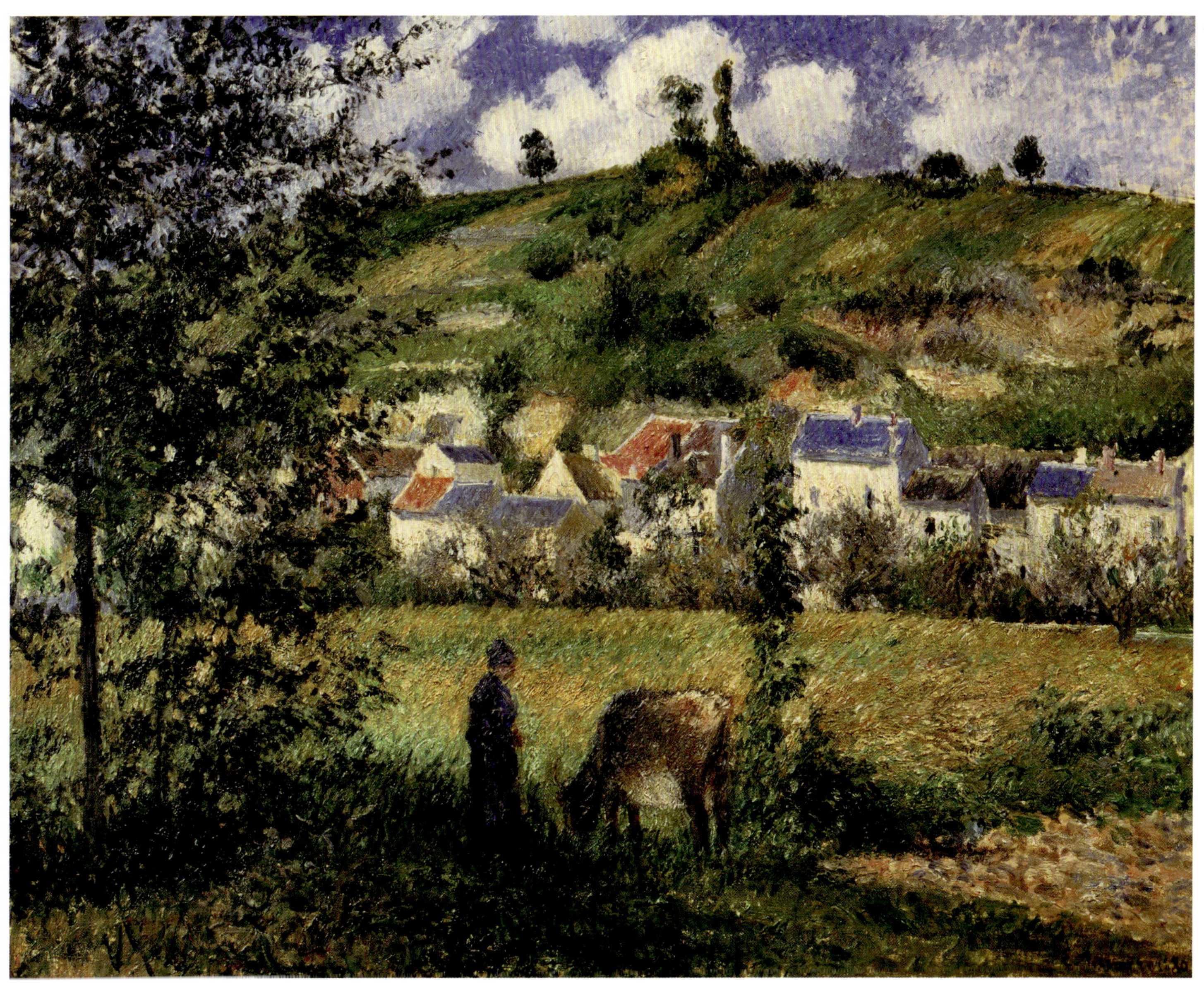

Camille Pissarro (1830–1903)

Landscape at Chaponval

Paysage à Chaponval

Landschaft bei Chaponval

Paisaje en Chaponval

Paesaggio a Chaponval

Landschap bij Chaponval

1880, Oil on canvas/Huile sur toile, 54,5 × 65 cm, Musée d'Orsay, Paris

Monet rarely painted cityscapes, but in 1875 began to follow the fashion of representing the newly created boulevards. Here he captures the vibrancy of contemporary life in the urban streets.

Monet peignait peu de paysages urbains, mais en 1875 il commença à suivre la mode pour représenter les boulevards nouvellement créés. Ici, il capte le dynamisme de la vie contemporaine dans les rues urbaines.

Monet malte selten Stadtansichten, folgte aber 1875 der Mode, die neu geschaffenen Boulevards darzustellen. Hier hält er sehr lebendig das zeitgenössische Leben in diesen großen Straßenzügen fest.

Monet raramente pintaba vistas de la ciudad, pero siguió a partir de 1875 la moda de representar los nuevos *Boulevards*. Aquí captura de manera muy vital la vida moderna en estas grandes arterias de la ciudad.

Monet dipingeva raramente paesaggi urbani, ma nel 1875 decise di seguire la moda dell'epoca e raffigurò i *boulevards* appena costruiti, vivace palcoscenico della vita contemporanea parigina.

Monet schilderde zelden stadsgezichten, maar in 1875 sloot hij zich aan bij de rage om de nieuwe boulevards uit te beelden. Hier legt hij het sfeervolle straatleven van deze brede straten vast.

Claude Monet (1840–1926)
Boulevard des Capucines
Boulevard des Capucines
Boulevard des Capucines
El Boulevard des Capucines
Boulevard des Capucines
De Boulevard des Capucines
1873/74, Oil on canvas/Huile sur toile, 80,33 × 60,33 cm, Nelson-Atkins Museum of Art, Kansas City

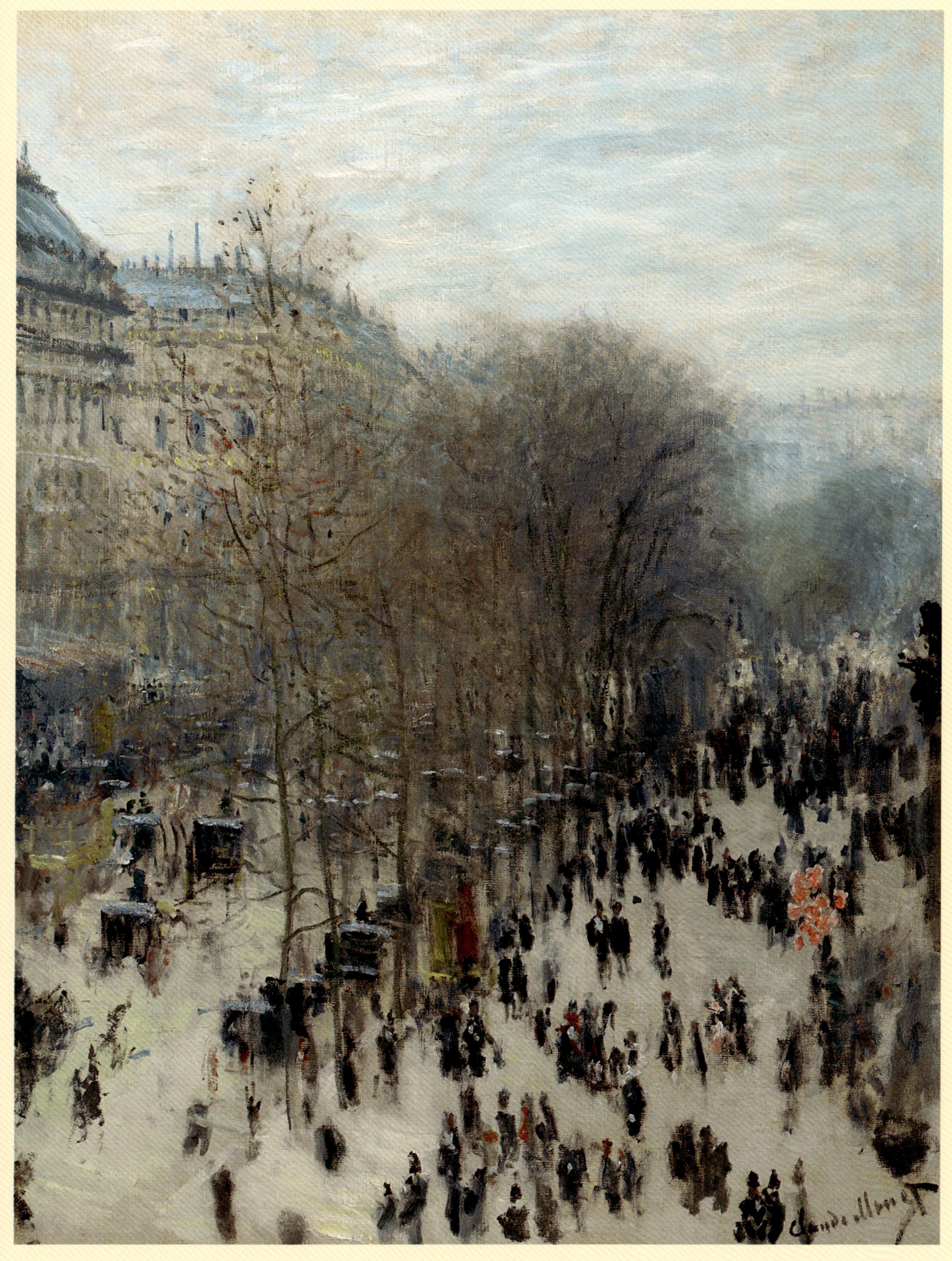

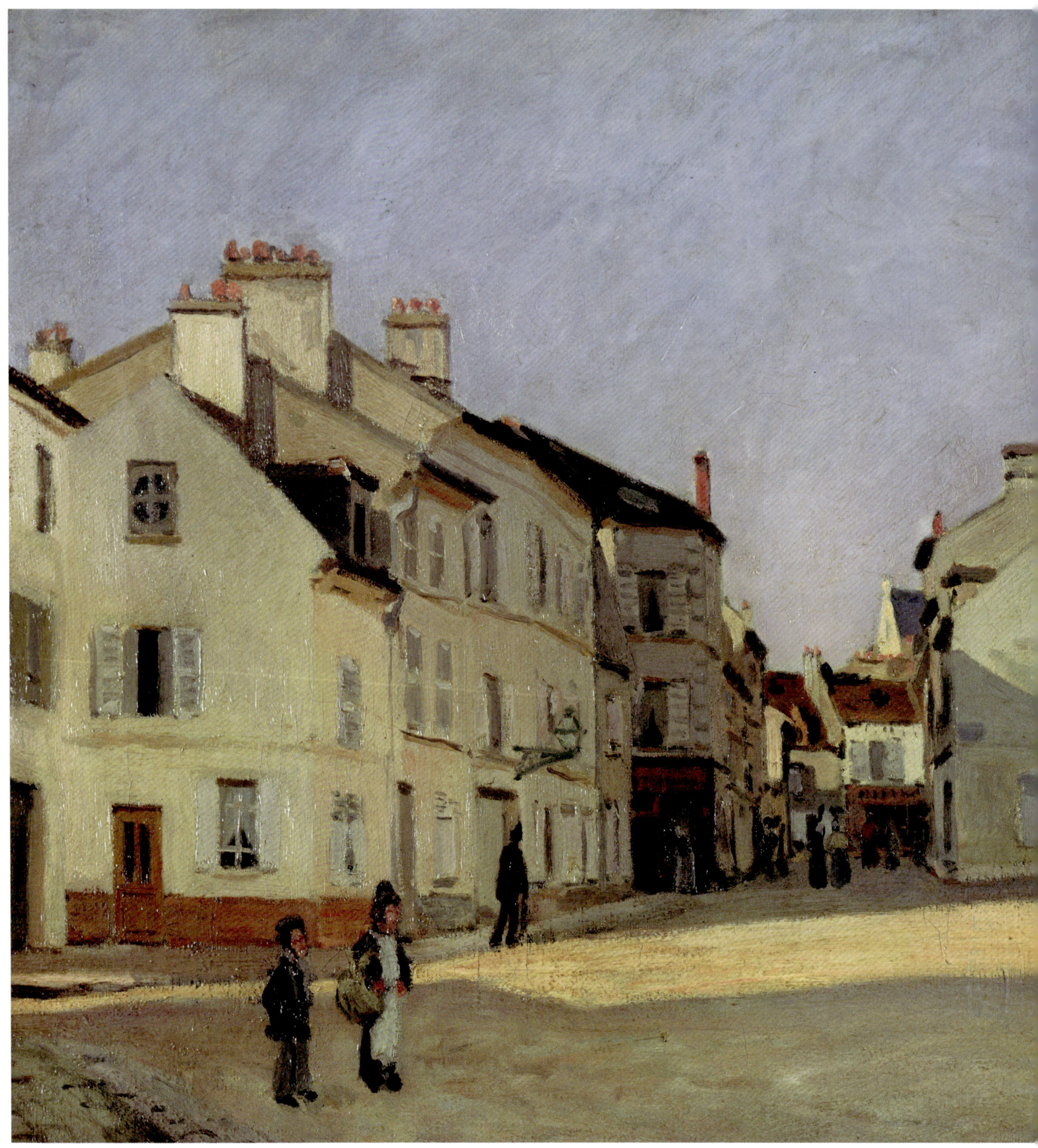

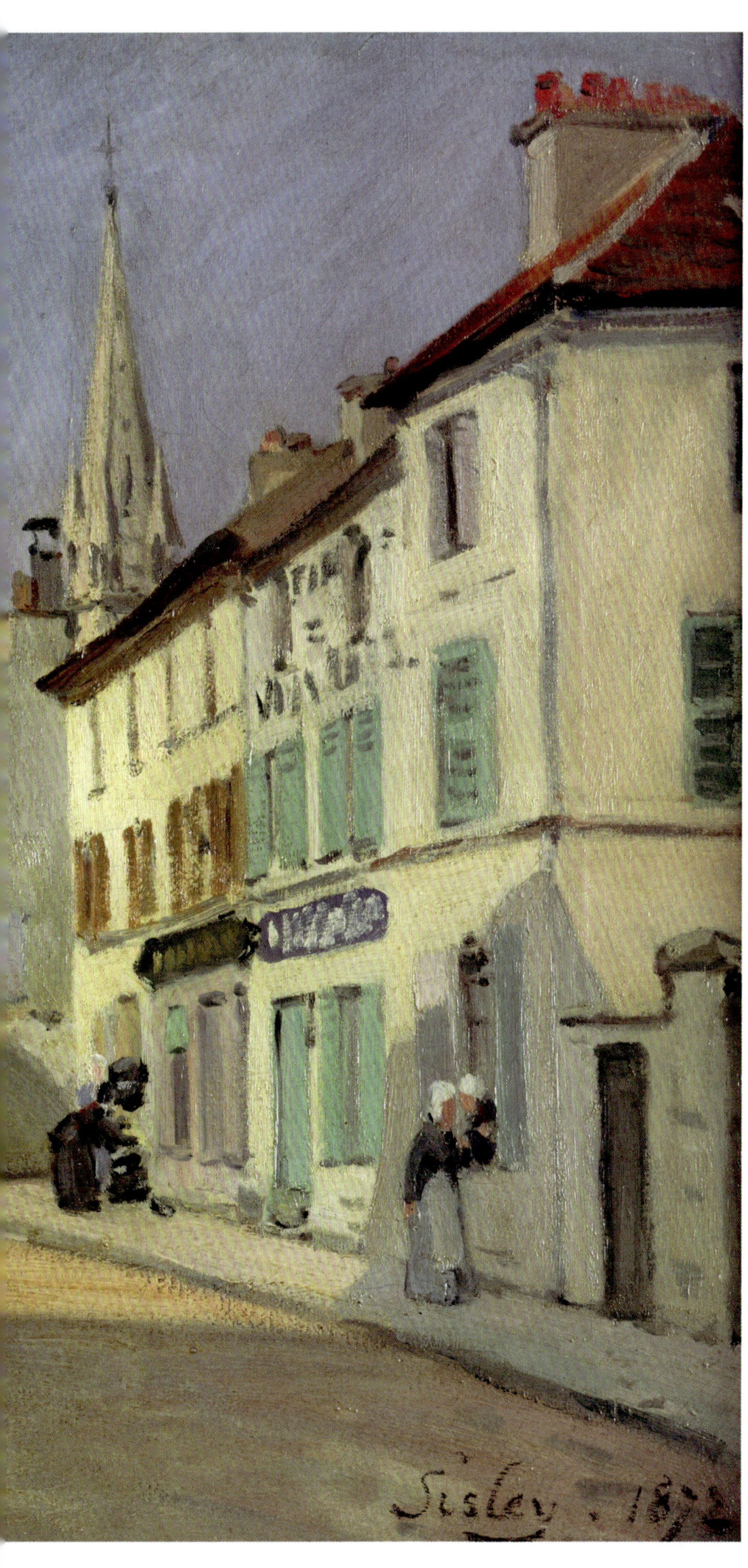

Alfred Sisley (1839–99)

Rue de la Chaussee at Argenteuil

Rue de la Chaussée à Argenteuil

Rue de la Chaussee in Argenteuil

Calle de la Chaussee en Argenteuil

Rue de la Chaussée ad Argenteuil

De Rue de la Chaussee in Argenteuil

1872, Oil on canvas/Huile sur toile, 46,5 × 66 cm, Musée d'Orsay, Paris

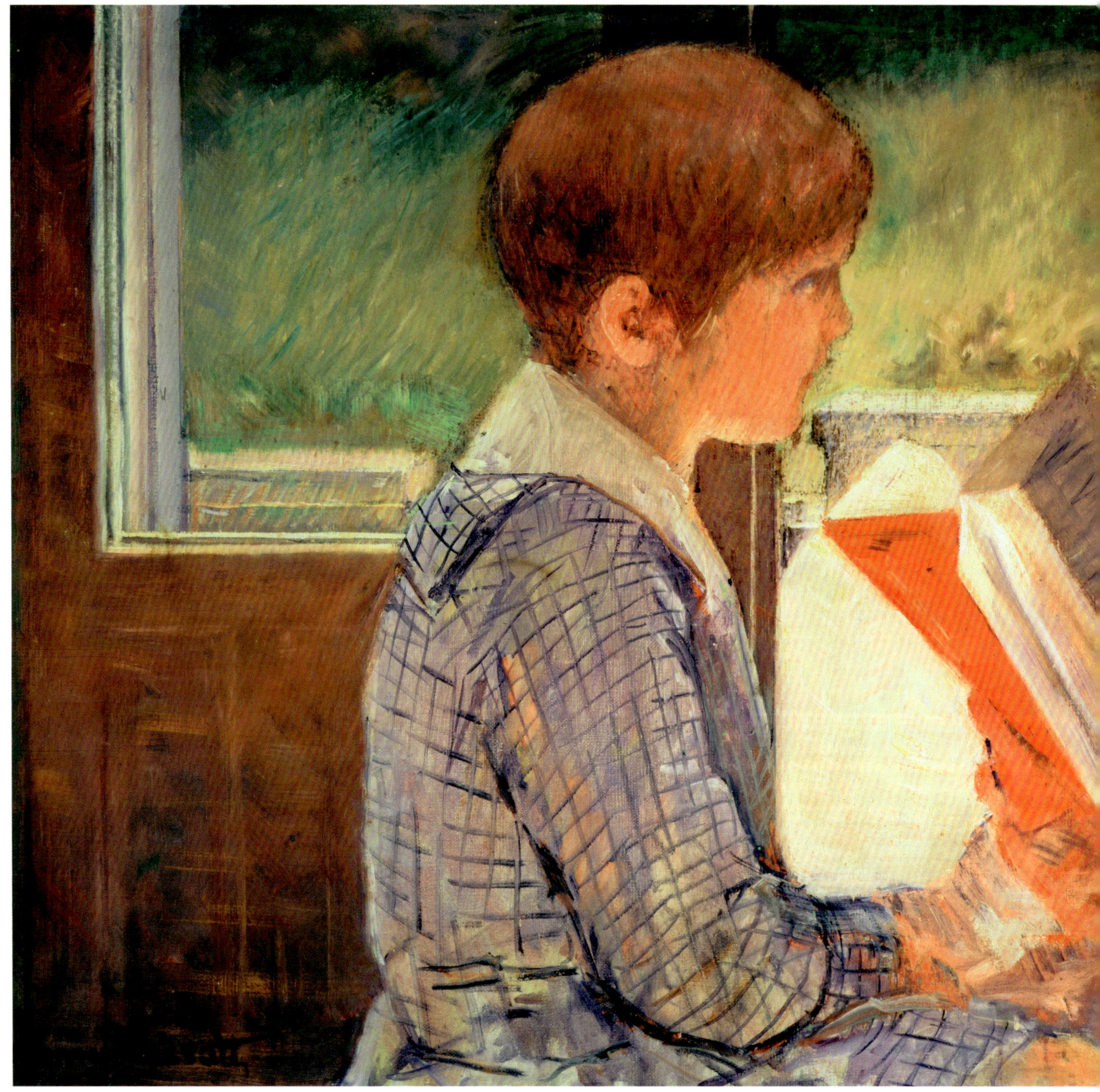

Mary Stevenson Cassatt (1844–1926)

Mrs Cassatt Reading to her Grandchildren

Madame. Cassatt lisant à ses petits-enfants

Mrs. Cassatt liest ihren Enkelkindern vor

Mrs. Cassatt leyendo a sus nietos

Khaterine Cassatt mentre legge ai suoi nipoti

Madame Cassatt leest haar kleinkinderen voor

1888, Oil on canvas/Huile sur toile, 12,7 × 17,8 cm, Private collection

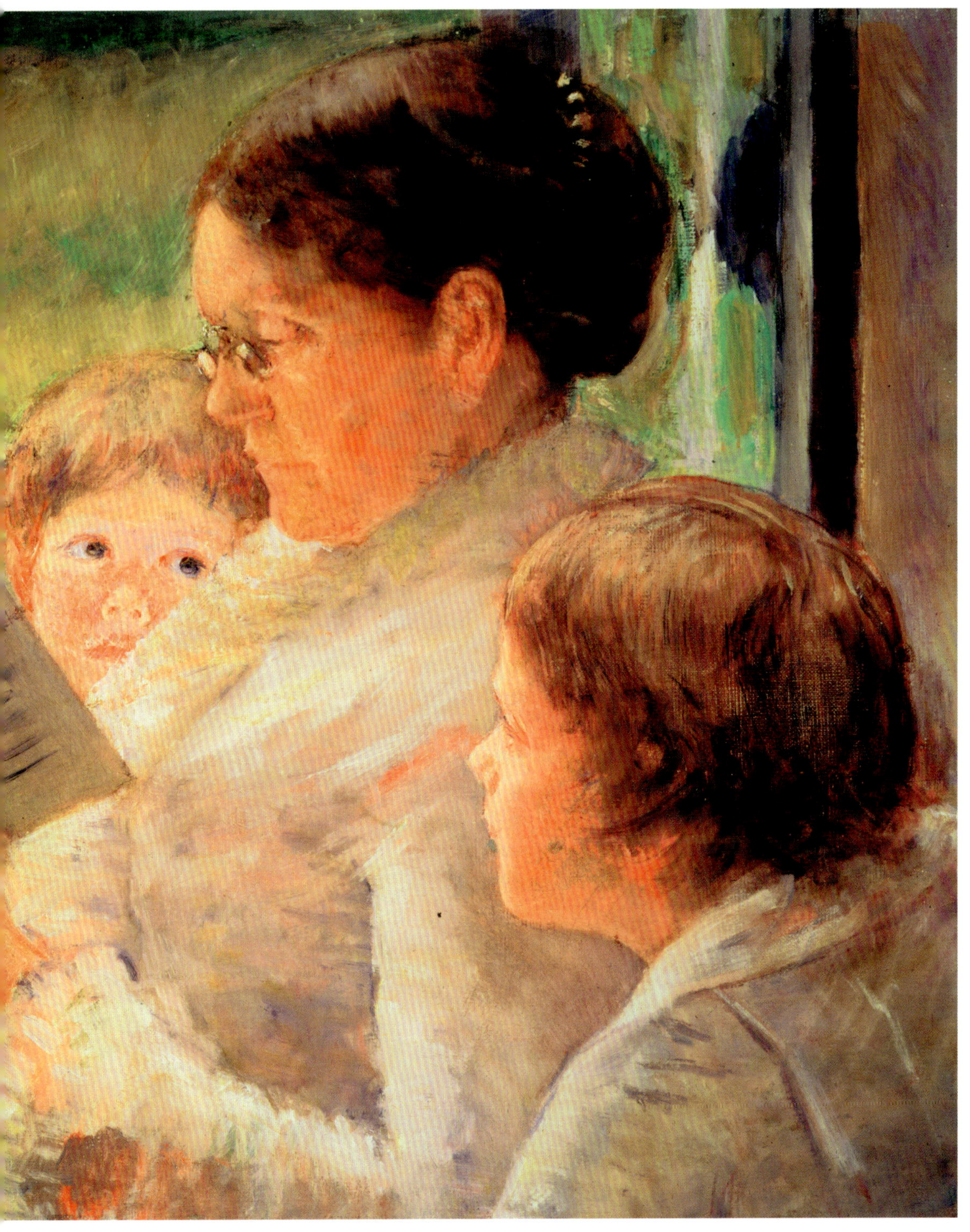

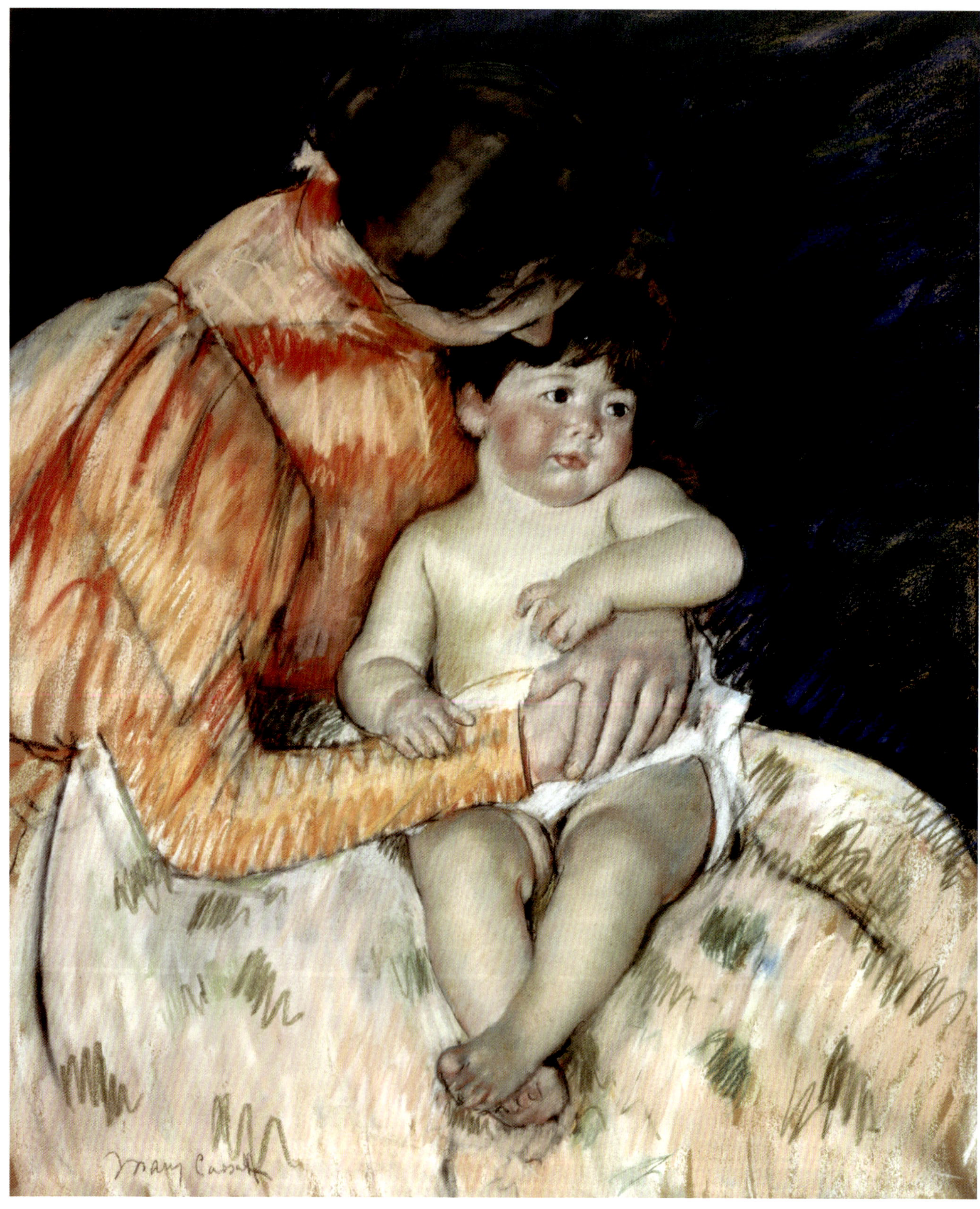

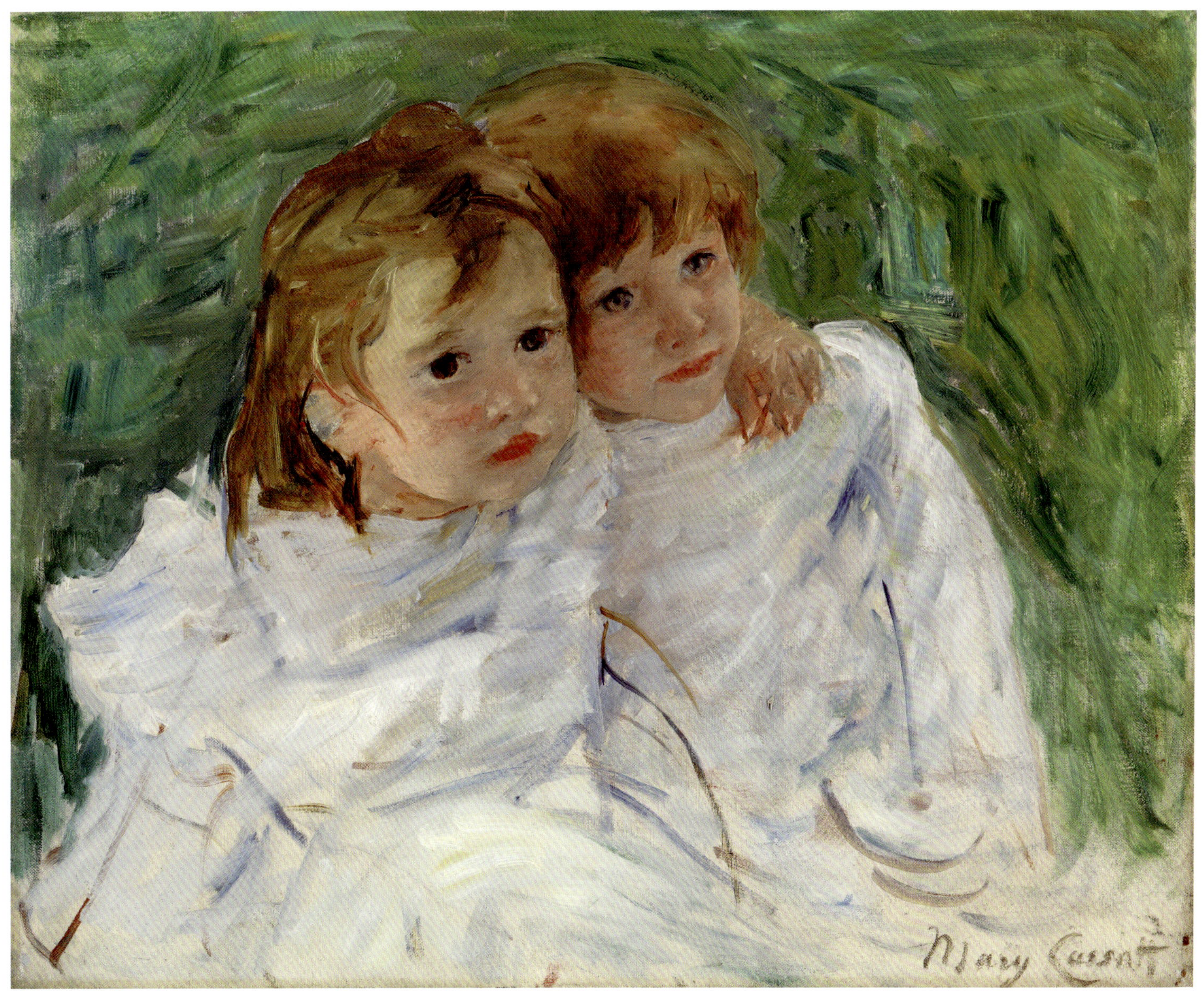

Mary Stevenson Cassatt (1844–1926)

Mother and Child

Mère et enfant

Mutter und Kind

Mujer e hijo

Madre e figlio

Moeder en kind

c. 1890, Pastel on paper/Pastel sur papier, 80 × 64 cm, Pushkin State Museum of Fine Arts, Moscow

Mary Stevenson Cassatt (1844–1926)

The Sisters

Les sœurs

Die Schwestern

Las hermanas

Le sorelle

De zusters

c. 1885, Oil on canvas/Huile sur toile, 46,3 × 55,5 cm, Kelvingrove Art Gallery and Museum, Glasgow

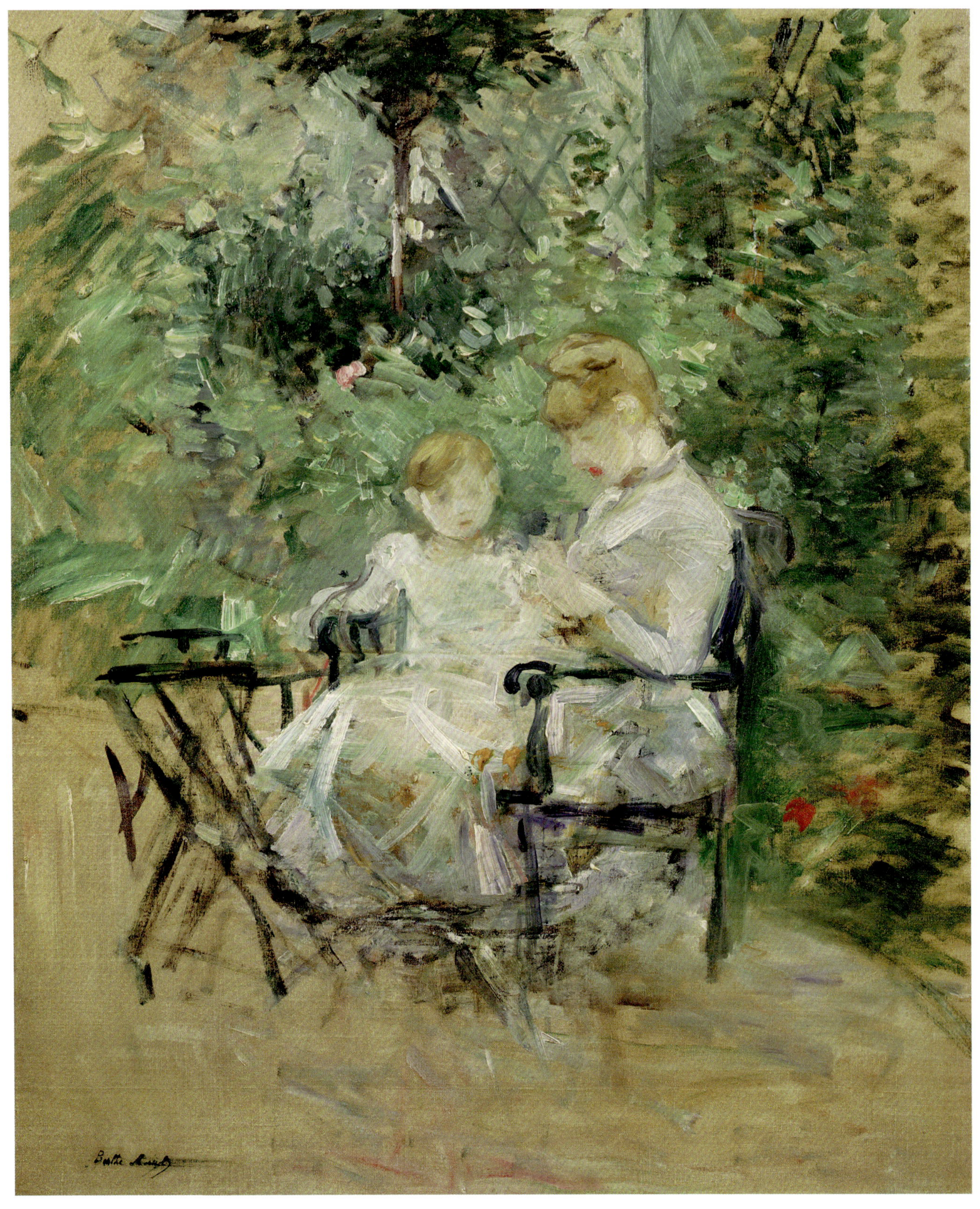

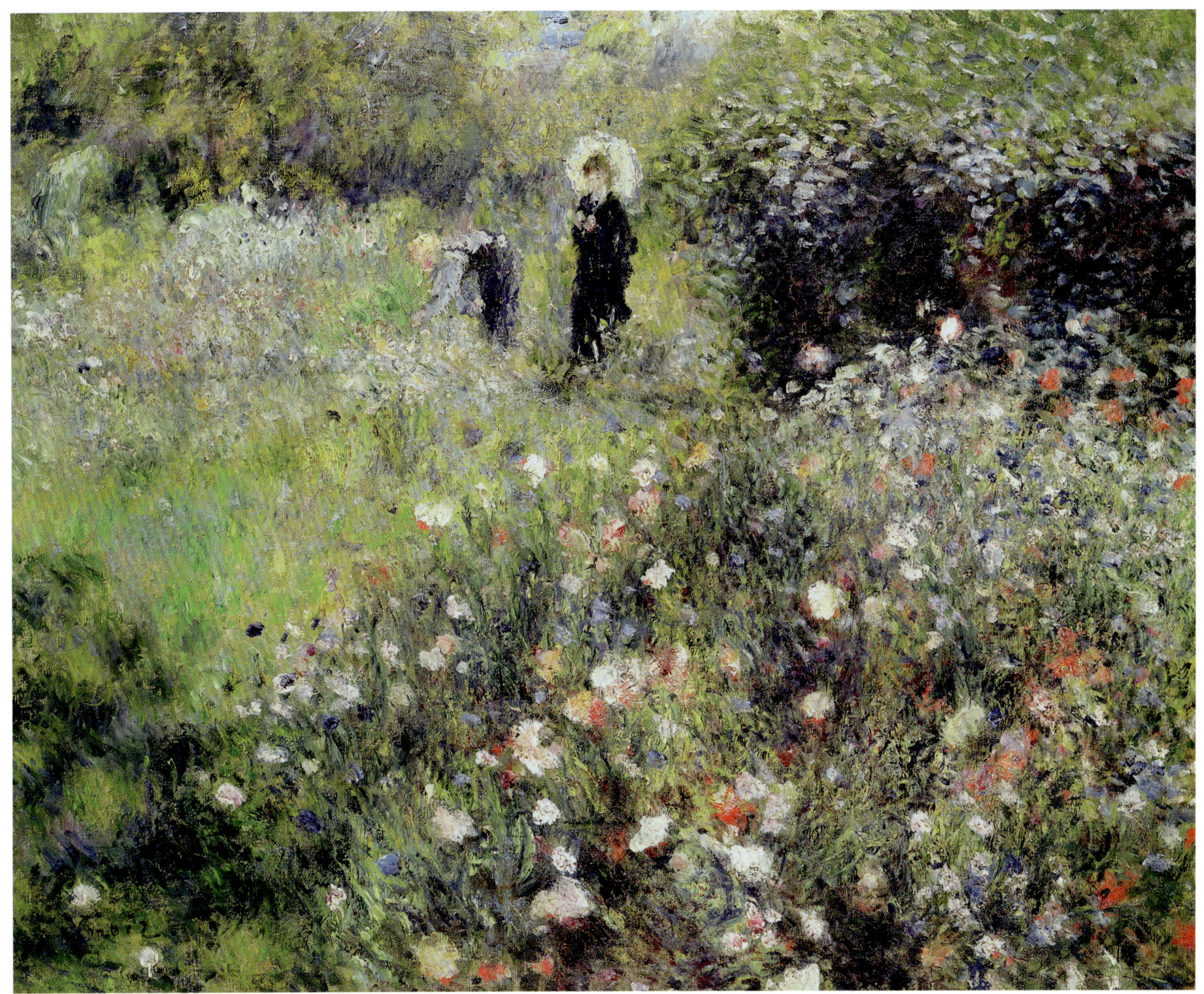

Berthe Morisot (1841–95)

In the Garden

Le Jardin

Im Garten

En el jardín

Nel giardino

In de tuin

c. 1885, Oil on canvas/Huile sur toile, 65 × 54 cm, Private collection

Pierre-Auguste Renoir (1841–1919)

Woman with a Parasol in a Garden

Femme à l'ombrelle dans un jardin

Frau mit Schirm im Garten

Mujer con sombrilla en el jardín

Donna con parasole in giardino

Vrouw met parasol in de tuin

1875, Oil on canvas/Huile sur toile, 54,5 × 65 cm, Museo Thyssen-Bornemisza, Madrid

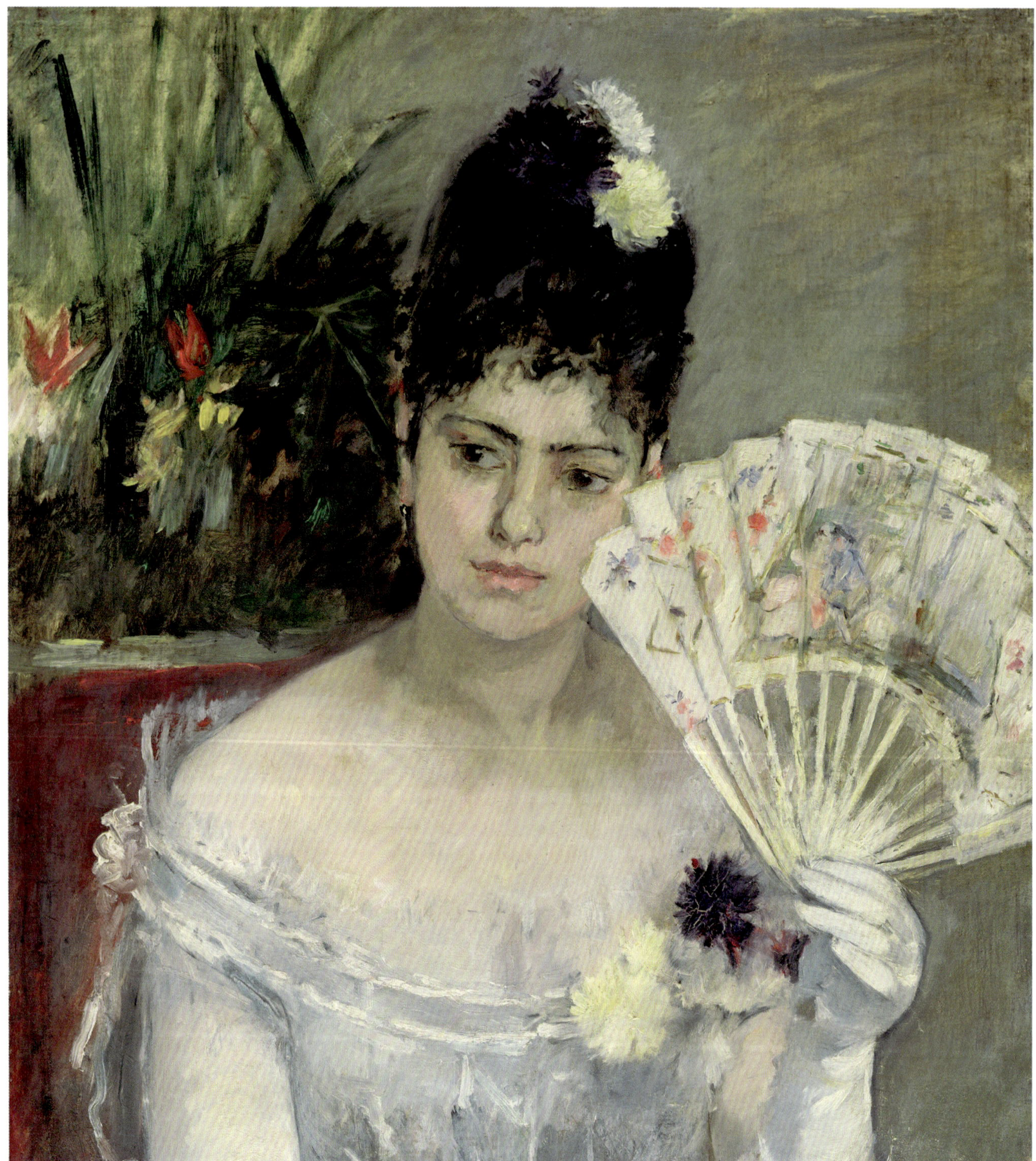

Berthe Morisot (1841–95)

At the Ball	Auf dem Ball	Ragazza al ballo
Au Bal	En el baile	In de balzaal

1875, Oil on canvas/Huile sur toile, 65 × 52 cm, Musée Marmottan Monet, Paris

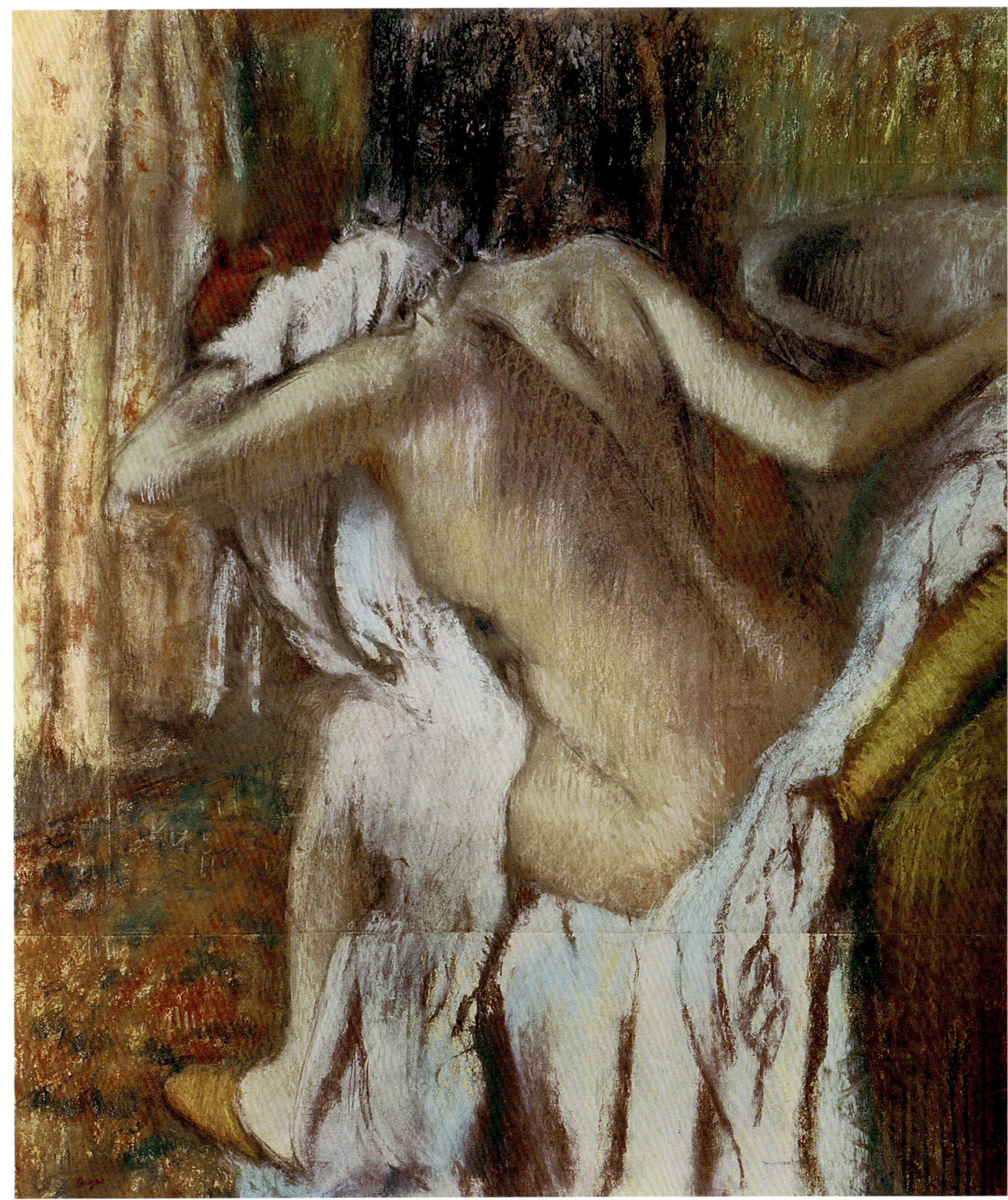

Edgar Degas (1834–1917)

Woman drying herself   Frau, sich abtrocknend   Donna che si asciuga

Après le bain, femme s'essuyant   Mujer secándose   Vrouw die zich afdroogt

c. 1890–95, Pastel/Pastel, 103,5 × 98,5 cm, National Gallery, London

In the foreground Renoir has portrayed
his friends. In the background couples are
dancing to the music of a dance band. The
intimate closeness between the pairs is
emphasized by the light of the gas lamps and
the flickering spots of light on the costumes
and jackets.

Renoir a peint ses amis au premier plan. Au
fond, des couples dansent sur la musique
d'un orchestre. La proximité entre les couples
est accentuée par la lumière des becs de gaz
et les taches vacillantes de la lumière sur les
costumes et les vestes.

Im Vordergrund hat Renoir seine Freunde
porträtiert. Im Hintergrund tanzen die Paare
zur Musik einer Tanzkapelle. Die intime
Nähe zwischen den Paaren wird durch
die Beleuchtung der Gaslampen und die
flirrenden Lichtflecken auf den Kostümen und
Jacken unterstrichen.

Renoir retrata en primer plano a sus
amigos. Detrás las parejas bailan al son
de la música de una banda de baile. La
intimidad de las parejas se enfatiza por
la iluminación de lámparas de gas y los
destellos resplandecientes en sus vestidos y
chaquetas.

Renoir ritrasse in primo piano i suoi amici
e sullo sfondo delle coppie che ballano al
ritmo della musica suonata dall'orchestrina.
L'intimità tra le coppie viene messa in risalto
dalla luce emessa dalle lampade a gas e
dai tremolanti punti luce sui vestiti e sulle
giacche.

Op de voorgrond heeft Renoir zijn vrienden
geportretteerd. Op de achtergrond dansen
paartjes op de muziek van een danskapel.
De intimiteit van de paren wordt versterkt
door het licht van de gaslampen en de
beweeglijke vlekjes zonlicht op de kleding
van de dansers.

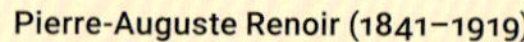

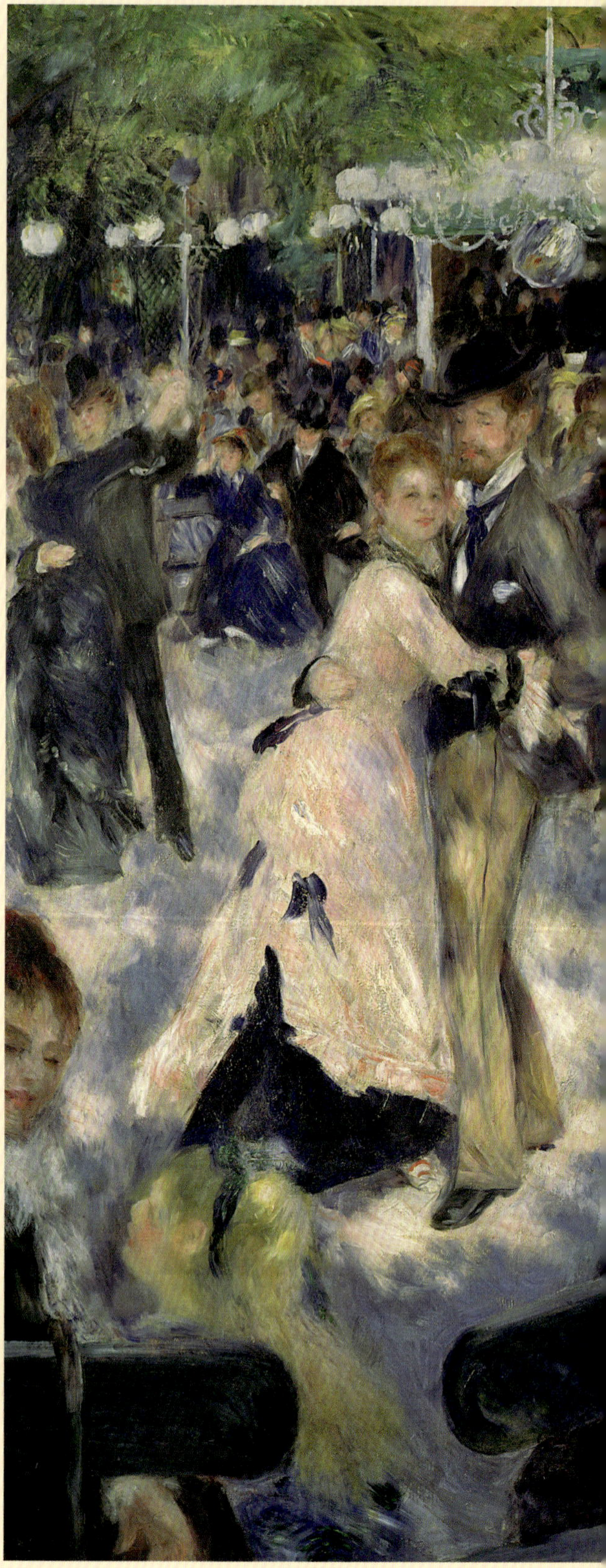

Pierre-Auguste Renoir (1841–1919)
Ball at the Moulin de la Galette
Le Bal du moulin de la Galette
Der Ball im Moulin de la Galette
Baile en el Moulin de la Galette
Ballo al Moulin de la Galette
Dans in de de Moulin de la Galette, detail
1876, Oil on canvas/Huile sur toile,
131,5 × 176,5 cm, Musée d'Orsay, Paris

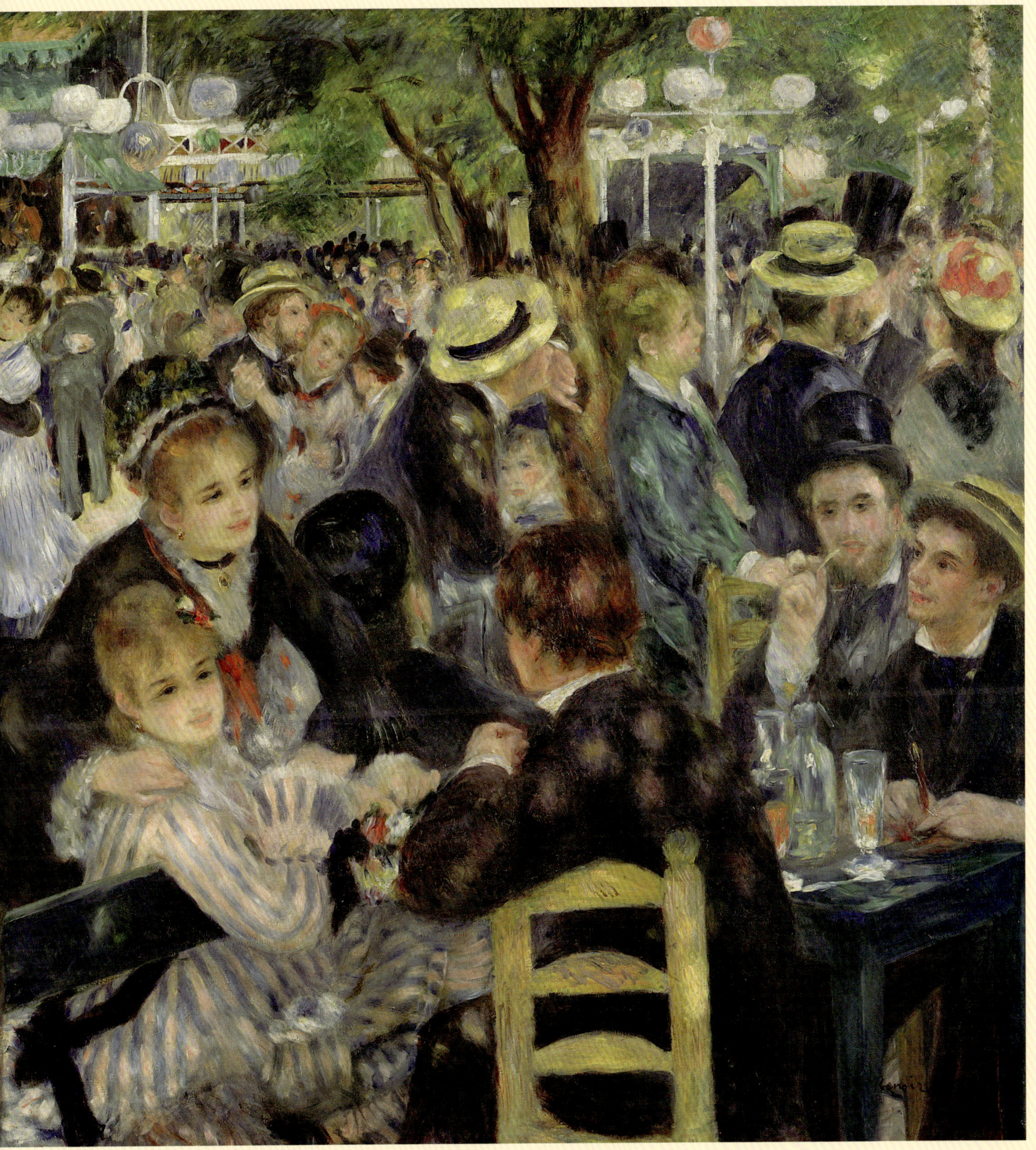

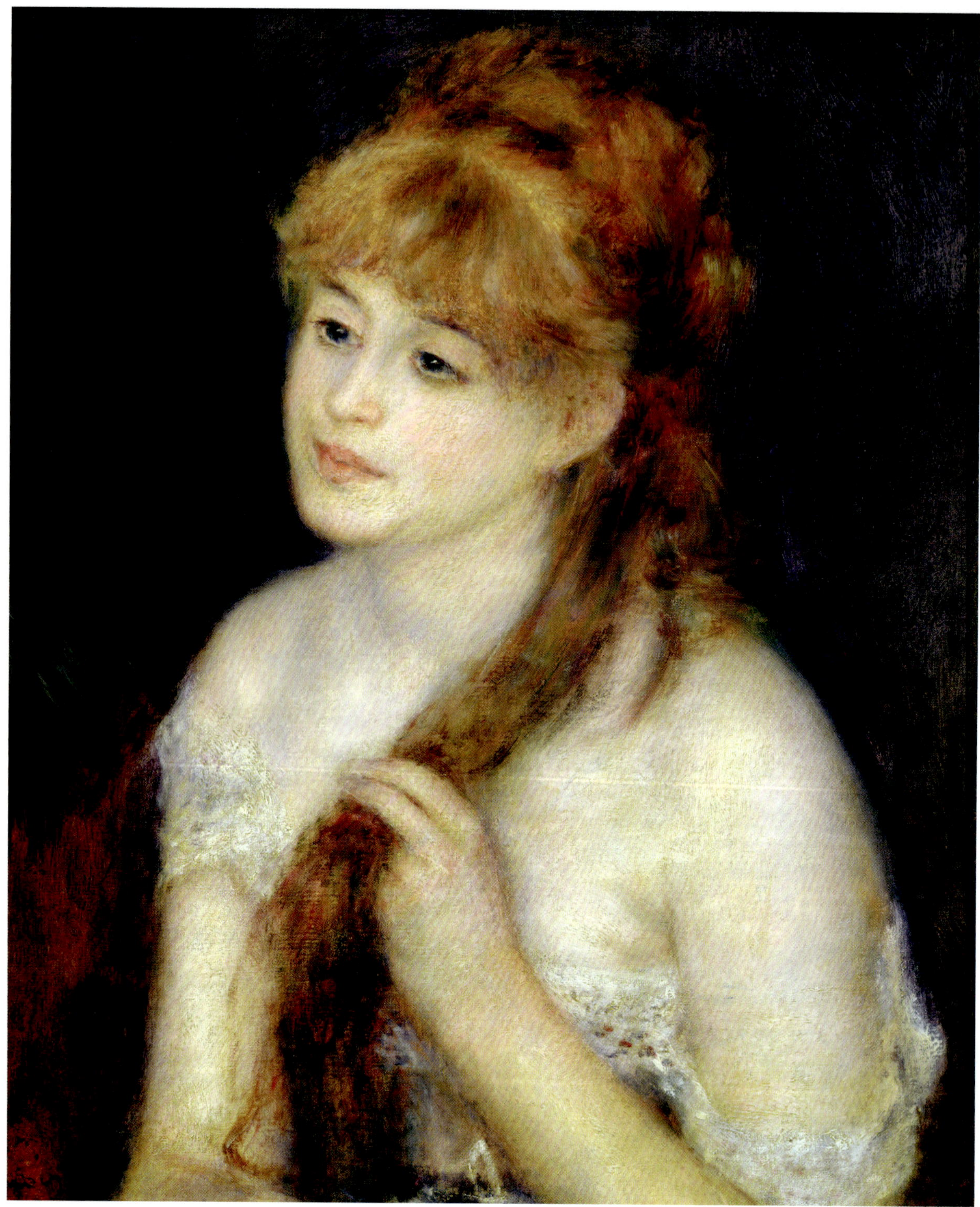

Pierre-Auguste Renoir (1841–1919)

Young Woman Braiding her Hair

Jeune fille coiffant ses cheveux

Frau, ihr Haar flechtend

Mujer trenzando su pelo

Giovane donna che si intreccia i capelli

Vrouw die haar haar vlecht

1876, Oil on canvas/Huile sur toile, 55,5 × 46 cm, National Gallery of Art, Washington

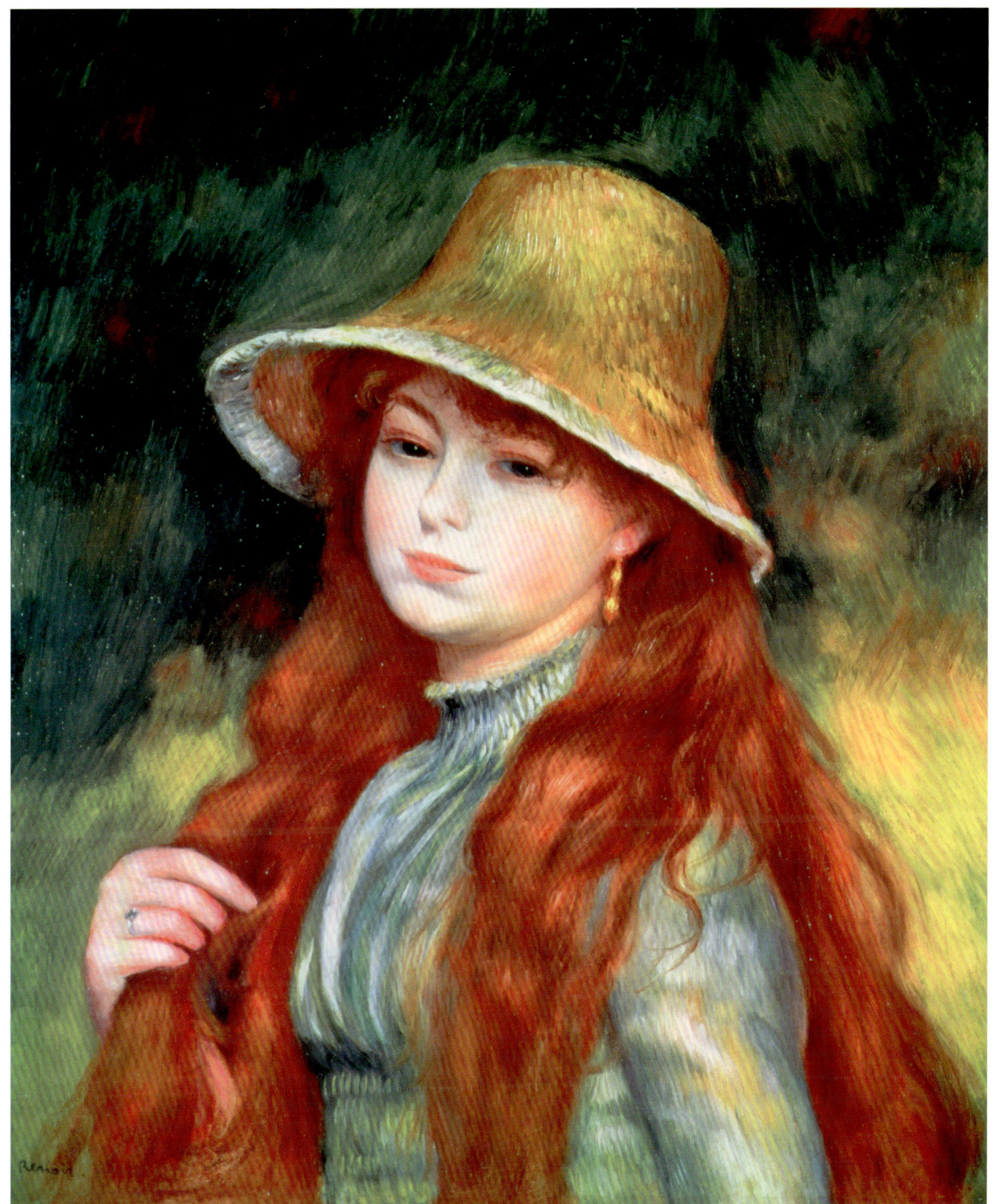

Pierre-Auguste Renoir (1841–1919)

Young girl with long hair *or* Young girl in a straw hat

Jeune fille aux cheveux longs,
ou Jeune fille au chapeau de paille

Mädchen mit langem Haar (Mädchen mit Strohhut)

Joven con pelo largo (joven con sombrero de paja)

Ragazza coi capelli lunghi (Ragazza con cappello di paglia)

Meisje met lang haar (Meisje met strohoed)

1884, Oil on canvas/Huile sur toile, 54 × 43 cm, Mitsubishi Ichigokan Museum, Tokyo

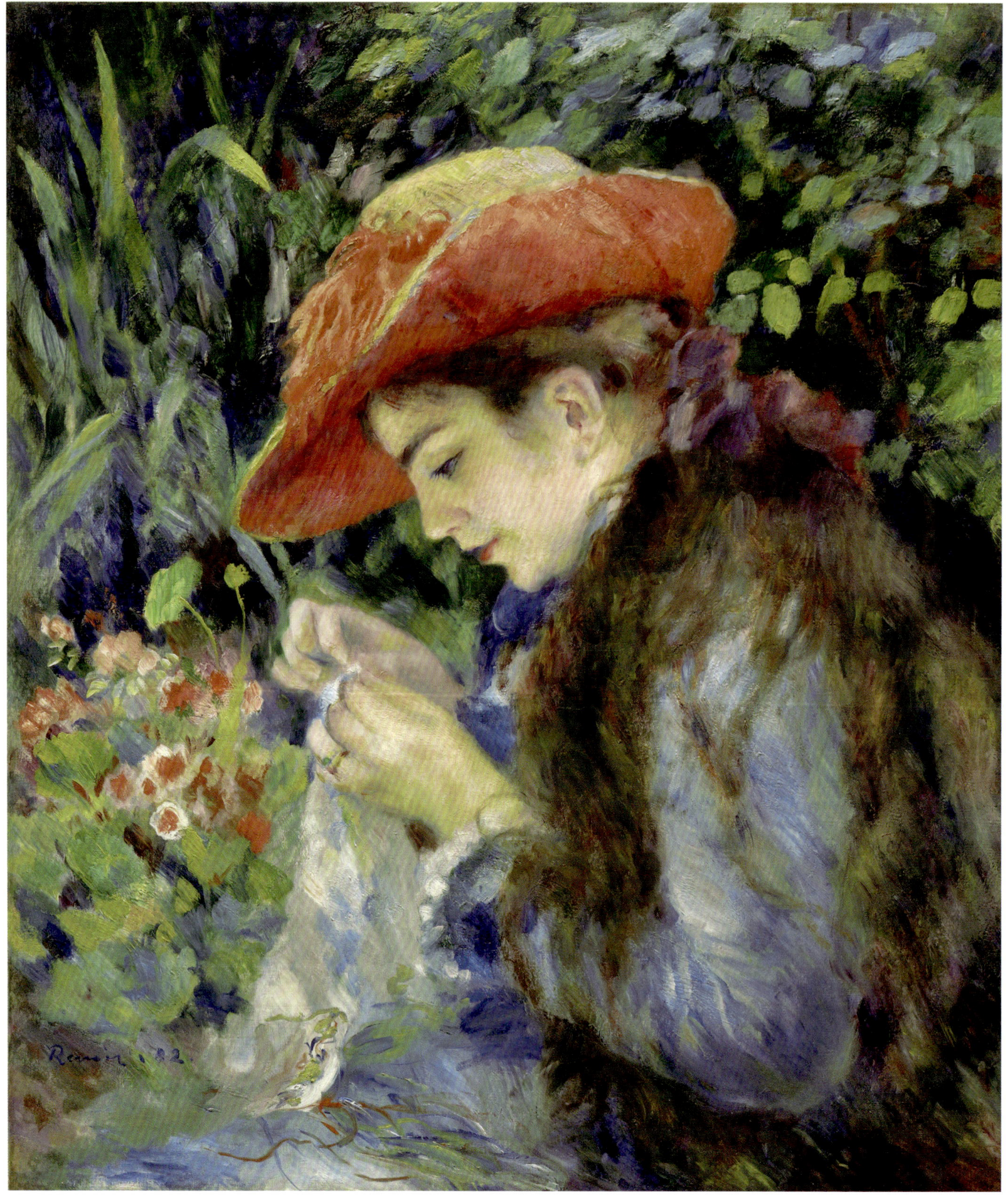

Pierre-Auguste Renoir (1841–1919)

In the Garden

Au jardin

Im Garten

En el jardín

Nel giardino

In de tuin

1885, Oil on canvas/Huile sur toile,
170,5 × 112,5 cm, State
Hermitage, St. Petersburg

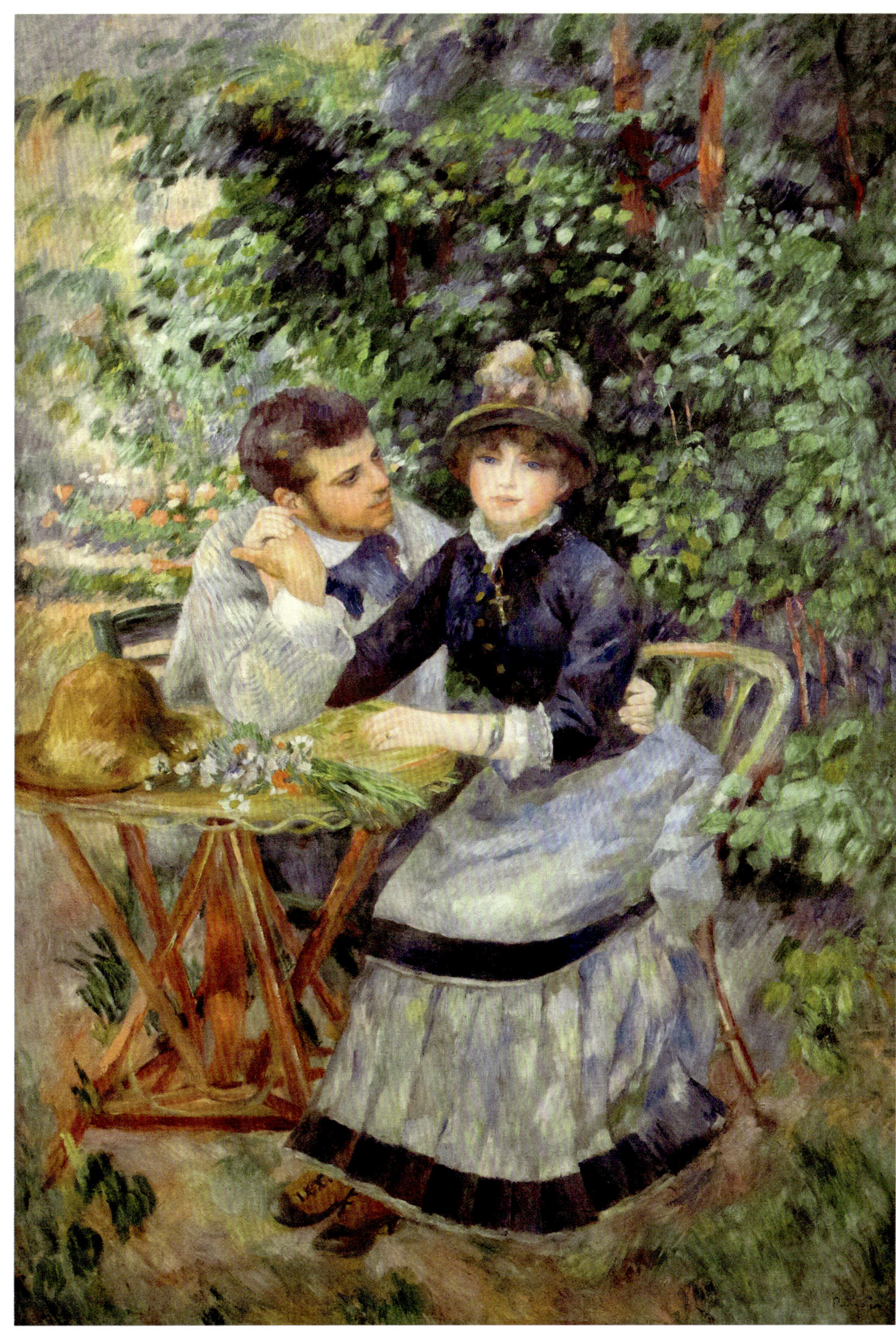

Pierre-Auguste Renoir (1841–1919)

Marie–Therese Durand–Ruel Sewing

Marie-Therese Durand-Ruel cousant

Marie-Thérèse Durand-Ruel, nähend

Marie-Thérèse Durand-Ruel, cosiendo

Marie-Thérèse Durand-Ruel che cuce

Marie-Thérèse Durand-Ruel, naaiend

1882, Oil on canvas/Huile sur toile,
64,8 × 53,8 cm, Clark Art Institute,
Williamstown

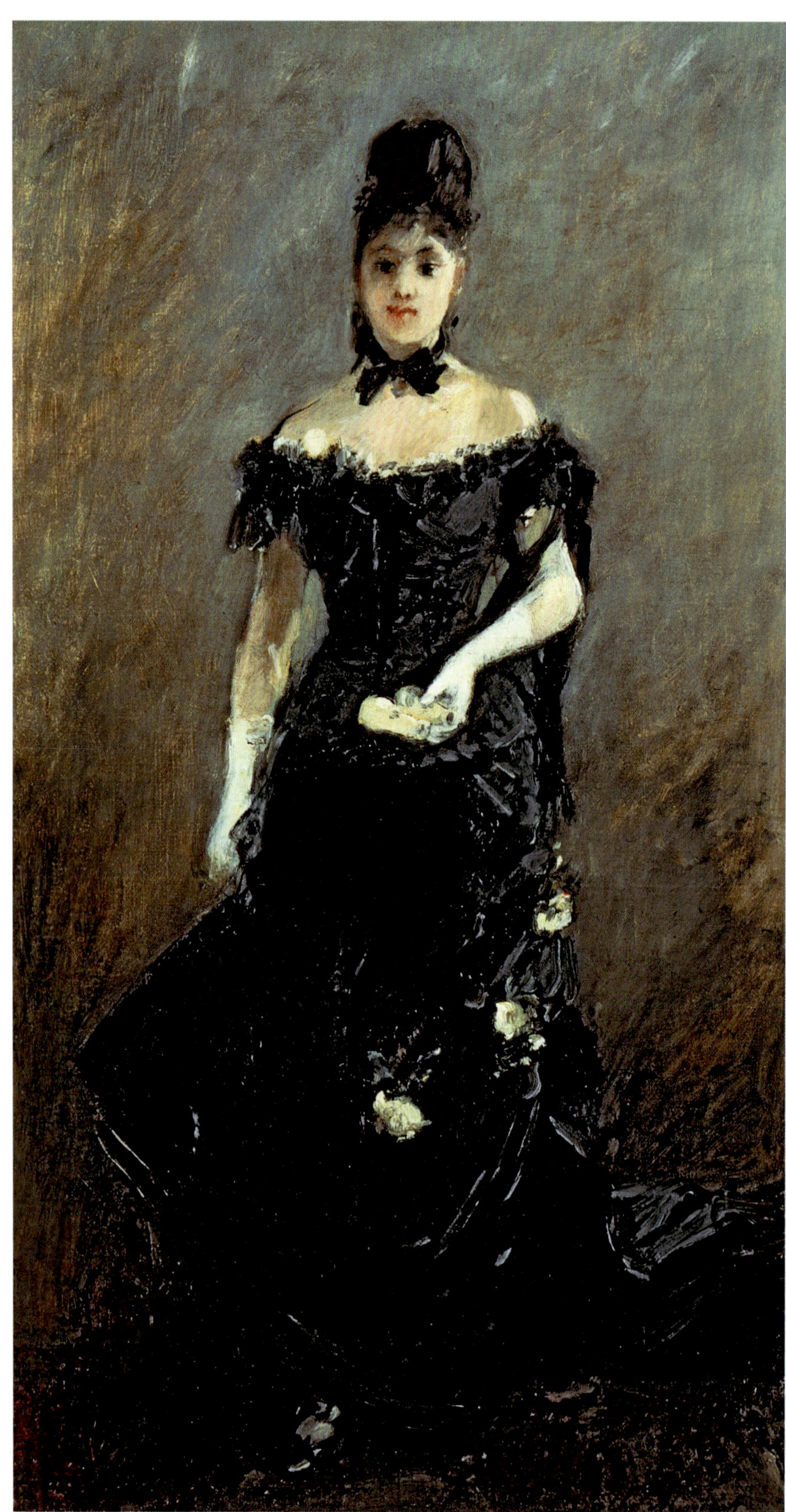

Pierre-Auguste Renoir (1841–1919)

A French Girl with a Fan

Jeune fille avec un éventail

Mädchen mit Fächer

Niña con abanico

Ragazza con ventaglio

Meisje met waaier

c. 1879, Oil on canvas/Huile sur toile, 65,4 × 54 cm,
Clark Art Institute, Williamstown

Berthe Morisot (1841–95)

Before the Theater

Avant le théâtre

Vor dem Theater

Antes del teatro

Prima del teatro

Voor het theater

c. 1875, Oil on canvas/Huile sur toile, 57 × 31 cm, Private collection

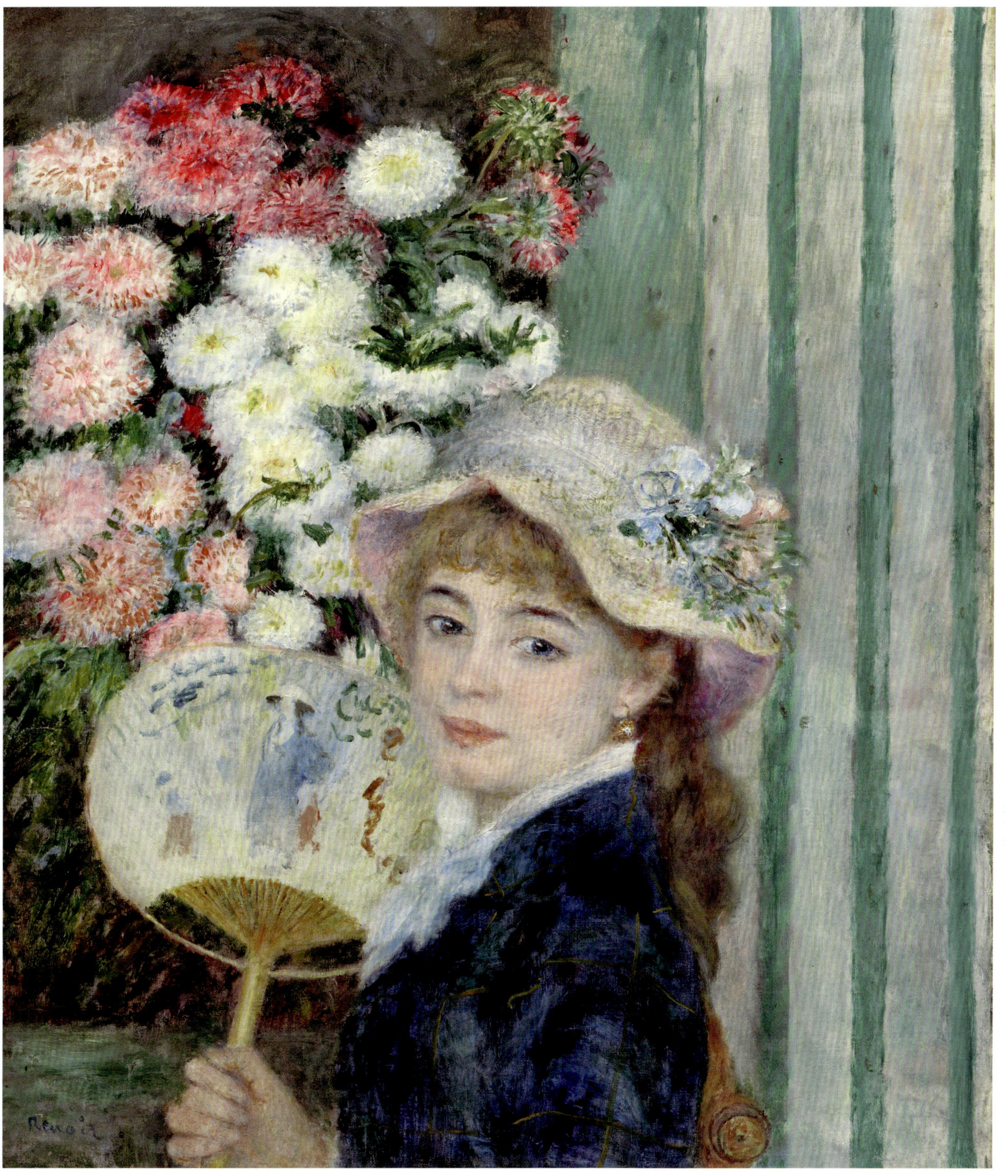

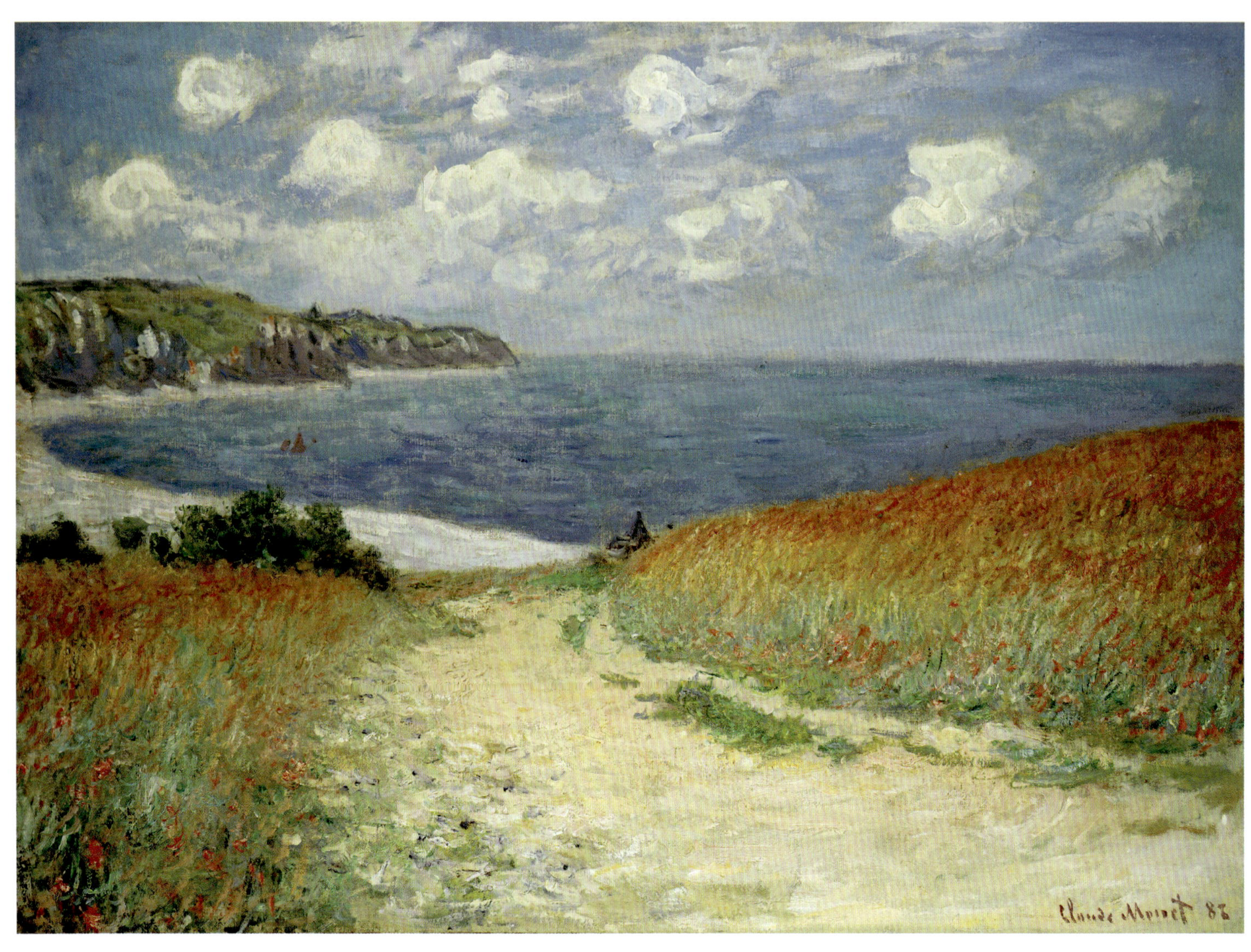

Claude Monet (1840–1926)

Path in the Wheat at Pourville

Chemin dans les blés à Pourville

Pfad durch ein Weizenfeld bei Pourville

Camino por el trigo en Pourville

Sentiero in mezzo al grano a Pourville

Pad door een tarweveld bij Pourville

1882, Oil on canvas/Huile sur toile, 58,2 × 78 cm, Private collection

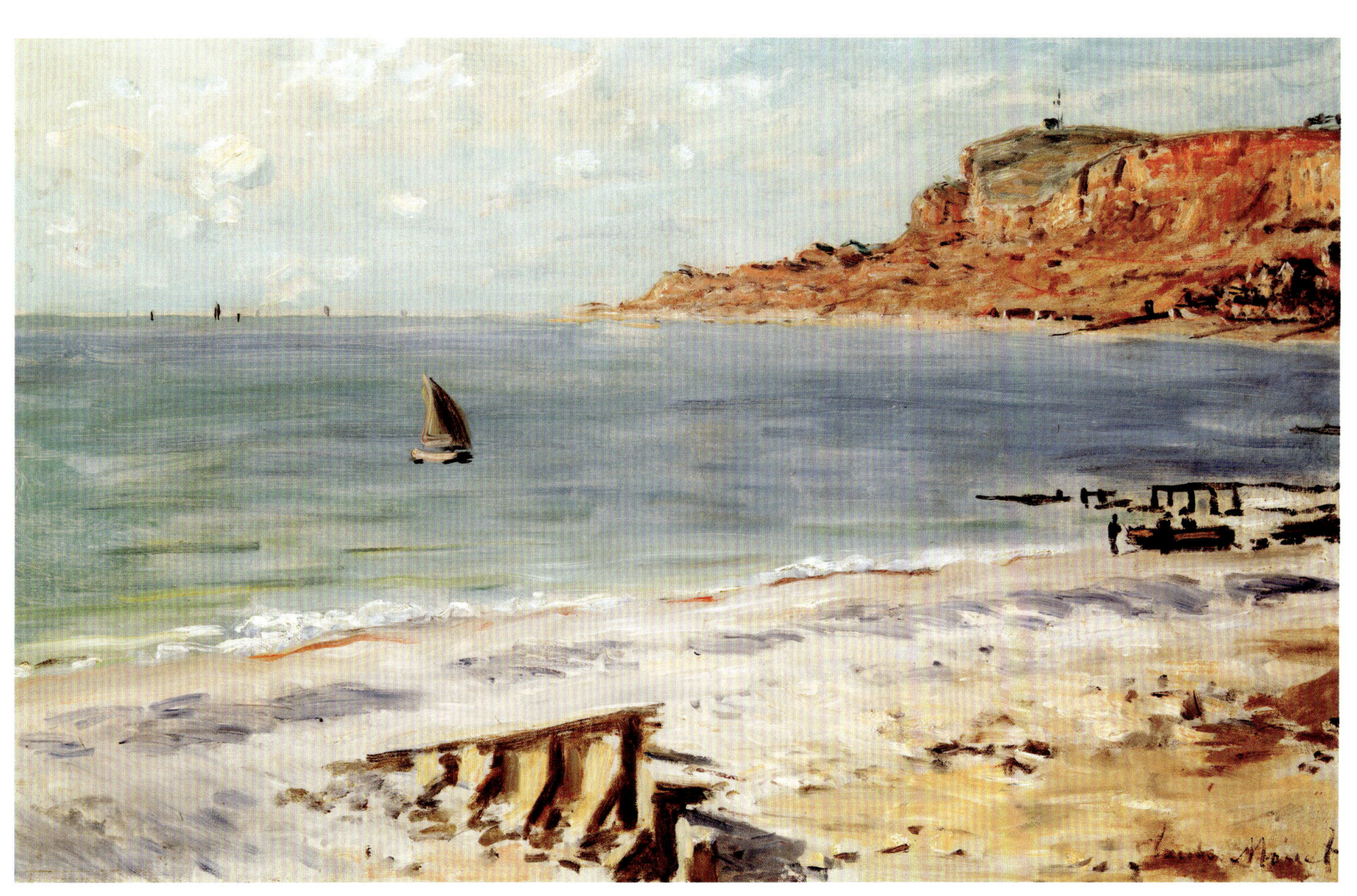

Claude Monet (1840–1926)

Seascape at Sainte–Adresse

Sainte-Adresse

Seestück bei Sainte-Adresse

Paisaje marítimo en Sainte-Adresse

Paesaggio marino a Sainte-Adresse

Zeegezicht bij Sainte-Adresse

1873, Oil on canvas/Huile sur toile, 48 × 74 cm, Private collection

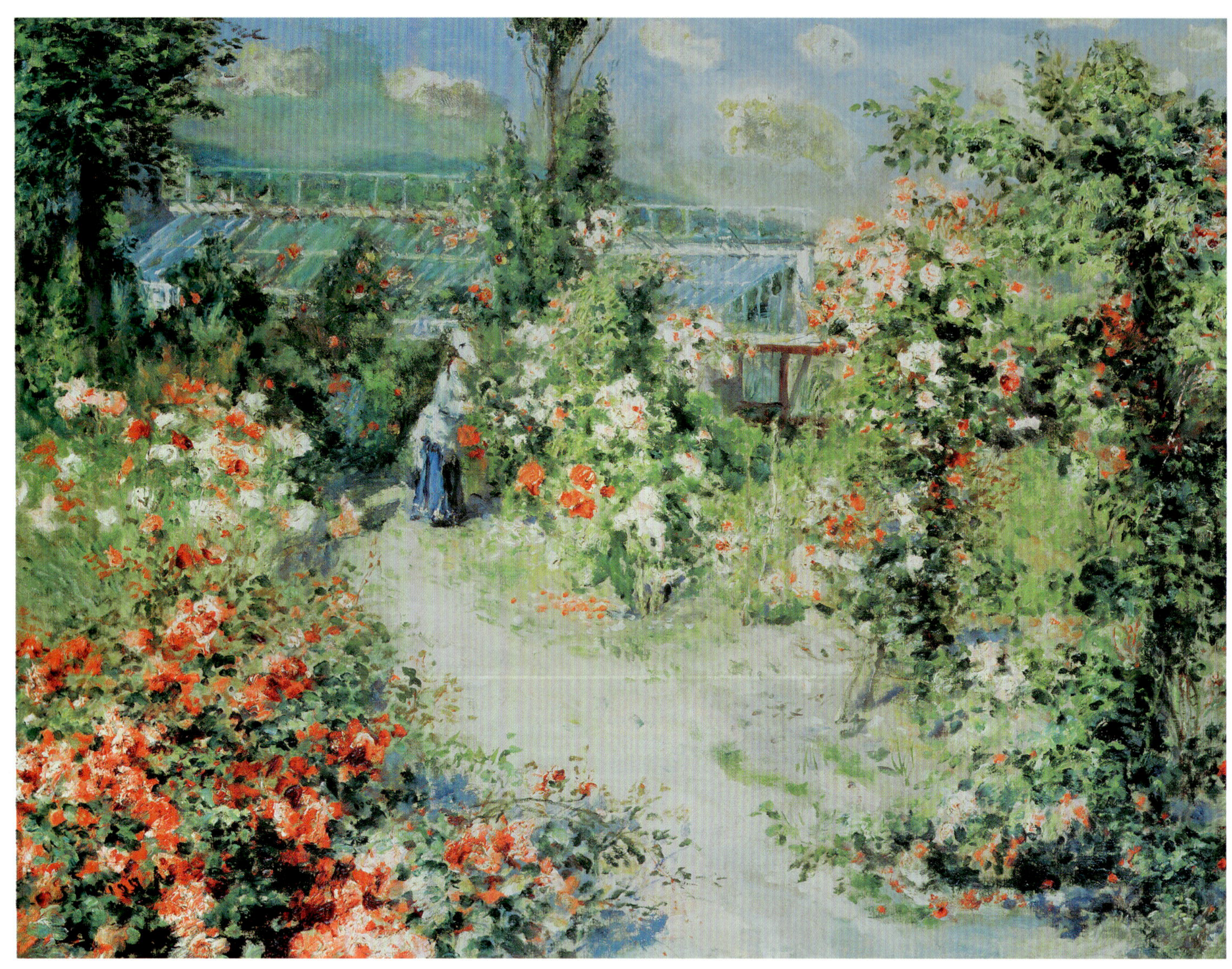

Pierre-Auguste Renoir (1841–1919)

The Conservatory

La serre

Das Gewächshaus

El invernadero

La serra

De kas

c. 1870, Oil on canvas/Huile sur toile, 60 × 74 cm, Private collection

Pierre-Auguste Renoir (1841–1919)

Self Portrait

Autoportrait

Selbstporträt

Autorretrato

Autoritratto

Zelfportret

1899, Oil on canvas/Huile sur toile, 41,4 × 33,7 cm, Clark Art Institute, Williamstown

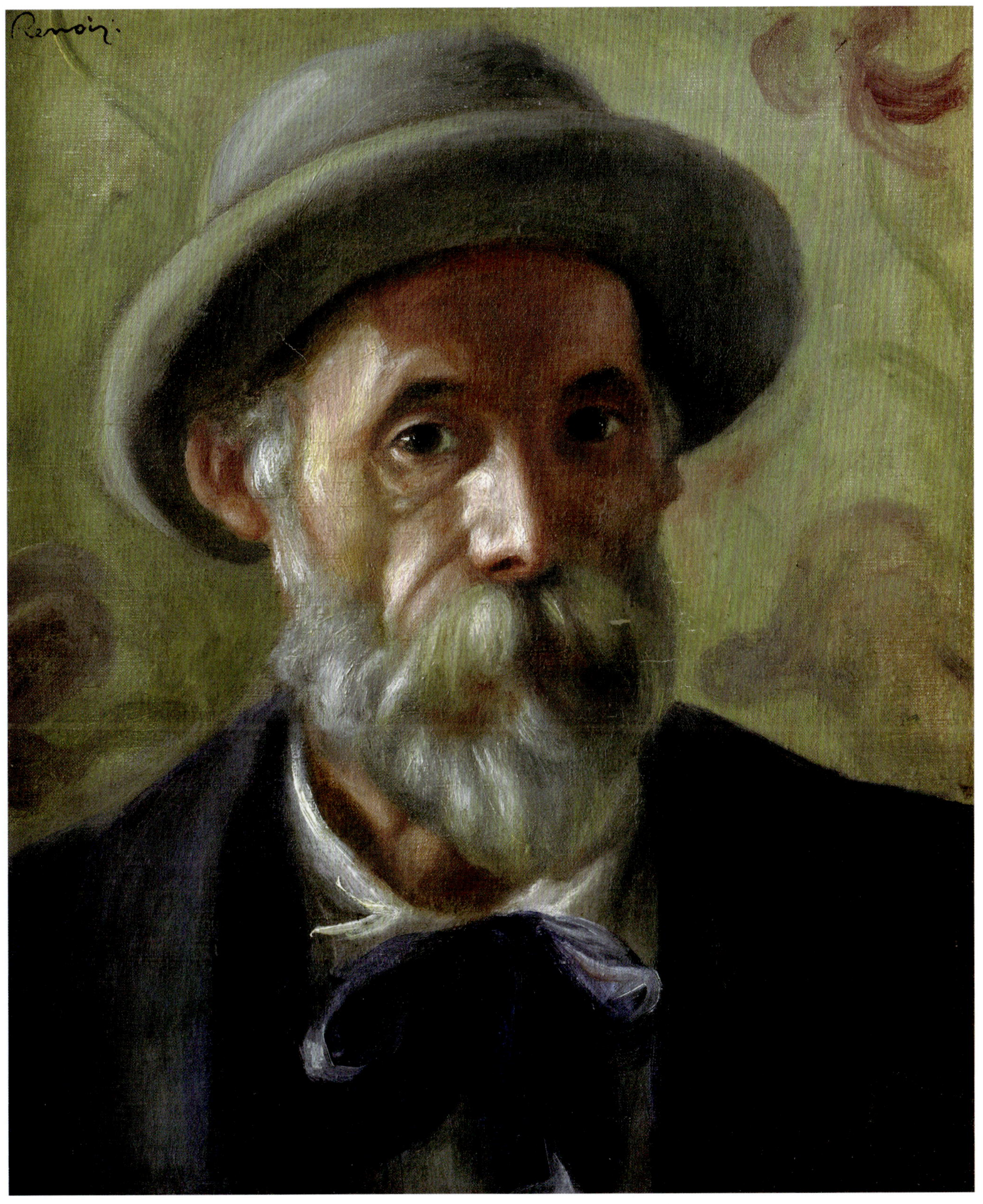
Renoir.

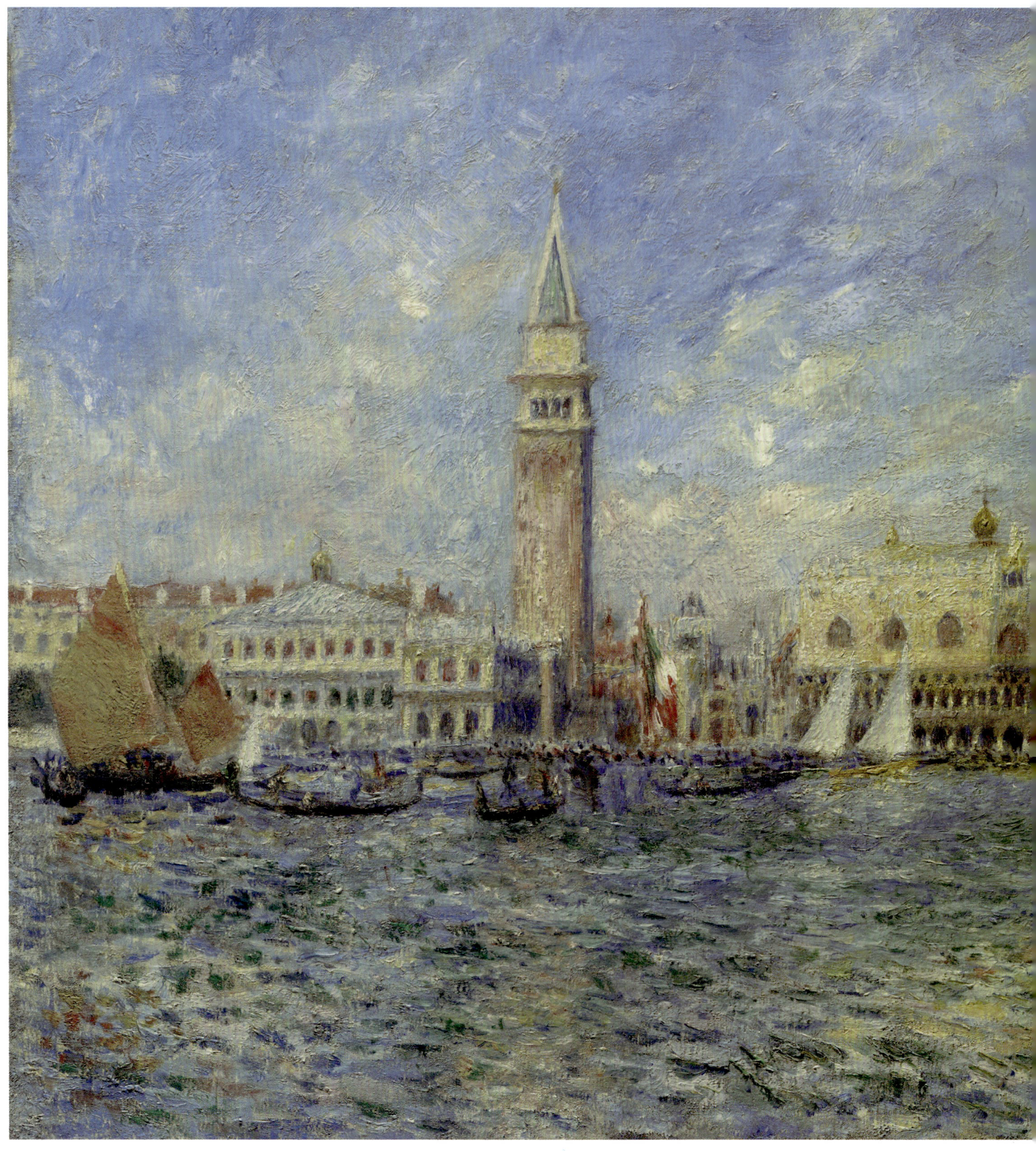

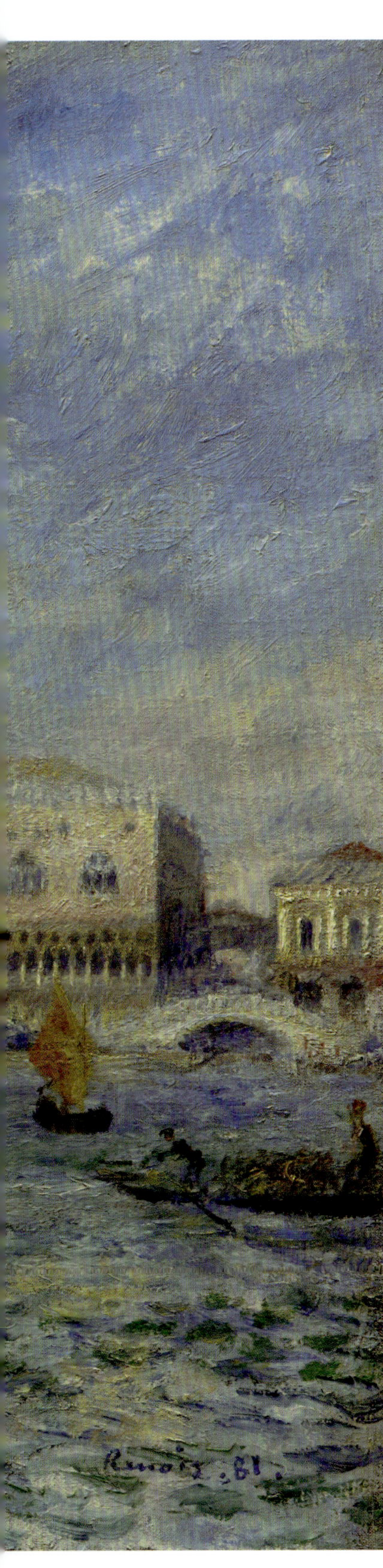

Pierre-Auguste Renoir (1841–1919)

Venice, the Doge's Palace

Le Palais des Doges à Venise

Der Dogenpalast in Venedig

El palacio ducal en Venecia

Il Palazzo Ducale di Venezia

Het Dogenpaleis in Venetië

1881, Oil on canvas/Huile sur toile, 54,5 × 65,7 cm, Clark Art Institute, Williamstown

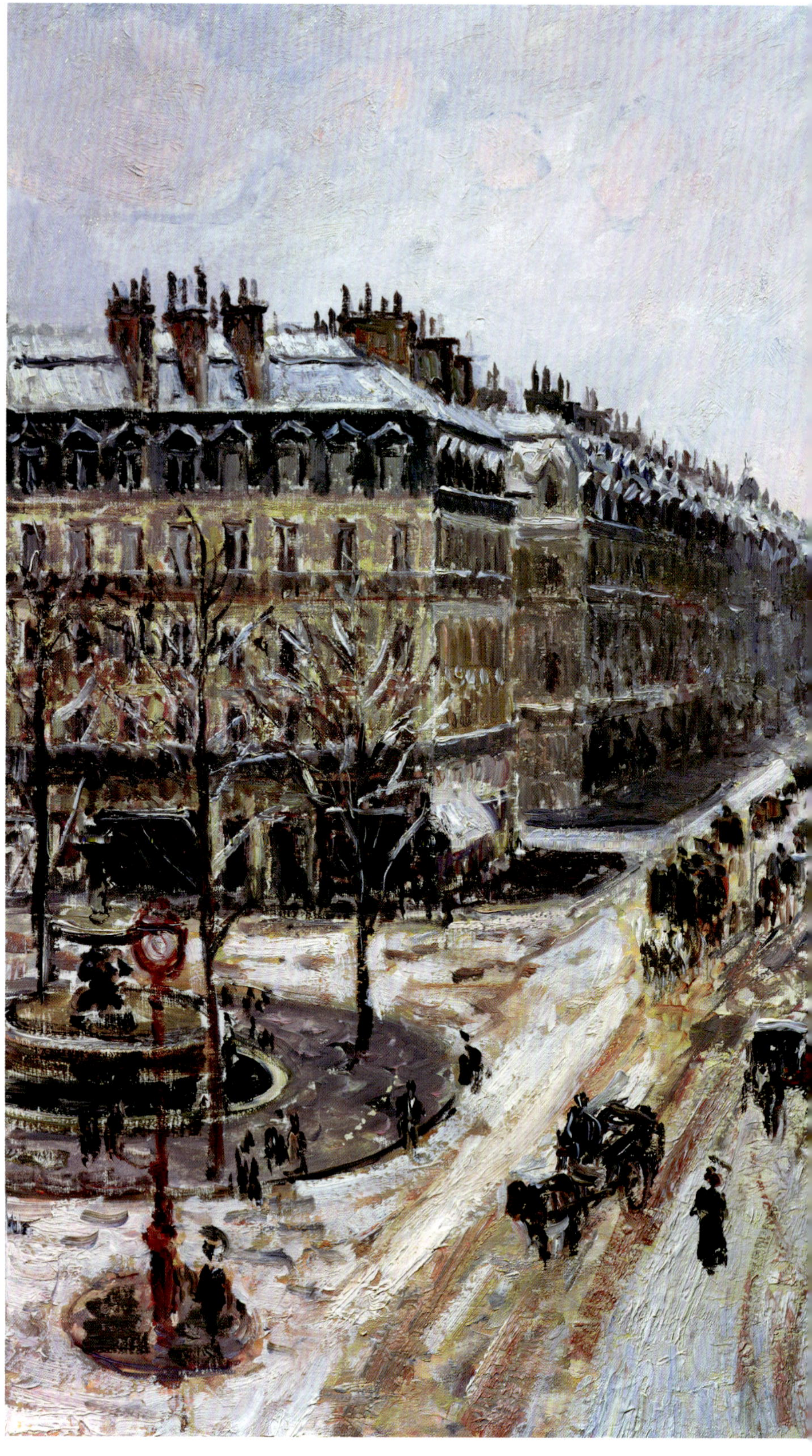

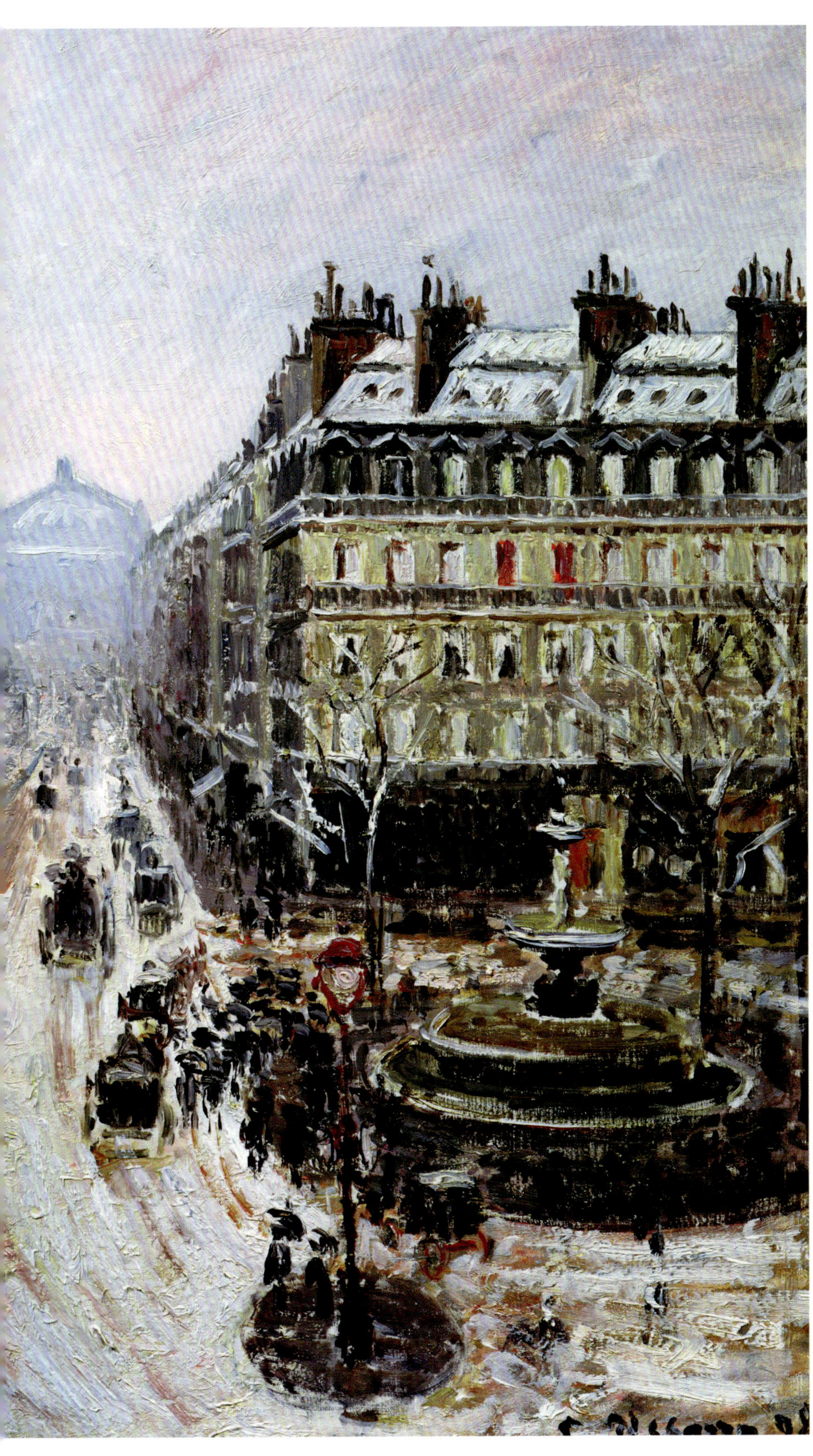

Camille Pissarro (1830–1903)

Avenue de l'Opera – Effect of Snow

Avenue de l'Opéra effet de neige

Avenue de l'Opera – Schnee

Avenue de l'Opera – Nieve

Avenue de l'Opéra, effetto di neve

De Avenue de l'Opera – sneeuw

1898, Oil on canvas/Huile sur toile, 54 × 65 cm, Private collection

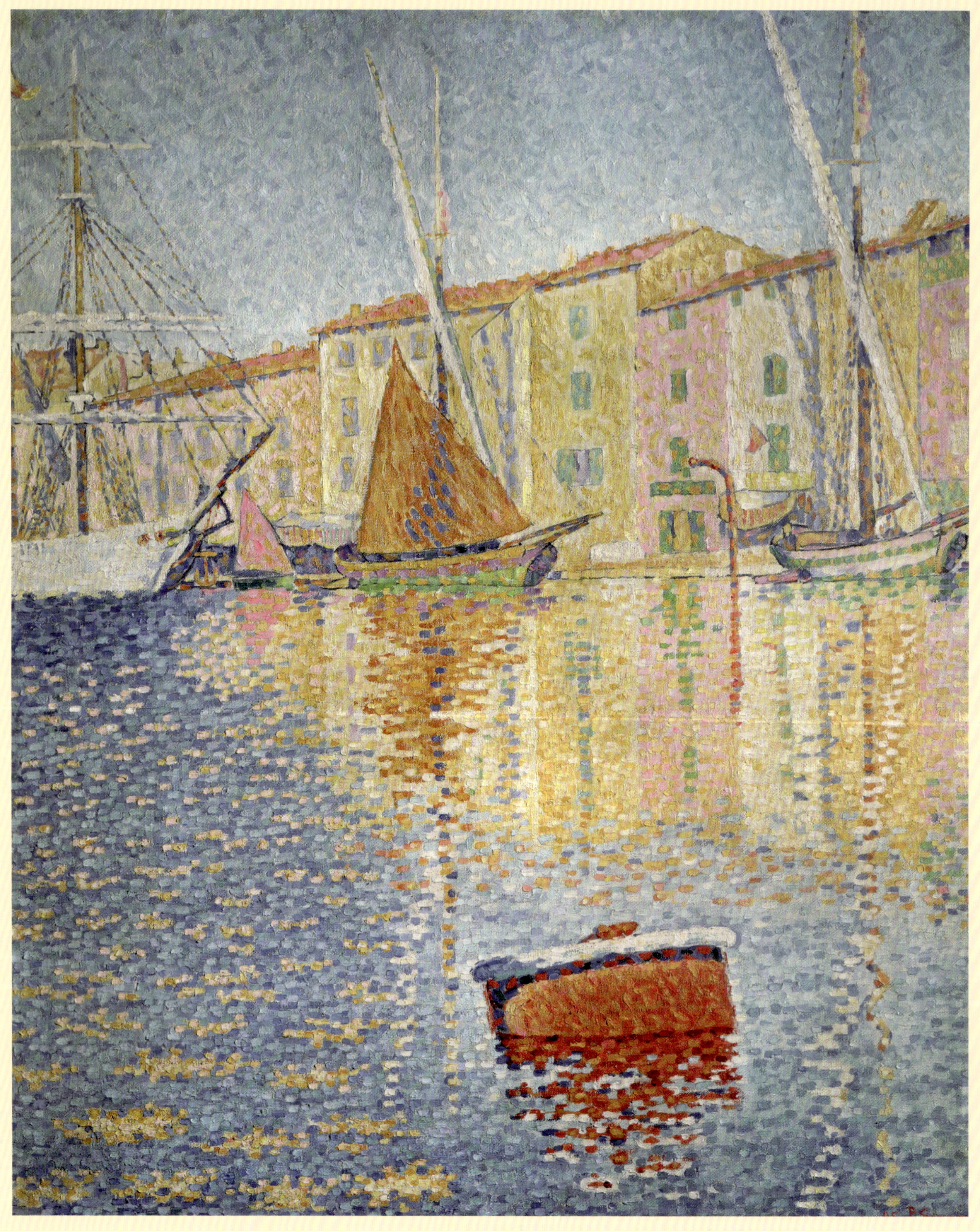

This masterpiece from Signac exhibits an exceptional atmosphere. The harbor entrance of Saint-Tropez lies quietly in the bright midday sun. No breath of wind ruffles the surface of the water, which in its representation through numerous dots nevertheless suggests movement. The red buoy creates an intensively colored accent in the otherwise well-balanced color scheme.

Ce chef-d'œuvre de Signac présente une atmosphère exceptionnelle. L'entrée du port de Saint-Tropez est paisible sous la lumière ensoleillée de midi. Aucun souffle de vent ne ride la surface de l'eau, qui dans sa représentation par de nombreux points suggère néanmoins un mouvement. La bouée rouge crée un accent intensément coloré dans une palette de couleurs par ailleurs bien équilibrée.

Dieses Meisterwerk von Signac zeigt eine außergewöhnliche Stimmung. Die Hafeneinfahrt von Saint-Tropez liegt ruhig in der hellen Mittagssonne. Kein Windhauch kräuselt die Wasseroberfläche, das in zahlreichen Punkten dennoch Bewegung suggeriert. Die rote Boje schafft einen intensiven farbigen Akzent in der sonst ausgewogenen Farbgebung.

Esta obra maestra de Signac muestra una atmósfera extraordinaria. La entrada al puerto de Saint-Tropez está bañada por el tranquilo sol de mediodía. No sopla el viento sobre la superficie del agua, que sin embargo sugiere movimiento en múltiples puntos. La boya roja supone un acento de color intenso en una composición cromática por lo demás equilibrada.

Questo capolavoro di Signac raffigura un'atmosfera eccezionale. Il porto di Saint-Tropez giace tranquillamente sotto il luminoso sole di mezzogiorno. Nemmeno un alito di vento increspa la superficie dell'acqua, il cui movimento è tuttavia suggerito in molti punti. La boa rossa crea un accento di colore intenso nel cromatismo equilibrato del quadro.

Dit meesterwerk van Signac ademt een buitengewone sfeer. De haveningang van Saint-Tropez glinstert in de felle middagzon. Geen zuchtje wind verruwt het wateroppervlak, dat door de talloze kleurpuntjes toch beweging lijkt te suggereren. De rode boei vormt een intens kleurcontrast met het uitgewogen kleurpalet in de rest van het doek.

Paul Signac (1863–1935)
The Red Buoy, Saint Tropez
La bouée rouge
Die rote Boje in Saint-Tropez
La boya roja en Saint-Tropez
La boa rossa, Saint-Tropez
De rode boei (Saint-Tropez)
1895, Oil on canvas/Huile sur toile, 81,2 × 65 cm, Musée d'Orsay, Paris

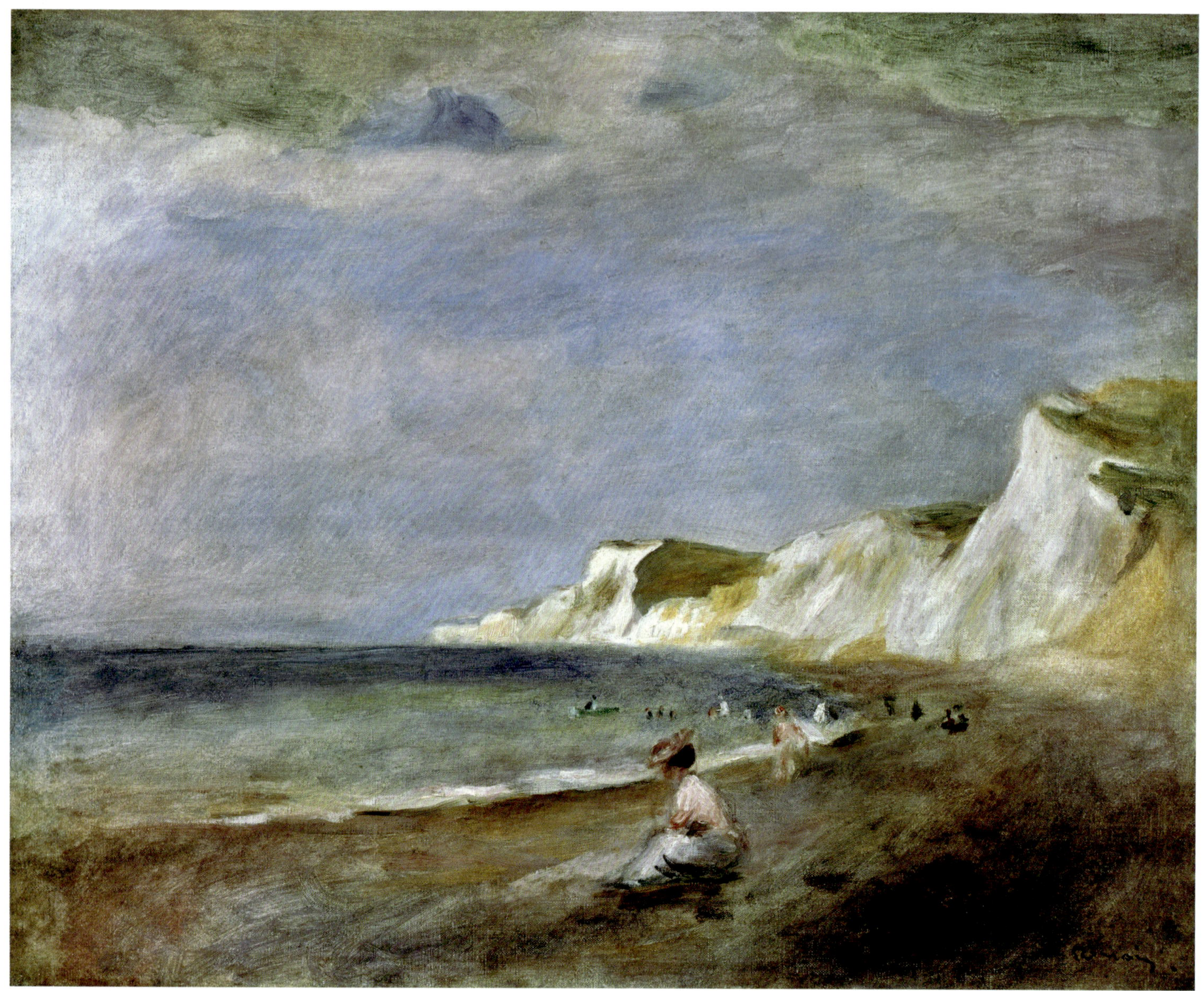

Pierre-Auguste Renoir (1841–1919)

The Beach at Varangeville

La plage de Varangéville

Der Strand von Varengeville

La playa de Varengeville

La spiaggia di Varengeville

Het strand van Varengeville

c. 1880, Oil on canvas/Huile sur toile, 44,4 × 54 cm, Private collection

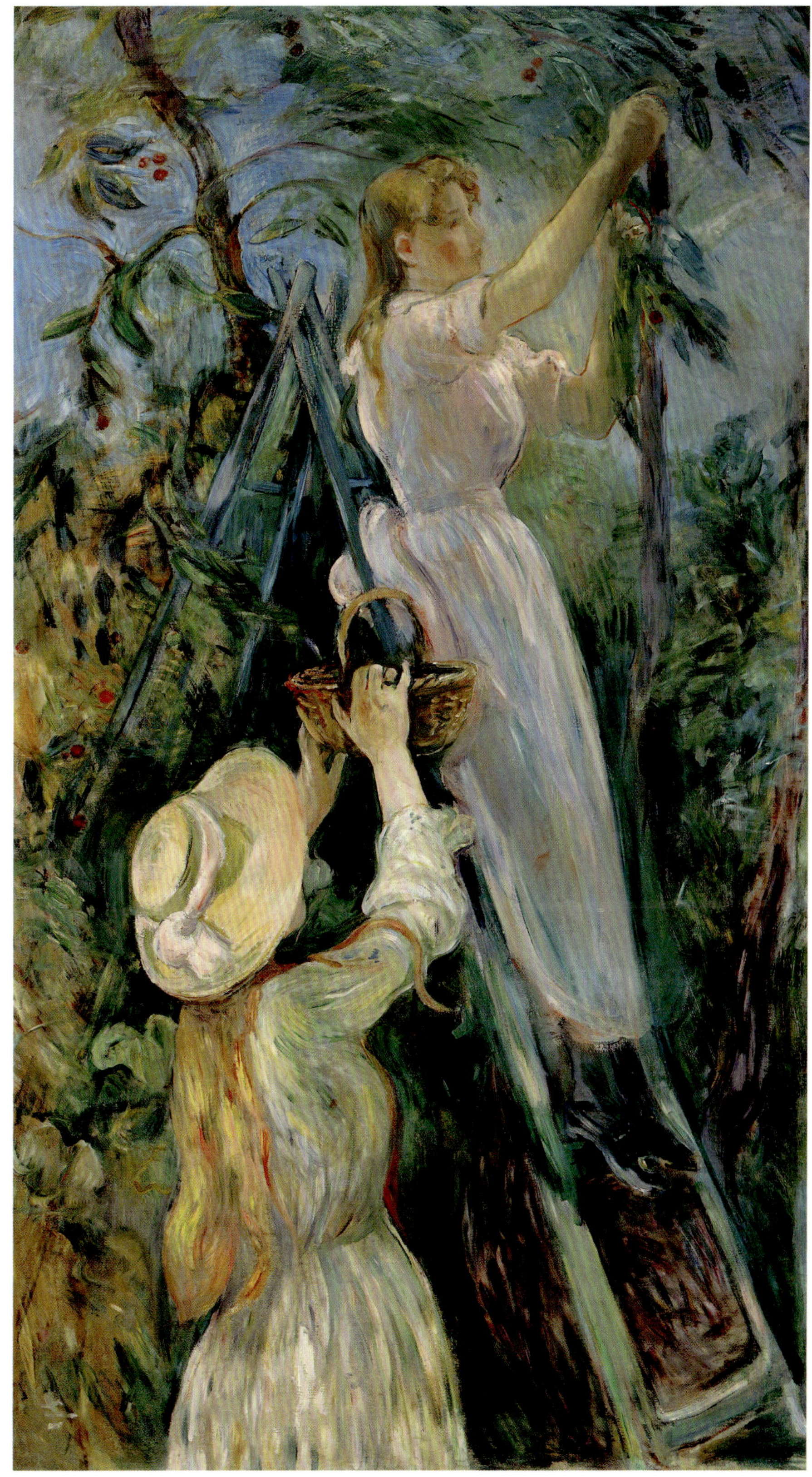

Berthe Morisot (1841–95)

The Cherry Picker

La cueillette des cerises

Die Kirschenpflückerinnen

La recogedora de cerezas

Raccolta delle ciliegie

De kersenpluksters

n.d., Oil on canvas/Huile sur toile, 154 × 84 cm, Private collection

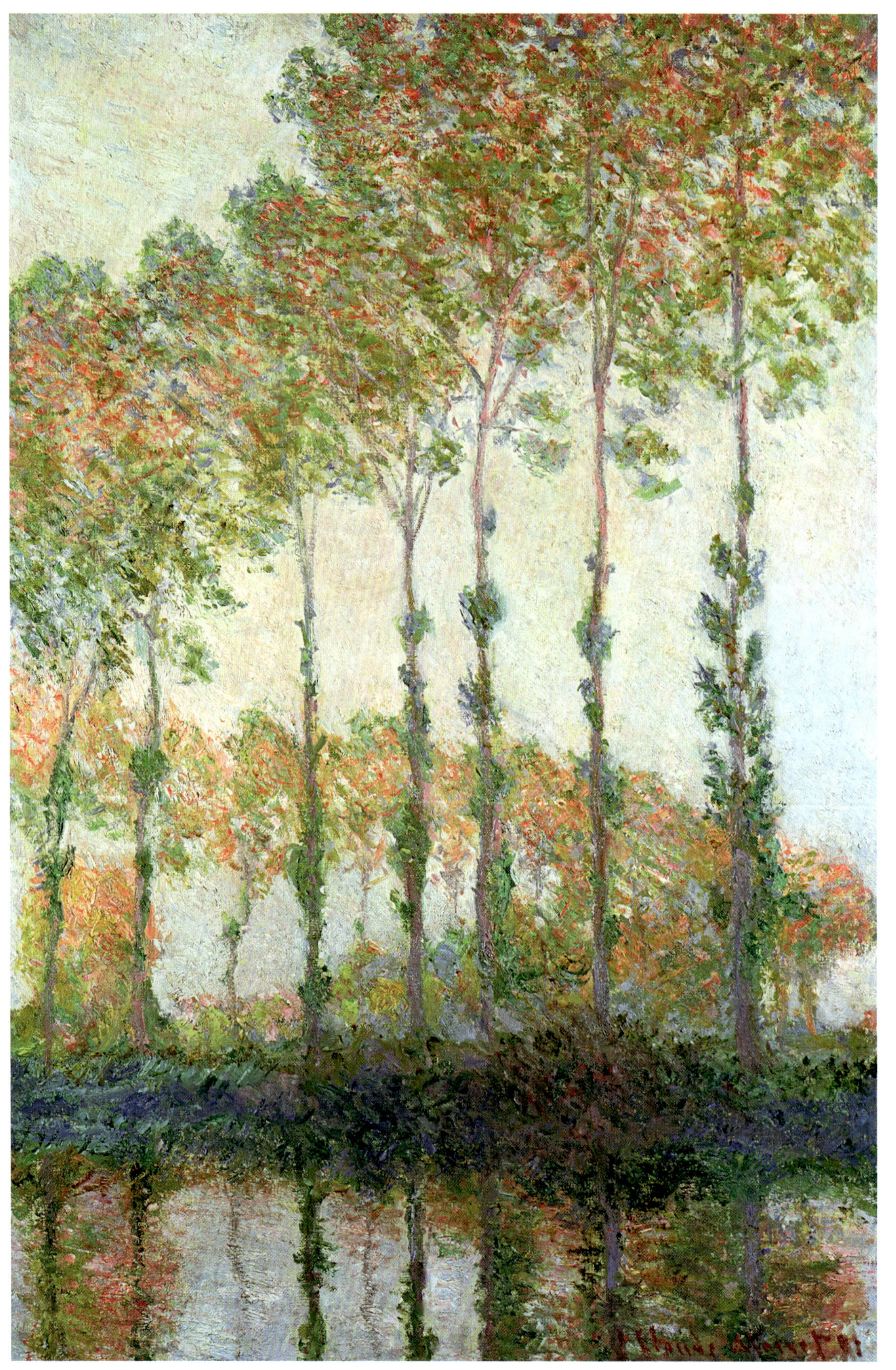

Claude Monet (1840–1926)

Poplars on the Banks of the Epte, Autumn

Peupliers au bord de l'Epte

Pappeln an der Epte, Herbst

Álamos a la orilla del Epte

Pioppi sulla riva dell'Epte

Populieren aan de oever van de Epte

1891, Oil on canvas/Huile sur toile,
101 × 66 cm, Private collection

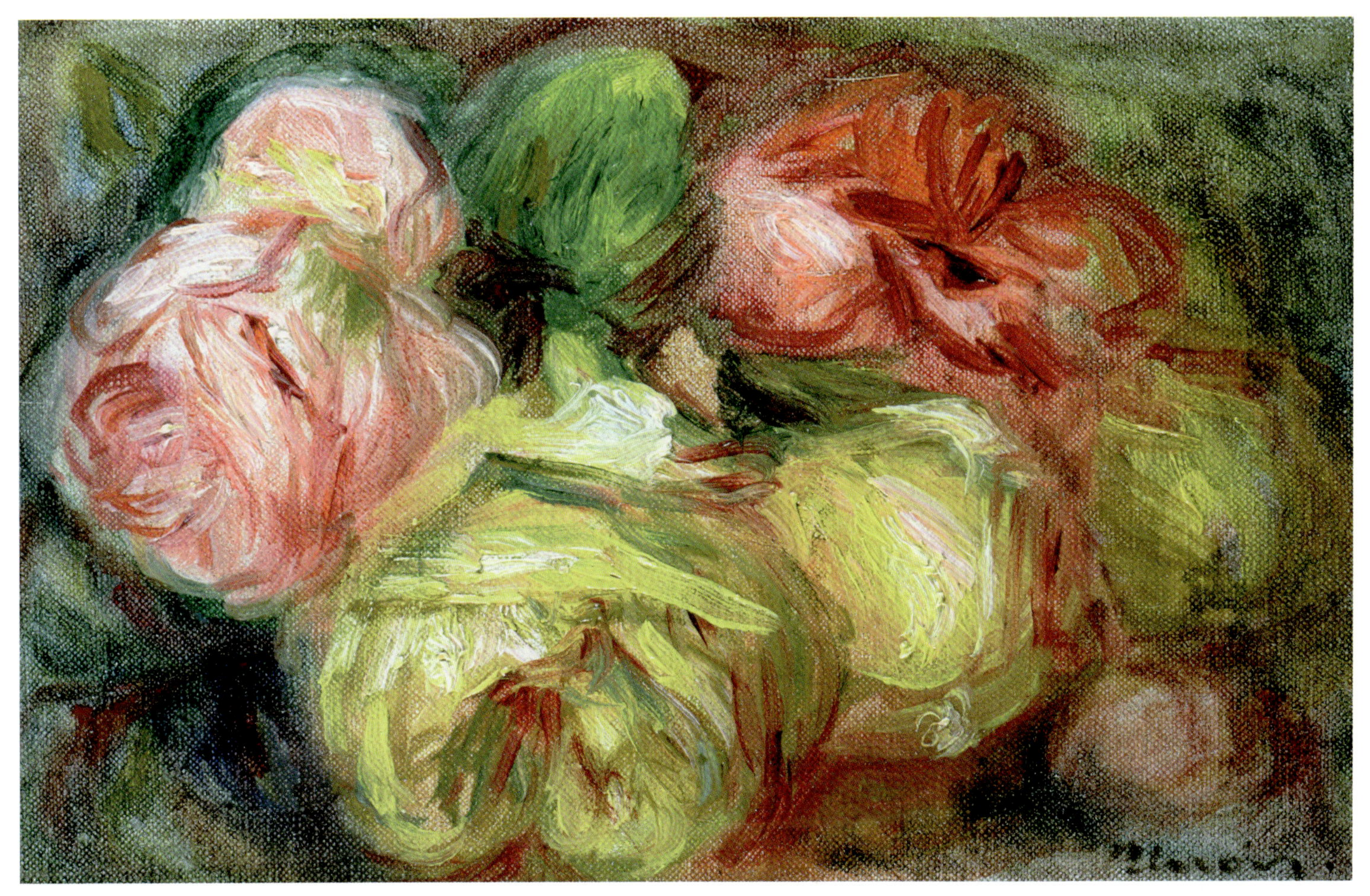

Pierre-Auguste Renoir (1841–1919)

Roses

Roses

Rosen

Rosas

Rose

Rozen

n.d., Oil on canvas/Huile sur toile, 14 × 21,3 cm, Private collection, Amsterdam

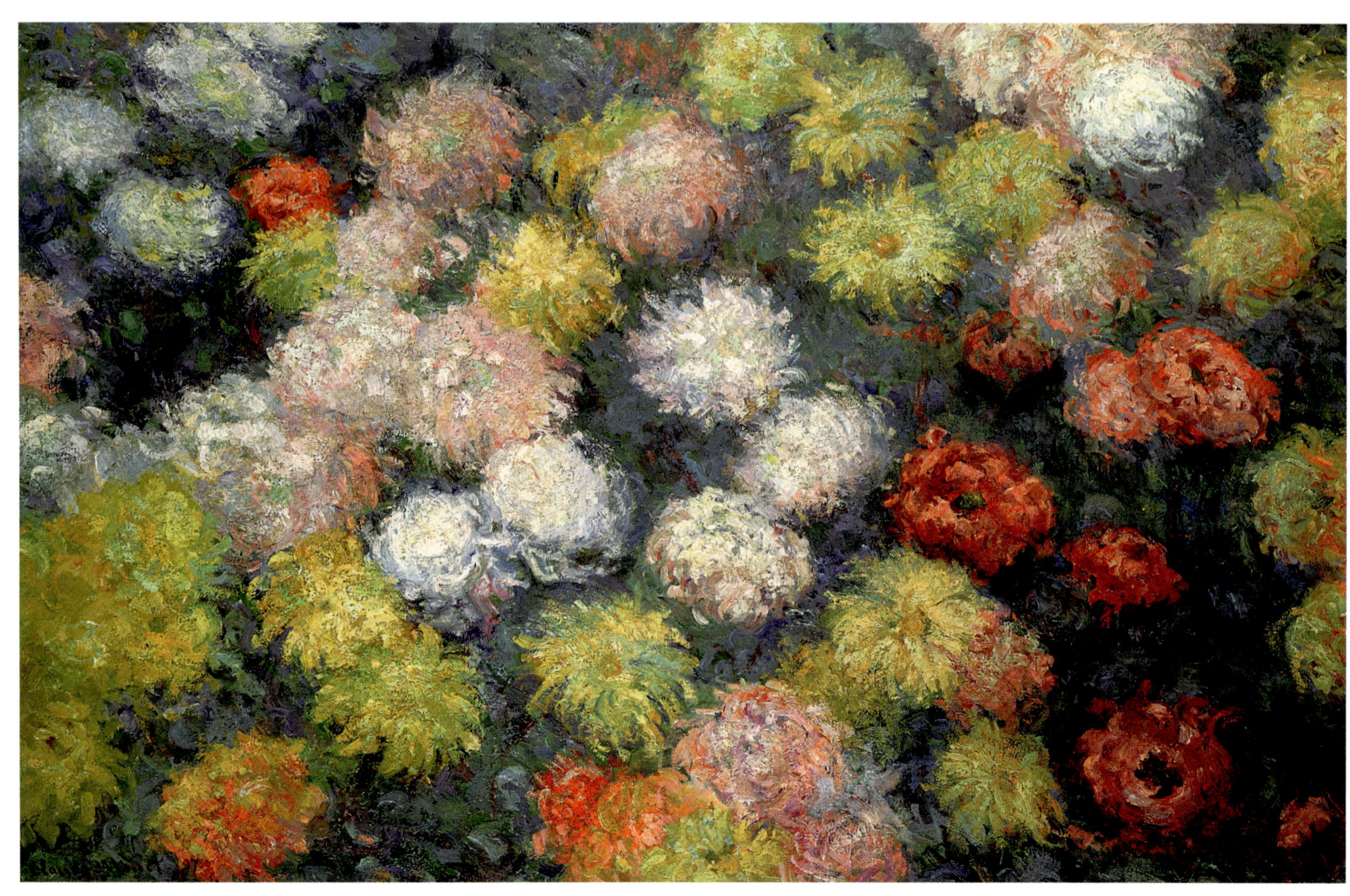

Claude Monet (1840–1926)

Chrysanthemums

Chrysanthèmes

Chrysanthemen

Crisantemos

Crisantemi

Chrysanten

1897, Oil on canvas/Huile sur toile, 80,3 × 120 cm, Private collection

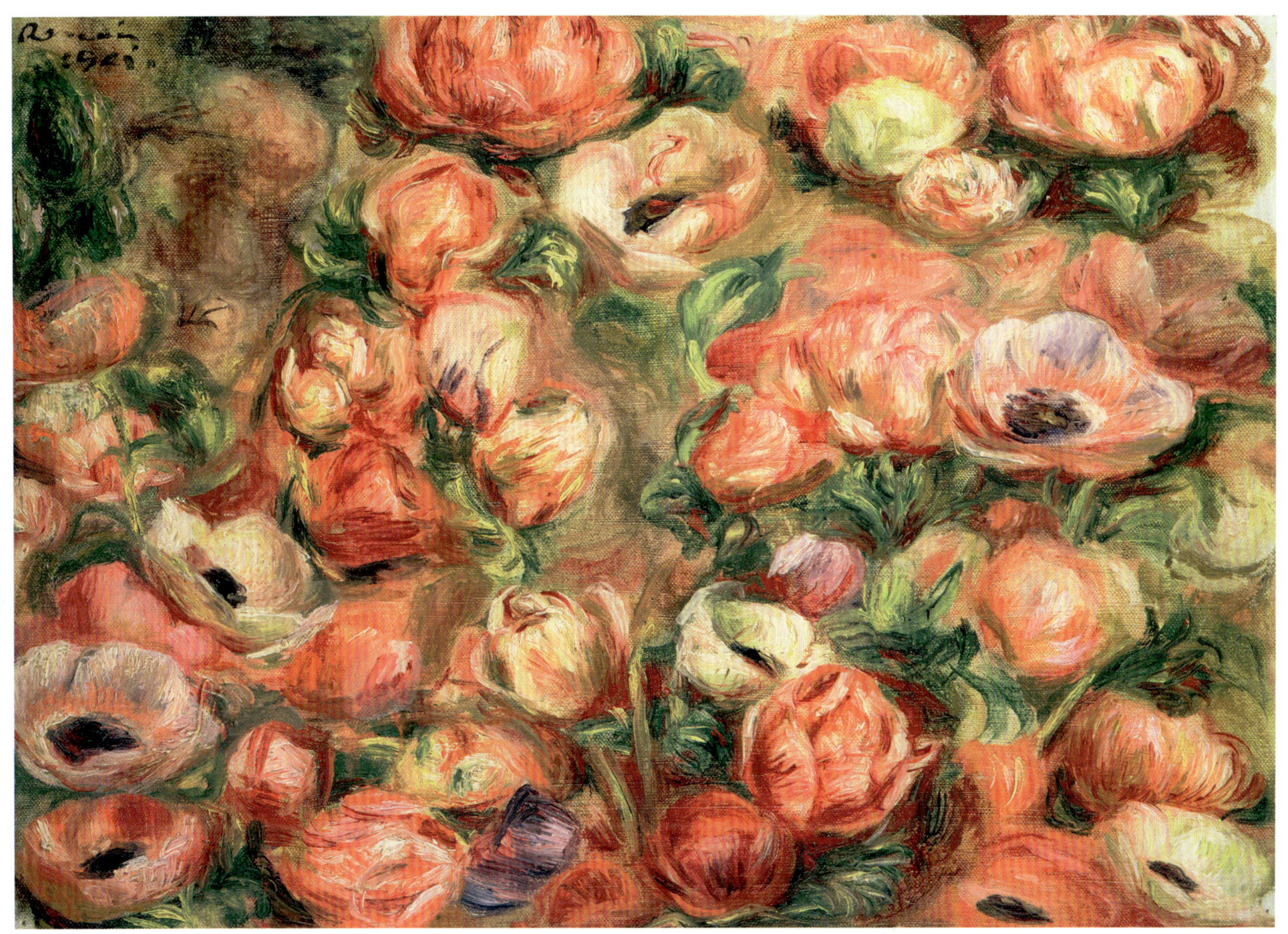

Pierre-Auguste Renoir (1841–1919)

Bed of anemones

Lit d'anémones

Anemonenbeet

Lecho de anemones

Letto di anemoni

Bed van anemonen

1901, Oil on canvas/Huile sur toile, 33 × 44 cm, Private collection, Amsterdam

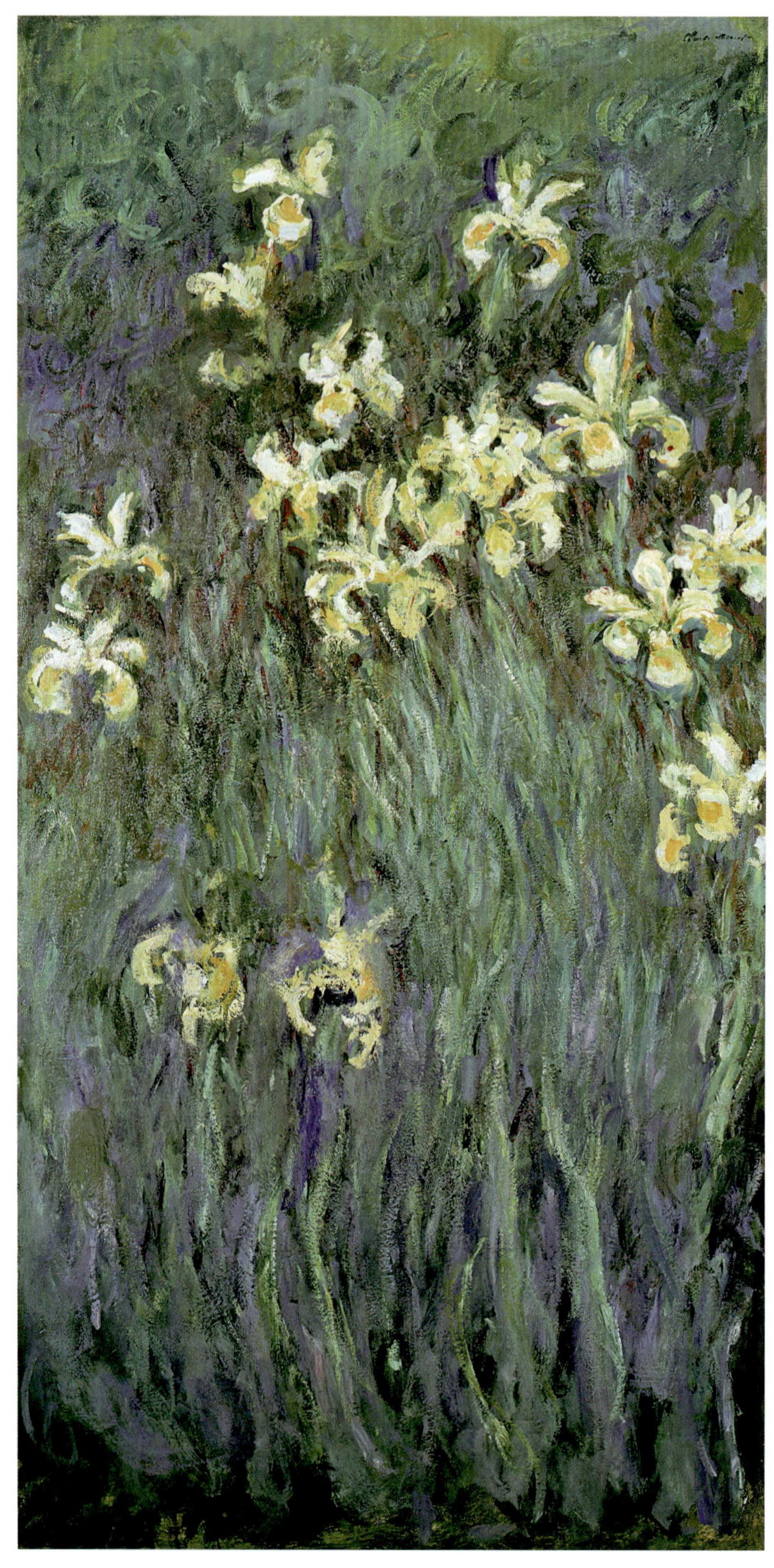

Claude Monet (1840–1926)

The Yellow Irises

Iris jaunes

Gelbe Iris

El lirio amarillo

Iris gialli

De gele irissen

1914–17, Oil on canvas/Huile sur toile,
200 × 101 cm, Private collection

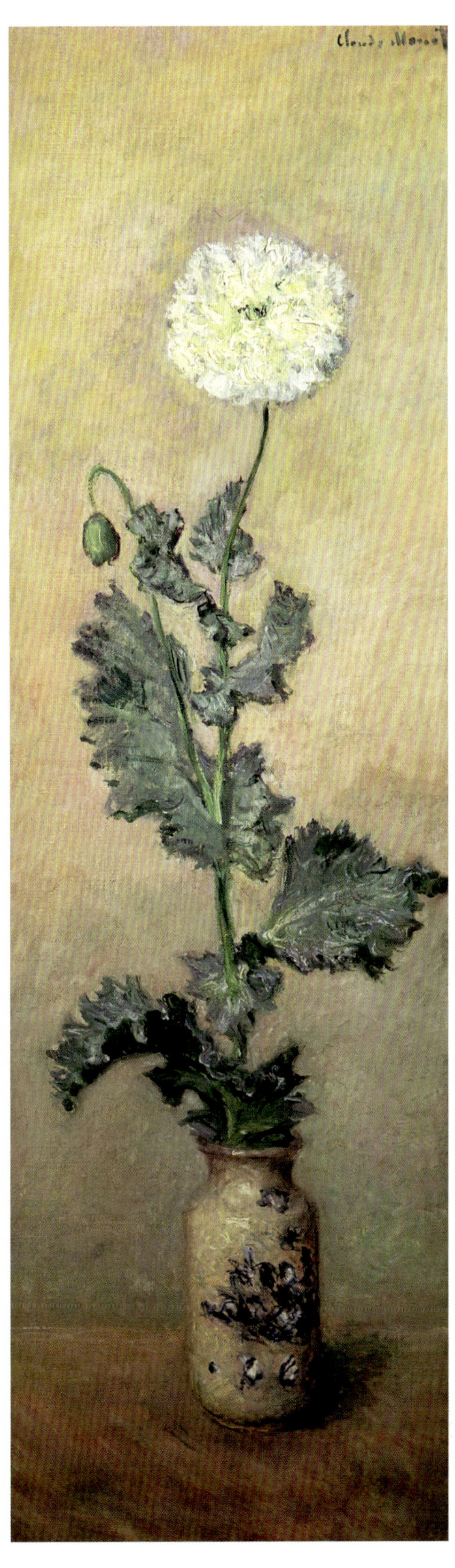

Claude Monet (1840–1926)

White Poppy

Coquelicot blanc

Weißer Mohn

Amapola blanca

Papavero bianco

Witte papaverbloem

1883, Oil on canvas/Huile sur toile, 117,5 × 37,2 cm,
Private collection

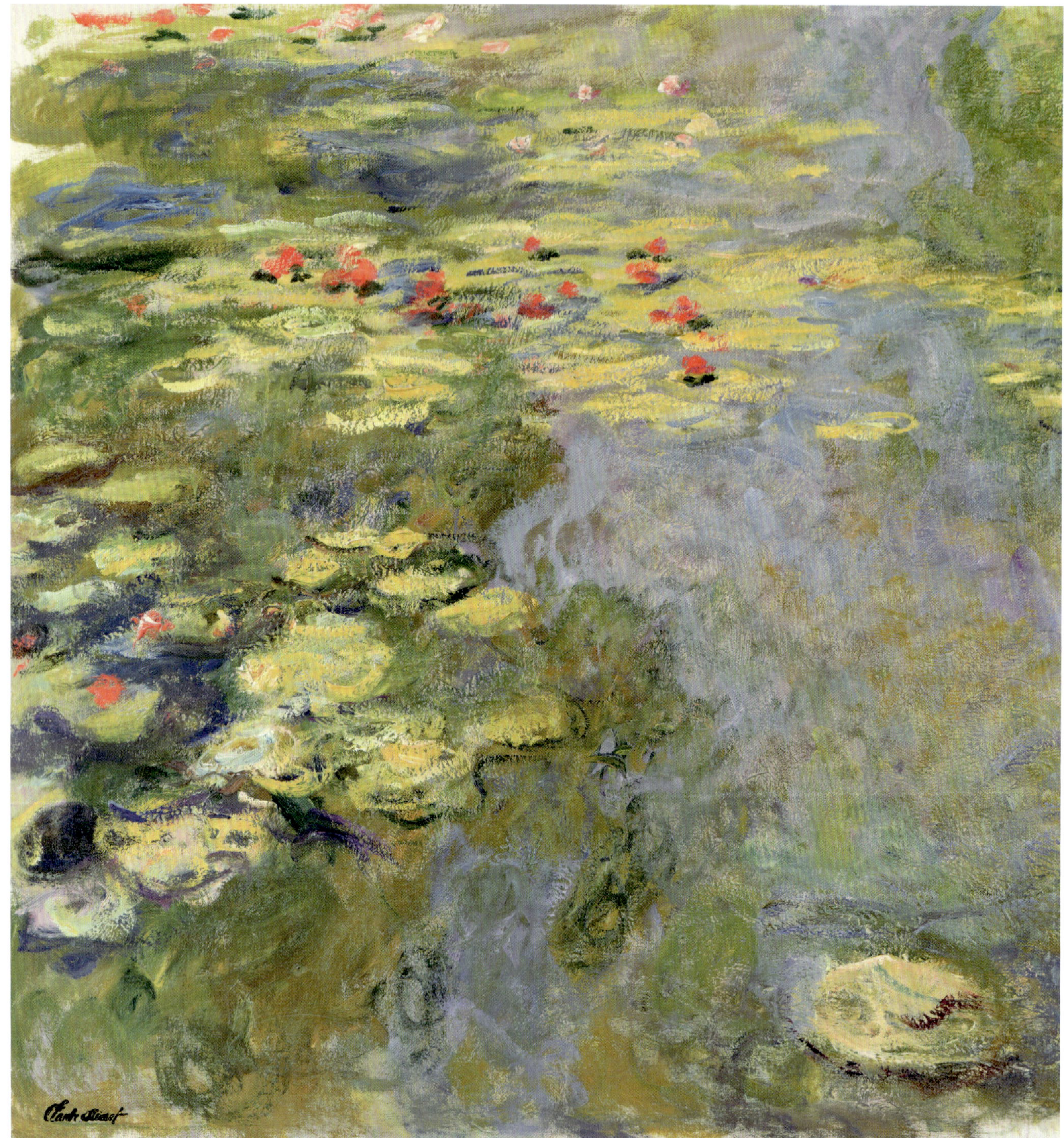

Claude Monet (1840–1926)

The Waterlily Pond   Der Seerosenteich   Lo sto di ninfee

Le bassin aux Nymphéas   El estanque de nenúfares   De waterlelievijver

1917–19, Oil on canvas/Huile sur toile, 130 × 120 cm, Musée Marmottan Monet, Paris

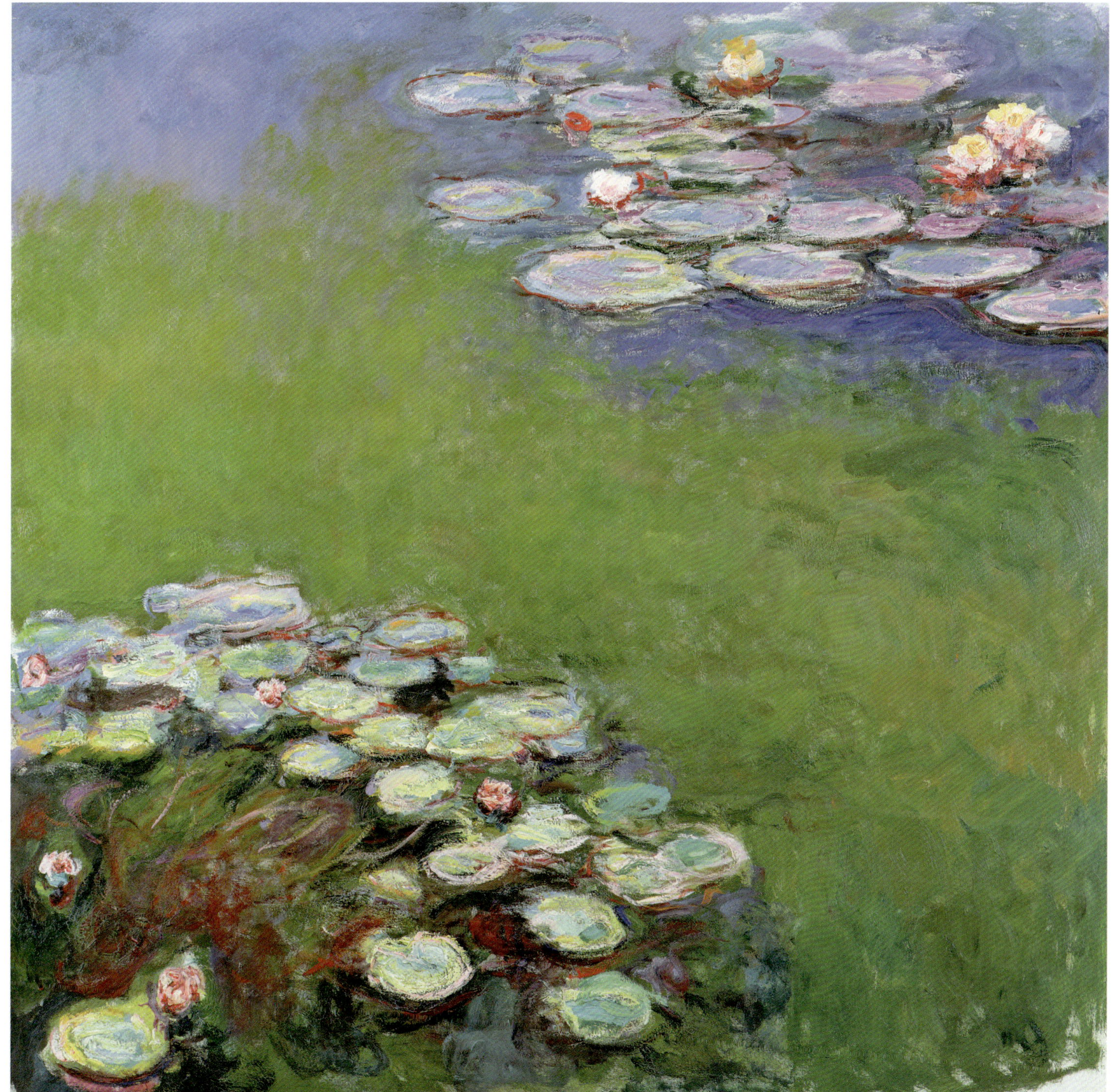

Claude Monet (1840–1926)

Waterlilies	Seerosen	Ninfee
Nymphéas	Nenúfares	Waterlelies

1914–17, Oil on canvas/Huile sur toile, 200 × 200 cm, Musée Marmottan Monet, Paris

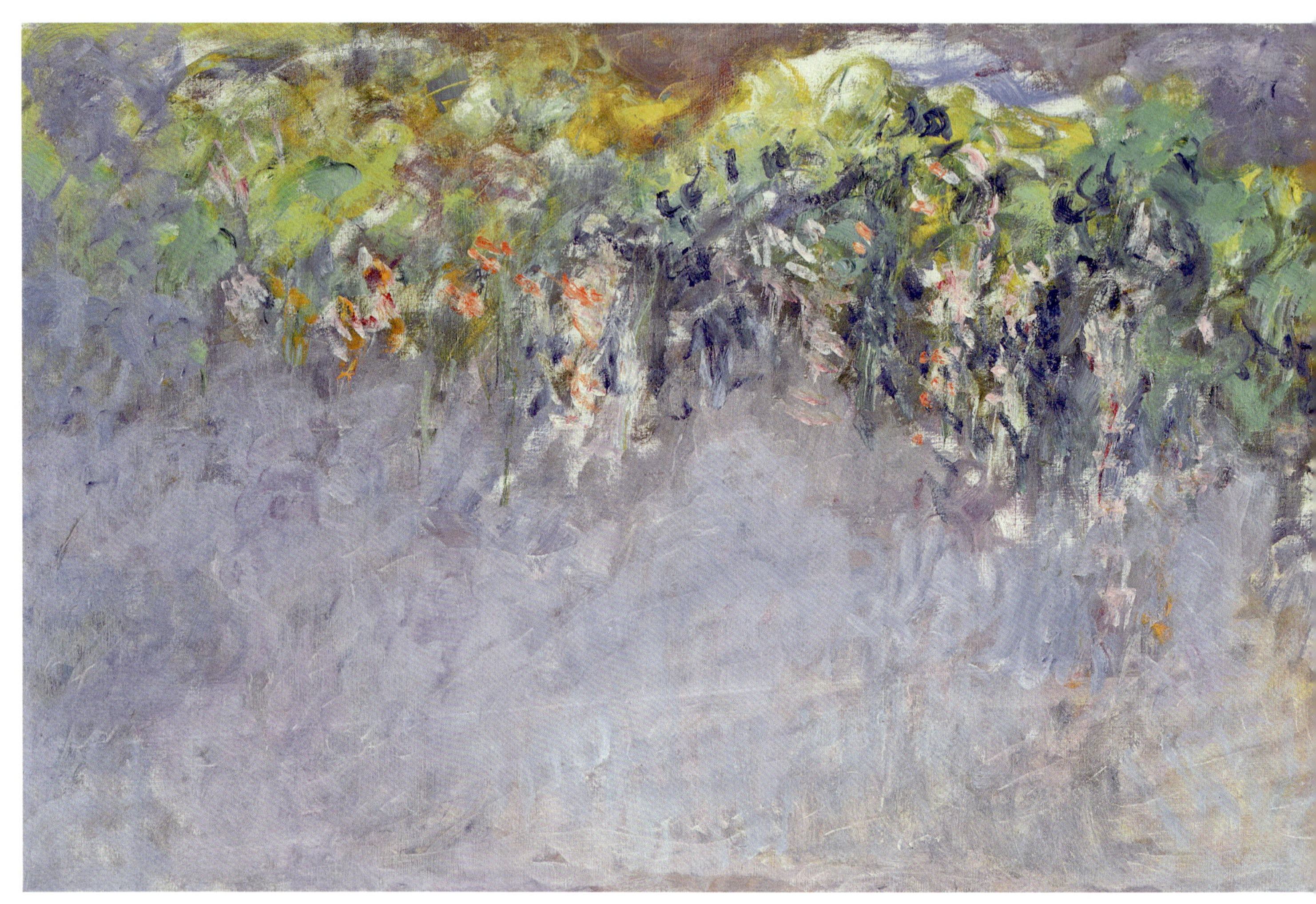

Claude Monet (1840–1926)

Wisteria

Glycine

Glyien

Glicinias

Glicine

Blauweregen

1919/20, Oil on canvas/Huile sur toile, 100 × 300 cm, Musée Marmottan Monet, Paris

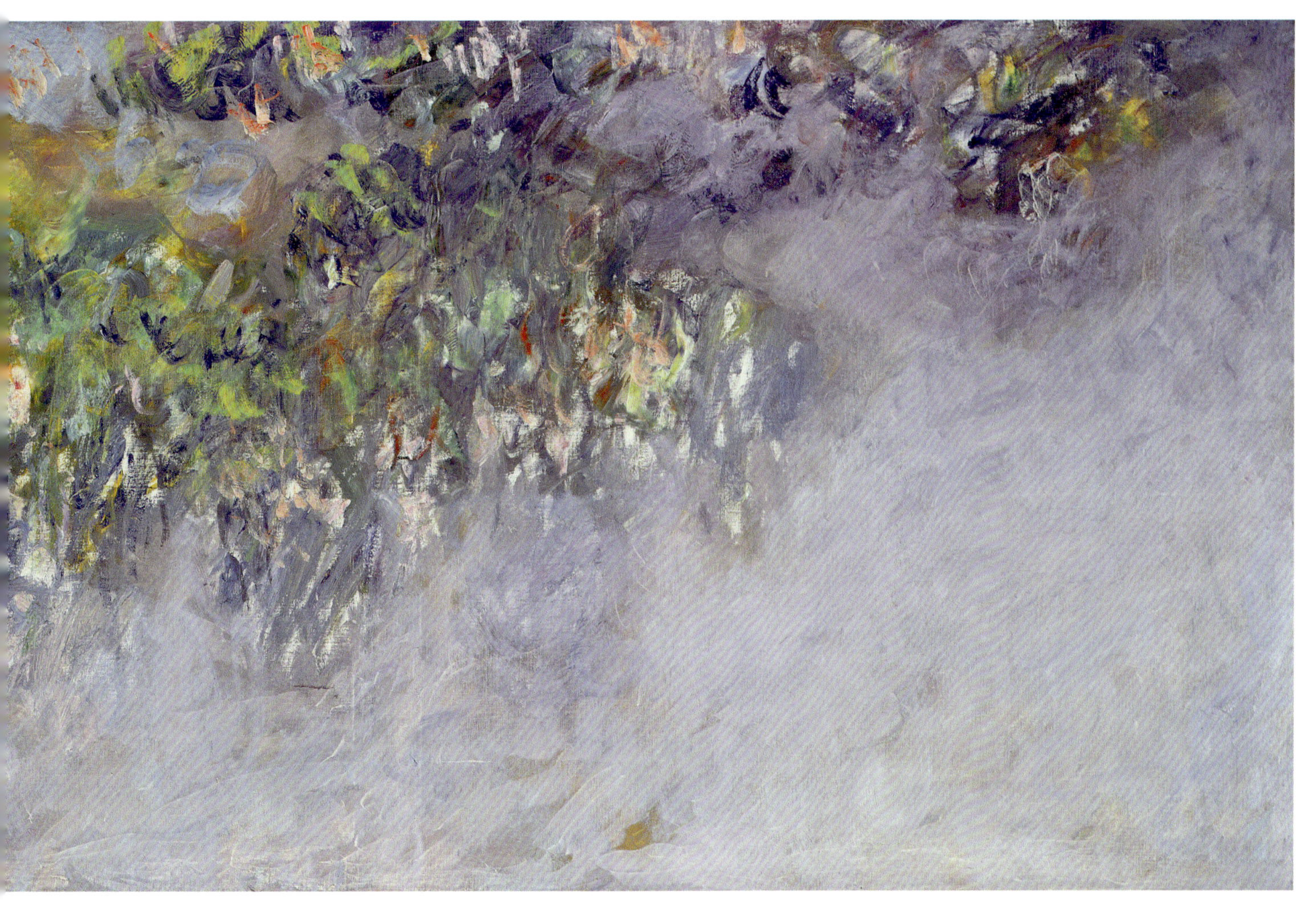

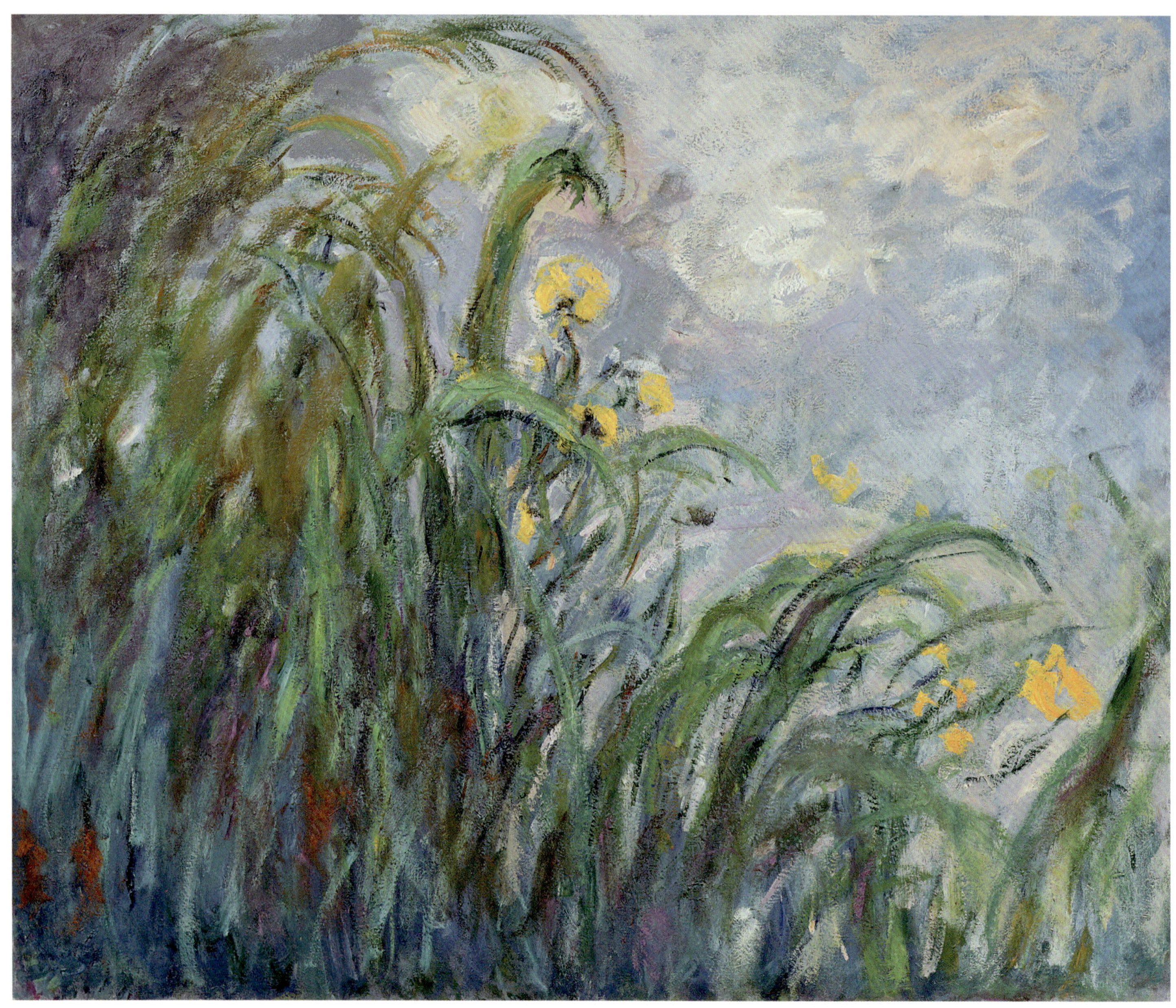

Claude Monet (1840–1926)

The Yellow Iris

Iris jaunes

Gelbe Iris

El lirio amarillo

Iris gialli

De gele irissen

1914–17, Oil on canvas/Huile sur toile, 130 × 152 cm, Musée Marmottan Monet, Paris

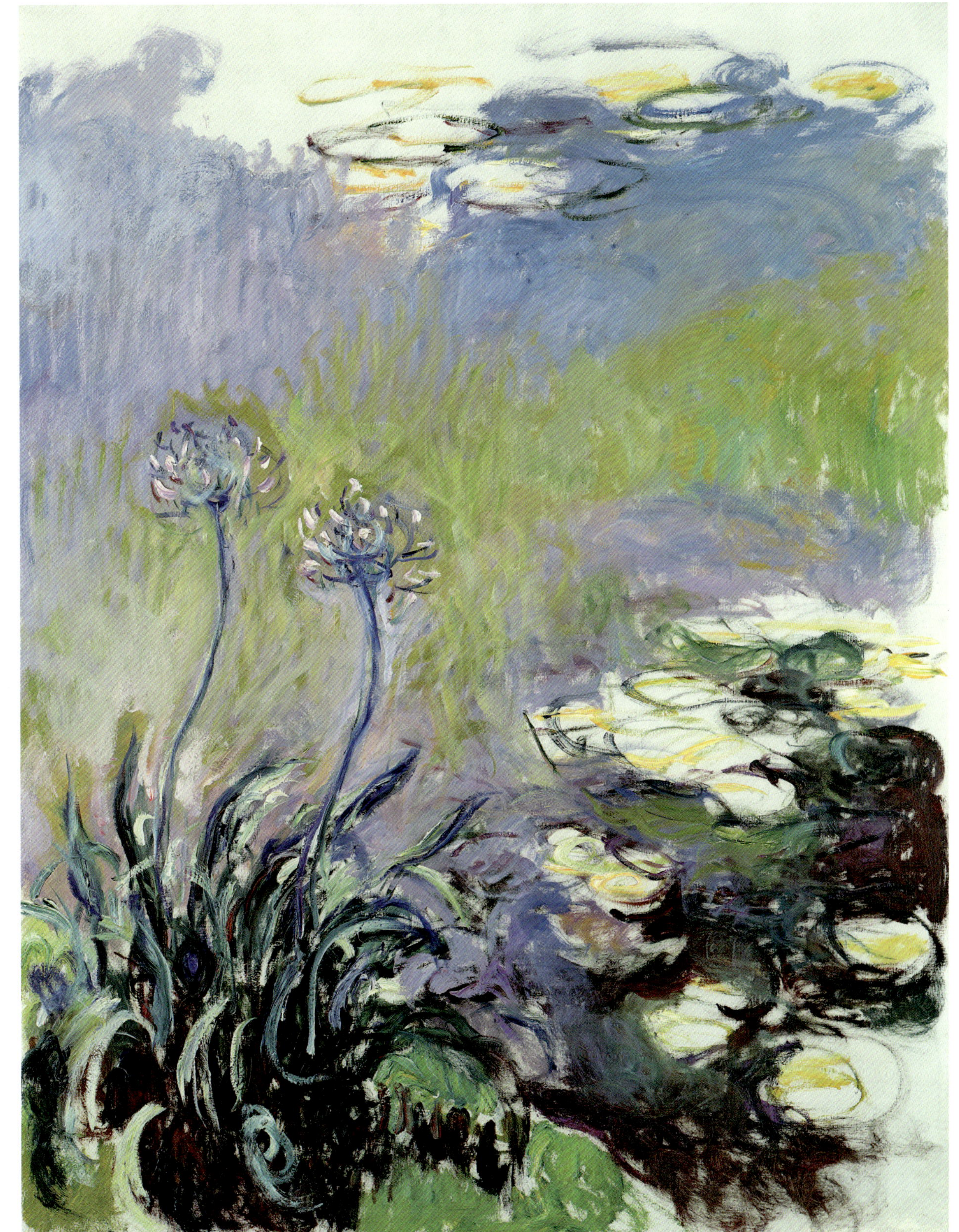

Claude Monet
(1840–1926)

The Agapanthus

Les agapanthes

Agapanthus

Agapanto

L'agapanto

De Afrikaanse lelies

1914–17, Oil on canvas/
Huile sur toile,
200 × 150 cm, Musée
Marmottan Monet, Paris

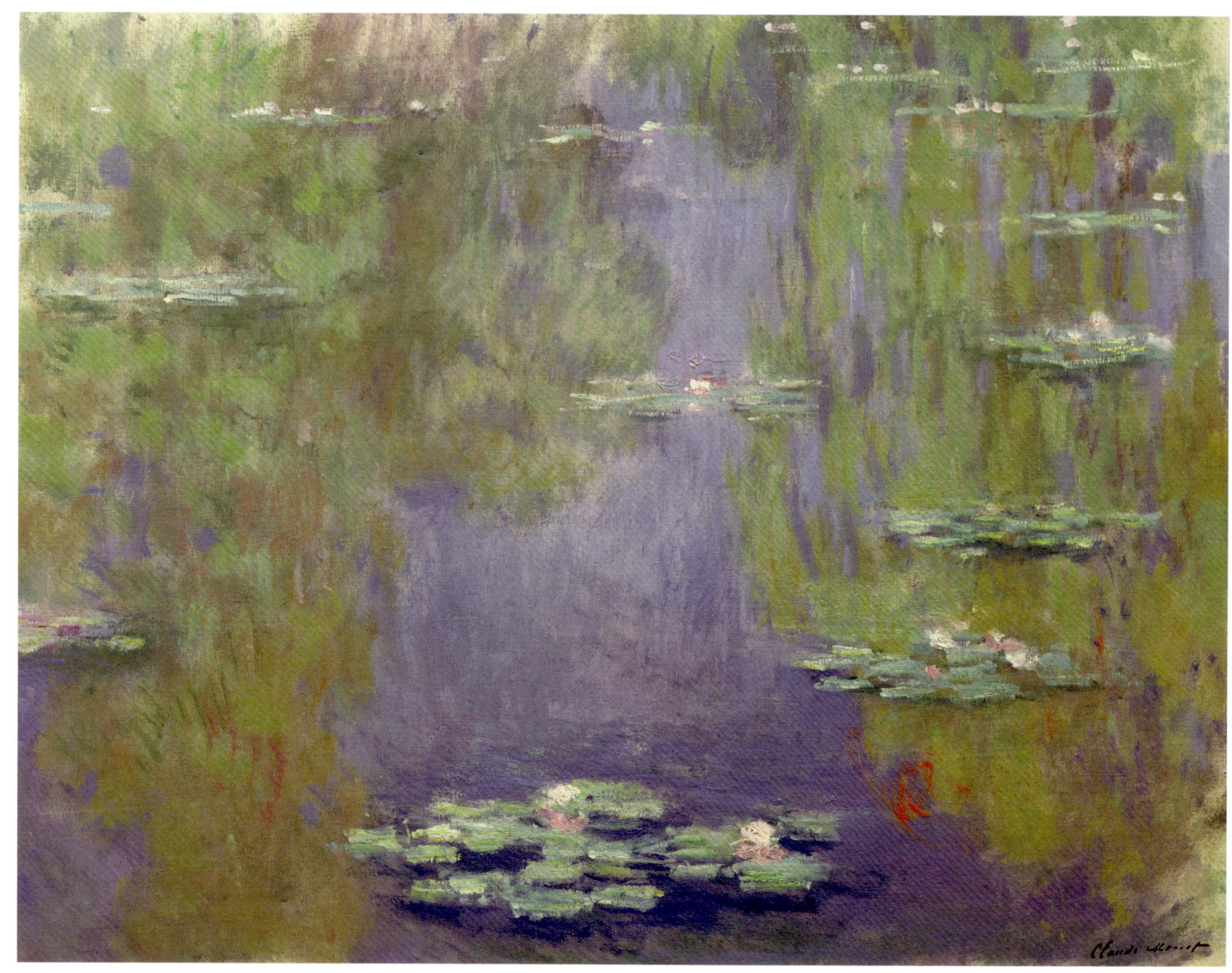

Claude Monet (1840–1926)

Waterlilies

Nymphéas

Seerosen

Nenúfares

Ninfee

Waterlelies

1903, Oil on canvas/Huile sur toile, 73 × 92 cm, Musée Marmottan Monet, Paris

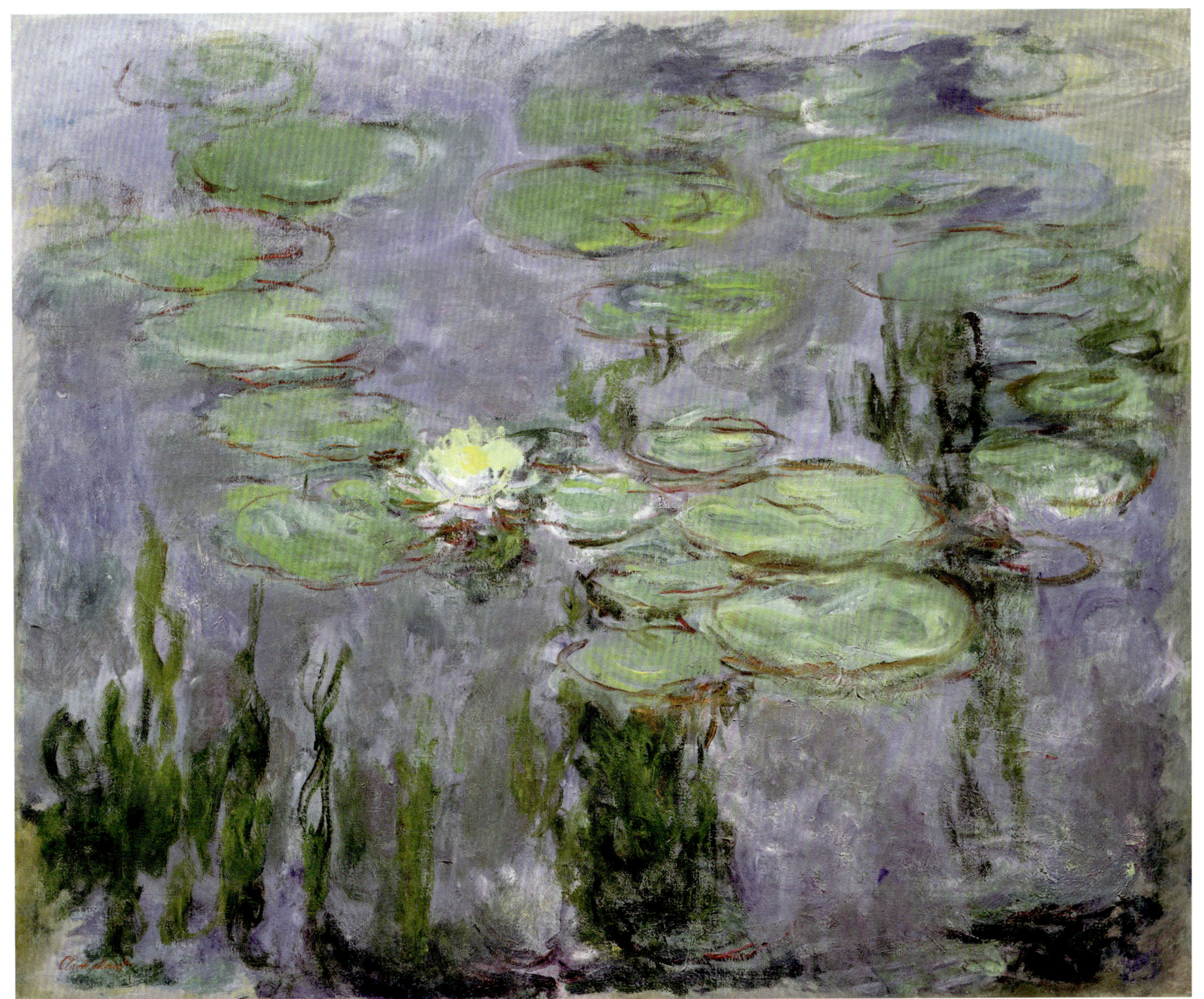

Claude Monet (1840–1926)

Waterlilies

Nymphéas

Seerosen

Nenúfares

Ninfee

Waterlelies

1915, Oil on canvas/Huile sur toile, 130 × 153 cm, Musée Marmottan Monet, Paris

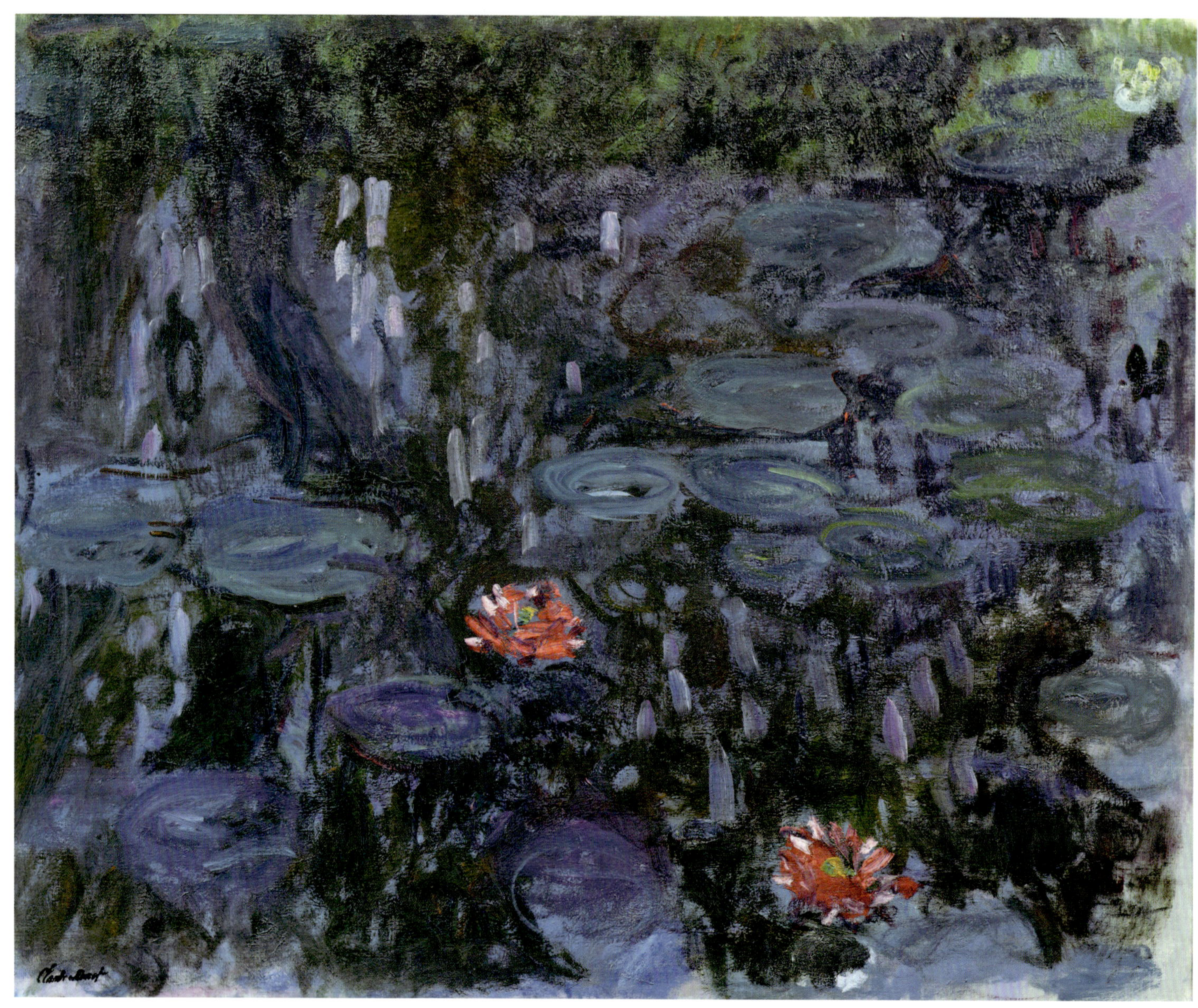

Claude Monet (1840–1926)

Waterlilies with Reflections of a Willow Tree

Nymphéas avec reflets de hautes herbes

Seerosen mit Reflexionen einer Trauerweide

Nenúfares con reflejos de un sauce llorón

Ninfee con riflessi di salici

Waterlelies met weerkaatsingen van treurwilgen

1916–19, Oil on canvas/Huile sur toile, 131 × 155 cm, Musée Marmottan Monet, Paris

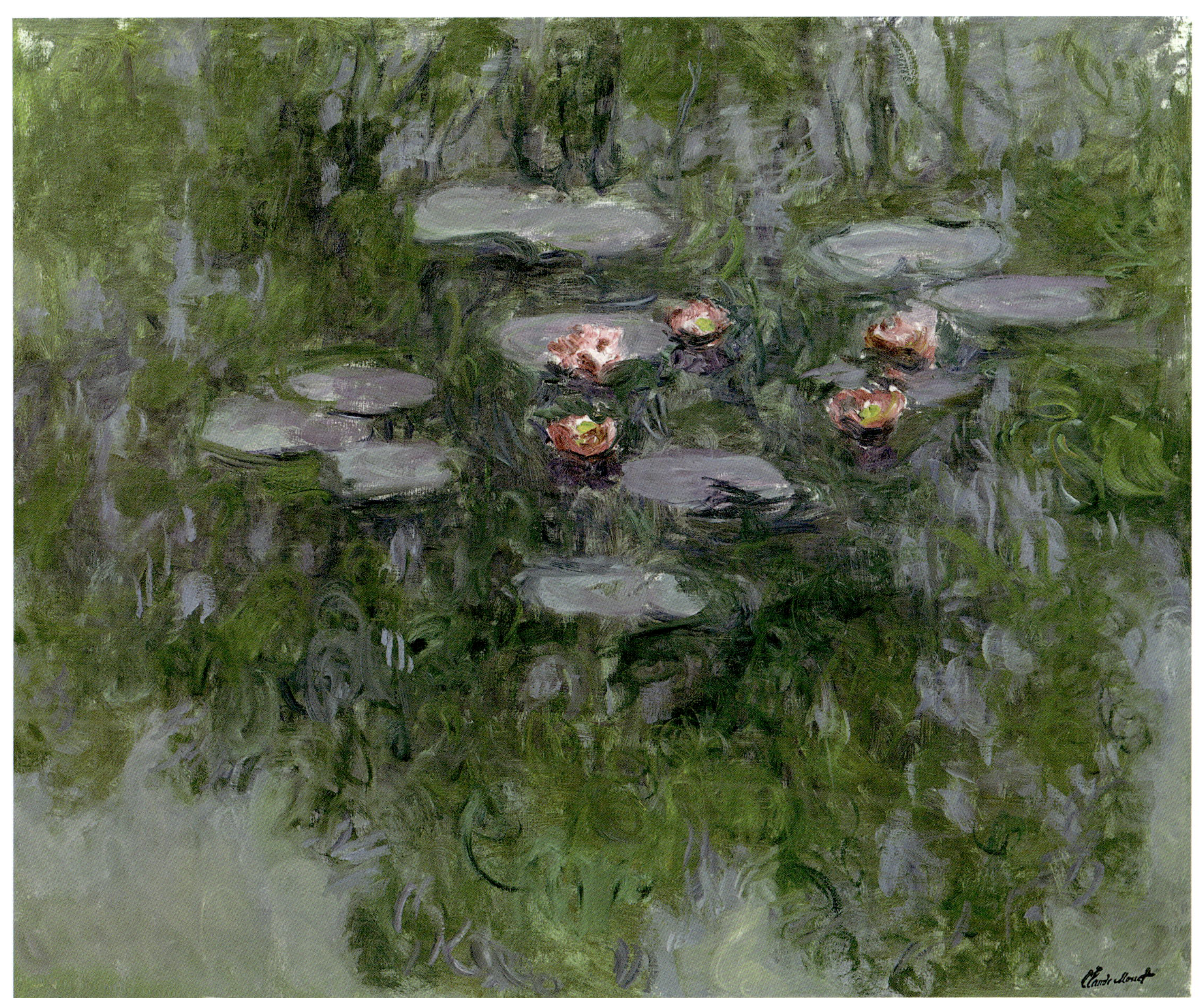

Claude Monet (1840−1926)

Waterlilies

Nymphéas

Seerosen

Nenúfares

Ninfee

Waterlelies

1916–19, Oil on canvas/Huile sur toile, 130 × 152 cm, Musée Marmottan Monet, Paris

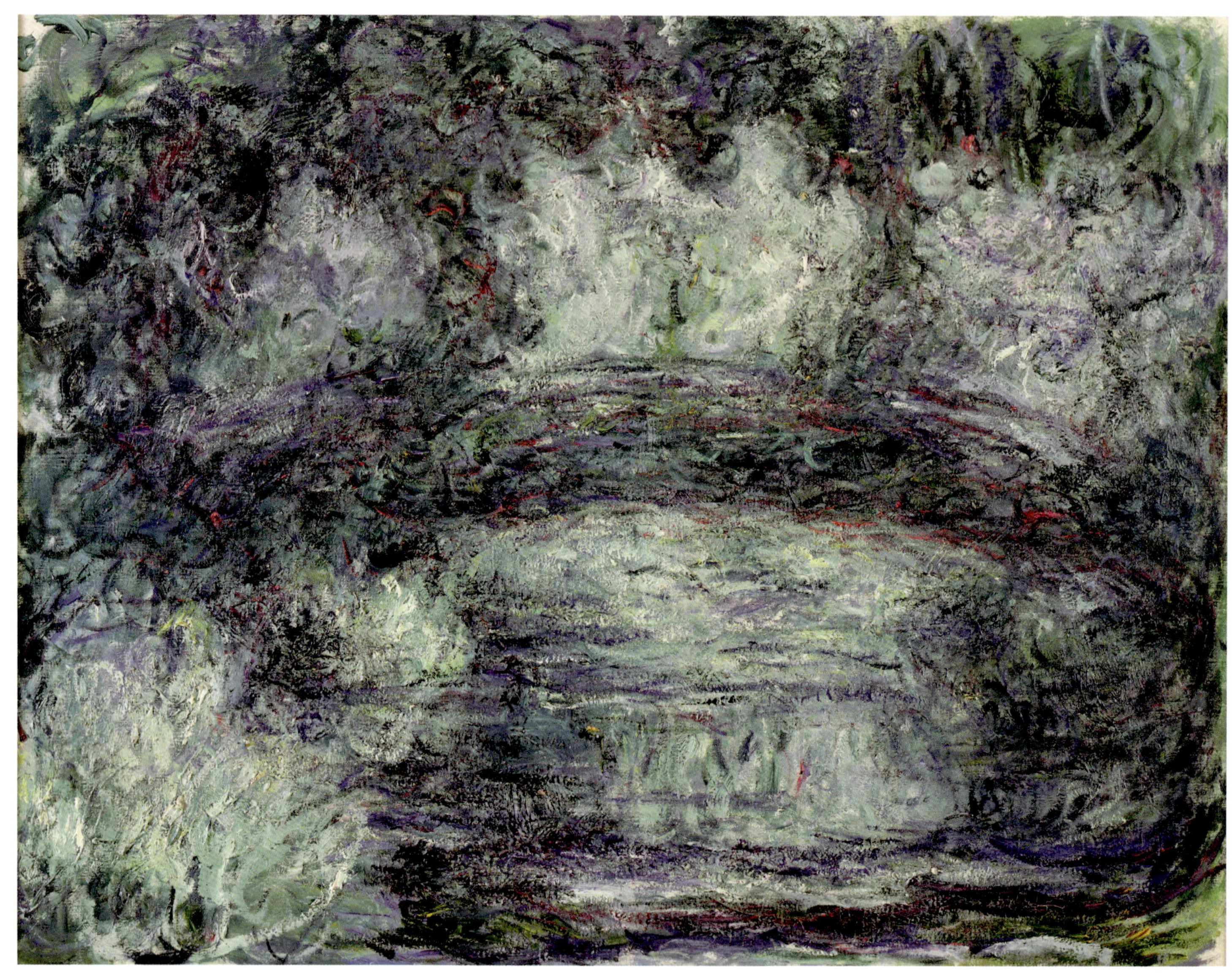

Claude Monet (1840–1926)

The Japanese Bridge

Le pont japonais

Die japanische Brücke

El puente japonés

Ponte giapponese

De Japanse brug

1918/19, Oil on canvas/Huile sur toile, 74 × 92 cm, Musée Marmottan Monet, Paris

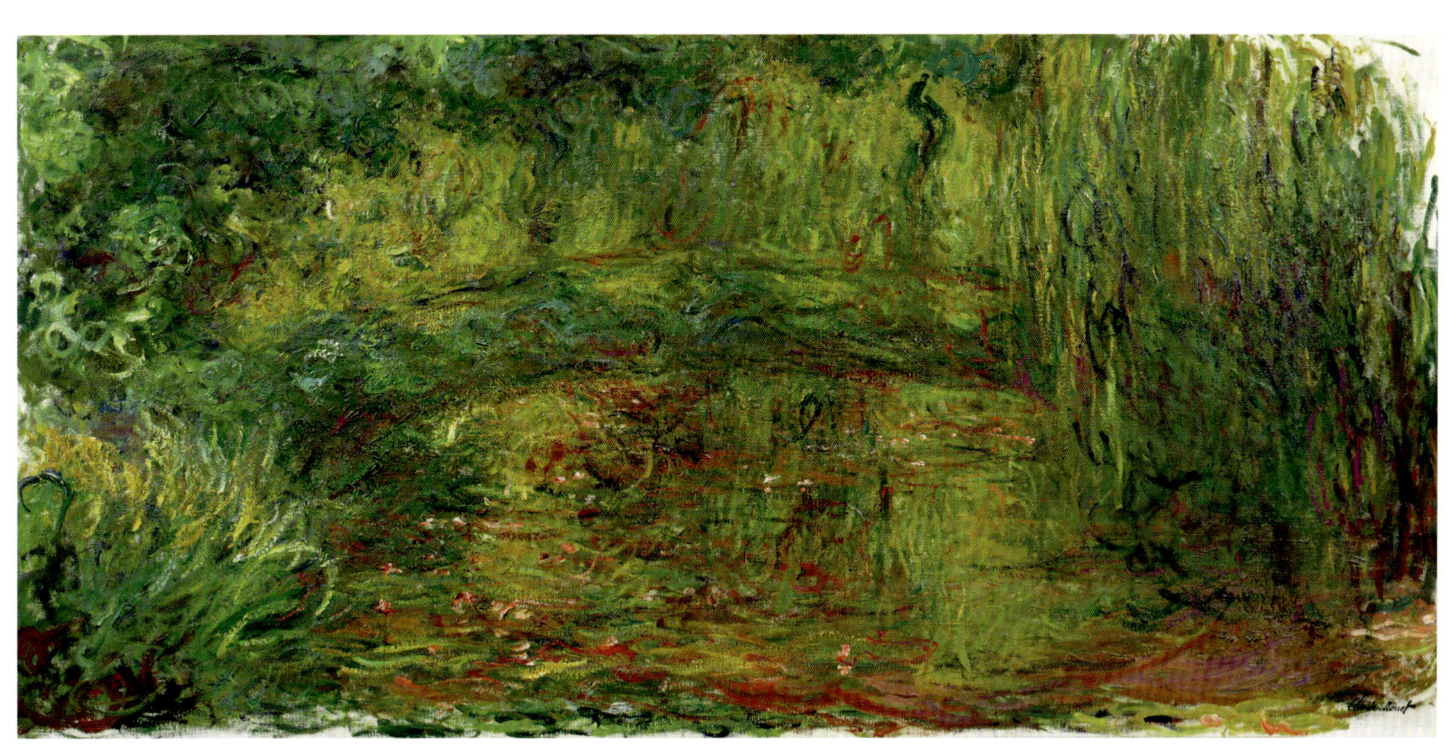

Claude Monet (1840–1926)

The Japanese Bridge

Le pont japonais

Die japanische Brücke

El puente japonés

Ponte giapponese

De Japanse brug

1918, Oil on canvas/Huile sur toile, 100 × 200 cm, Musée Marmottan Monet, Paris

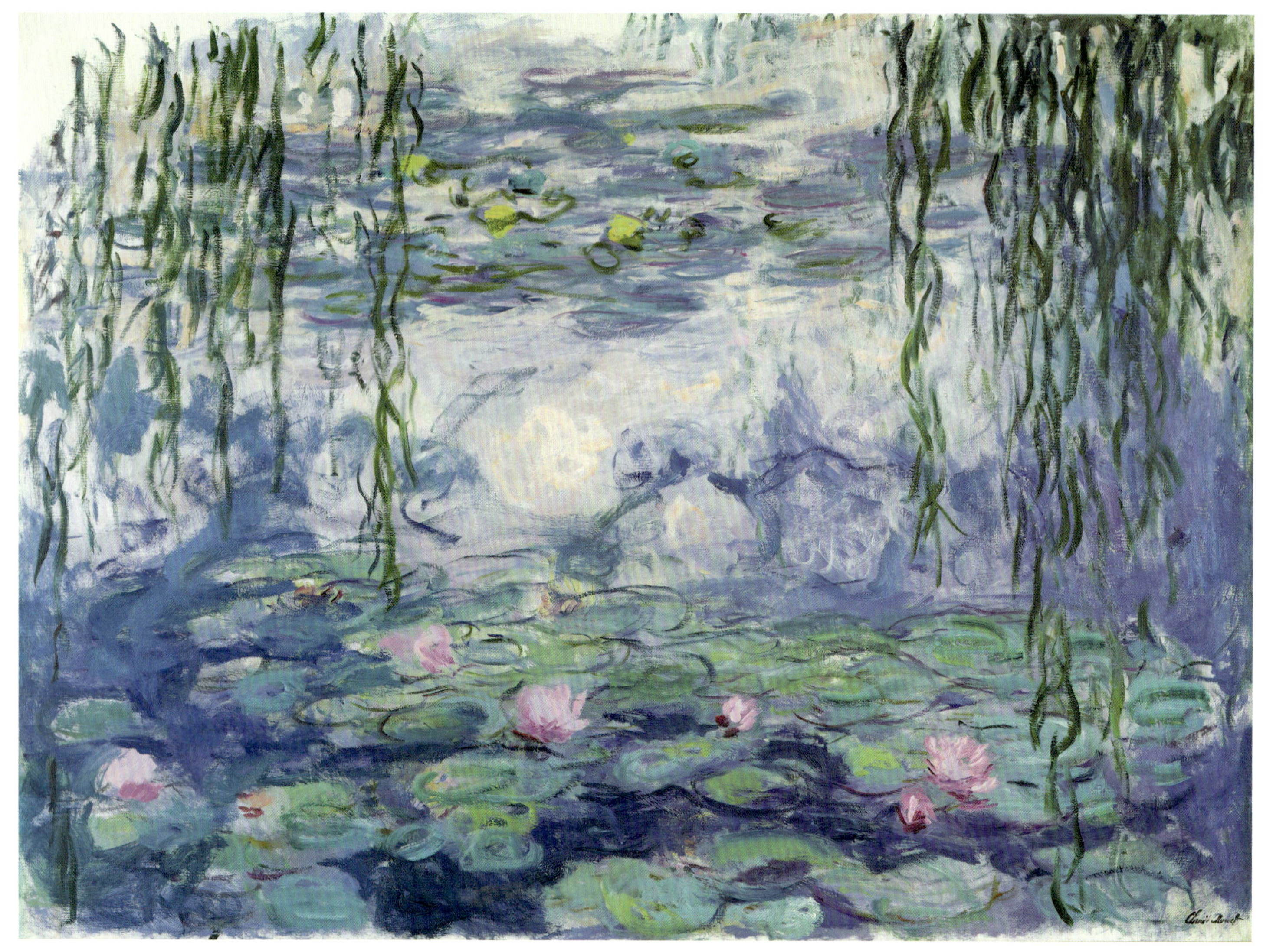

Claude Monet (1840–1926)

Waterlilies

Nymphéas

Seerosen

Nenúfares

Ninfee

Waterlelies

1916–19, Oil on canvas/Huile sur toile, 150 × 197 cm, Musée Marmottan Monet, Paris

Claude Monet (1840–1926)

Waterlilies

Nymphéas

Seerosen

Nenúfares

Ninfee

Waterlelies

1916–19, Oil on canvas/Huile sur toile, 200 × 180 cm, Musée Marmottan Monet, Paris

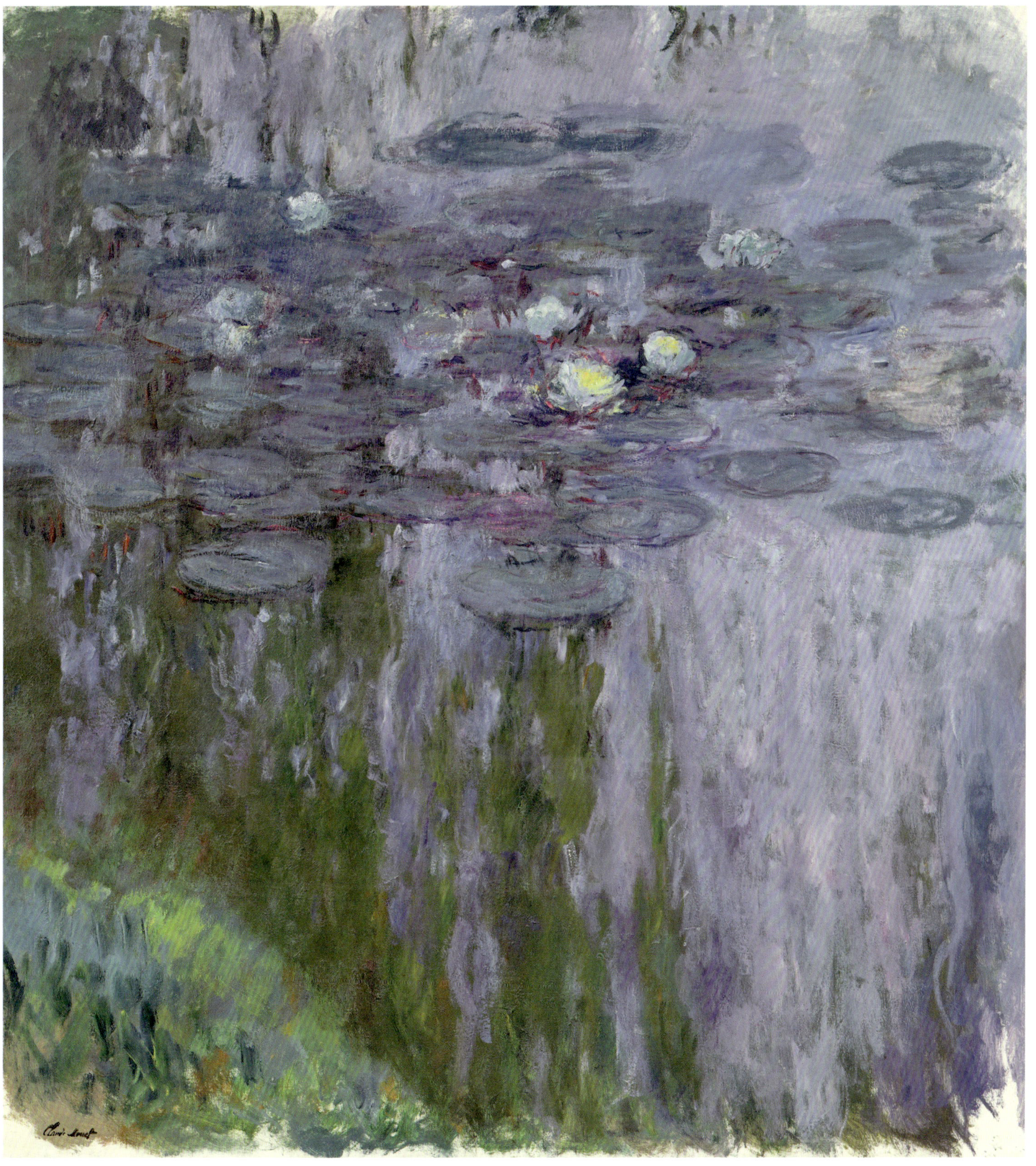

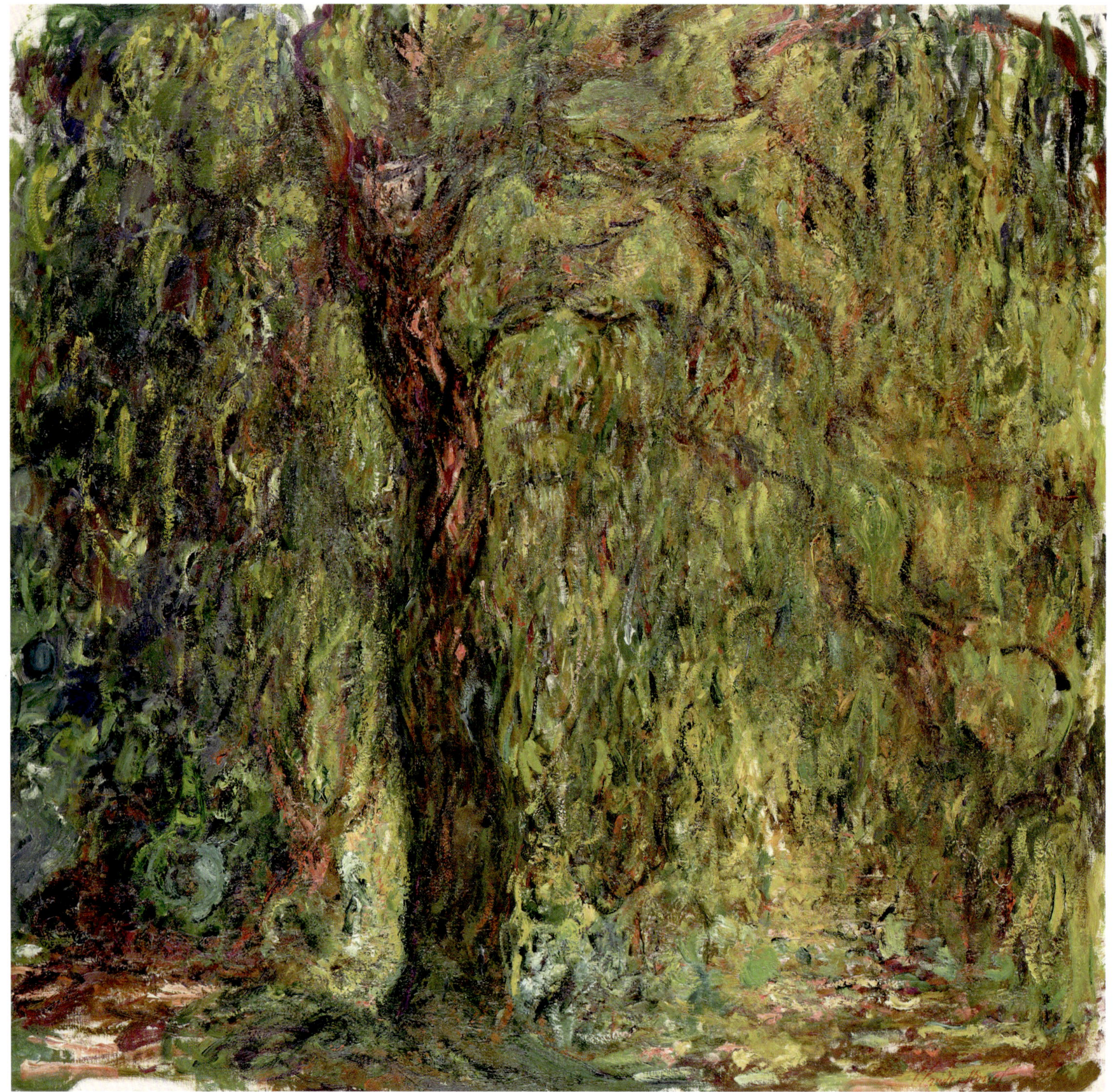

Claude Monet (1840–1926)

Weeping Willow   Trauerweide   Salice piangente

Saule pleureur   El sauce llorón   Treurwilg

1918/19, Oil on canvas/Huile sur toile, 100 × 100 cm, Musée Marmottan Monet, Paris

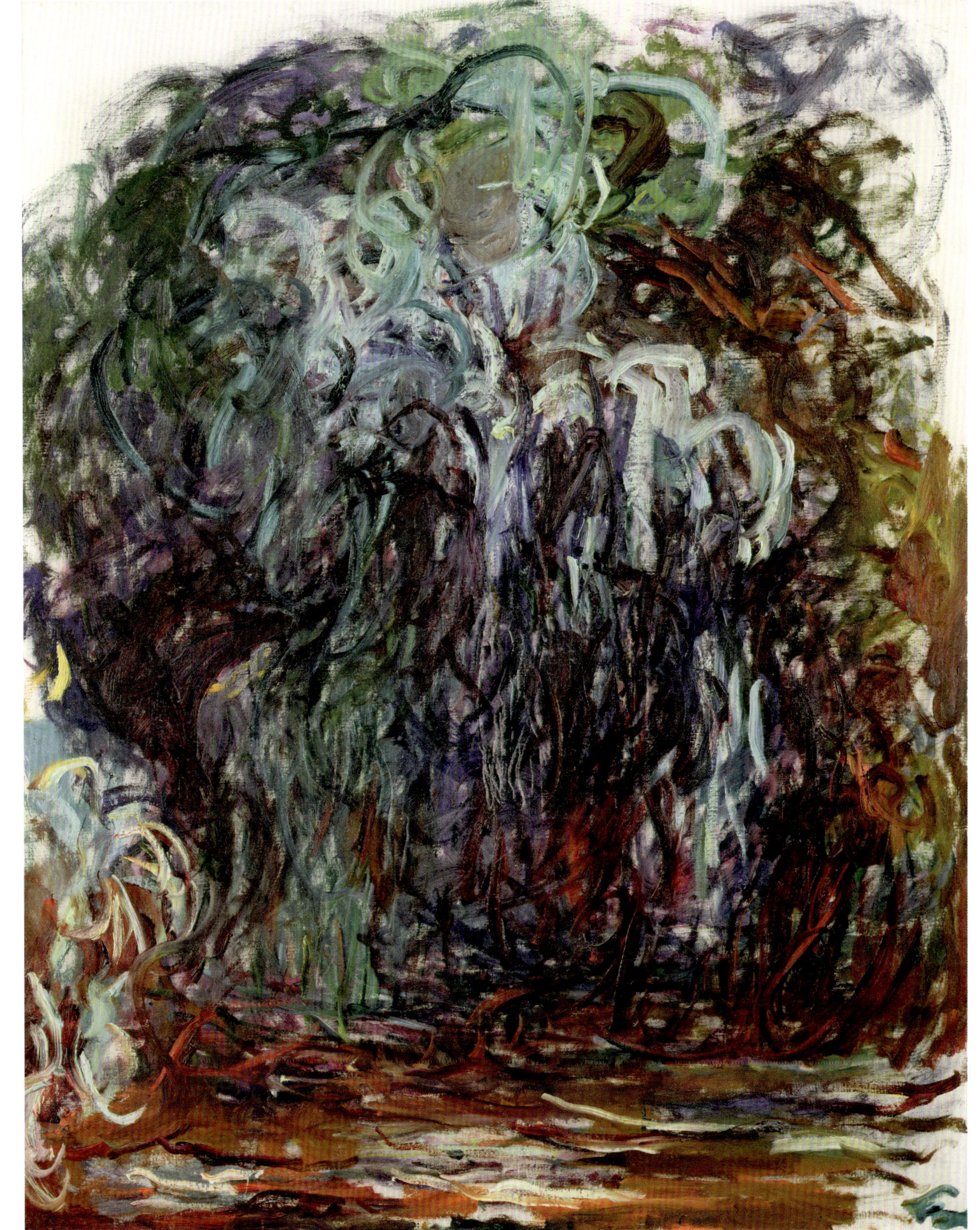

Claude Monet
(1840–1926)

Weeping Willow

Saule pleureur

Trauerweide

El sauce llorón

Salice piangente

Treurwilg

1921/22, Oil on canvas/Huile sur toile, 116 × 89 cm, Musée Marmottan Monet, Paris

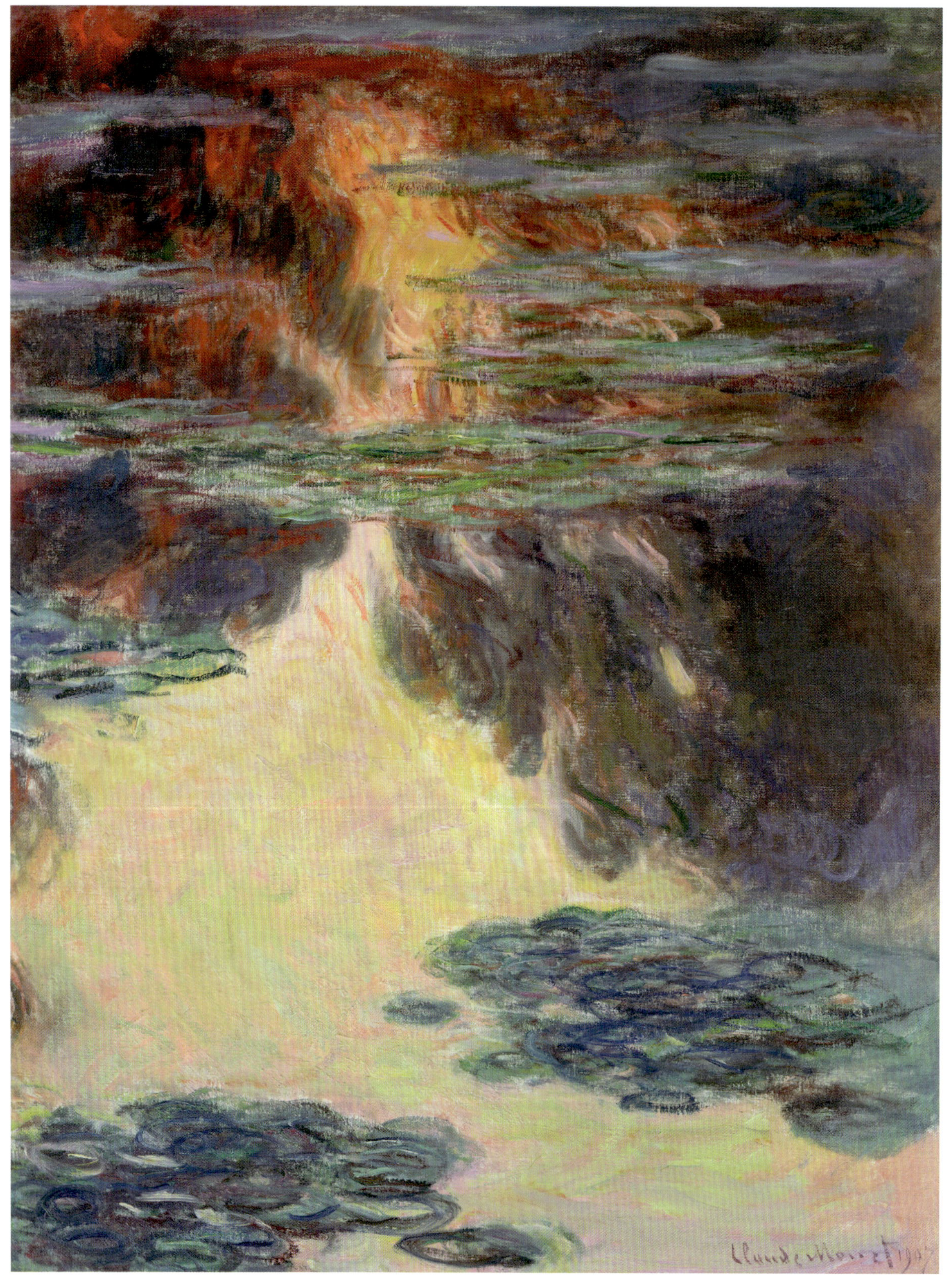

Claude Monet (1840–1926)

Waterlilies

Nymphéas

Seerosen

Nenúfares

Ninfee

Waterlelies

1907, Oil on canvas/Huile sur toile, 100 × 73 cm, Musée Marmottan Monet, Paris

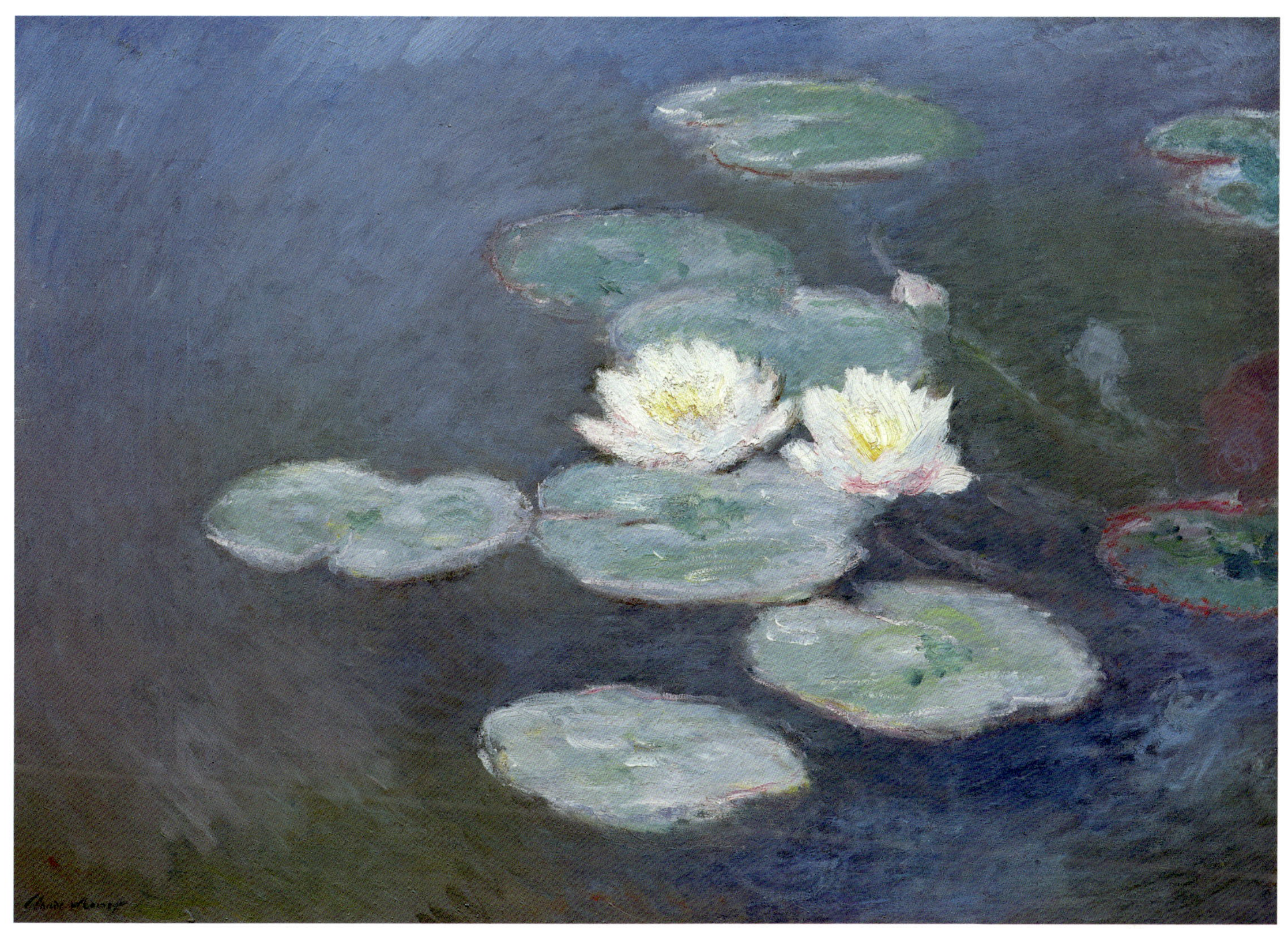

Claude Monet (1840–1926)

Waterlilies

Nymphéas

Seerosen, Wirkung des Abends

Nenúfares

Ninfee

Waterlelies

1897–99, Oil on canvas/Huile sur toile, 81 × 100 cm, Neue Pinakothek, München

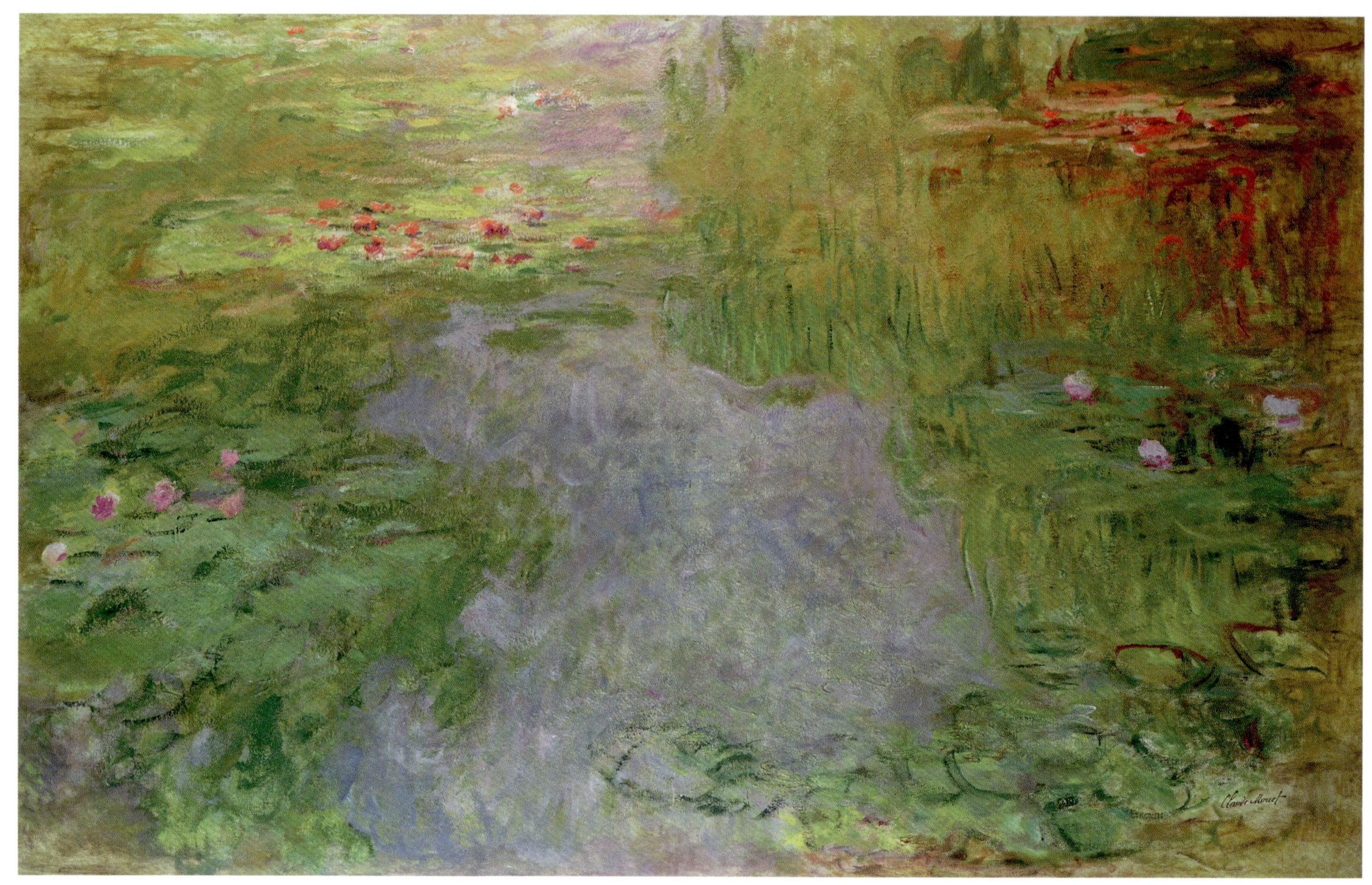

Claude Monet (1840−1926)

Waterlilies

Nymphéas

Seerosen

Nenúfares

Ninfee

Waterlelies

c. 1919, Oil on canvas/Huile sur toile, 132 × 201 cm, Private collection

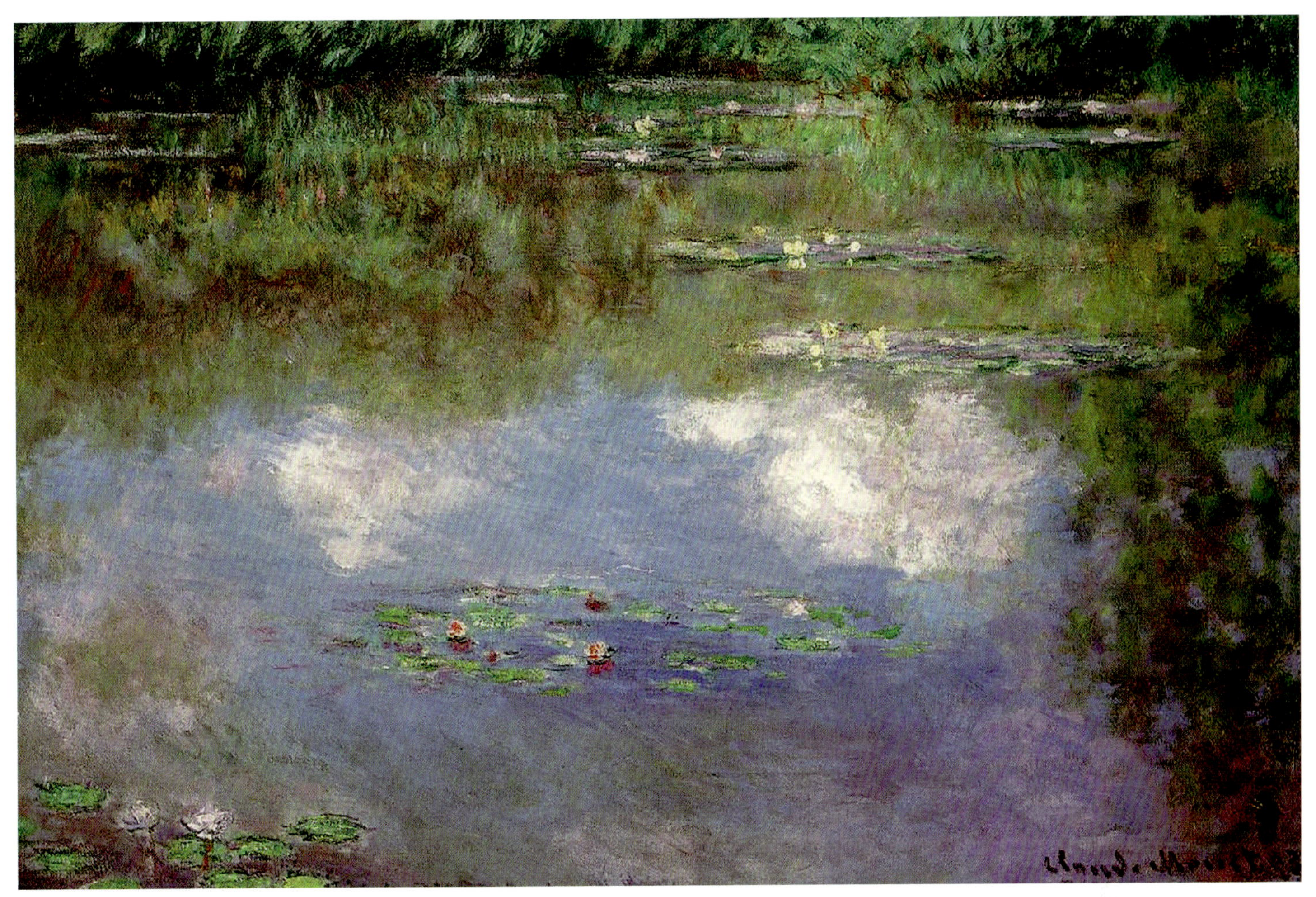

Claude Monet (1840–1926)

Water Lilies, the Cloud

Nymphéas, paysage d'eau, les nuages

Seerosen mit Wolke

Nenúfares con nubes

Ninfee con nuvole

Waterlelies met wolk

1903, Oil on canvas/Huile sur toile, 74,5 × 105,5 cm, Private collection

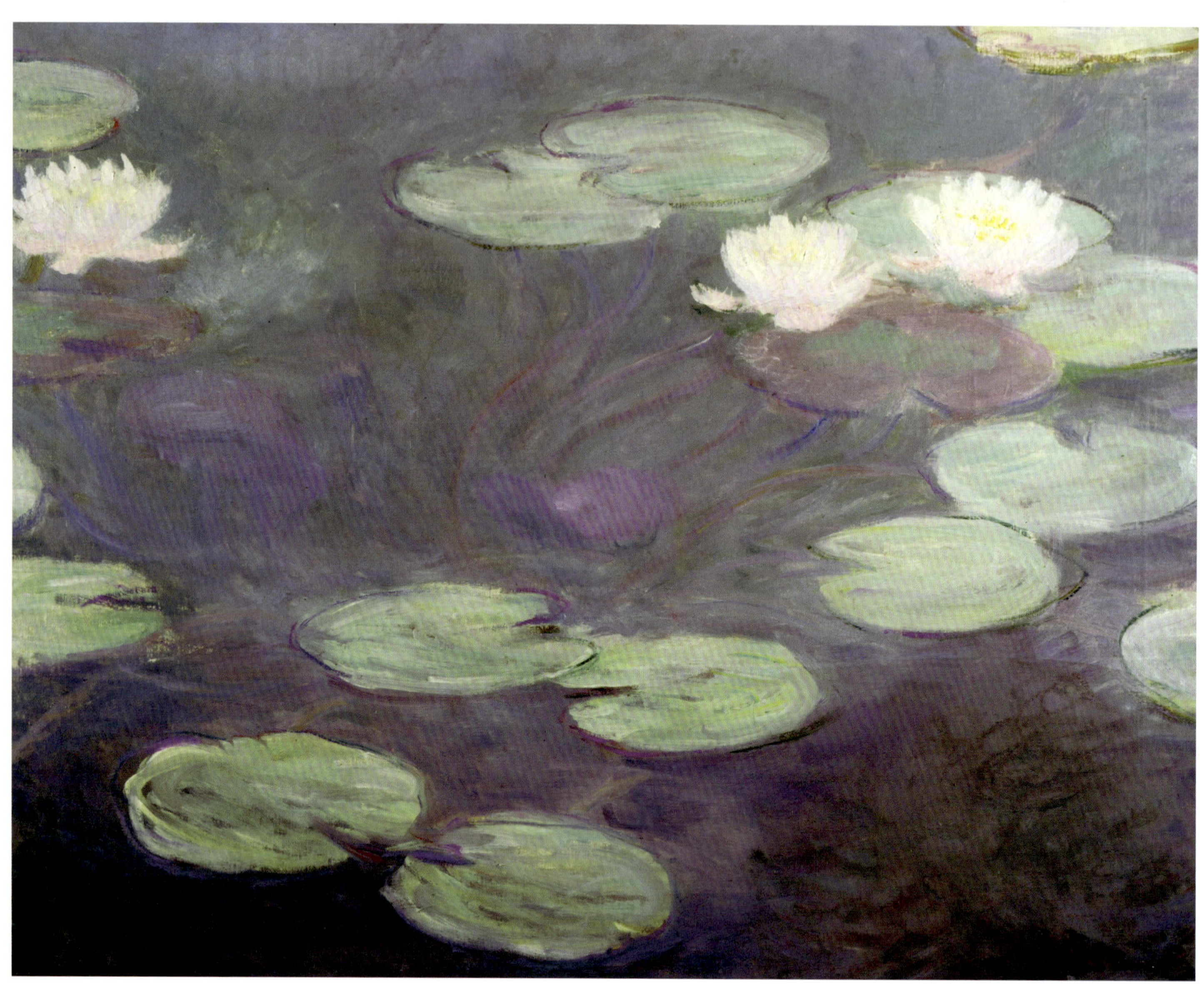

Claude Monet (1840–1926)

Waterlilies	Seerosen, rosa	Ninfee
Nymphéas	Nenúfares	Waterlelies

1897–99, Oil on canvas/Huile sur toile, 81 × 100 cm, Galleria Nazionale d'Arte Moderna, Rom

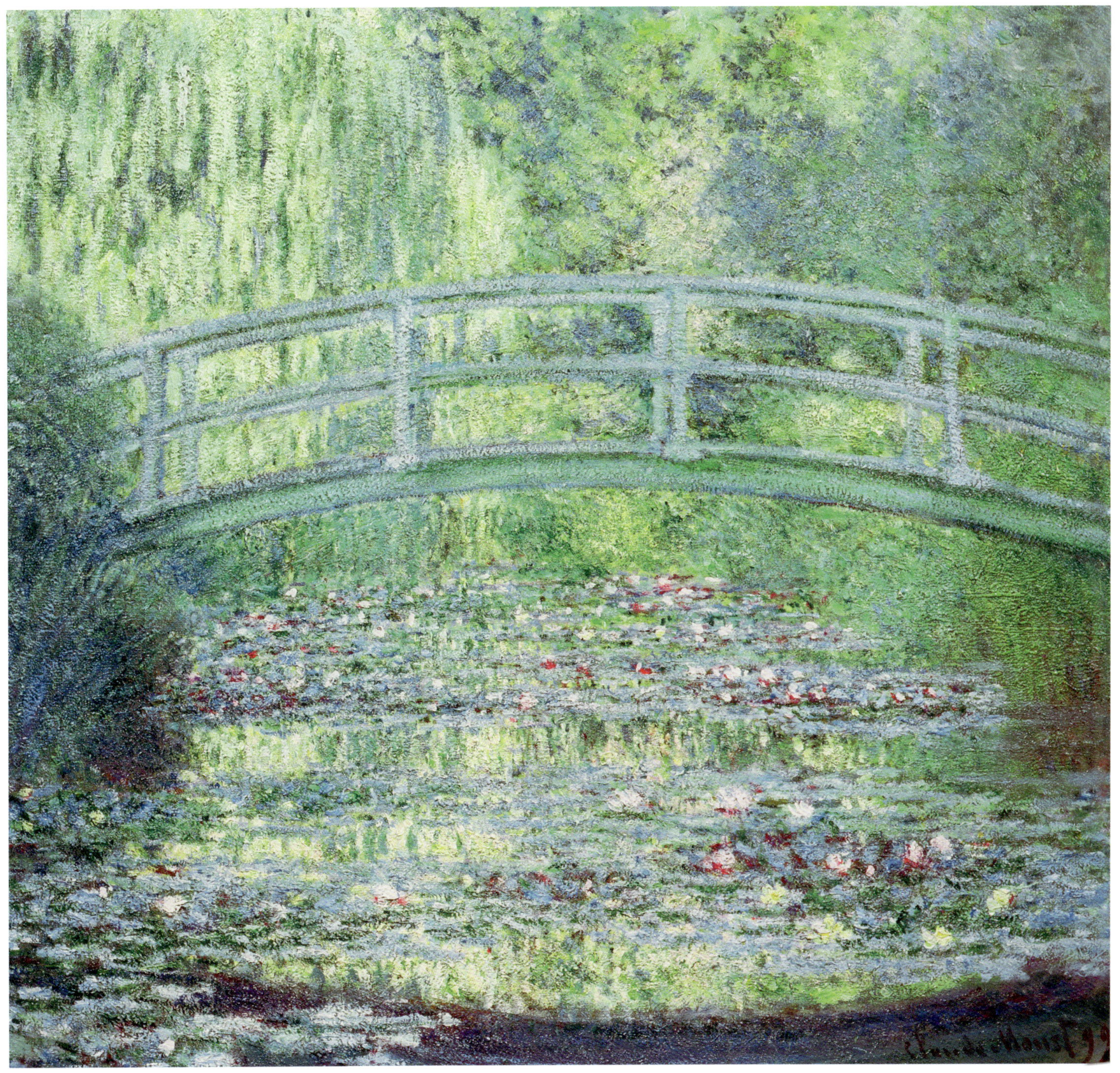

Claude Monet (1840–1926)

The Waterlily Pond with the Japanese Bridge   Der Seerosenteich mit japanischer Brücke   Lo sto di ninfee con ponte giapponese

Le bassin aux Nymphéas et le pont japonais   El estanque de nenúfares con el puente japonés   De waterlelievijver met de japanse brug

1899, Oil on canvas/Huile sur toile, 89,5 × 91,5 cm, Private collection

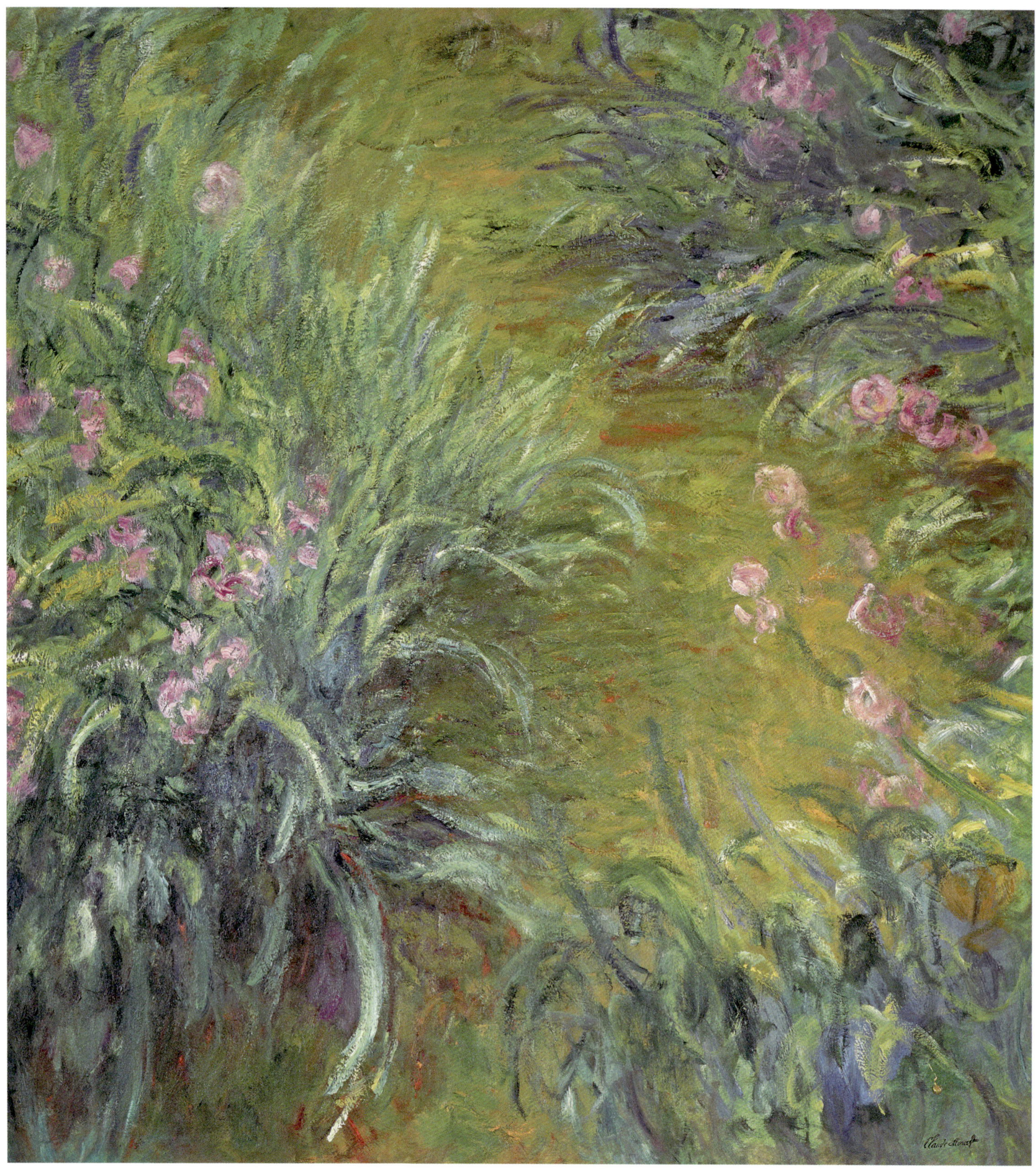

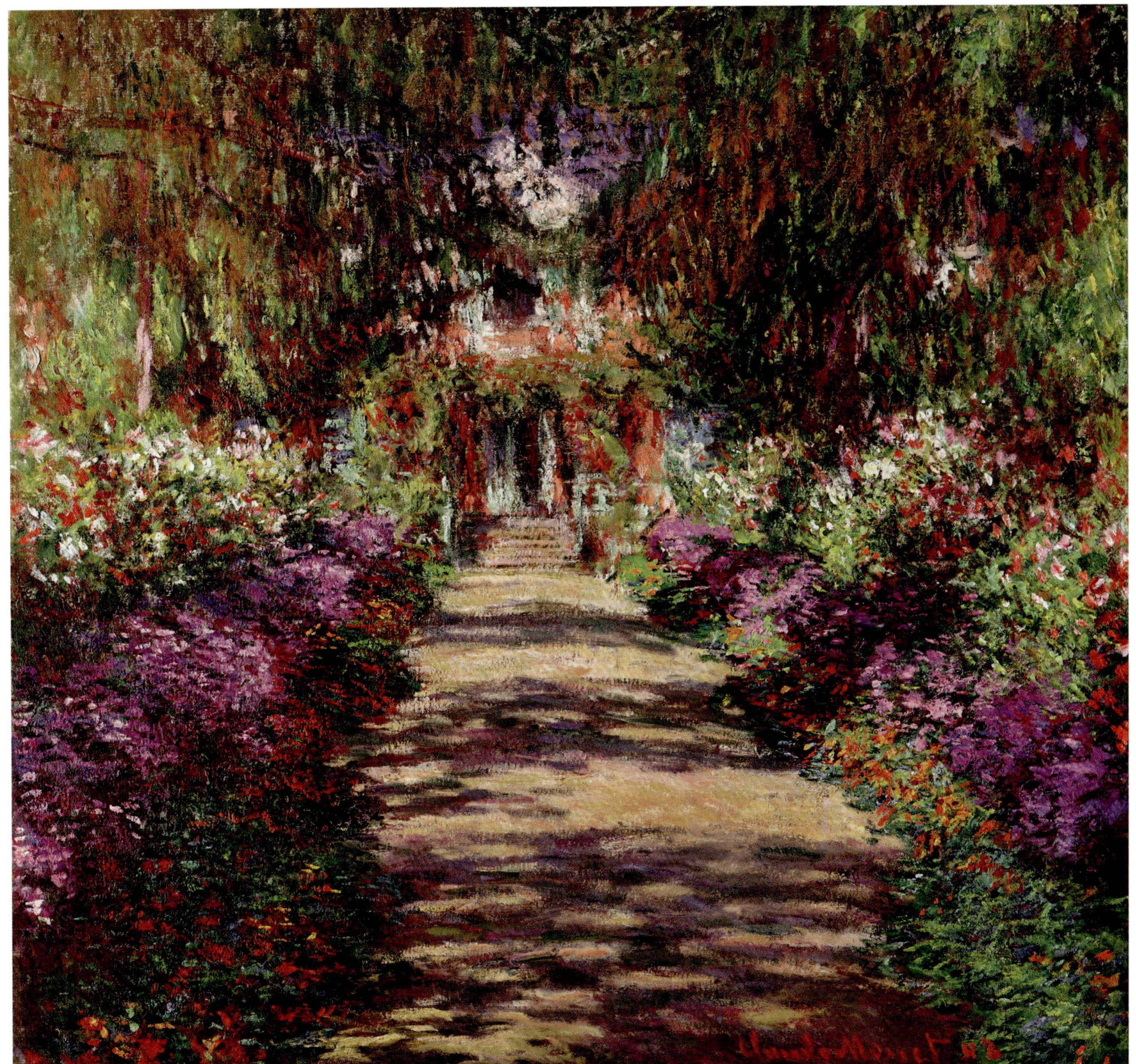

Claude Monet (1840–1926)

The Path through the Irises

Le chemin à travers les iris

Der Pfad durch die Schwertlilien

Iris

Iris

Irissen

1914–17, Oil on canvas/Huile sur toile, 200,3 × 180 cm, Metropolitan Museum of Art, New York

Claude Monet (1840–1926)

A Pathway in Monet's Garden, Giverny

Allée dans le jardin de Monet à Giverny

Weg in Monets Garten in Giverny

Un camino en el jardín de Giverny

Sentiero nel giardino di Monet a Giverny

Pad in Monets tuin te Giverny

1902, Oil on canvas/Huile sur toile, 89 × 92 cm, Belvedere, Wien

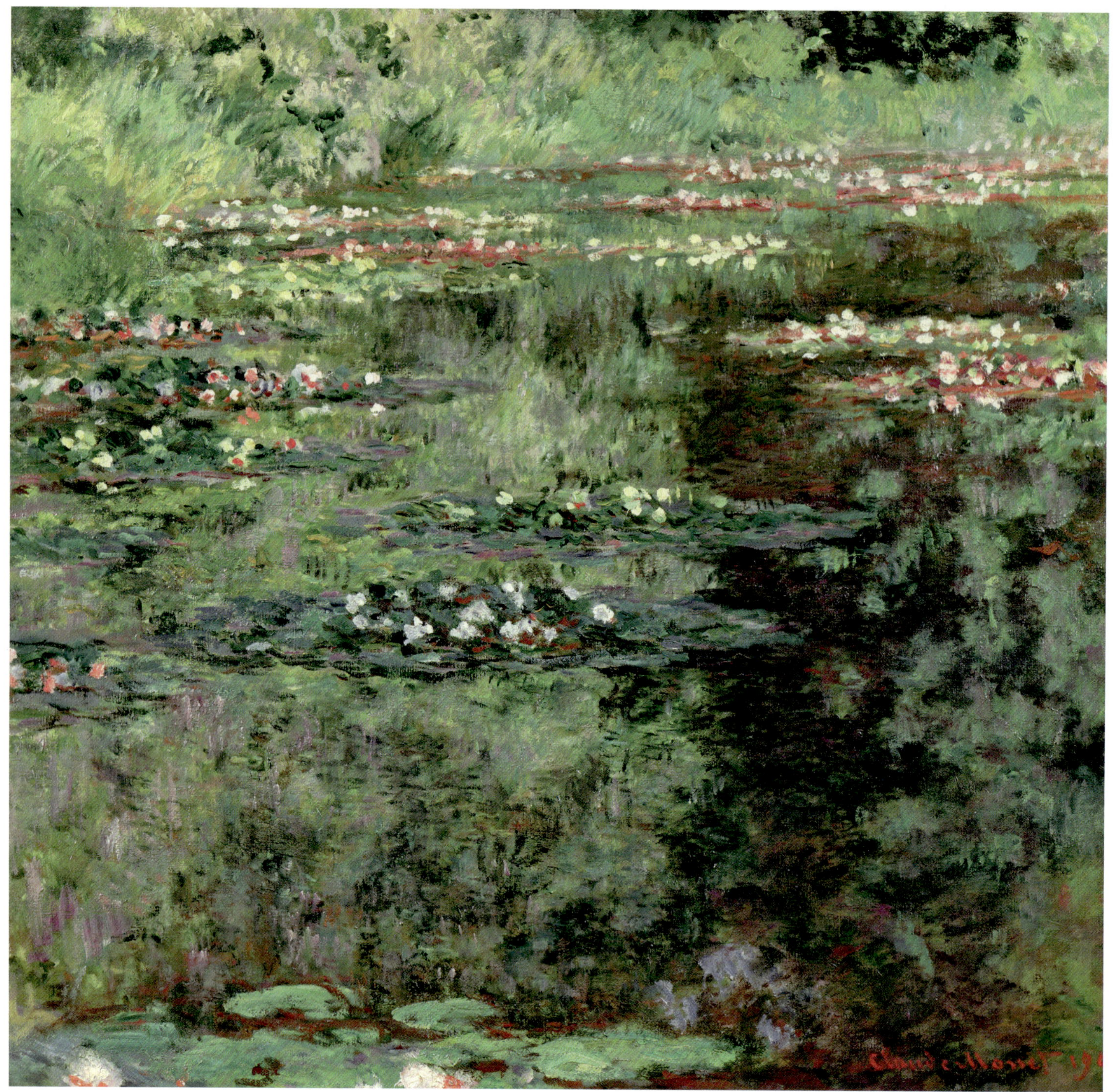

Claude Monet (1840–1926)

The Waterlily Pond	Der Seerosenteich	Lo sto di ninfee
Le bassin aux Nymphéas	El estanque de nenúfares	De waterlelievijver

1904, Oil on canvas/Huile sur toile, 90 × 92 cm, Private collection

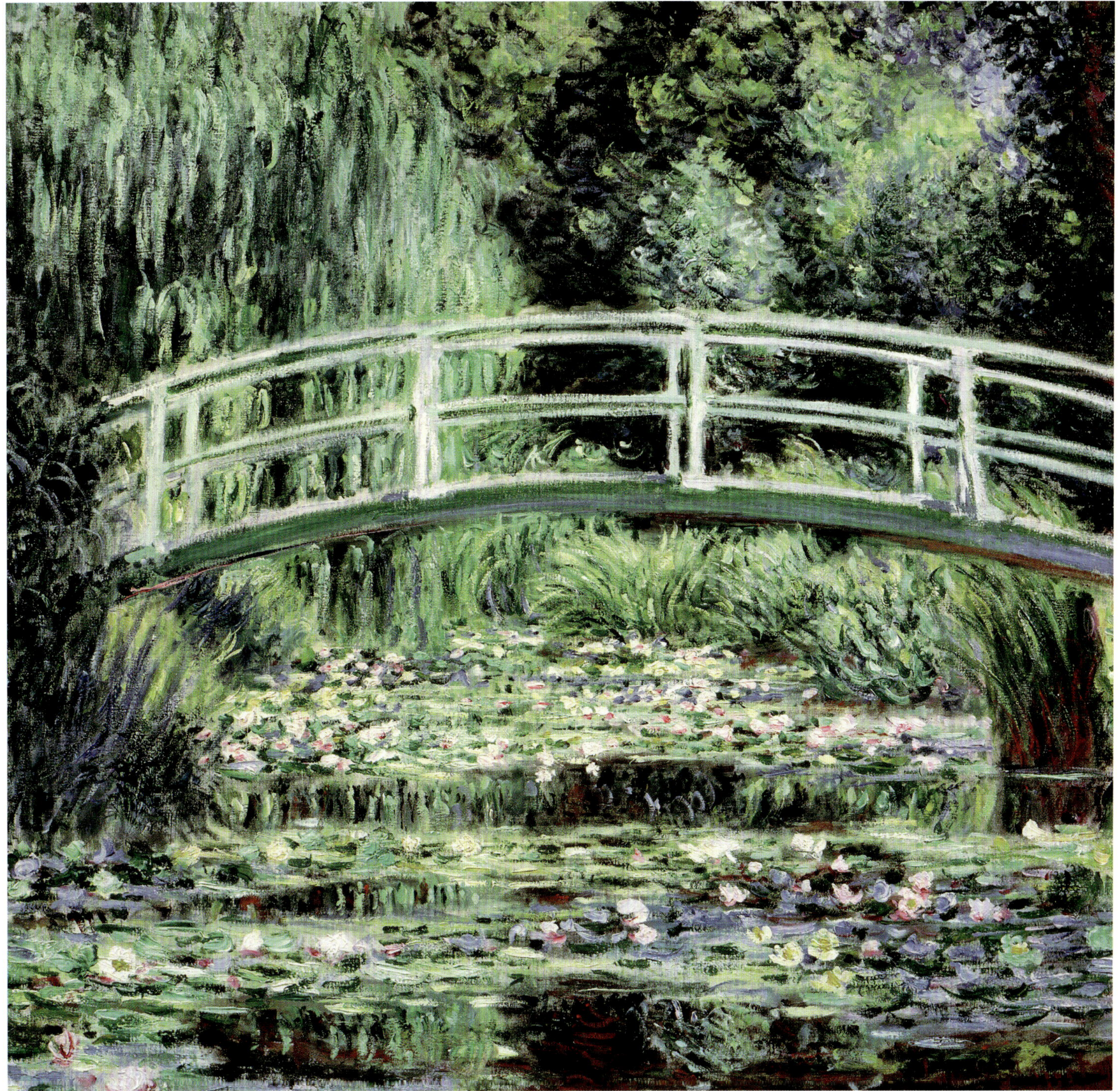

Claude Monet (1840–1926)

The Waterlily Pond   Der Seerosenteich   Lo sto di ninfee

Le bassin aux Nymphéas   El estanque de nenúfares   De waterlelievijver

1899, Oil on canvas/Huile sur toile, 89 × 93 cm, Pushkin State Museum of Fine Arts, Moscow

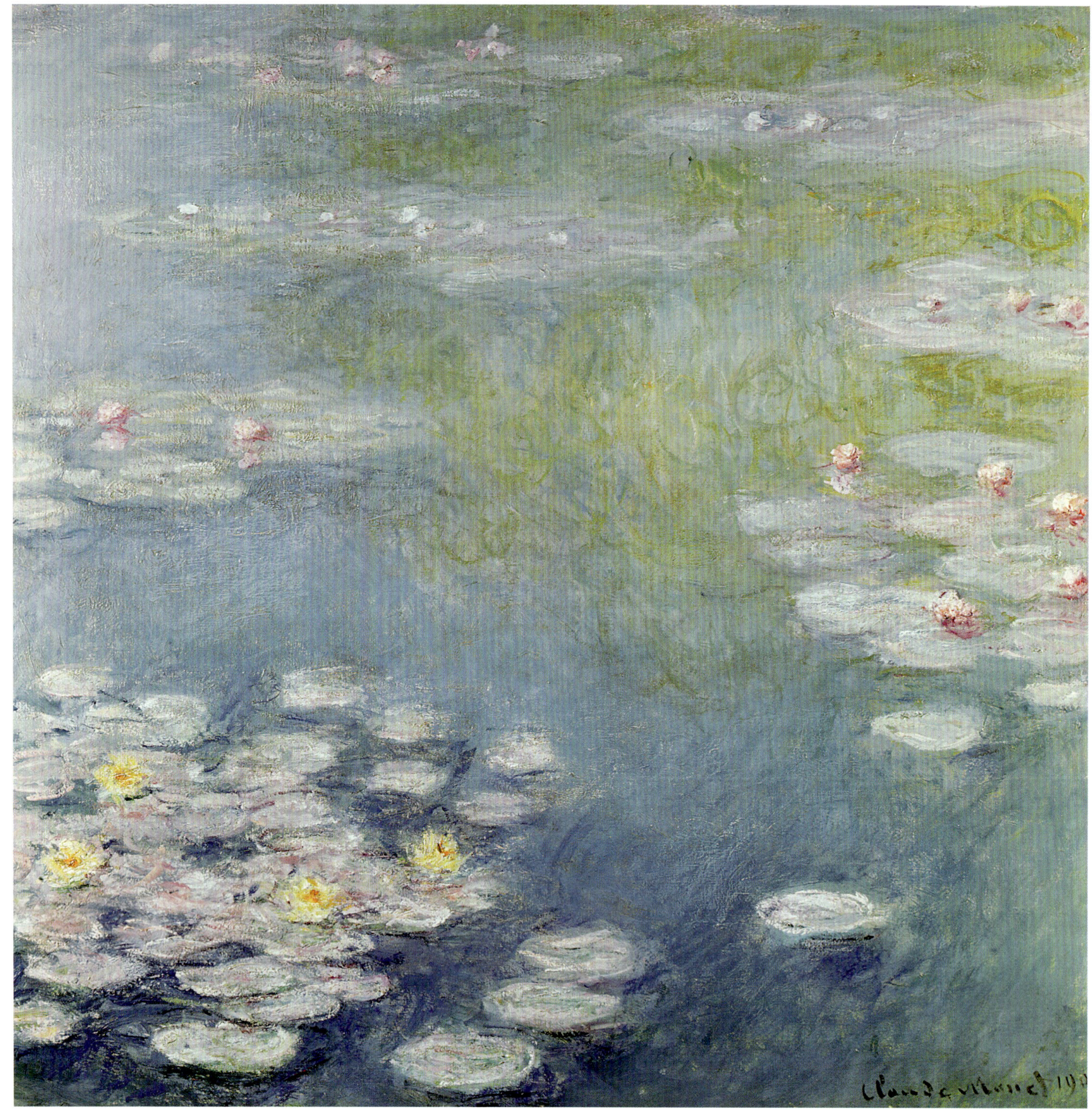

Claude Monet (1840−1926)

Nympheas at Giverny	Seerosen in Giverny	Ninfee a Giverny
Nymphéas à Giverny	Nenúfares en Giverny	Waterlelies in Giverny

1908, Oil on canvas/Huile sur toile, 92 × 89 cm, Private collection

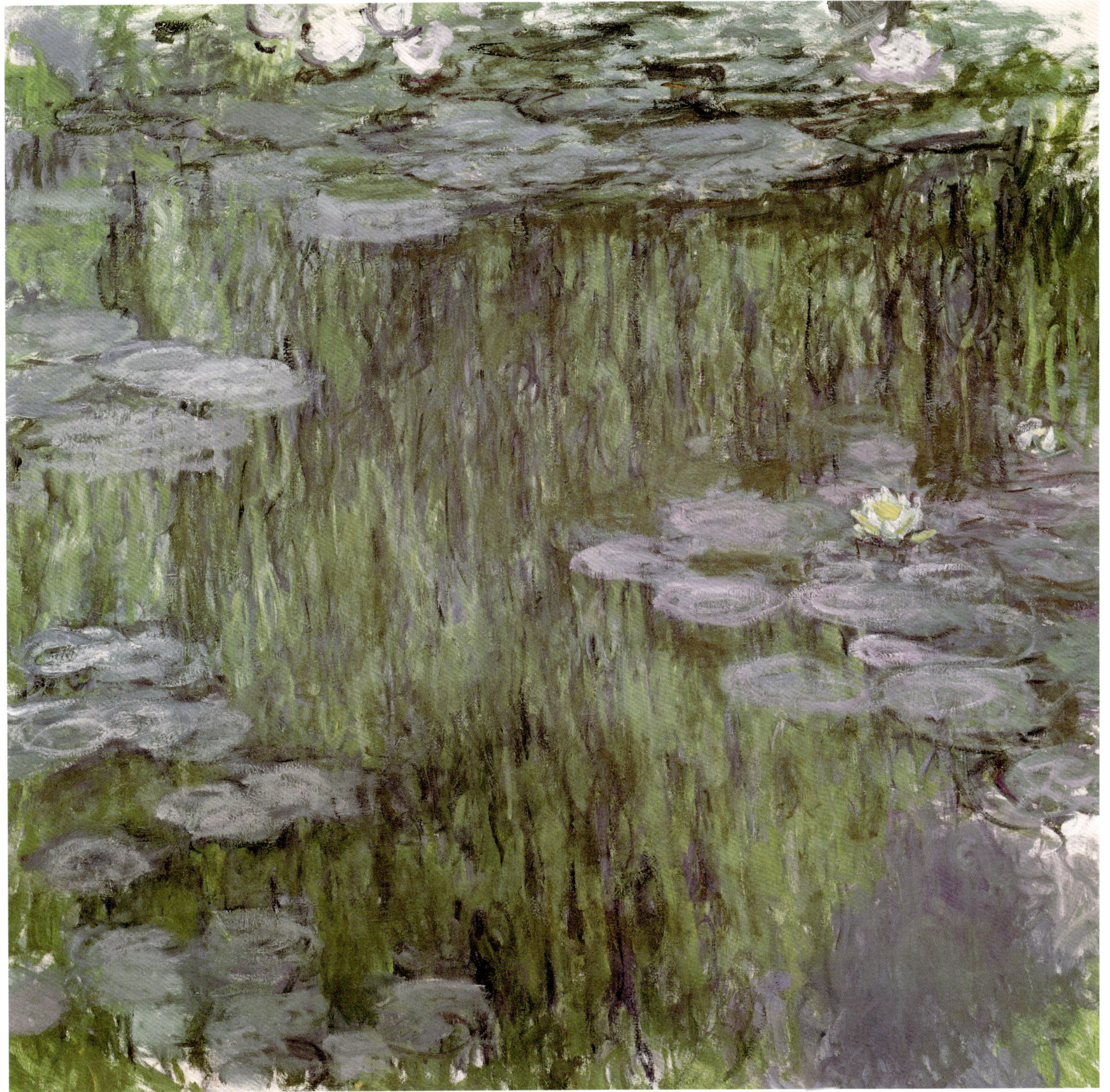

Claude Monet (1840–1926)

Nympheas at Giverny	Seerosen in Giverny	Ninfee a Giverny
Nymphéas à Giverny	Nenúfares en Giverny	Waterlelies in Giverny

1918/19, Oil on canvas/Huile sur toile, 194 × 200 cm, Private collection

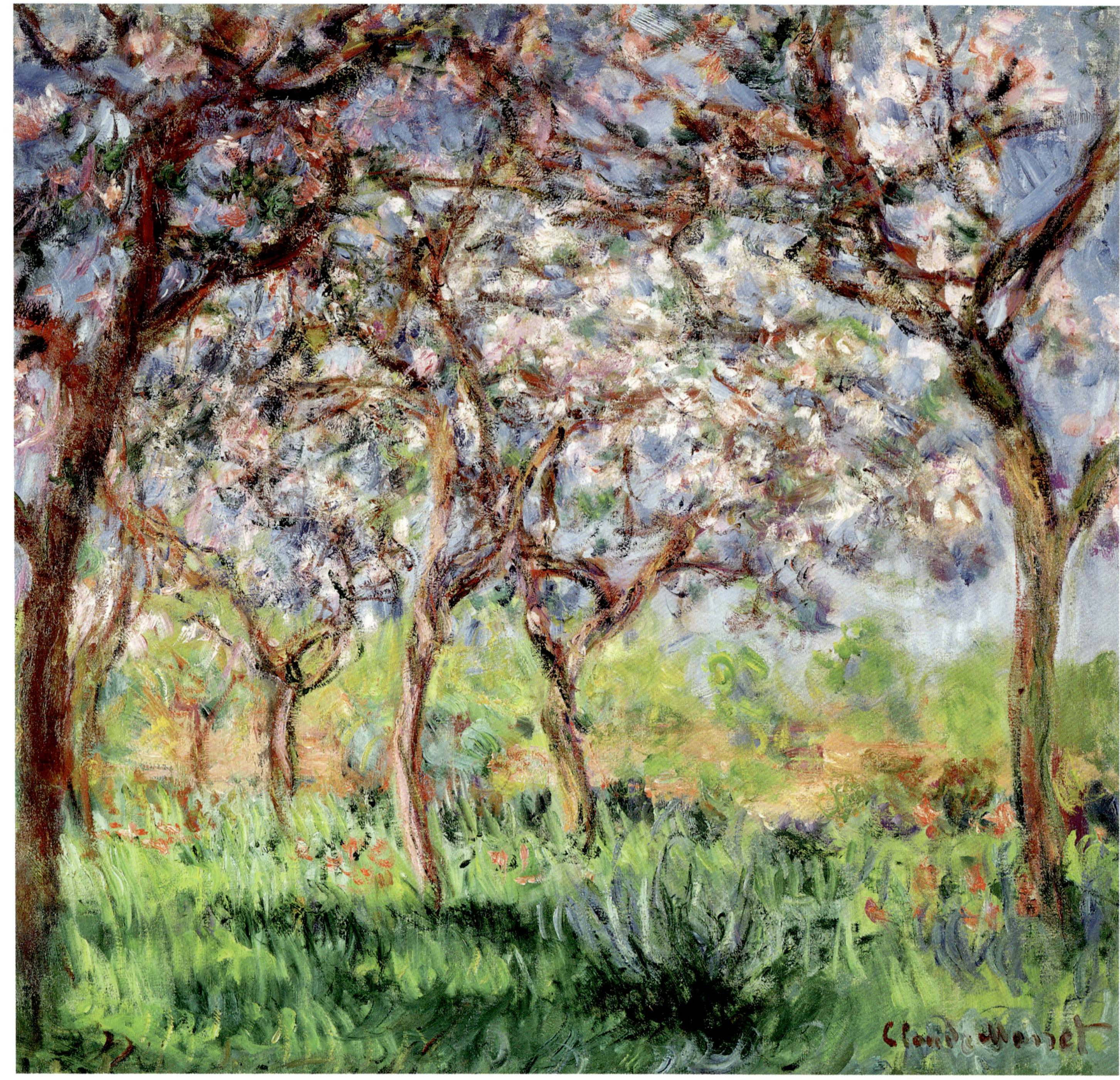

Claude Monet (1840–1926)

Printemps a Giverny   Frühling in Giverny   Primavera a Giverny

Le printemps à Giverny   Primavera en Giverny   Voorjaar in Giverny

1903, Oil on canvas/Huile sur toile, 89 × 93 cm, Private collection

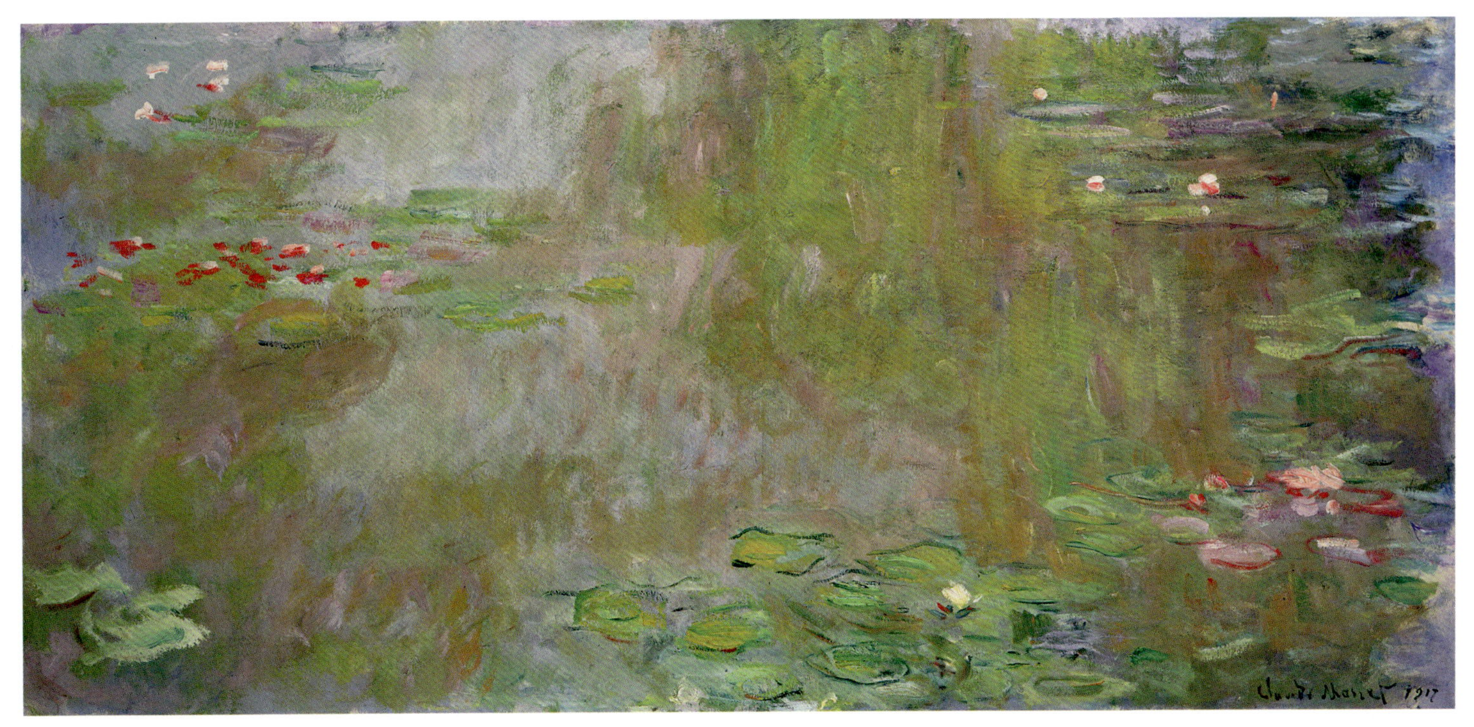

Claude Monet (1840–1926)

Waterlilies at Giverny

Les Nymphéas à Giverny

Seerosen in Giverny

Nenúfares en Giverny

Ninfee a Giverny

Waterlelies in Giverny

1917–19, Oil on canvas/Huile sur toile, 100 × 200 cm, Musée des Beaux-Arts, Nantes

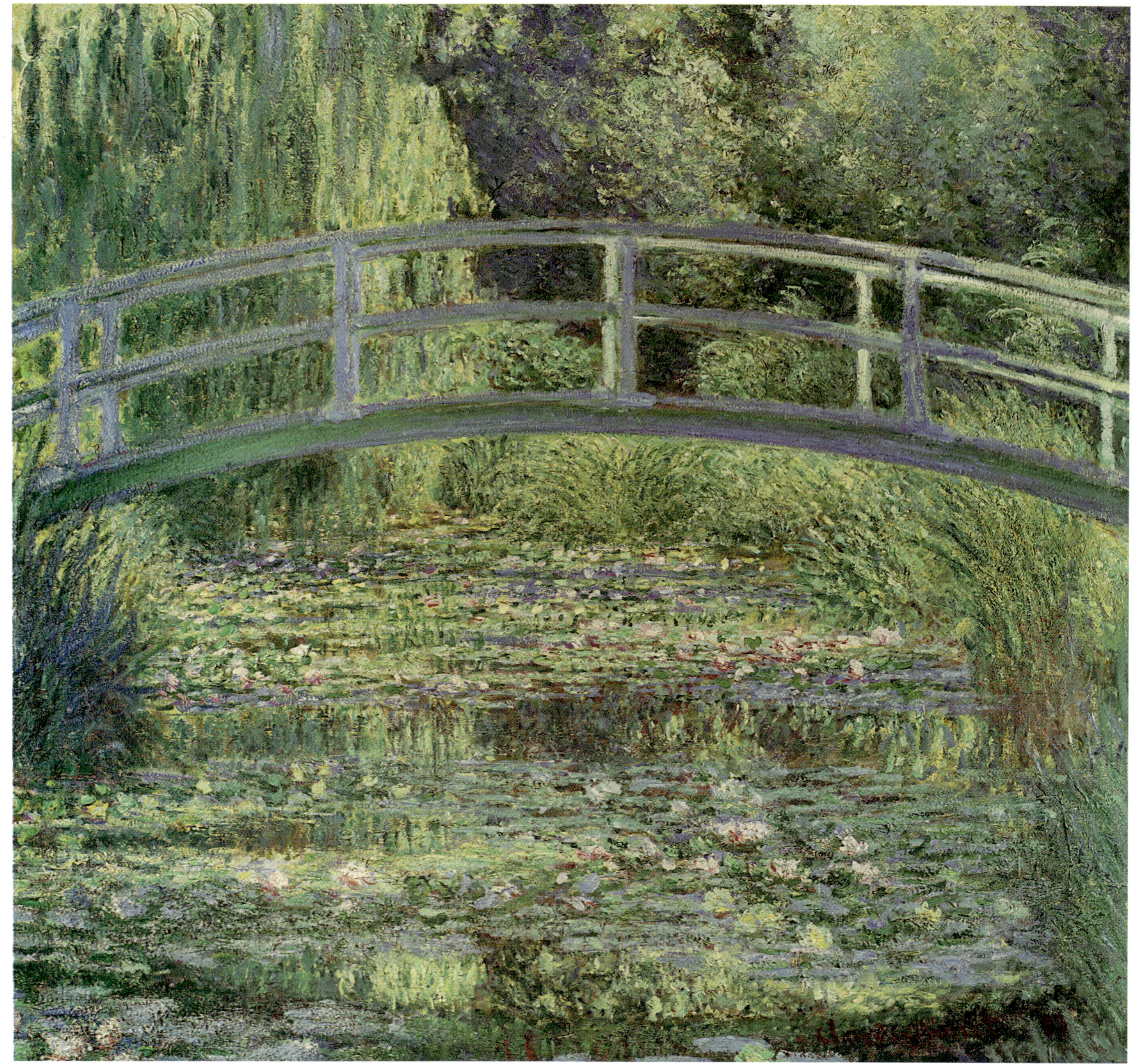

Claude Monet (1840−1926)

Waterlily Pond	Seerosenteich	Sto di ninfee
Le bassin aux Nymphéas	El estanque de nenúfares	De waterlelievijver

1899, Oil on canvas/Huile sur toile, 88,3 × 93,1 cm, National Gallery, London

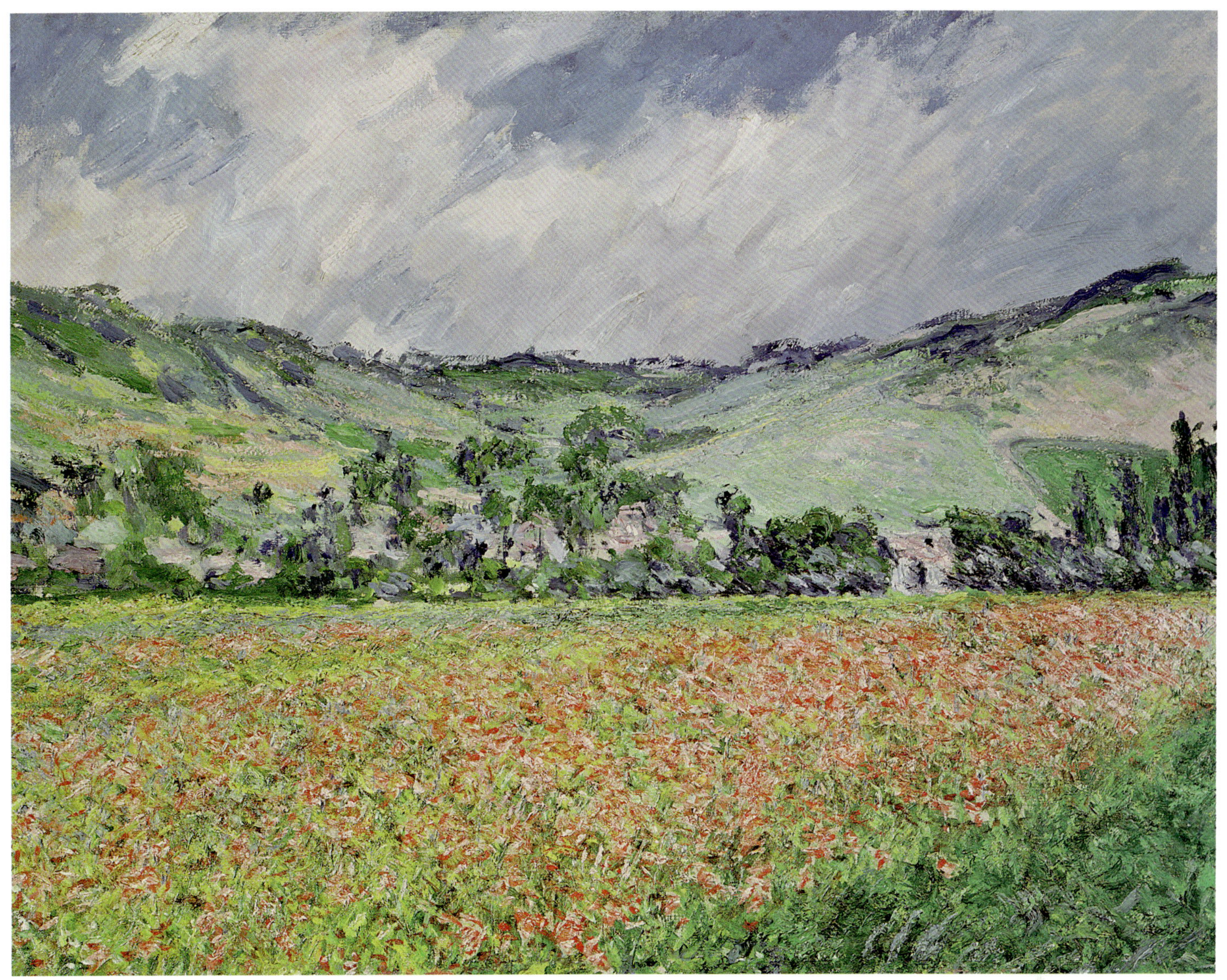

Claude Monet (1840–1926)

The Poppy Field near Giverny

Champ de coquelicots à Giverny

Mohnfeld bei Giverny

Campo de amapolas en Giverny

Campo di papaveri presso Giverny

Papaverveld bij Giverny

1885, Oil on canvas/Huile sur toile, 65 × 82 cm, Musée des beaux-arts, Rouen

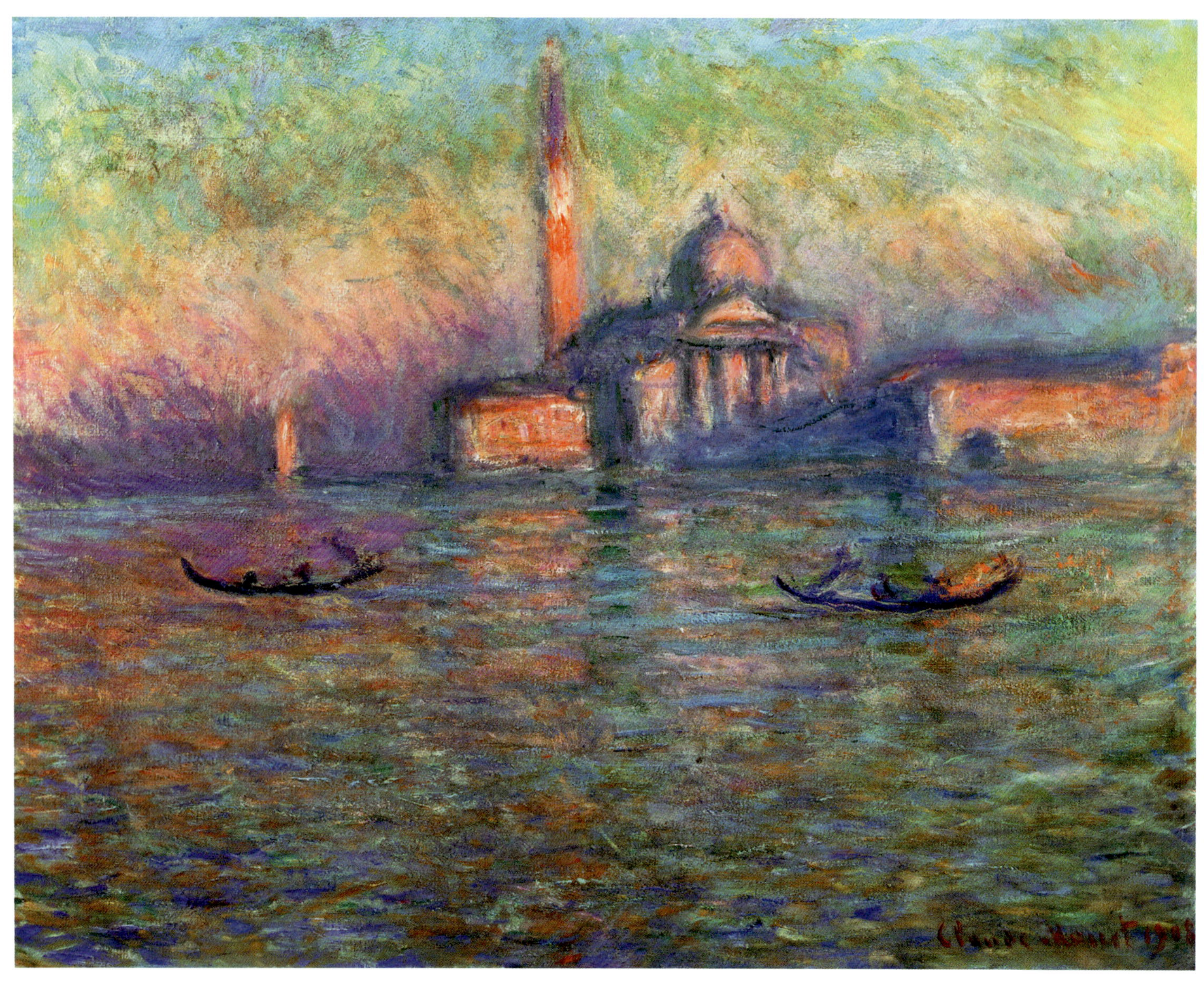

Claude Monet (1840–1926)

San Giorgio Maggiore, Venice

Saint Georges Majeur, Venise

San Giorgio Maggiore, Venedig

San Giorgio Maggiore, Venecia

Vista di San Giorgio Maggiore, Venezia

San Giorgio Maggiore, Venetië

1908, Oil on canvas/Huile sur toile, 60 × 73 cm, Private collection

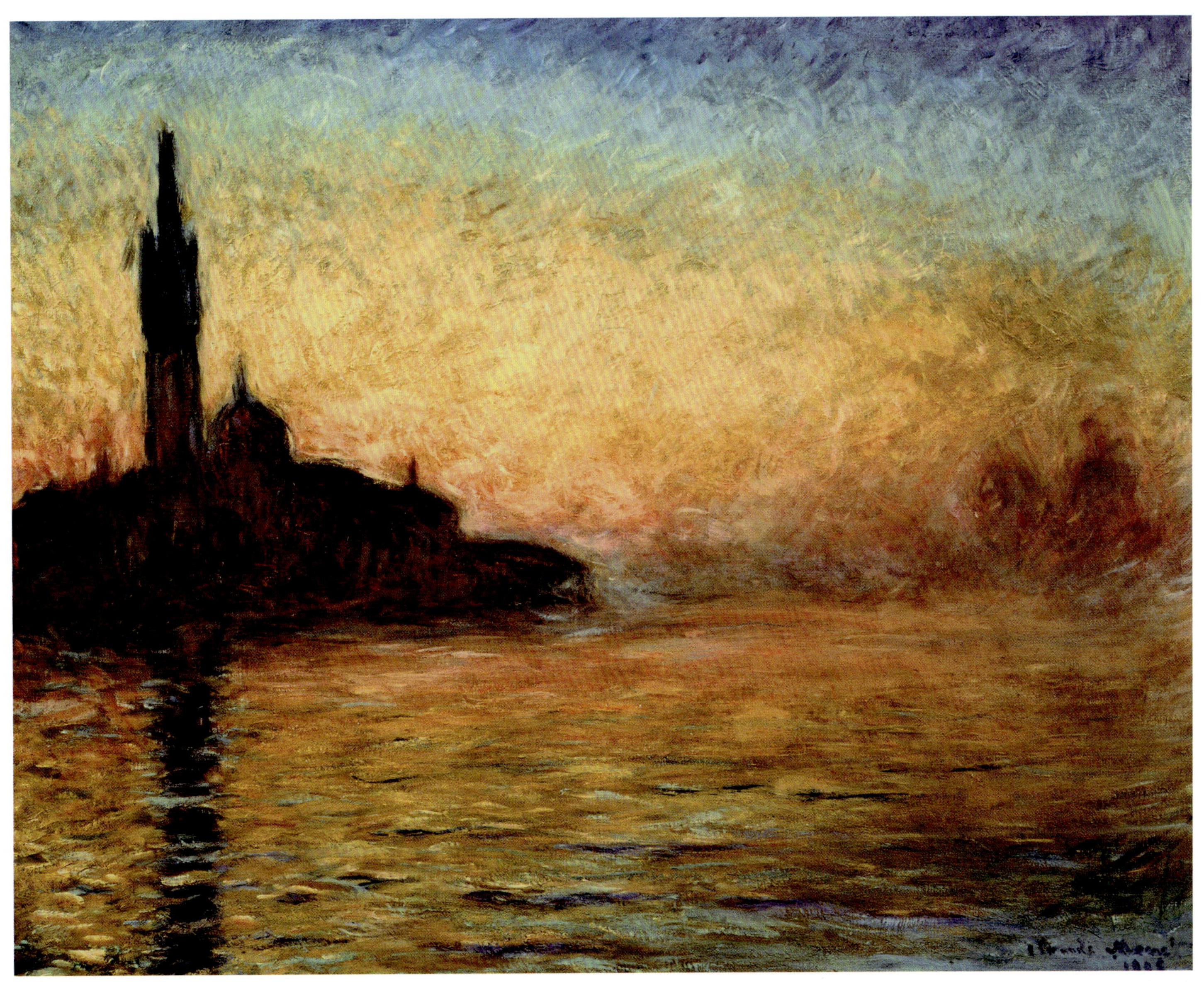

Claude Monet (1840–1926)

View of San Giorgio Maggiore, Venice by Twilight

Saint Georges Majeur au crépuscule

San Giorgio Maggiore im Abendlicht

San Giorgio Maggiore en la luz del crepúsculo

San Giorgio Maggiore al crepuscolo

De San Giorgio Maggiore bij avondlicht

1908, Oil on canvas/Huile sur toile, 74 × 93 cm, Bridgestone Museum of Art, Tokyo

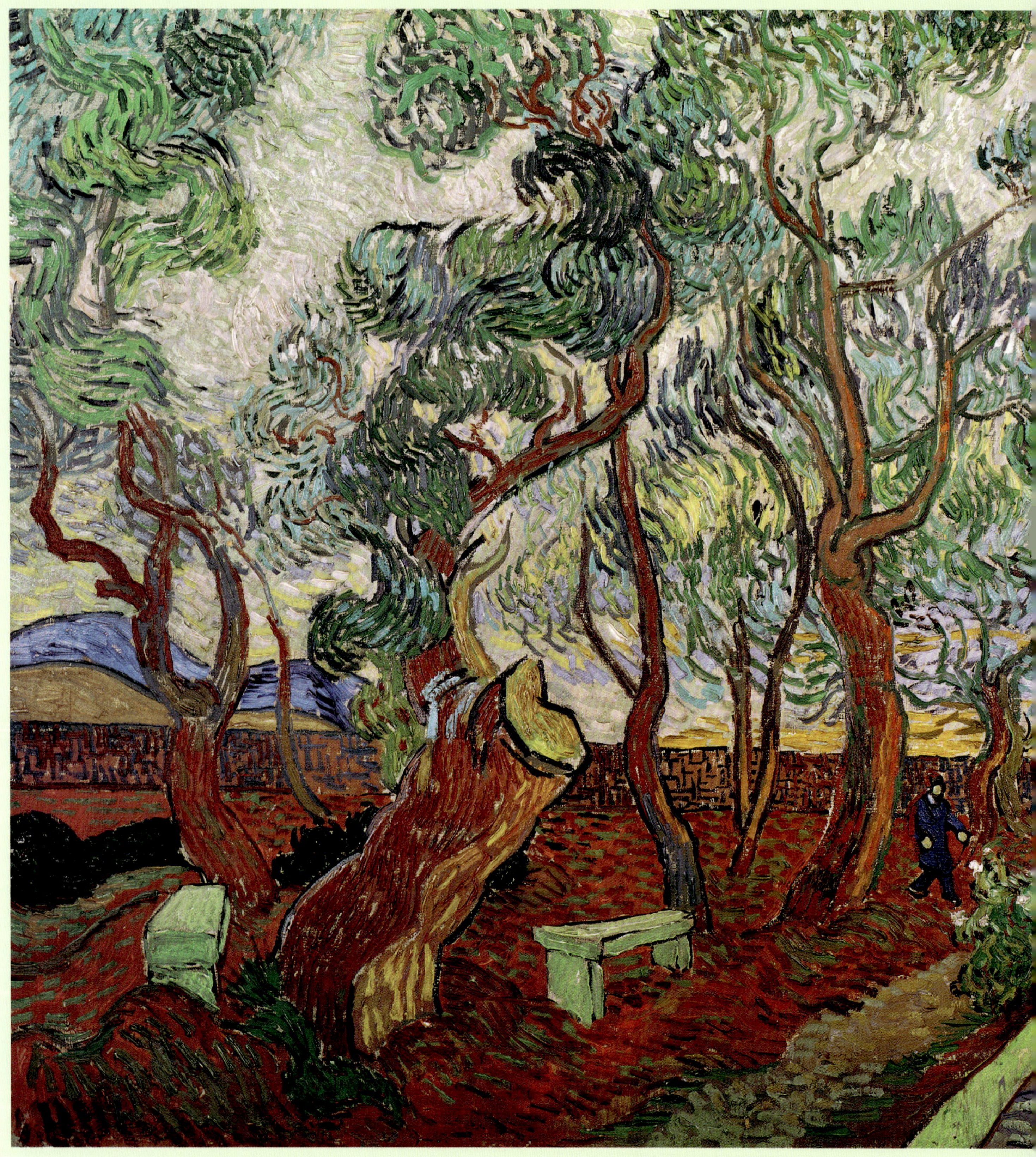

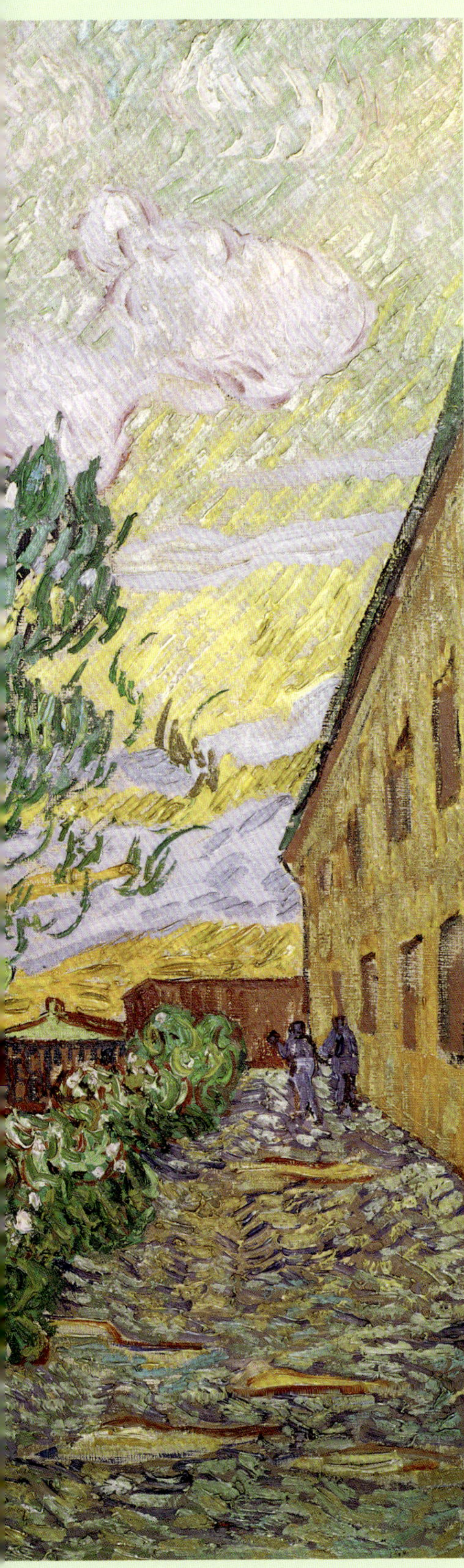

Vincent van Gogh (1853–90)
The Garden of St. Paul's Hospital at St. Remy
Le jardin de l'Hôpital Saint-Paul à Saint-Rémy
Der Garten des Hospitals von Saint-Rémy
El jardín del hospital de St. Paul en Saint-Rémy
Il giardino dell'ospedale di Saint-Paul a Saint-Rémy
Der Garten des St.-Paul-Krankenhauses in Saint-Rémy

1889, Oil on canvas/Huile sur toile, 75 × 93,5 cm, Museum Folkwang, Essen

Impressionism and afterwards

Up until 1886, the artists had organized a total of
eight group exhibitions, after which the community
dissolved in order to develop their more individual
styles. There began a thematic and stylistic
specialization, which sought to accommodate the
burgeoning and diversifying art market, but also to
take into account personal artistic development.

In the 1890s Monet painted the various picture
series of *haystacks, poplars, cathedrals* and finally *water
lilies,* in which the subject of the water lilies' pond
in Giverny gave way in importance to compositions
completely invented from color. It was not until 1945
that the abstract artists grappled again with this
autonomy of color in which Monet was a forerunner.

In France itself there was very soon opposition to
the artistic perception of interest in appearance only,
firstly by a group of painters who called themselves
neo-impressionists and who saw their renewal as a
radical improvement. The head of this group, the
young painter Georges Seurat (1859–1891), did not
rely solely upon the perception of color shades, but

L'impressionnisme et ensuite

Jusqu'en 1886, les artistes organisèrent au total de huit
expositions de groupe. La communauté fut ensuite
dissoute afin de développer des styles plus individuels.
Commença alors une spécialisation thématique et
stylistique, pour s'adapter au marché de l'art en plein
essor et qui se diversifiait, mais aussi afin de tenir
compte du développement artistique personnel.

Dans les années 1890 Monet peignit les différentes
séries de tableaux *Meules de foin, Peupliers, Cathédrales*
et enfin les *Nymphéas,* dans laquelle le sujet du bassin
aux nymphéas de Giverny met l'accent sur l'importance
des compositions complètement inventées de la couleur.
Il fallut attendre 1945 pour que les artistes abstraits
s'attaquent à cette autonomie de la couleur dont Monet
fut un précurseur.

En France, il y eut bientôt une opposition à la
perception artistique du seul intérêt de l'apparence,
tout d'abord de la part d'un groupe de peintres qui
s'étaient autobaptisés néo-impressionnistes et voyaient
son renouvellement comme un progrès radical. Le chef
de file de ce groupe, le jeune peintre Georges Seurat

Der Impressionismus und die Folgen

Bis 1886 organisierten die Künstler insgesamt
acht Gruppenausstellungen, dann löste sich die
lockere Gemeinschaft auf, um individuellere Stile
auszubilden. Es begann eine thematische wie
stilistische Spezialisierung, die den Erfordernissen
des aufblühenden und sich verzweigenden
Kunstmarkts entgegenzukommen suchte, aber auch
den persönlichen Entwicklungen Rechnung trug.

Monet malte in den 1890er-Jahren die Serien der
Heuschober, Pappeln, Kathedralen und schließlich der
Seerosen, die den Gegenstand des Seerosenteiches in
Giverny immer stärker zugunsten freier, ganz aus der
Farbe erfundener Kompositionen zurückdrängen. Mit
dieser Autonomie der Farbe setzten sich erst wieder
die abstrakten Künstler nach 1945 auseinander, die in
Monet einen Vorläufer sahen.

In Frankreich selbst wurde gegen die nur
am „Augen-Schein" interessierte künstlerische
Wahrnehmung sehr bald opponiert, zunächst
von einer Gruppe von Malern, die sich Neo-
Impressionisten nannten, diese Erneuerung

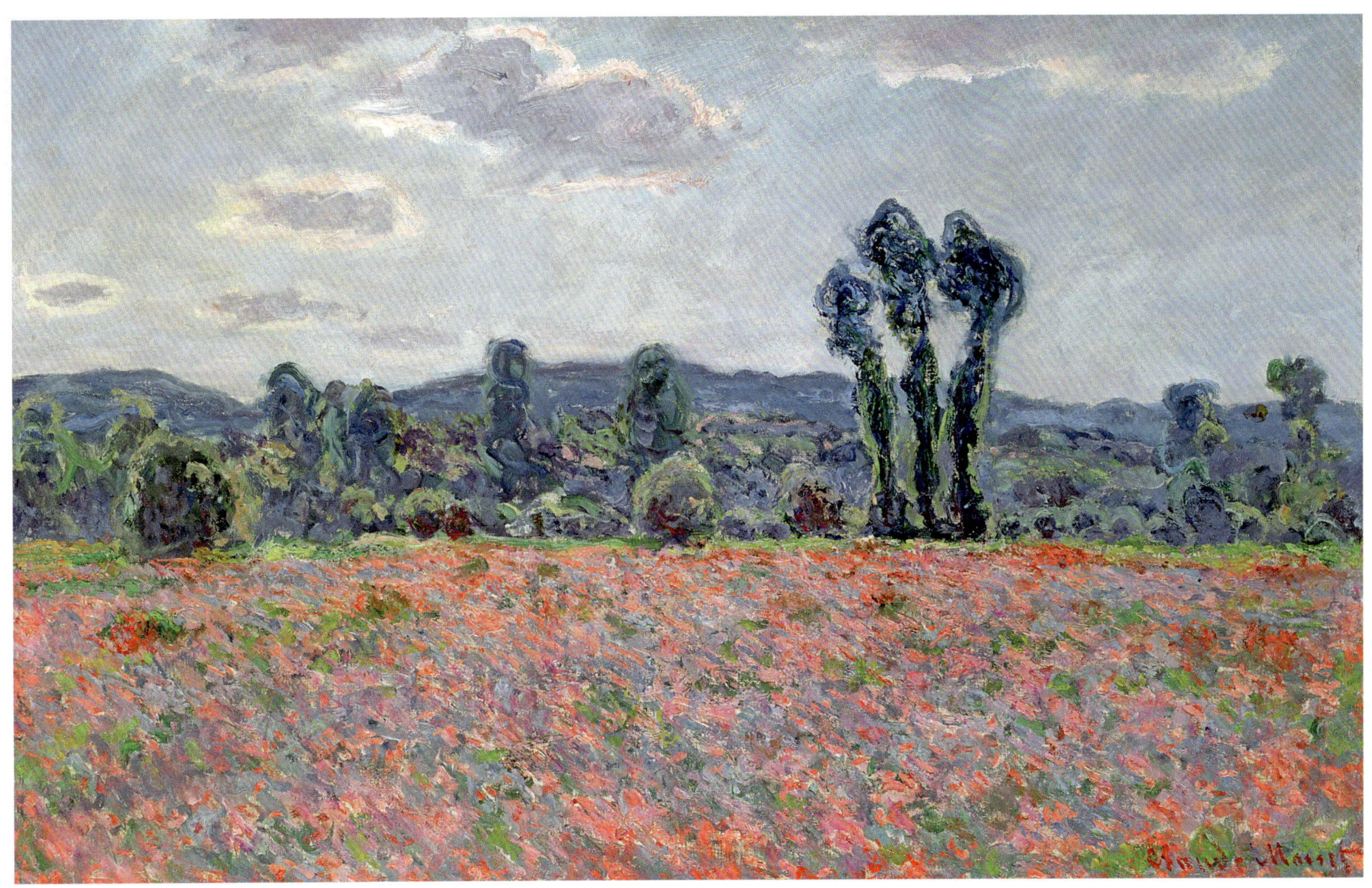

El impresionismo y su continuación

Hasta 1886 los artistas organizaron un total de ocho exposiciones grupales, tras las cuales esta puntual asociación se disolvió, dando paso a la creación de estilos personales. Comenzó entonces una especialización temática y estilística que buscaba satisfacer el creciente y diversificado mercado de arte, pero cuidando a la vez el desarrollo artístico personal.

Monet pintó en los años 1890 las series de *Montones de heno, Álamos, Catedrales* y por último los *Nenúfares,* en los que el motivo de los estanques de nenúfares de Giverny iban perdiendo importancia a favor de una composición más libre y basada en el color. Los artistas abstractos, después de 1945, trabajarían con esta autonomía del color haciendo de Monet un precursor.

En la propia Francia rápidamente creció un movimiento de oposición a la percepción del arte únicamente como impresión óptica, en un primer momento liderado por un grupo de pintores que se denominaban neoimpresionistas y entendían su propuesta como una mejora radical. El líder de

L'Impressionismo e la sua eredità

Fino al 1886 gli artisti organizzarono un totale di otto mostre collettive. Successivamente, iniziarono a seguire percorsi diversi e a sviluppare stili più individuali. Ebbe così inizio una specializzazione tematica e stilistica che cercò di soddisfare le esigenze del mercato dell'arte fiorente e diversificato, così come dello sviluppo personale dei pittori.

Monet dipinse nel 1890 le serie *Covoni, Pioppi, Cattedrali* e, infine, *Ninfee,* che portarono sempre più in secondo piano il soggetto degli stagni di ninfee a Giverny a favore di composizioni più libere e con cromatismi completamente inventati. Monet è dunque un precursore dell'autonomia del colore che sarà ripresa solo dopo il 1945 dagli artisti dell'Astrattismo.

Tuttavia, in Francia nacque ben presto un'opposizione a questa percezione artistica basata esclusivamente sull'apparenza, inizialmente formata da un gruppo di pittori che si definivano neo-impressionisti ma che tuttavia interpretavano questo rinnovamento come miglioramento radicale. Il leader del gruppo, il giovane pittore Georges Seurat

De invloed van het impressionisme

Tot 1886 organiseerden de kunstenaars in totaal acht exposities, waarna de losse groep uiteenviel en ieder zijn individuele stijl verder ontwikkelde. Er begon zich een stilistische specialisering af te tekenen, waarbij de kunstenaars niet alleen tegemoet kwamen aan de opkomende en steeds verder vertakkende kunstmarkt, maar ook hun persoonlijke ontwikkeling lieten zien.

In de jaren negentig van de negentiende eeuw creëerde Monet series over *hooibergen, populieren* en *kathedralen.* In zijn laatste serie, over de *waterlelies* in zijn tuin te Giverny, loste het onderwerp steeds verder op in composities die uit een vrij kleurgebruik voortkwamen. Op dit autonome kleurgebruik sloten zich pas na 1945 de abstracte kunstenaars aan, die in Monet dan ook een voorloper zagen.

In Frankrijk ontstond al snel weerstand tegen de impressionistische blik, waarin het – letterlijk 'ogenschijnlijk' – om een aanblik van de natuur ging; de eerste kritiek kwam van de 'neo-impressionisten', die zich als radicale verbeteraars

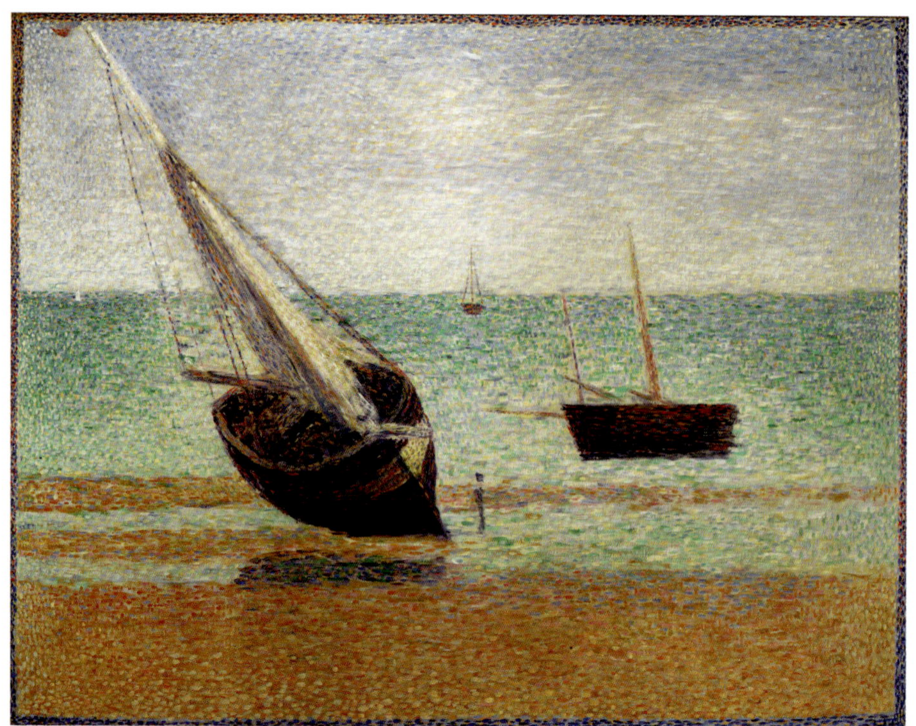

developed from scientific principles and theories of color a system of juxtaposed small dots, or pointillism, which in the eye of the viewer from a particular distance should present a unified optical mix. Despite the positivist-inspired and scientifically derived optical illusion, the deconstruction of colors produced a purer and brighter color mixture, and regardless of the later dogmatically fixed aesthetics, Seurat had created from a variety of sources a new vision of art. This would have a great influence on the further development of modern painting through, for instance, Mondrian, Kandinsky and Matisse.

After a brief impressionist phase, Paul Cézanne systematically developed a new painting technique from modulations of color which would represent the motifs, landscapes, portraits and figures in a new formal clarity and strength. Cézanne wanted 'something solid and lasting, like the art of museums', from impressionism. That meant for Cézanne reclaiming a solid composition and vivid result with maximum richness of color. The landscape around the Montagne Sainte-Victoire in Aix-en-Provence was his primary subject in his last years. In a dense fabric of color spots *(taches colorées)* the motif is, as it were, cancelled out in the larger rhythm of the composition. Painting had freed itself from the "naive" view of the observation of nature, to reveal the "essence" behind the appearance. From here on, modern art unfolded itself with the cubists, Fauves and constructivists.

(1859–1891), ne se référait pas uniquement à la perception des nuances de couleurs, mais développa à partir des principes et des théories scientifiques sur la couleur un système de petits points juxtaposés, ou pointillisme, que l'œil de l'observateur devrait voir, à partir d'une certaine distance, comme un ensemble optique unifié. Malgré l'illusion d'optique, d'origine positiviste et établie de manière scientifique, la déconstruction des couleurs produisit un mélange de couleur plus pur et plus clair, et indépendamment des critères esthétiques qui seraient fixés de manière dogmatique ensuite, Seurat créa une nouvelle vision de l'art à partir d'une variété de sources. Cela aurait une grande influence sur le développement de la peinture moderne et sur des peintres comme Mondrian, Kandinsky et Matisse.

Après une brève phase impressionniste, Paul Cézanne mit au point une nouvelle technique de peinture à partir des modulations de la couleur pour représenter les motifs, paysages, portraits et visages avec une clarté formelle et une force nouvelle. Cézanne voulait faire de l'impressionnisme « quelque chose de solide et durable, comme les œuvres d'art des musées ». Cela signifiait pour Cézanne d'obtenir une composition solide et un résultat éclatant avec une richesse de la couleur maximale. Le paysage autour de la Montagne Sainte-Victoire à Aix-en-Provence fut son principal sujet pendant les dernières années de sa vie. Dans une structure dense de points de couleur (taches colorées), c'est pour ainsi dire comme si le motif se fondait dans

aber als radikale Verbesserung verstanden. Der Kopf der Gruppe, der junge Maler Georges Seurat (1859–1891), verließ sich nicht allein auf die Wahrnehmung der Farbnuancen, sondern entwickelte aus wissenschaftlichen Regeln und Farbtheorien ein System nebeneinandergesetzter kleiner Punkte (Pointillismus), die im Auge des Betrachters aus einiger Entfernung zur „optischen Mischung" gelangen sollten. Trotz der durch die positivistische Wissenschaftsgläubigkeit verursachten Täuschung, die Zerlegung der Farben erzeuge eine reinere und hellere Farbmischung, und der später dogmatisch festgelegten Ästhetik hatte Seurat aus den verschiedensten Quellen eine neue Kunstanschauung geschaffen, die auf die weitere Entwicklung der modernen Malerei (Mondrian, Kandinsky, Matisse) großen Einfluss hatte.

Nach einer kurzen impressionistischen Phase erarbeitete Paul Cézanne systematisch eine neuartige Maltechnik aus Modulationen der Farbe, die das Motiv, Landschaften, Porträts, Figuren in neuartiger formaler Klarheit und Festigkeit darstellen. Cézanne wollte aus dem Impressionismus „etwas Festes und Beständiges machen, wie die Kunst der Museen". Das bedeutete für Cézanne die Wiedergewinnung einer festen Komposition und plastischer Werte bei größtmöglichem Farbreichtum. Die Landschaft um die Montagne Sainte-Victoire bei Aix-en-Provence war in den letzten Jahren das Hauptmotiv. In einem

este grupo, el joven Georges Seurat (1859–1891), no confiaba únicamente en la percepción de los matices cromáticos, sino que diseñó un sistema de reglas científicas y teorías cromáticas en el que pequeños puntos (puntillismo) formarían una "mezcla óptica" en el ojo del espectador, a una cierta distancia. A pesar del equívoco, producido por una fe positivista en la ciencia, la descomposición de los colores generó una mezcla cromática más pura y brillante, y con su estética de construcción dogmática Seurat había construido a través de sus diversas fuentes una nueva forma de entender el arte, que tendría una gran influencia en el desarrollo posterior de la pintura moderna (Mondrian, Kandinsky, Matisse).

Tras un corto período impresionista Paul Cézanne desarrolló de manera sistemática una nueva técnica pictórica con modulaciones del color que presentaban el motivo o tema, paisajes, retratos, personajes, con una nueva solidez y claridad formal. Cézanne quería hacer del impresionismo "algo sólido y estable, como el arte de los museos". Esto suponía para Cézanne la recuperación de una composición más sólida y un carácter más plástico manteniendo la mayor riqueza cromática posible. El paisaje alrededor del Monte Sainte-Victoire en Aix-en-Provence fue su motivo central en los últimos años. El motivo central se suspende aquí en el ritmo general de la composición, una tupida red de manchas cromáticas *(taches colorées)*. La pintura se ha liberado de la observación

(1859–1891), abbandonò la pittura basata esclusivamente sulla percezione delle sfumature di colore e sviluppò, sulla base di principi scientifici e teorie del colore, un sistema di piccoli punti giustapposti (Puntillismo) che portavano ad una "mescolanza ottica" negli occhi degli osservatori quando ammiravano i quadri da una certa distanza. Nonostante l'"inganno" dello scientismo positivista, la separazione dei colori produsse una più pura e più luminosa miscelazione cromatica, e l'estetica di Seurat, nata da una varietà di fonti e in seguito fissata dogmaticamente, creò una nuova visione dell'arte, che ebbe una grande influenza sull'ulteriore sviluppo della pittura moderna (Mondrian, Kandinsky, Matisse ecc.).

Dopo una breve fase impressionista, Paul Cézanne sviluppò sistematicamente una tecnica pittorica a partire dalle modulazioni cromatiche, mediante le quali motivi, paesaggi, ritratti e figure venivano rappresentati con una solidità e chiarezza formale tutta nuova. Cézanne voleva "fare dell'Impressionismo qualcosa di solido e duraturo come l'arte dei musei". Ciò significava per Cézanne il recupero di una composizione solida e di valori plastici conservando la massima ricchezza di colore. Il paesaggio intorno alla montagna Sainte-Victoire ad Aix-en-Provence fu il soggetto principale dell'artista negli ultimi anni. In un tessuto fitto di macchie di colore *(taches colorées)*, il motivo si fonde in certo qual modo nel grande ritmo della composizione.

van de impressionistische stijl opwierpen. De leider van de groep, de jonge schilder Georges Seurat (1859–1891), wilde de waarneming van kleurnuances verder ontwikkelen. Op basis van wetenschappelijke regels en kleurtheorieën plaatste hij kleurvlekjes of -puntjes (pointillisme) naast elkaar, zodat ze op enige afstand in het oog van de beschouwer een 'optisch mengsel' zouden vormen. Hoewel Seurat door zijn positivistische geloof in de wetenschap tot de onjuiste overtuiging kwam dat naast elkaar geplaatste kleuren een grotere puurheid en helderheid opleverden en later een dogmatische esthetiek opstelde, had zijn zienswijze grote invloed op de ontwikkeling van de moderne schilderkunst (Mondriaan, Kandinsky, Matisse).

Na een korte impressionistische fase werkte Paul Cézanne systematisch zijn eigen schildertechniek uit, waarbij hij in kleurmodulaties zijn thema's, landschappen en figuren een nieuwe formele helderheid en stabiliteit verleende. Cézanne wilde van het impressionisme "iets stevigs en houdbaars maken, zoals de kunst in de musea". Hij zocht naar een stabiele compositie en naar een plastische uitstraling, met behoud van een zo groot mogelijke kleurenrijkdom. Aan het eind van zijn leven vormde het landschap rond de berg Sainte-Victoire bij Aix-en-Provence zijn hoofdmotief. In een dicht weefsel van kleurvlakken *(taches colorées)* lost hij dat motief in het bredere ritme van de compositie op. Volgens

Paul Gauguin (1848–1903) also emerged from impressionism, but soon missed the world of ideas excluded by the impressionist perception. In Brittany and later in the South Seas Gauguin was searching for the concealed sources of art, for simplicity and yet at the same time the mystery and meanings of long-forgotten myths and symbols. By connecting various sources of inspiration, including the technique of sacred stained glass as well as Japanese woodcuts and the intense colors of Fauvism (Matisse), Gauguin created a new type of painting, of intense, solid colors and simplified forms which was no longer subject to unconditional observations of nature, but rather a desire to reveal a decorative "synthesis" (synthetism).

The so-called Nabis (hebrew: *prophet*) continued further in this direction; a circle of friends from the Académie Julian was established in 1888, amongst whose number included Maurice Denis (1870–1943), Pierre Bonnard (1867–1947), Édouard Vuillard (1868–1940) and Félix Vallotton (1865–1925). Similarly to Gauguin, their admired ideal, these artists were united in their rejection of the natural model and the mysterious correspondence between colors, shapes, emotions and beings hidden behind images. The atmospherically relaxed and richly colored paintings in the late works of Bonnard and Vuillard, after 1900, connects late impressionism with the international movement of "art nouveau" (Jugendstil, Modern Style).

le rythme global de la composition. La peinture s'est libérée du regard « naïf » de l'observation de la nature pour révéler l'« essence » derrière l'apparence. Ensuite, l'art moderne a suivi avec les Cubistes, Fauves et Constructivistes.

Cézanne a peint la montagne provençale de nombreuses fois selon la même perspective : dominant la plaine d'Arc, beaucoup plus grande que dans la réalité, elle domine un paysage composé de taches de couleur. Pas de maison, pas de buissons et surtout aucun être humain, seule l'application uniforme des couleurs crée un réseau dense de références colorées et formelles dans lesquelles le sujet principal se dresse comme un cristal.

Paul Gauguin (1848–1903) est également issu de l'impressionnisme, mais le monde des idées exclu par la perception impressionniste va bientôt lui manquer. En Bretagne et plus tard dans les mers du Sud, Gauguin rechercha des sources cachées de l'art, de la simplicité et pourtant en même temps du mystère et des significations de mythes et symboles oubliés depuis longtemps. En reliant différentes sources d'inspiration, y compris la technique du vitrail sacré, ainsi que des estampes japonaises et les couleurs intenses du fauvisme (Matisse), Gauguin créa une nouvelle façon de peindre – faite de couleurs intenses et unies et de formes simplifiées– qui ne dépendait plus des observations inconditionnelles de la nature, mais plutôt d'un désir de révéler une « synthèse » décorative (synthétisme).

dichten Gewebe von Farbflecken *(taches colorées)* ist das Motiv gleichsam in dem größeren Rhythmus der Bildkomposition aufgehoben. Die Malerei hat sich von der „naiven" Naturbetrachtung freigemacht, um das „Wesentliche" hinter der Erscheinung zu erkennen. Von hier aus entfaltet sich die moderne Kunst bei Kubisten, Fauvisten und Konstruktivisten.

Auch Paul Gauguin (1848–1903) war vom Impressionismus ausgegangen, vermisste aber bald die von der impressionistischen Wahrnehmung ausgesparte Ideenwelt. In der Bretagne und später in der Südsee suchte Gauguin nach den verschütteten Quellen der Kunst, nach Einfachheit und zugleich Geheimnisvollem, Bedeutsamen, nach vergessenen Mythen und Symbolen. Aus der Verbindung verschiedener Inspirationsquellen, wozu die Technik der sakralen Glasmalerei genauso gehörte wie der japanische Holzschnitt und die intensiven Farben des Fauvismus (Matisse), schuf Gauguin eine neuartige Malerei aus intensiven, flächigen Farben und vereinfachten Formen, die nicht mehr der unbedingten Naturbeobachtung unterworfen sind, sondern einen Willen zur dekorativen „Synthese" offenbaren (Synthetismus).

In diese Richtung gingen die sogenannten Nabis (hebräisch *Propheten*) weiter, ein 1888 zusammengefundener Freundeskreis aus der Académie Julian, dem unter anderem Maurice Denis

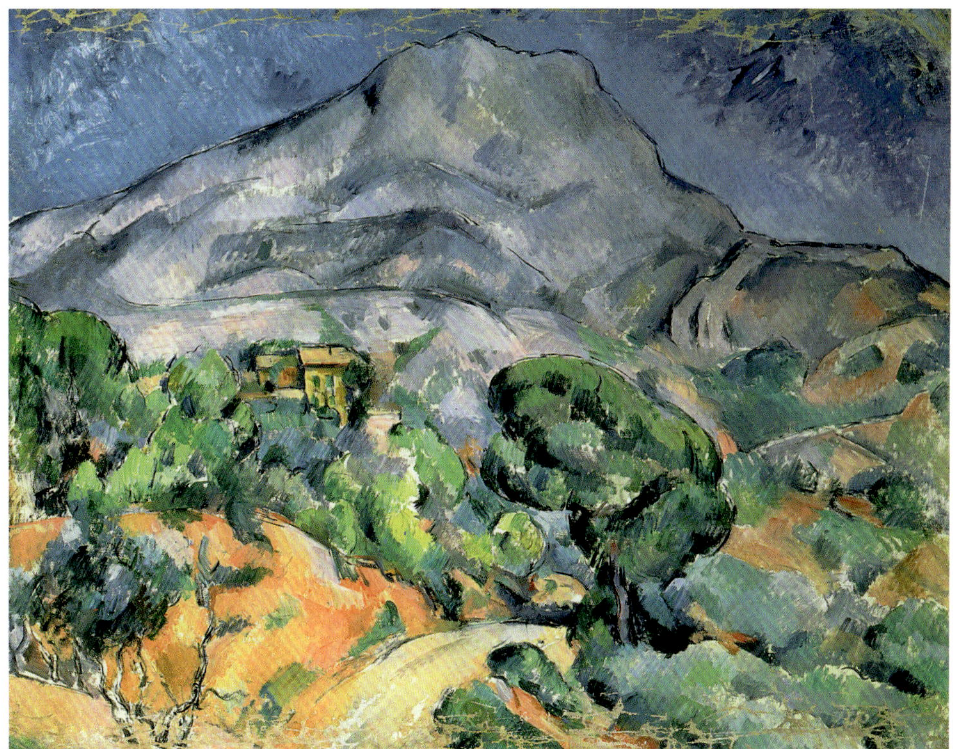

Paul Cézanne (1839–1906)

The Mountain Sainte-Victoire

La monte Sainte-Victoire

Der Berg Sainte-Victoire

Monte Sainte-Victoire

La monta Sainte-Victoire

De berg Sainte-Victoire

1900, Oil on canvas/Huile sur toile, 78 × 99 cm,
State Hermitage, St. Petersburg

"ingenua" de la naturaleza, para capturar lo "esencial" detrás de su apariencia. A partir de aquí se desarrolló el arte moderno con los cubistas, fauvistas y constructivistas.

También Paul Gauguin (1848–1903) partió del impresionismo, pero pronto echó en falta el mundo simbólico que el trabajo perceptivo impresionista dejaba a un lado. En la Bretaña, y después en el Mar del Sur, Gauguin fue en busca de las fuentes escondidas del arte, en busca de lo sencillo y a la vez secreto y significativo, en busca de mitos y símbolos olvidados. De la conexión entre diversas fuentes de inspiración entre las que se contaban tanto las vidrieras religiosas como la xilografía japonesa y los intensos colores del fauvismo (Matisse), Gauguin creó una nueva pintura de colores intensos y planos y de formas sencillas, que no quedaban sometidas a la observación necesaria de la naturaleza, sino que representaban una voluntad de síntesis decorativa (sintetismo).

Los denominados Nabis (del hebreo *profetas*) continuaron por este camino: eran un grupo de amigos creado en 1888 en la Académie Julian y al que pertenecían entre otros Maurice Denis (1870–1943), Pierre Bonnard (1867–1947), Édouard Vuillard (1868–1940) y Félix Vallotton (1865–1925). Al igual que Gauguin, su admirado predecesor, estos artistas rechazaban el motivo de la naturaleza en favor de

La pittura si era dunque liberata dalla "naïve" osservazione della natura per riconoscere l'"essenza" nascosta dietro l'apparenza. Da qui, l'arte moderna si svilupperà attraverso il Cubismo, il Fauvismo e il Costruttivismo.

Anche Paul Gauguin (1848–1903) si affiliò dall'Impressionismo, ma ben presto sentì nostalgia per il mondo di idee eluso dalla percezione della realtà della corrente. In Bretagna e poi nei mari del sud, Gauguin si dedicò alla ricerca delle fonti sepolte dell'arte, della semplicità e, al contempo, del misterioso e significativo, dei simboli e dei miti dimenticati. Mediante la combinazione di diverse fonti di ispirazione, tra cui la tecnica del vetro colorato sacrale, la xilografia giapponese e i colori intensi del Fauvismo (Matisse), Gauguin creò un nuovo stile pittorico caratterizzato da colori intensi e solidi e da forme semplificate che non sono più soggette all'osservazione incondizionata della natura bensì esprimono il desiderio di "sintesi" decorativa (Sintetismo).

In questa stessa direzione si mossero anche i cosiddetti *nabis* ("profeti" in ebraico), un circolo di amici fondato nel 1888 da artisti dell'Académie Julian, al quale appartenevano, tra gli altri, Maurice Denis (1870–1943), Pierre Bonnard (1867–1947), Édouard Vuillard (1868–1940) e Félix Vallotton (1865–1925). Come Gauguin, il loro ammirato modello, questi

Cézanne moest de schilderkunst zich van de "naïeve" natuurbeschouwing losmaken om het "essentiële" achter de verschijningsvormen te herkennen. Uit deze zienswijze ontwikkelden zich het moderne kubisme, fauvisme en constructivisme.

Ook Paul Gauguin (1848–1903) begon als impressionist, waarna hij echter al snel heimwee kreeg naar een ideeënwereld die in het impressionisme niet aan de orde kwam. In Bretagne en later in de Stille Oceaan zocht hij naar de verloren gegane bronnen van de kunst, naar eenvoud en mysterie, naar de zingeving en betekenis van vergeten mythen en symbolen. Uit zijn verbindingen tussen verschillende inspiratiebronnen, waaronder de sacrale glasschilderkunst, de Japanse houtsnede en het intense kleurgebruik van het fauvisme (Matisse), schiep Gauguin een nieuwe schilderkunst van heldere kleurvelden en vereenvoudigde vormen, die niet langer aan de waarneming van de werkelijkheid waren gebonden maar getuigden van een ontwikkeling naar 'decoratieve synthese' (cloisonnisme).

In deze richting ontwikkelden zich de zogenaamde Nabis (Hebreeuws voor *profeten*), een in 1888 ontstane vriendenkring van schilders van de Académie Julian, waartoe ook Maurice Denis (1870–1943), Pierre Bonnard (1867–1947), Édouard Vuillard (1868–1940) en Félix Vallotton (1865–1925) behoorden.

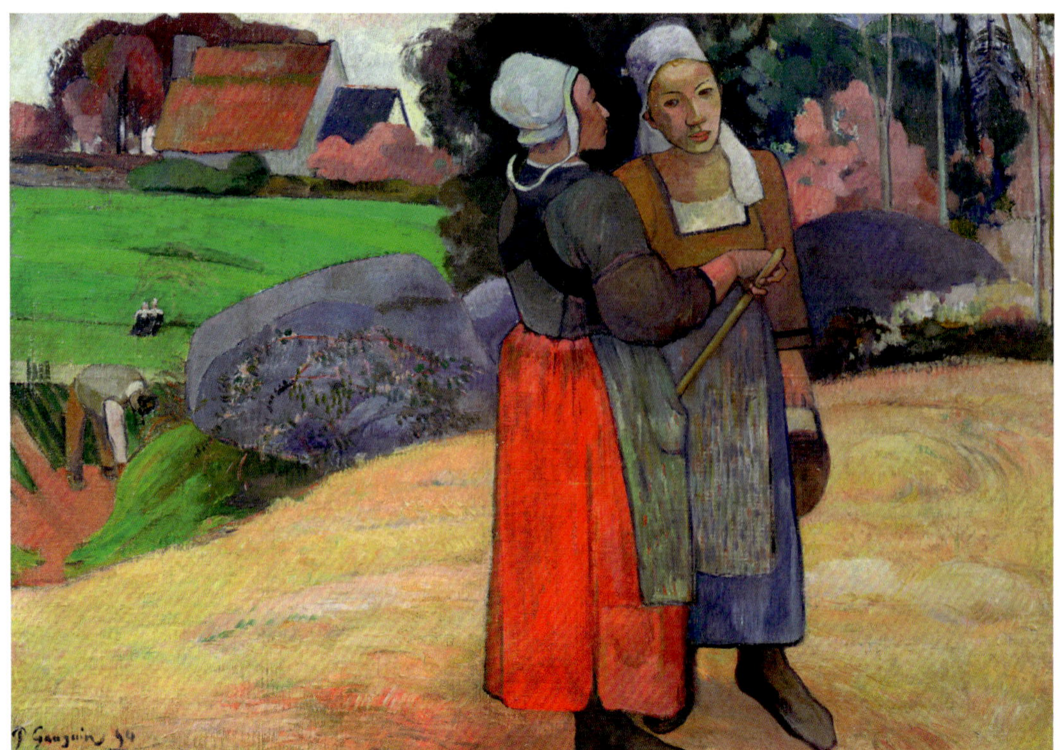

Paul Gauguin (1848–1903)

Breton Peasants

Paysannes bretonnes

Bretonische Bäuerinnen

Campesinas bretonas

Contadini bretoni

Bretonse boerinnen

1894, Oil on canvas/Huile sur toile,
66,5 × 9,7 cm, Musée d'Orsay, Paris

Although Henri de Toulouse-Lautrec (1864–1901) shared in these endeavors, he did not join any of these groups. After 1884 he lived on the Montmartre, drawing his themes from the world of cafes and cabarets, theaters, dance halls and brothels, creating atmospherically dense scenes of the 'fin de siècle', whereby he attached particular importance to the sometimes acerbic and characteristic human representation.

The artist had been closely observing the goings-on in one of the most famous night clubs of Paris and reproduced this in an impressive composition. The depth of the space is largely suggested by the staggered arrangement of the figures. In the center are the dancer La Goulue (the glutton) and Valentin le désossé (Valentin the contortionist), two cabaret stars preserved forever by Toulouse-Lautrec in the history of art.

Another loner was the Dutchman Vincent van Gogh (1853–1890), who emerged from the Hague School and the painters of Barbizon, only to find himself in disagreement with impressionism, leading to his very distinctive and expressive works from glowing, complementarily positioned colors. Van Gogh saw colors not only as simple visual material, but also as having their own suggestive language capable of direct interaction with the human soul. Unlike the impressionists, Van Gogh did not show in

Les Nabis (qui signifie prophète en hébreu) continuèrent dans cette direction. Un cercle d'amis de l'Académie Julian se forma en 1888, avec, entre autres membres, Maurice Denis (1870–1943), Pierre Bonnard (1867–1947), Édouard Vuillard (1868–1940) et Félix Vallotton (1865–1925). Comme Gauguin, leur modèle tant admiré, ces artistes étaient unis par un rejet commun du modèle naturel et par la correspondance mystérieuse entre les couleurs, les formes, les émotions et les êtres cachés derrière les images. Les peintures atmosphériquement détendues et richement colorées des œuvres tardives de Bonnard et Vuillard, après 1900, font le lien entre la fin de l'impressionnisme et le mouvement international « art nouveau » (Jugendstil, Modern Style).

Bien que Henri de Toulouse-Lautrec (1864–1901) ait partagé cet intérêt, il ne rejoignit aucun de ces groupes. Après 1884, il vécut à Montmartre, tirant ses thèmes du monde des cafés et cabarets, théâtres, salles de bal et maisons closes, représentant des scènes à l'atmosphère dense de la « fin de siècle », montrant qu'il attache une importance particulière à la représentation humaine parfois acerbe et caractéristique.
L'artiste avait observé de près les allées et venues dans l'un des plus célèbres dancings de Paris et les reproduisit dans une composition impressionnante. La profondeur de l'espace est largement suggérée par la disposition décalée des personnages. Au centre, se trouvent la danseuse La Goulue et Valentin le désossé, deux stars

(1870–1943), Pierre Bonnard (1867–1947), Édouard Vuillard (1868–1940) und Félix Vallotton (1865–1925) angehörten. Ähnlich wie Gauguin, das bewunderte Vorbild, waren sich diese Künstler in der Ablehnung des Naturvorbildes und der geheimnisvollen Korrespondenz zwischen Farben, Formen, Emotionen und den hinter den Erscheinungen verborgenen Wesenheiten einig. Die atmosphärisch lockere buntfarbige Malweise im Spätwerk von Bonnard und Vuillard ab 1900 verbindet den Spätimpressionismus mit der internationalen Bewegung des „Art Nouveau" (Jugendstil, Modern Style).

Der diesen Bestrebungen nahestehende Henri de Toulouse-Lautrec (1864–1901) schloss sich keiner dieser Gruppen an. Seit 1884 auf dem Montmartre lebend bezog er seine Themen aus der Welt der Cafés und Cabarets, der Theater, Tanzlokale und Bordelle und schuf atmosphärisch dichte Szenen des Fin de Siècle, wobei er besonderen Wert auf die manchmal karikierende und charakterisierende Menschendarstellung legte.

Ein anderer Einzelgänger war der Niederländer Vincent van Gogh (1853–1890), der zunächst von der Haager Schule sowie den Malern von Barbizon ausging, um dann in der Auseinandersetzung mit dem Impressionismus zu ganz eigenständigen expressiven Werken aus glühenden, komplementär gesetzten Farben zu gelangen. Van Gogh sah in

correspondencias más secretas entre formas, colores y emociones, escondidas tras las apariencias. La técnica pictórica de la etapa tardía de Bonnard y Vuillard, atmosférica, suelta y muy colorida, establece relaciones entre el impresionismo tardío y el movimiento internacional del *"Art Nouveau"* (Modernismo).

Henri de Toulouse-Lautrec (1864–1901), cercano a todas estas aspiraciones, no se adhirió a ninguno de estos grupos. Desde que se instaló en Montmartre en 1884 se dedicó a los temas del mundo de los cafés y cabarets, el teatro, salas de baile y burdeles, y creó densas y atmosféricas escenas de fin de siglo, prestando especial atención a la representación a veces caricaturesca del ser humano.

Otro espíritu individual fue el del holandés Vincent van Gogh (1853–1890), que partió en un principio de la escuela de la Haya y los pintores de Barbizon, para crear después mediante su confrontación con el impresionismo obras expresivas y personales compuestas de colores brillantes y complementarios. Van Gogh veía los colores no solo como un simple medio pictórico, sino como un sugestivo lenguaje propio que podía hablar directamente al alma humana. Al contrario que los impresionistas Van Gogh no mostraba en sus paisajes y retratos la mirada deambulante del hombre de ciudad en busca de relajación, sino que mostraba

artisti respingevano il prototipo naturale e riconoscevano la misteriosa corrispondenza tra colori, forme, emozioni e l'essenza nascosta dietro le apparenze. La pittura altamente cromatica e rilassata delle ultime opere di Bonnard e Vuillard a partire dal 1900 collega il Post-impressionismo con il movimento internazionale dell'Art Nouveau (Stile Liberty).

Sebbene condividesse il loro stesso impegno, Henri de Toulouse-Lautrec (1864–1901) non si unì a nessuno di questi gruppi. Nel 1884 si trasferì nel vivace quartiere di Montmartre e iniziò a trarre i motivi dei suoi quadri dal mondo del caffè e dei cabaret, dei teatri, delle sale da ballo e dei bordelli, creando scene dense dell'atmosfera *fin de siècle* in cui attribuiva particolare importanza alla rappresentazione umana, a volte aspra e caratterizzante.

Un altro solitario era l'olandese Vincent van Gogh (1853–1890), il quale si discostò dalla Scuola dell'Aia e dai pittori del Barbizon per arrivare, allontanandosi dall'Impressionismo, a opere espressive molto particolari caratterizzate dall'accostamento di colori brillanti e complementari. Van Gogh vedeva nei colori non solo dei semplici mezzi visivi, ma anche un linguaggio suggestivo capace di interagire direttamente con l'anima umana. A differenza degli impressionisti, van Gogh non mostrava nei suoi paesaggi e ritratti lo sguardo vagante dei cittadini alla ricerca di relax, bensì la natura nel suo complesso,

Evenals Gauguin, hun grote voorbeeld, wezen ze een strikte weergave naar de natuur af en gingen op zoek naar de mysterieuze verbanden tussen kleuren, vormen en emoties en naar de essentie achter de verschijningsvormen. De sfeervolle en vrije schildertechniek waarin Bonnard en Vuillard in hun latere werk een bont kleurenpalet gebruiken, verbindt het late impressionisme na 1900 met de internationale stijl van de Art Nouveau of Jugendstil.

Ook Henri de Toulouse-Lautrec (1864–1901) streefde deze nieuwe stijl na, maar hij sloot zich bij geen van deze stromingen aan. Vanaf 1884 woonde hij in Montmartre en ontleende zijn motieven aan cafés, het theater, danslokalen en bordelen, die hij in sfeervolle en drukke fin de siècle-scènes uitbeeldde, waarbij hij veel aandacht schonk aan de – soms karikaturale – typering van zijn figuren.

Een andere eenling was de Nederlander Vincent van Gogh (1853–1890), die aanvankelijk onder invloed van de Haagse School en de kunstenaars van Barbizon schilderde, maar vervolgens in een levendige uitwisseling met het impressionisme geheel eigen, expressieve doeken in zinderende, complementaire kleuren creëerde. Van Gogh beschouwde kleur niet louter als schilderkunstig middel, maar als een beeldtaal die direct op de ziel van de beschouwer inwerkte. Anders dan de impressionisten toonde Van Gogh in zijn landschappen en portretten niet de verre

his landscapes and portraits the sweeping views of the recreation-seeking city dweller, but nature as a whole in which people appear as part of a greater integrated framework. With the complementary relationship of the pure colors and the expressive brushwork, van Gogh reached an intensity and eloquence, particularly with his later pictures, which would in the future be adopted by Fauvism and expressionism.

de cabaret immortalisées pour l'histoire de l'art par Toulouse-Lautrec.

Le Néerlandais Vincent Van Gogh (1853–1890) était un autre solitaire, issu de l'école de La Haye et des peintres de Barbizon. Son désaccord avec l'impressionnisme conduisit à ses œuvres très particulières et expressives, du fait du positionnement éclatant et complémentaire de leurs couleurs. Van Gogh considérait les couleurs non seulement comme matériel visuel simple, mais aussi comme ayant leur propre langue suggestive capable d'interaction directe avec l'âme humaine. Contrairement aux impressionnistes, Van Gogh n'a pas montré dans ses paysages et portraits de vues panoramiques de citadins en quête de loisirs, mais la nature dans son ensemble, les personnages faisant d'un cadre intégré plus grand. Avec la relation de complémentarité de ses couleurs pures et son coup de pinceau expressif, Van Gogh a atteint une intensité et une éloquence, en particulier avec ses dernières peintures, qui serait à l'avenir adopté par le fauvisme et l'expressionnisme.

den Farben nicht nur einfache bildnerische Mittel, sondern eine eigene suggestive Sprache, die direkt auf die Seele des Menschen einzuwirken vermag. Anders als die Impressionisten zeigte van Gogh in seinen Landschaften und Porträts nicht den schweifenden Blick des Entspannung suchenden Städters, sondern die Natur als Ganzes, in die der Mensch als Teil einer übergeordneten sinnvollen Gliederung integriert erscheint. Mit den komplementären Beziehungen der reinen Farben und dem expressiven Pinselduktus hat van Gogh vor allem in seinen späten Bildern eine Intensität und Ausdruckskraft erreicht, die später vom Fauvismus und Expressionismus übernommen wurde.

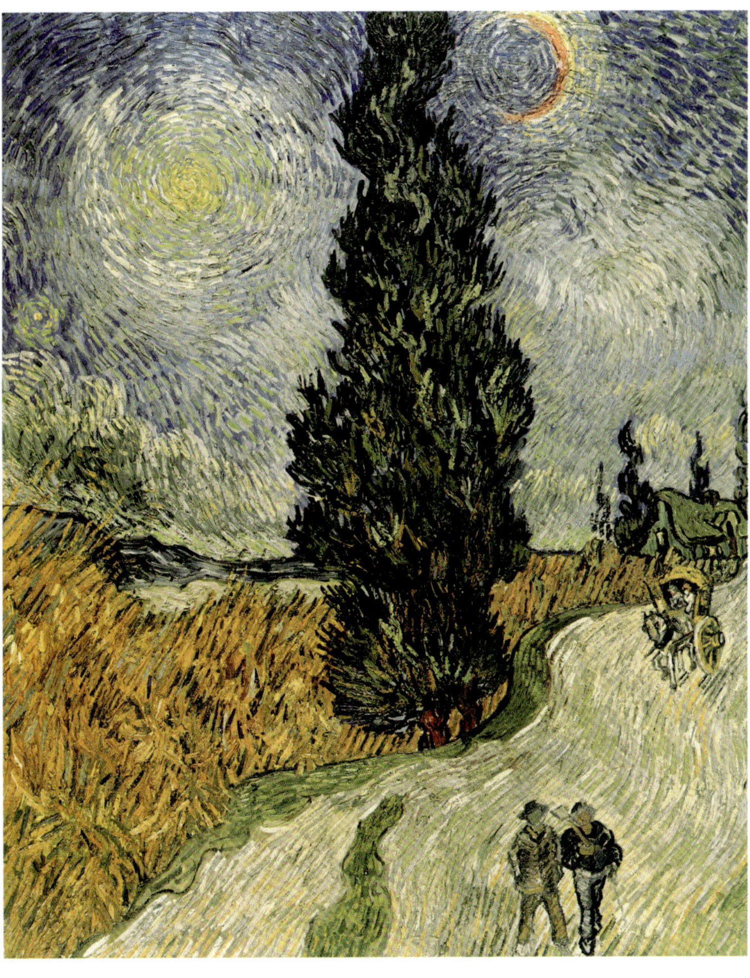

una naturaleza en su totalidad, en la que el hombre parece integrado como parte de una estructura lógica que todo lo ordena. Las relaciones complementarias entre los colores puros y el trazo expresivo de su pincel permiten a Van Gogh alcanzar, sobre todo en sus trabajos tardíos, una intensidad y expresividad que sería después retomada por el fauvismo y el expresionismo.

in cui l'uomo appare integrato come parte di un tutto superiore e sensato. Grazie al rapporto di complementarietà dei colori puri e della pennellata espressiva, van Gogh raggiunse nei suoi quadri un'intensità ed espressività che saranno poi acquisite dal Fauvismo ed dall'Espressionismo.

blik van de stedeling op zoek naar ontspanning, maar de natuur als een geheel waarin de mens slechts als onderdeel van een hogere, betekenisvolle ordening lijkt te zijn opgenomen. Met zijn complementaire wisselwerkingen tussen pure kleuren en zijn expressieve penseelvoering wist Van Gogh vooral in zijn latere werk een uitdrukkingskracht te leggen die later door het fauvisme en het expressionisme werd overgenomen.

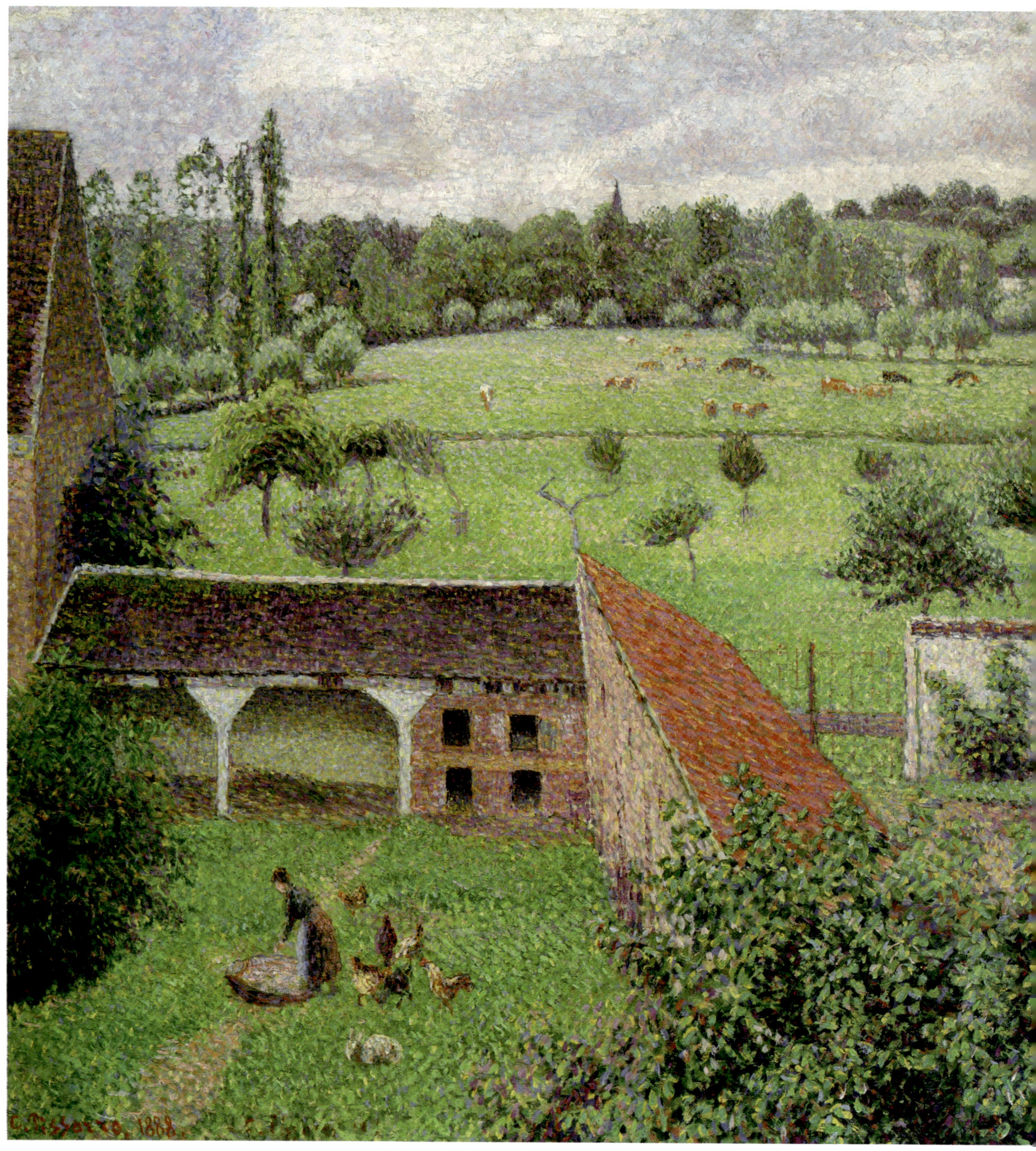

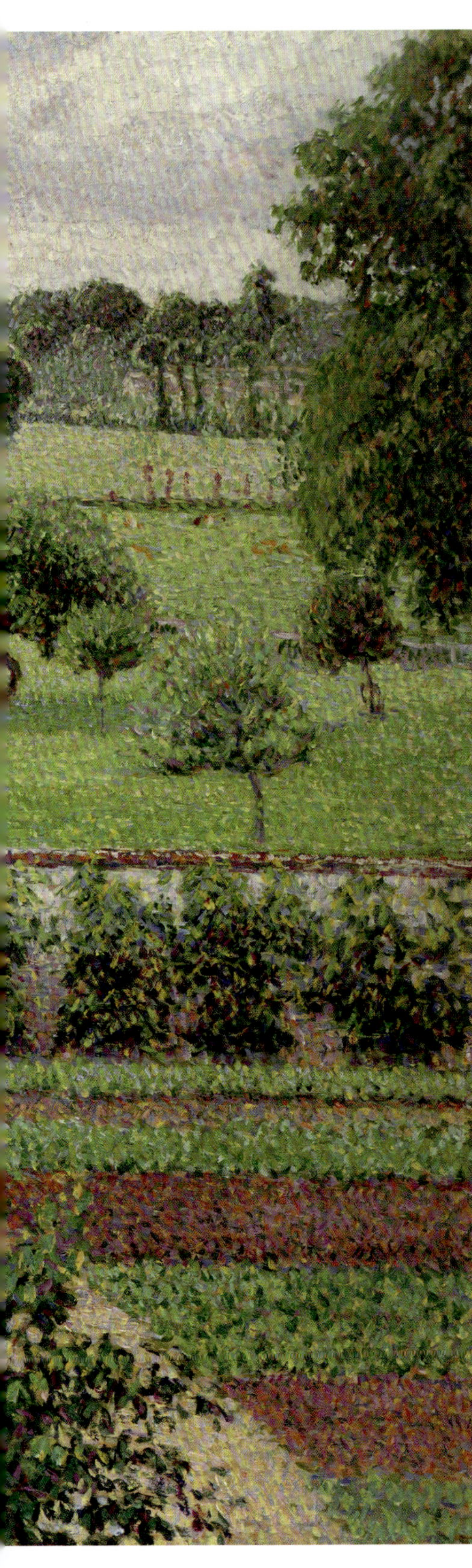

Camille Piccarro (1830 1903)

View Through a Window, Ery

Vue de ma Fenêtre, Éry

Blick aus dem Fenster in Éry

Vista desde la ventana en Ery

Veduta dalla finestra dell'artista, Ery

Blik uit het raam in Ery

1888, Oil on canvas/Huile sur toile, 65 × 81 cm, Ashmolean Museum, Oxford

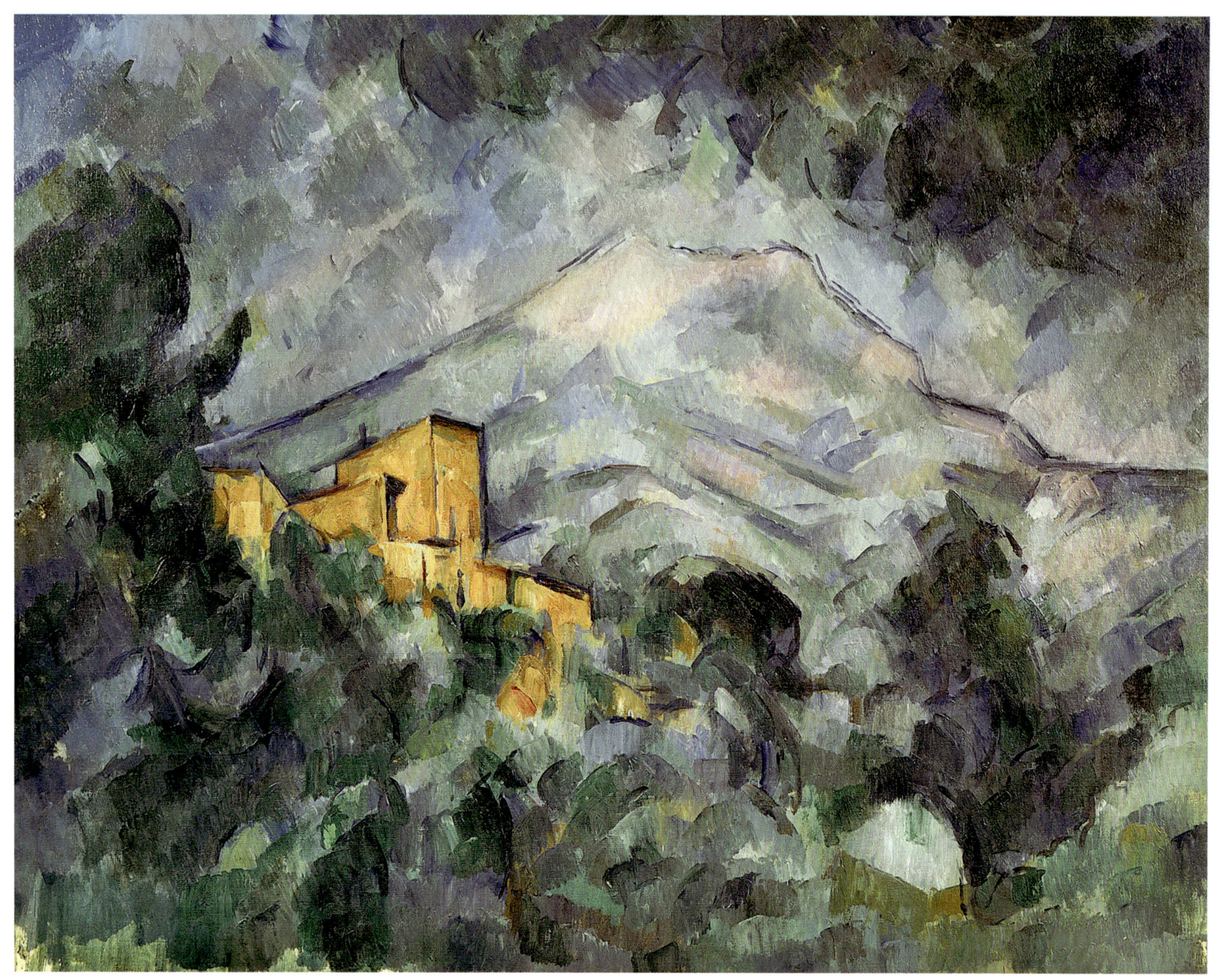

Paul Cézanne (1839–1906)

The Mountain Sainte–Victoire and the Black Chateau

La monte Sainte-Victoire et le château noir

Der Berg Sainte-Victoire und das Château Noir

Monte Sainte-Victoire y el Château Noir

La monta Sainte-Victoire e lo Château Noir

De berg Sainte-Victoire en het Château Noir

1904–06, Oil on canvas/Huile sur toile, 65,5 × 81 cm, Bridgestone Museum of Art, Tokyo

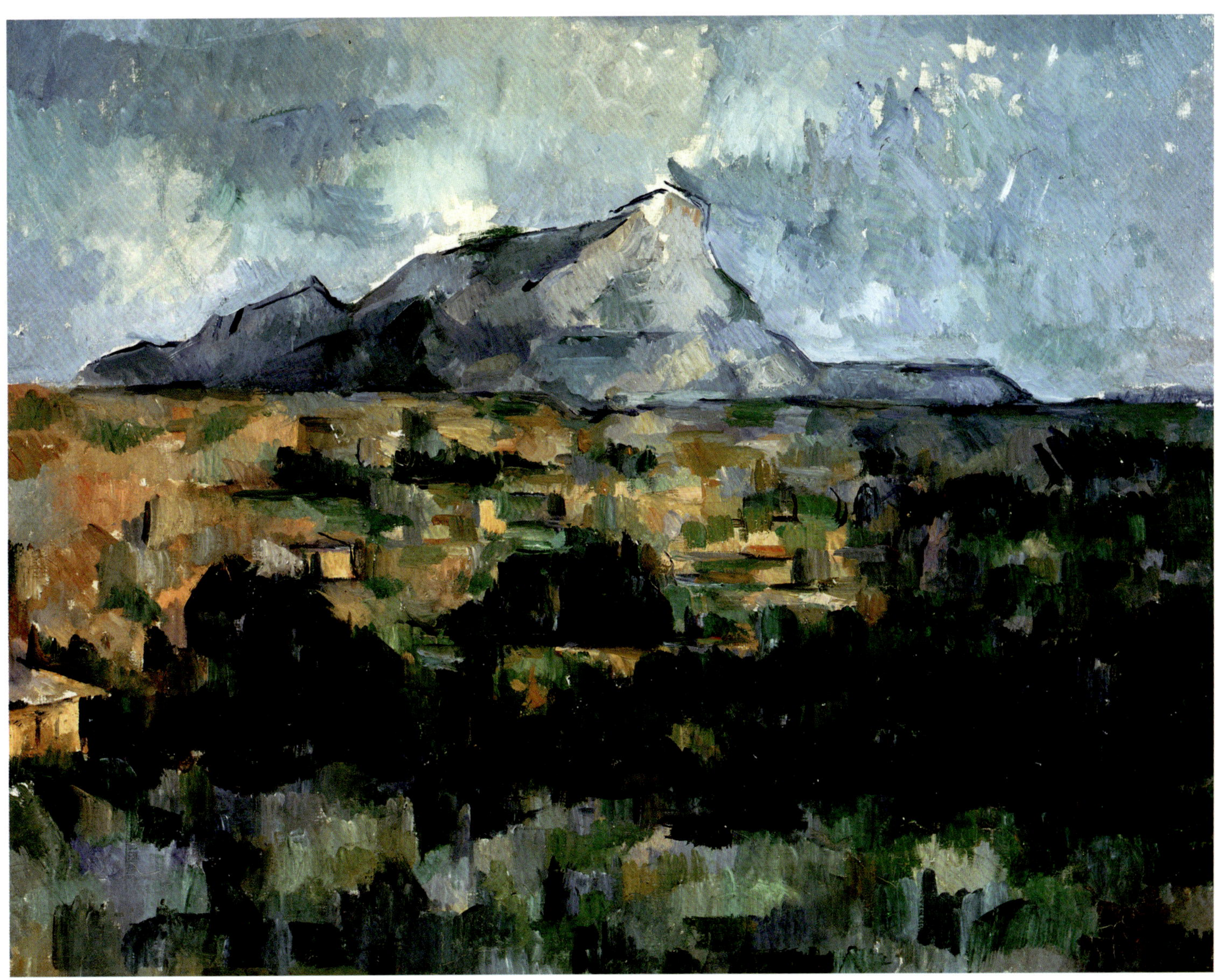

Paul Cézanne (1839–1906)

The Mountain Sainte–Victoire

La monte Sainte-Victoire

Der Berg Sainte-Victoire

Monte Sainte-Victoire

La monta Sainte-Victoire

De berg Sainte-Victoire

1904–06, Oil on canvas/Huile sur toile, 66 × 81,5 cm, Stiftung Sammlung E. G. Bührle, Zürich

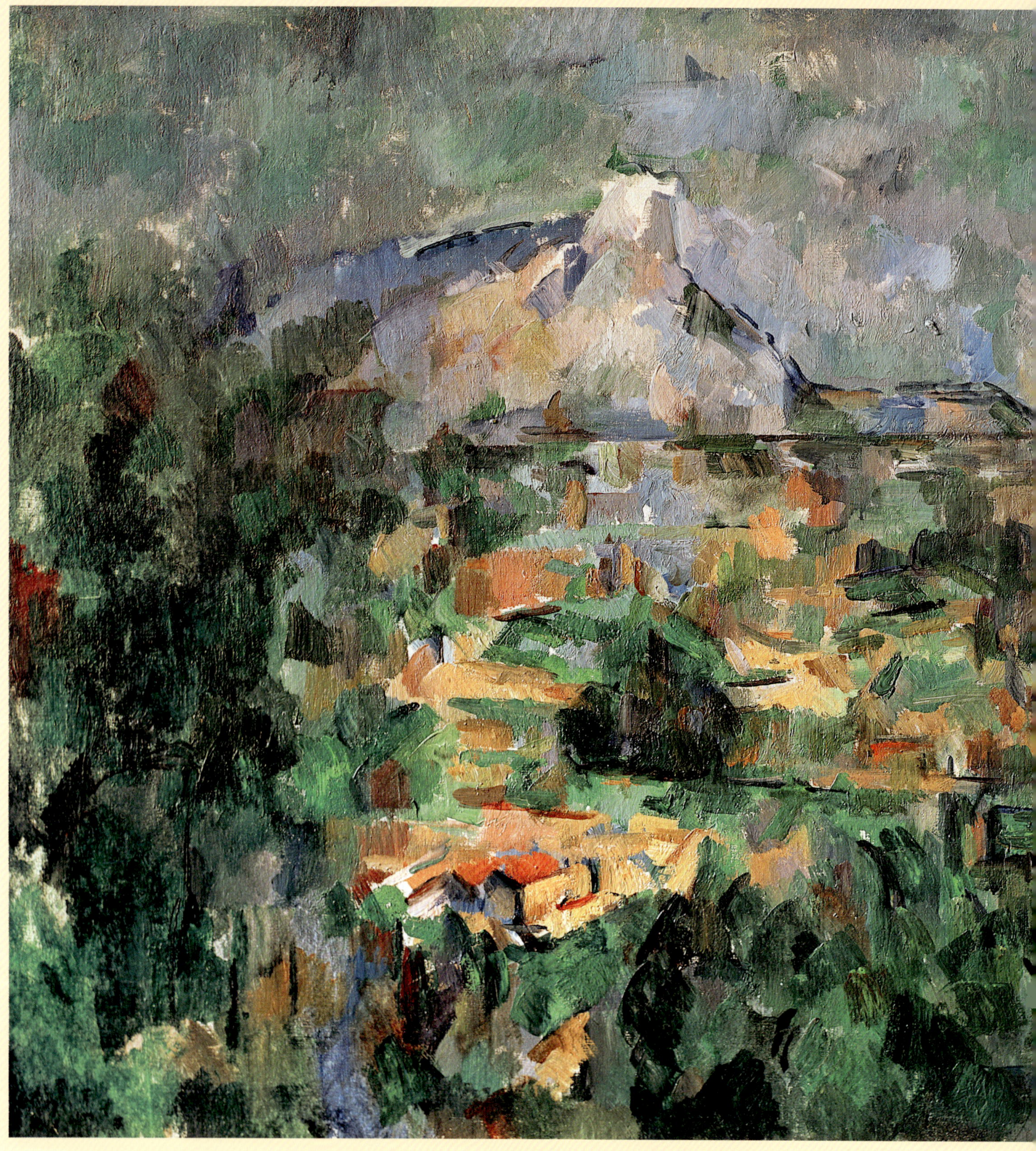

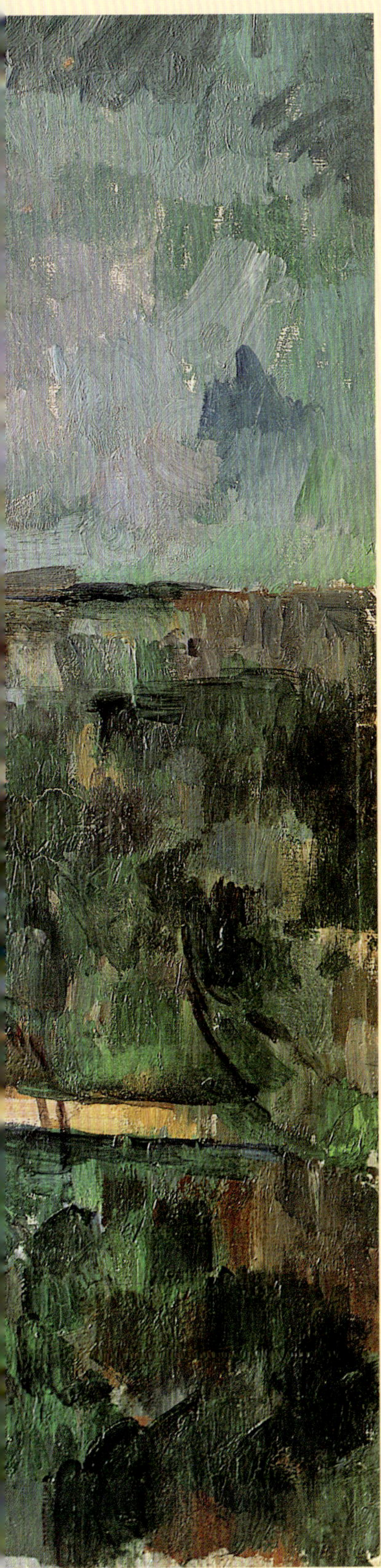

Cézanne painted the Provencal mountain many times from the same perspective: towering over the plain of Arc, much larger than in reality, it dominates a landscape consisting of patches of color. No house, no bushes and above all no human being can be seen, only the uniform application of colors creates a dense network of colored and formal references in which the main subject rises up appearing like a crystal.

Cézanne a peint la montagne provençale de nombreuses fois selon la même perspective : dominant la plaine d'Arc, beaucoup plus grande que dans la réalité, elle domine un paysage composé de taches de couleur. Pas de maison, pas de buissons et surtout aucun être humain, seule l'application uniforme des couleurs crée un réseau dense de références colorées et formelles dans lesquelles le sujet principal se dresse comme un cristal.

Cézanne malte den provenzalischen „Hausberg" viele Male unter dem gleichen Blickwinkel: hoch aufragend über der Ebene von Arc, viel größer als in Wirklichkeit dominiert er eine Landschaft aus Farbflecken. Kein Haus, kein Strauch, erst recht kein Mensch ist zu erkennen, nur die gleichmäßige Setzung von Farben schafft ein dichtes Netz von farbigen und formalen Bezügen, in dem das eigentliche Motiv wie in einem Kristall aufgegangen ist.

Cézanne pintó este conocido monte de la Provenza repetidas veces con la misma perspectiva: coronando el valle de Arc, mucho más grande que en la realidad, domina un paisaje de manchas cromáticas. No se reconoce ninguna casa, arbusto o persona, solo la colocación regular de colores formando una tupida red de relaciones cromáticas y formales, de las que el motivo principal parece cristalizar.

Cézanne dipinse molte volte questa montagna provenzale dalla stessa angolazione: molto più grande della realtà, domina la pianura del fiume Arc, un paesaggio costituito da macchie di colore. Non vi sono case né arbusti o esseri umani, bensì solo la distribuzione uniforme dei colori che crea una fitta rete di riferimenti colorati e formali in cui il soggetto principale è aumentato come attraverso una lente.

Cézanne schilderde zijn Provençaalse 'huisberg' keer op keer, vanuit hetzelfde perspectief: veel groter dan normaal en oprijzend boven de vlakte van Arc overheerst hij een landschap van kleurvlakken. Er zijn geen huizen, struiken en al helemaal geen mensen te zien. De gelijkmatig opgebrachte kleurvlakken creëren een dicht netwerk van kleurige en formele verbanden, waarbinnen het eigenlijke onderwerp als facetten van een kristal zijn opgelost.

Paul Cézanne (1839–1906)
The Mountain Sainte–Victoire viewed from Lauves
La monte Sainte-Victoire vue des Lauves
Der Berg Sainte-Victoire, von Lauves aus gesehen
Monte Sainte-Victoire, visto desde Lauves
La monta Sainte-Victoire vista da Lauves
De berg Sainte-Victoire, gezien vanuit Lauves
1904–06, Oil on canvas/Huile sur toile, 59,9 × 72,2 cm, Kunstmuseum, Basel

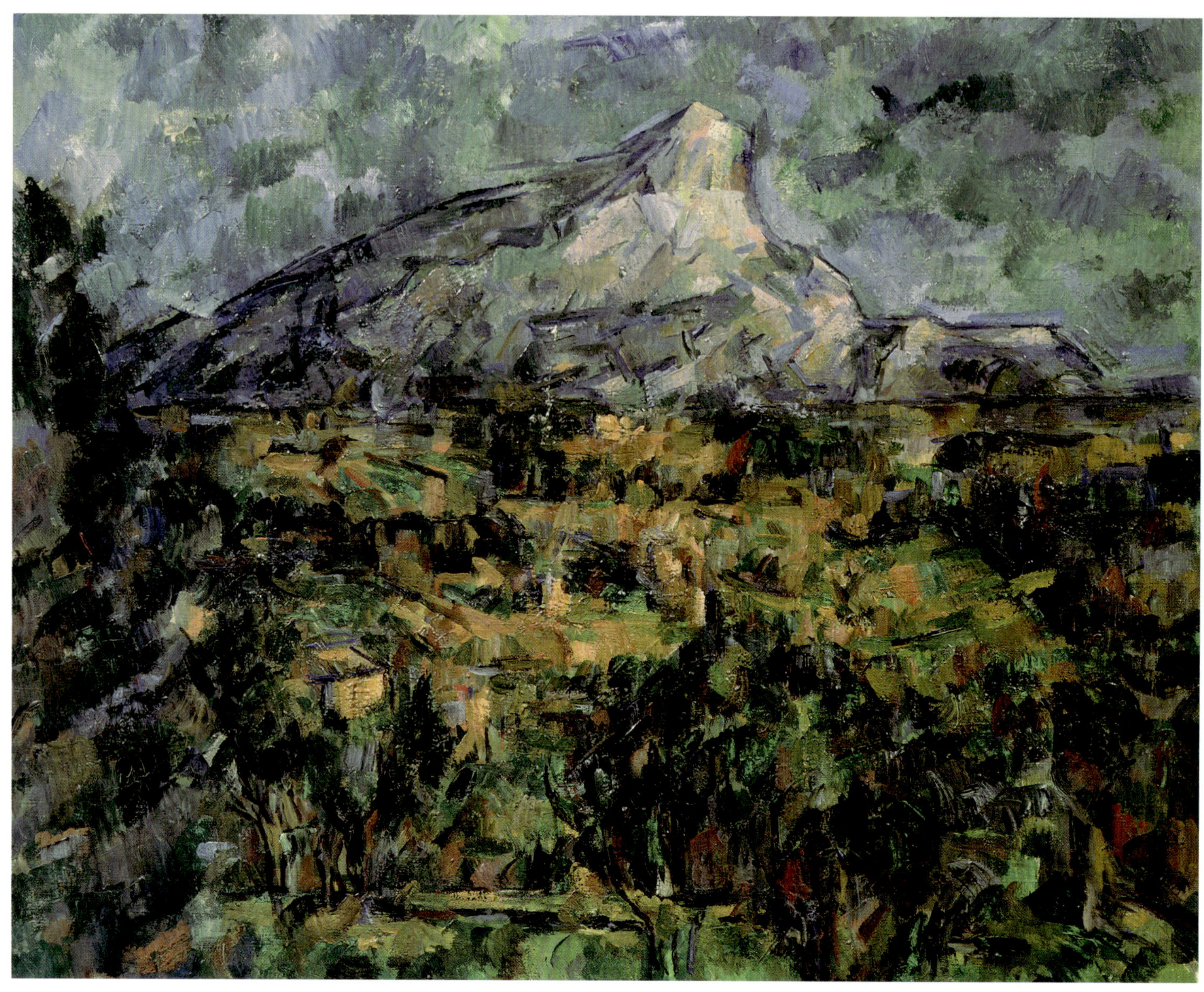

Paul Cézanne (1839–1906)

Montagne Sainte-Victoire

La Montagne Sainte-Victoire, vue des Lauves

Montagne Sainte-Victoire, von Les Lauves aus gesehen

Montaña Sainte-Victoire, vista desde Les Lauves

Monte Sainte-Victoire visto da Les Lauves

De Montagne Sainte-Victoire gezien vanuit Les Lauves

c. 1906, Oil on canvas/Huile sur toile, 60 × 73 cm, Pushkin State Museum of Fine Arts, Moscow

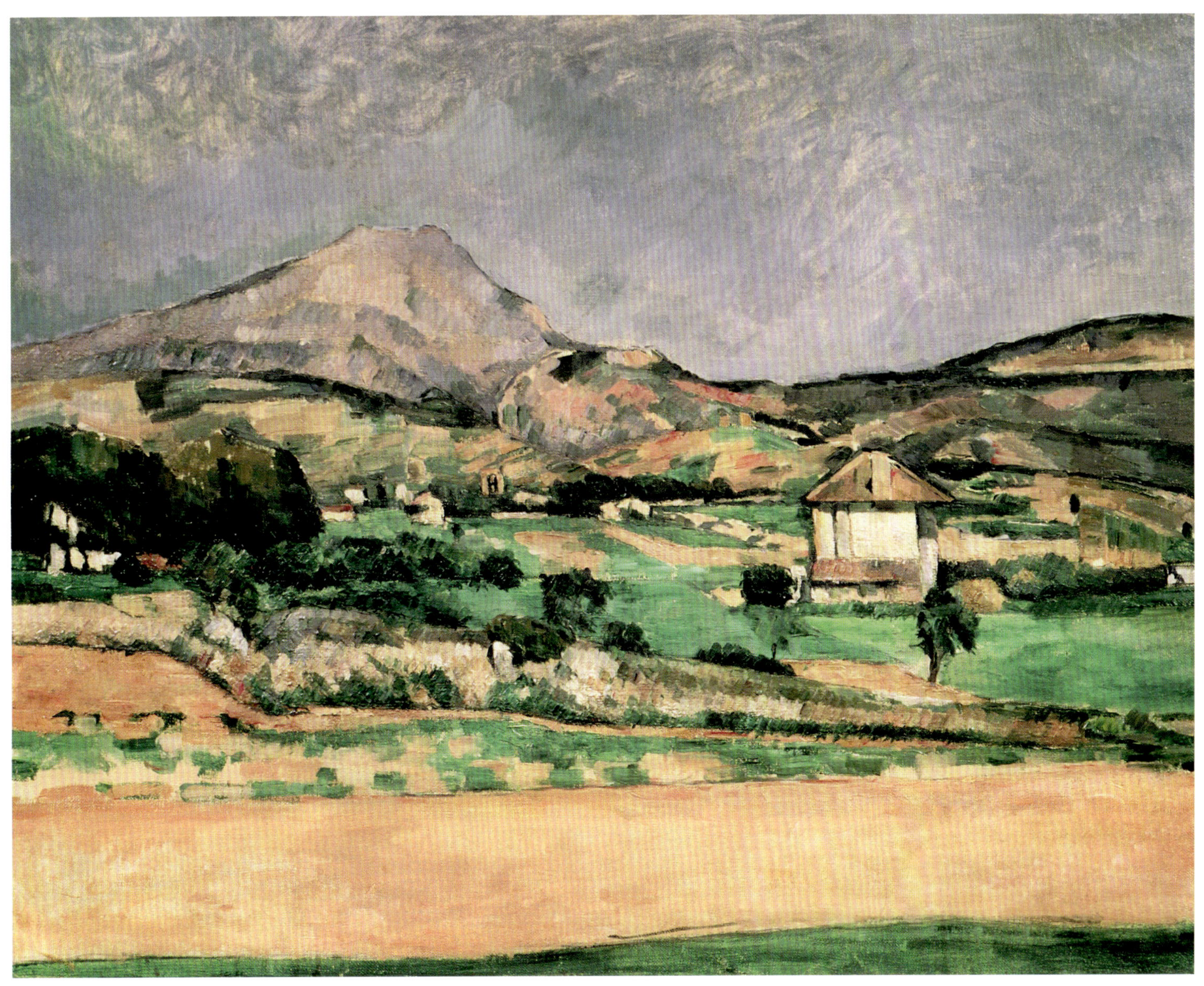

Paul Cézanne (1839–1906)

The Plain by Mont Sainte-Victoire, View from Valcros

La Montagne Sainte-Victoire vue du chemin de Valcros

Der Berg Sainte-Victoire, Blick von Valcros

Montaña Sainte-Victoire, vista desde Valcros

Monte Sainte-Victoire visto da Valcros

De Montagne Sainte-Victoire gezien vanuit Valcros

1882–85, Oil on canvas/Huile sur toile, 58 × 72 cm, Pushkin State Museum of Fine Arts, Moscow

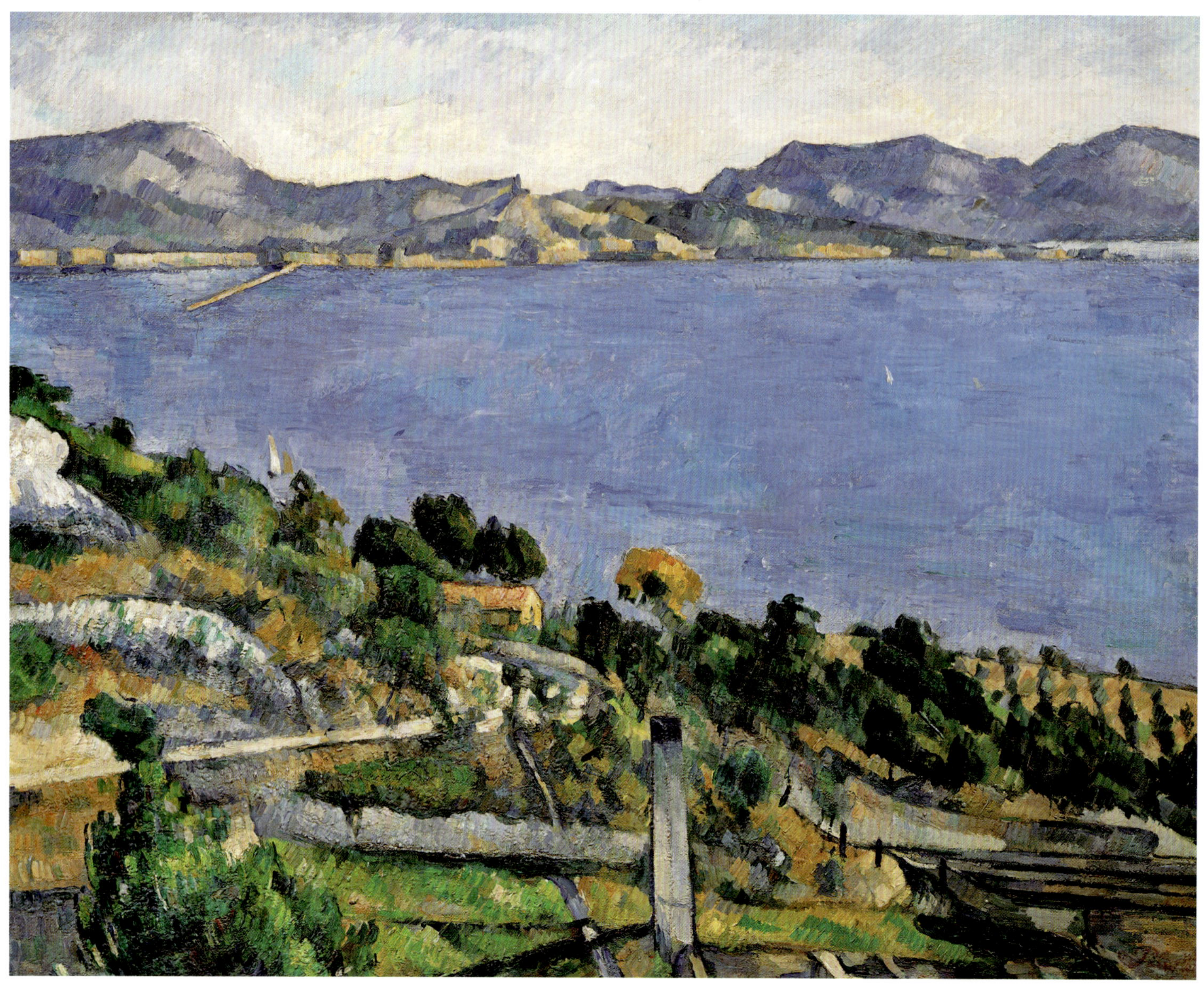

Paul Cézanne (1839–1906)

L'Estaque, View of the Bay of Marseilles

Le golfe de Marseille vu de l'Estaque

L'Estaque mit Blick auf die Bucht von Marseille

L'Estaque, vistas a la bahía de Marsella

Il golfo di Marsiglia visto dall'Estaque

L'Estaque met geizcht op de Baai van Marseille

c. 1878/79, Oil on canvas/Huile sur toile, 59,5 × 73 cm, Musée d'Orsay, Paris

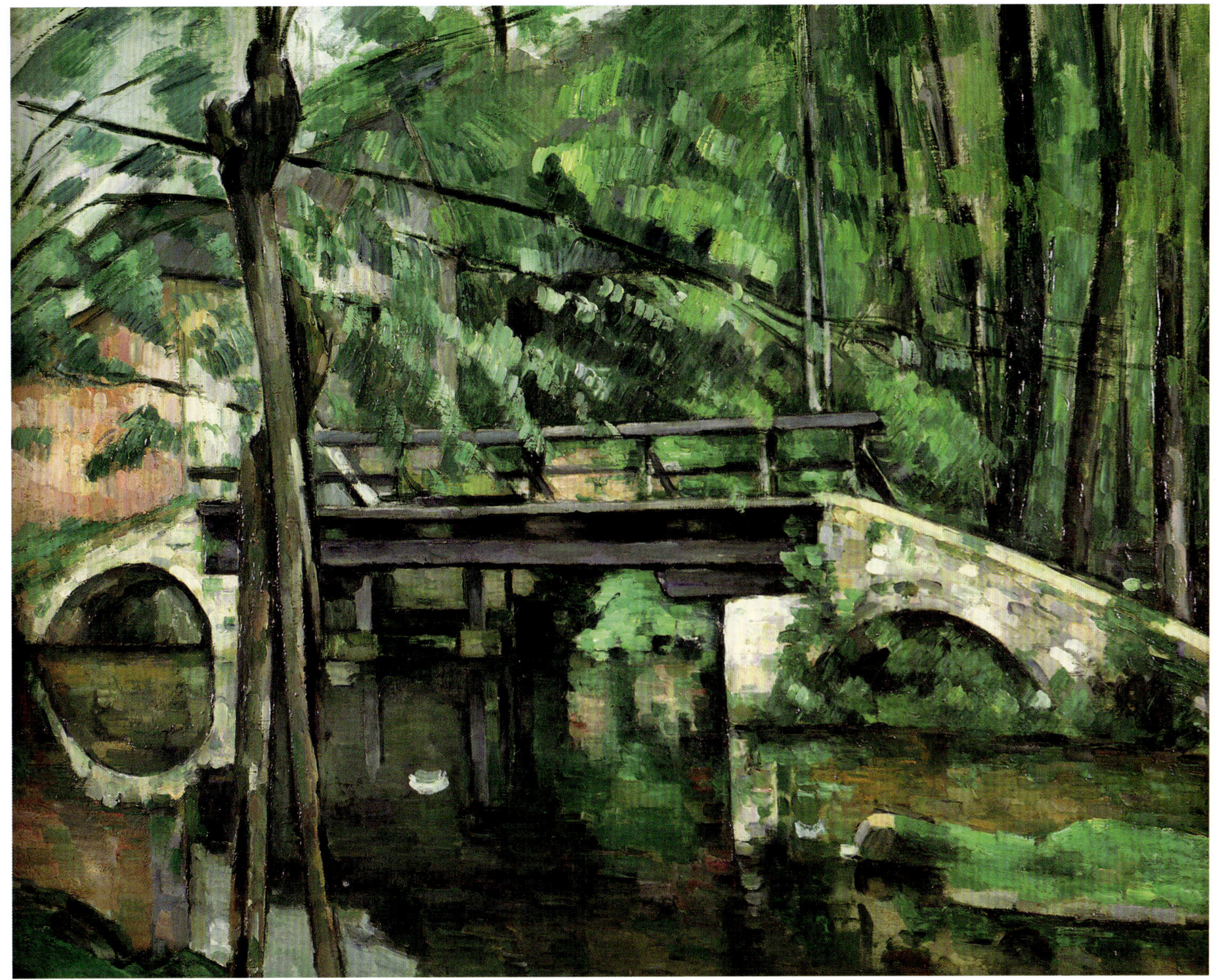

Paul Cézanne (1839–1906)

The Bridge at Maincy, or The Bridge at Mennecy, or The Little Bridge

Pont de Maincy

Die Brücke von Maincy

El puente de Maincy

Il ponte di Maincy

De brug van Maincy

c. 1879, Oil on canvas/Huile sur toile, 58,4 × 72,4 cm, Musée d'Orsay, Paris

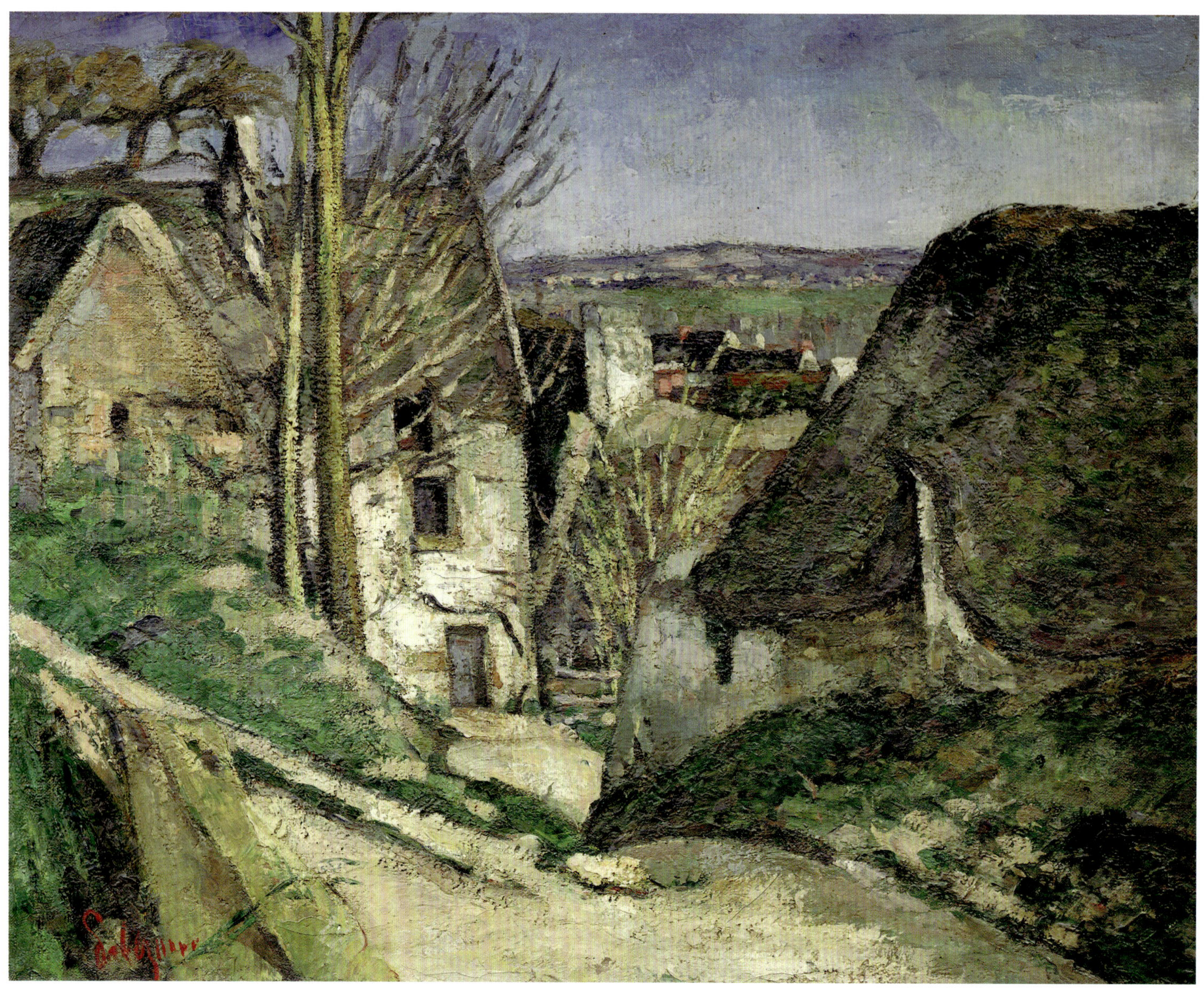

Paul Cézanne (1839–1906)

The House of the Hanged Man, Auvers–sur–Oise

La maison du pendu

Das Haus des Gehängten, Auvers-sur-Oise

La casa del ahorcado

La casa dell'impiccato

Het huis van de gehangene

1873, Oil on canvas/Huile sur toile, 55,5 × 663 cm, Musée d'Orsay, Paris

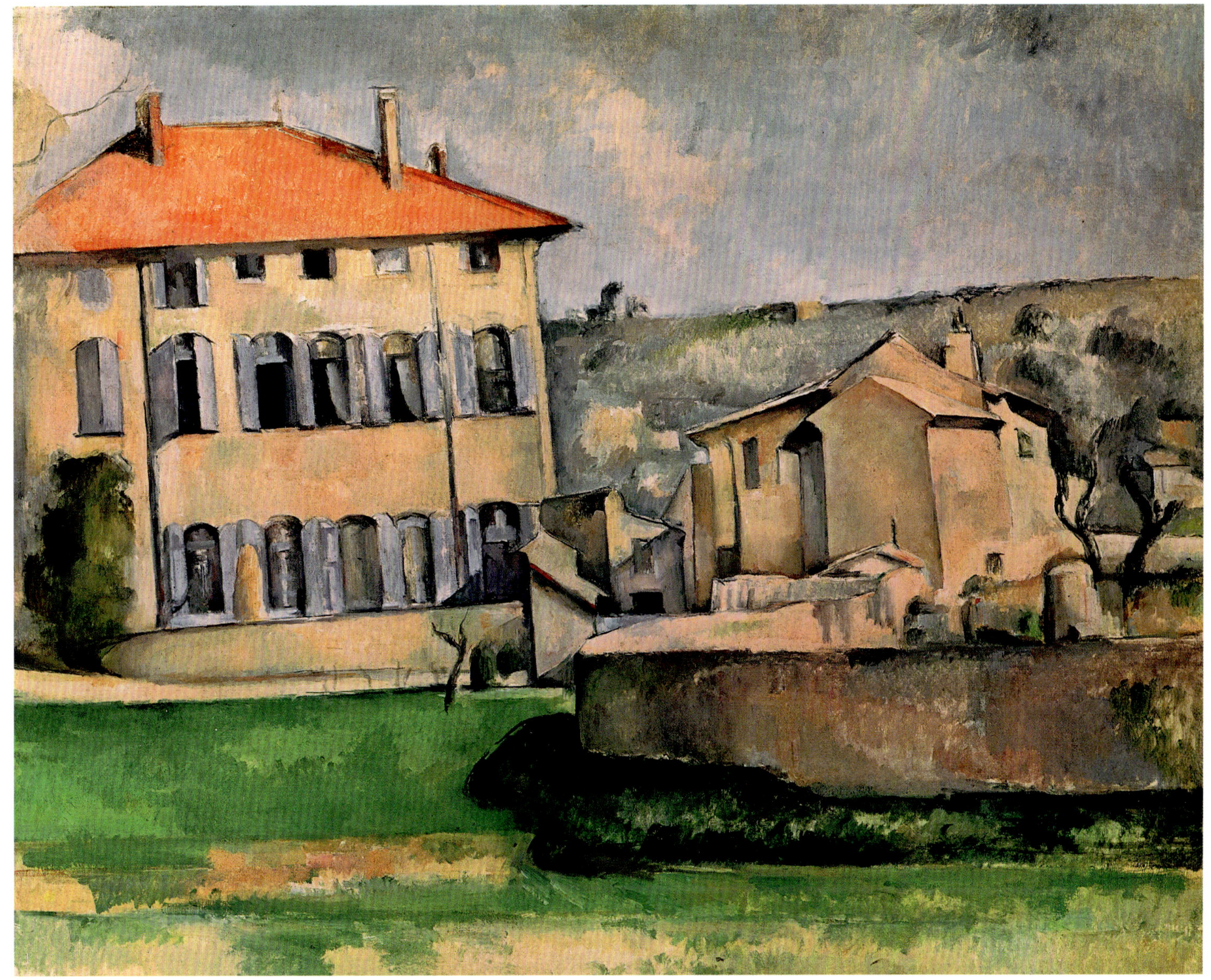

Paul Cézanne (1839–1906)

Jas de Bouffan

Le Jas de Bouffan

Der Jas de Bouffan

El Jas de Bouffan

Jas de Bouffan

De Jas de Bouffan

1885– 87, Oil on canvas/Huile sur toile, 60,8 × 73,8 cm, Narodni Gallery, Prague

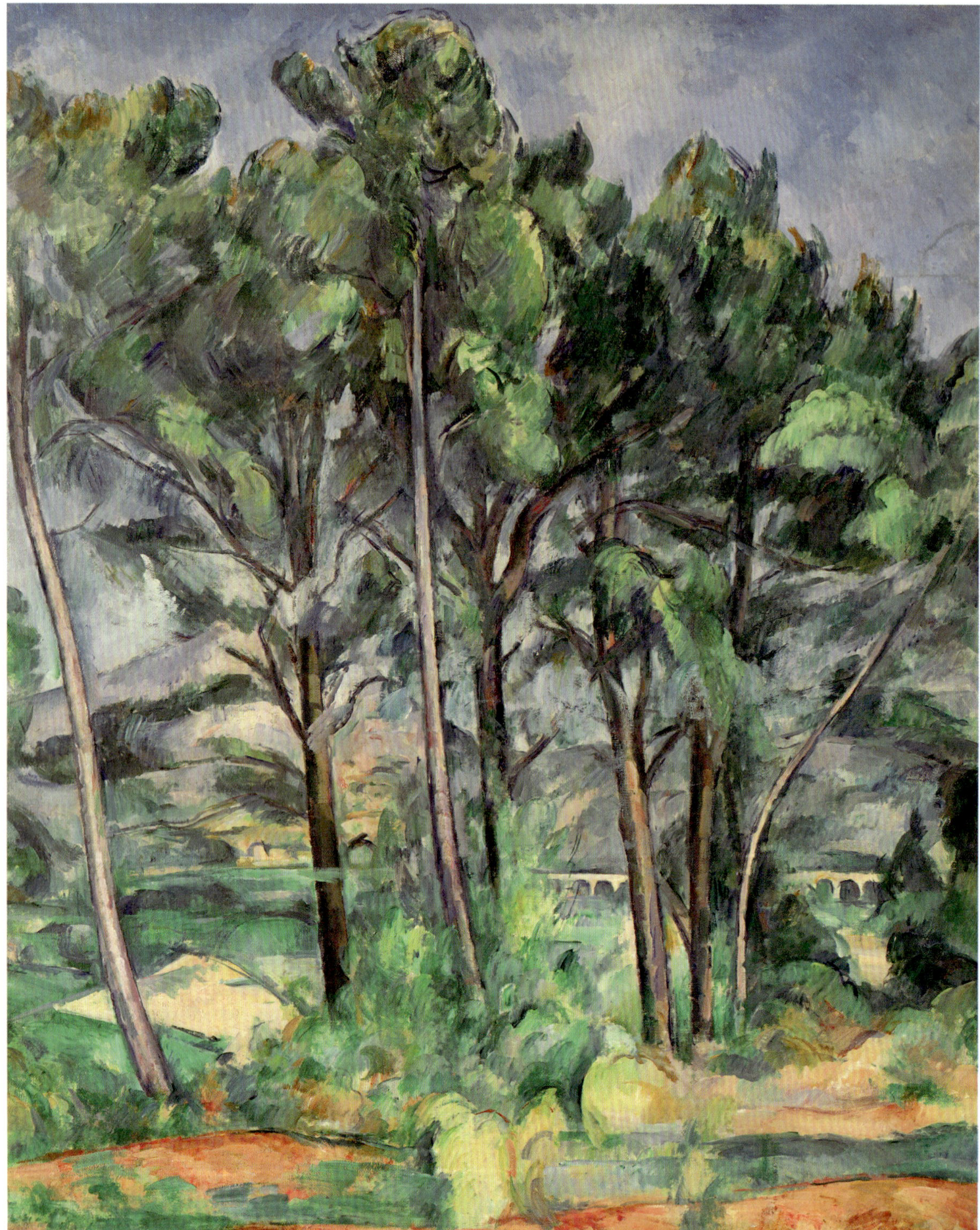

Paul Cézanne (1839–1906)

The Aqueduct (Monte Sainte-Victoire
seen through Trees)

L'aqueduc. La monte Ste-Victoire
vue à travers les arbres

Der Aquädukt. Monte Sainte-Victoire
durch Bäume gesehen

El acueducto. Monte Sainte-Victoire
visto desde los árboles

L'acquedotto. La monta Sainte-Victoire
vista attraverso gli alberi

Het aquaduct. Gezicht door de bomen
op de berg Sainte-Victoire

1900, Oil on canvas/Huile sur toile, 91 × 72 cm, Pushkin State Museum of Fine Arts, Moscow

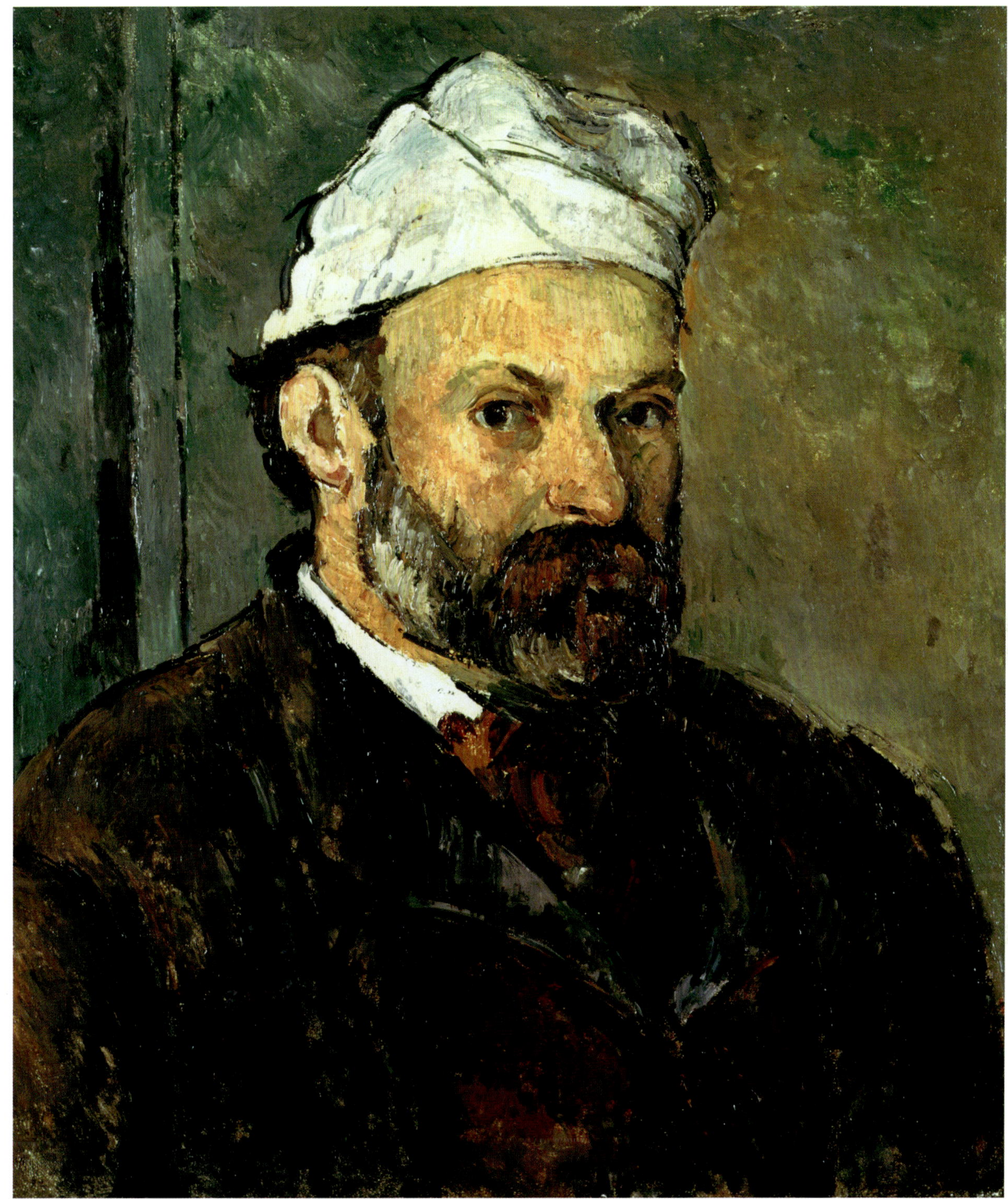

Paul Cézanne (1839–1906)

Self portrait Selbstporträt mit weißem Turban Autoritratto

Autoportrait Autorretrato Zelfportret

1881/82, Oil on canvas/Huile sur toile, 55,5 × 46 cm, Neue Pinakothek, München

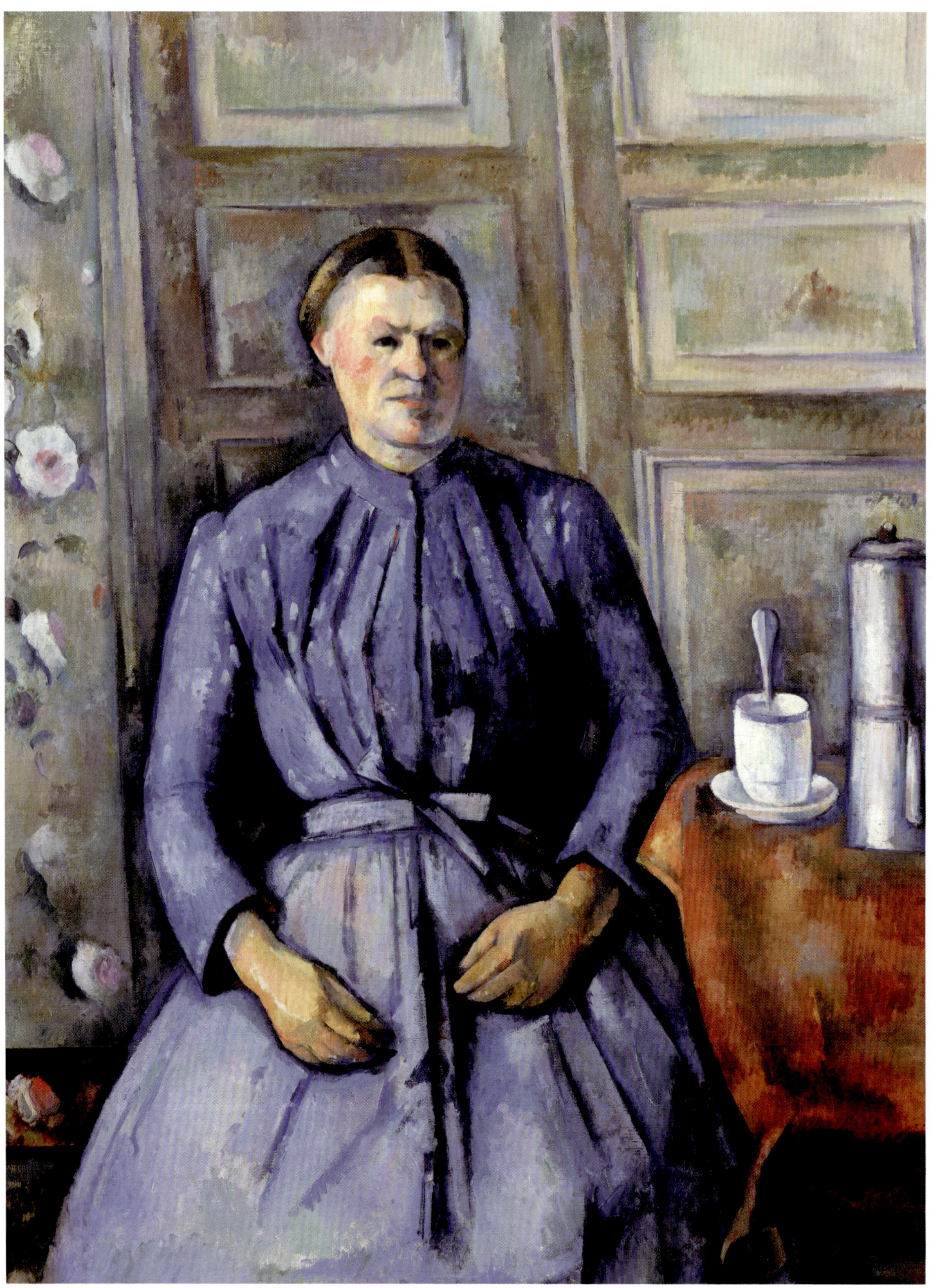

Paul Cézanne (1839–1906)

Woman with a Coffee Pot

La femme à la cafetière

Frau mit Kaffeekanne

Mujer con cafetera

Donna con caffettiera

Vrouw met koffiekan

1890–95, Oil on canvas/
Huile sur toile, 130 × 97 cm,
Musée d'Orsay, Paris

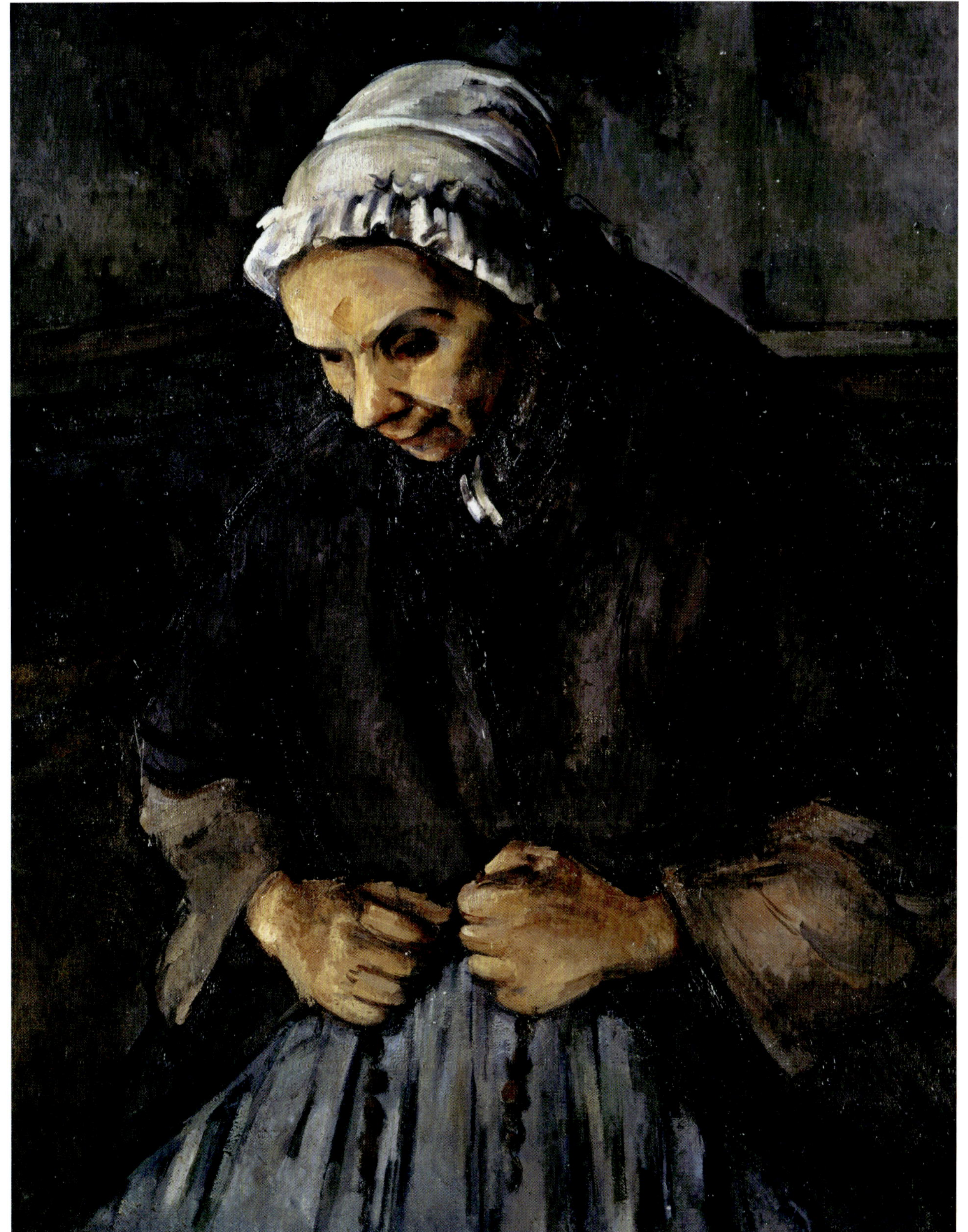

Paul Cézanne
(1839–1906)

Old Woman
with a Rosary

Vieille femme
au rosaire

Alte Frau mit
Rosenkranz

Anciana con rosario

Vecchia con rosario

Oude vrouw met
rozenkrans

c. 1895/96, Oil on
canvas/Huile sur
toile, 80,6 × 65,5 cm,
National Gallery,
London

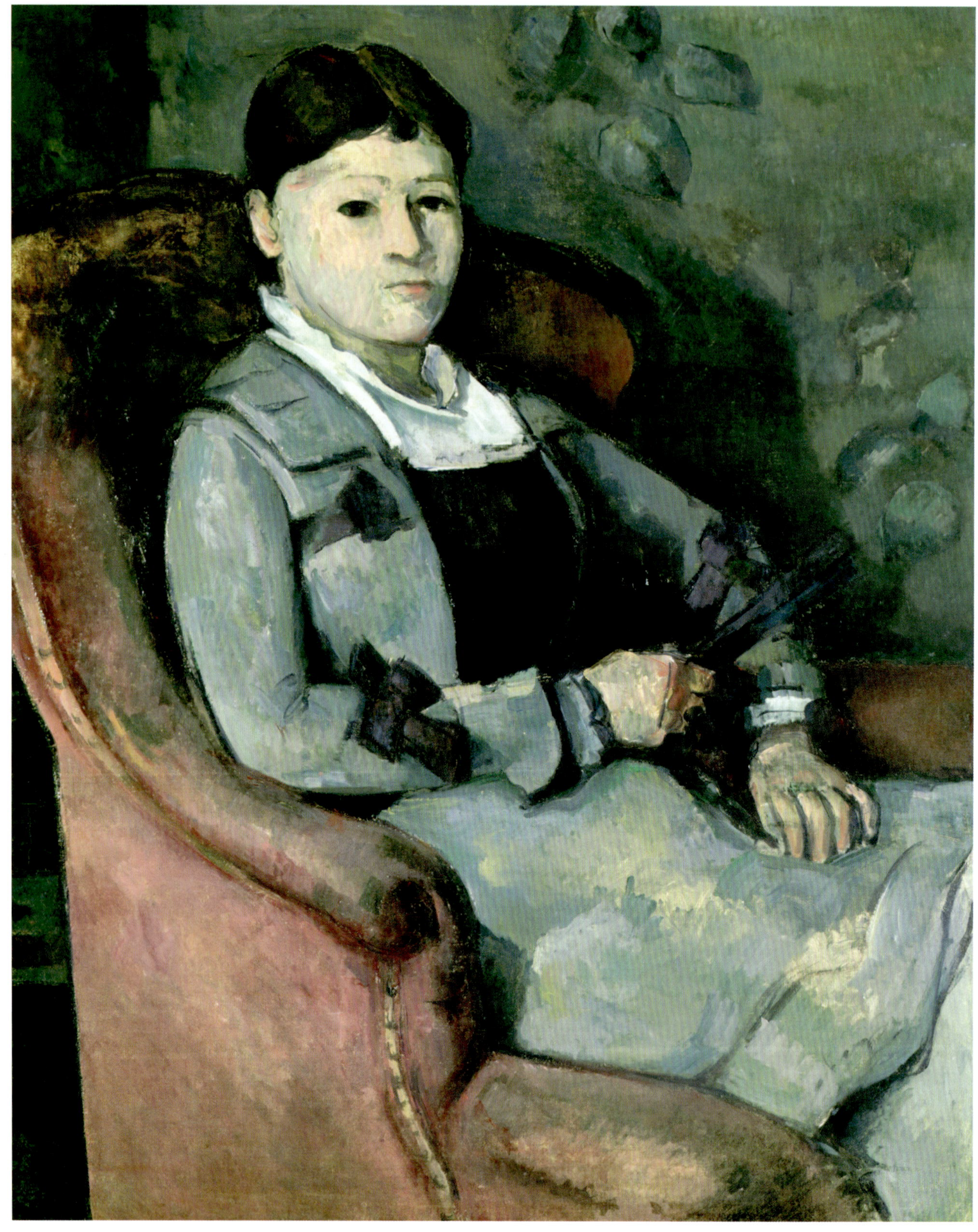

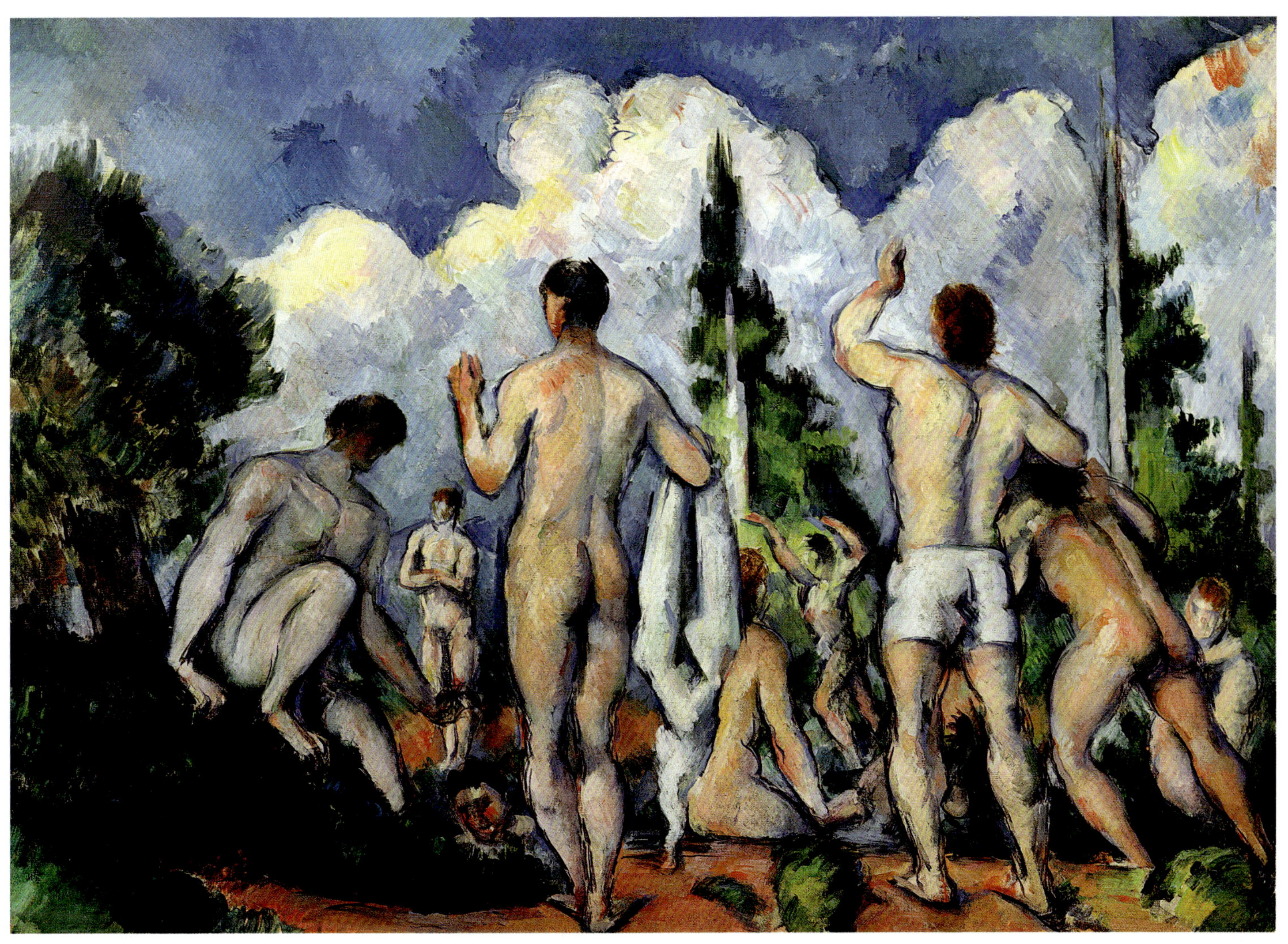

Paul Cézanne (1839–1906)

The Artist's Wife in an Armchair

La Femme de l'artiste dans un fauteuil

Die Frau des Künstlers im Lehnstuhl

La mujer del artista en un sillón

La moglie dell'artista seduta in poltrona

De vrouw van de kunstenaar in een leunstoel

c. 1881/82, Oil on canvas/Huile sur toile, 92,5 × 73,5 cm, Stiftung Sammlung E. G. Bührle, Zürich

Paul Cézanne (1839–1906)

The Bathers

Baigneurs

Die Badenden

Las bañistas

Banti

De baders

c. 1890, Oil on canvas/Huile sur toile, 60,5 × 82,5 cm, Musée d'Orsay, Paris

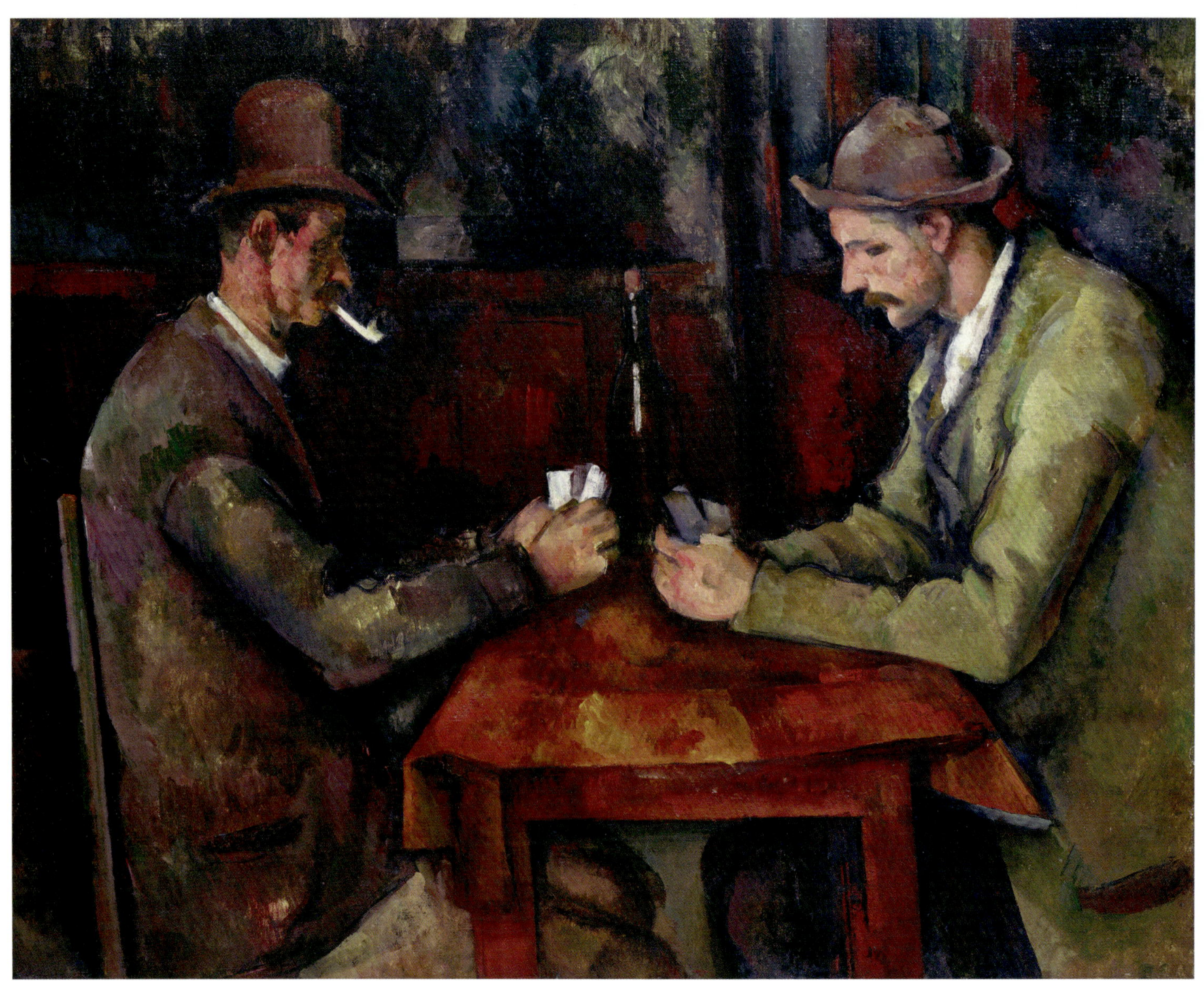

Paul Cézanne (1839–1906)

The Card Players

Les joueurs de cartes

Die Kartenspieler

Los jugadores de cartas

I giocatori di carte

De kaartspelers

1890–95, Oil on canvas/Huile sur toile, 47 × 56,5 cm, Musée d'Orsay, Paris

Paul Cézanne (1839–1906)

The Smoker

Le fumeur

Der Raucher

El fumador

Fumatore di pipa

De roker

c. 1890–92, Oil on canvas/Huile sur toile, 92,5 × 73,5 cm, State Hermitage, St. Petersburg

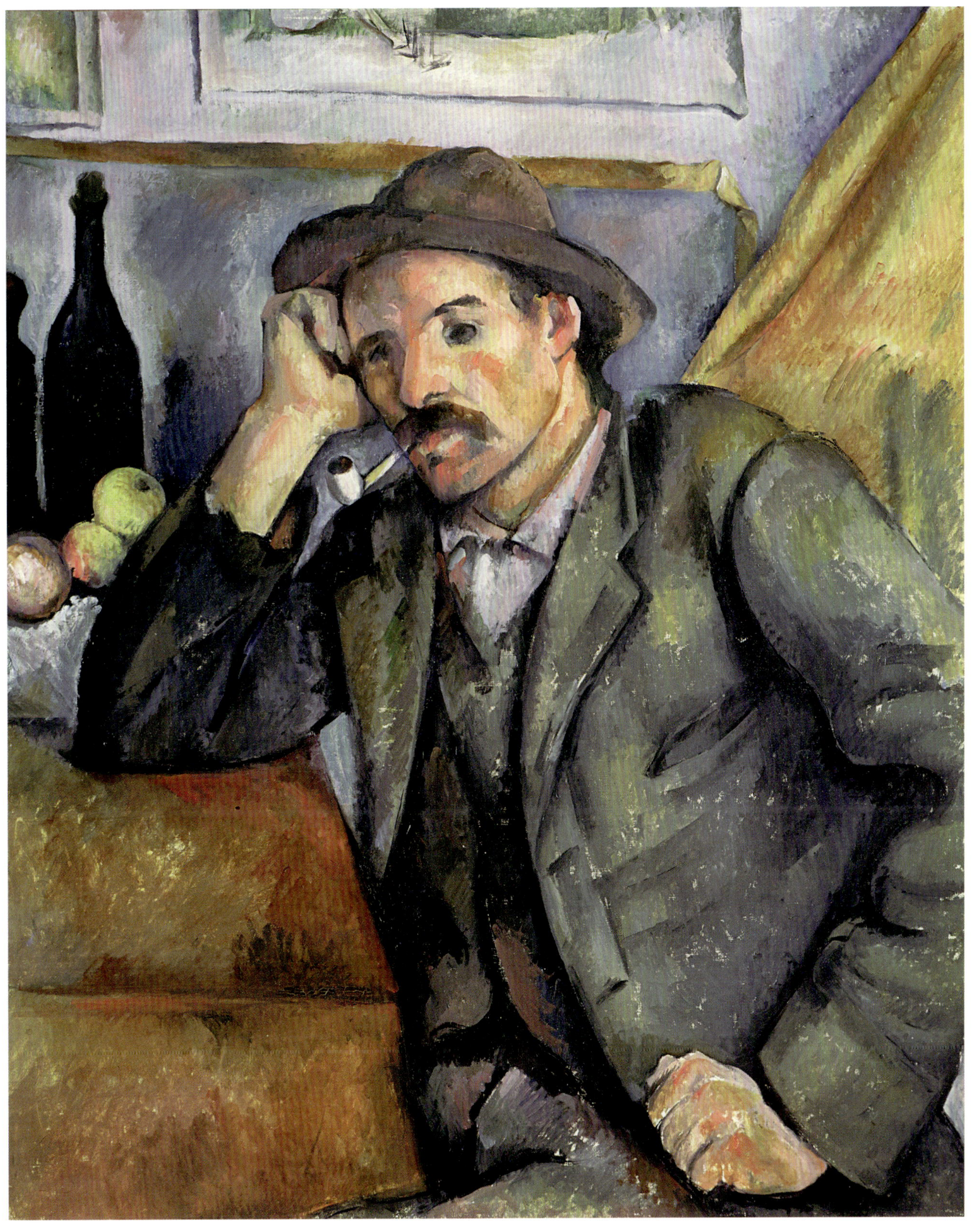

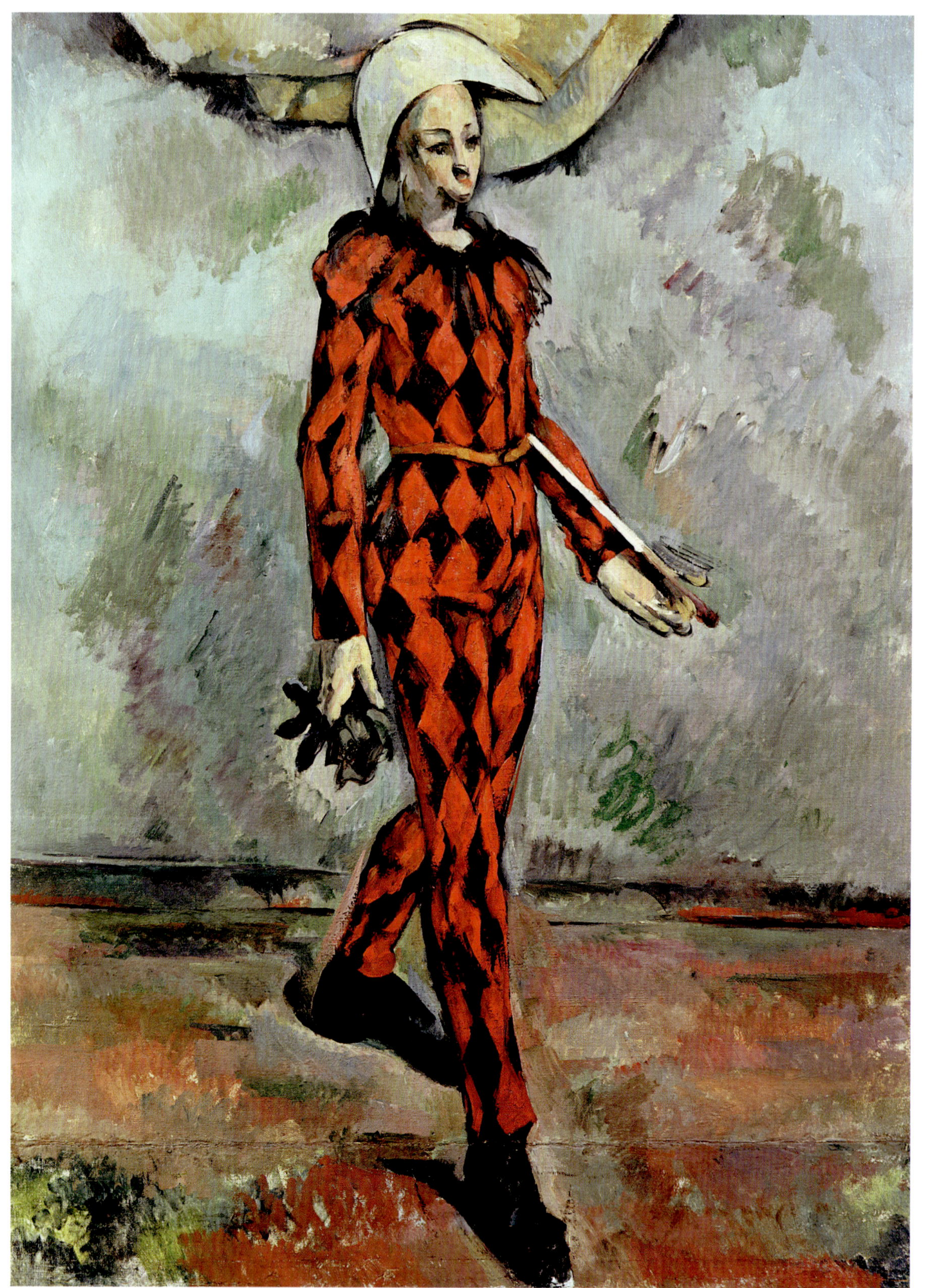

Paul Cézanne (1839–1906)
Harlequin
Arlequin
Harlekin
El arlequín
Arlecchino
De harlekijn
1890, Oil on canvas/Huile sur toile,
92 × 65 cm, Private collection

Paul Cézanne (1839–1906)
Pierrot and Harlequin
(Mardi Gras)
Mardi Gras (Pierrot et Arlequin)
Pierrot und Harlekin
Pierrot y Arlequín
Pierrot e Arlecchino
Pierrot en harlekijn
1888, Oil on canvas/Huile sur toile,
102 × 81 cm, The Pushkin State
Museum of Fine Art, Moscow

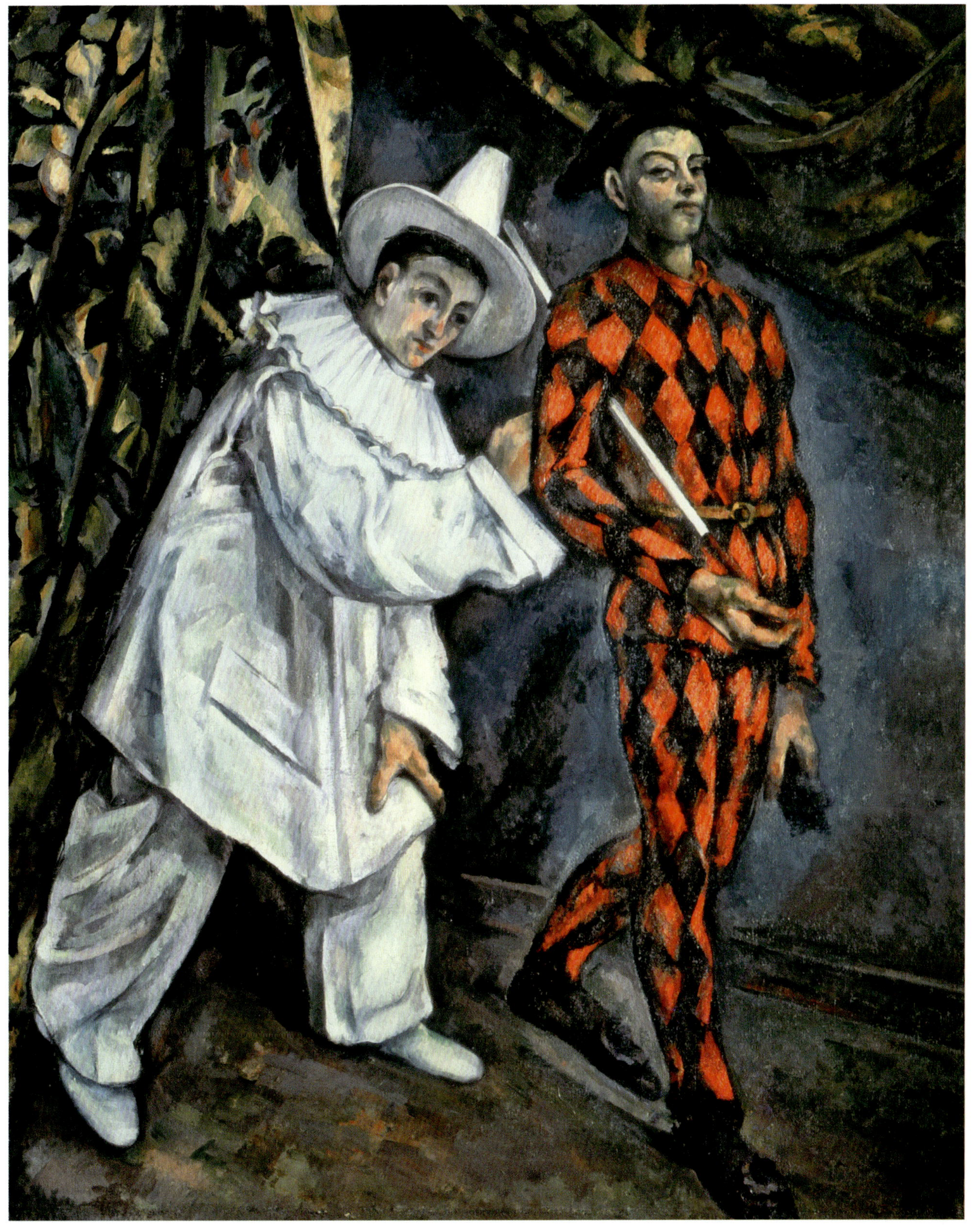

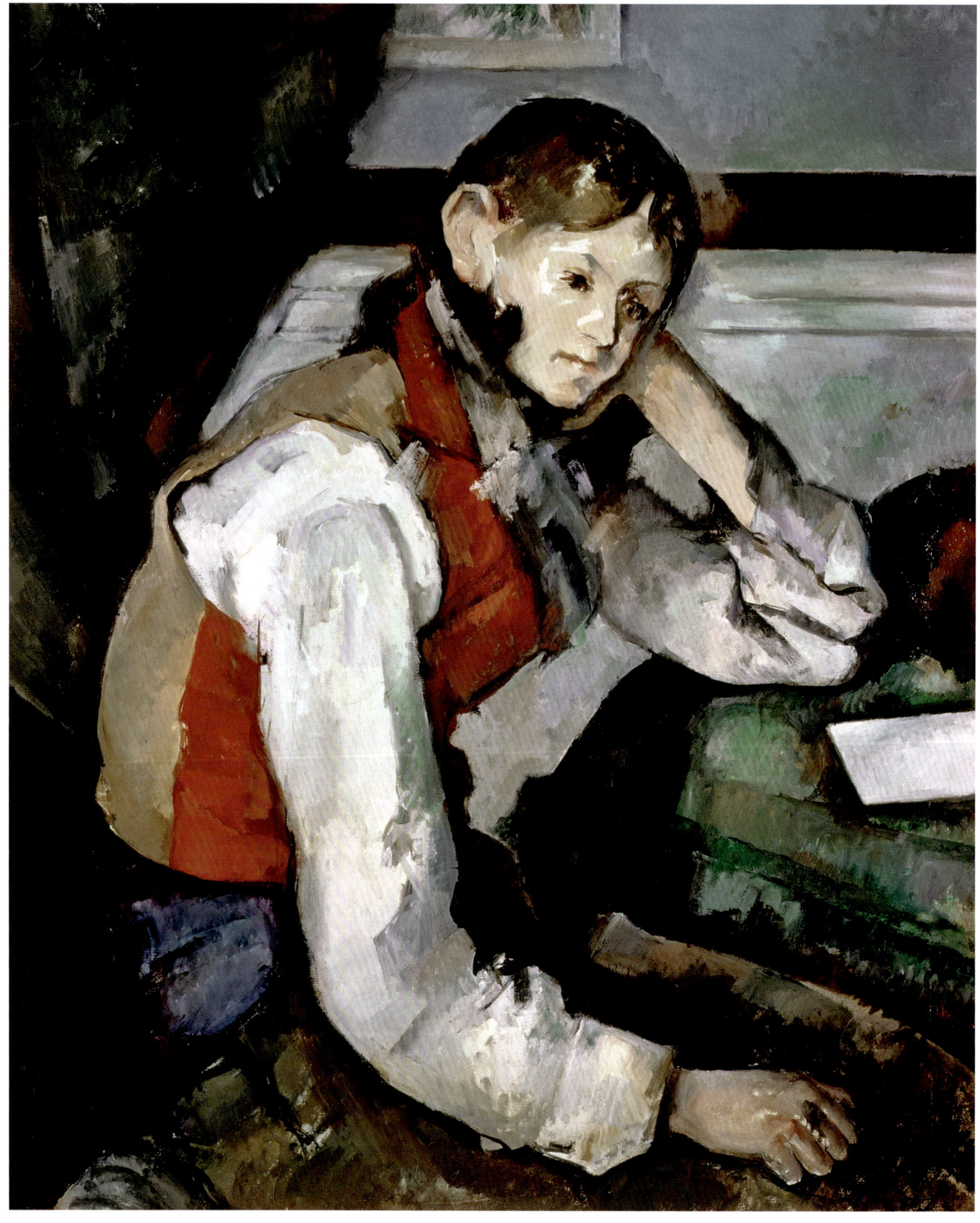

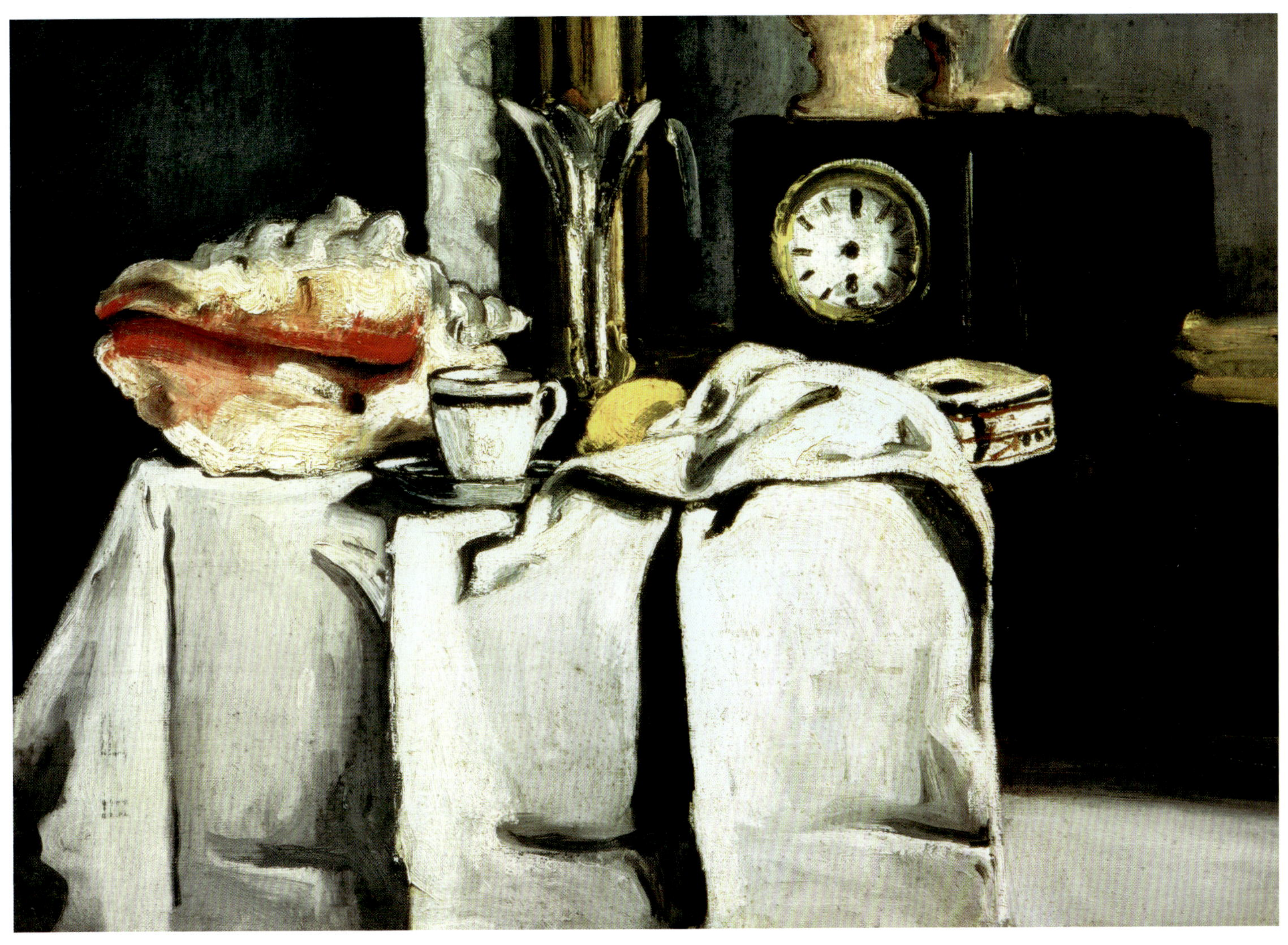

Paul Cézanne (1839–1906)

The Boy in the Red Waistcoat

Le Garçon au gilet rouge

Der Knabe in der roten Weste

El joven del chaleco rojo

Il ragazzo con il panciotto rosso

De knaap in het rode vest

c. 1889/90, Oil on canvas/Huile sur toile, 79,5 × 64 cm, Stiftung Sammlung E. G. Bührle, Zürich

Paul Cézanne (1839–1906)

The Black Marble Clock

La pendule noire

Die schwarze Uhr

El reloj negro

L'orologio in marmo nero

De zwarte klok

c. 1870, Oil on canvas/Huile sur toile, 55,2 × 74,3 cm, Private collection, Paris

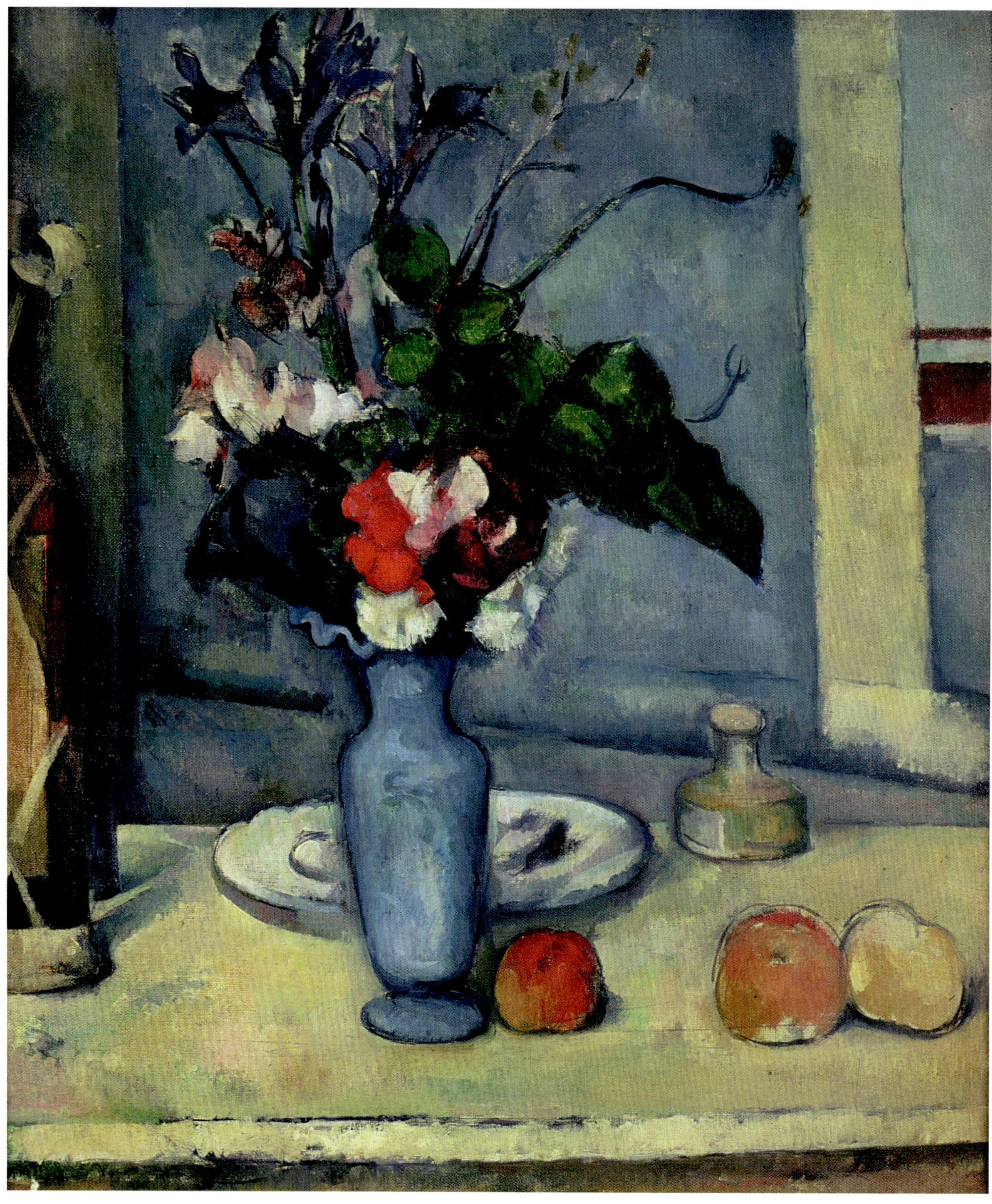

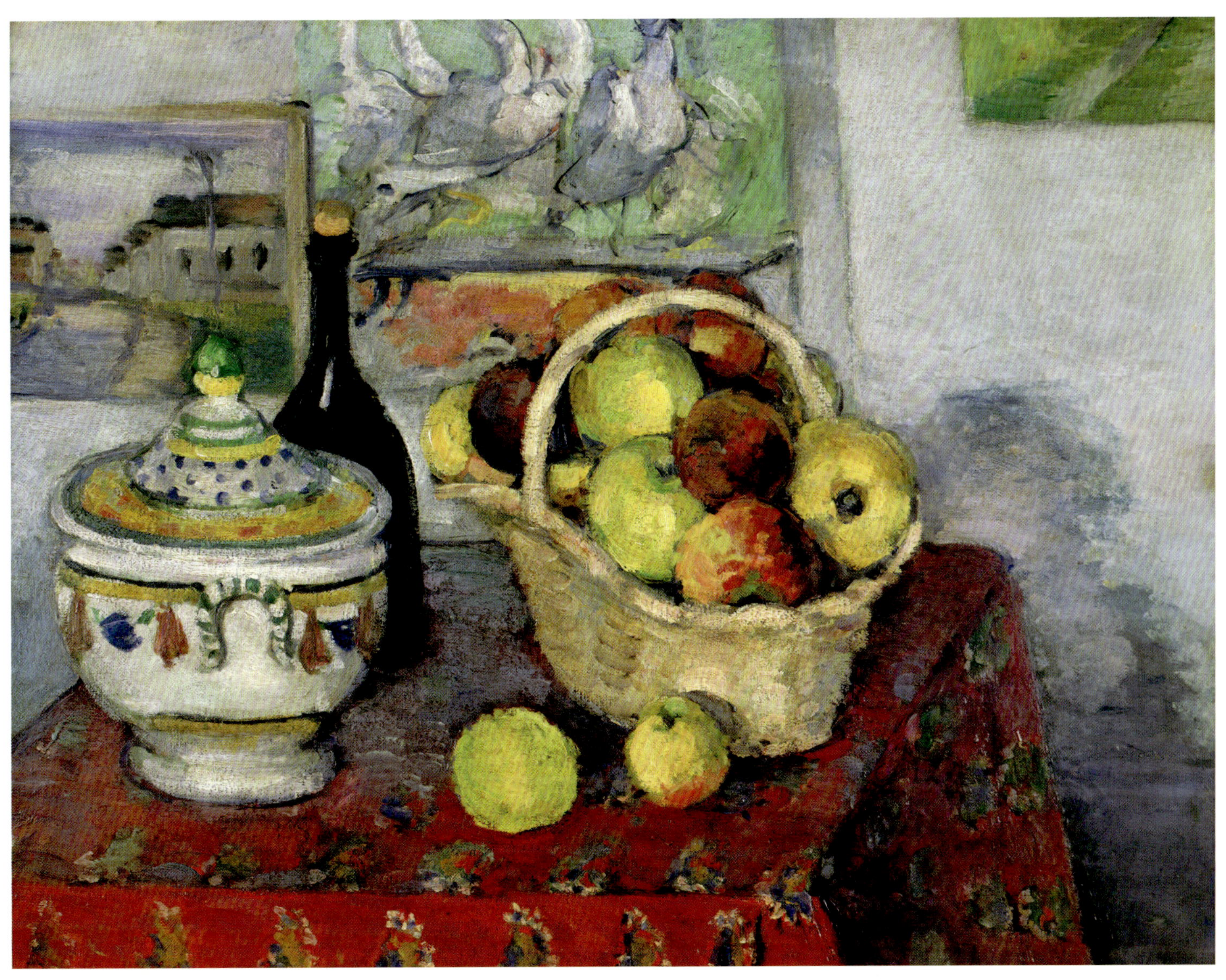

Paul Cézanne (1839–1906)

The Blue Vase

Le vase bleu

Die blaue Vase

El jarrón azul

Il vaso blu

De blauwe vaas

1889/90, Oil on canvas/Huile sur toile, 61,2 × 50 cm, Musée d'Orsay, Paris

Paul Cézanne (1839–1906)

Still Life with Tureen

Nature morte à la soupière

Stillleben mit Suppenterrine

Bodegón con sopera

Natura morta con zuppiera

Stilleven met soepterrine

c. 1877, Oil on canvas/Huile sur toile, 65 × 81,5 cm, Musée d'Orsay, Paris

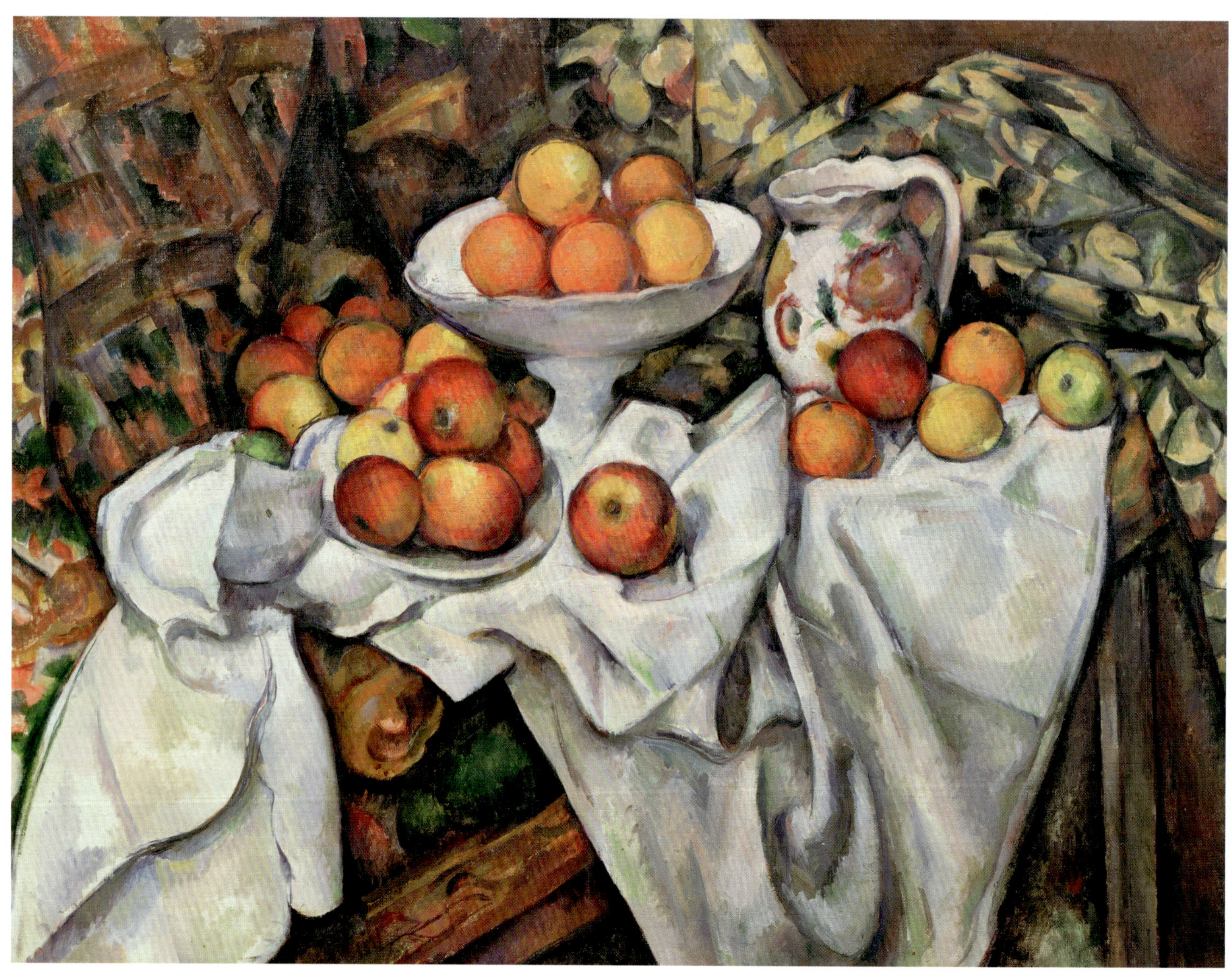

Paul Cézanne (1839–1906)

Apples and Oranges

Pommes et oranges

Stillleben mit Äpfeln und Orangen

Bodegón con manzanas y naranjas

Natura morta con mele e arance

Stilleven met appels en sinaasappels

c. 1899, Oil on canvas/Huile sur toile, 74 × 93 cm, Musée d'Orsay, Paris

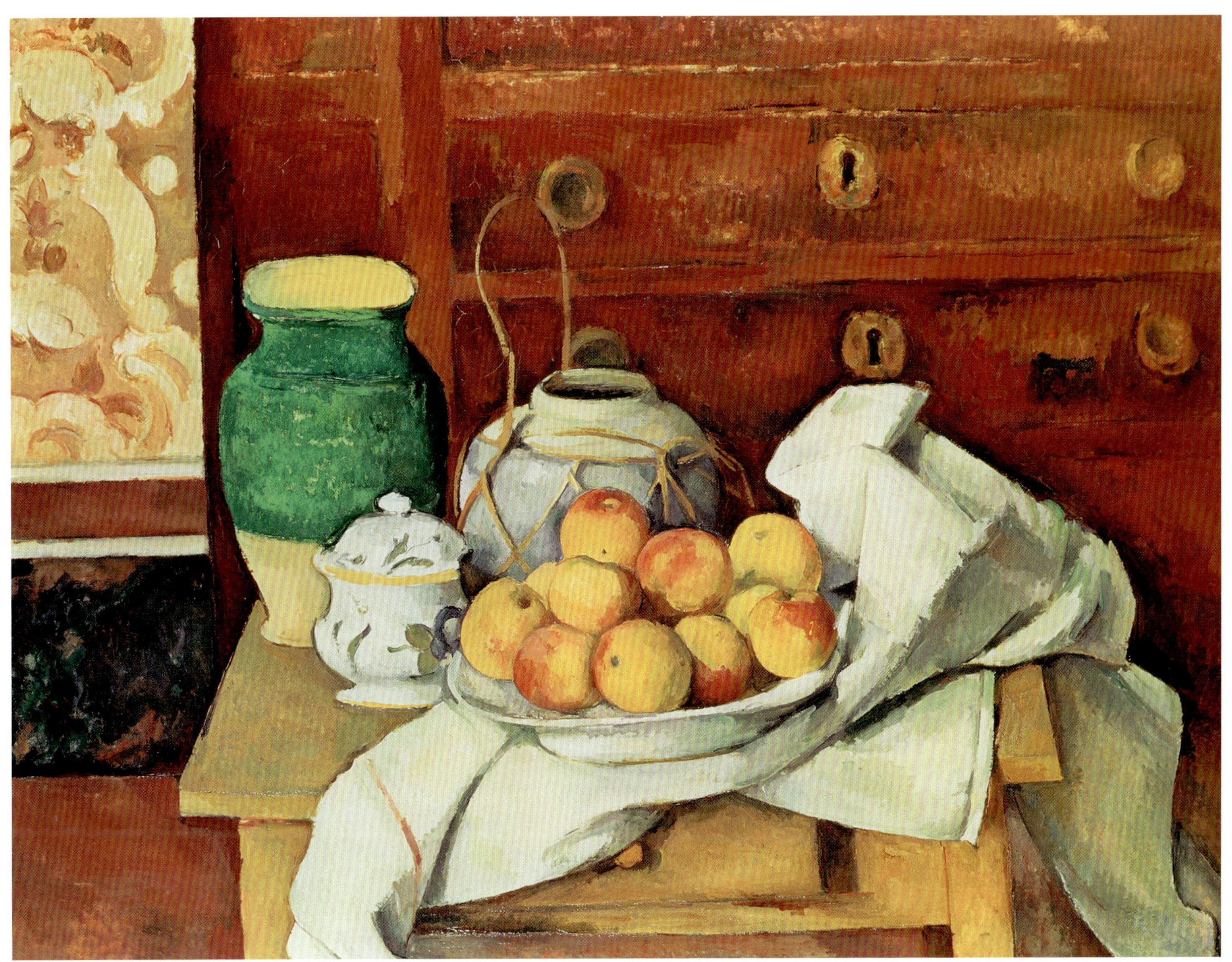

Paul Cézanne (1839–1906)

Still Life with a Chest of Drawers

Nature morte à la commode

Stillleben mit Kommode

Bodegón con cómoda

Natura morta con cassettone

Stilleven met commode

1883–87, Oil on canvas/Huile sur toile, 73,3 × 92,2 cm, Neue Pinakothek, München

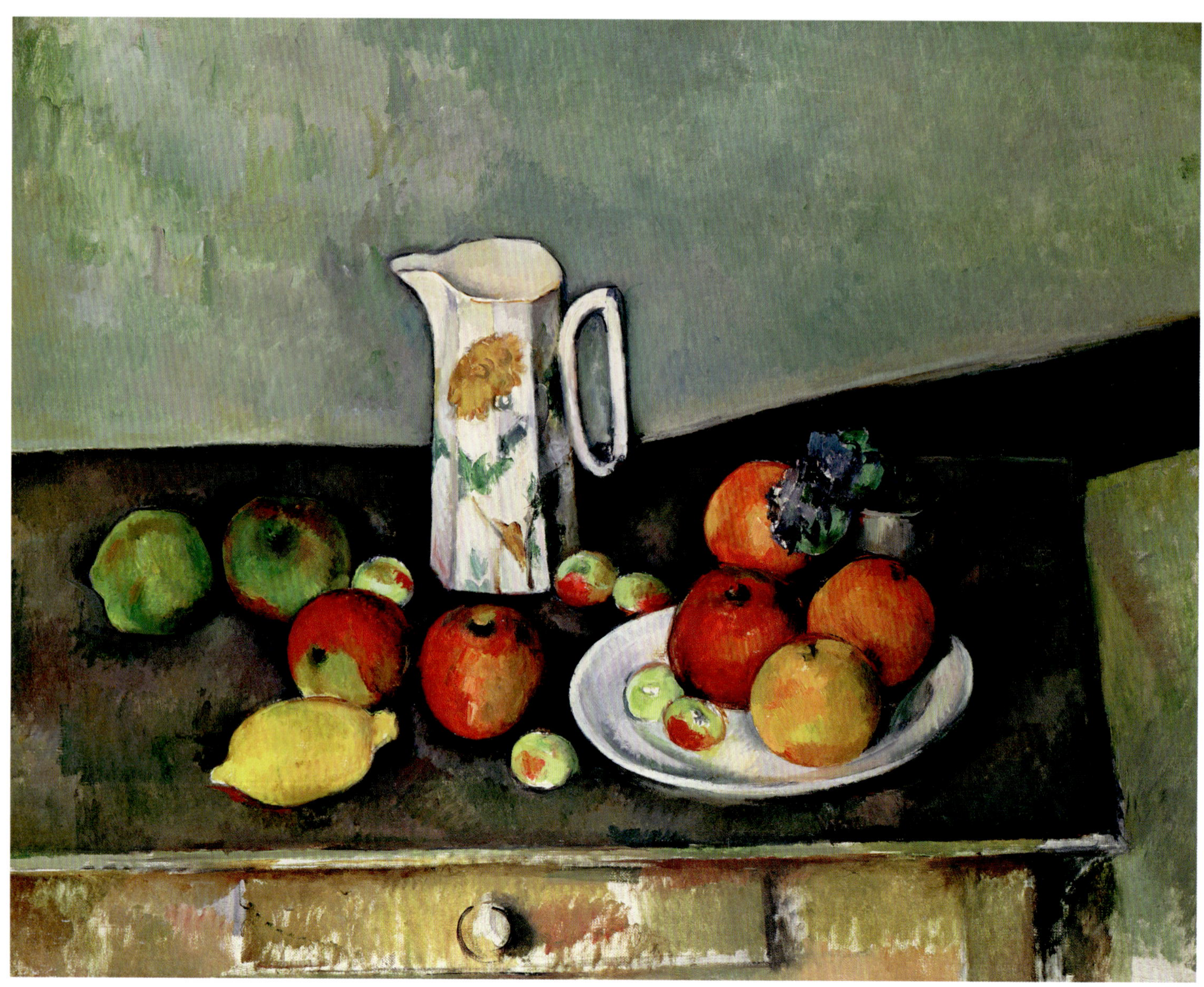

Paul Cézanne (1839–1906)

Still life with milk jug and fruit

Nature morte – Pot à lait et fruits

Stillleben mit Milchkrug und Früchten

Bodegón con jarra de leche y fruta

Natura morta con brocca di latte e frutta

Stilleven met melkkan en vruchten

c. 1890, Oil on canvas/Huile sur toile, 59,5 × 73 cm, Nasjonalmuseet, Oslo

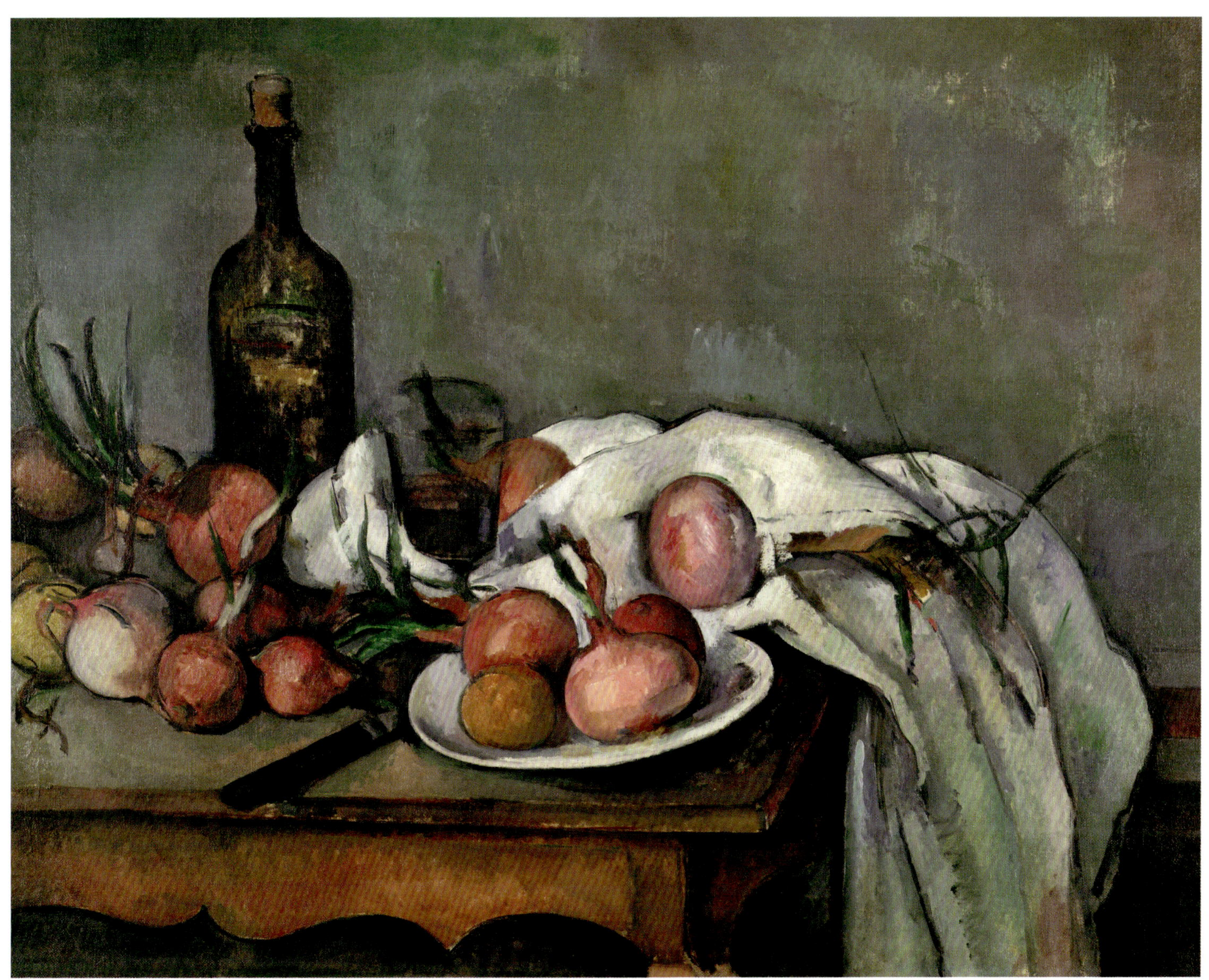

Paul Cézanne (1839–1906)

Still Life with Onions

Nature morte aux oignons

Stillleben mit Zwiebeln

Bodegón con cebollas

Natura morta con cipolle

Stilleven met uien

1896–98, Oil on canvas/Huile sur toile, 66 × 82 cm, Musée d'Orsay, Paris

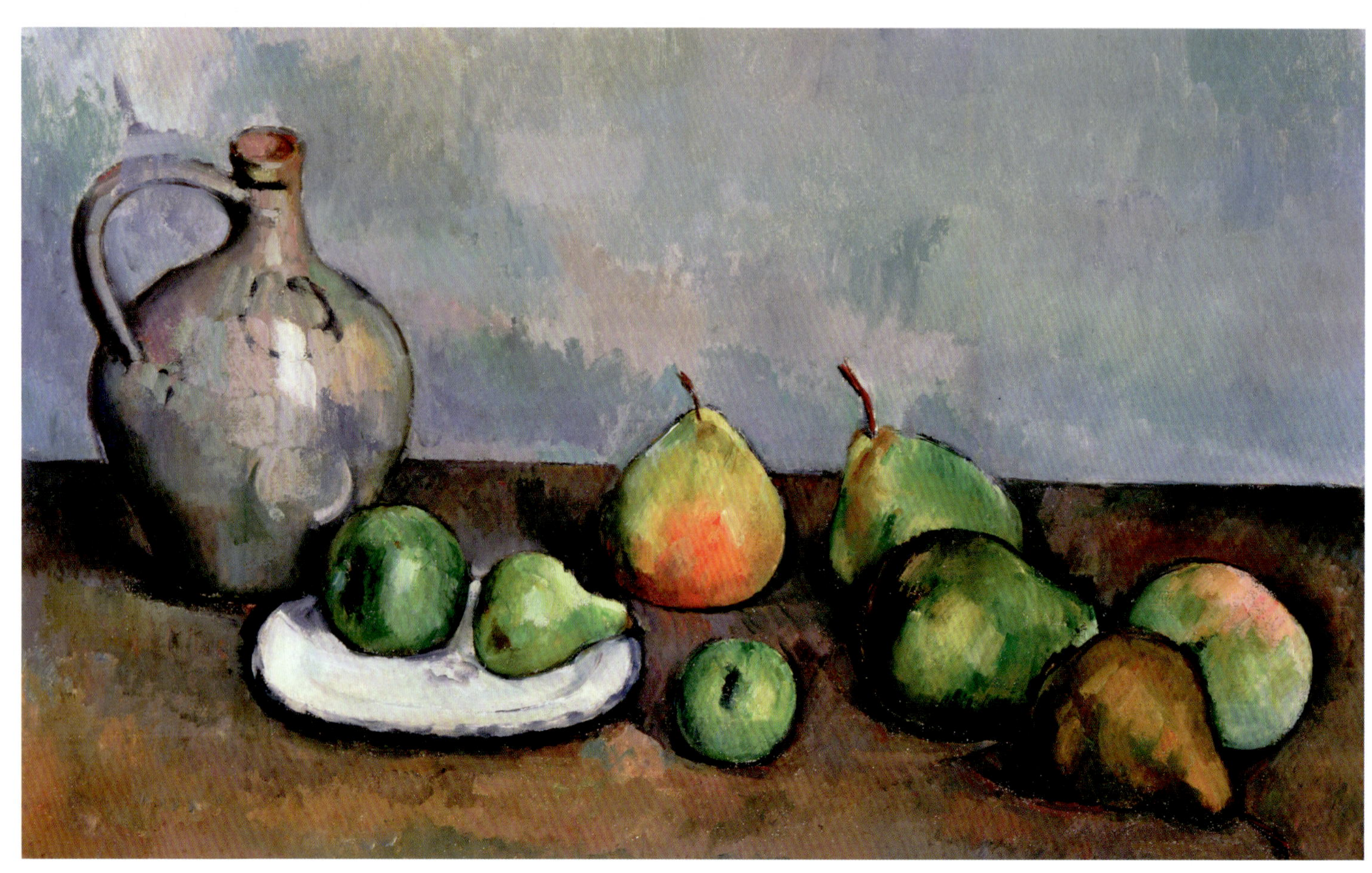

Paul Cézanne (1839–1906)

Still Life with Pitcher and Fruit

Nature morte avec pichet et fruits

Stillleben mit Krug und Früchten

Bodegón con jarra y fruta

Natura morta con brocca e frutta

Stilleven met kruik en vruchten

1893/94, Oil on canvas/Huile sur toile, 43,2 × 62,8 cm, Private collection

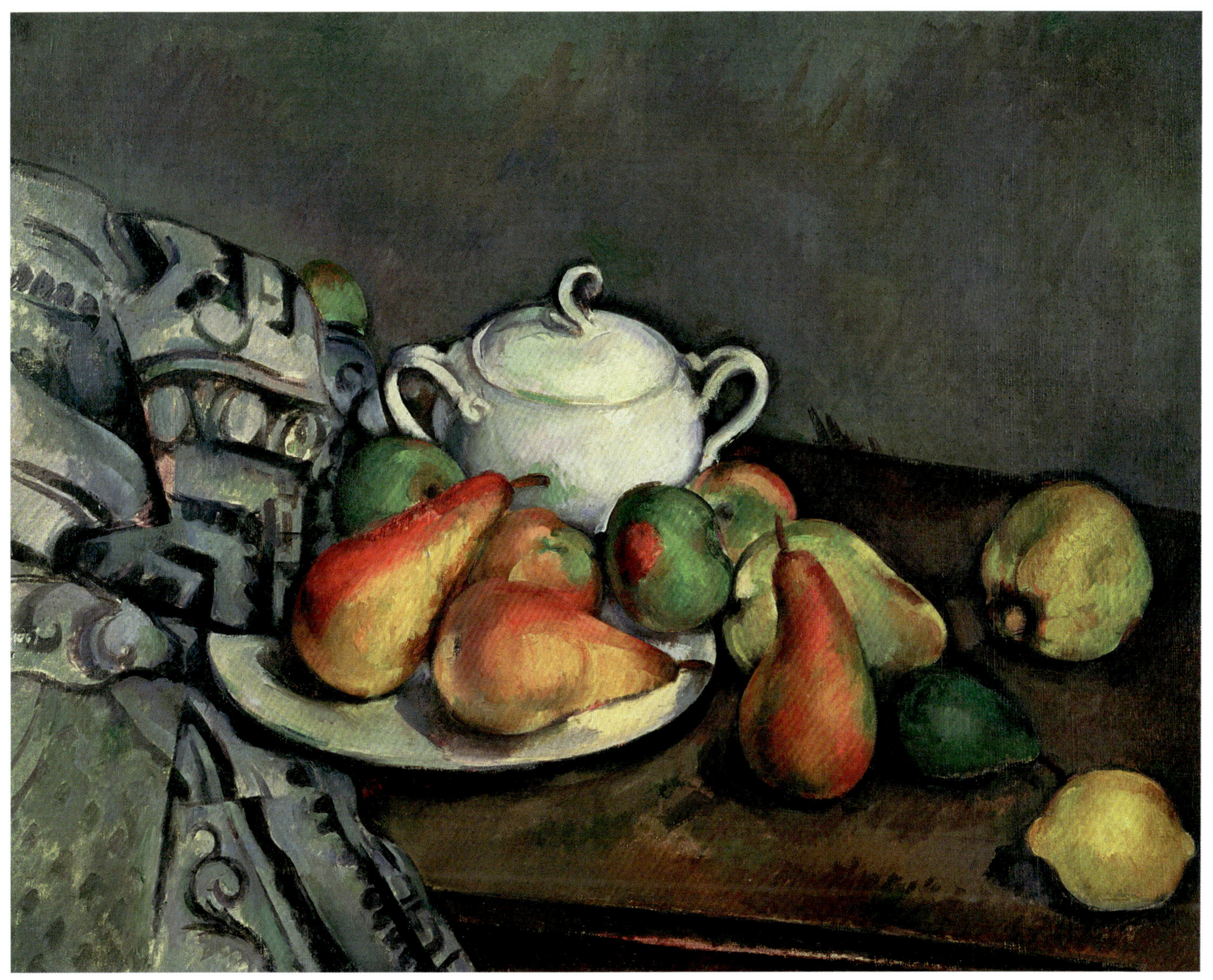

Paul Cézanne (1839–1906)

Still life with sugar basin and fruit

Nature morte avec sucrier, poires et nappe

Stillleben mit Zuckerdose und Früchten

Bodegón con azucarero y frutas

Natura morta con zuccheriera

Stilleven met

c. 1880, Oil on canvas/Huile sur toile, 45,7 × 35,6 cm, Private collection

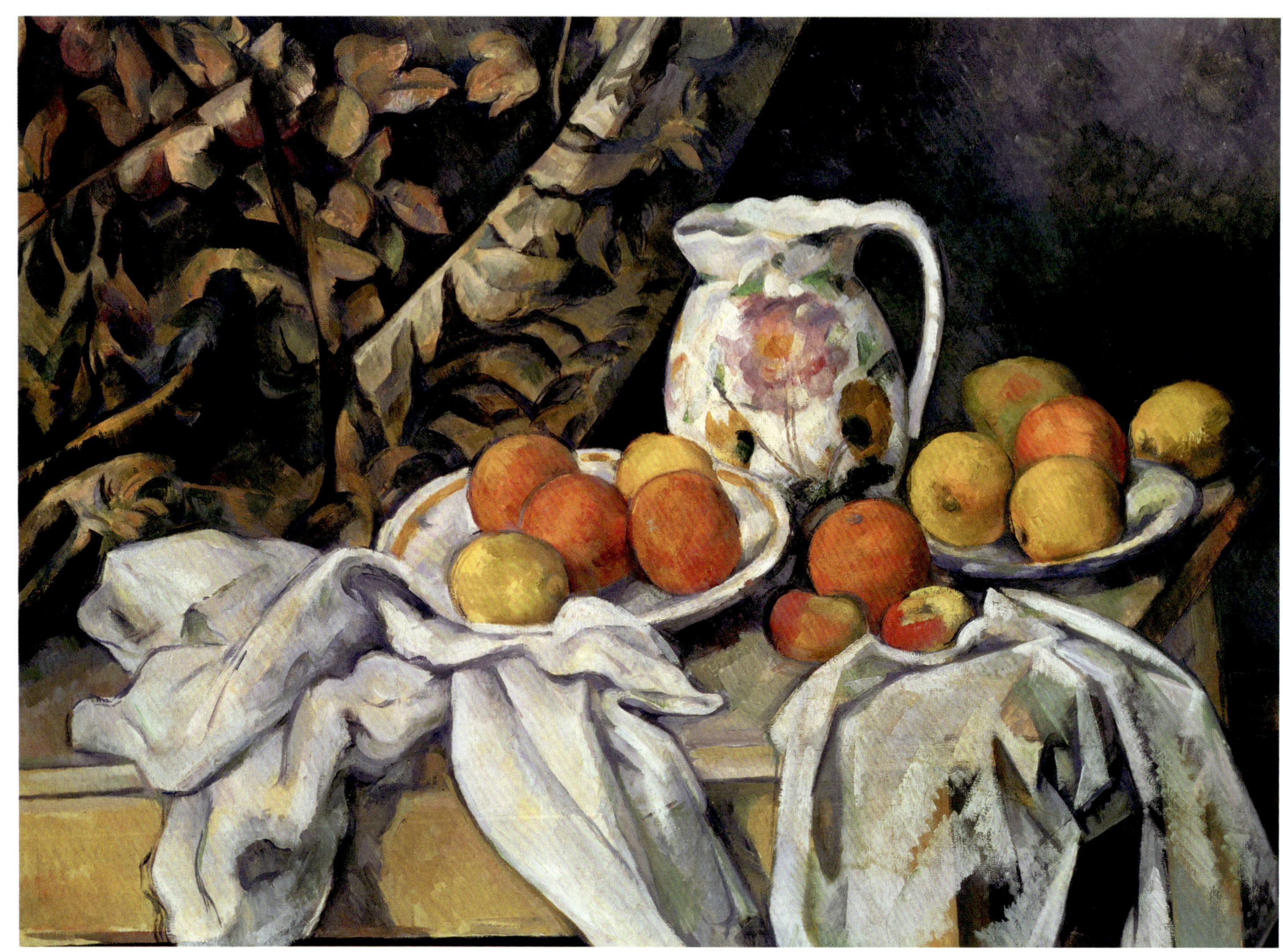

Paul Cézanne (1839–1906)

Still life with drapery

Nature morte au rideau

Stillleben mit Vorhang

Bodegón con cortina

Natura morta con drappeggio

Stilleven met gordijn

c. 1895, Oil on canvas/Huile sur toile, 55 × 74,5 cm, State Hermitage, St. Petersburg

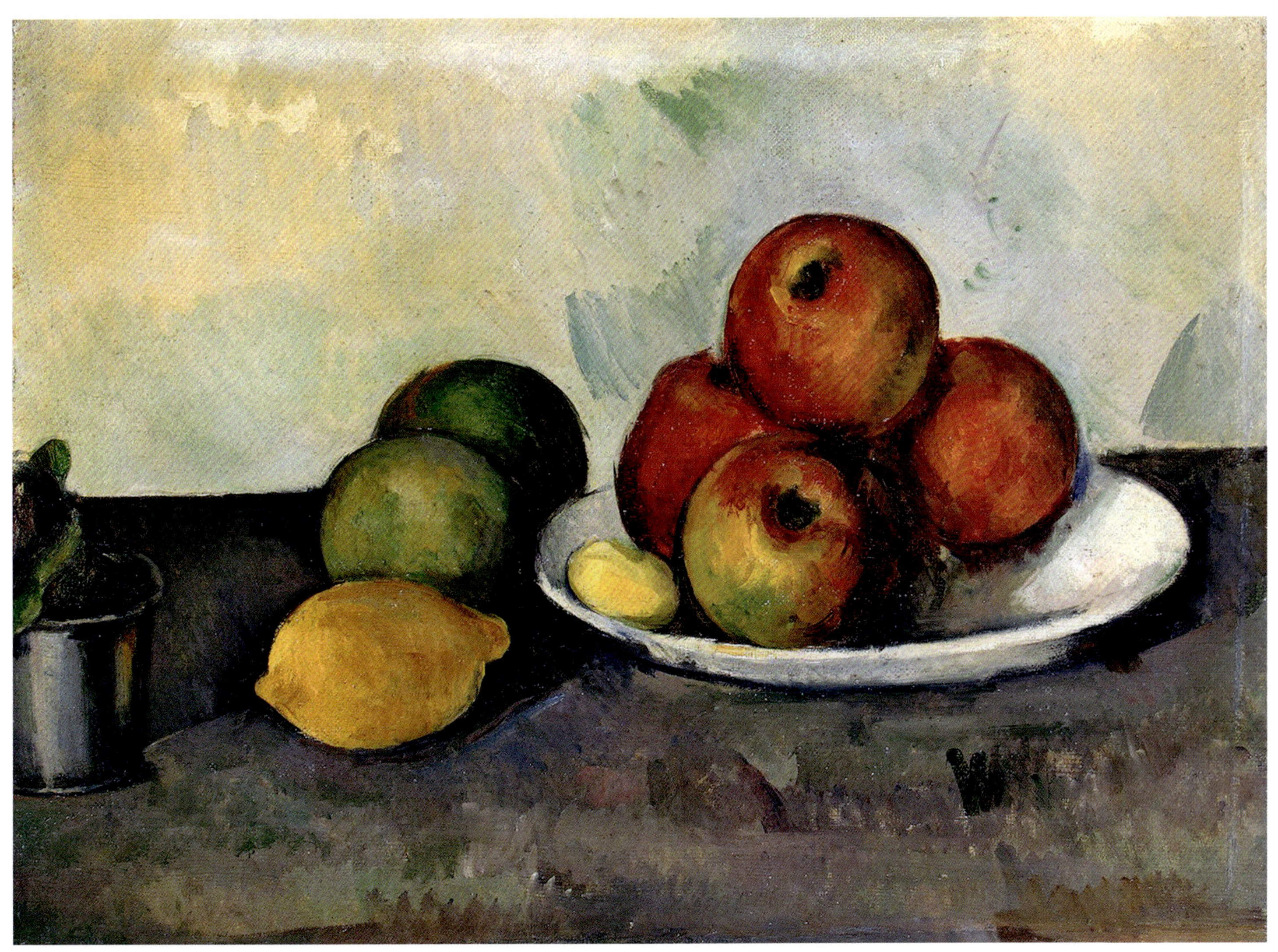

Paul Cézanne (1839–1906)

Still life with Apples

Nature morte aux pommes

Stillleben mit Äpfeln

Bodegón con manzanas

Natura morta con mele

Stilleven met appels

c. 1890, Oil on canvas/Huile sur toile, 35,2 × 46,2 cm, State Hermitage, St. Petersburg

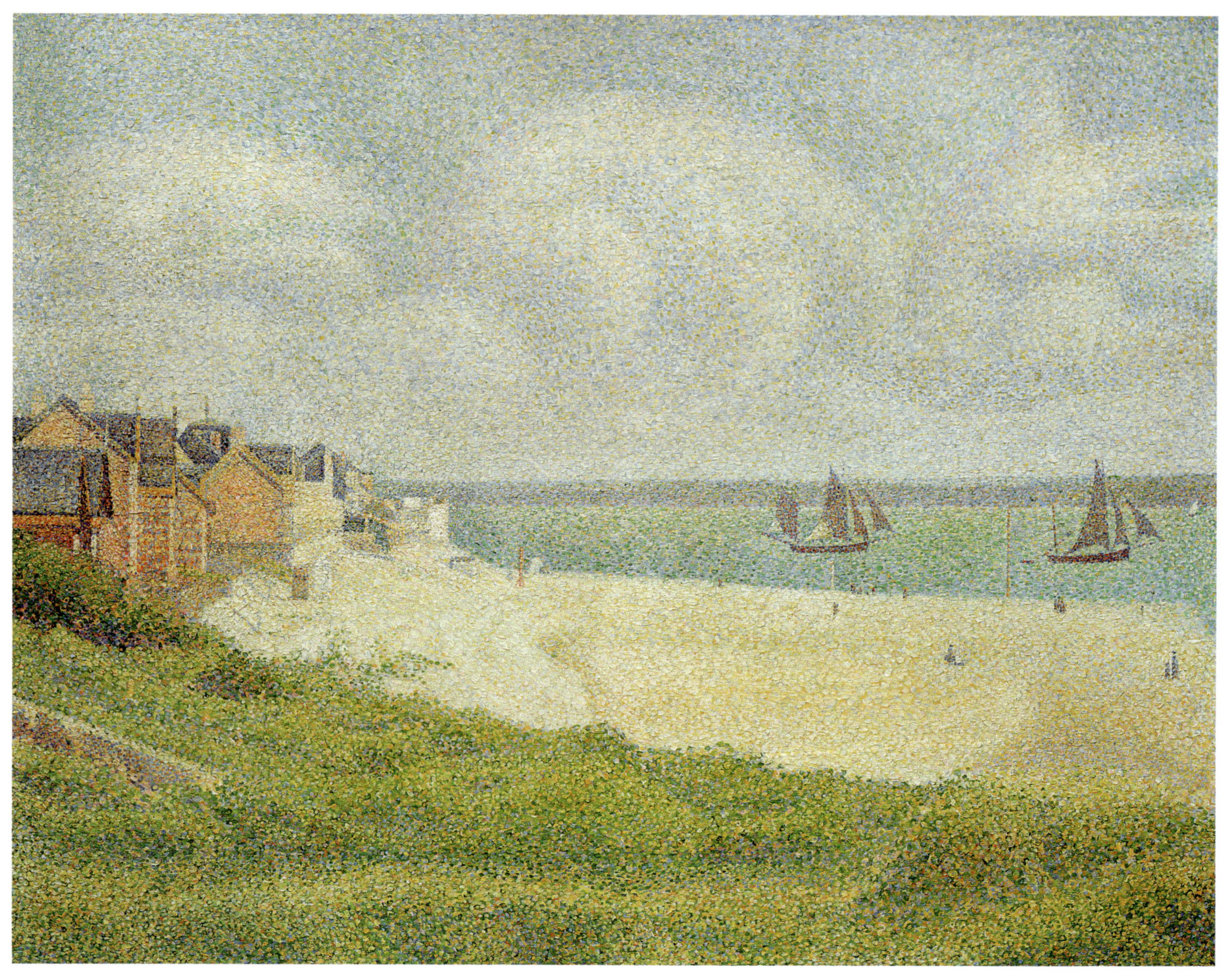

Georges-Pierre Seurat (1859–91)

Le Crotoy looking Upstream

Le Crotoy, amont

Le Crotoy flussabwärts

El Crotoy visto río arriba

Le Crotoy a monte

Le Crotoy, stroomopwaarts

1889, Oil on canvas/Huile sur toile, 70,5 × 86,5 cm, Private collection

widersprüchliche Dimension: 54.5 × 48.2 cm - falscher Titel, korrekt: Le Crotoy, downstream

Georges-Pierre Seurat (1859–91)

The Seine at Courbevoie

La Seine à Courbevoie

Die Seine bei Courbevoie

El Sena de Courbevoie

Donna in riva alla Senna a Courbevoie

De Seine bij Courbevoie

1885, Oil on canvas/Huile sur toile, 81 × 65 cm, Private collection

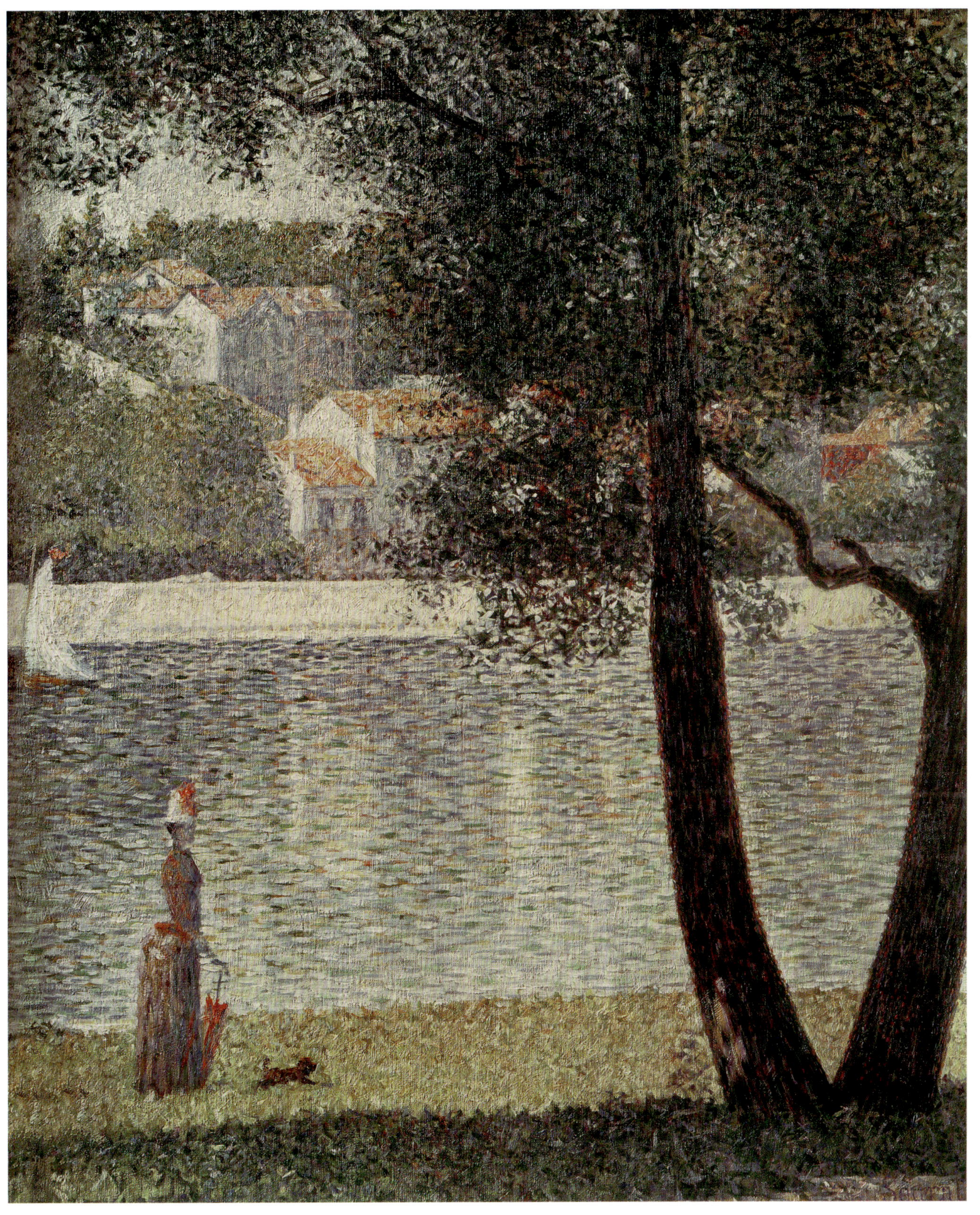

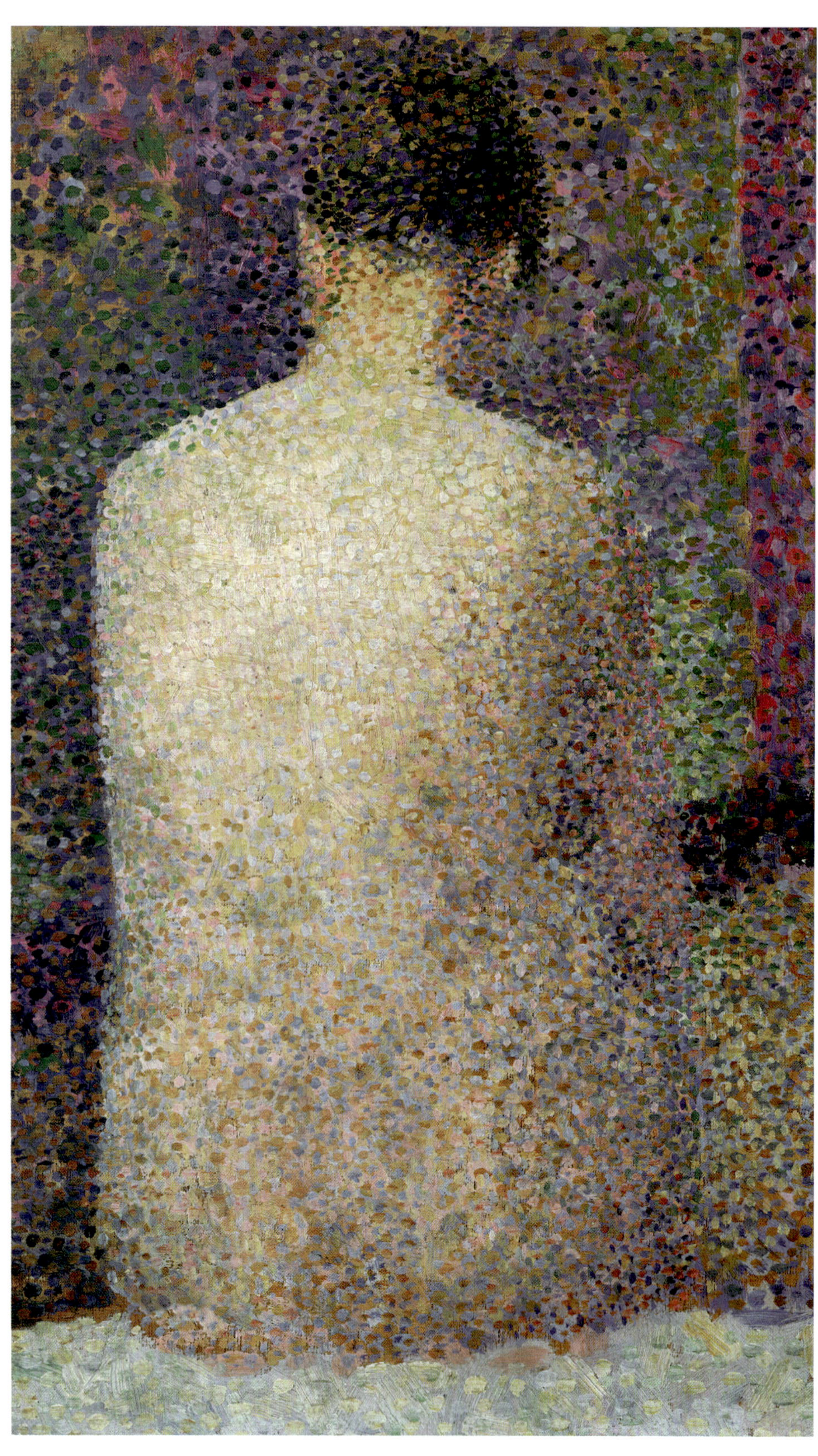

Georges-Pierre Seurat (1859–91)

Model from the Back

Poseuse de dos

Modell von hinten

Modelo de espaldas

Modella seduta, di spalle

Model van achteren

1886, Oil on panel/Huile sur bois, 24,3 × 15,3 cm, Musée d'Orsay, Paris

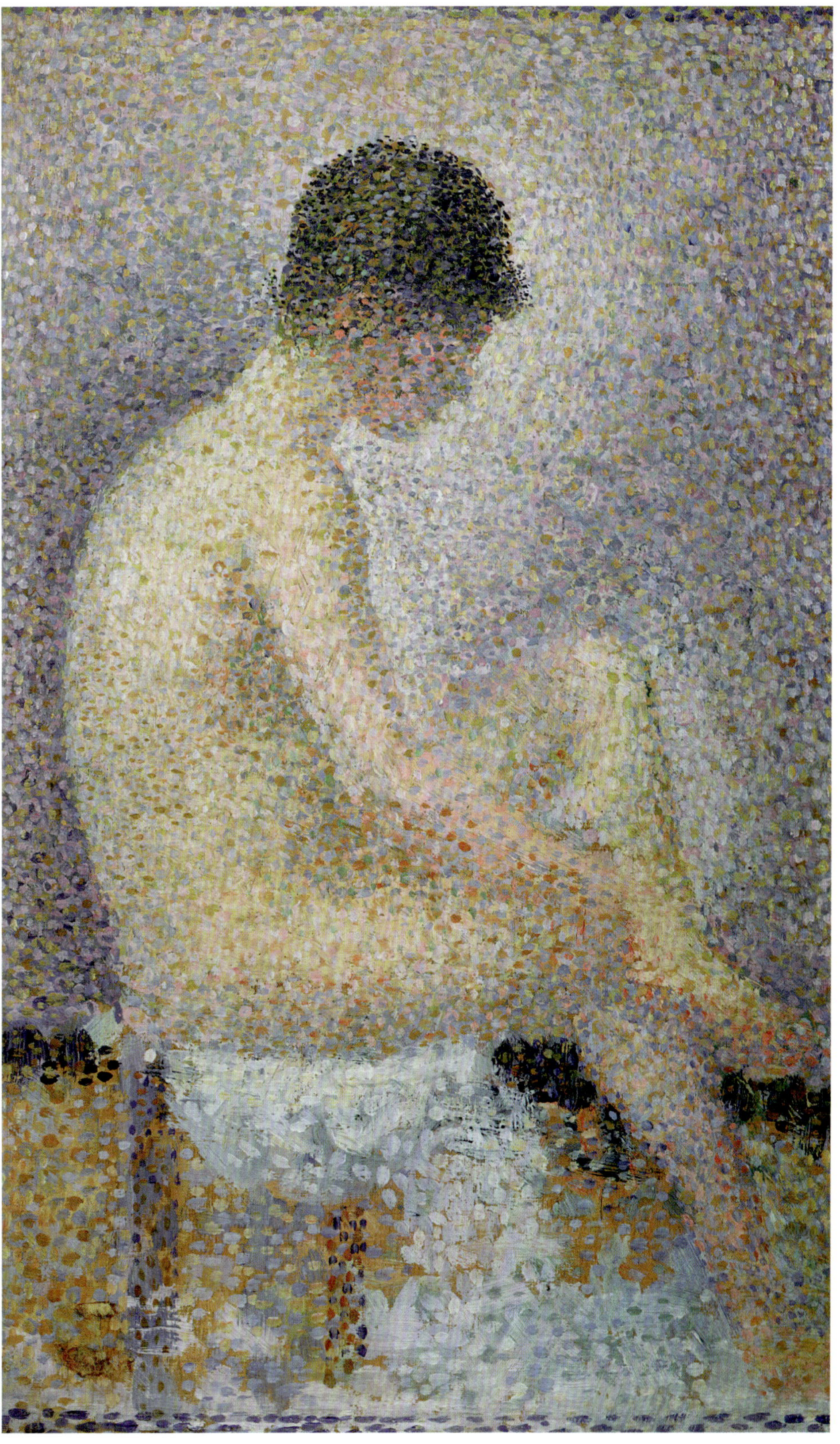

Georges-Pierre Seurat (1859–91)
Model in Profile
Poseuse de profil
Modell im Profil
Modelo de perfil
Modella seduta, di profilo
Model en profil
1886, Oil on panel/Huile sur bois, 25 × 16 cm, Musée d'Orsay, Paris

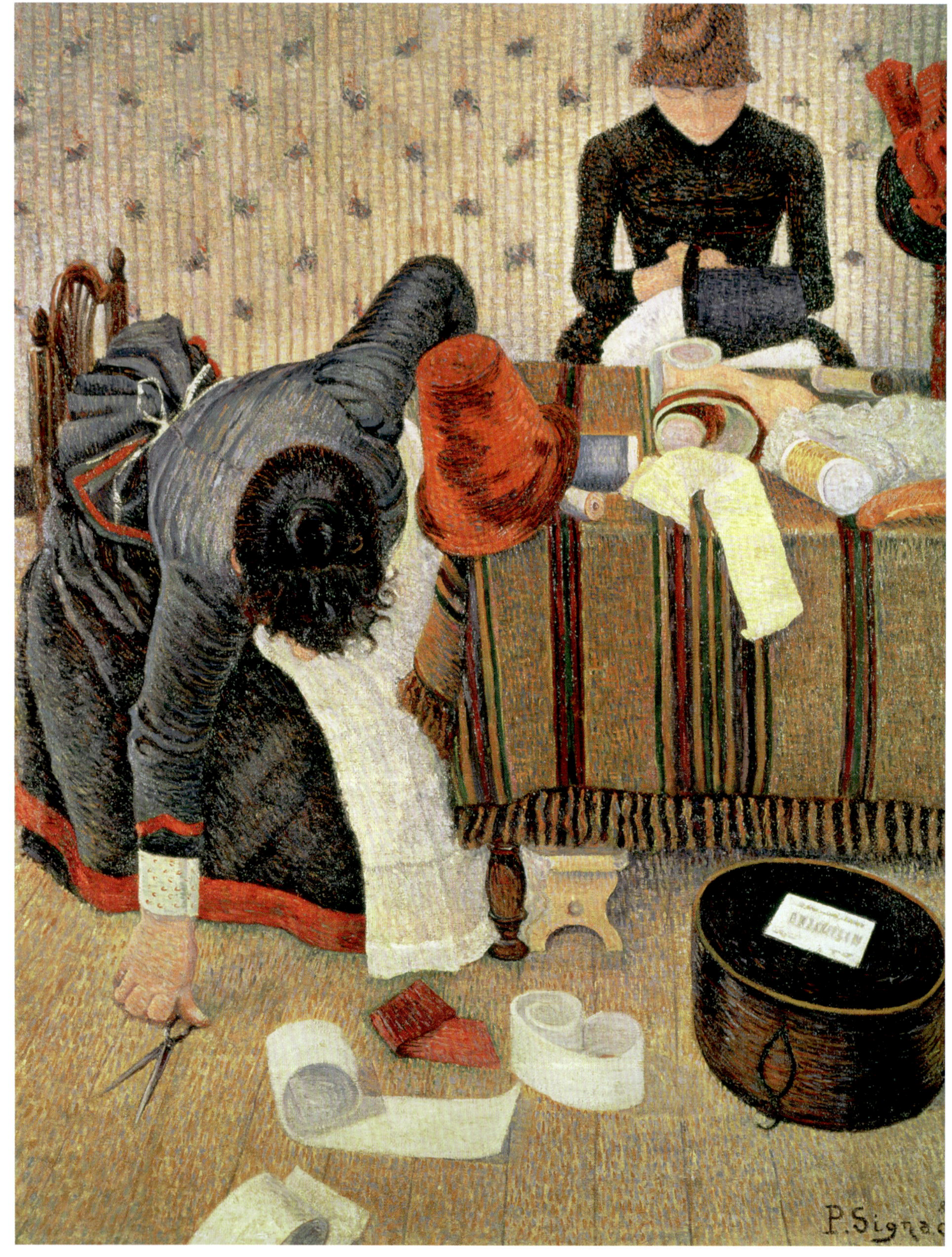

P.Signac

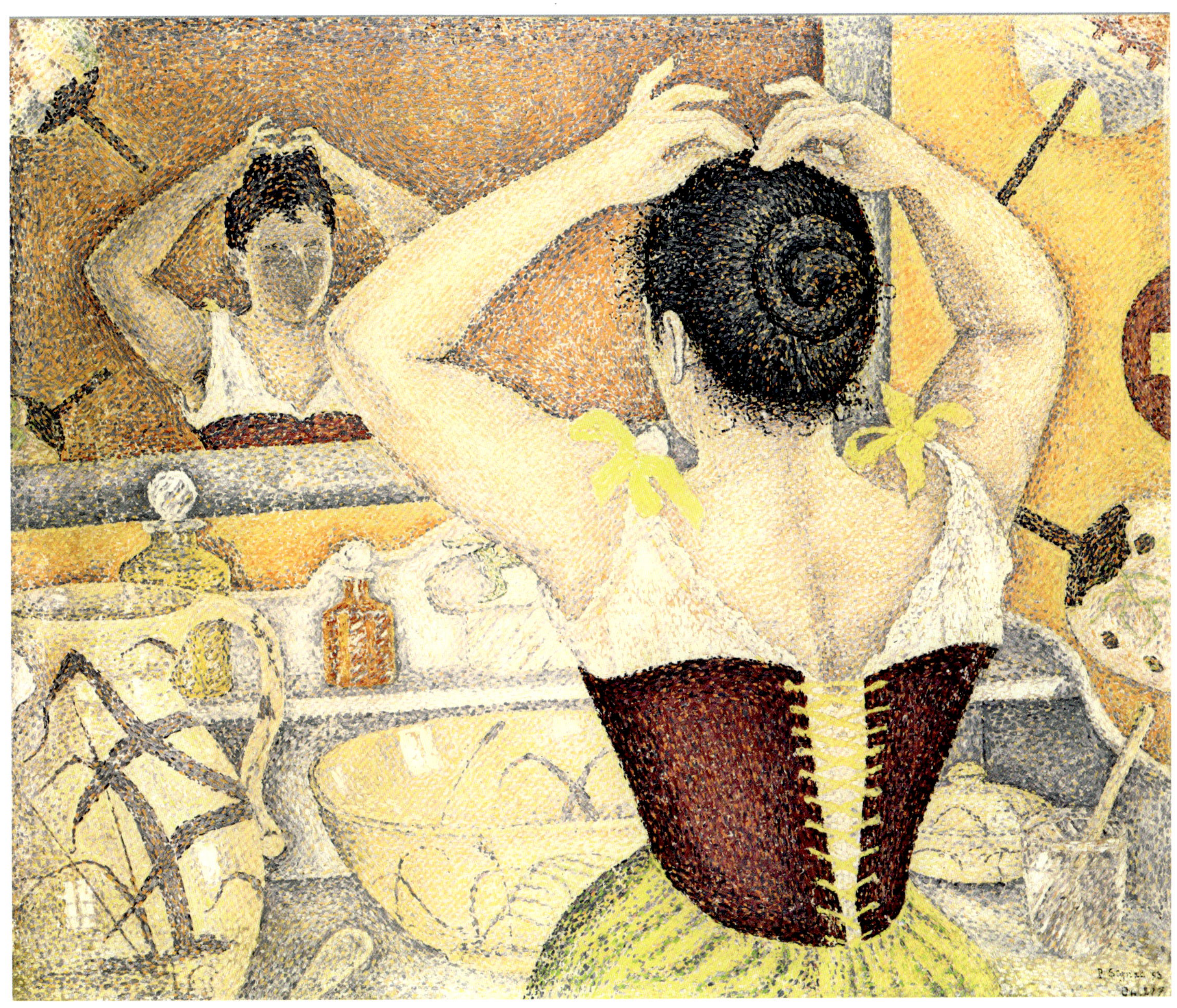

Paul Signac (1863–1935)

The Milliner

Les modistes

Die Modistinnen

La sombrerera

La cappellaia

De hoedenmaakster

1885/86, Oil on canvas/Huile sur toile, 116 × 89 cm, Stiftung Sammlung E. G. Bührle, Zürich

Paul Signac (1863–1935)

Woman at her toilette wearing a purple corset

Femme à son cabinet de toilette portant un corset violet

Frau bei der Toilette mit einem violetten Korsett

Mujer en el aseo con corsé violeta

Donna alla sua toilette con un corsetto viola

Vrouw met paars korset bij het toilet

1893, Oil on canvas/Huile sur toile, 59 × 70 cm, Private collection

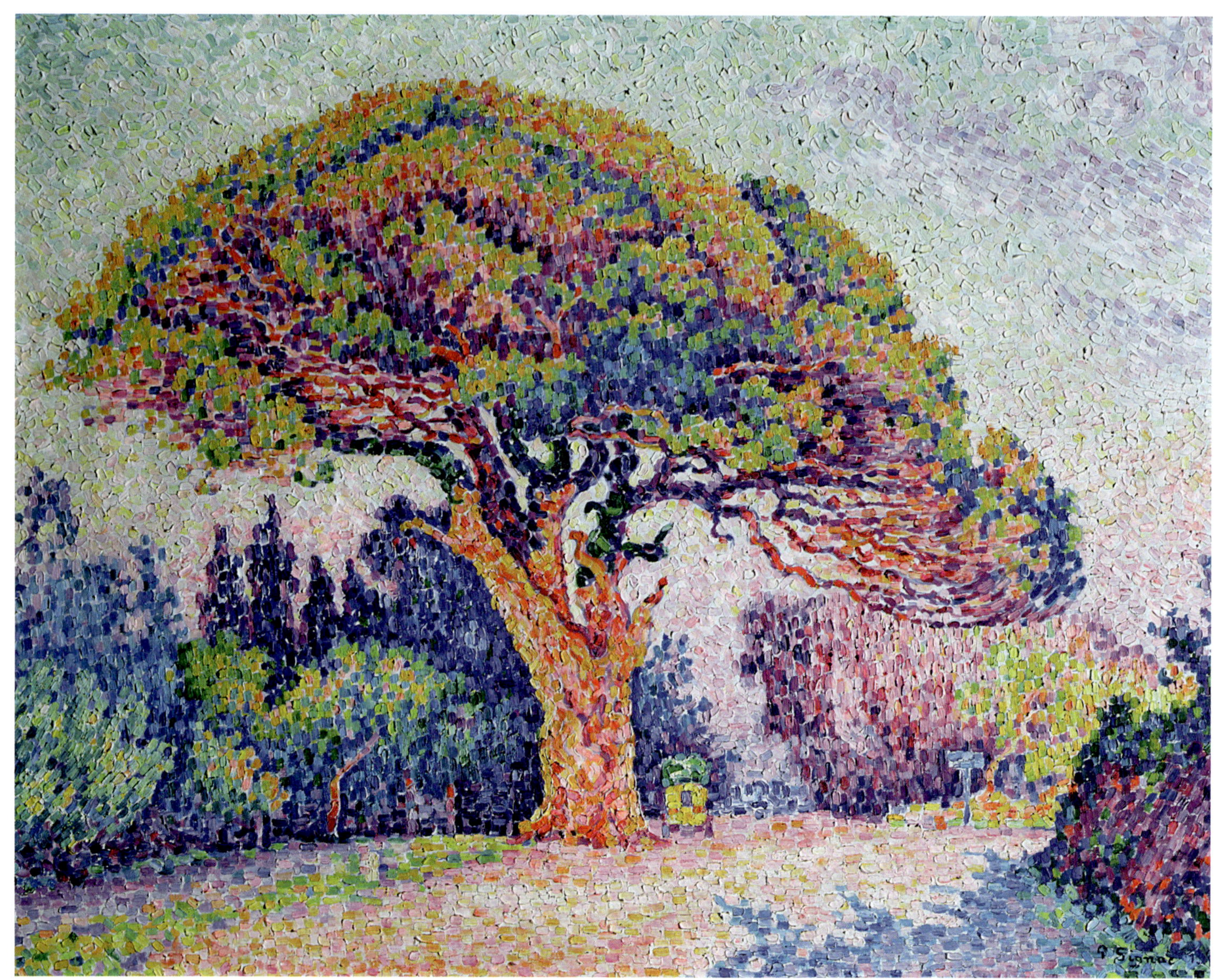

Paul Signac (1863–1935)

The Pine Tree at St. Tropez

Le Grand Pin Saint-Tropez

Die Pinie in St. Tropez

El gran pino en Saint-Tropez

Grande pino a Saint Tropez

De grote pijnboom in Saint-Tropez

1909, Oil on canvas/Huile sur toile, 72 × 92 cm, The Pushkin State Museum of Fine Art, Moscow

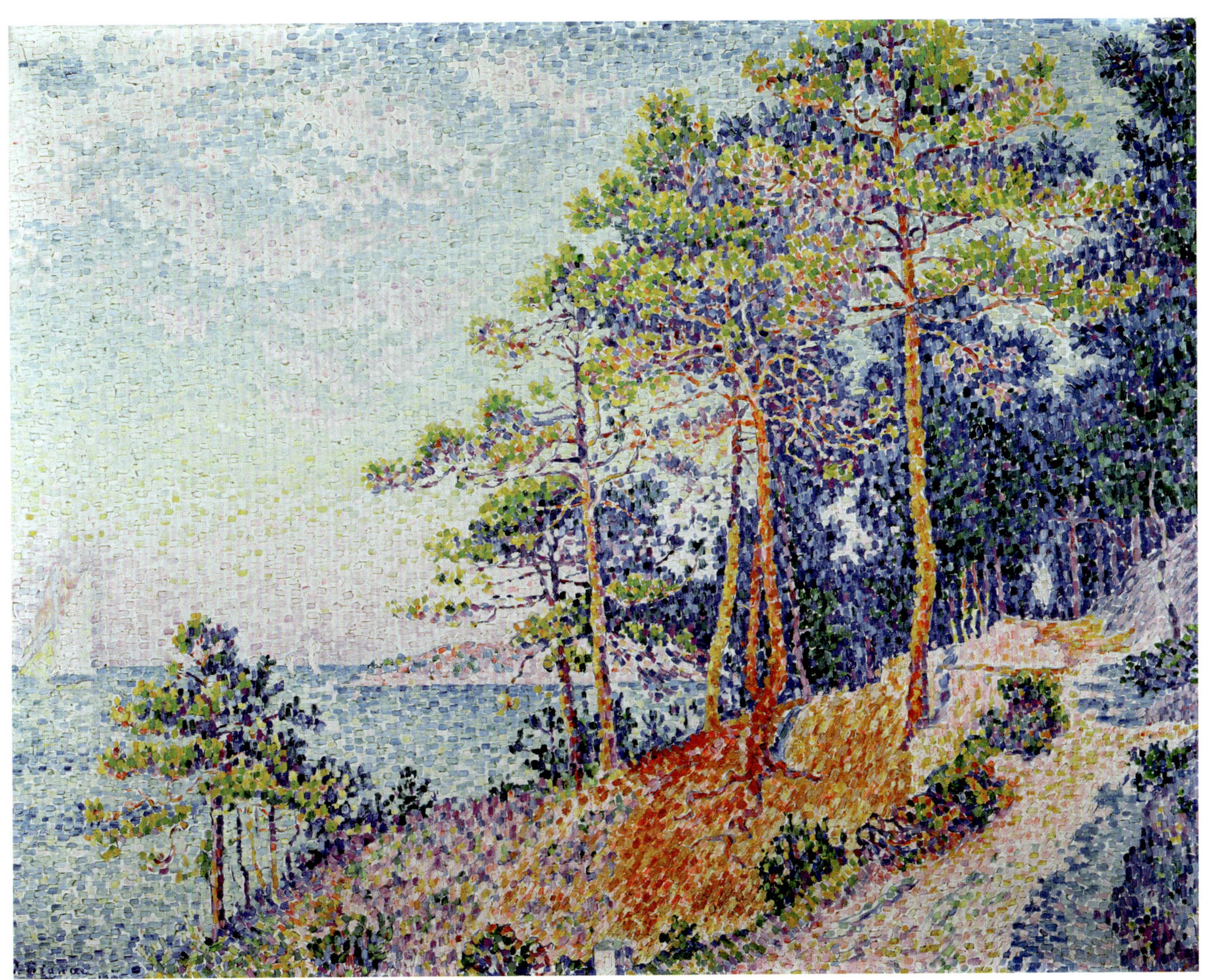

Paul Signac (1863–1935)

St. Tropez, the Custom's Path

Saint-Tropez, le sentier de douane

Wanderweg bei Saint-Tropez

Sendero en Saint-Tropez

Sentiero a Saint-Tropez

Wandelpad bij Saint-Tropez

1905, Oil on canvas/Huile sur toile, 72 × 92,5 cm, Musée de Grenoble, Grenoble

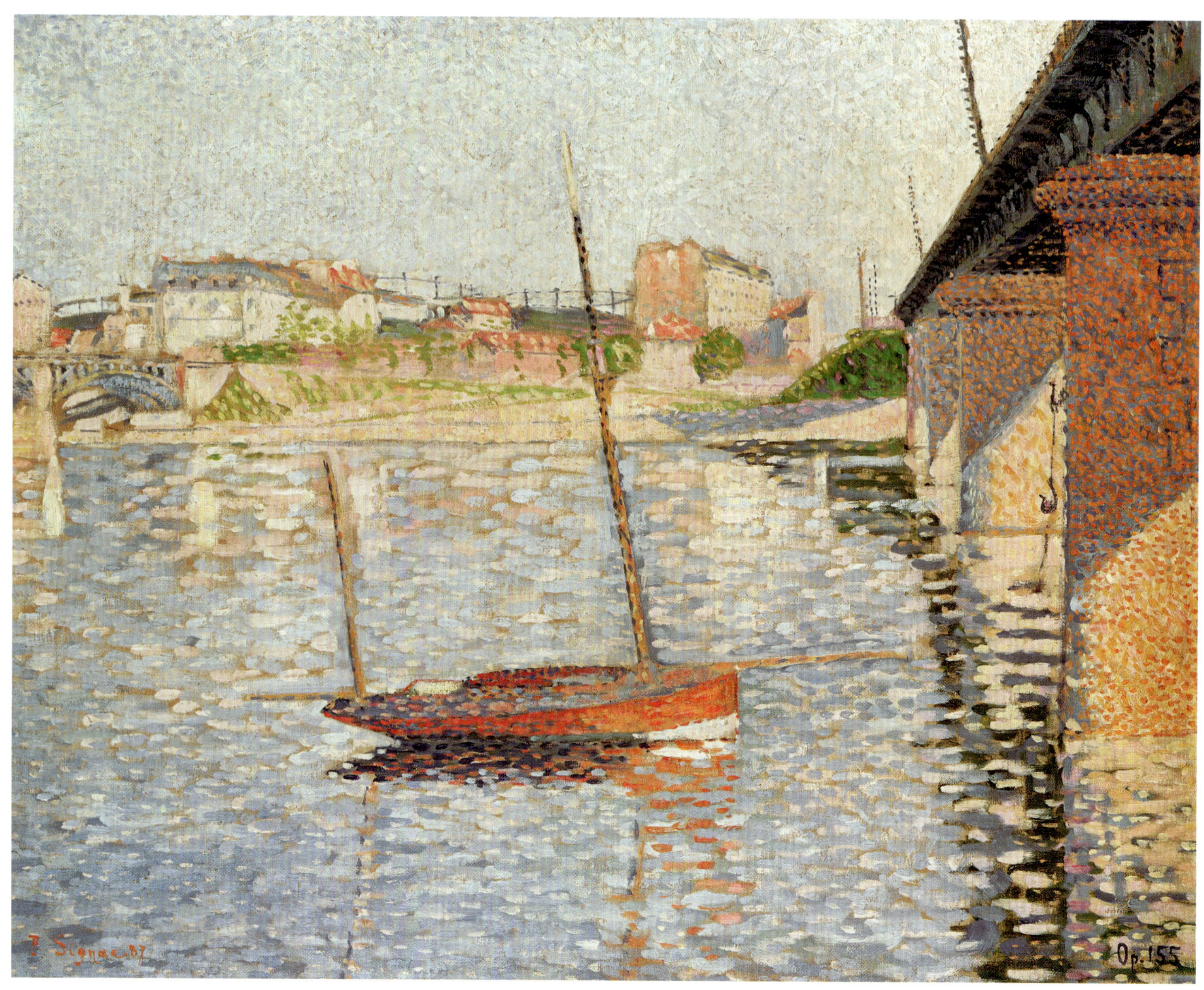

Paul Signac (1863–1935)

Le Clipper, Asnieres

Le Clipper, Asnières

Segelboot in Asnières

Bote de vela en Asnières

Barca a vela ad Asnières

Zeilboot in Asnières

1887, Oil on canvas/Huile sur toile, 43,8 × 54,9 cm, Private collection

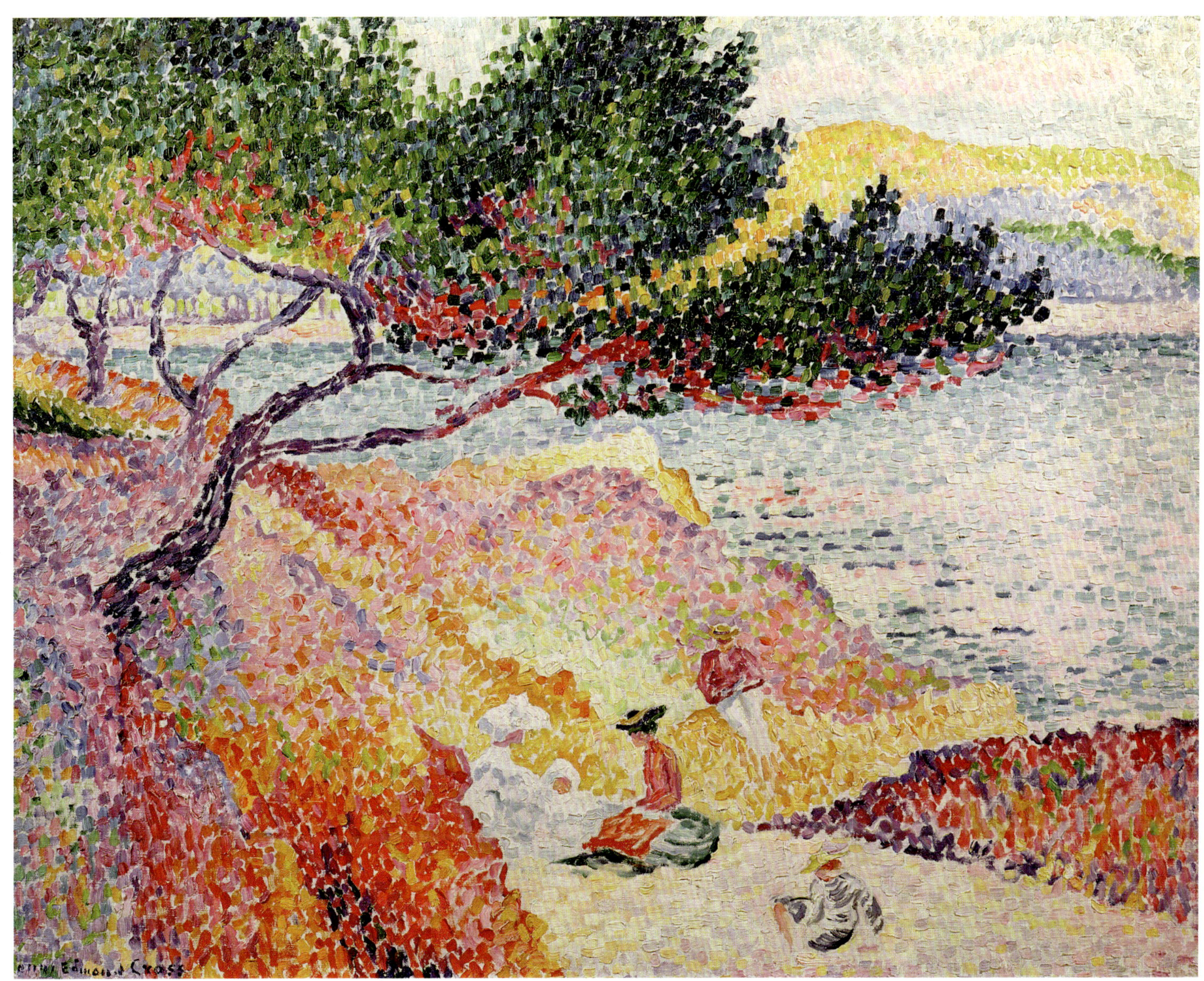

Henri-Edmond Cross (1856–1910)

La Plage de Saint–Clair

La plage de Saint-Clair

Der Strand von Saint-Clair

La playa de Saint-Clair

La spiaggia di Saint-Clair

Het strand van Saint-Clair

1906/07, Oil on canvas/Huile sur toile, 65 × 81 cm, Musée de l'Annonciade, Saint-Tropez

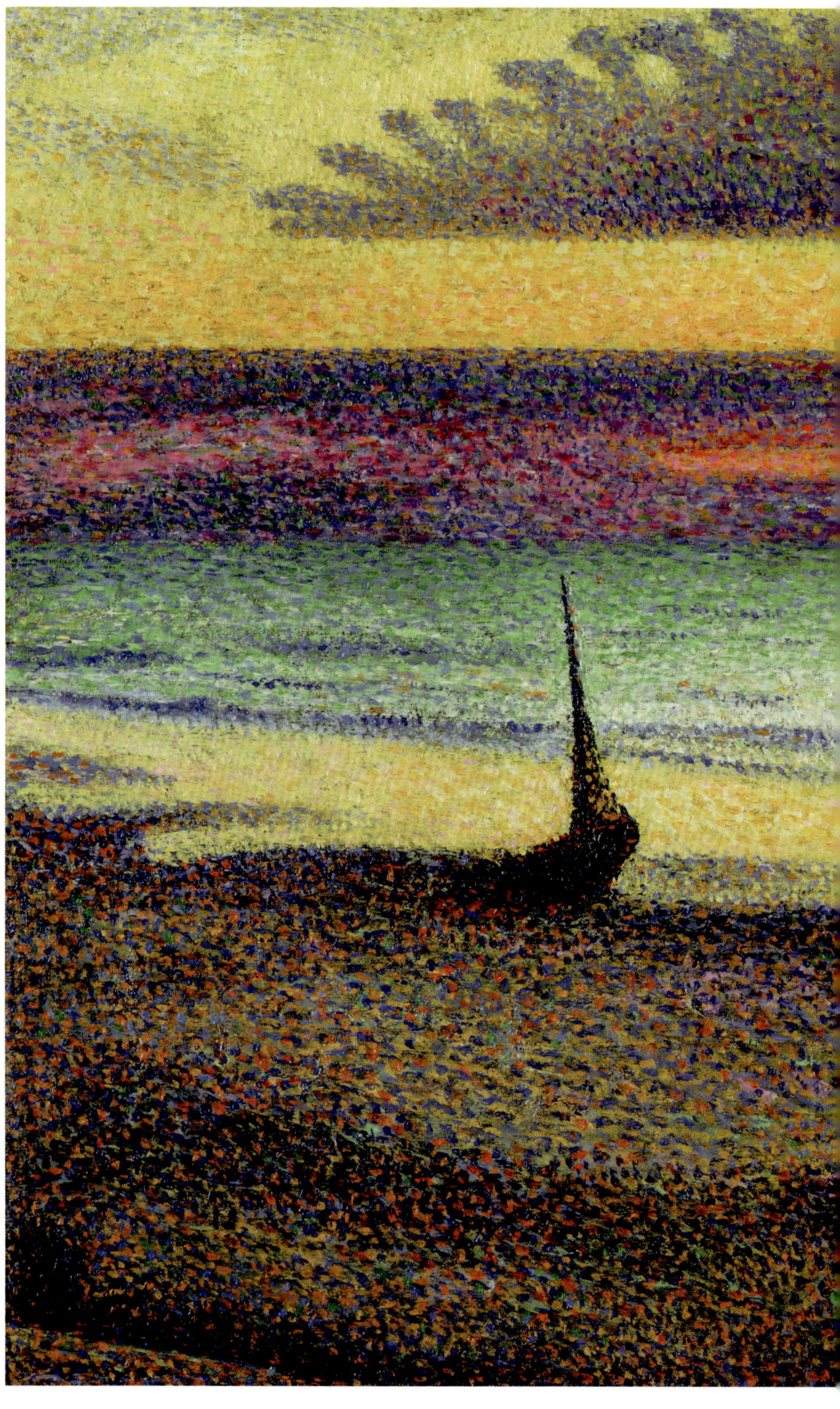

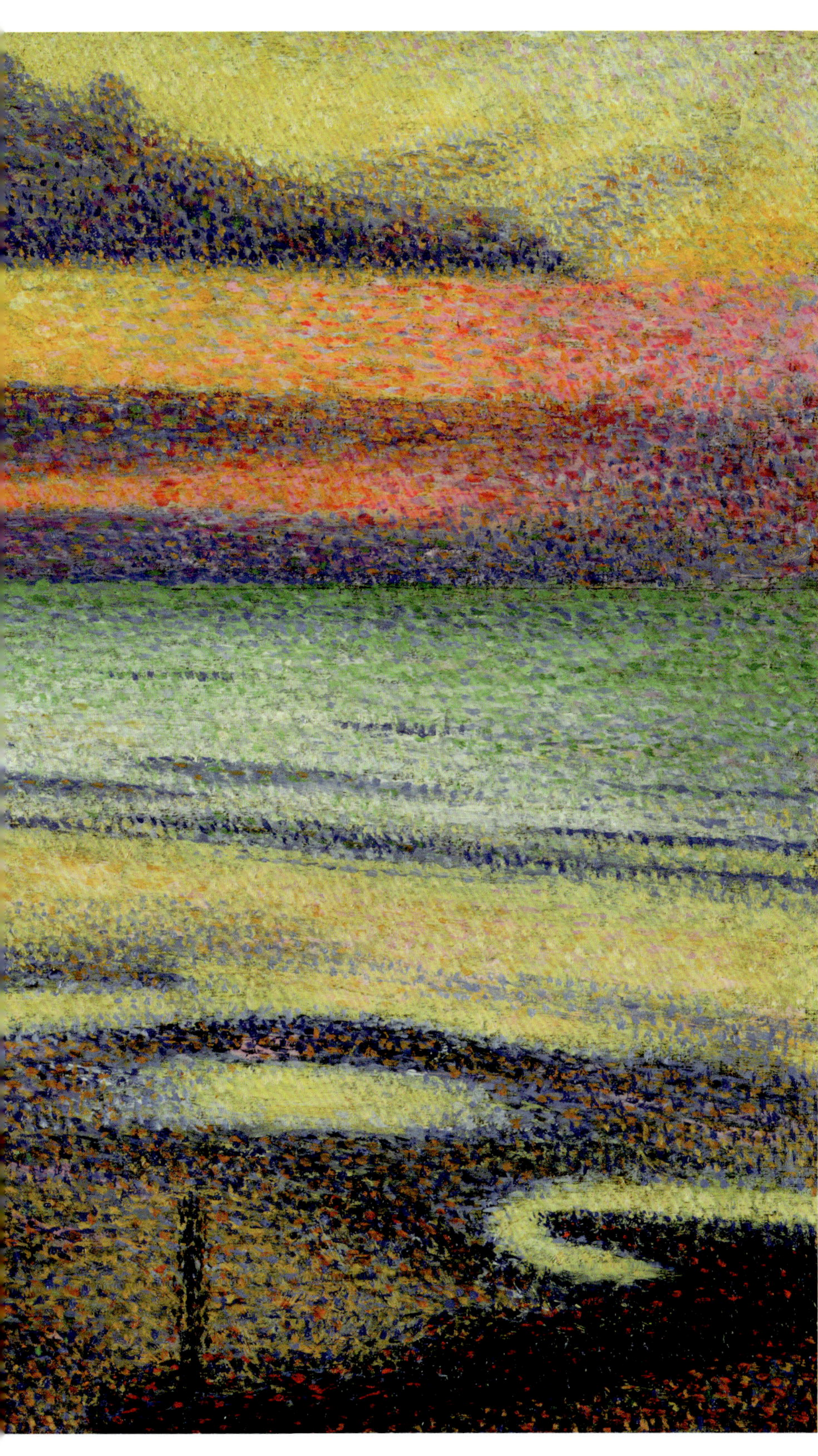

Georges Lemmen (1865–1916)

The Beach at Heist

Plage à Heist

Der Strand von Heist

La playa en Heist

La spiaggia di Heist

Het strand van Heist

1891/92, Oil on panel/Huile sur toile, 37,5 × 46 cm, Musée d'Orsay, Paris

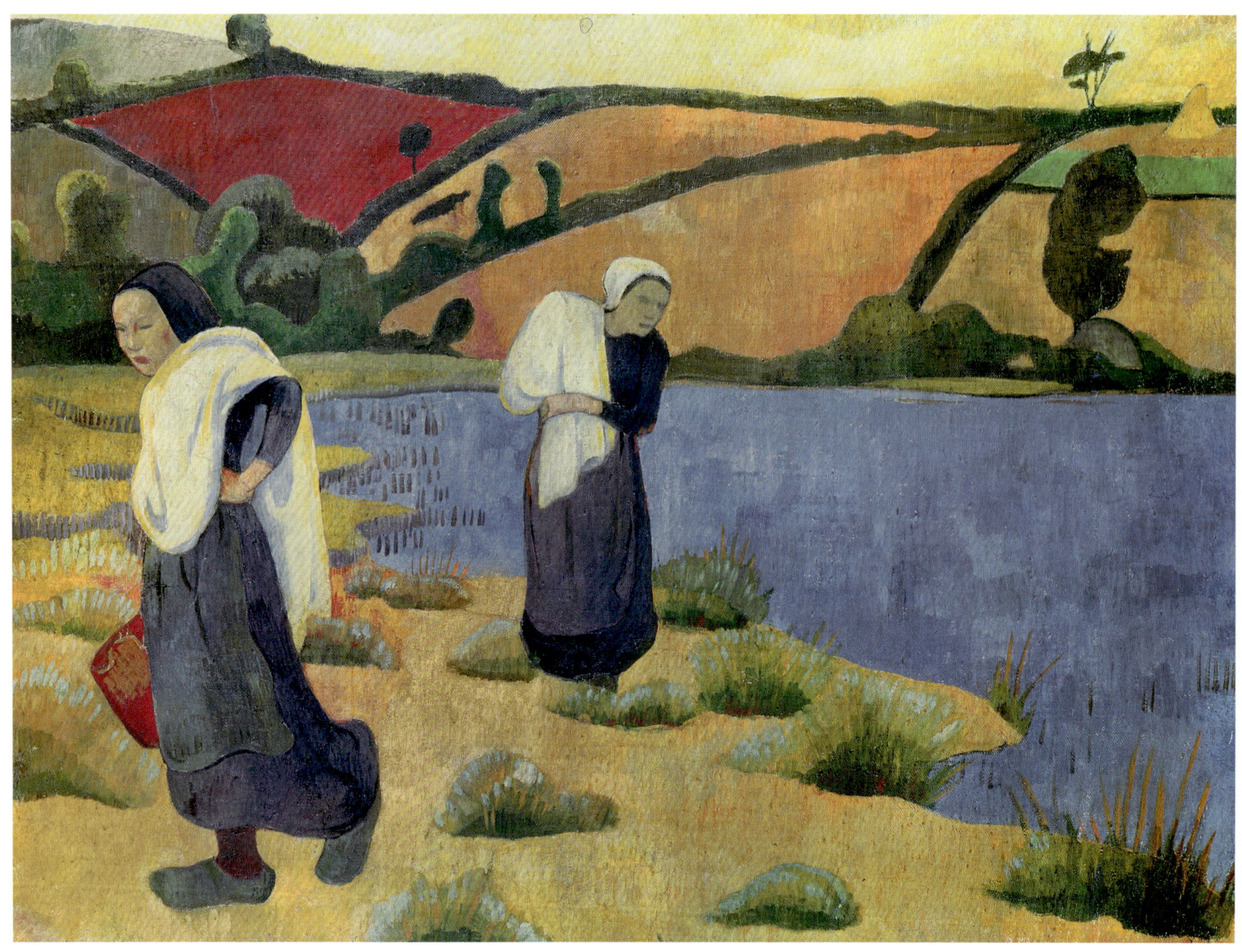

Paul Sérusier (1864–1927)

Washerwomen at the Laita River, near Pouldu

Lavandières à La Laïta, Près Pouldu

Wäscherinnen an der Laïta bei Pouldu

Lavanderas en el río Laïta cerca de Pouldu

Lavandaie presso La Laïta a Pouldu

Wasvrouwen aan de Laïta bij Pouldu

1892, Oil on canvas/Huile sur toile, 73,2 × 92,2 cm, Musée d'Orsay, Paris

Paul Sérusier (1864–1927)

The Incantation *or* The Holy Wood

L'Incantation *ou* Le Bois sacré

Das Ritual *oder* Der Heilige Wald

La encantación *o* El bosque santo

L'incantesimo *o* Il bosco sacro

Het ritueel, *of:* Het heilige woud

1891/92, Oil on canvas/Huile sur toile, 91,5 × 72 cm, Musée des Beaux-Arts, Quimper

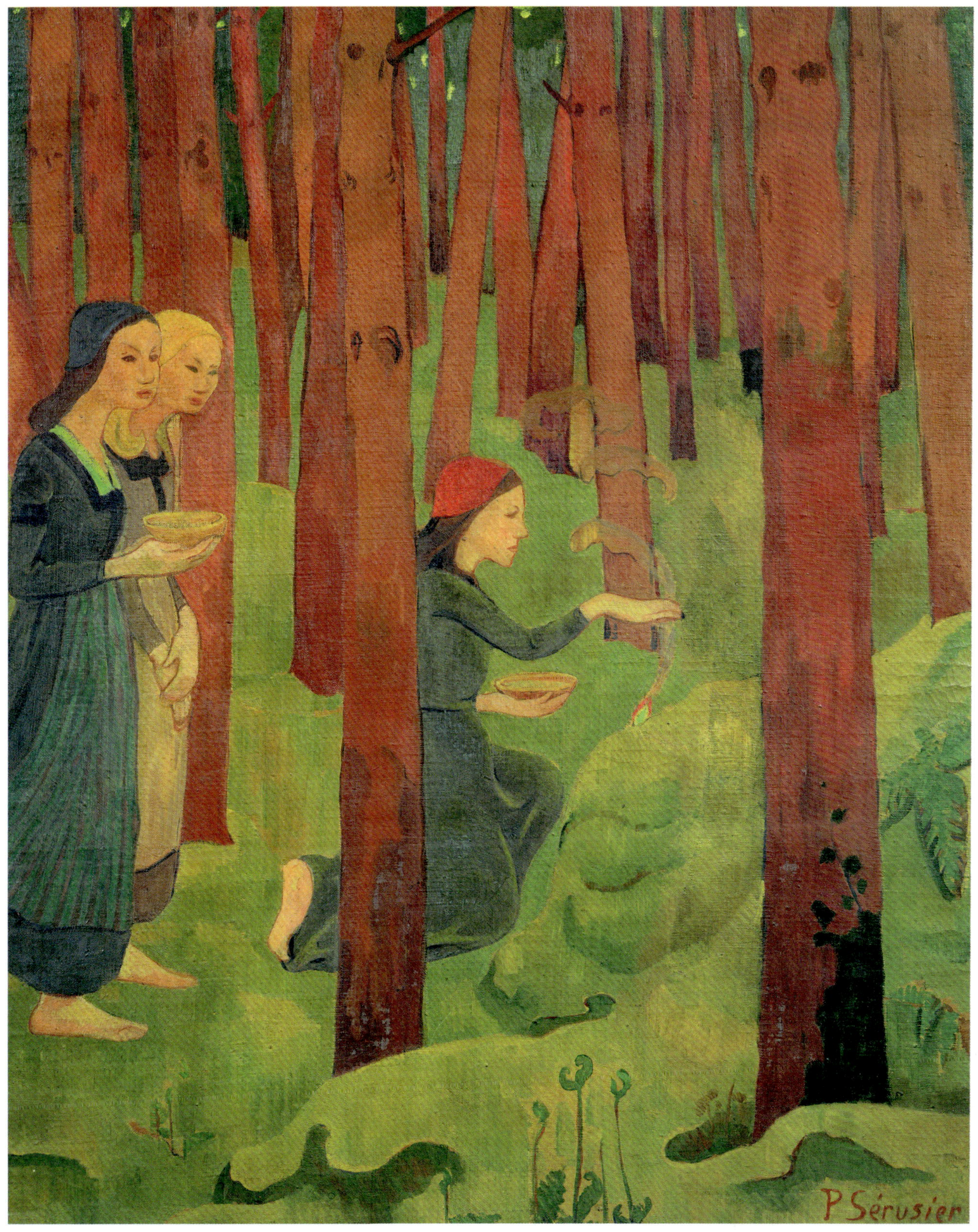

P. Sérusier

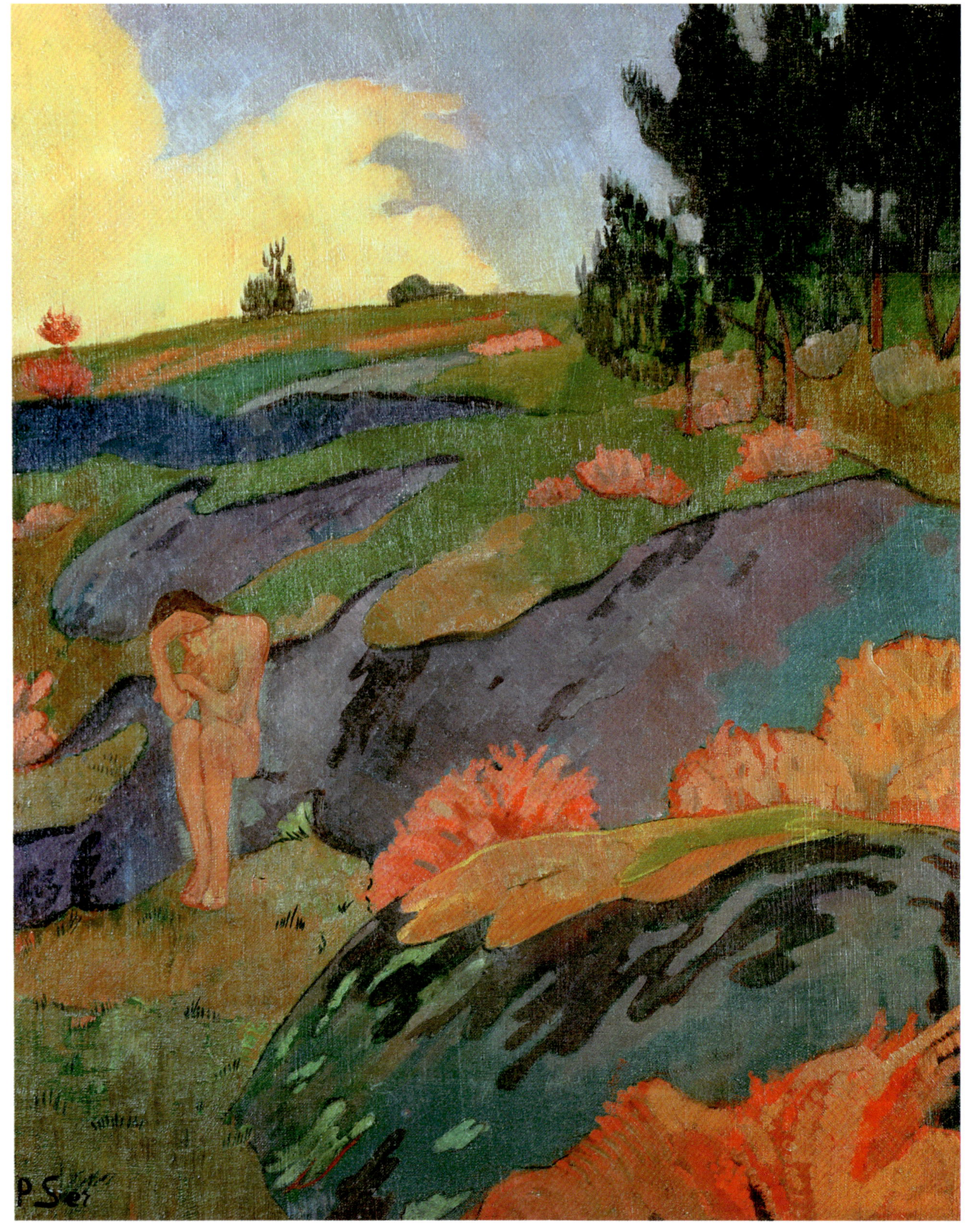

P Ser

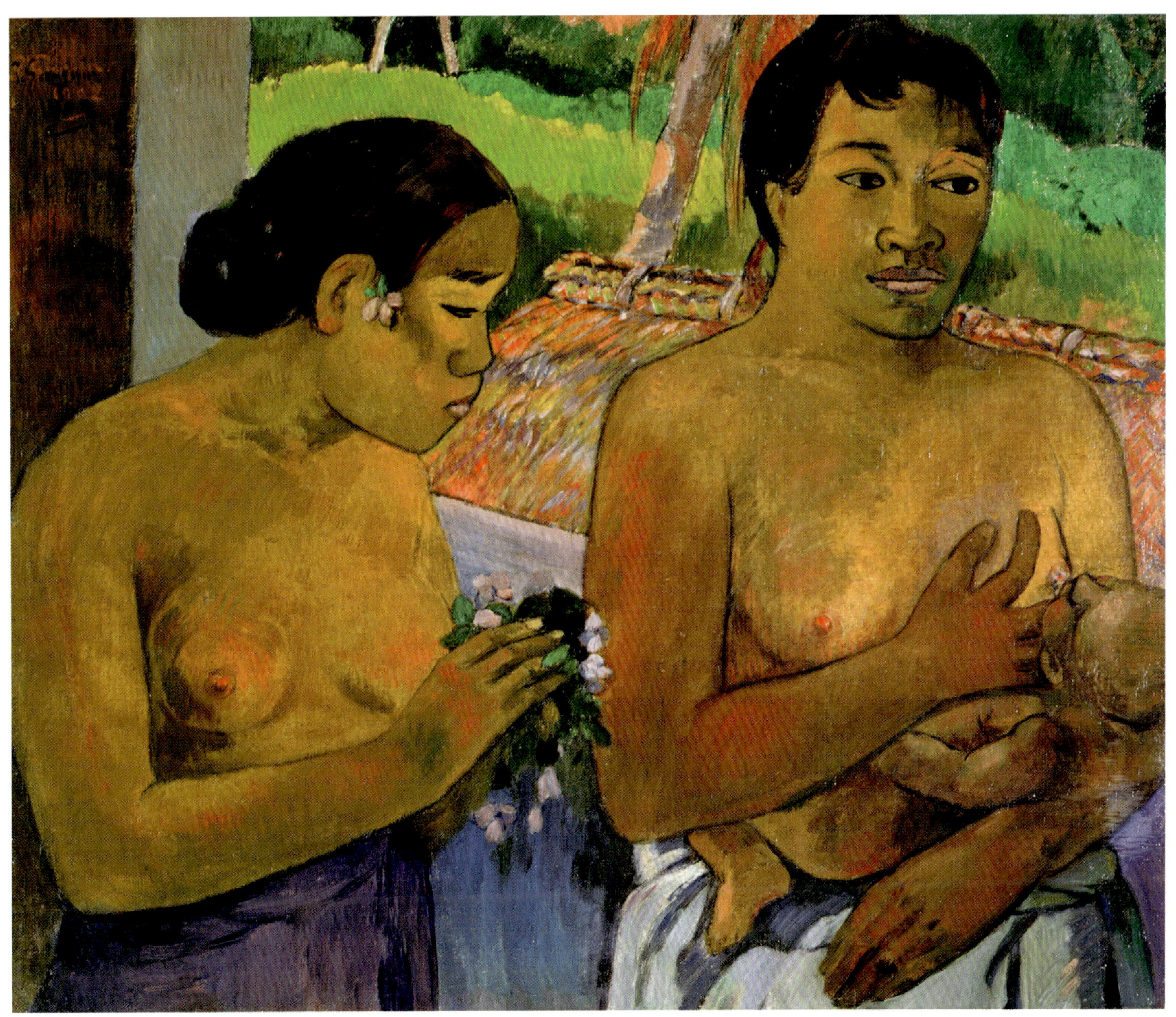

Paul Sérusier (1864–1927)

Breton Eve *or* Melancholy

Ève bretonne *ou* Mélancolie

Bretonische Eva *oder* Die Melancholie

Eva bretona *o* La melancolía

Eva bretone *o* Malinconia

Bretonse Eva, *of:* De melancholie

1890, Oil on canvas/Huile sur toile, 72,6 × 58,3 cm, Musée d'Orsay, Paris

Paul Gauguin (1848–1903)

The Offering

L'Offrande

Die Opfergabe

La ofrenda

Il dono

De gave

1902, Oil on canvas/Huile sur toile, 68,5 × 78,5 cm, Stiftung Sammlung E. G. Bührle, Zürich

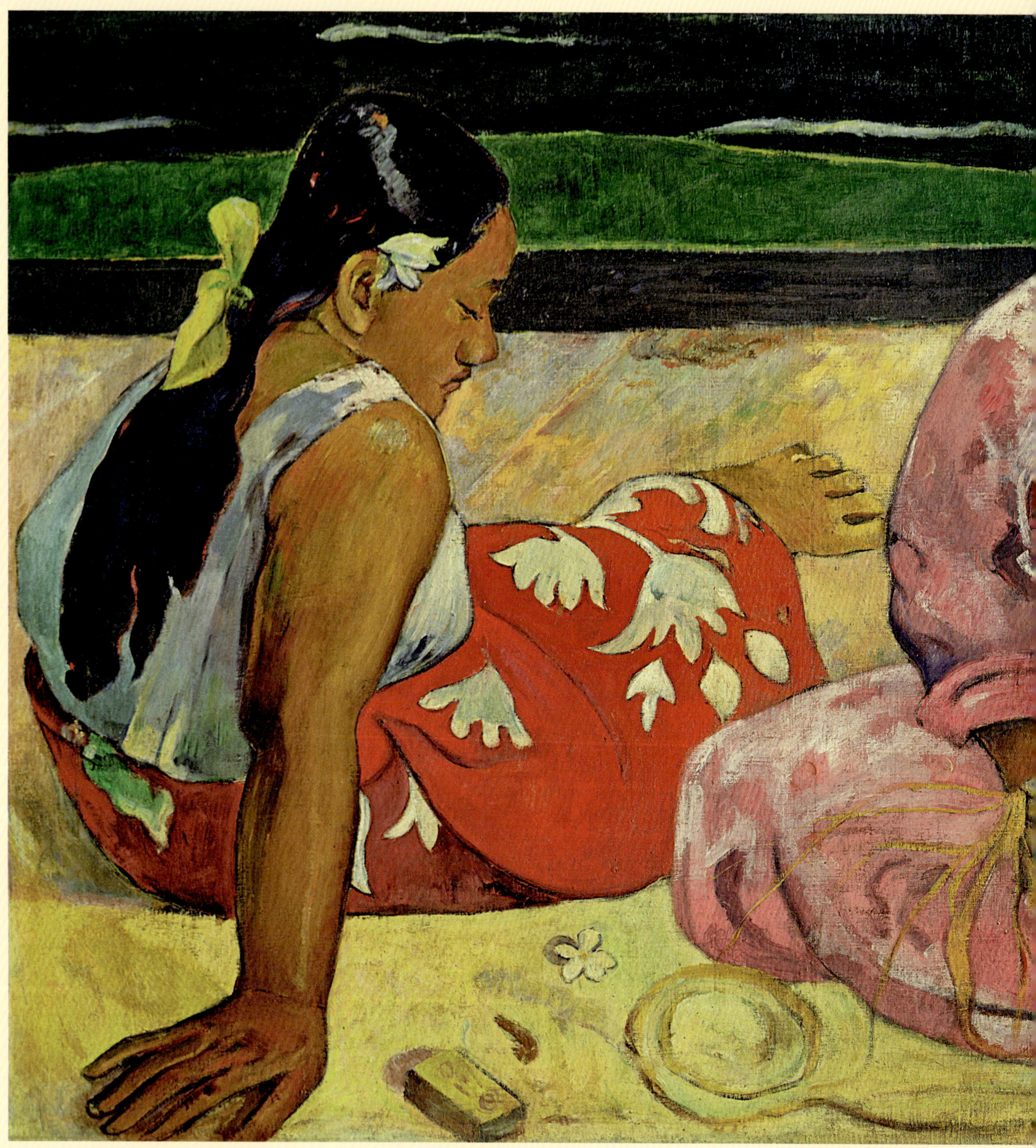

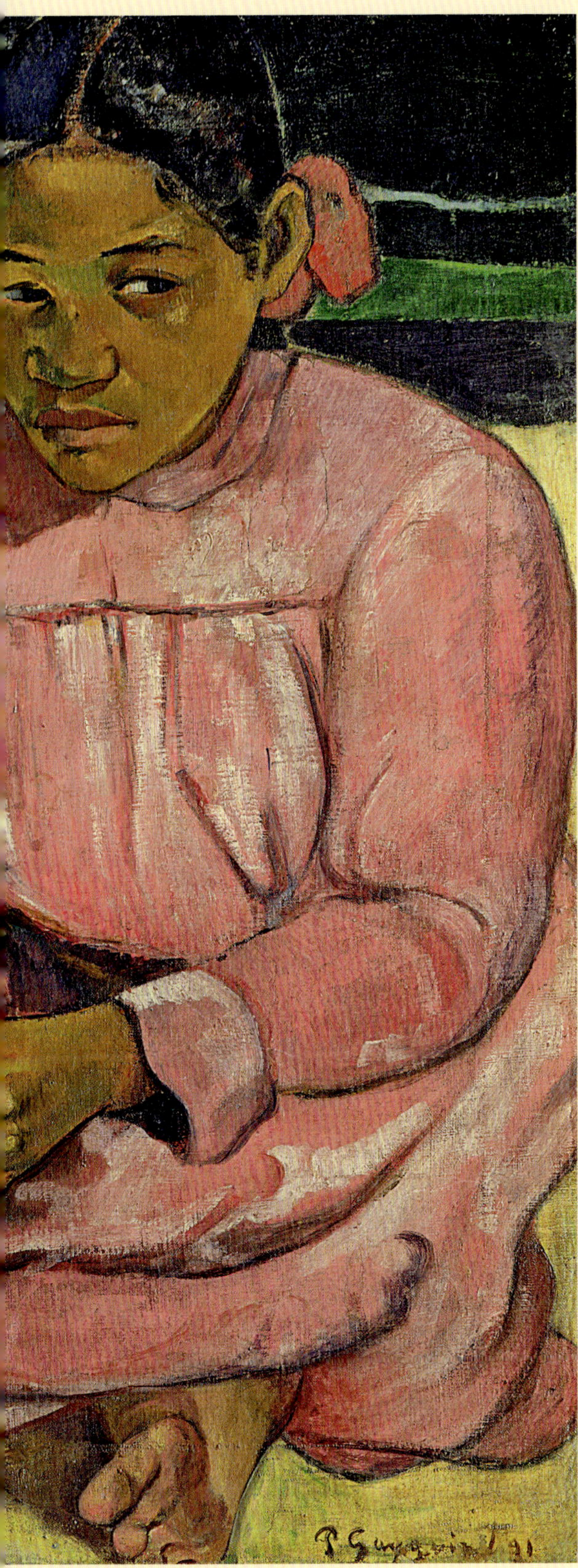

In a close-up view, Gauguin has painted two local women wearing their traditional dress. The sea shimmers green and forms a strong contrast to the intense red and pink tones in the image. The simple but very vivid representation impresses by the naturalness and grace of the women, to whom Gauguin was not only artistically attracted.

Gauguin a peint en gros plan deux Tahitiennes portant leur costume traditionnel. La mer se miroite en vert et forme un fort contraste avec les tons intenses rouges et roses du tableau. La représentation simple, mais très colorée, impressionne par le naturel et la grâce de ces femmes qui attiraient Gauguin pour des raisons qui n'étaient pas uniquement artistiques.

In starker Nahsicht hat Gauguin hier zwei einheimische Frauen in ihrer traditionellen Tracht gemalt. Das Meer schillert grün und bildet einen kräftigen Kontrast zu den intensiven Rot- und Rosatönen im Bild. Die einfache, aber sehr plastische Darstellung beeindruckt durch die Natürlichkeit und Anmut der Frauen, denen Gauguin nicht nur als Künstler zugeneigt war.

Gauguin pinta aquí a dos mujeres locales con traje tradicional en un intenso primer plano. El mar ofrece destellos verdes, que generan un potente contraste con los rojos y rosas intensos de la imagen. La representación, sencilla pero muy plástica, impresiona por la naturalidad y gracia de las mujeres, que atraían a Gauguin no solo como artista.

In questo quadro Gauguin raffigura da vicino due donne del posto con indosso i loro abiti tradizionali. Il mare, di colore verde, luccica e crea un forte contrasto con gli intensi toni rossi e rosa presenti nel dipinto. La rappresentazione semplice ma molto vivida colpisce per la sua naturalezza e la grazia delle donne, dalle quali Gauguin era attratto non solo come artista.

Van dichtbij heeft Gauguin twee inheemse vrouwen in traditionele klederdracht geschilderd. De zee glinstert groen en contrasteert met de intens rode en roze tonen in het schilderij. De simpele maar zeer plastische weergave is des te indrukwekkender door de natuurlijkheid en bevalligheid van de vrouwen, met wie Gauguin niet alleen artistieke relaties onderhield.

Paul Gauguin (1848–1903)
Women of Tahiti, On the Beach
Femmes de Tahiti
Frauen von Tahiti am Strand
Mujeres de Tahití en la playa
Due donne tahitiane
Vrouwen van Tahiti aan het strand
1891, Oil on canvas/Huile sur toile, 69 × 91,5 cm, Musée d'Orsay, Paris

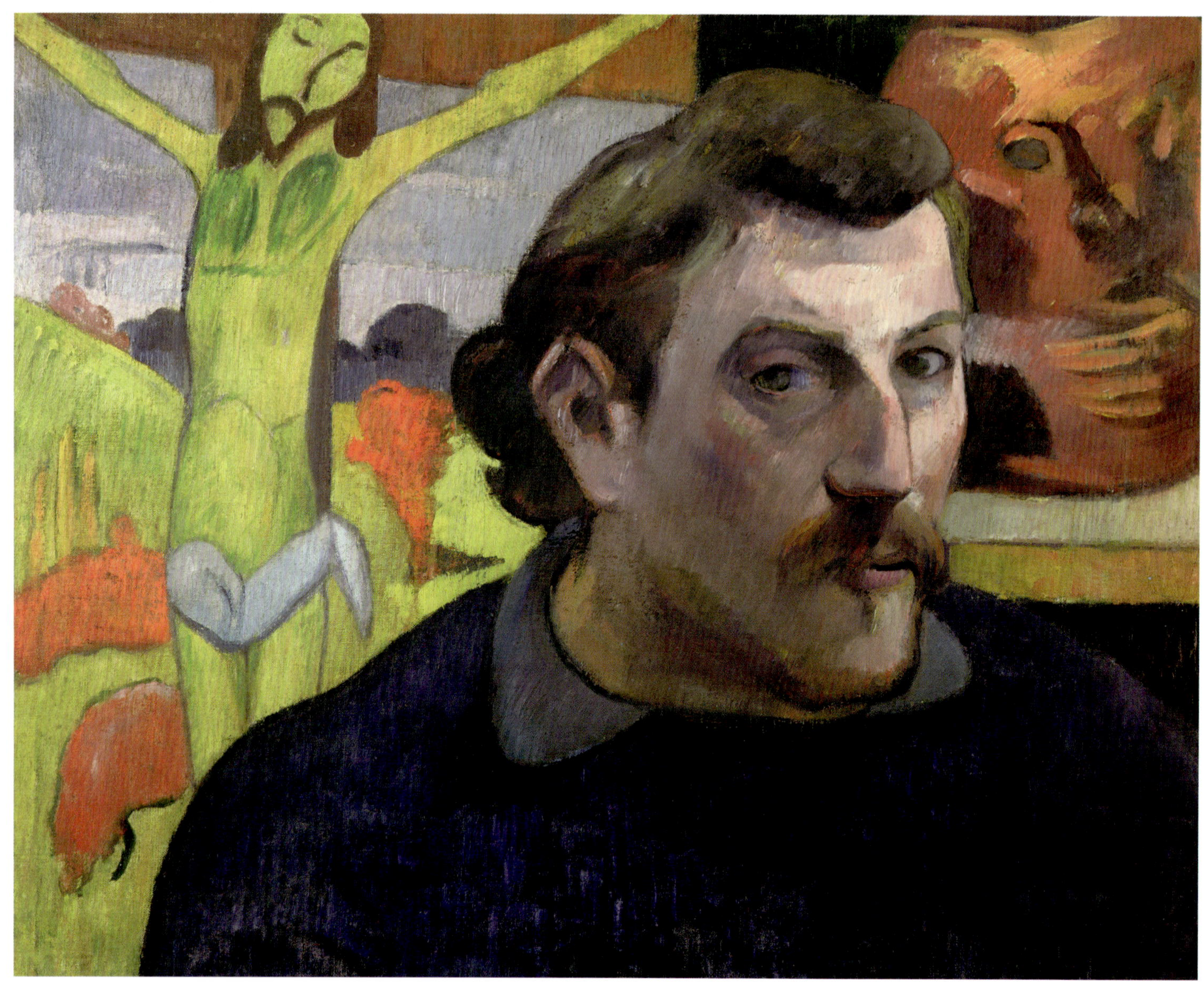

Paul Gauguin (1848–1903)

Self Portrait with the Yellow Christ

Autoportrait au Christ Jaune

Selbstporträt mit dem gelben Christus

Autorretrato con el Cristo amarillo

Autoritratto con Il Cristo giallo

Zelfportret met de gele Christus

1890/91, Oil on canvas/Huile sur toile, 38 × 46 cm, Musée d'Orsay, Paris

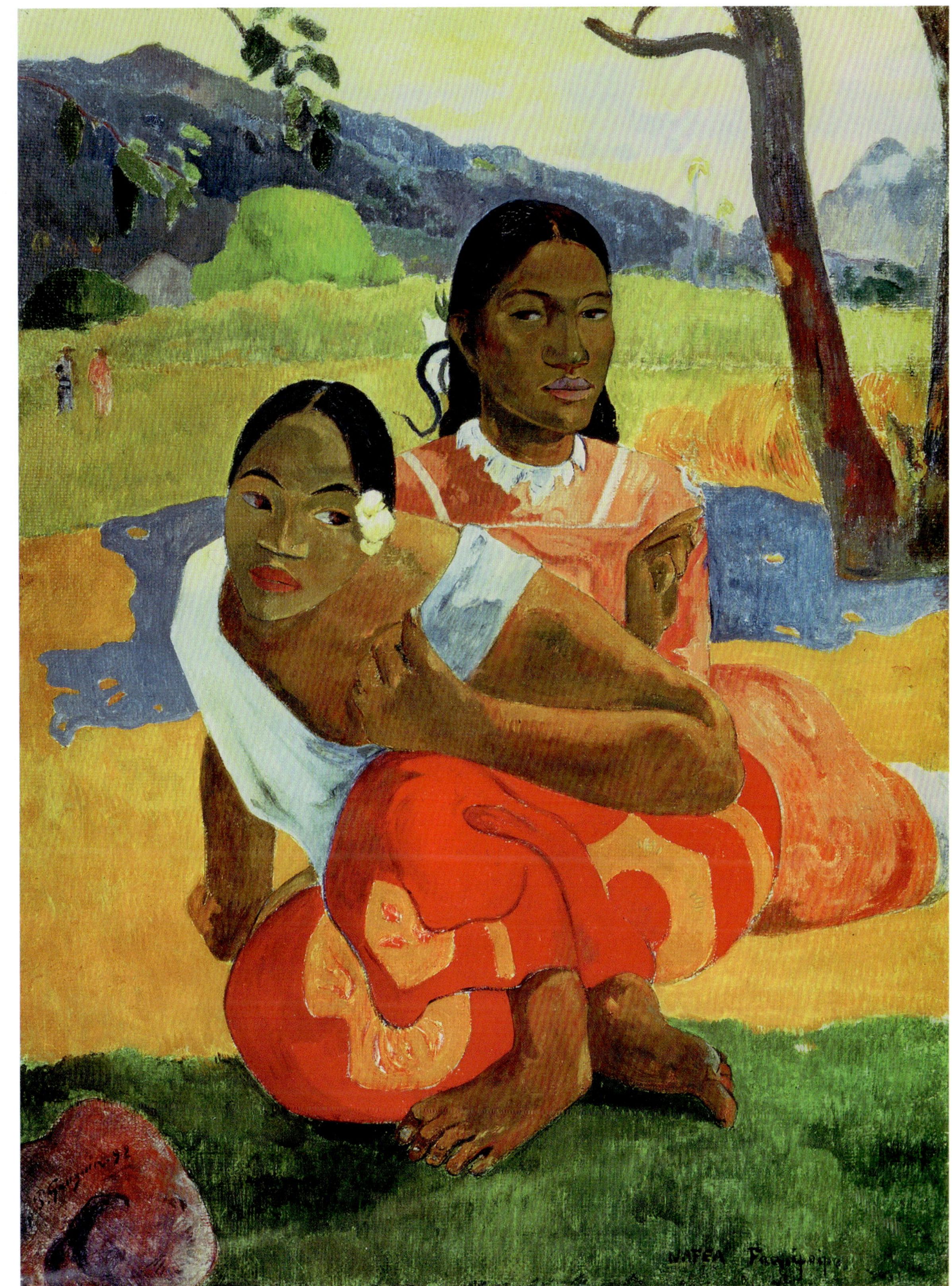

Paul Gauguin (1848–1903)

Nafea Faaipoipo (When are
you Getting Married?)

Nafea faa ipoipo ?
(Quand te maries-tu ?)

Nafea Faaipoipo (Wann
heiratest Du?)

Nafea Faaipoipo
(¿Cuándo te casas?)

Nafea faa ipoipo
(Quando ti sposi?)

Nafea Faaipoipo (Wanneer
ga je trouwen?)

1892, Oil on canvas/Huile
sur toile, 105 × 77,5 cm,
Private collection

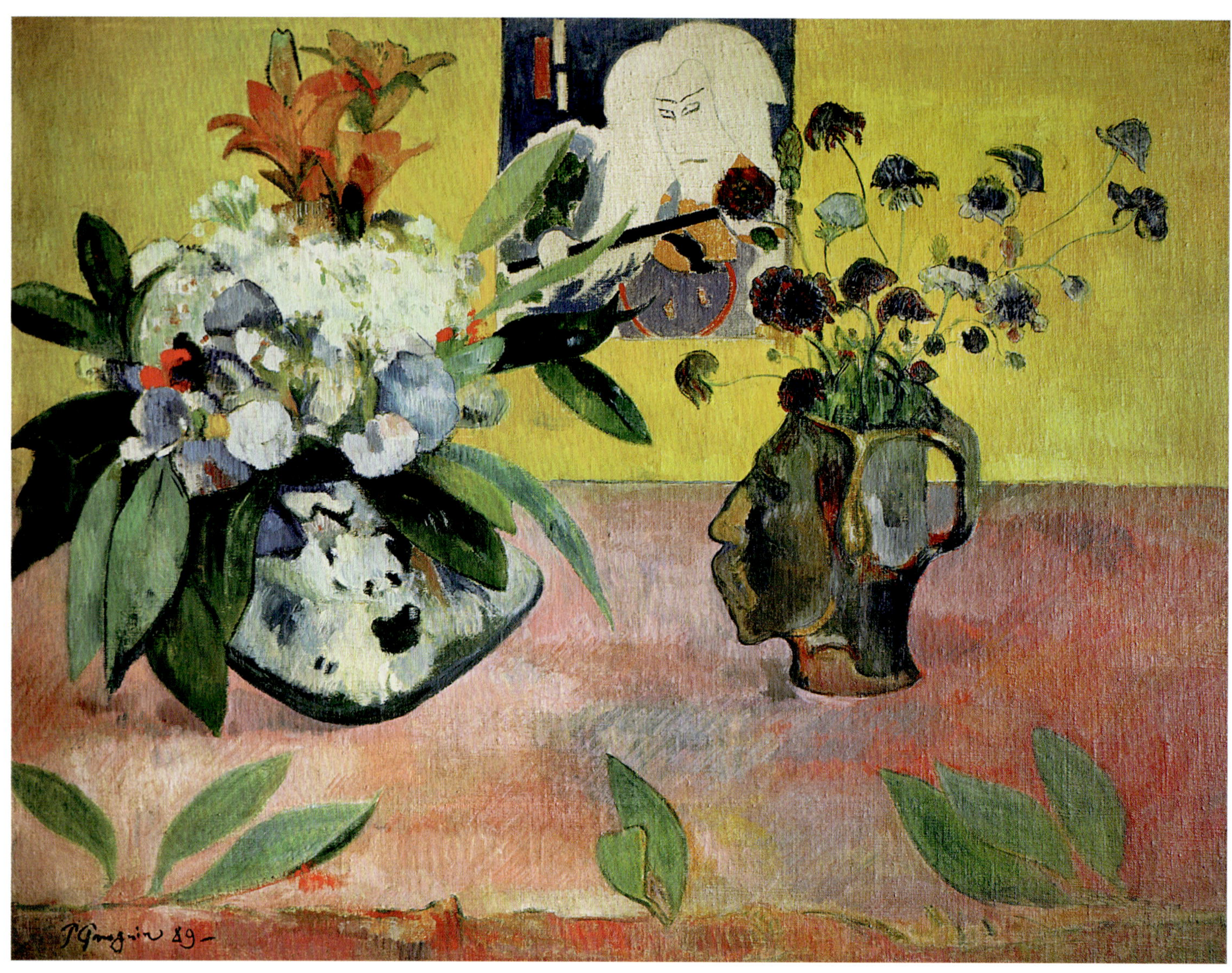

Paul Gauguin (1848–1903)

Flowers and a Japanese Print

Nature Morte à l'estampe japonaise

Stillleben mit Blumen und japanischem Holzschnitt

Bodegón con flores y xilografía japonesa

Natura morta con xilografia giapponese

Stilleven met bloemen en Japanse houtsnede

1889, Oil on canvas/Huile sur toile, 85 × 115 cm, Private collection

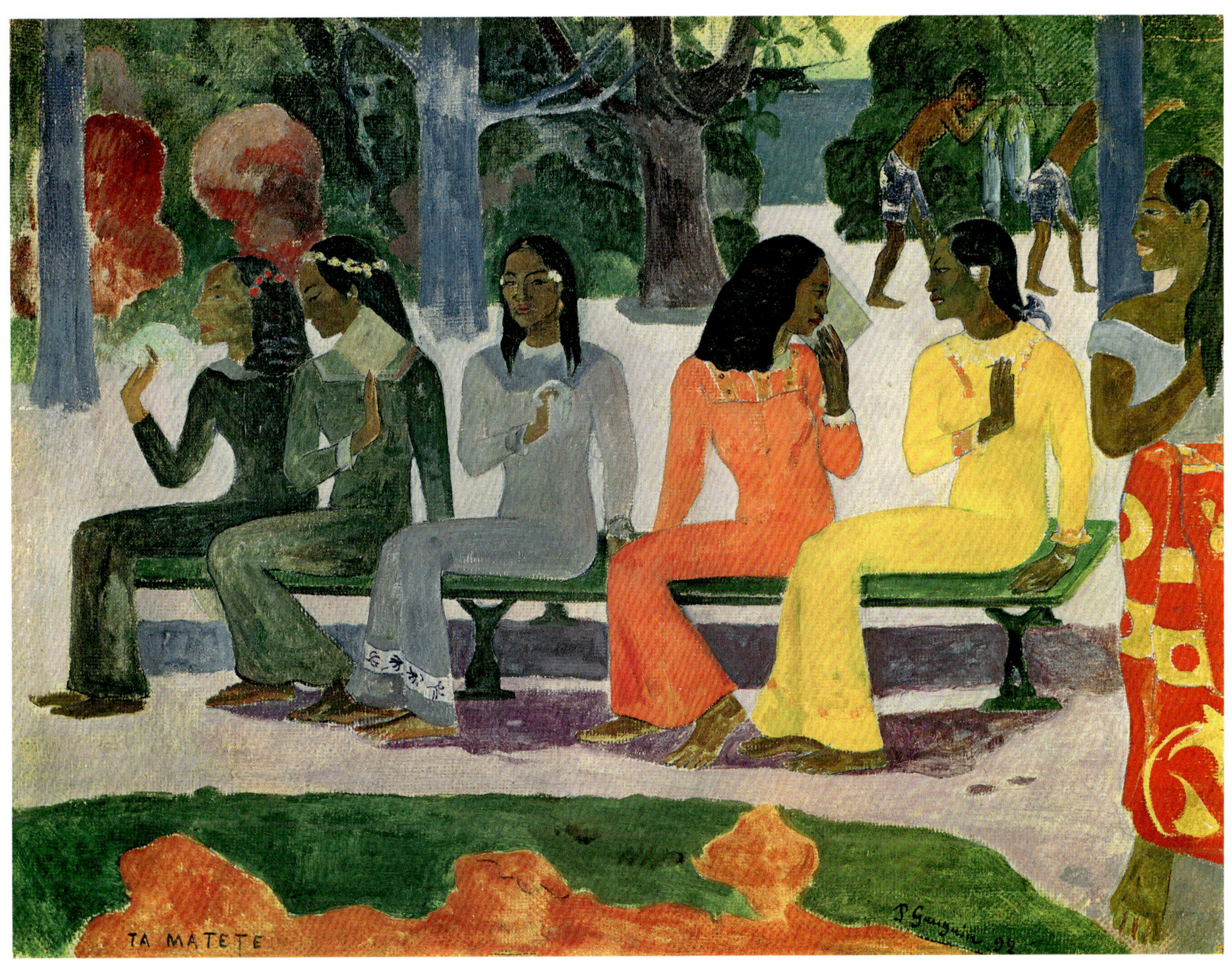

Paul Gauguin (1848–1903)

Ta Matete (We Shall Not Go to Market Today)

Ta Matete

Ta Matete (Der Markt)

Ta Matete

Ta Matete

Ta Matete

1892, Oil on canvas/Huile sur toile, 73,2 × 91,5 cm, Kunstmuseum, Basel

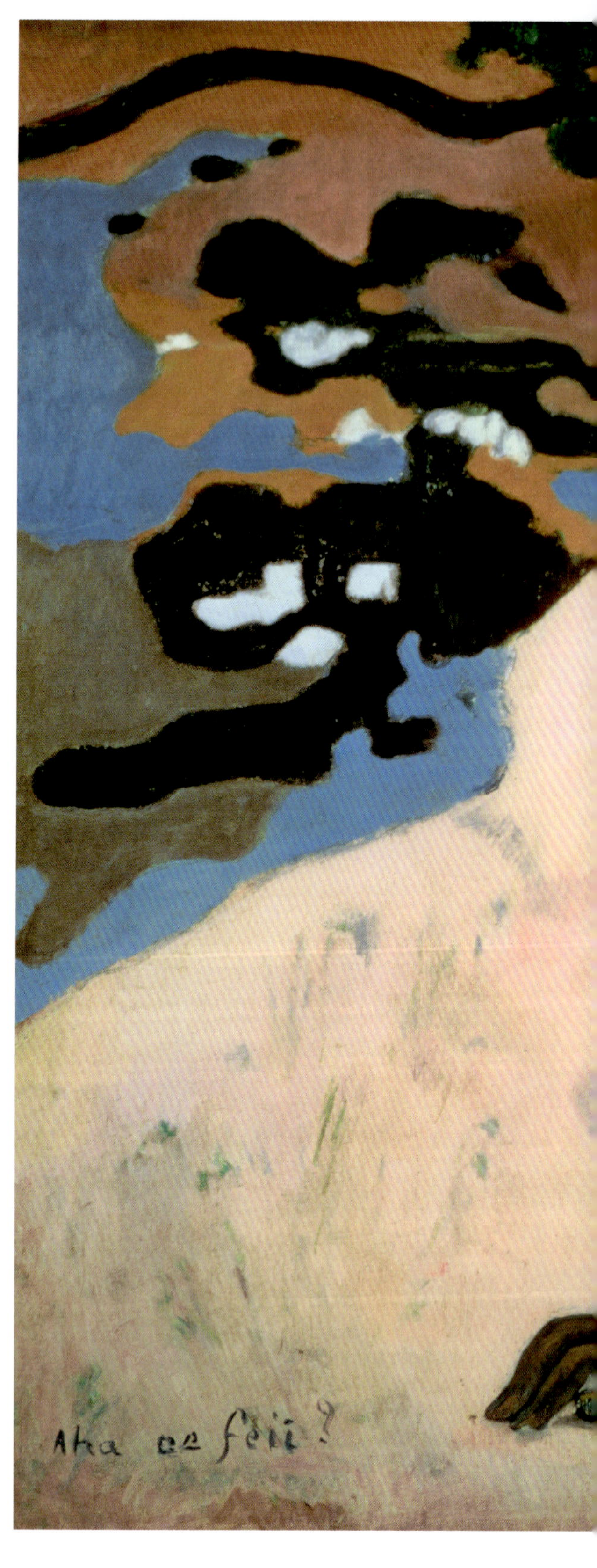

Paul Gauguin (1848–1903)

Aha oe Feii? (Are You Jealous?)

Aha oe Feii ? (Eh quoi, tu es jalouse ?)

Aha oe Feii? (Bist du eifersüchtig?)

Aha oe Feii? (¿Eres celoso?)

Aha oe feii? (Come, sei gelosa?)

Aha oe Feii? (Ben je jaloers?)

1892, Oil on canvas/Huile sur toile, 66,2 × 89,3 cm, Pushkin State Museum of Fine Arts, Moscow

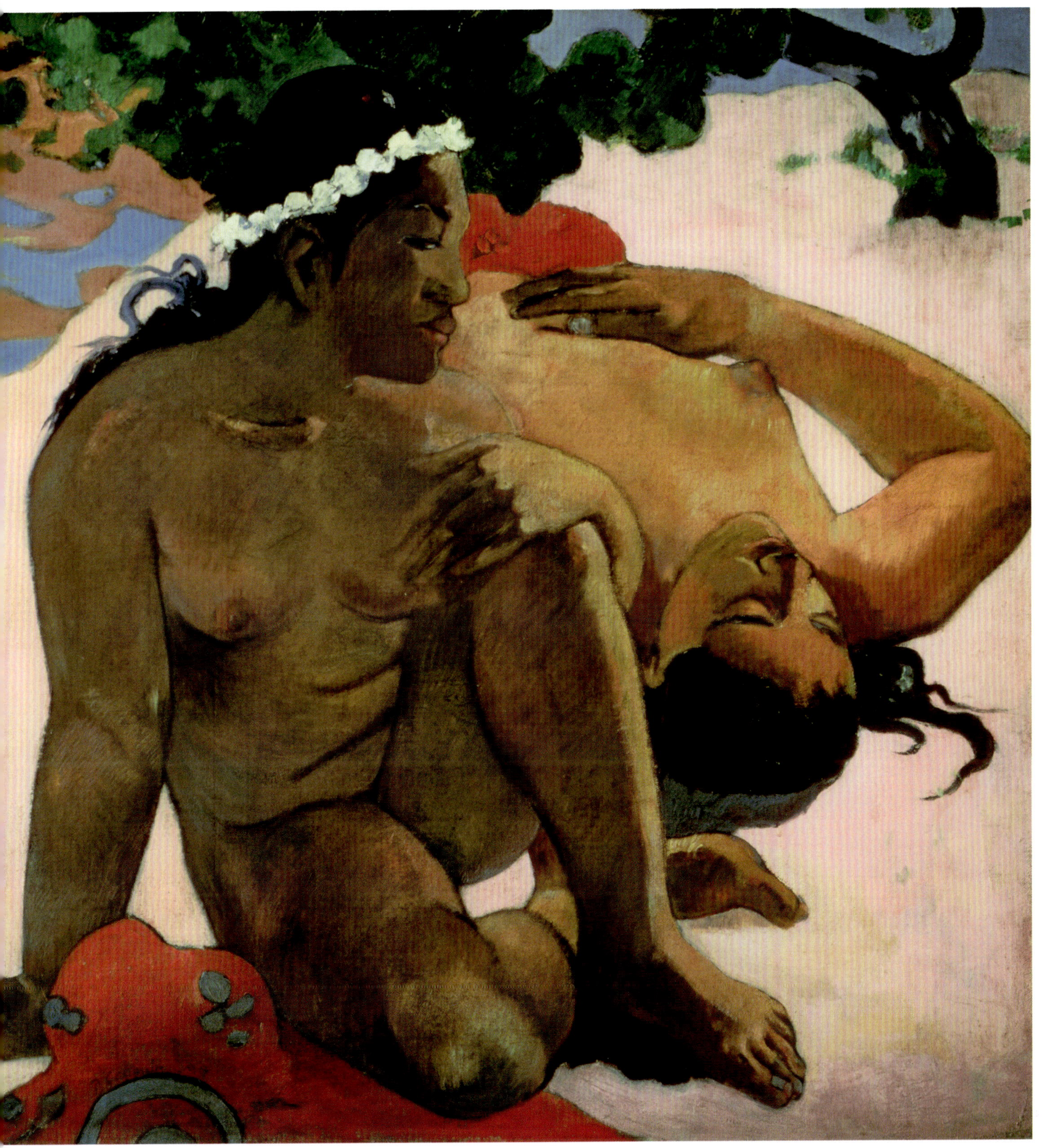

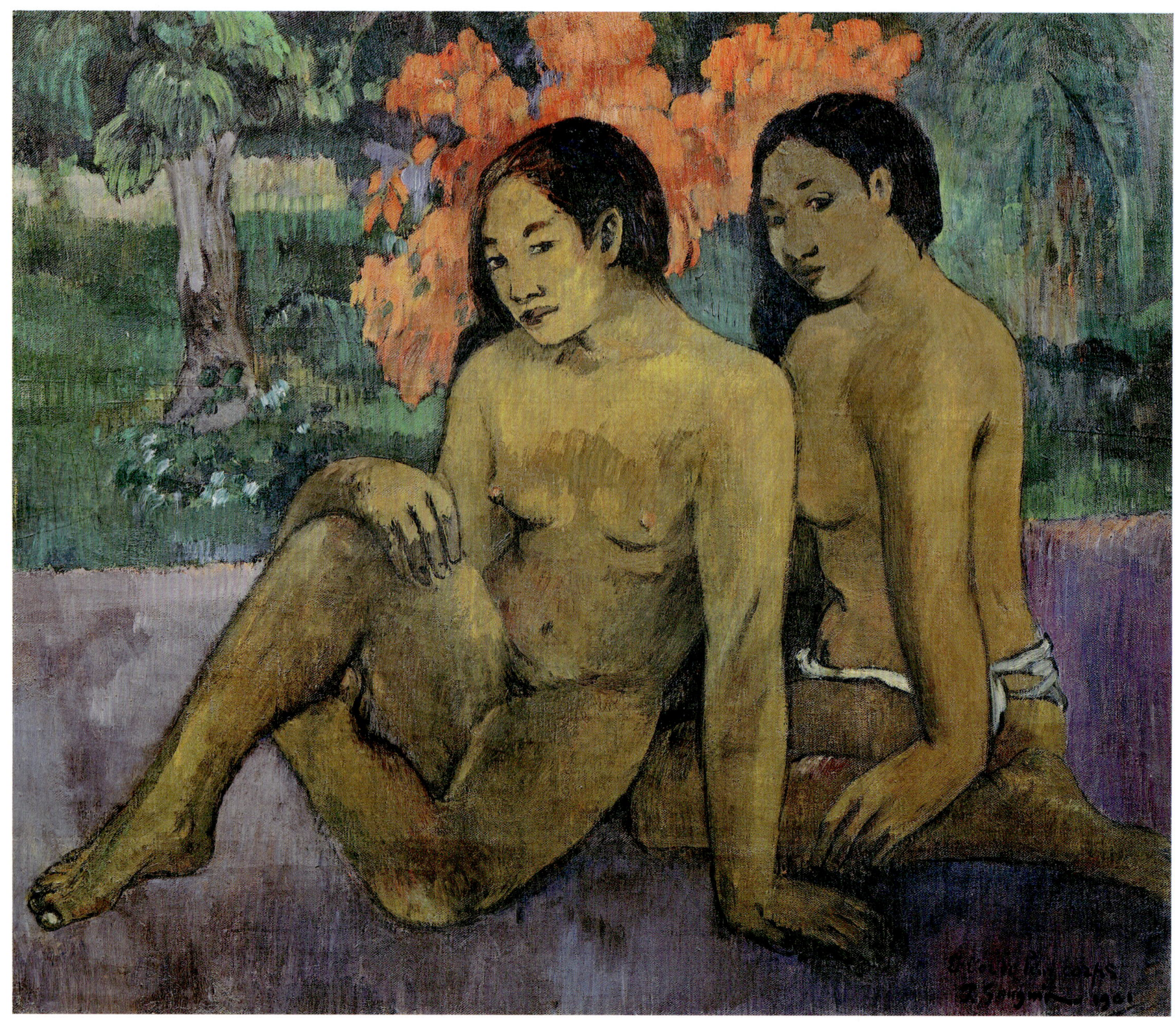

Paul Gauguin (1848–1903)

And the Gold of their Bodies

Et l'or de leur corps

Und das Gold ihrer Körper

Y el oro de sus cuerpos

Due donne tahitiane sedute (...E l'oro dei loro corpi)

En het goud van hun lichamen

1901, Oil on canvas/Huile sur toile, 67 × 76,5 cm, Musée d'Orsay, Paris

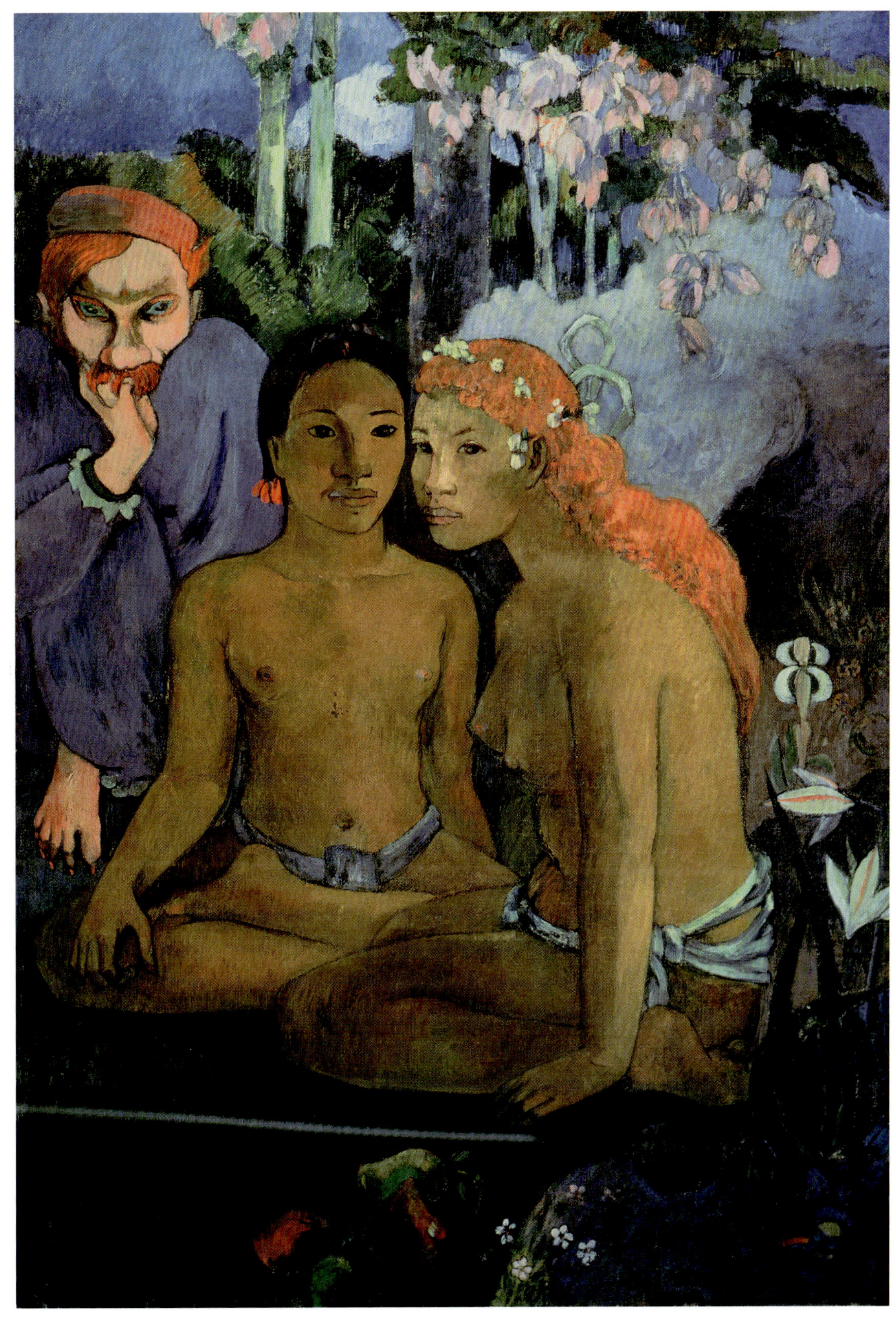

Paul Gauguin (1848–1903)
Contes Barbares
Contes Barbares
Contes Barbares
Contes Barbares
Racconti barbari
Contes Barbares ('Barbaarse vertellingen')
1902, Oil on canvas/Huile sur toile, 130 × 91,5 cm, Museum Folkwang, Essen

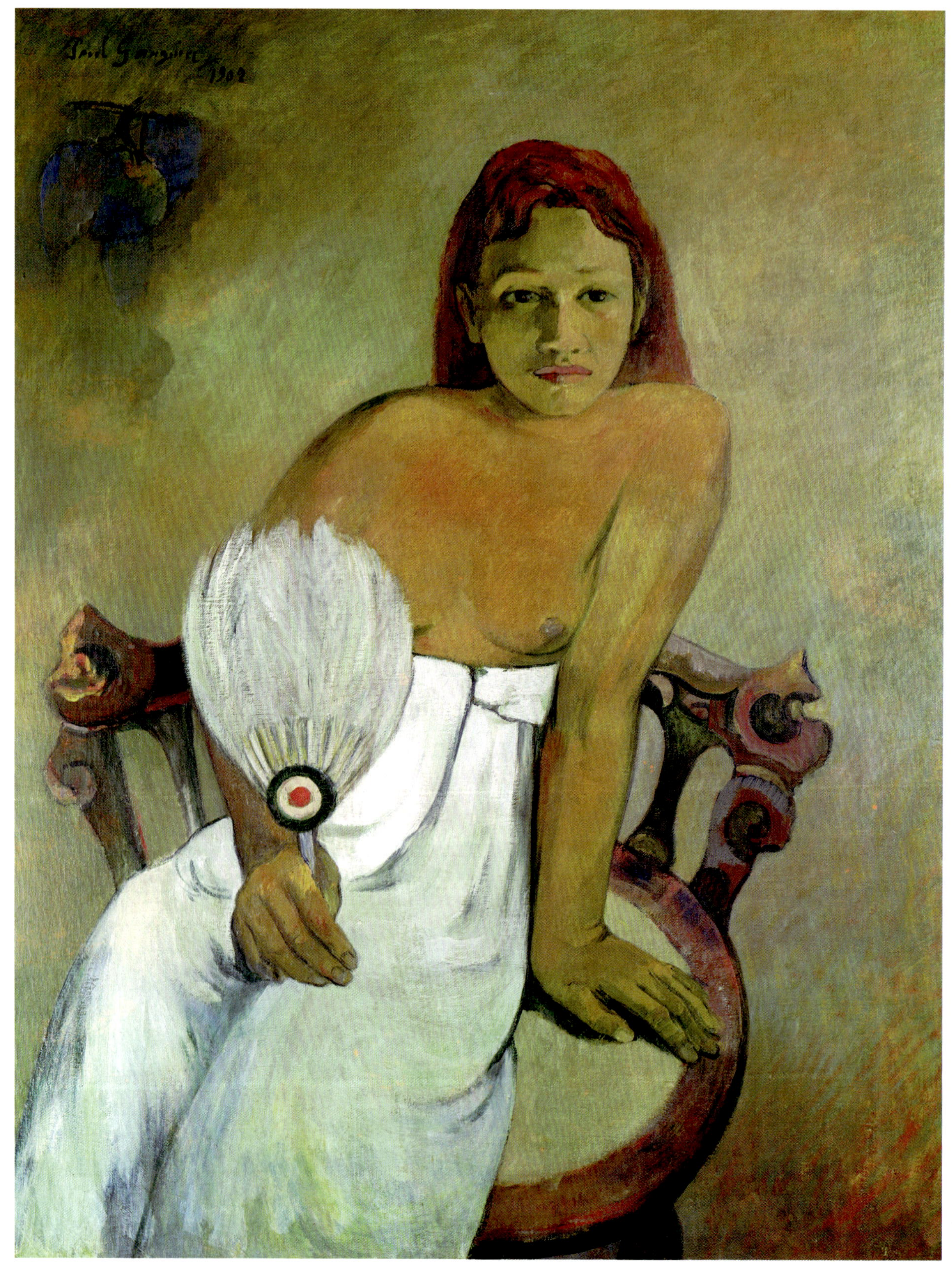

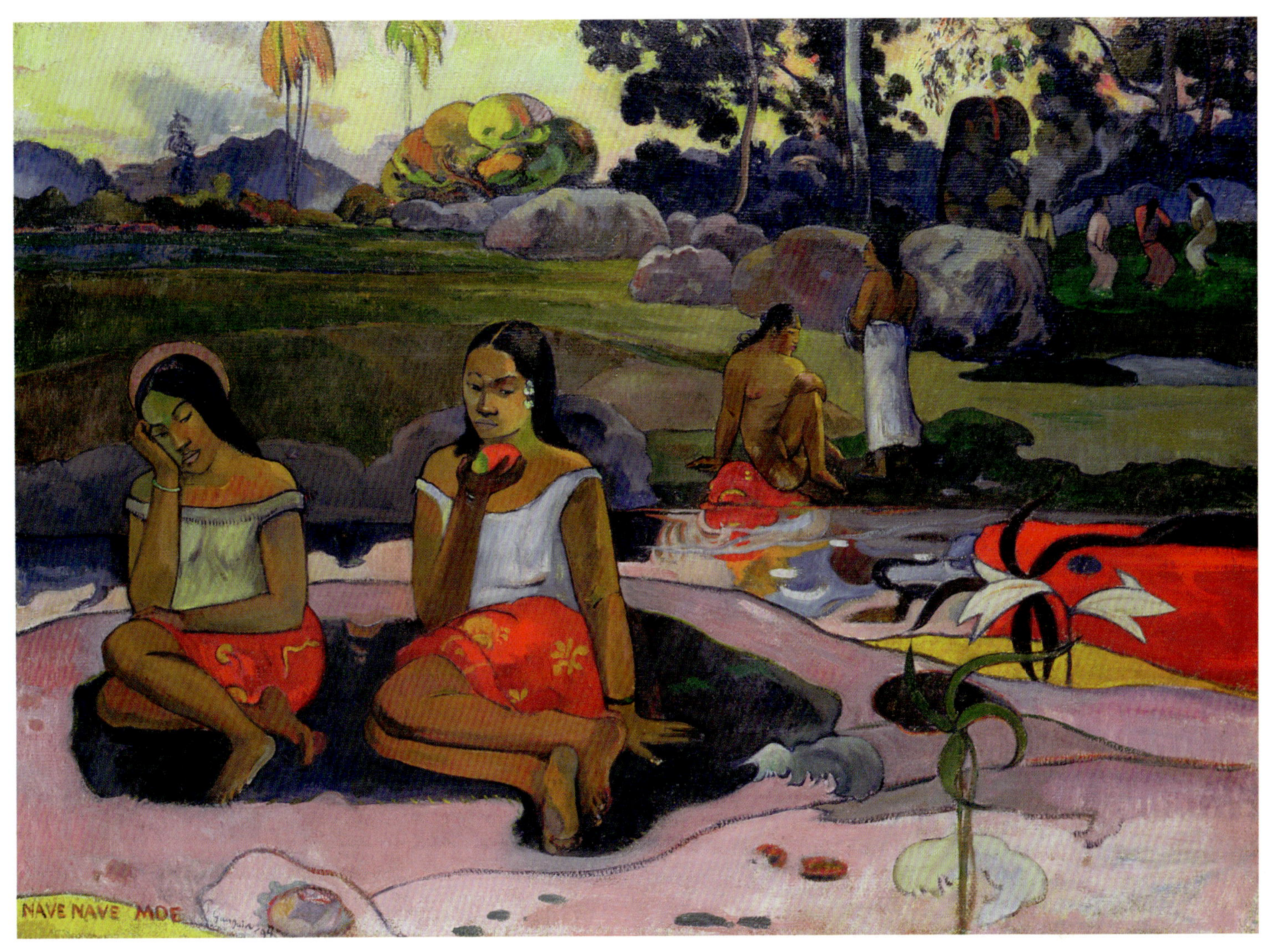

Paul Gauguin (1848–1903)

Girl with fan

Jeune fille à l'éventail

Mädchen mit Fächer

Niña con abanico

Giovane tahitiana col ventaglio

Het meisje met de waaier

1902, Oil on canvas/Huile sur toile, 91 × 73 cm, Museum Folkwang, Essen

Paul Gauguin (1848–1903)

Nave Nave Moe (Sacred Spring)

Nave Nave Moe (Printemps Sacré)

Nave Nave Moe (Heiliger Frühling: Süße Träume)

Nave Nave Moe (Primavera Santa)

Nave Nave Moe (Primavera sacra)

Nave Nave Moe (Heilig voorjaar)

1894, Oil on canvas/Huile sur toile, 74 × 100 cm, State Hermitage, St. Petersburg

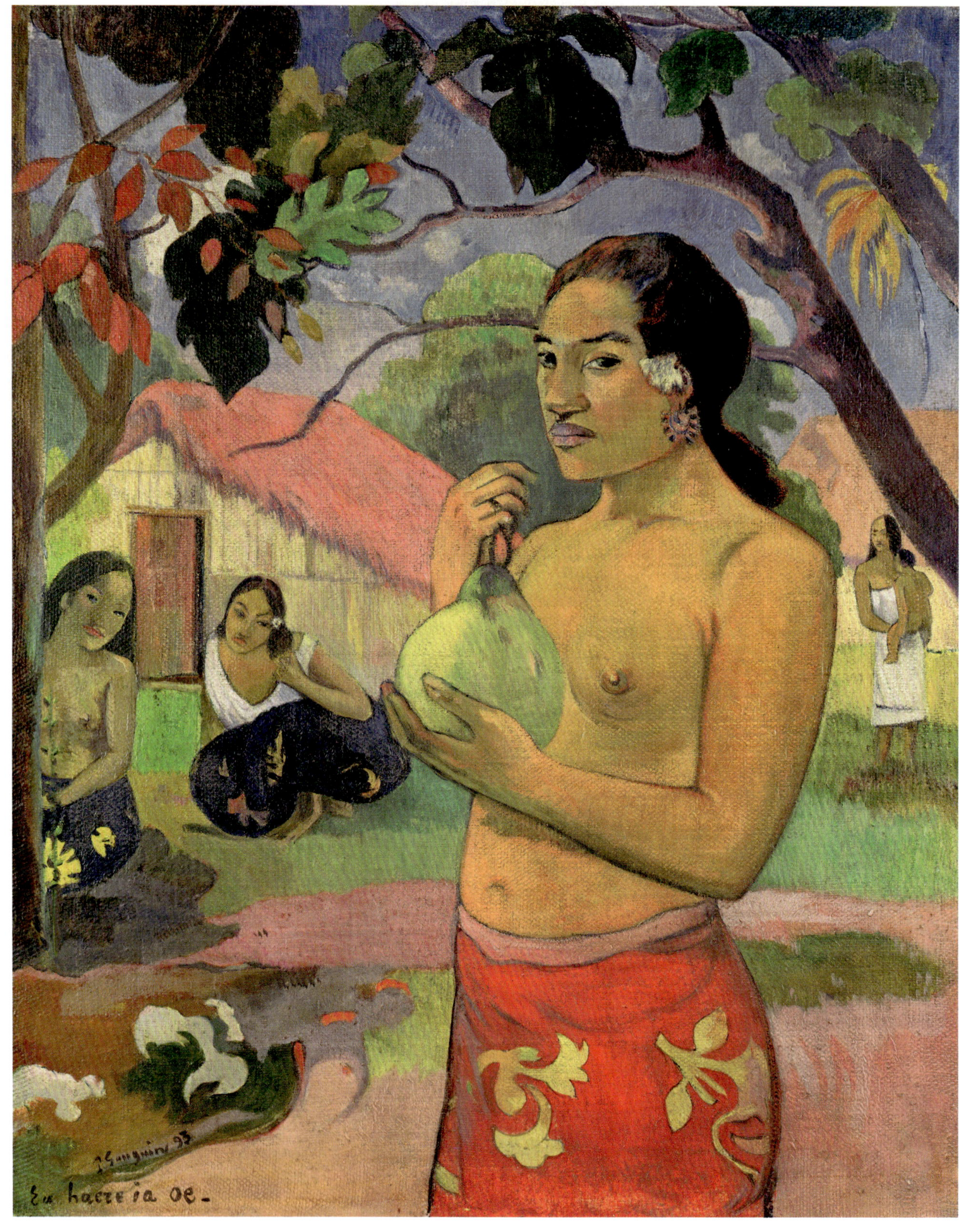

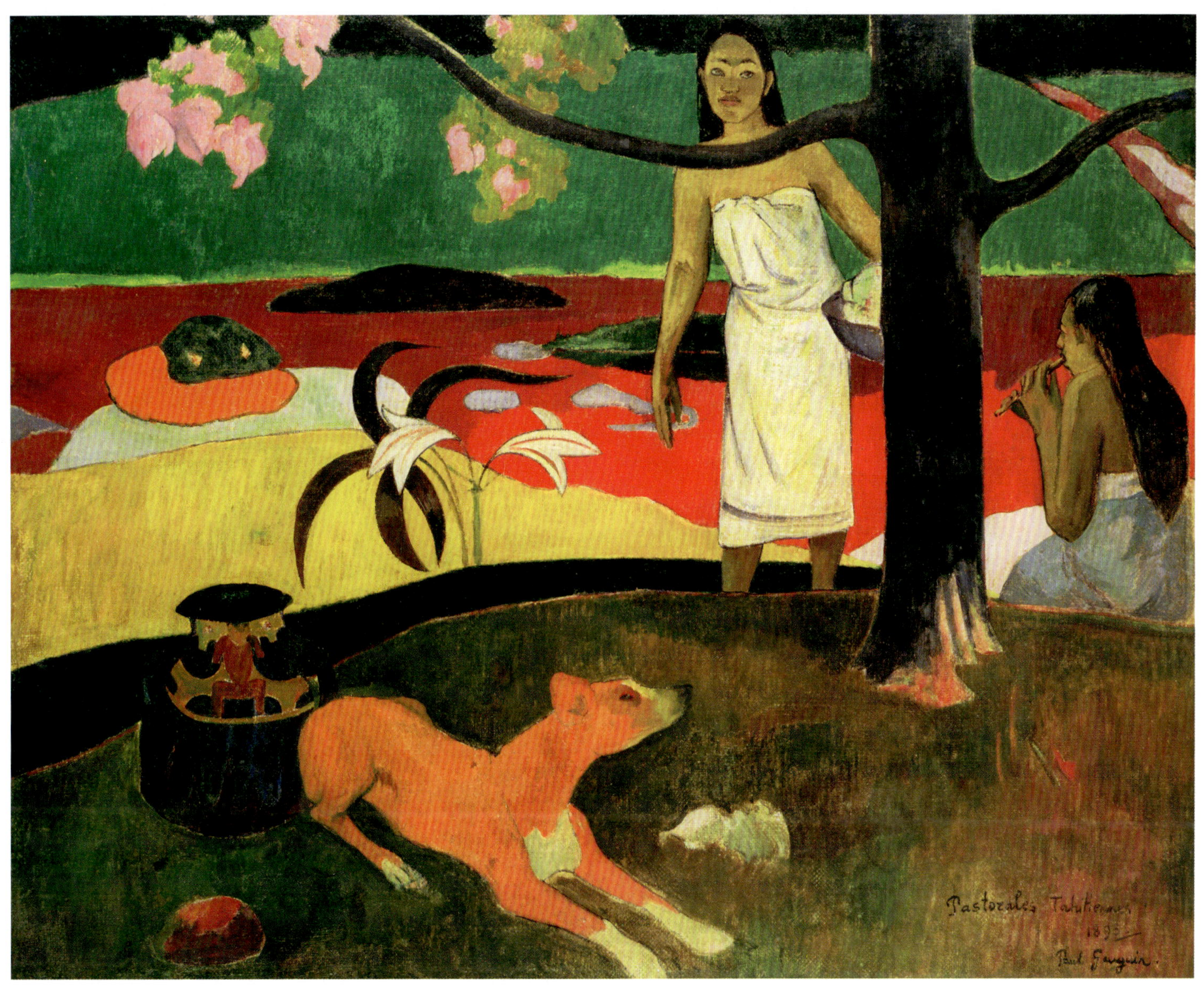

Paul Gauguin (1848–1903)

Woman with Mango

Femme à la mangue

Eu haere ia oe (Wo gehst du hin?) – Frau mit Mango

Mujer con mango

Donna con mango

Vrouw met mango

1893, Oil on canvas/Huile sur toile, 92,5 × 73,5 cm, State Hermitage, St. Petersburg

Paul Gauguin (1848–1903)

Pastorales Tahitiennes

Pastorales Tahitiennes

Pastorale auf Tahiti

Pastorale auf Tahiti

Pastorale tahitiana

Pastorale op Tahiti

1893/94, Oil on canvas/Huile sur toile, 87,5 × 113,7 cm, State Hermitage, St. Petersburg

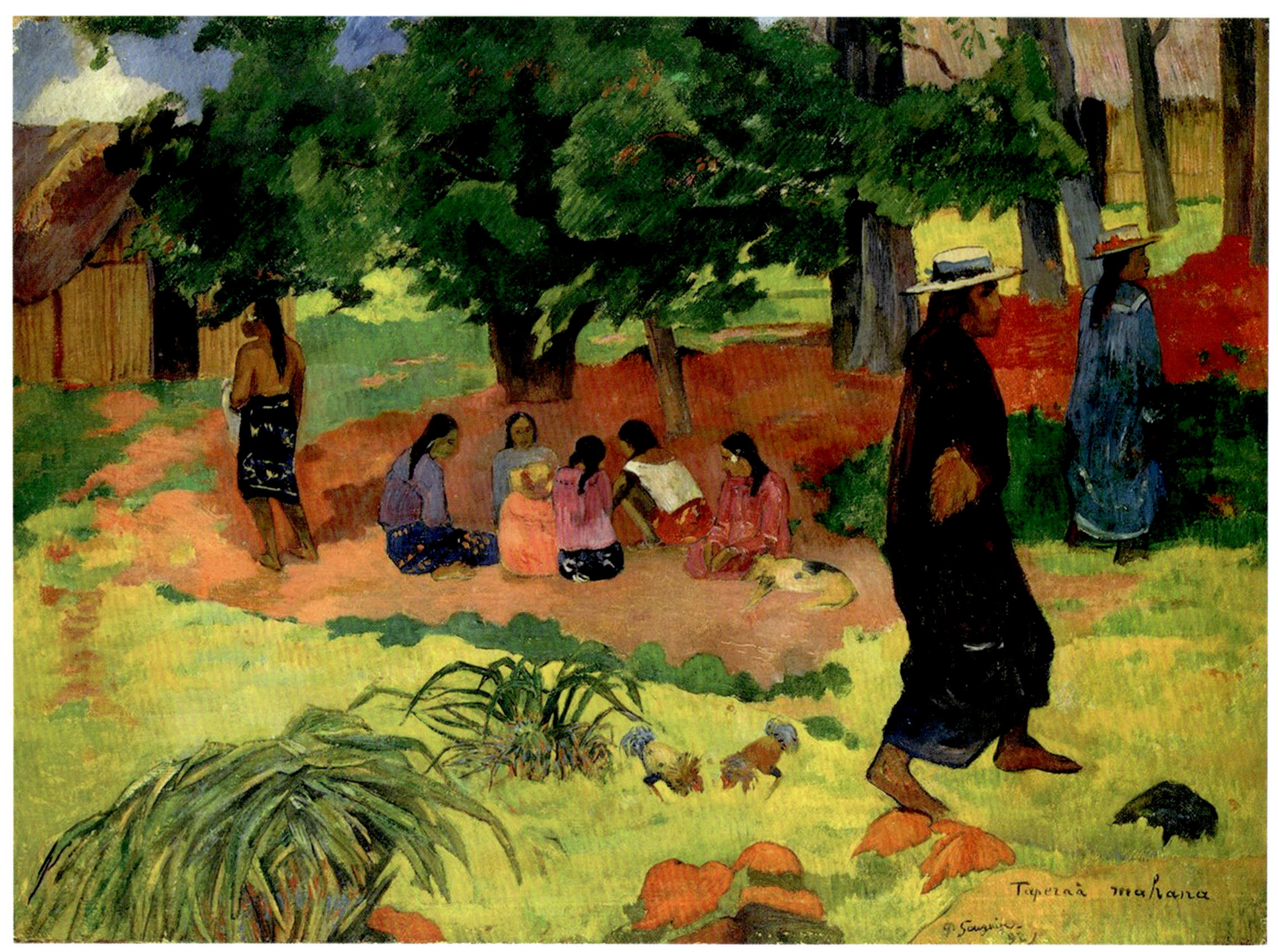

Paul Gauguin (1848–1903)

Taperaa Mahana

1892, Oil on canvas/Huile sur toile, 72,3 × 97,5 cm, State Hermitage, St. Petersburg

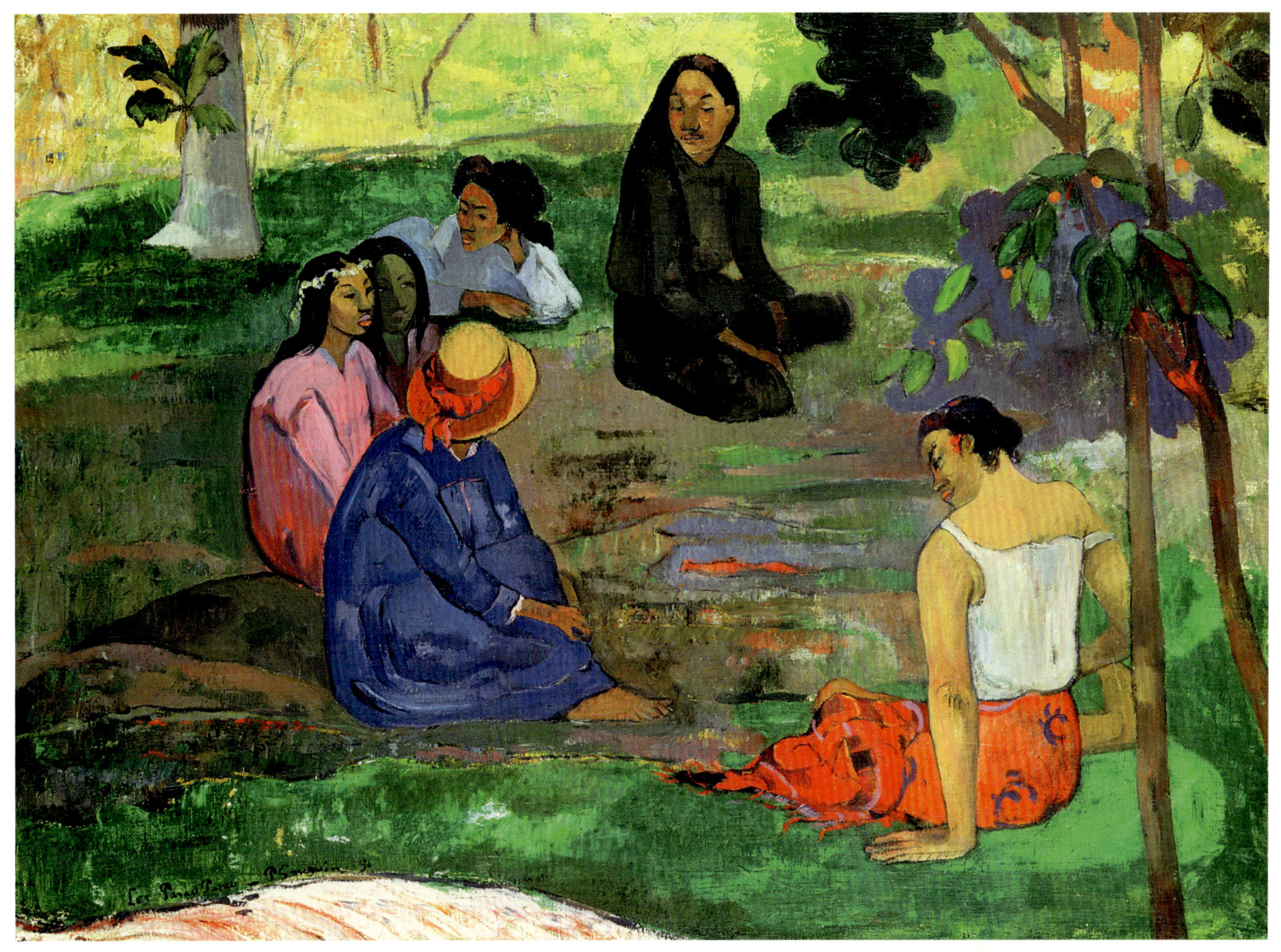

Paul Gauguin (1848–1903)

Les Parau Parau (The Gossipers) *or* Conversation

Parau Parau (Les potins)

Les Parau Parau (Die Unterhaltung)

Parau Parau (La conversación)

Parau Parau (La conversazione)

Parau Parau (Het gesprek)

1891, Oil on canvas/Huile sur toile, 70,5 × 90,3 cm, State Hermitage, St. Petersburg

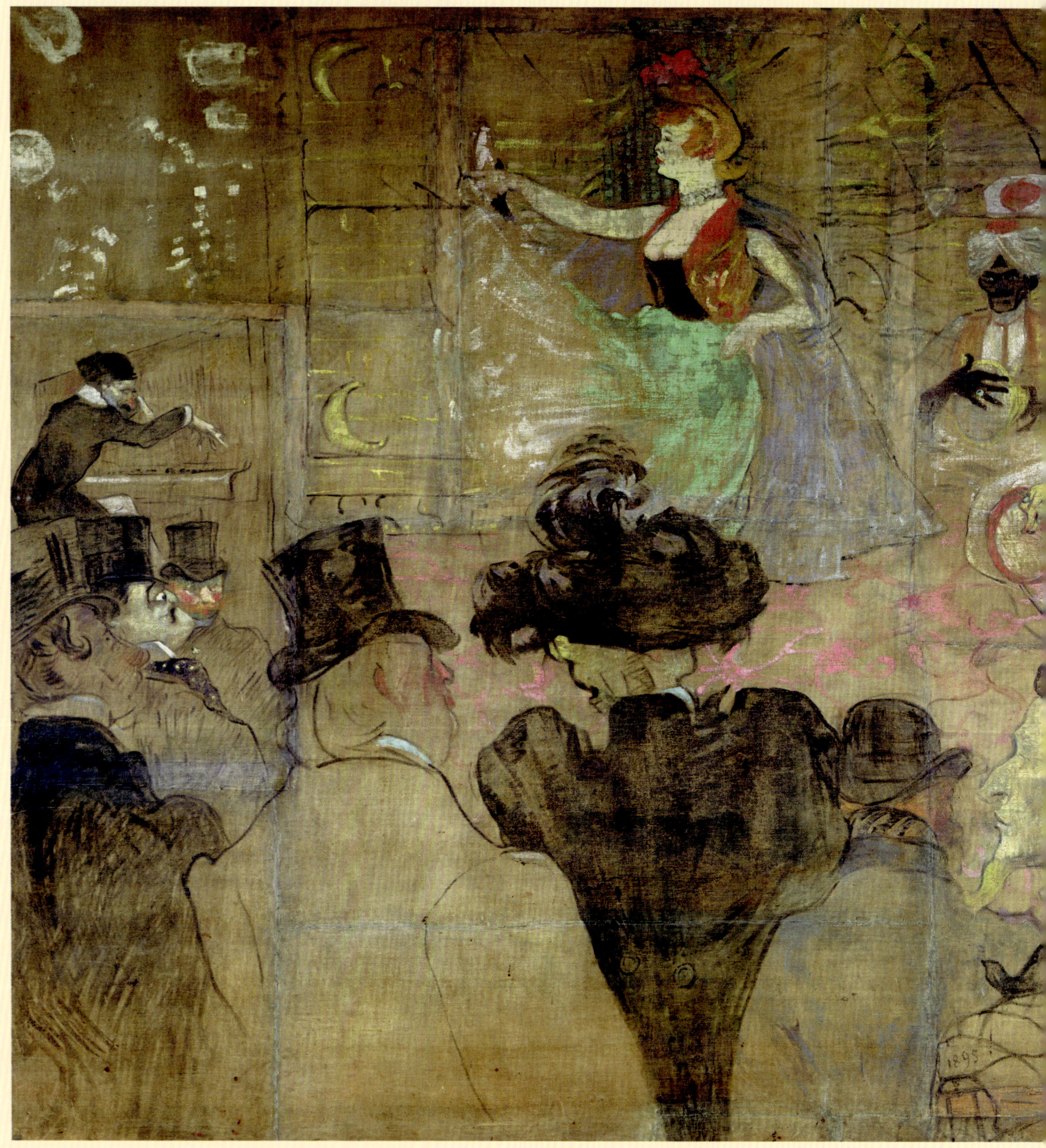

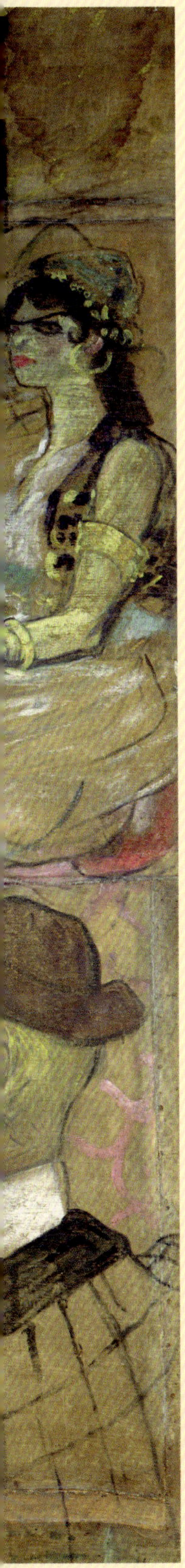

The artist had been closely observing the goings-on in one of the most famous night clubs of Paris and reproduced this in an impressive composition. The depth of the space is largely suggested by the staggered arrangement of the figures. In the center are the dancer La Goulue (the glutton) and Valentin le désossé (Valentin the contortionist), two cabaret stars preserved forever by Toulouse-Lautrec in the history of art.

L'artiste avait observé de près les allées et venues dans l'un des plus célèbres dancings de Paris et les reproduisit dans une composition impressionnante. La profondeur de l'espace est largement suggérée par la disposition décalée des personnages. Au centre, se trouvent la danseuse La Goulue et Valentin le désossé, deux stars de cabaret immortalisées pour l'histoire de l'art par Toulouse-Lautrec.

Der Künstler hat das Treiben in einem der berühmtesten Nachtlokale von Paris genau beobachtet und in einer eindrucksvollen Komposition wiedergegeben. Die Tiefe des Raums wird weitgehend von der Staffelung der Figuren suggeriert. In der Bildmitte tanzen La Goulue (die Gefräßige) und Valentin le Désossé (Valentin der Schlangenmensch), zwei Cabaretstars, die durch Toulouse-Lautrec in die Kunstgeschichte eingingen.

El artista ha observado meticulosamente la actividad de uno de los locales nocturnos más famosos de París y lo ha representado en una impresionante composición. La profundidad del espacio se sugiere apilando las figuras. En el medio de la imagen bailan La Goulue (la glotona) y Valentin le Désossé (el deshuesado), dos estrellas del cabaret que pasaron a la historia del arte de la mano de Toulouse-Lautrec.

In quest'opera l'artista riproduce in una potente composizione uno degli eventi osservati da vicino in uno dei più famosi locali notturni di Parigi. La profondità dello spazio è ampiamente suggerita dalle figure. Al centro ballano La Goulue (La Gola) e Valentin le Désossé (Valentin il Contorsionista), due stelle del teatro che sono entrate nella storia proprio grazie a Toulouse-Lautrec.

De kunstenaar heeft de gezellige drukte in een van de beroemdste nachtlokalen van Parijs goed geobserveerd en in een gedurfde compositie uitgebeeld. De diepte van de ruimte wordt door de opstelling van de figuren gecreëerd. In het midden dansen La Goulue ('de Gulzige') en Valentin le Désossé ('de Slangenmens'), twee cabaretiers die dankzij Toulouse-Lautrec in de annalen van de kunstgeschiedenis zijn opgenomen.

Henri de Toulouse-Lautrec (1864–1901)

Dancing at the Moulin Rouge: La Goulue

La danse au Moulin Rouge (*dit aussi* La Goulue)

Tanz im Moulin Rouge: La Goulue

Baile en el Moulin Rouge: La Goulue

Ballo al Moulin Rouge: La Goulue

Dans in de Moulin Rouge: La Goulue

1895, Oil on canvas/Huile sur toile, 289 × 316 cm, Musée d'Orsay, Paris

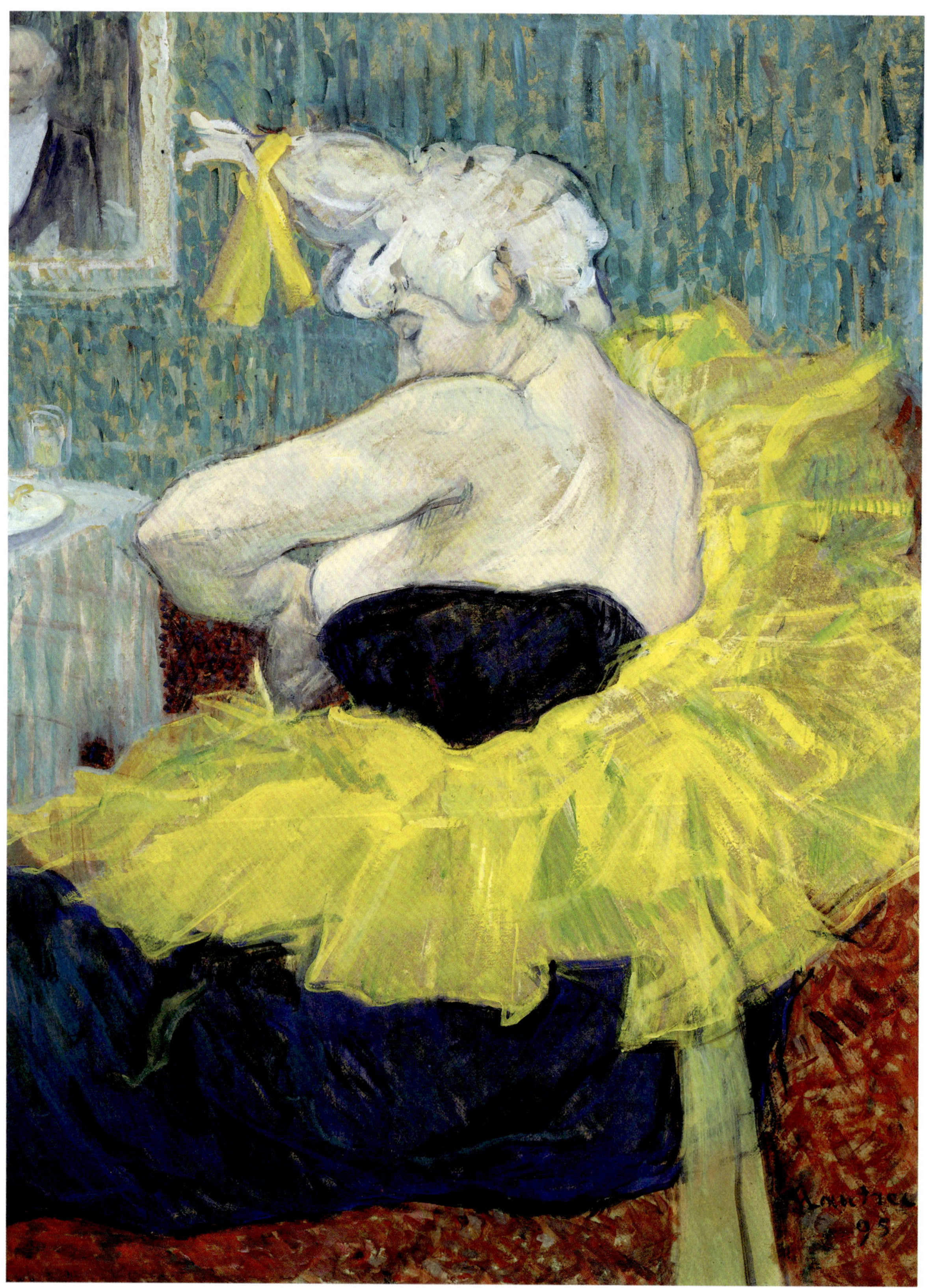

**Henri de Toulouse-Lautrec
(1864–1901)**

The Clowness
Cha–U–Kao in a Tutu

La Clownesse Cha-U-Kao

Die Clownin
Cha-U-Kao im Tutu

La clown Cha-U-Kao
en un tutú

La clownessa Cha-U-Kao

De clown Cha-U-Kao
in een tutu

1895, Oil on canvas/Huile
sur carton, 58 × 43 cm,
Musée d'Orsay, Paris

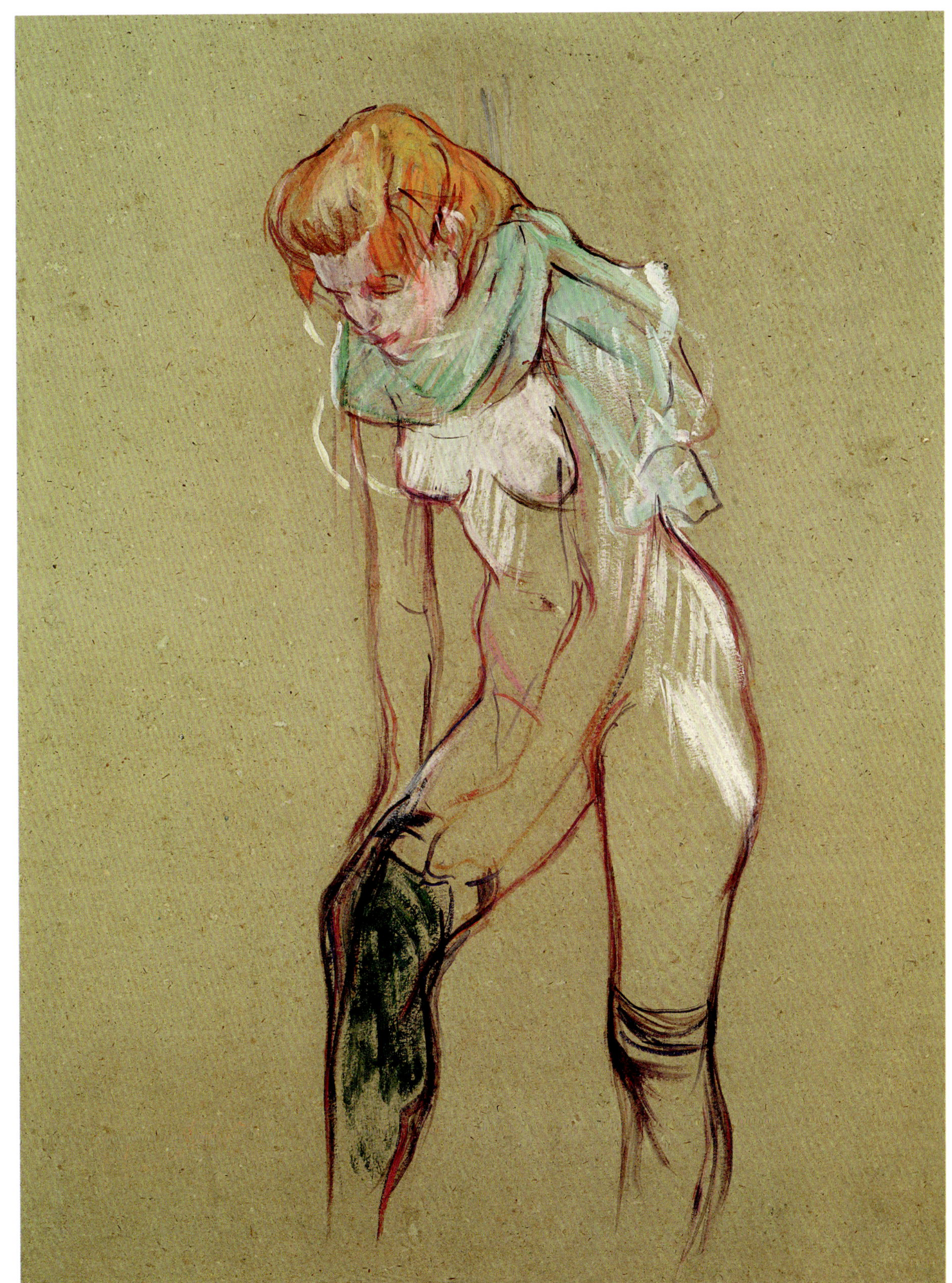

**Henri de Toulouse-Lautrec
(1864–1901)**

Woman Pulling Up
her Stocking

Femme qui tire son bas

Frau, sich die Strümpfe
hochziehend

Mujer poniéndose
las medias

Donna che s'infila le calze

Vrouw die kousen aantrekt

1894, Oil on cardboard/Huile
sur toile, 61,5 × 44,5 cm,
Musée Toulouse-Lautrec, Albi

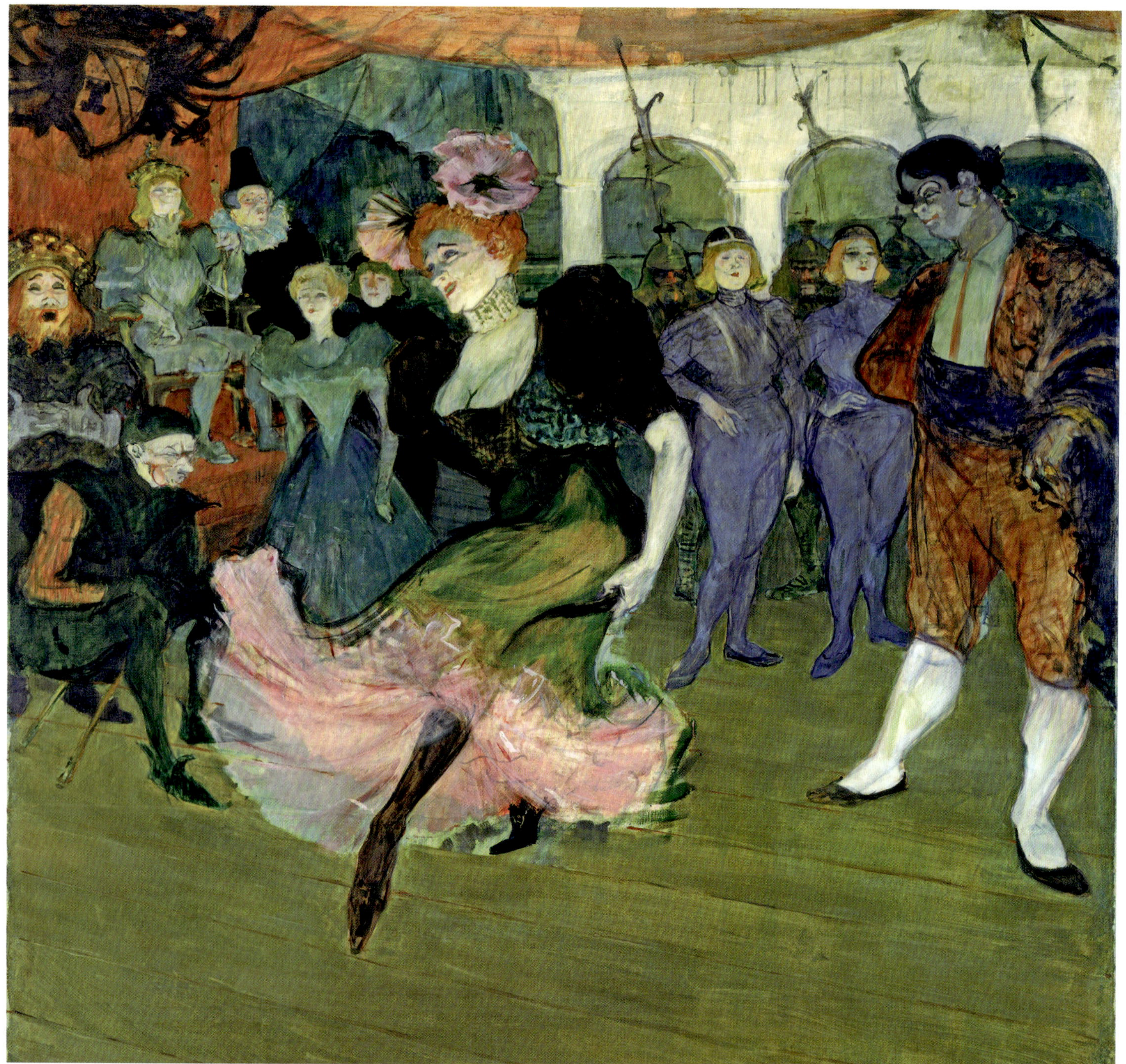

Henri de Toulouse-Lautrec (1864–1901)

Marcelle Lender Dancing the Bolero in 'Chilperic'

Marcelle Lender danse le boléro au « Chilpéri c»

Marcelle Lender tanzt den Bolero in „Chilpéric"

Marcelle Lender baila el Bolero en "Chilpéric"

Marcelle Lender balla il bolero al "Chilpéric"

Marcelle Lender danst de Boléro in de "Chilpéric"

1895/96, Oil on canvas/Huile sur toile, 145 × 149 cm, National Gallery of Art, Washington

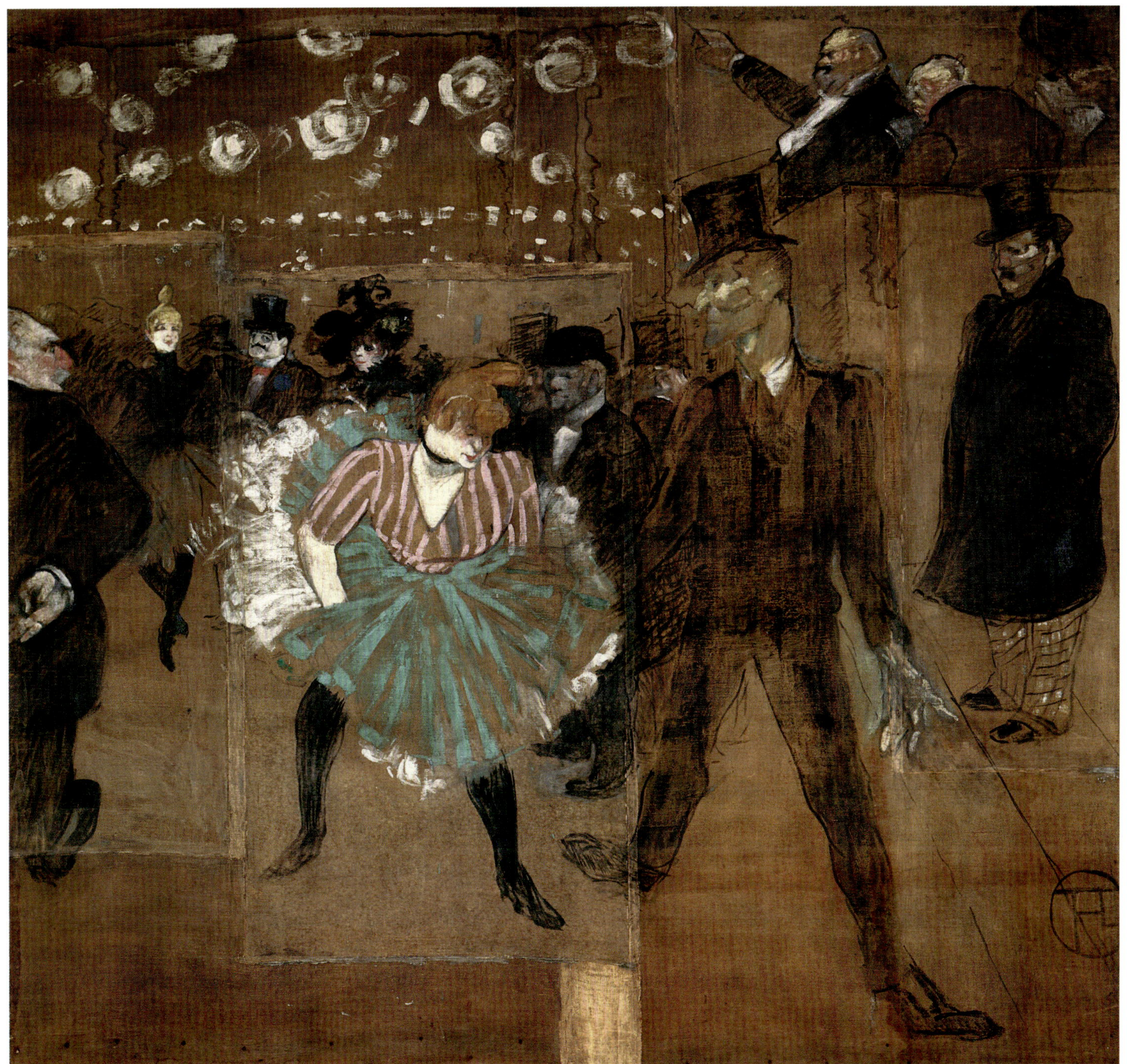

Henri de Toulouse-Lautrec (1864–1901)

Dancing at the Moulin Rouge: La Goulue (1870–1927) and Valentin le Desosse (1843–1907)

La danse au Moulin Rouge, dit aussi La Goulue et Valentin de désossé

Tanz im Moulin Rouge: La Goulue und Valentin le Desossé

Baile en el Moulin Rouge: La Goulue y Valentin le Desossé

Ballo al Moulin Rouge: La Goulue e Valentin-le-Desossé

Dansen in de Moulin Rouge: La Goulue en Valentin le Desossé

1895, Oil on canvas/Huile sur toile, 298 × 316 cm, Musée d'Orsay, Paris

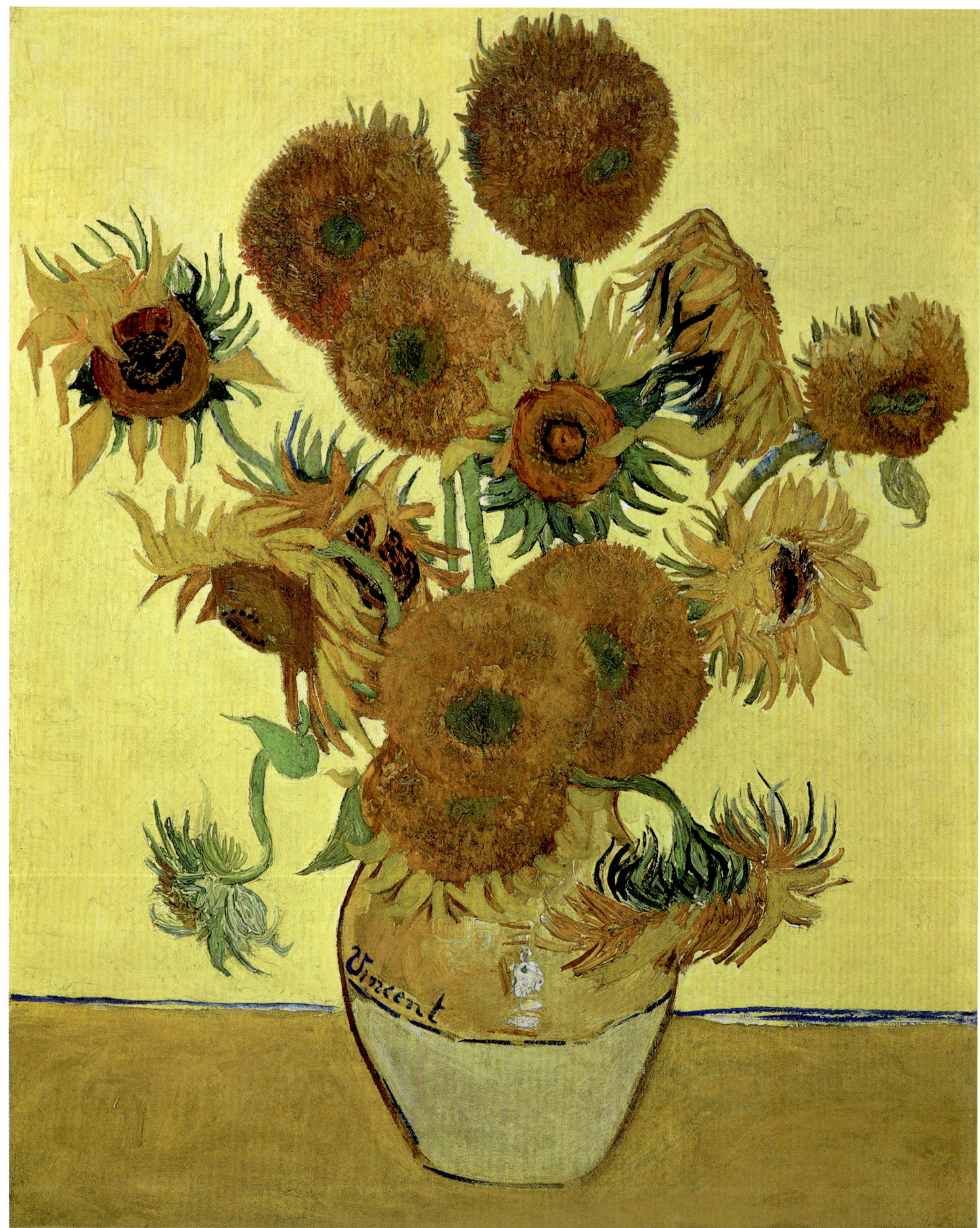

Vincent van Gogh (1853–90)

Sunflowers	Vase mit Sonnenblumen	I girasoli
Les Tournesols	Girasoles	Vaas met zonnebloemen

1888, Oil on canvas/Huile sur toile, 92,1 × 73 cm, National Gallery, London

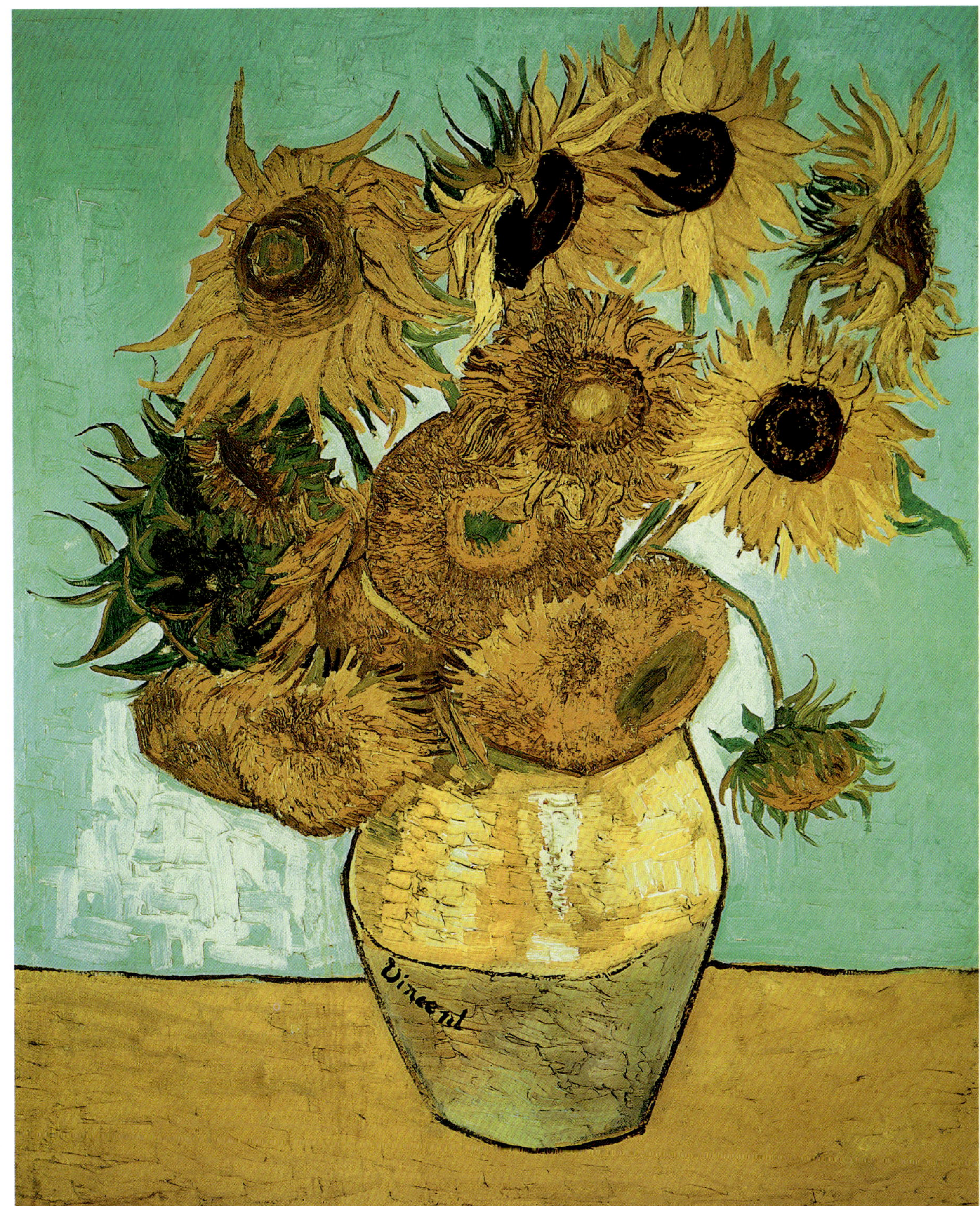

Vincent van Gogh (1853–90)

Sunflowers	Vase mit Sonnenblumen	I girasoli
Les Tournesols	Girasoles	Vaas met zonnebloemen

1888, Oil on canvas/Huile sur toile, 91 × 72 cm, Neue Pinakothek, München

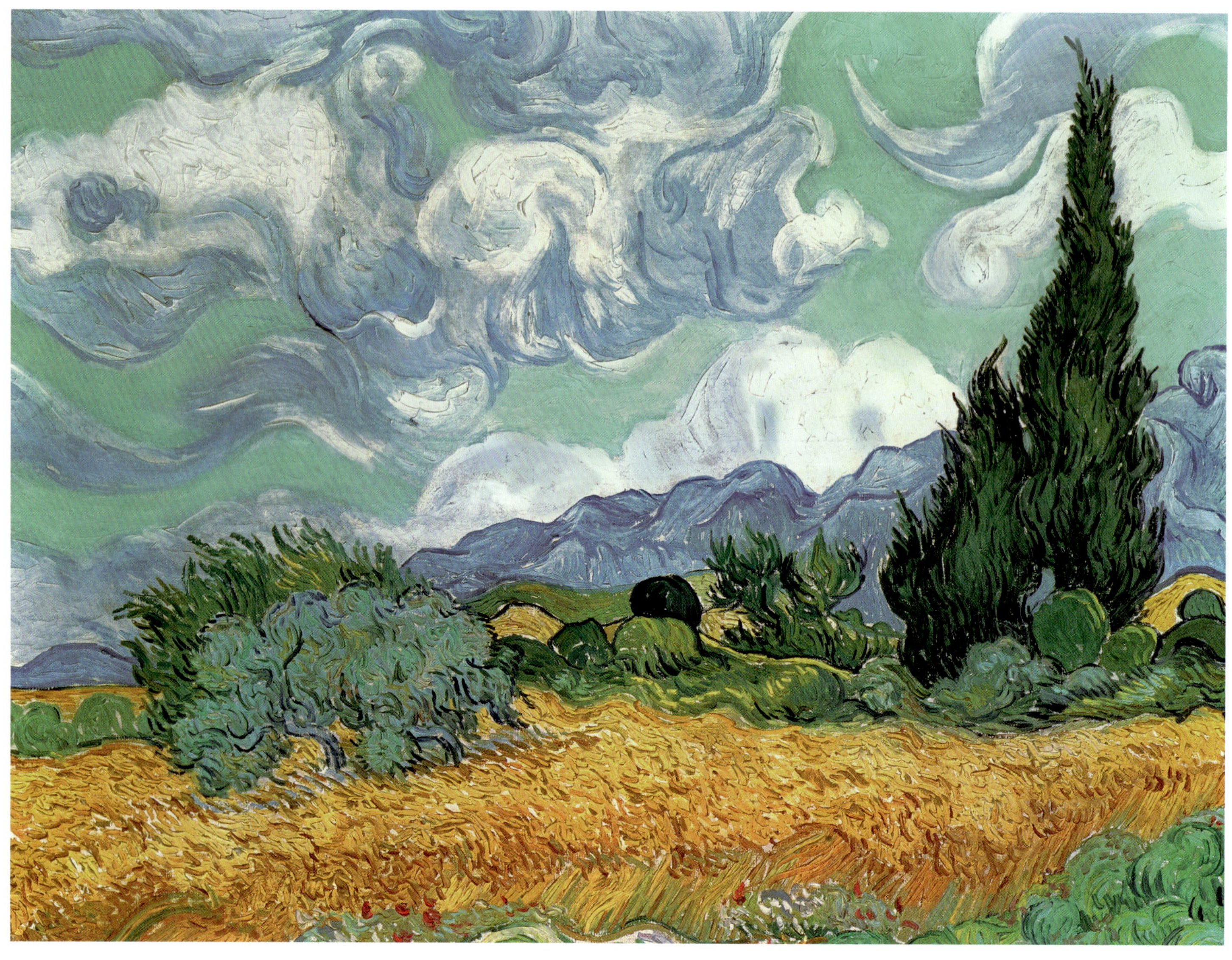

Vincent van Gogh (1853–90)

Wheatfield with Cypresses

Champ de blé avec cyprès

Weizenfeld mit Zypressen

Campo de trigo con cipreses

Campo di grano con cipressi

Tarweveld met cipressen

1889, Oil on canvas/Huile sur toile, 72,1 × 90,9 cm, National Gallery, London

Vincent van Gogh (1853–90)

Cypresses and Two Women

Cyprès avec deux femmes

Zypressen und zwei Frauen

Cipreses y dos mujeres

Cipressi con due figure femminili

Cipressen en twee vrouwen

c. 1889/90, Oil on canvas/Huile sur toile, 65 × 49 cm, Kröller-Müller Museum, Otterlo

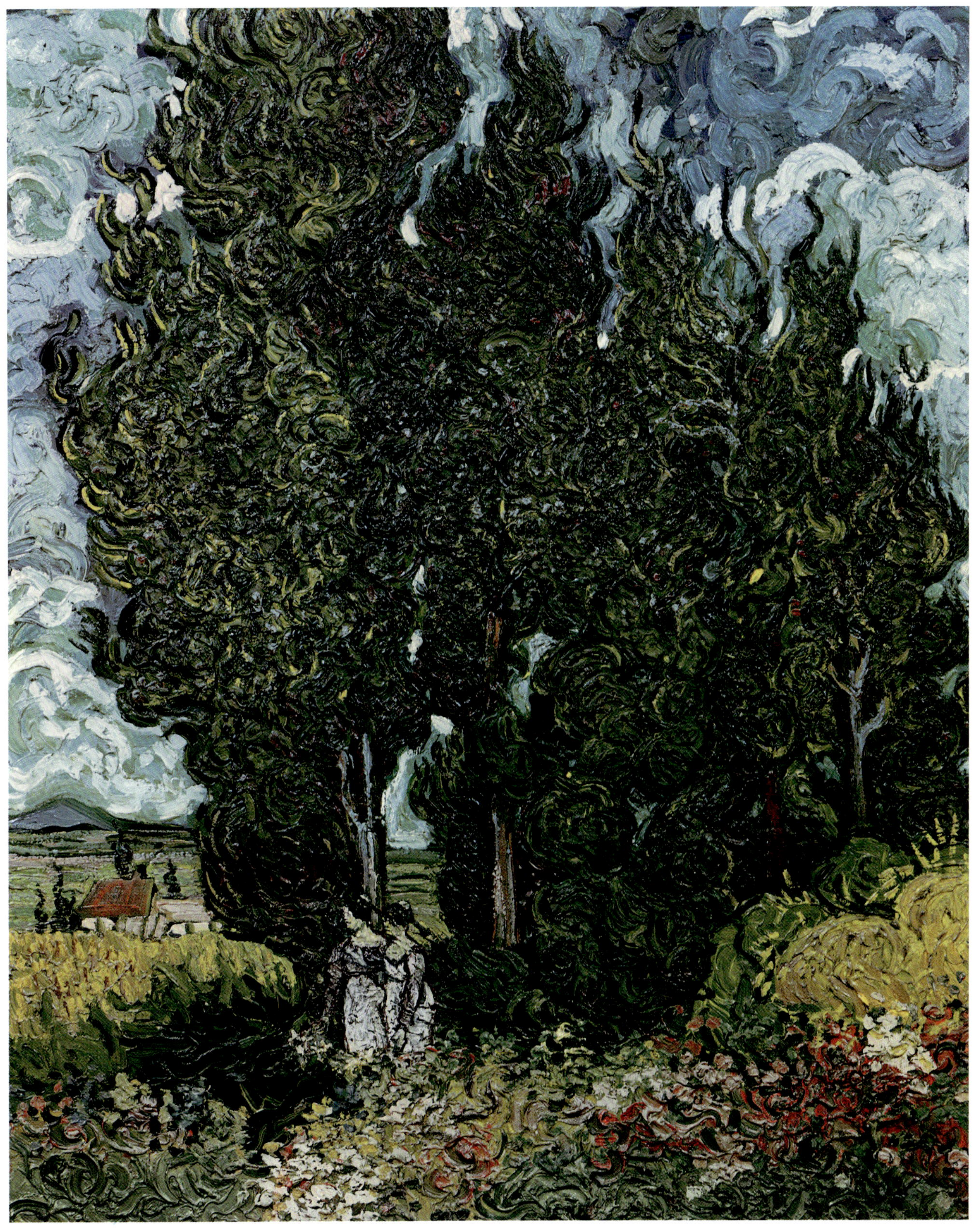

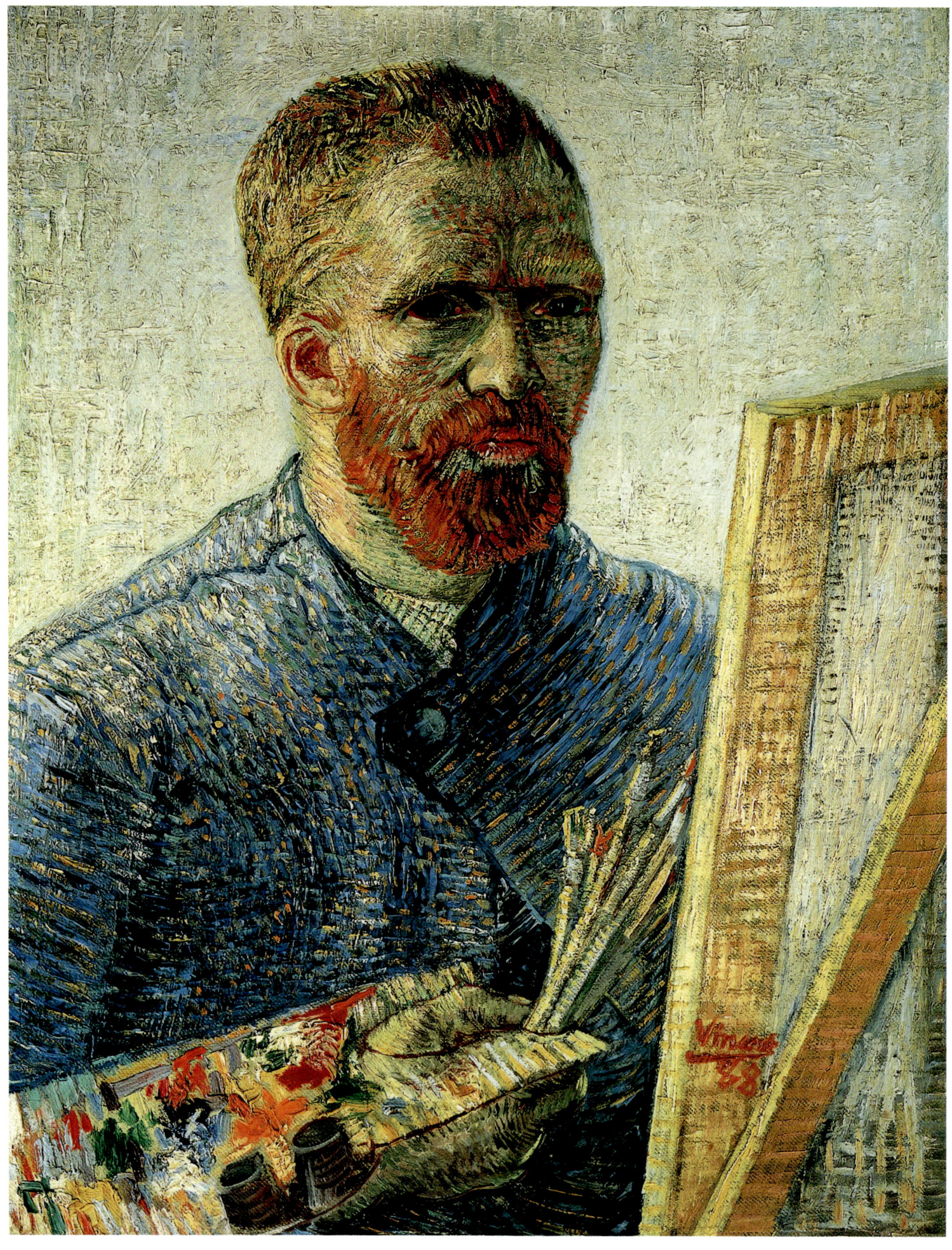

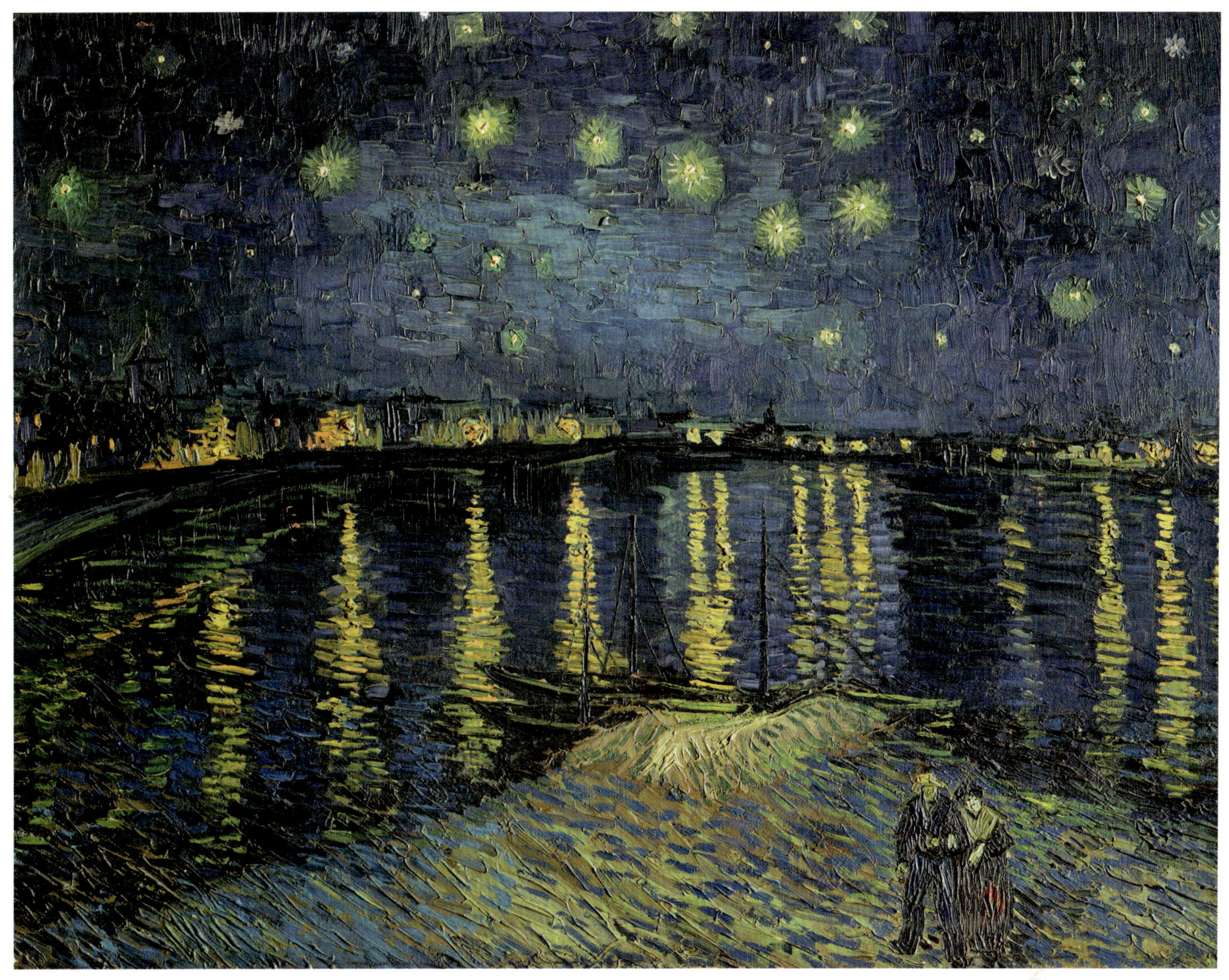

Vincent van Gogh (1853–90)

Self Portrait as a Painter

Autoportrait au chevalet

Selbstbildnis als Maler

Autorretrato como pintor

Autoritratto come pittore

Zelfportret als schilder

1888, Oil on canvas/Huile sur toile, 65,5 × 50 cm, Van Gogh Museum, Amsterdam

Vincent van Gogh (1853–90)

Starry Night over the Rhone

Nuit étoilée sur le Rhône

Sternennacht über der Rhône

Noche estrellada sobre el Rhône

Notte stellata sul Rodano

Sterrenhemel boven de Rhône

1888, Oil on canvas/Huile sur toile, 73 × 92 cm, Musée d'Orsay, Paris

The most famous painting by van Gogh shows his hometown Arles under a blazing night sky with comet tails. The dark cypresses leap from below like wild tongues towards this natural spectacle. Man is at the mercy of the cosmic forces, but simultaneously safe within them.

Le tableau le plus célèbre de Van Gogh montre sa ville natale, Arles, sous un ciel de nuit flamboyant avec des queues de comète. Les cyprès sombres s'élancent comme des langues sauvages depuis le sol vers ce spectacle naturel. L'homme est à la merci des forces cosmiques, mais en même temps en toute sécurité en leur sein.

Das berühmteste Bild von van Gogh zeigt seine Wahlheimat Arles unter einem glühenden Sternenhimmel mit Kometenschweifen. Wild züngeln von unten die dunklen Zypressen diesem Naturschauspiel entgegen. Der Mensch ist den kosmischen Mächten ausgeliefert, gleichzeitig aber auch in ihnen geborgen.

La obra más famosa de Van Gogh muestra su casa de Arles bajo un brillante cielo estrellado con colas de cometa. Los cipreses se retuercen desde abajo contra este fondo de naturaleza. El hombre se ve sometido a los poderes cósmicos, y a la vez se encuentra protegido por ellos.

Nel suo quadro più famoso, van Gogh raffigura Arles, il suo paese nativo, sotto un cielo notturno sfavillante illuminato da code di comete. A contrasto con questo spettacolo naturale spunta dal basso il cipresso. L'uomo è al contempo in balia e al sicuro dai poteri cosmici.

Het beroemdste werk van Gogh toont een stralende sterrenhemel met komeetachtige wervelingen boven Saint-Rémy-en-Provence, samen met een denkbeeldig dorp. Donkere cipressen rijzen naar de sterren op. De mens is overgeleverd aan kosmische krachten, maar voelt zich daarin ook geborgen.

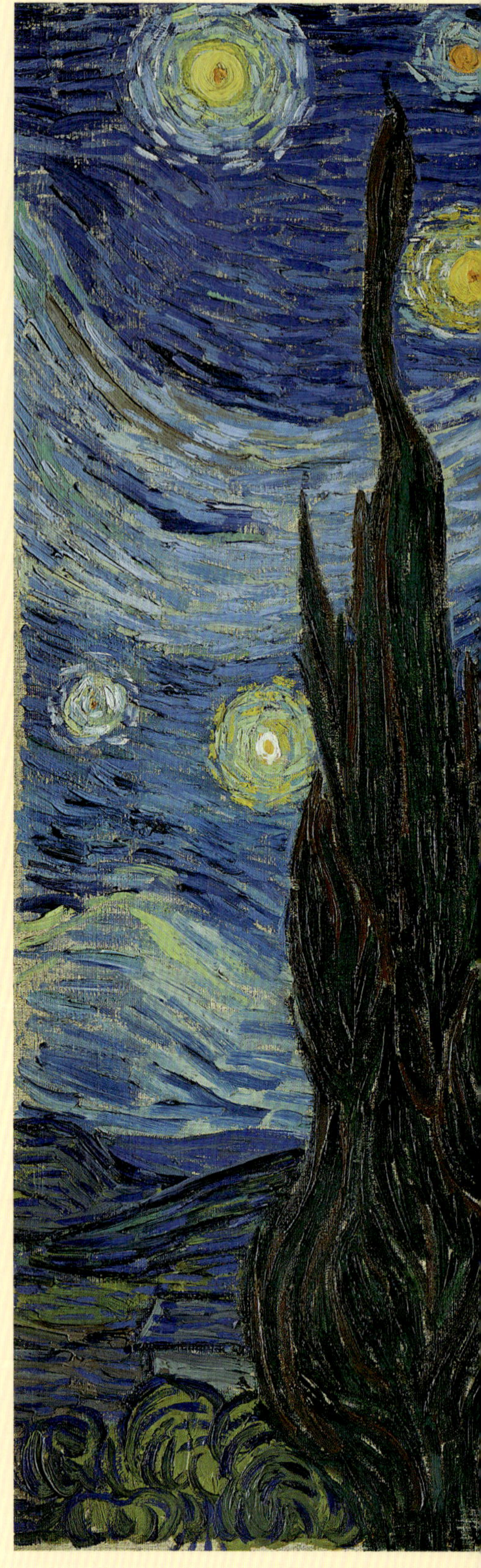

Vincent van Gogh (1853–90)
The Starry Night
La nuit étoilée
Die Sternennacht (Zypressen und Dorf)
La noche estrellada
Notte stellata (cipresso e paese)
De sterrennacht (Cipressen en dorp)
1889, Oil on canvas/Huile sur toile, 73,7 × 92,1 cm, Museum of Modern Art, New York

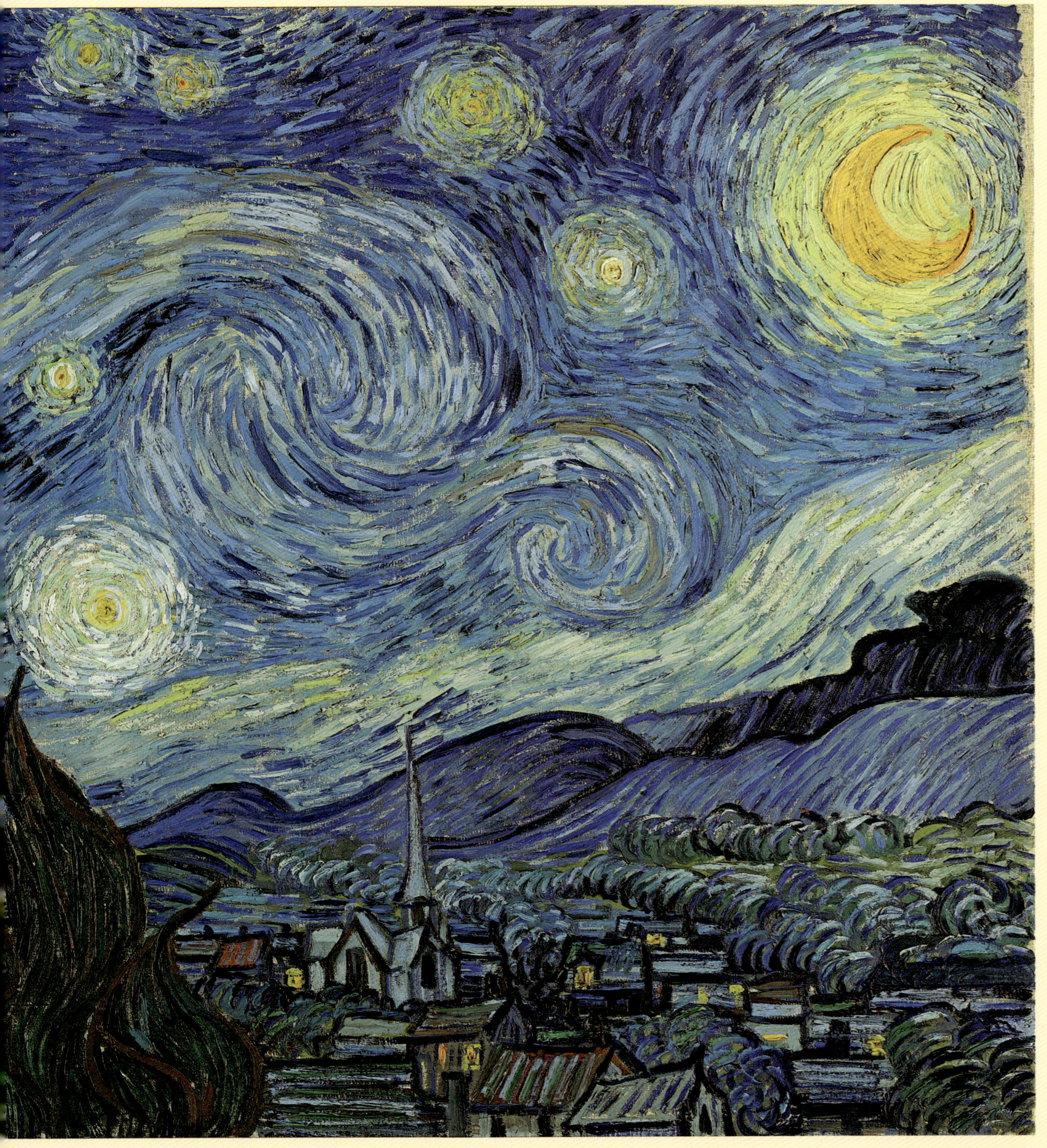

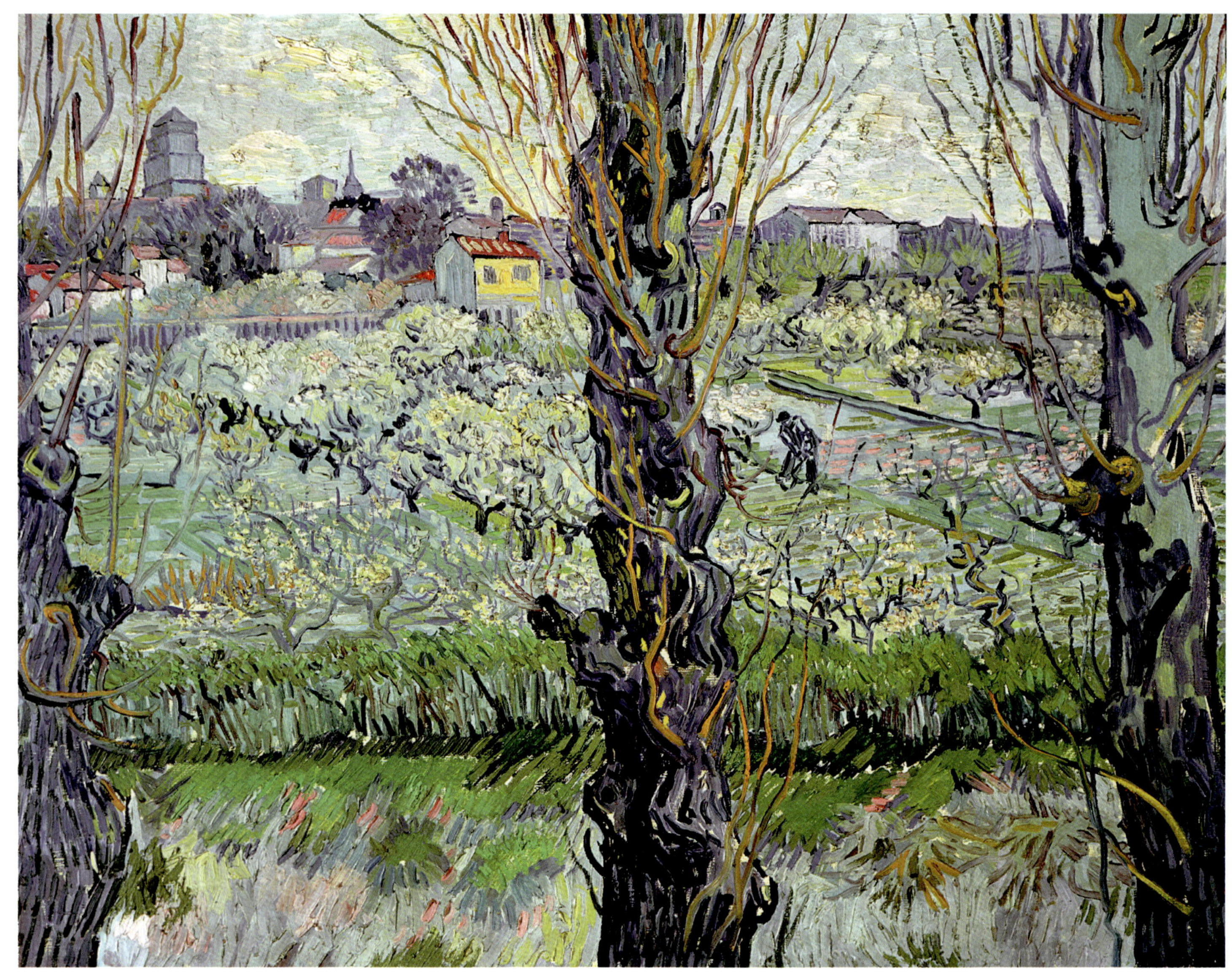

Vincent van Gogh (1853–90)

View of Arles

Vue d'Arles

Blick auf Arles

Vista de Arles

Veduta di Arles

Gezicht op Arles

1889, Oil on canvas/Huile sur toile, 72 × 92 cm, Neue Pinakothek, München

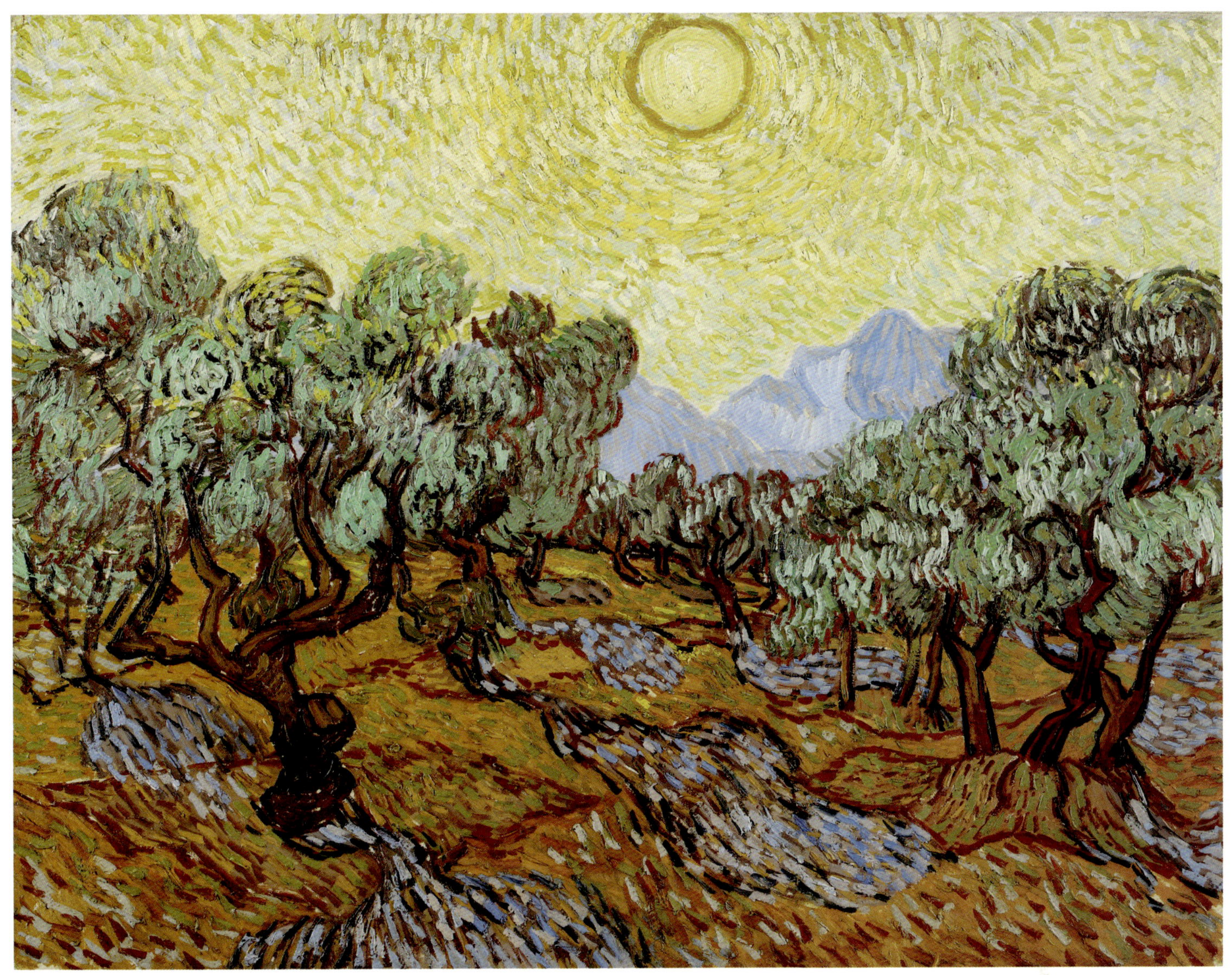

Vincent van Gogh (1853–90)

Olive Trees

Oliviers

Olivenbäume

Olivos

Ulivi

Olijfbomen

1889, Oil on canvas/Huile sur toile, 72,4 × 91,4 cm, Minneapolis Institute of Arts, Minneapolis

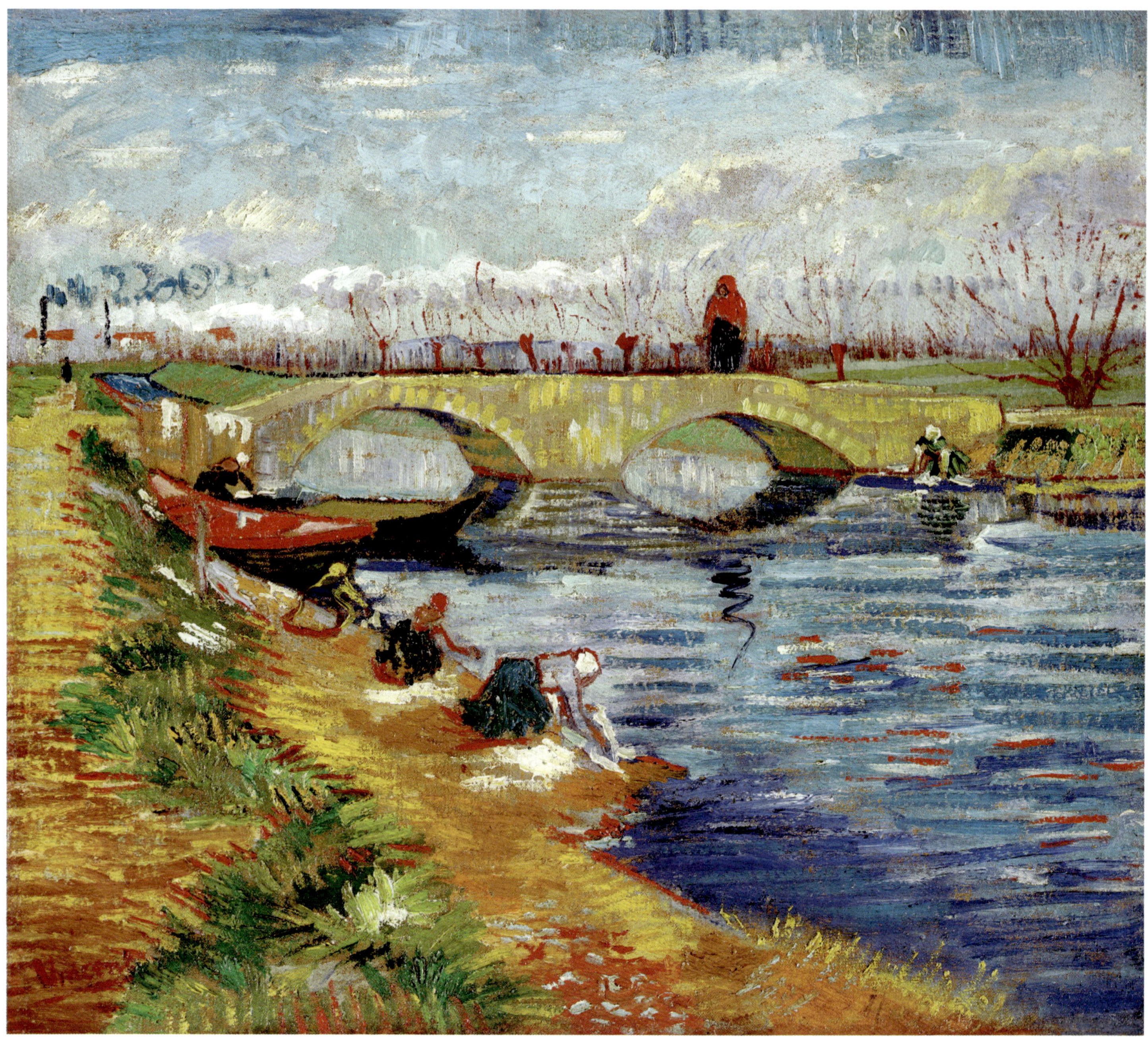

Vincent van Gogh (1853–90)

The Gleize Bridge over the Vigneyret Canal, near Arles

Le pont sur le canal Gleize Vigneyret

Die Gleize-Brücke über den Kanal Vigneyret bei Arles

El puente Gleize sobre el canal de Vigneyret en Arles

Il ponte Gleize sul canale Vigneyret ad Arles

De Gleize-brug over het kanaal van Vigneyret bij Arles

n.d., Oil on canvas/Huile sur toile, 45,7 × 48,9 cm, Private collection

Vincent van Gogh (1853–90)

Le Pont de Langlois a Arles

Le pont de Langlois à Arles

Die Pont de Langlois in Arles

El puente de Langlois de Arles

Il ponte di Langlois ad Arles

De Pont de Langlois in Arles

1888, Watercolor, gouache, chalk and ink on paper/Aquarelle, gouache,
craie et encre sur papier, 30,5 × 30,2 cm, Private collection

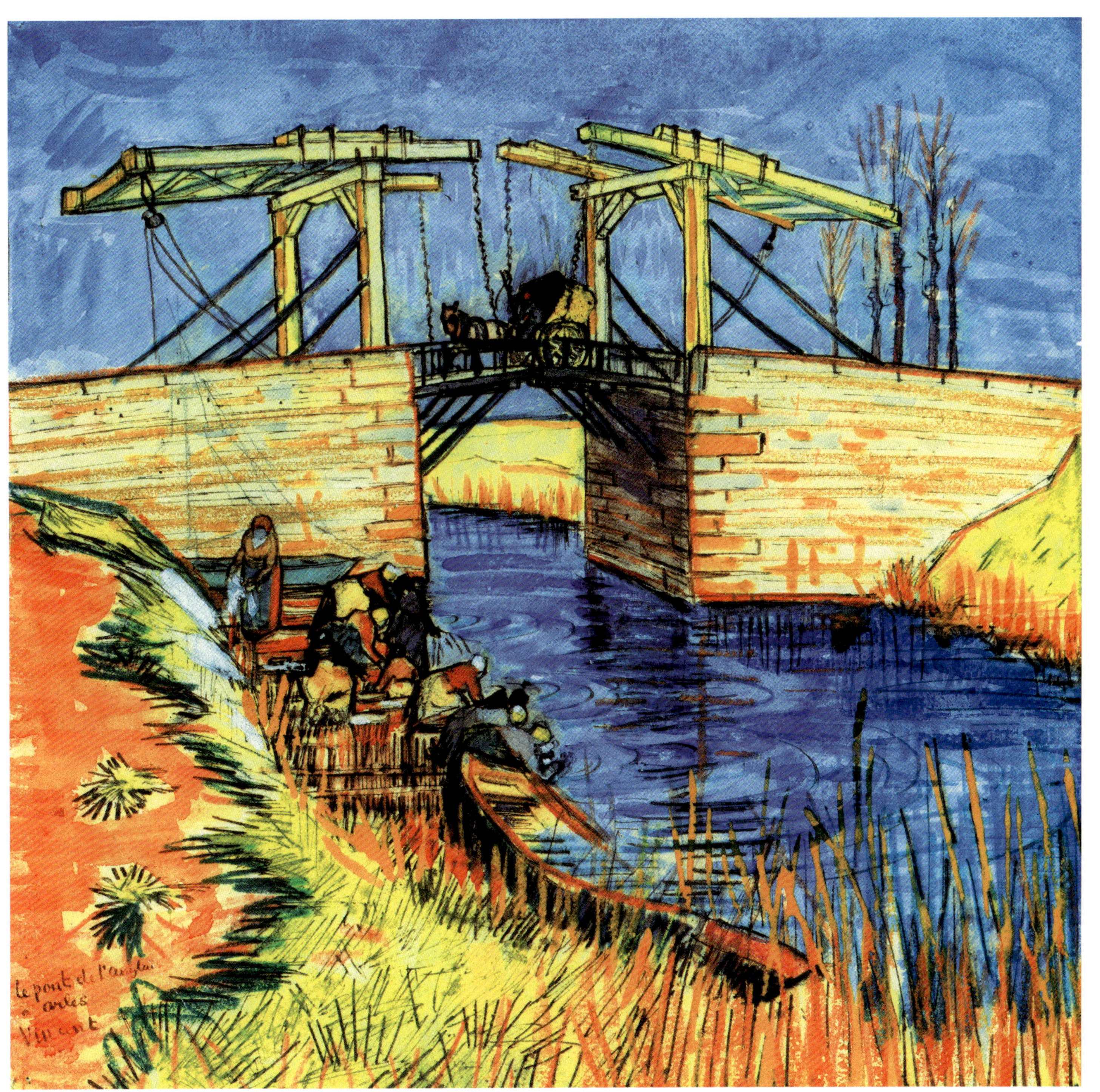

le pont de l'anglais
à arles
Vincent

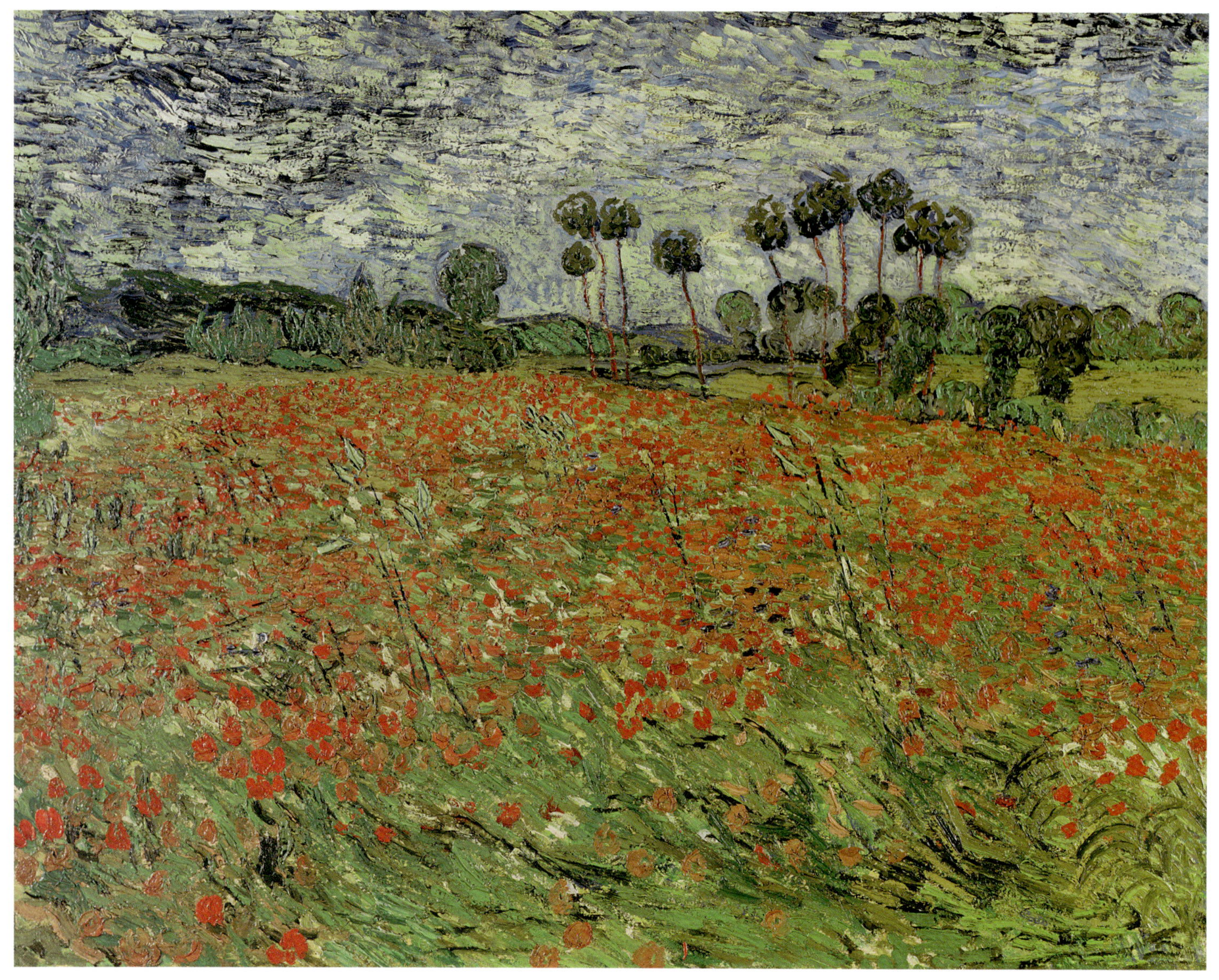

Vincent van Gogh (1853–90)

Field of Poppies, Auvers–sur–Oise

Champ de coquelicots, Auvers-sur-Oise

Mohnfeld, Auvers-sur-Oise

Campo de amapolas, Auvers-sur-Oise

Campo di papaveri, Auvers-sur-Oise

Papaverveld, Auvers-sur-Oise

1890, Oil on canvas/Huile sur toile, 73 × 91,5 cm, Gemeentemuseum, The Hague

Vincent van Gogh (1853–90)

The Harvesters

Les moissonneurs

Die Ährenpflückerinnen

Los cosechadores

Campo di grano con convoni

Akker met korenschoven

1888, Oil on canvas/Huile sur toile, 73 × 54 cm, Musée Rodin, Paris

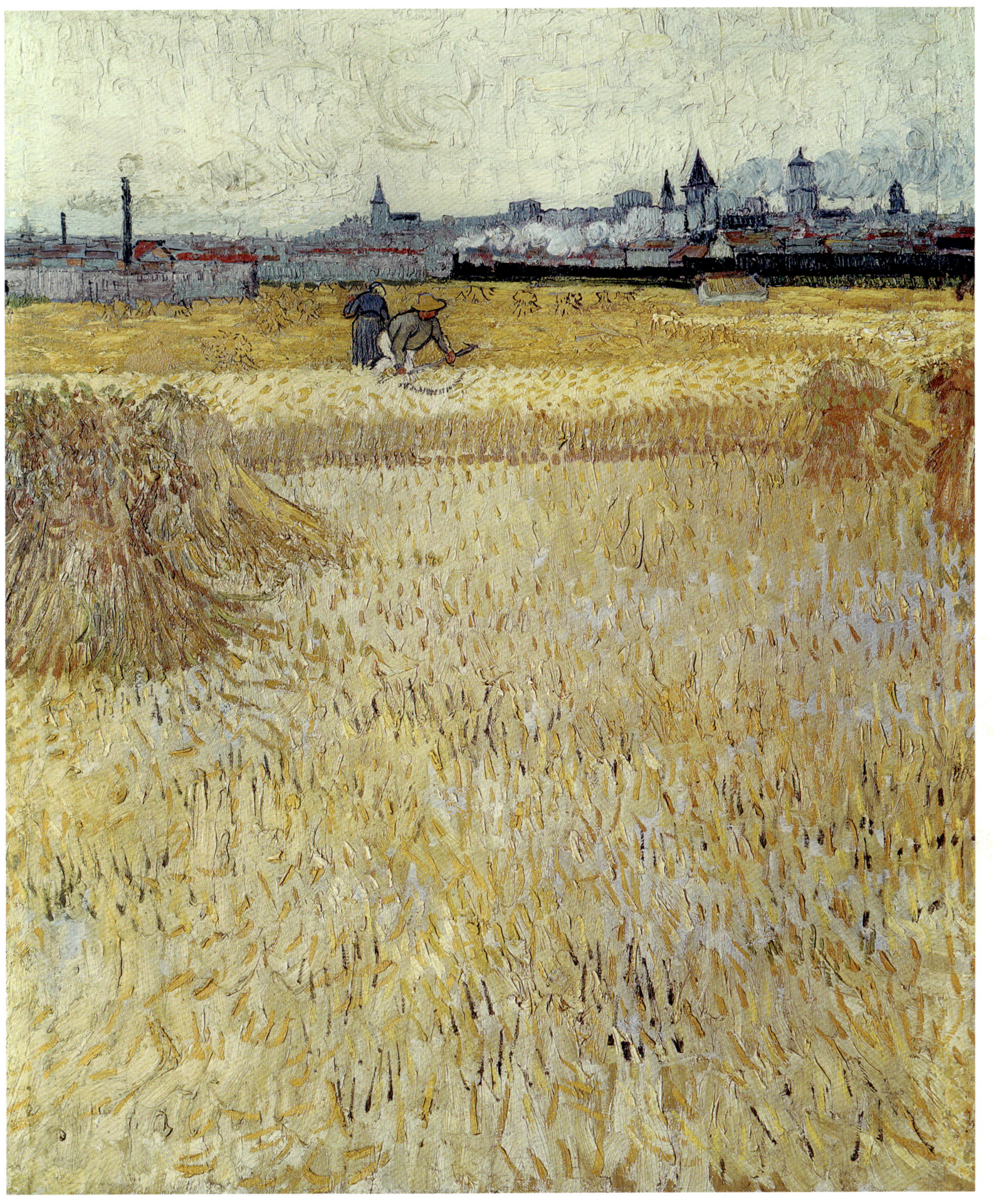

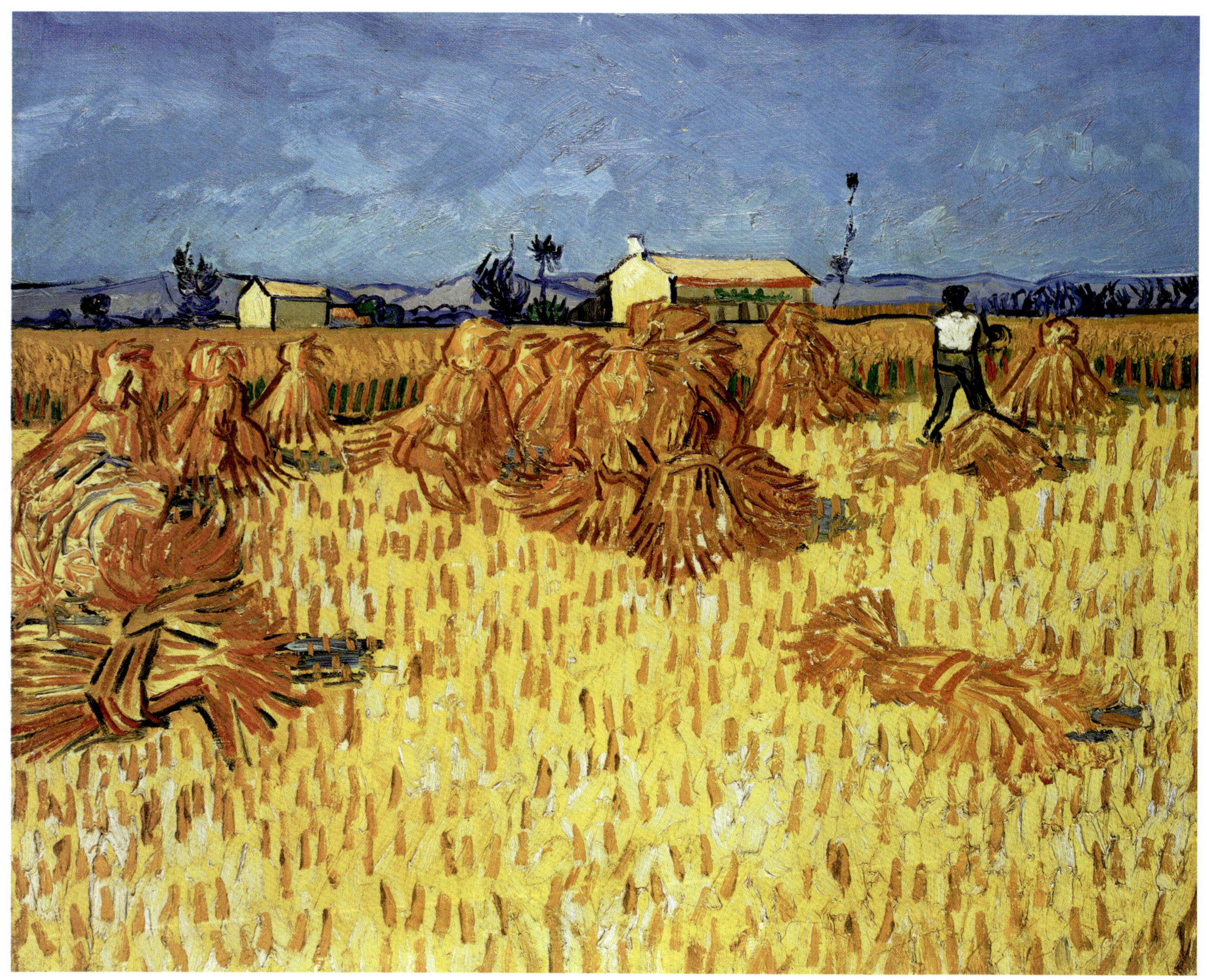

Vincent van Gogh (1853–90)

Harvest in Provence

Moisson en Provence

Ernte in der Provence

La cosecha en la Provenza

Raccolto in Provenza

Oogst in de Provence

1888, Oil on canvas/Huile sur toile, 51 × 60 cm, Israel Museum, Jerusalem

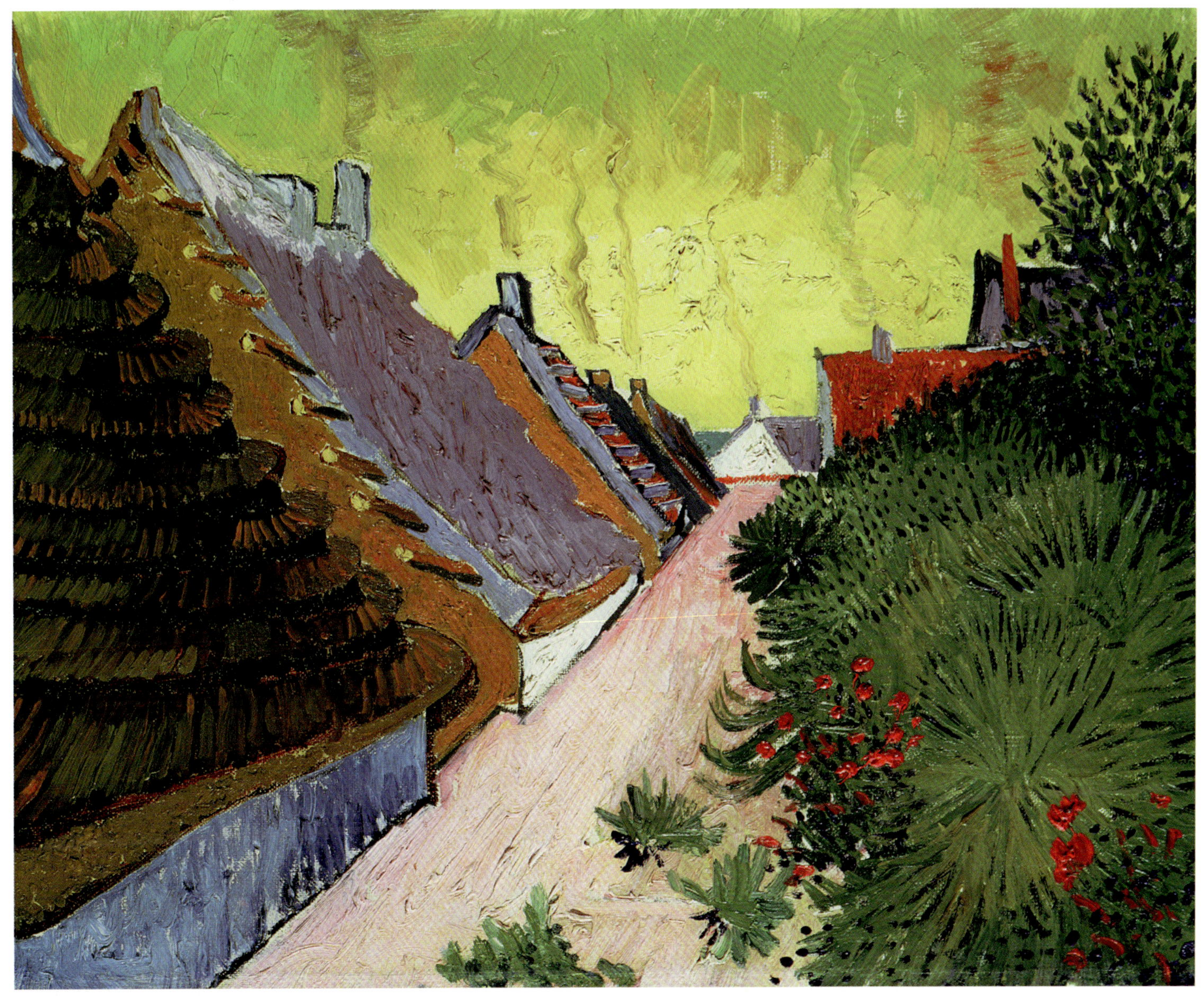

Vincent van Gogh (1853–90)

Mas at Saintes–Mairies

Cabanes aux Saintes-Maries

Hütten in Saintes-Maries

Cabañas en Saintes-Maries

Capanna di paglia a Saintes-Maries

Hutten in Saintes-Maries

1888, Oil on canvas/Huile sur toile, 38,3 × 46,1 cm, Private collection

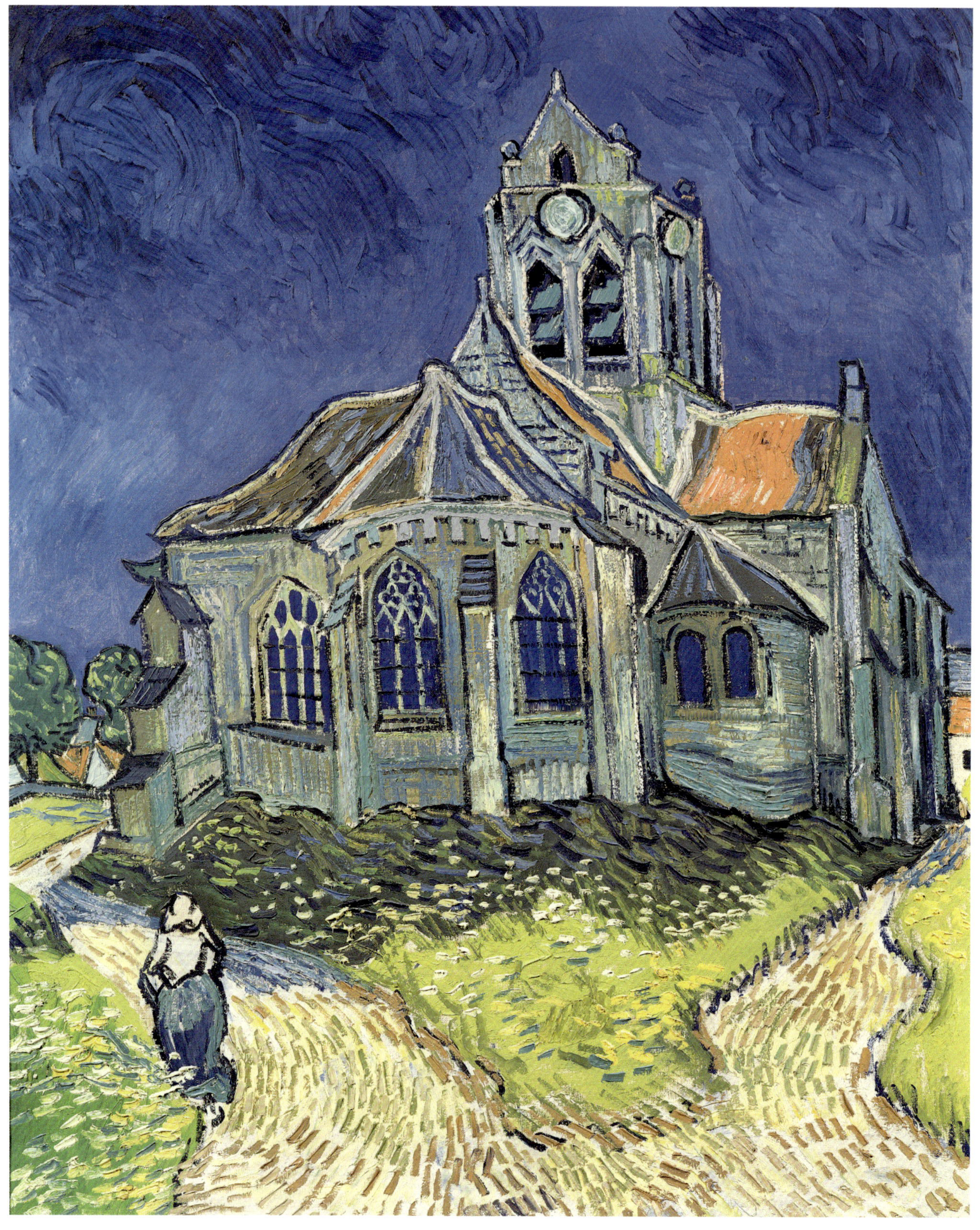

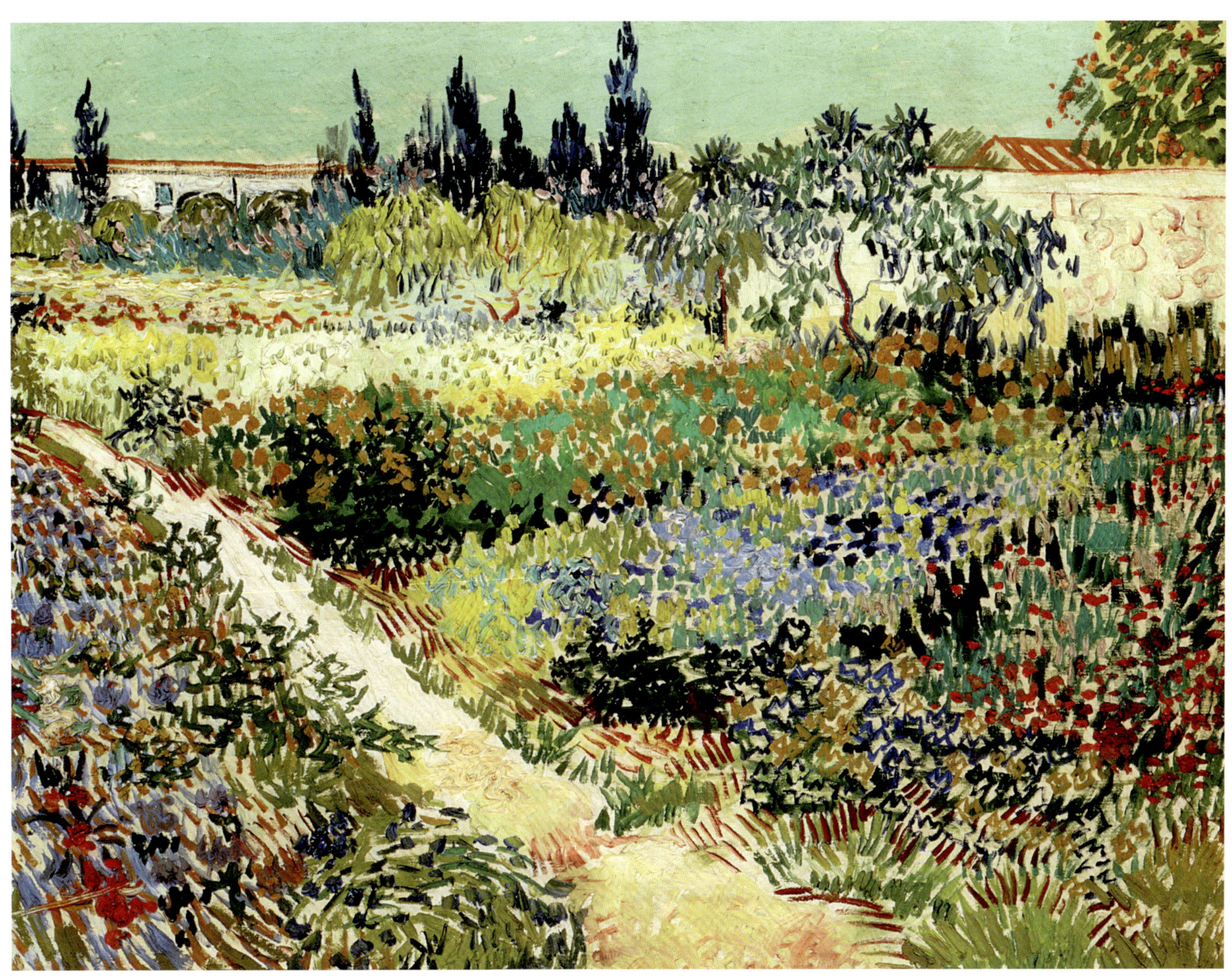

<table>
<tr><td>

Vincent van Gogh (1853–90)

The Church at Auvers–sur–Oise

L'église d'Auvers-sur-Oise

Die Kirche in Auvers-sur-Oise

La iglesia en Auvers-sur-Oise

La chiesa di Auvers-sur-Oise

De kerk van Auvers-sur-Oise

1890, Oil on canvas/Huile sur toile, 93 × 74,5 cm, Musée d'Orsay, Paris

</td><td>

Vincent van Gogh (1853–90)

The Garden at Arles

Le jardin à Arles

Der Garten in Arles

El jardín de Arles

Il giardino ad Arles

De tuin in Arles

1888, Oil on canvas/Huile sur toile, 73 × 92 cm, Gemeentemuseum, The Hague

</td></tr>
</table>

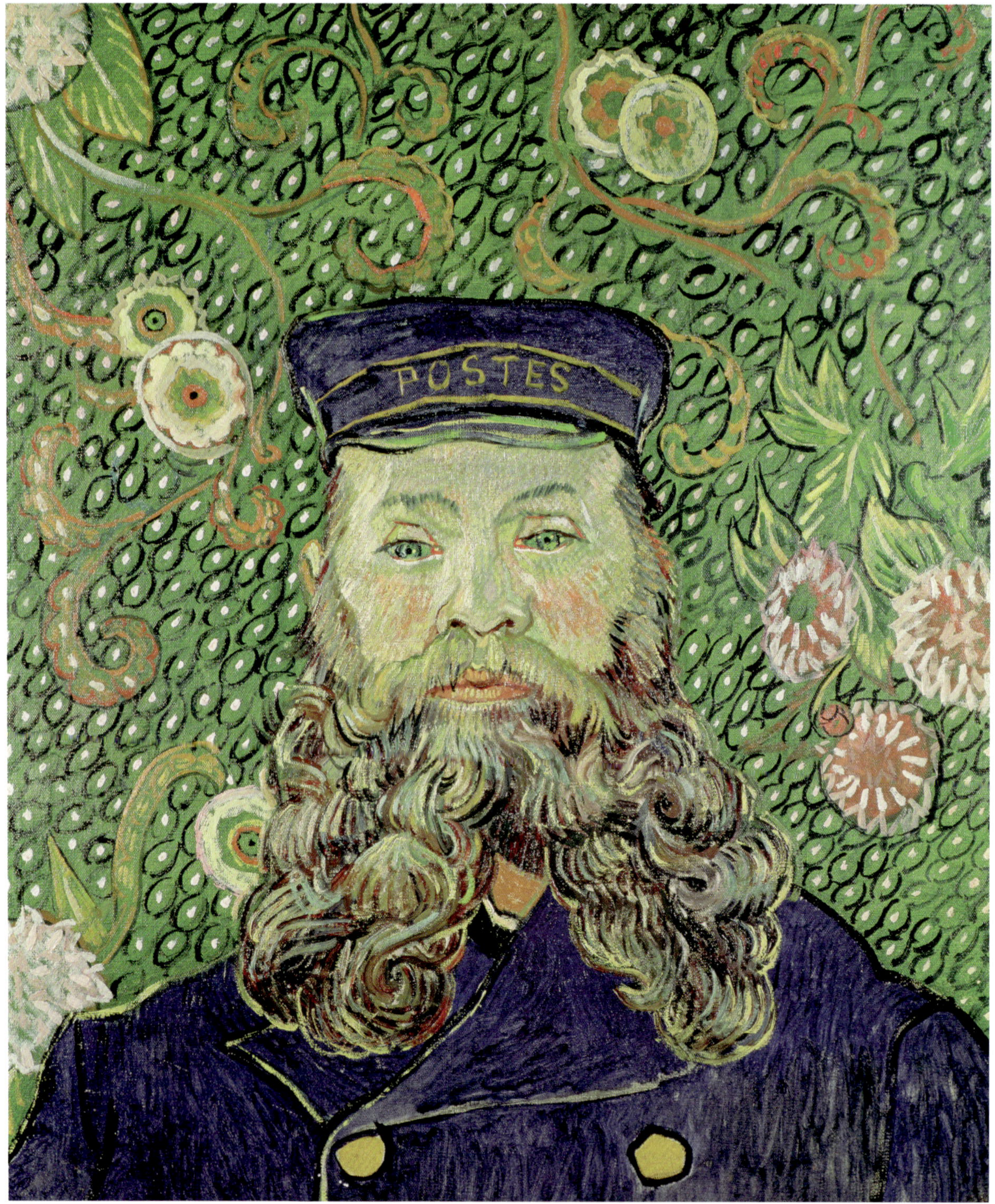

Vincent van Gogh (1853–90)

Portrait of the Postman Joseph Roulin Bildnis des Postboten Joseph Roulin Ritratto del postino Joseph Roulin

Portrait du facteur Joseph Roulin Retrato del cartero Joseph Roulin Portret van postbode Joseph Roulin

1889, Oil on canvas/Huile sur toile, 64,4 × 55,2 cm, Museum of Modern Art, New York

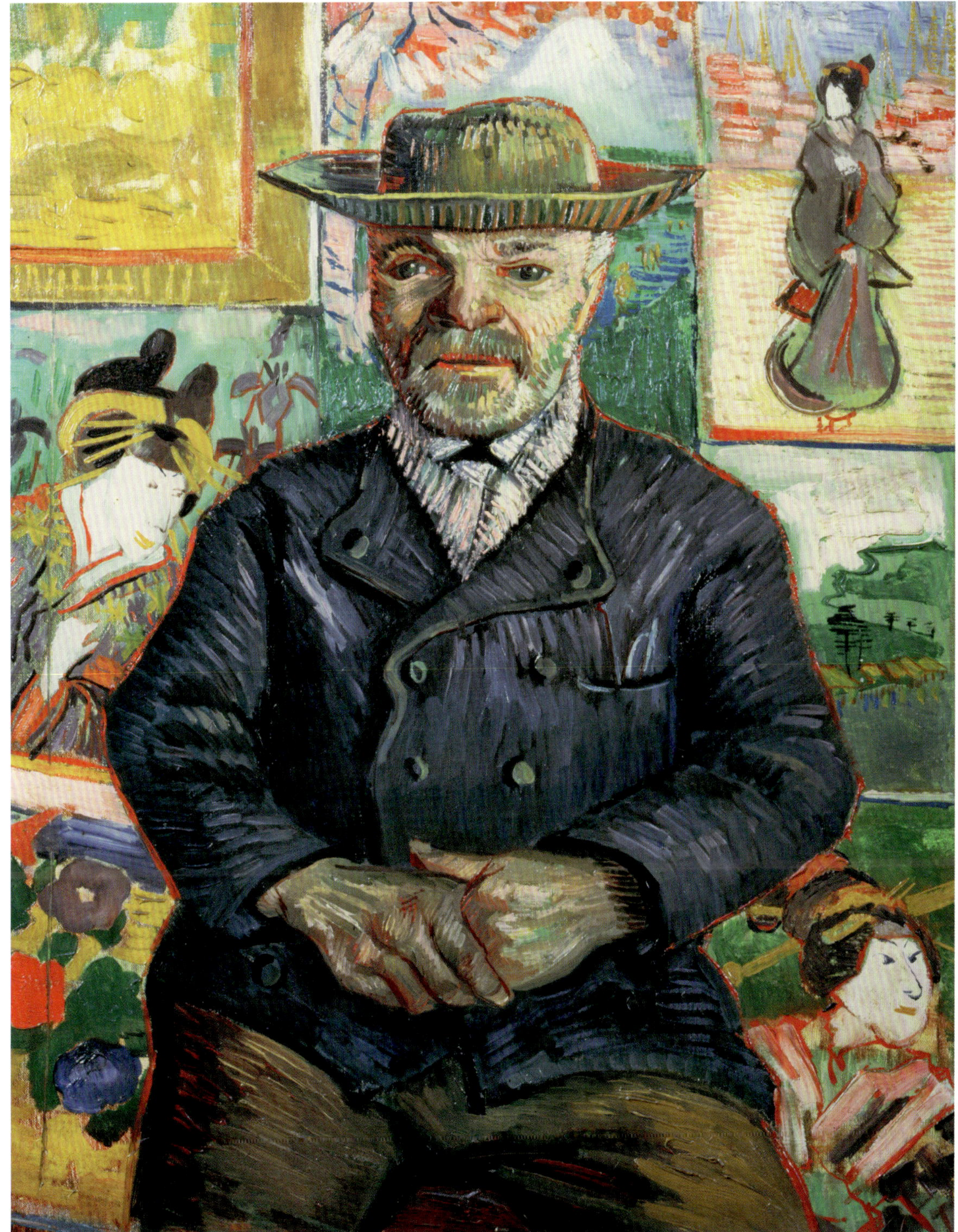

Vincent van Gogh (1853–90)

Père Tanguy   Bildnis Père Tanguy   Ritratto di Père Tanguy

Père Tanguy   Retrato de Père Tanguy   Portret van Père Tanguy

1887/88, Oil on canvas/Huile sur toile, 65 × 51 cm, Private collection

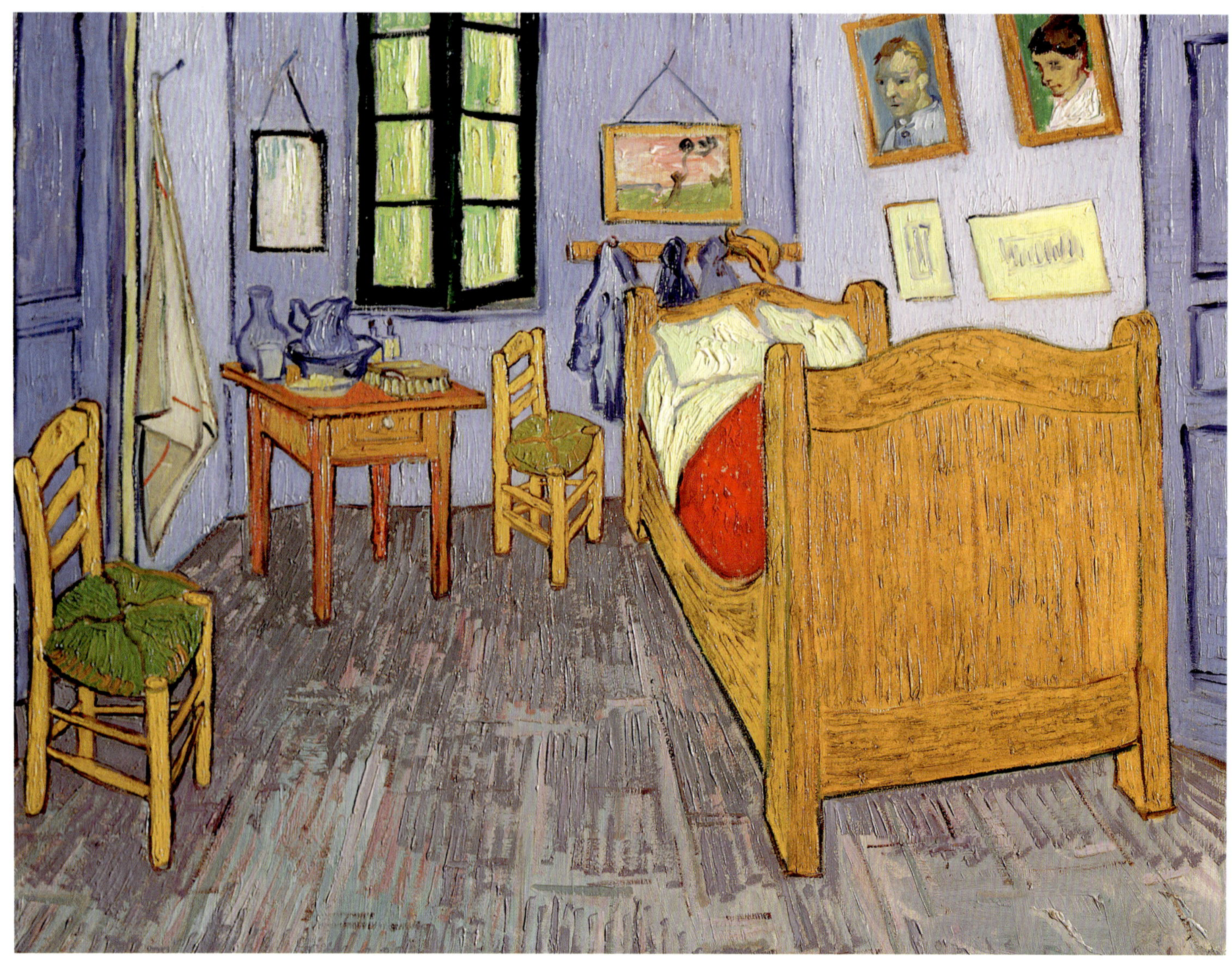

Vincent van Gogh (1853–90)

Van Gogh's Bedroom at Arles,

La chambre de Van Gogh à Arles

Das Schlafzimmer in Arles

El dormitorio de Arles

La camera di Vincent ad Arles

De slaapkamer in Arles

1889, Oil on canvas/Huile sur toile, 57,3 × 73,5 cm, Musée d'Orsay, Paris

Vincent van Gogh (1853–90)

Self Portrait with Bandaged Ear and Pipe

Autoportrait à l'oreille bandée (ou L'Homme à la pipe)

Selbstporträt mit verbundenem Ohr und Pfeife

Autorretrato con oreja vendada y pipa

Autoritratto con orecchio dato e pipa

Zelfportret met verbonden oor en pijp

1889, Oil on canvas/Huile sur toile, 51 × 45 cm, Private collection

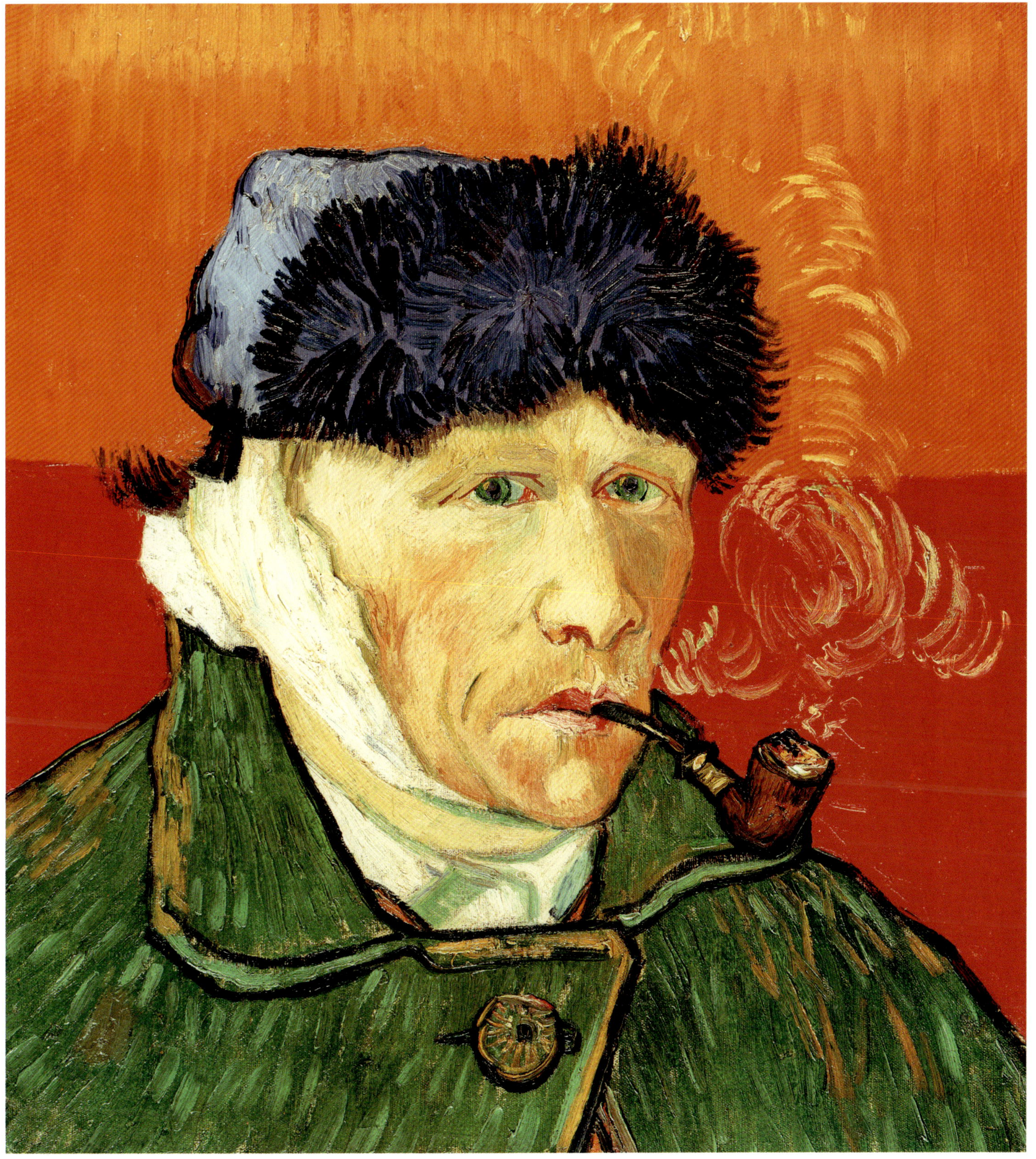

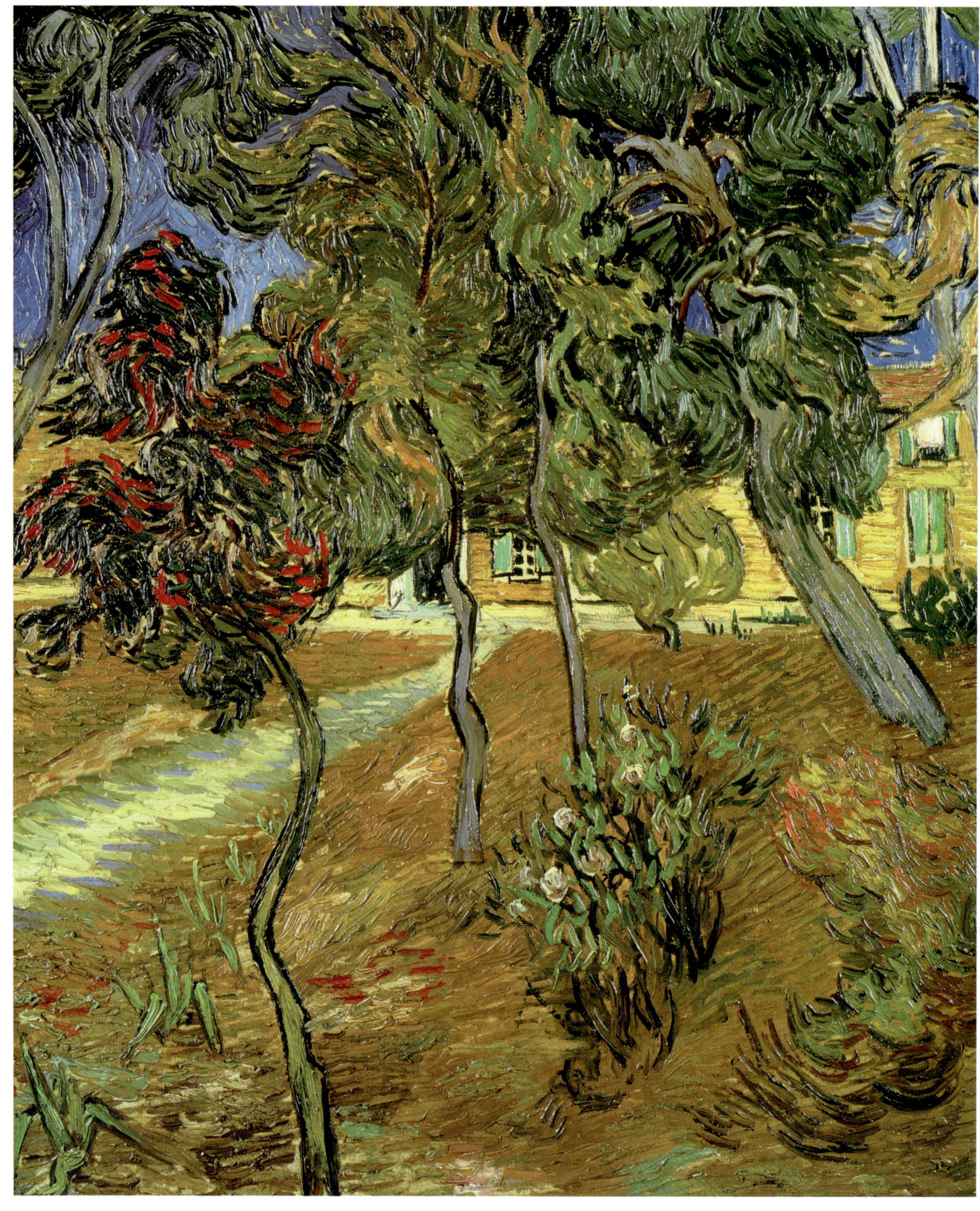

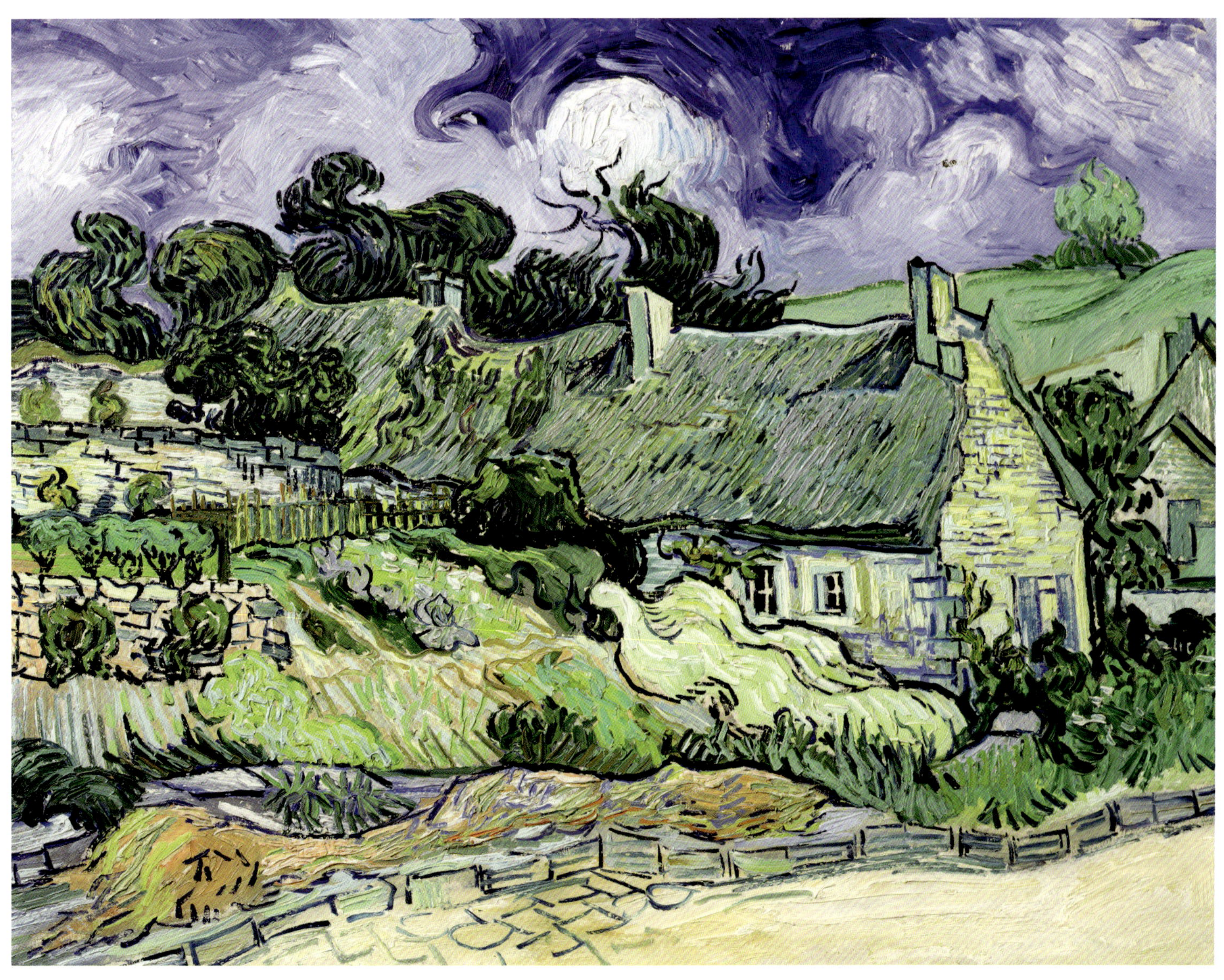

Vincent van Gogh (1853–90)

Garden of St. Paul's Hospital

Le jardin de l'Hôpital Saint-Paul

Garten des St. Paul-Krankenhauses

Jardín del hospital de St. Paul

Il giardino dell'ospedale di Saint-Paul

Tuin in het hospitaal van St.-Paul

1889, Oil on canvas/Huile sur toile, 73 × 60 cm, Private collection

Vincent van Gogh (1853–90)

Thatched cottages at Cordeville, Auvers–sur–Oise

Chaumières à Auvers-sur-Oise

Riedgedeckte Häuser in Cordeville, Auvers-sur-Oise

Casas rurales con tejado de paja en Cordeville, Auvers-sur-Oise

Tetti di paglia di Cordeville ad Auvers-sur-Oise

Huizen met rieten daken in Cordeville, Auvers-sur-Oise

1890, Oil on canvas/Huile sur toile, 73 × 92 cm, Musée d'Orsay, Paris

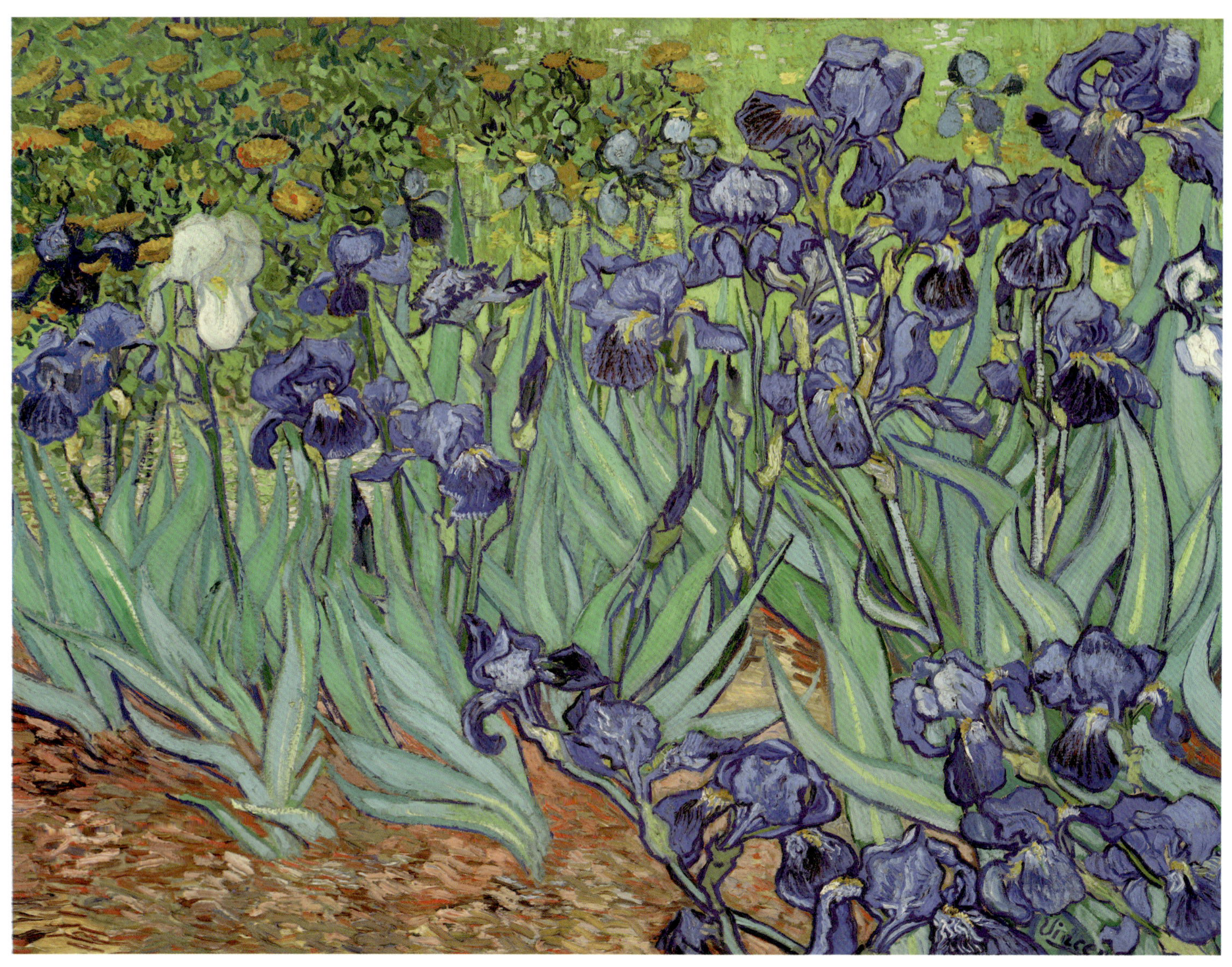

Vincent van Gogh (1853–90)

Irises

Iris

Blaue Iris

Iris

Iris blu

Blauwe irrissen

1889, Oil on canvas/Huile sur toile, 74,3 × 94,3 cm, Getty Center, Los Angeles

Vincent van Gogh (1853–90)

Dr. Paul Gachet

Portrait du docteur Gachet avec branche de digitale

Bildnis Dr. Paul Gachet

Retrato del Dr. Paul Gachet

Ritratto del dottor Gachet

Portret van dr. Paul Gachet

1890, Oil on canvas/Huile sur toile, 68,2 × 57 cm, Musée d'Orsay, Paris

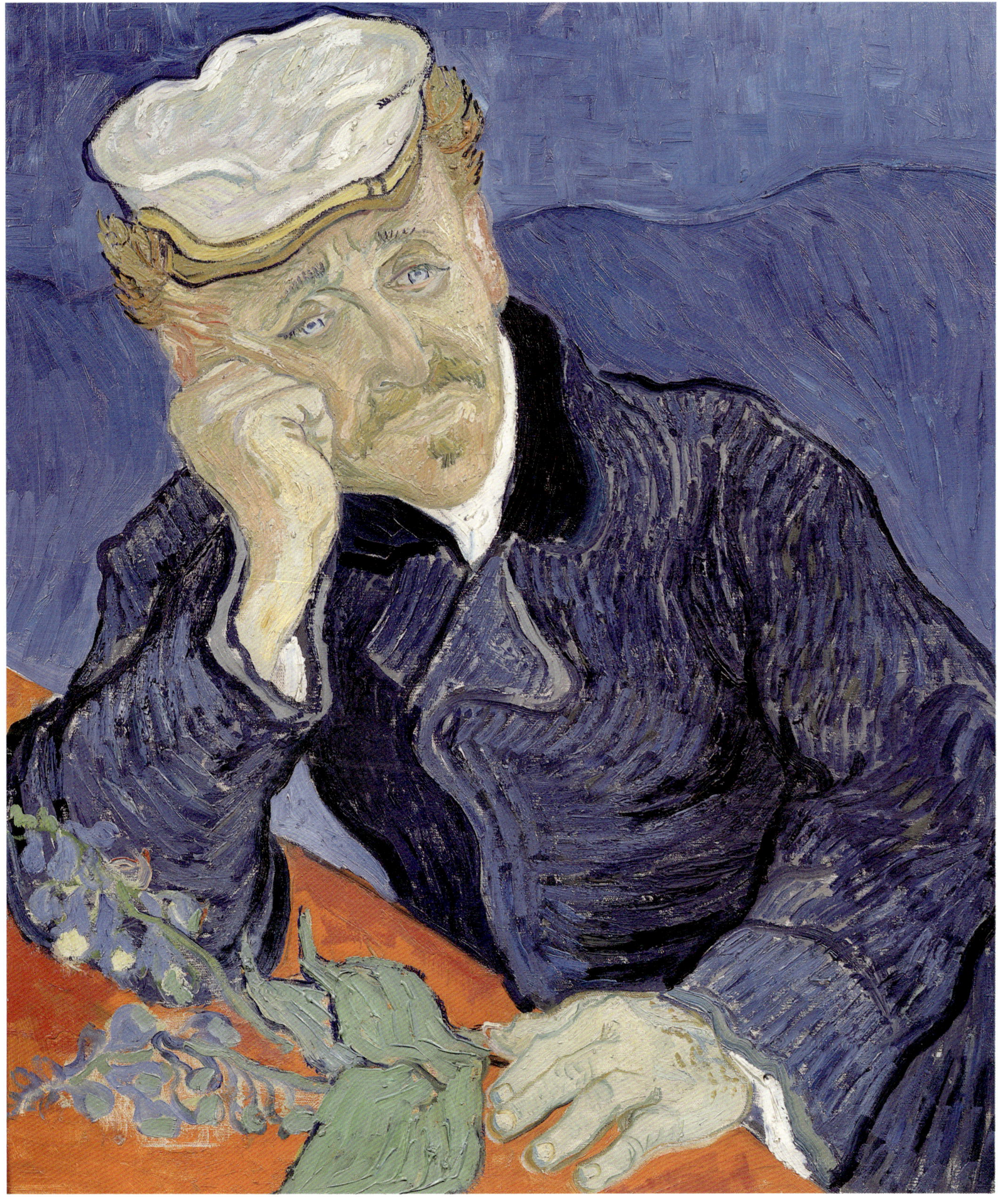

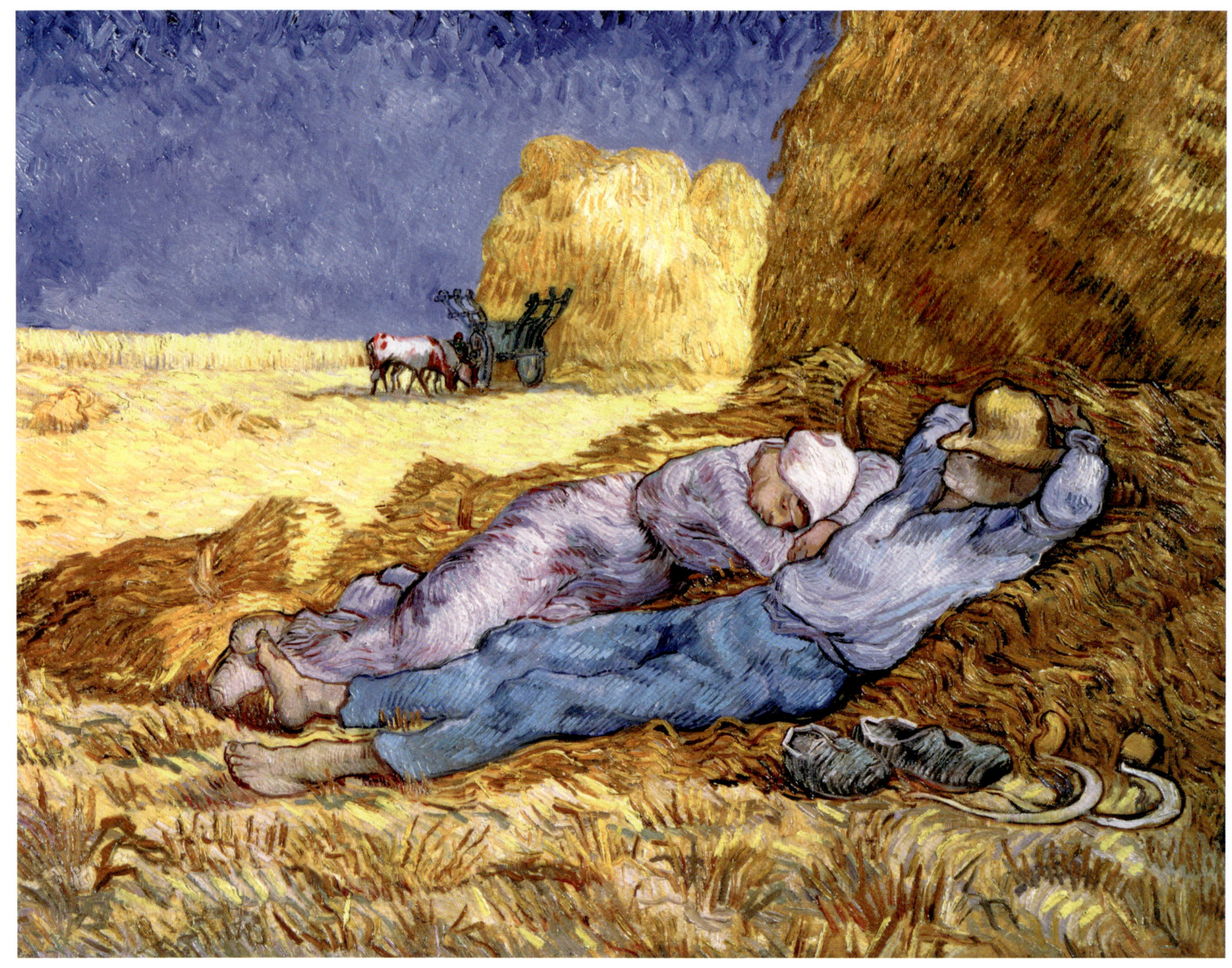

Vincent van Gogh (1853–90)

Noon *or* The Siesta, after Millet

La méridienne, *dit aussi* La sieste (d'après Millet)

Mittagsschlaf *oder* Die Siesta (nach Millet)

La meridiana *o* La siesta (basado en Millet)

La meridiana *o* La siesta (da Millet)

Middagrust, *of*: De siësta (naar Millet)

1889/90, Oil on canvas/Huile sur toile, 73 × 91 cm, Musée d'Orsay, Paris

Vincent van Gogh (1853–90)

Self portrait

Autoportrait

Selbstbildnis

Autorretrato

Autoritratto

Zelfportret

1889, Oil on canvas/Huile sur toile, 65 × 54,2 cm, Musée d'Orsay, Paris

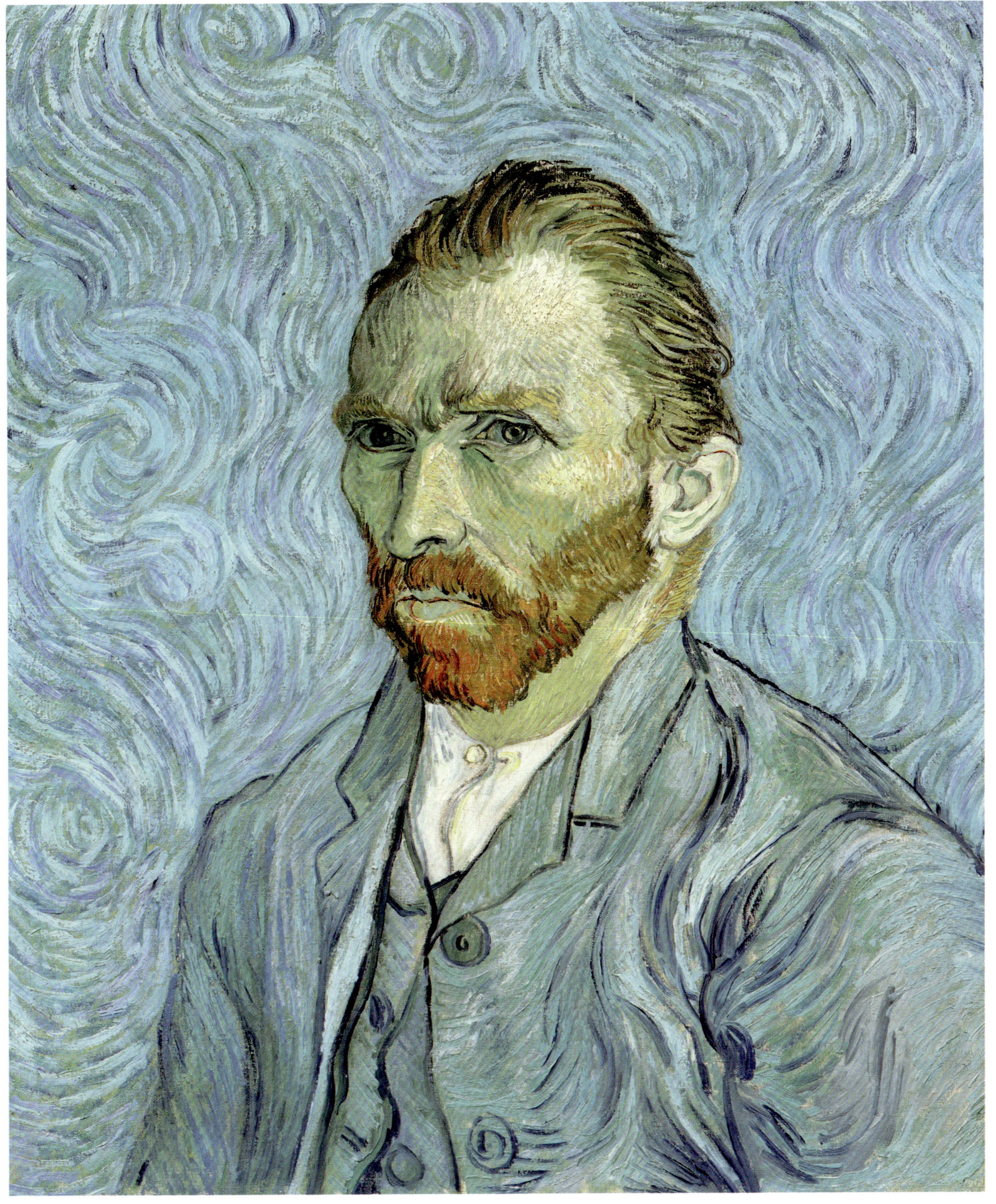

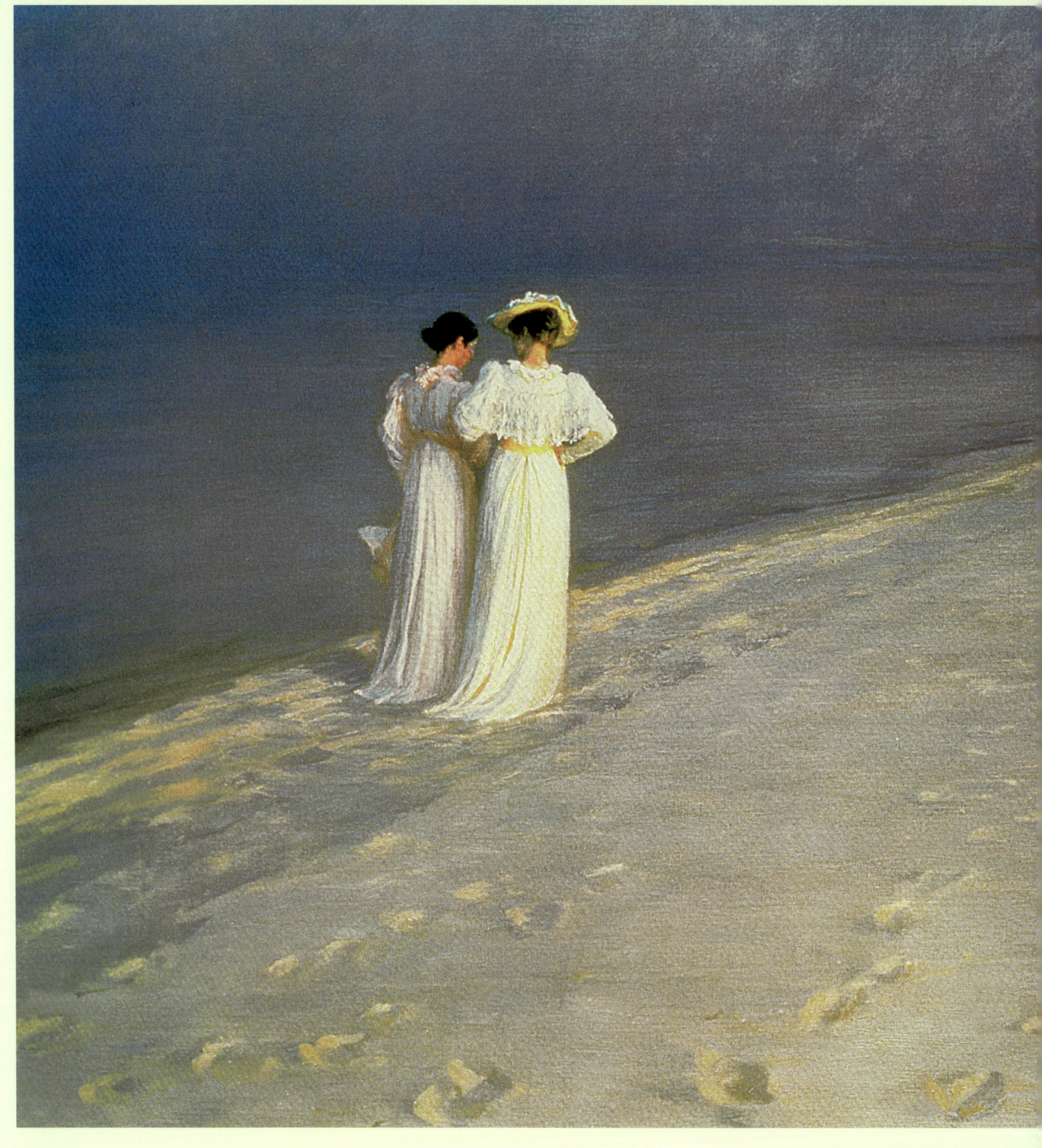

IMPRESSIONISM AS AN INTERNATIONAL ART MOVEMENT

L'IMPRESSIONNISME EN TANT QUE MOUVEMENT ARTISTIQUE INTERNATIONAL

DER IMPRESSIONISMUS ALS INTERNATIONALE KUNSTBEWEGUNG

EL IMPRESIONISMO COMO MOVIMIENTO ARTÍSTICO INTERNACIONAL

L'IMPRESSIONISMO COME MOVIMENTO ARTISTICO INTERNAZIONALE

HET IMPRESSIONISME ALS INTERNATIONALE BEWEGING

Peder Severin Krøyer (1851–1909)
Summer Evening on the Skagen Southern Beach with Anna Ancher and Marie Kroyer
Soir d'été sur la plage de Skagen avec Anna Ancher et Marie Krøyer
Sommerabend am Skagener Südstrand mit Anna Ancher und Marie Krøyer
Noche de verano en la playa meridional de Skagen con Anna Ancher y Marie Krøyer
Sera d'estate sulla spiaggia di Skagen con Anna Ancher e Marie Krøyer
Zomeravond op het zuidstrand van Skagen met Anna Ancher en Marie Krøyer
1893, Oil on canvas/Huile sur toile, 100 × 150 cm, Skagens Museum, Skagen

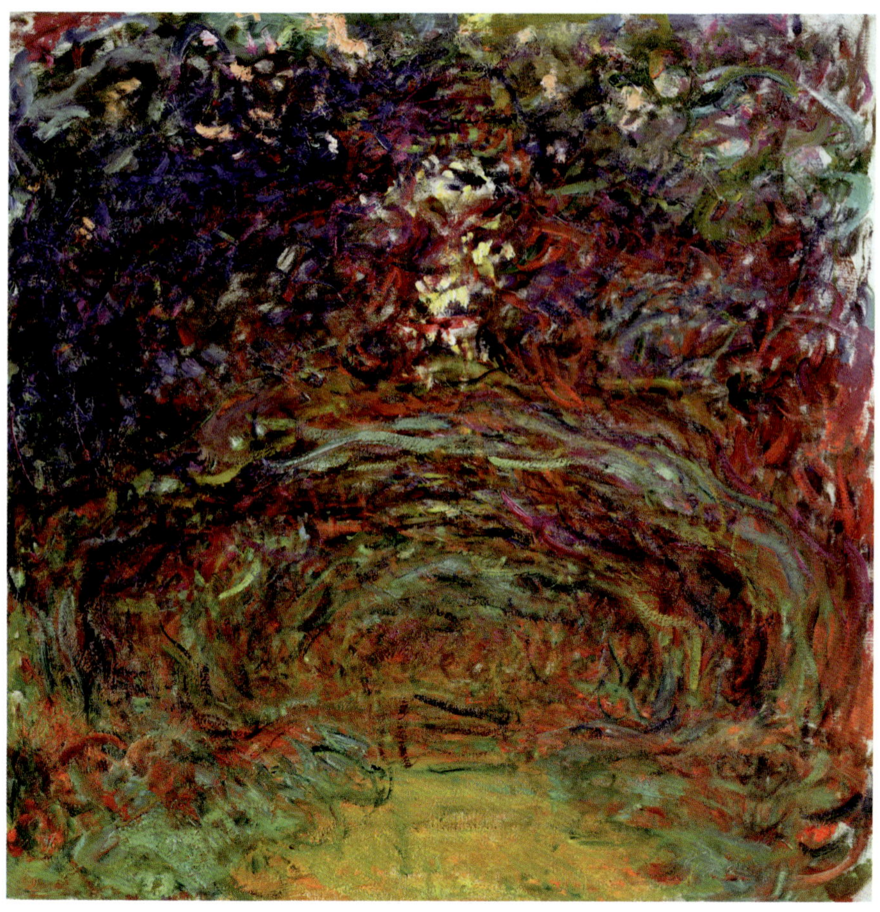

Impressionism as an international art movement

The impressionist impulse was also felt in other countries, leading to a renewal in painting, so that today we may speak of an international art movement which encompassed not only the whole of Europe, but also America, Russia and Japan.

With a delay of 15 years, this impulse also had an effect upon a number of hitherto naturalistic-working painters in Germany, of whom the most important were Max Liebermann (1847-1935), Max Slevogt (1868-1932) and Lovis Corinth (1858-1925). As the "triumvirate of German impressionism" these artists sought, within the Berlin "Secession", founded in 1898, to gain acceptance for the new outdoor painting, which was in opposition to the Wilhelminian art dogma. Showing less interest in the color and form experiments of their French counterparts, they took on the bright palette, the loose brushwork and naturalism, which had certainly been prepared for by German romanticism and by the Dachau school and the Leibl circle. The themes of German impressionists also included

L'impressionnisme en tant que mouvement artistique international

L'impulsion impressionniste a également été ressentie dans d'autres pays, ce qui a conduit à un renouveau de la peinture, de sorte qu'aujourd'hui, nous pouvons parler d'un mouvement d'art international qui a englobé non seulement l'ensemble de l'Europe, mais aussi l'Amérique, la Russie et le Japon.

Avec 15 ans de retard, cette impulsion a également eu un effet sur un certain nombre de peintres jusqu'ici naturalistes et travaillant en Allemagne, dont les plus importants étaient Max Liebermann (1847–1935), Max Slevogt (1868–1932) et Lovis Corinth (1858–1925). En tant que « triumvirat de l'impressionnisme allemand », ces artistes ont cherché, avec le mouvement berlinois « Secession », fondé en 1898, à obtenir l'acceptation de la nouvelle peinture en plein air, qui était en opposition au dogme wilhelmien de l'art. Affichant moins d'intérêt pour la couleur et les formes d'expérimentation que leurs homologues français, ils leur empruntèrent leur palette lumineuse, leurs coups de pinceau et le naturalisme, qui avait certainement été préparé par le romantisme allemand et par l'école de Dachau et le

Der Impressionismus als internationale Kunstbewegung

Auch in anderen Ländern machte sich der impressionistische Impuls bemerkbar und führte zu einer Neubelebung der Malerei, sodass man heute von einer internationalen Kunstbewegung spricht, die ganz Europa, aber auch Amerika, Russland und Japan erfasste.

Mit 15 Jahren Verspätung traf dieser Impuls auch in Deutschland auf eine Reihe von bis dahin naturalistisch arbeitenden Malern, von denen die bedeutendsten Max Liebermann (1847–1935), Max Slevogt (1868–1932) und Lovis Corinth (1858–1925) sind. Als „Triumvirat des deutschen Impressionismus" suchten diese Künstler innerhalb der 1898 gegründeten Berliner „Secession" die neue Freilichtmalerei gegen das wilhelminische Kunstdogma durchzusetzen. Weniger interessiert an den Farb- und Formexperimenten der Franzosen übernahmen sie die helle Palette, den lockeren Pinselduktus und den Naturlyrismus, der allerdings von der deutschen Romantik wie von der Dachauer Schule und dem Leibl-Kreis vorbereitet war. Die Themen der deutschen

Claude Monet (1840–1926)

The Rose Path at Giverny

L'allée aux roses à Giverny

Der Rosenweg in Giverny

El camino de rosas en Giverny

Il sentiero delle rose a Giverny

Het rozenpad in Giverny

1920–22, Oil on canvas/Huile sur toile, 92 × 89 cm, Musée Marmottan Monet, Paris

El impresionismo como movimiento artístico internacional

El impulso del impresionismo también se hizo palpable en otros países, llevando a una revitalización de la pintura, de modo que podemos hoy hablar de un movimiento internacional que incluyó a toda Europa, pero también a América, Rusia y Japón.

Este impulso llegó a Alemania con un retraso de 15 años de la mano de unos pintores que trabajaban hasta entonces con el naturalismo, siendo los más importantes Max Liebermann (1847–1935), Max Slevogt (1868–1932) y Lovis Corinth (1858–1925). Como "triunvirato del impresionismo alemán" estos artistas buscaron, dentro del grupo fundado en Berlín en 1898 "Secesión", una nueva pintura al aire libre para oponerla al dogma artístico de los tiempos de Guillermo I. Menos interesados en los experimentos de forma y color de los franceses, asumieron la paleta más clara, el trazo de pincel más ligero y el naturalismo, que ya había sido preparado durante el Romanticismo alemán por la escuela de Dachau y el circuito de Leibl. Los temas de los impresionistas alemanes incluían también motivos históricos

L'Impressionismo come movimento artistico internazionale

L'impulso impressionista si manifestò anche in altri Paesi, dove portò alla rinascita della pittura, tanto che oggi si parla di un movimento artistico internazionale diffusosi non solo in tutta Europa, ma anche in America, Russia e Giappone.

Con 15 anni di ritardo, l'Impressionismo raggiunse anche la Germania, manifestandosi nelle opere di un certo numero di pittori fino ad allora naturalistici, tra i quali spiccano Max Liebermann (1847–1935), Max Slevogt (1868–1932) e Lovis Corinth (1858–1925). Nell'ambito della "secessione" berlinese del 1898, gli artisti appartenenti a questo "triumvirato dell'impressionismo tedesco" cercarono di creare una nuova pittura all'aperto che si allontanasse dall'arte dogmatica wilhelmina. Meno interessati agli esperimenti cromatici e formali rispetto ai pittori francesi, ne acquisirono la tavolozza brillante, la pennellata fluida e il lirismo della natura, di cui fu precursore il Romanticismo tedesco con, ad esempio, la Scuola di Dachau e il circolo di Leibl. Tuttavia, gli impressionisti tedeschi trattavano anche argomenti

Het impressionisme als internationale beweging

Ook elders was de impuls van het impressionisme merkbaar en leidde tot een wederopleving van de schilderkunst zelf, zodat men tegenwoordig spreekt van een internationale kunststroming die niet alleen Europa maar ook Amerika, Rusland en Japan veroverde.

Met vijftien jaar vertraging bereikte deze impuls een groep Duitse kunstenaars die tot dan toe in een naturalistische stijl hadden gewerkt, onder wie Max Liebermann (1847–1935), Max Slevogt (1868–1932) en Lovis Corinth (1858–1925). Als 'triumviraat' van het Duitse impressionisme probeerden deze leden van de groep Berliner Secession (opgericht in 1898) het nieuwe schilderen in de vrije natuur te introduceren, tegen de dogma's van het wilhelminische establishment in. Ze richtten zich minder op het Franse experiment met kleur en vorm, maar namen wel het heldere palet, de losse penseelvoering en de lyrische verbeelding van de natuur over; hiervoor was al tijdens de Duitse Romantiek de basis gelegd, door de Dachauer Schule en de kring rond Wilhelm Leibl. Maar de Duitsers

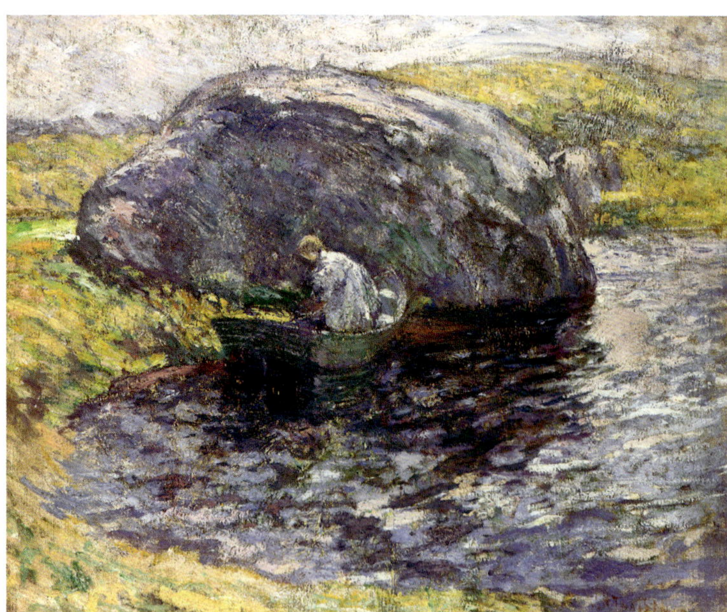

John Henry Twachtman (1853–1902)

A Summer Day

Une journée d'été

Ein Sommertag

Día de verano

Un giorno d'estate

Een zomerdag

c. 1900, Oil on canvas/Huile sur toile, 68,5 × 76,2 cm, Indianapolis Museum of Art, Indianapolis

historical, religious and sentimental subjects which were taboo for the impressionist avant-garde in France.

Through the English national tradition of landscape painting (Constable and Turner), the country remained closed for a long time to the ideas of impressionism. This changed, firstly through the maverick James McNeill Whistler (1834-1903), who carried on a friendship with the French impressionists and exhibited his famous *Nocturnes* (night paintings) in London, and then through the founding in 1886 of the New English Art Club, which became the platform for English impressionism. What remained important was the solid image composition and the representation of the figure, while only a few painters, such as John Singer Sargent, (1856–1925) who had experienced temporarily direct contact with Monet, developed a similarly colored and atmospheric painting style.

Through the contacts of Paul Durand-Ruel to the American art scene, impressionism also became known there in the late 1880s. In 1886 the art dealer organized a major exhibition of impressionist art in New York's American Art Association. It became fashionable for American painters to visit Paris and other places where the impressionists had painted. Amongst these pioneers of American Impressionism were Theodore Robinson (1852-1896), John Twachtman (1853-1902) and Julian Alden Weir (1852-1919). Upon their return to America, they spread the new style of painting through exhibitions and teaching. Impressionism in northern Europe is primarily associated with the artists' colony at Skagen. Situated at the northernmost tip of Denmark, the small fishing port of Skagen was, in 1834, the meeting place for

cercle Leibl. Les thèmes des impressionnistes allemands comprenaient aussi des sujets historiques, religieux et sentimentaux qui étaient tabou pour l'avant-garde impressionniste en France.

Du fait la tradition nationale anglaise de la peinture de paysage (Constable et Turner), ce pays est resté longtemps fermé aux idées de l'impressionnisme. Cela changea, d'abord avec le franc-tireur James McNeill Whistler (1834–1903), qui s'était lié d'amitié avec les impressionnistes français et exposa son fameux *Nocturnes* à Londres, puis fonda en 1886 le New English Art Club, qui devint la plate-forme de l'impressionnisme anglais. Il en resta la solide composition de l'image et la représentation de la figure, alors que seuls quelques peintres, comme John Singer Sargent (1856–1925) qui avait eu un contact temporairement direct avec Monet, développèrent un style de peinture similaire en termes de couleur et d'atmosphère.

Grâce aux contacts de Paul Durand-Ruel avec la scène artistique américaine, l'impressionnisme y fut également connu à la fin des années 1880. En 1886, le marchand d'art organisa une grande exposition d'art impressionniste à l'American Art Association de New York. Il devint à la mode pour les peintres américains de visiter Paris et d'autres endroits où les impressionnistes avaient peint. Theodore Robinson (1852–1896), John Twachtman (1853–1902) et Julian Alden Weir (1852–1919) faisaient partie ces pionniers de l'impressionnisme américain. À leur retour en Amérique, ils propagèrent ce nouveau style de peinture par des expositions et à travers l'enseignement. L'impressionnisme en Europe du Nord est principalement associé au village d'artistes de Skagen.

Impressionisten schlossen aber auch historische, religiöse und sentimentale Sujets ein, die in Frankreich bei der impressionistischen Avantgarde verpönt waren.

Durch die nationale Tradition des Landschaftsbildes (Constable und Turner) blieb in England der Blick auf den Impressionismus lange Zeit verschlossen. Erst durch den Einzelgänger James McNeill Whistler (1834–1903), der freundschaftlich mit den französischen Impressionisten verkehrte und in London seine berühmten *Nocturnes* (Nachtbilder) ausstellte, kam es 1886 zur Gründung des New English Art Club, der zur Plattform des englischen Impressionismus wurde. Wichtig blieb der feste Bildaufbau und die Darstellung der Figur, während nur wenige Maler, wie John Singer Sargent (1856–1925) durch den direkten Kontakt zum Beispiel mit Monet zumindest zeitweise, eine ähnliche farbige, atmosphärische Malerei entwickelten.

Durch die Kontakte Paul Durand-Ruels zur amerikanischen Kunstszene wurde der Impressionismus auch dort Ende der 1880er-Jahre bekannt. 1886 veranstaltete der Kunsthändler in der New Yorker American Art Association eine umfassende Ausstellung impressionistischer Kunst. Es wurde unter amerikanischen Malern bald zur Mode, Paris und andere Orte, an denen die Impressionisten gemalt hatten, zu besuchen. Zu diesen Pionieren des amerikanischen Impressionismus gehörten Theodore Robinson (1852–1896), John Twachtman (1853–1902) und Julian Alden Weir (1852–1919). Nach ihrer Rückkehr verbreiteten sie durch Ausstellungen und Lehrtätigkeit die neue Malweise in Amerika. Der Impressionismus im Norden Europas wird in erster Linie mit der Künstlerkolonie von Skagen

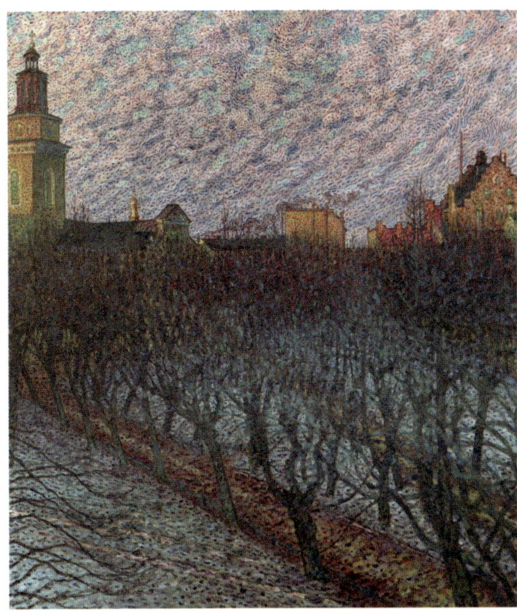

Nils Kreuger (1858–1930)

Evening Sun over Maria Magdalena Church Stockholm
Coucher de soleil sur l'église Marie-Madeleine à Stockholm
Abendsonne über der Maria Magdalena Kirche in Stockholm
Sol de la tarde sobre la iglesia de María Magdalena, en Estocolmo
Sole al tramonto sopra la chiesa di Santa Maria Maddalena a Stoccolma
Avondzon over de Maria Magdelena Kerk in Stockholm

c. 1902, Oil on canvas/Huile sur toile, 100 × 85,5 cm, Private collection

religiosos y sentimentales, mal vistos en Francia por la vanguardia impresionista.

Debido a su tradición nacional de paisajistas (Constable y Turner), Inglaterra no mostró interés por el impresionismo durante un largo período. Solo con la llegada de James McNeill Whistler (1834–1903), que estableció amistad con los impresionistas franceses y expuso sus famosos *Nocturnes* en Londres, se fundó en 1866 el "New English Art Club", que se convertiría en la plataforma del impresionismo inglés. La composición de la imagen y la representación de las figuras mantuvieron su importancia, con tan solo algunos pintores como John Singer Sargent (1856–1925), tal vez mediante su contacto directo con p. ej. Monet, desarrollando una pintura similarmente cromática y atmosférica.

Mediante los contactos de Paul Durand-Ruels con la escena artística americana también el impresionismo se hizo conocido allí a finales de la década de 1880. En 1886 el marchante de arte organizó una exhaustiva exposición de arte impresionista en la "New Yorker American Art Association". Entre los pintores norteamericanos se puso de moda visitar París y otros lugares donde los impresionistas habían pintado. Entre estos pioneros del impresionismo norteamericano podemos contar a Theodore Robinson (1852–1896), John Twachtman (1853–1902) y Julian Alden Weir (1852–1919). A su regreso difundieron, mediante exposiciones y seminarios, la nueva técnica pictórica en los Estados Unidos. El impresionismo en el norte de Europa está relacionado principalmente con la colonia de artistas en Skagen. Este pequeño pueblo pesquero, en la punta más septentrional de Dinamarca,

storici, religiosi e sentimentali, che erano invece tabù in Francia presso l'avanguardia impressionista.

Poiché possedeva già una lunga tradizione nazionale paesaggistica (Constable e Turner), l'Inghilterra resistette a lungo al fascino dell'Impressionismo. Fu solo nel 1866, attraverso il solitario James McNeill Whistler (1834–1903), che aveva stretto amicizia con gli impressionisti francesi e aveva esposto a Londra i suoi famosi *Nocturnes* (quadri notturni), che venne fondato il New English Art Club, la piattaforma dell'Impressionismo inglese. Tuttavia, in Inghilterra continuarono ad avere una grande importanza la rigida composizione e la rappresentazione della figura umana, e solo pochi pittori, come John Singer Sargent (1856–1925), svilupparono per contatto diretto, ad esempio con Monet, al meno temporalmente, una pittura atmosferica e colorata simile a quella dell'Impressionismo francese.

Attraverso i contatti di Paul Durand-Ruel con la scena artistica americana, l'Impressionismo acquisì popolarità anche in questo Paese alla fine degli anni Ottanta dell'Ottocento. Nel 1886 il mercante d'arte organizzò presso l'American Art Association di New York un'importante mostra di arte impressionista. Tra i pittori americani scoppiò ben presto la moda di visitare Parigi e altri luoghi in cui operavano gli impressionisti. Tra i pionieri dell'Impressionismo americano si annoverano Theodore Robinson (1852-1896), John Twachtman (1853–1902) e Julian Alden Weir (1852–1919). Al loro ritorno diffusero in America, attraverso mostre e attività formative, il nuovo stile di pittura. L'Impressionismo nel nord Europa è associato principalmente alla colonia di artisti di Skagen. Situato sulla punta più settentrionale della Danimarca, questo

beeldden ook historische en religieuze thema's uit, die in het Franse impressionisme werden gemeden.

Door de eigen traditie van de landschapsschilderkunst (Constable en Turner) ging het impressionisme lange tijd aan Groot-Brittannië voorbij. Pas door de eenling James McNeill Whistler (1834–1903), die bevriend was met de Franse impressionisten en in Londen zijn beroemde *Nocturnes* exposeerde, ontstond in 1866 de New English Art Club, die tot hét platform voor het Britse impressionisme uitgroeide. Belangrijk bleef wel de gecomponeerde opbouw van het schilderij en de uitbeelding van de menselijke figuur, terwijl slechts enkele schilders, zoals John Singer Sargent (1856–1925), door hun contacten met bijvoorbeeld Monet een tijdlang een soortgelijke kleurrijke en sfeervolle stijl ontwikkelden.

Dankzij de kunsthandelaar Paul Durand-Ruel bereikte het impressionisme aan het einde van de jaren tachtig van de negentiende eeuw ook de VS. In 1886 organiseerde hij in de New Yorkse American Art Association een grote expositie van impressionistische kunst. Veel Amerikaanse schilders begonnen Parijs en andere plekken te bezoeken die de impressionisten hadden geschilderd. Tot deze eerste Amerikaanse impressionisten behoorden Theodore Robinson (1852–1896), John Twachtman (1853–1902) en Julian Alden Weir (1852–1919). Na terugkeer introduceerden ze de nieuwe stijl in de VS door middel van exposities en door les te geven. In Noord-Europa is het impressionisme vooral verbonden met de kunstenaarskolonie in Skagen. Dit vissersplaatsje aan de uiterste noordpunt van Denemarken werd vanaf 1834 een trefpunt voor kunstenaars uit Scandinavië, die

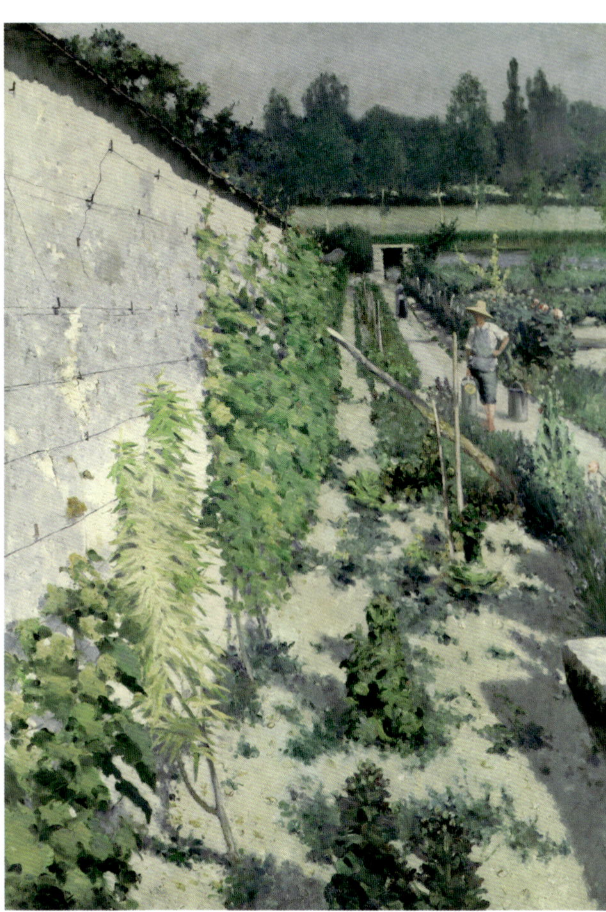

artists from all over Scandinavia who wanted to paint outdoors together. In the 1890s, the Swedish painters Karl Nordström (1855-1923) and Nils Kreuger (1858-1930), as well as the Norwegian Christian Krohg (1852-1925), developed there, and later in their home countries, a luminous painting style with a loose technique. In Italy, unlike in France, there was a lack of national statehood and hence no cultural center like Paris, which meant that a number of small towns all had their own traditions. In the mid-1850s a number of artists who frequented Florence's Caffè Michelangelo developed an artistic style which deviated from academicism, a kind of color-intensive spot painting. Thus, these painters who included Giovanni Fattori (1825–1908), Giuseppe De Nittis (1846–1884), Federico Zandomeneghi (1841–1917) und Telemaco Signorini (1835–1901) and were known as "Macchiaoli" (patches, or spots). The best-known of these was Giovanni Segantini (1858-1899) with his scenes of the Alpine landscape.

Situé à l'extrême nord du Danemark, le petit port de Skagen fut, en 1834, le lieu de rencontre d'artistes venus de toute la Scandinavie et qui voulaient peindre ensemble en plein air. Dans les années 1890, les peintres suédois Karl Nordström (1855–1923) et Nils Kreuger (1858–1930), ainsi que le norvégien Christian Krohg (1852–1925), développèrent à Skagen et plus tard dans leurs pays d'origine, un style de peinture lumineux avec une technique libre. Il y avait en Italie, contrairement à la France, un manque d'indépendance nationale et donc pas de centre culturel comme Paris, ce qui signifie qu'un certain nombre de petites villes avaient chacune leurs propres traditions. Au milieu des années 1850, un certain nombre d'artistes qui fréquentaient le Caffè Michelangelo de Florence développa un style artistique issu de l'académisme, une sorte de peinture par taches de couleurs intensives. Ainsi, ces peintres dont Giovanni Fattori (1825–1908), Giuseppe De Nittis (1846–1884), Federico Zandomeneghi (1841–1917) et Telemaco Signorini (1835–1901) étaient connus comme « Macchiaioli » (patches, ou taches). Le plus connu d'entre eux fut Giovanni Segantini (1858–1899) avec ses scènes de paysages alpins.

verbunden. Der an der nördlichsten Spitze Dänemarks gelegene kleine Fischerort Skagen wurde ab 1834 zum Treffpunkt für Künstler aus ganz Skandinavien, die gemeinsam im Freien malen wollten. Die schwedischen Maler Karl Nordström (1855–1923) und Nils Kreuger (1858–1930) sowie der Norweger Christian Krohg (1852–1925) entwickelten dort und anschließend in ihren Heimatländern in den 1890er Jahren eine lichthaltige Malerei in einer freien Technik. Im Unterschied zu Frankreich gab es in Italien infolge der fehlenden Nationalstaatlichkeit kein kulturelles Zentrum wie Paris, sondern eine Anzahl kleinerer Städte mit eigenen Traditionen. Mitte der 1850er Jahre entwickelten einige, im Florentiner Caffè Michelangelo verkehrende Künstler einen vom Akademismus abweichenden Malstil, eine Art farbintensiver Fleckenmalerei. Dahern wurde diese Maler, unter anderem Giovanni Fattori (1825–1908), Giuseppe De Nittis (1846–1884), Federico Zandomeneghi (1841–1917) und Telemaco Signorini (1835–1901) auch „Macchiaoli" (Fleckenmaler) genannt. Am bekanntesten wurde Giovanni Segantini (1858–1899) mit Szenen der Alpenlandschaft.

se convirtió a partir de 1834 en punto de encuentro para artistas de toda Escandinavia que querían pintar al aire libre. Los suecos Karl Nordström (1855–1923) y Nils Kreuger (1858–1930) así como el noruego Christian Krohg (1852–1925) desarrollaron allí y posteriormente en sus países de origen en 1890 y posteriormente una pintura luminosa de técnica libre. Al contrario que en Francia en Italia no había, dado que no era todavía una nación, un único centro cultural como París, sino más bien una multitud de ciudades más pequeñas con tradiciones propias. En la mitad de la década de 1850 un grupo de artistas que se reunían en el Caffè Michelangelo de Florencia desarrolló un estilo pictórico que se apartaba del academicismo, una especie de pintura de manchas cromáticas. Por esto se conoció a estos pintores, entre otros Giovanni Fattori (1825–1908), Giuseppe De Nittis (1846–1884), Federico Zandomeneghi (1841–1917) y Telemaco Signorini (1835–1901) como "Macchiaoli" (pintores de manchas). Giovanni Segantini (1858–1899) fue el más conocido de entre ellos gracias a sus paisajes de los Alpes.

piccolo villaggio di pescatori divenne, a partire dal 1834, il luogo d'incontro degli artisti provenienti da tutta la Scandinavia che volevano dipingere insieme all'aperto. Negli anni Novanta dell'Ottocento, i pittori svedesi Karl Nordström (1855–1923) e Nils Kreuger (1858–1930) e il norvegese Christian Krohg (1852–1925) svilupparono, dapprima a Skagen e poi nei loro Paesi d'origine, una pittura luminosa ottenuta mediante una tecnica libera. A differenza della Francia, in Italia mancava un centro culturale nazionale come Parigi a causa della mancanza di uno stato unitario. Al suo posto esistevano invece diverse piccole città con le proprie tradizioni. A metà degli anni Cinquanta dell'Ottocento, nel Caffè Michelangelo di Firenze, degli artisti in viaggio svilupparono uno stile pittorico antiaccademico, un tipo di pittura basato su macchie di colore intenso. Tra gli esponenti di questo movimento si annoverano Giovanni Fattori (1825–1908), Giuseppe De Nittis (1846–1884), Federico Zandomeneghi (1841–1917) e Telemaco Signorini (1835–1901), noti anche come "macchiaioli". L'artista più rinomato di questa corrente fu Giovanni Segantini (1858–1899), che dipinse scene del paesaggio alpino.

gezamenlijk in de openlucht werkten. Aan het einde van de eeuw ontwikkelden de Zweden Karl Nordström (1855–1923) en Nils Kreuger (1858–1930) en de Noor Christian Krohg (1852–1925) in Skagen en vervolgens in hun eigen landen een lichte en luchtige schilderstijl in een losse techniek. In Italië bestond er, anders dan in Frankrijk, door het ontbreken van één natiestaat geen cultureel centrum als Parijs, maar een groot aantal kleinere kunstcentra met elk een eigen traditie. Halverwege de eeuw ontwikkelden enkele kunstenaars die elkaar in het Florentijnse Caffè Michelangelo troffen, een nieuwe stijl die afweek van de academische normen; tot de groep behoorden Giovanni Fattori (1825–1908), Giuseppe De Nittis (1846–1884), Federico Zandomeneghi (1841–1917) en Telemaco Signorini (1835–1901). Hun stijl berustte op intense kleurvlekken, wat de schilders de groepsnaam 'Macchiaoli' ('vlekkenschilders') opleverde. De bekendste onder hen was Giovanni Segantini (1858–1899), die vooral Alpenlandschappen creëerde.

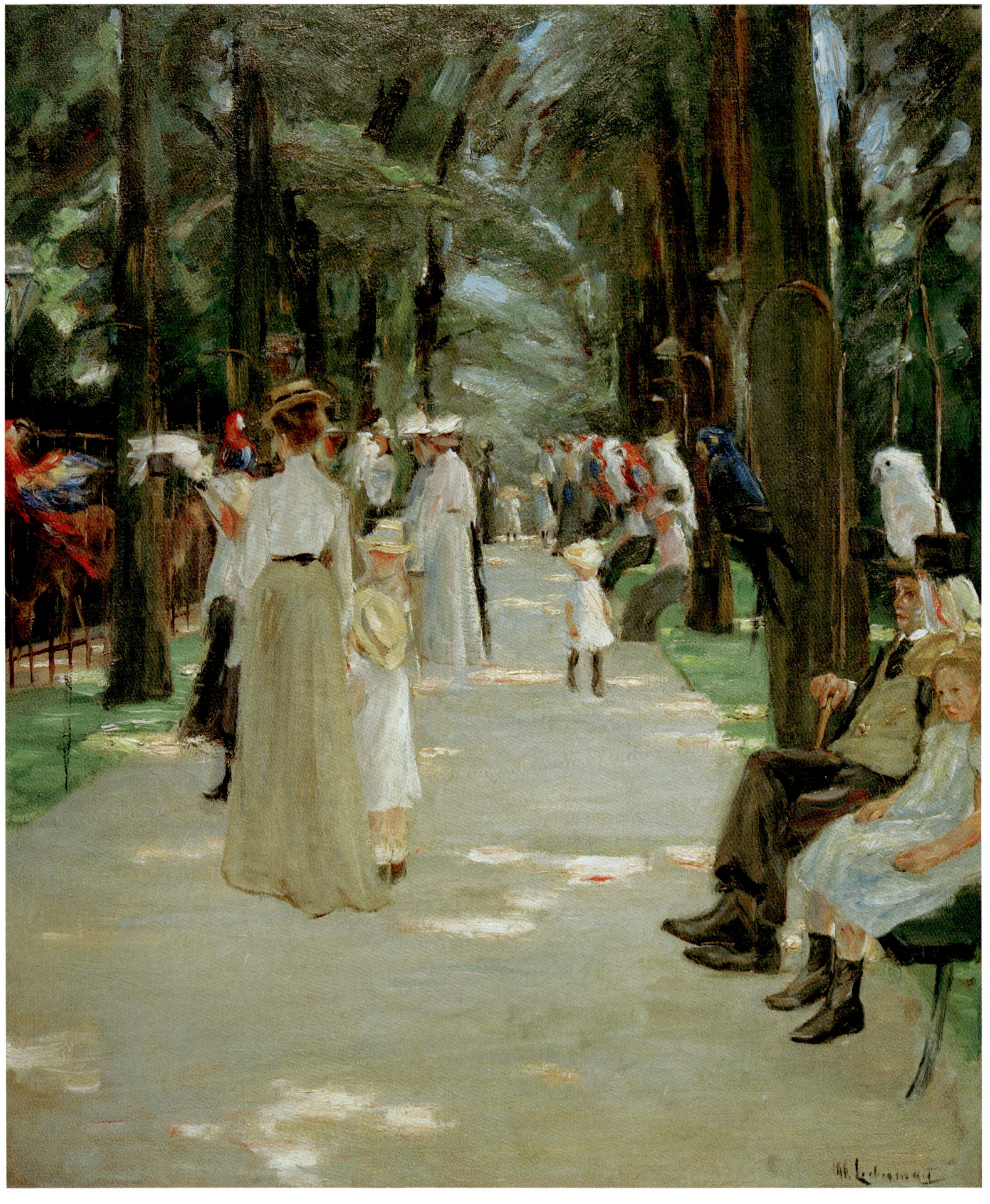

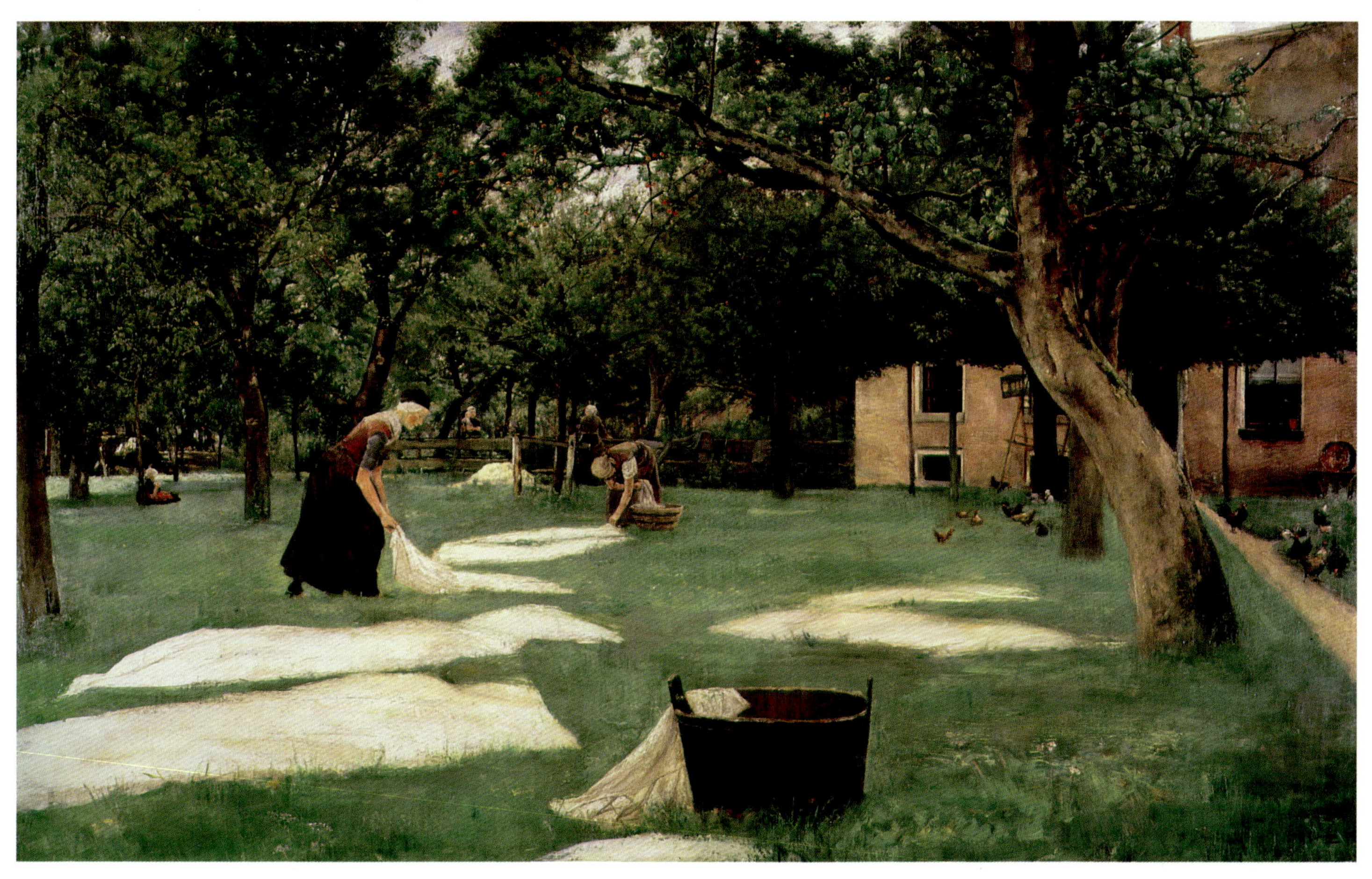

Max Liebermann (1847–1935)

Parrot Alley

Allée des Perroquets

Papageienallee

La avenida de los papagayos

Viale dei pappagalli

De papegaaienlaan

1902, Oil on canvas/Huile sur toile, 88,1 × 72,5 cm, Kunsthalle Bremen, Bremen

Max Liebermann (1847–1935)

The bleaching ground

La blanchisserie

Die Rasenbleiche

El blanqueo sobre la hierba

Il bucato sul prato

De bleekstraat

1882, Oil on canvas/Huile sur toile, 109 × 173 cm, Wallraf-Richartz-Museum & Fondation Corboud, Köln

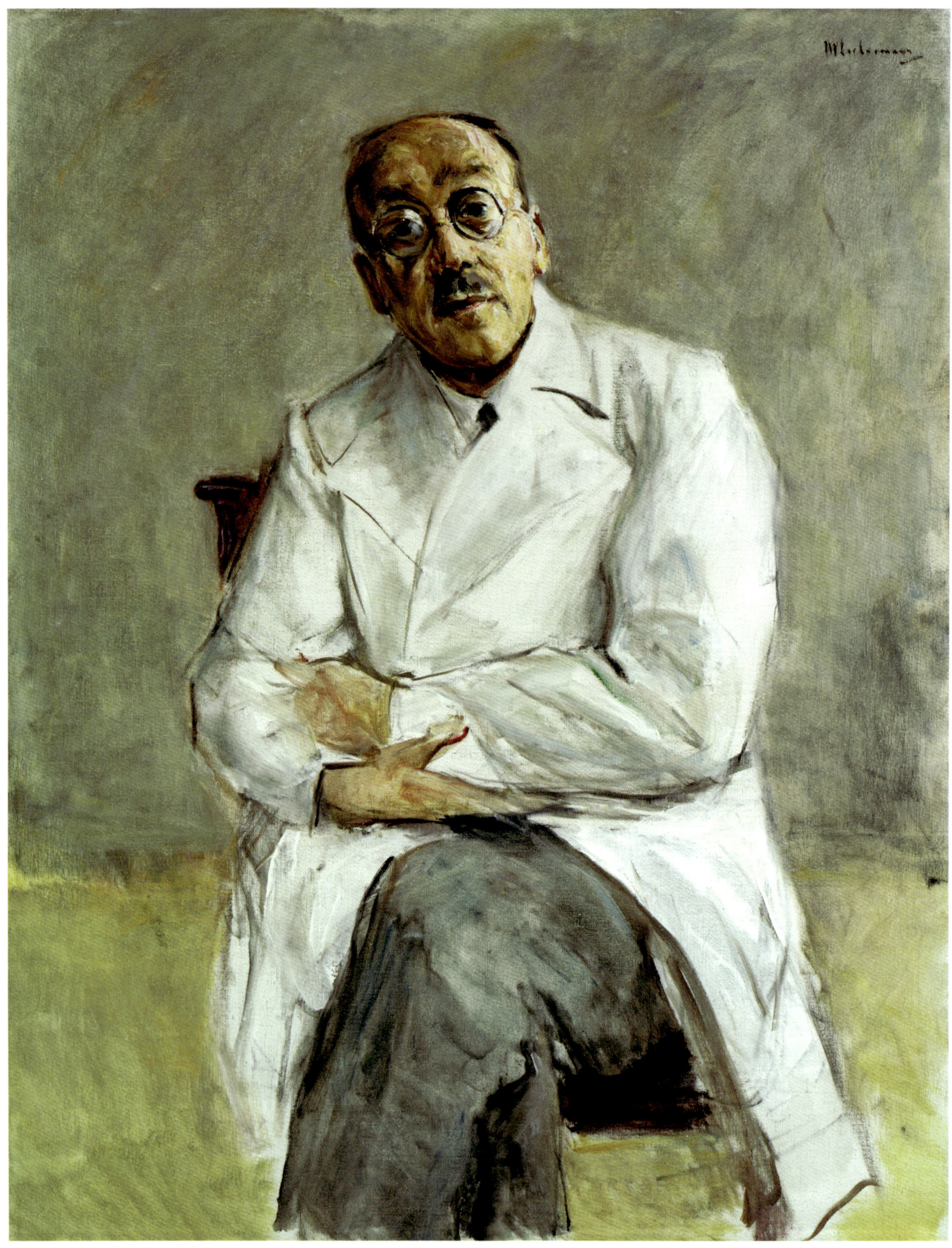

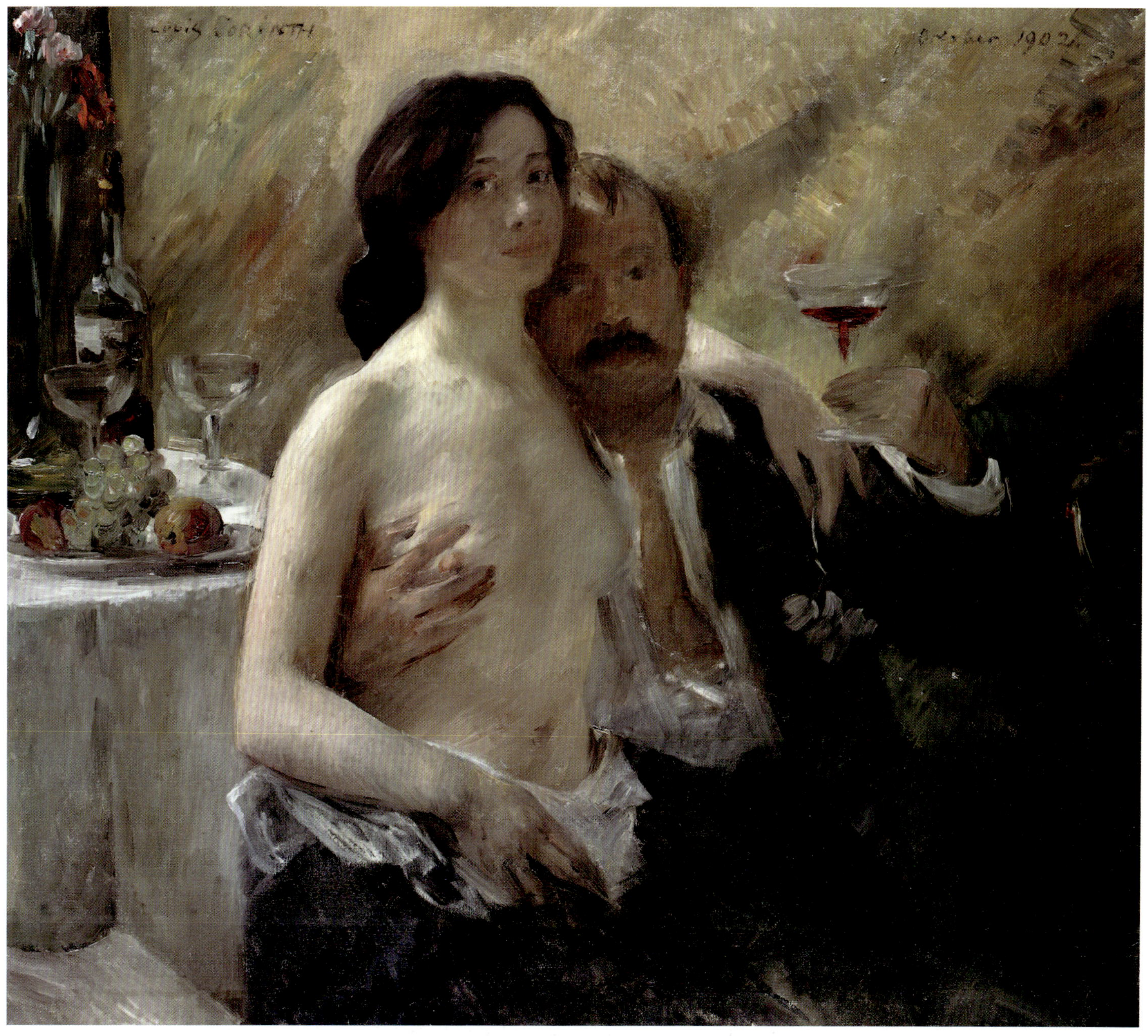

Max Liebermann (1847–1935)

The Surgeon, Ferdinand Sauerbruch

Portrait du chirurgien Ferdinand Sauerbruch

Der Chirurg Ferdinand Sauerbruch

El cirujano, Fernando Sauerbruch

Il chirurgo Ferdinand Sauerbruch

De chirurg, Fernando Sauerbruch

1932, Oil on canvas/Huile sur toile, 117,2 × 89,4 cm, Hamburger Kunsthalle, Hamburg

Lovis Corinth (1858–1925)

Self portrait with his wife and a sekt glass

Autoportrait au verre de champagne avec son épouse

Selbstporträt mit seiner Frau und Sektglas

Autorretrato con su esposa y copa de vino

Autoritratto con sua moglie e bicchiere di champagne

Zelfportret met zijn vrouw en een champagneglas

1902, Oil on canvas/Huile sur toile, 98,5 × 108,5 cm, Private collection

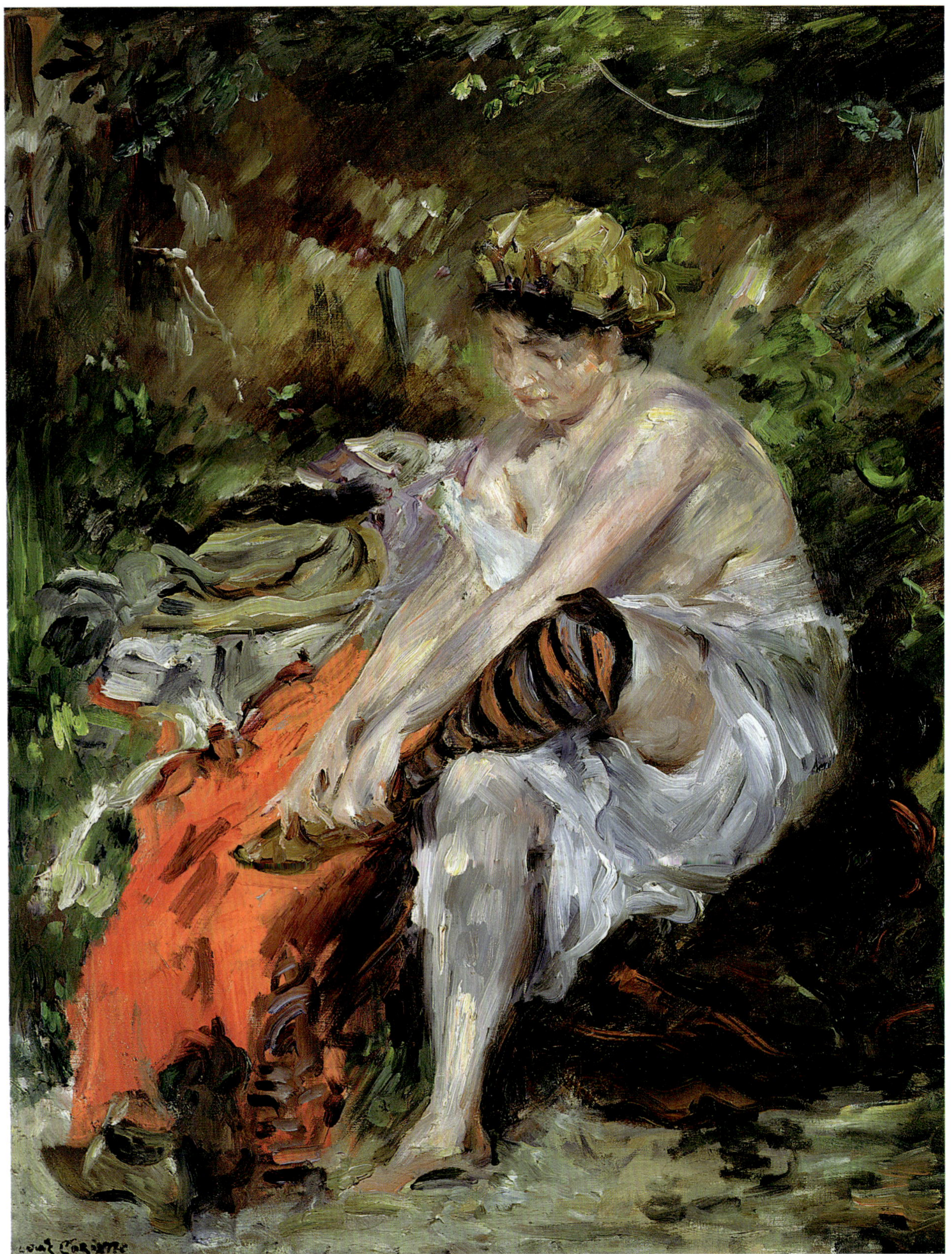

Lovis Corinth
(1858–1925)

After the swim

Après le bain

Nach dem Bade

Después del baño

Dopo il bagno

Na het baden

1907, Oil on canvas/
Huile sur toile,
80 × 60 cm, Hamburger
Kunsthalle, Hamburg

Max Slevogt
(1868–1932)

The Art Historian,
Professor Dr. Karl Voll

Portrait de l'historien
d'art, Prof Dr Karl Voll

Der Kunsthistoriker
Prof. Dr. Karl Voll

El historiador de arte,
Prof. Dr. Karl Voll

Lo storico dell'arte
Prof. Dr. Karl Voll

De kunsthistoricus,
Prof. Dr. Karl Voll

1911, Oil on canvas/
Huile sur toile,
120 × 93 cm, Hamburger
Kunsthalle, Hamburg

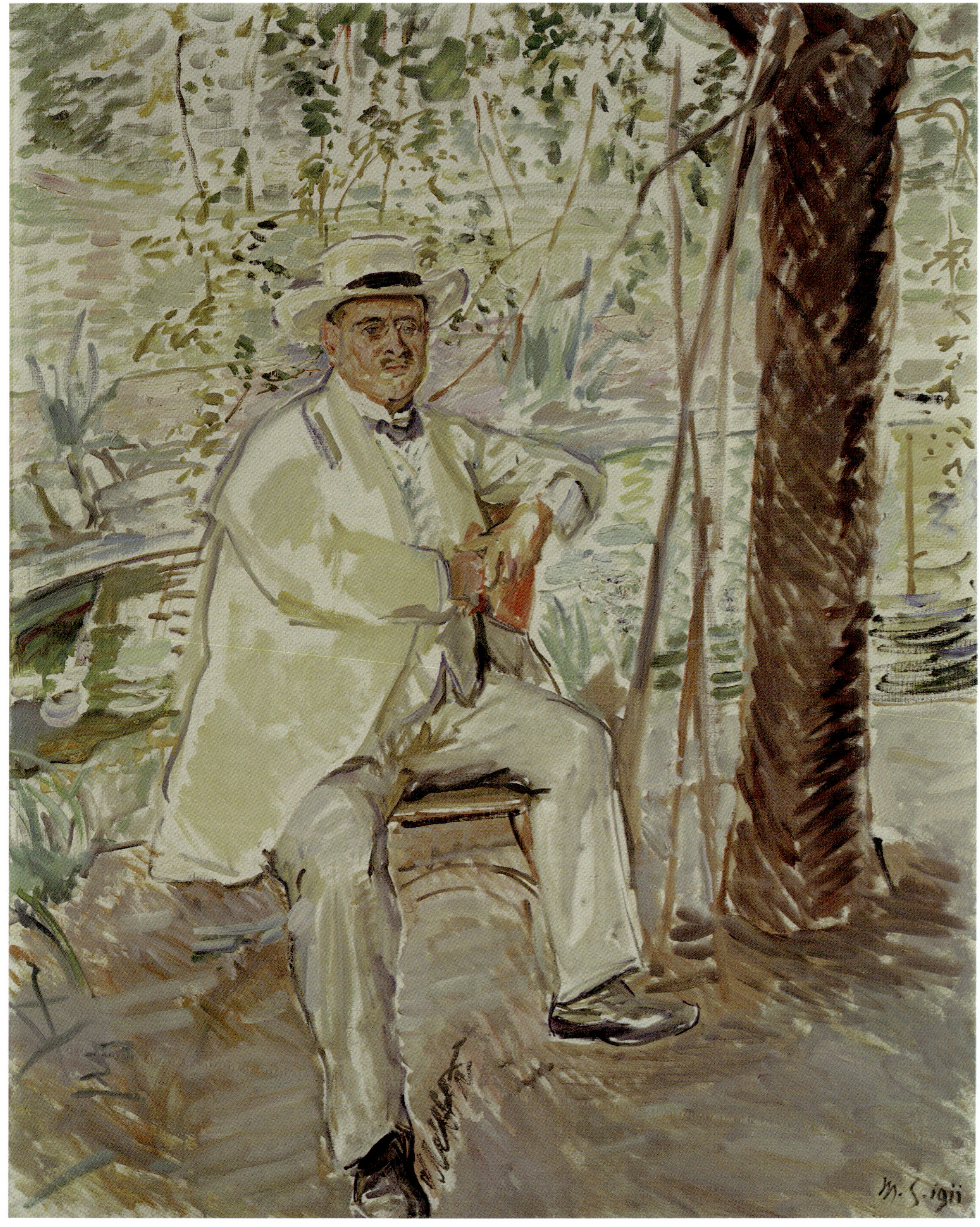

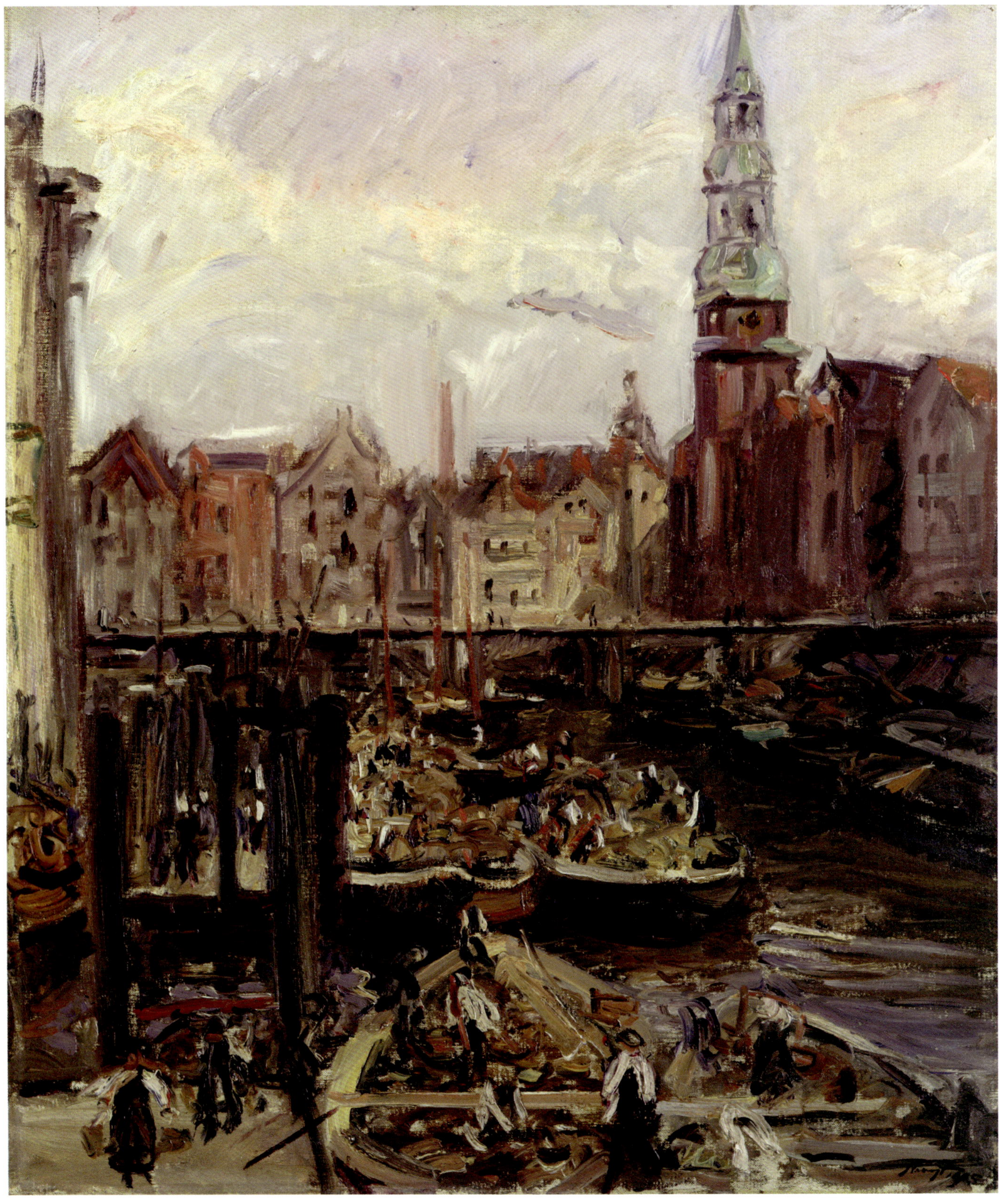

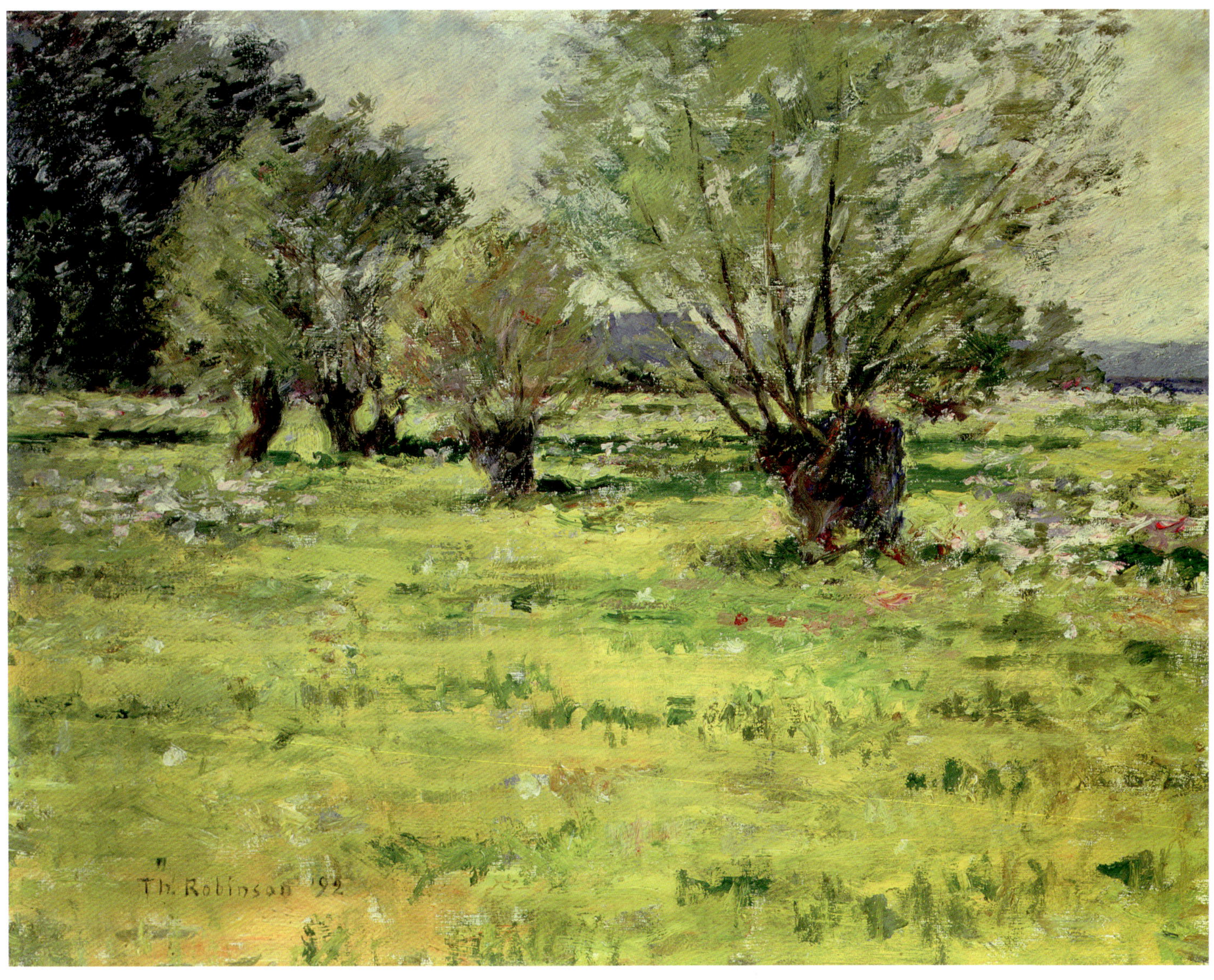

Max Slevogt (1868–1932)

Floating market on a canal in Hamburg

Marché flottant sur un canal à Hambourg

Schwimmender Markt auf einem Kanal in Hamburg

Mercado flotante en un canal de Hamburgo

Mercato galleggiante su un canale di Amburgo

Drijvende markt op een kanaal in Hamburg

1905, Oil on canvas/Huile sur toile, 75 × 62 cm, Hamburger Kunsthalle, Hamburg

Theodore Robinson (1852–96)

Springtime

Printemps

Frühling

Primavera

Primavera

Lente

1892, Oil on canvas/Huile sur toile, 44,5 × 55,3 cm, Private collection

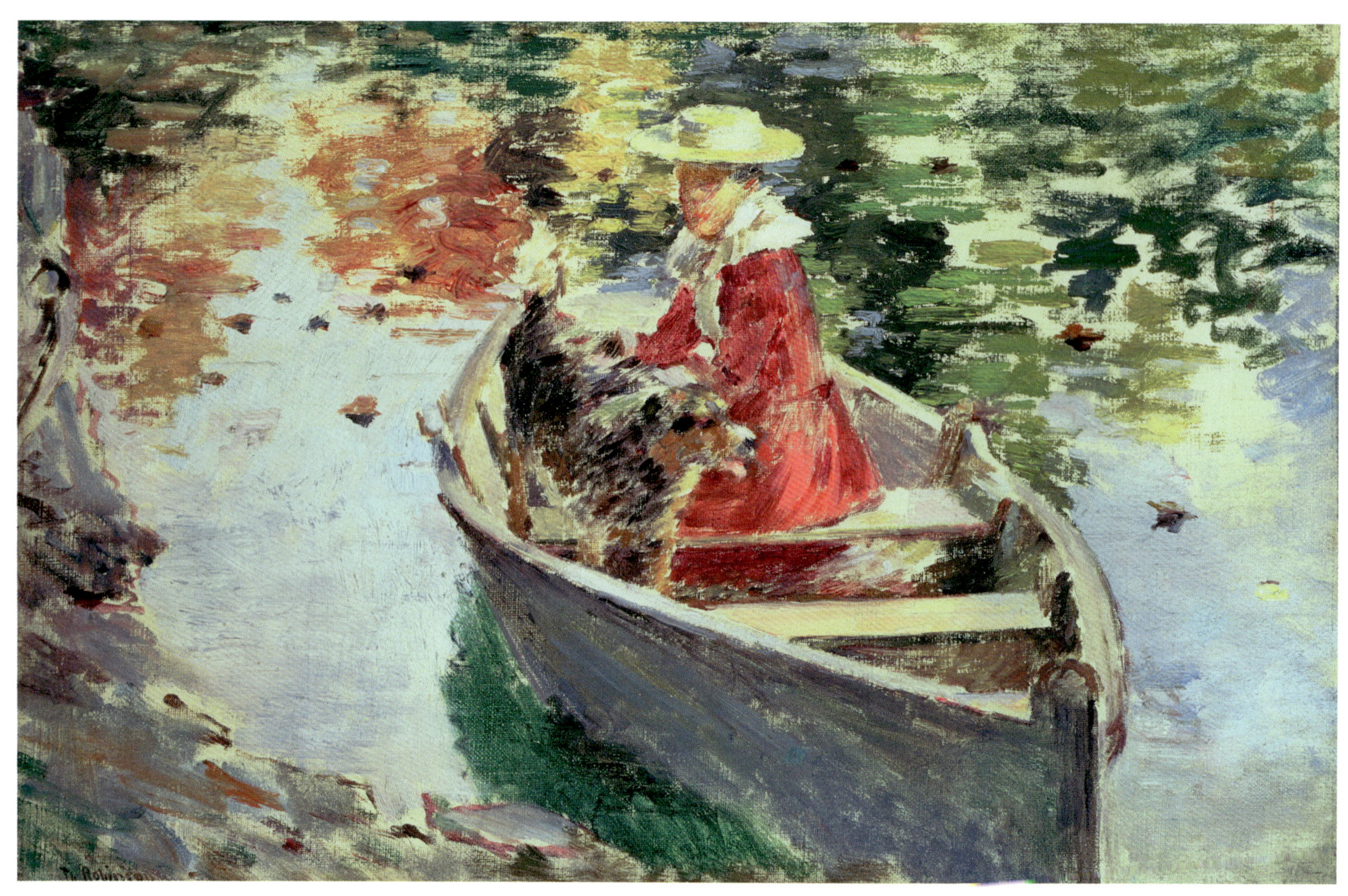

Theodore Robinson (1852–96)

Miss Motes and her Dog Shep

Mademoiselle Motes et son chien Shep

Miss Motes und ihr Hund Shep

Señorita Motes y su perro Shep

Miss Motes e il suo cane Shep

Mevrouw Motes en haar hond Shep

1893, Oil on canvas/Huile sur toile, 30,5 × 45,7 cm, Private collection

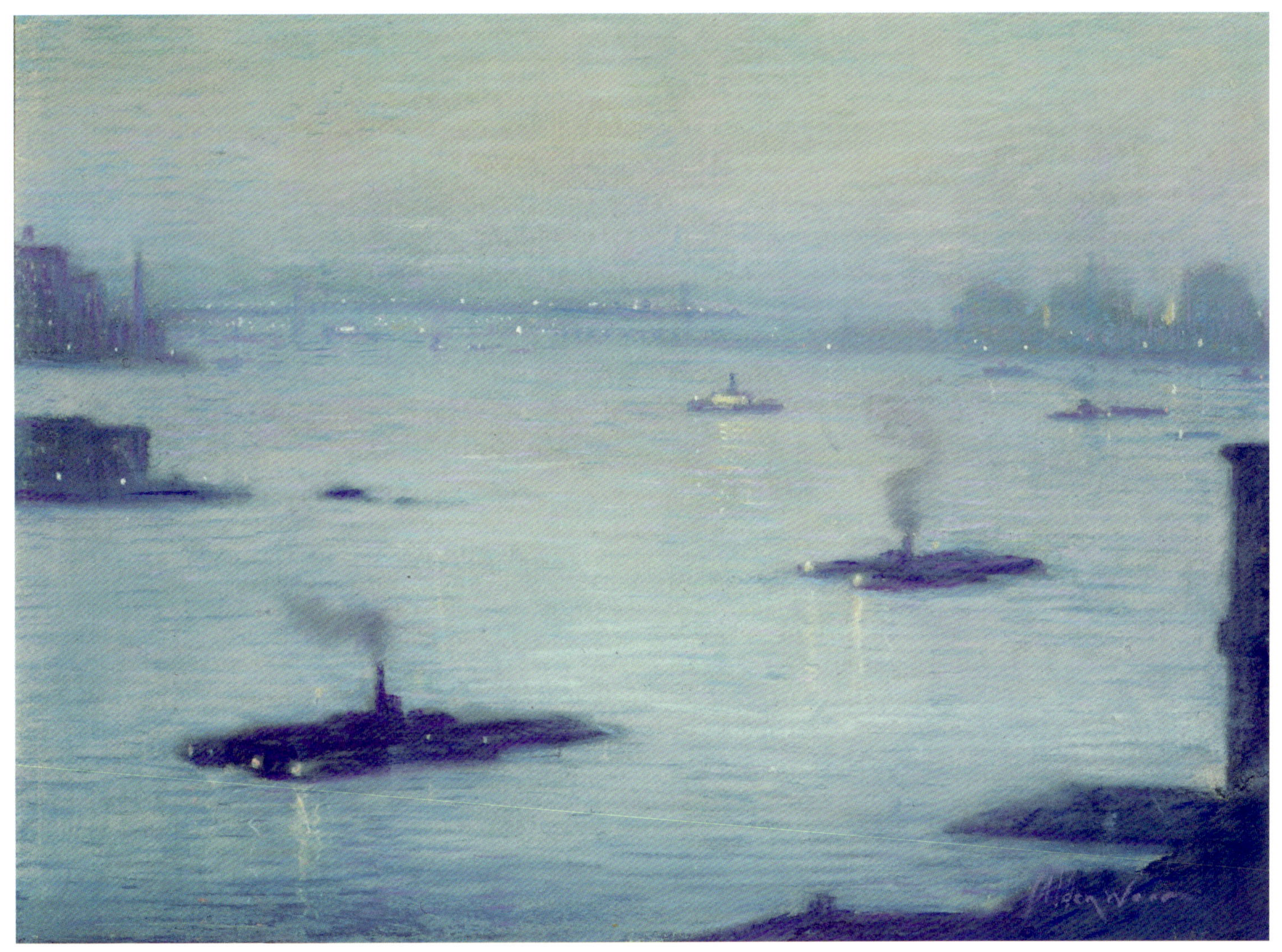

Julian Alden Weir (1852–1919)

The East River – Night Scene

L'East River de nuit

East River bei Nacht

El East River – Escena nocturna

L'East River di notte

East River bij nacht

1905, Pastel/Pastel, 30,5 × 40,6 cm, Mead Art Museum at Amherst College, Amherst

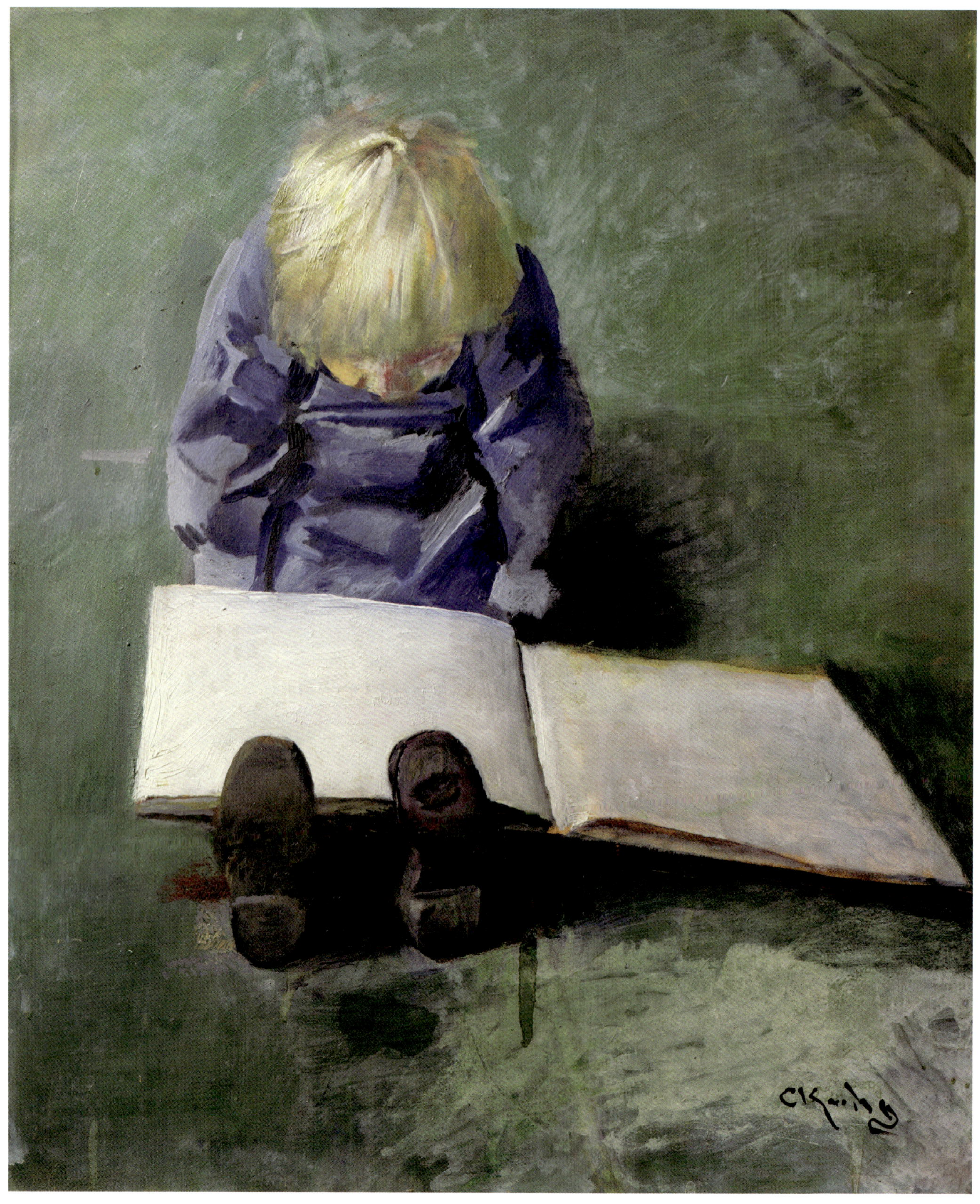

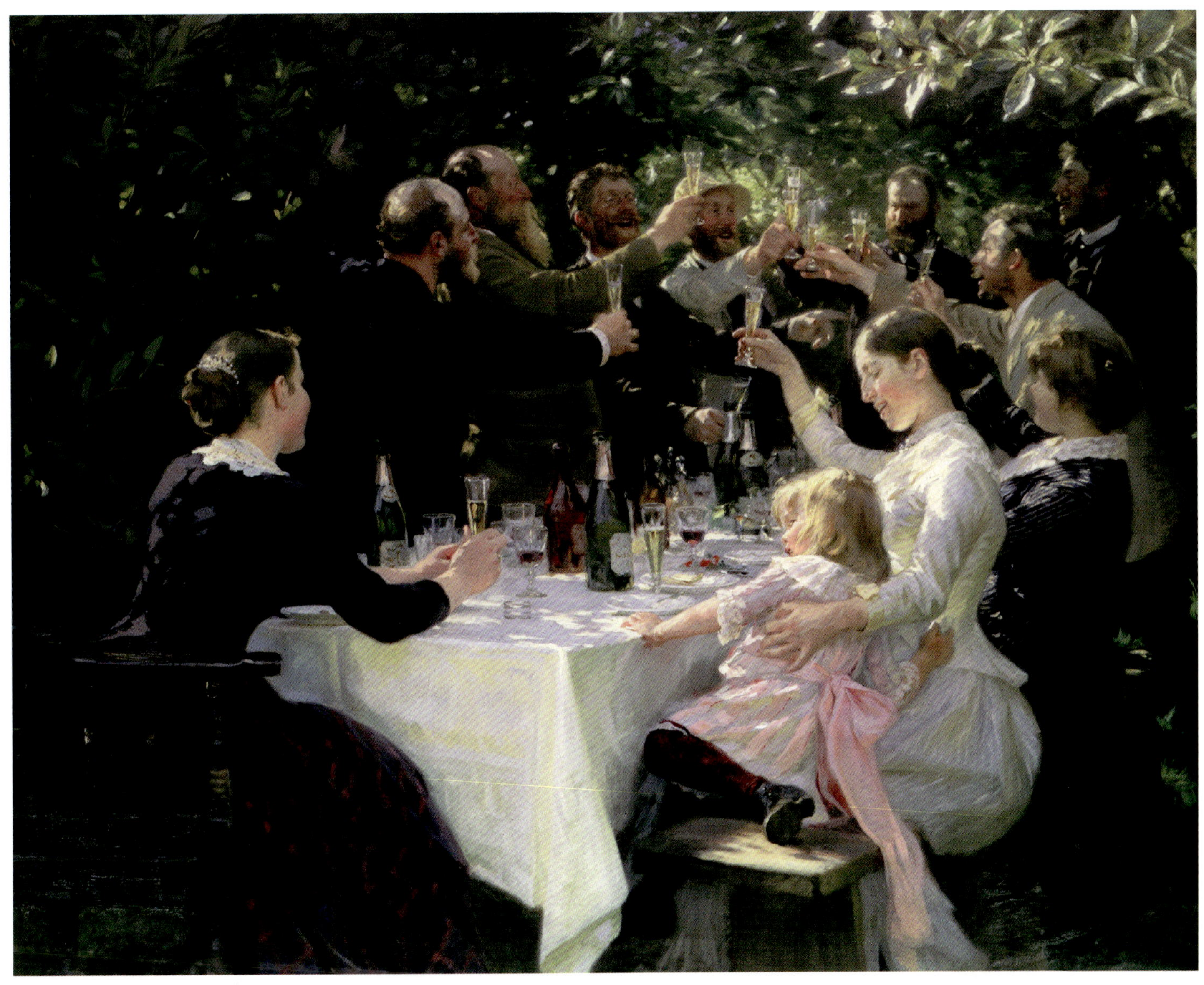

Christian Krohg (1852–1925)

Little Ebbe reading

Petite Ebbe lisant

Klein-Ebbe, lesend

Pequeña Ebbe leyendo

Bambino che legge

Kleine Ebbe, lezend

1920, Oil on canvas/Huile sur toile, 65 × 53 cm, Private collection

Peder Severin Krøyer (1851–1909)

"Hip Hip Hurrah!" Artists' Party at Skage

« Hip, hip, hourra ! » Fête d'artistes à Skagen

„Hip Hip Hurrah!" Künstlerfest in Skagen

"Hip Hip Hurrah!" Fiesta de artistas en Skagen

"Hip Hip Hurrà!" Festa degli artisti a Skage

"Hiep hiep hoera!" Kunstenaarsfeest in Skage

1887/88, Oil on canvas/Huile sur toile, 134,5 × 165,5 cm, Konstmuseet, Göteborg

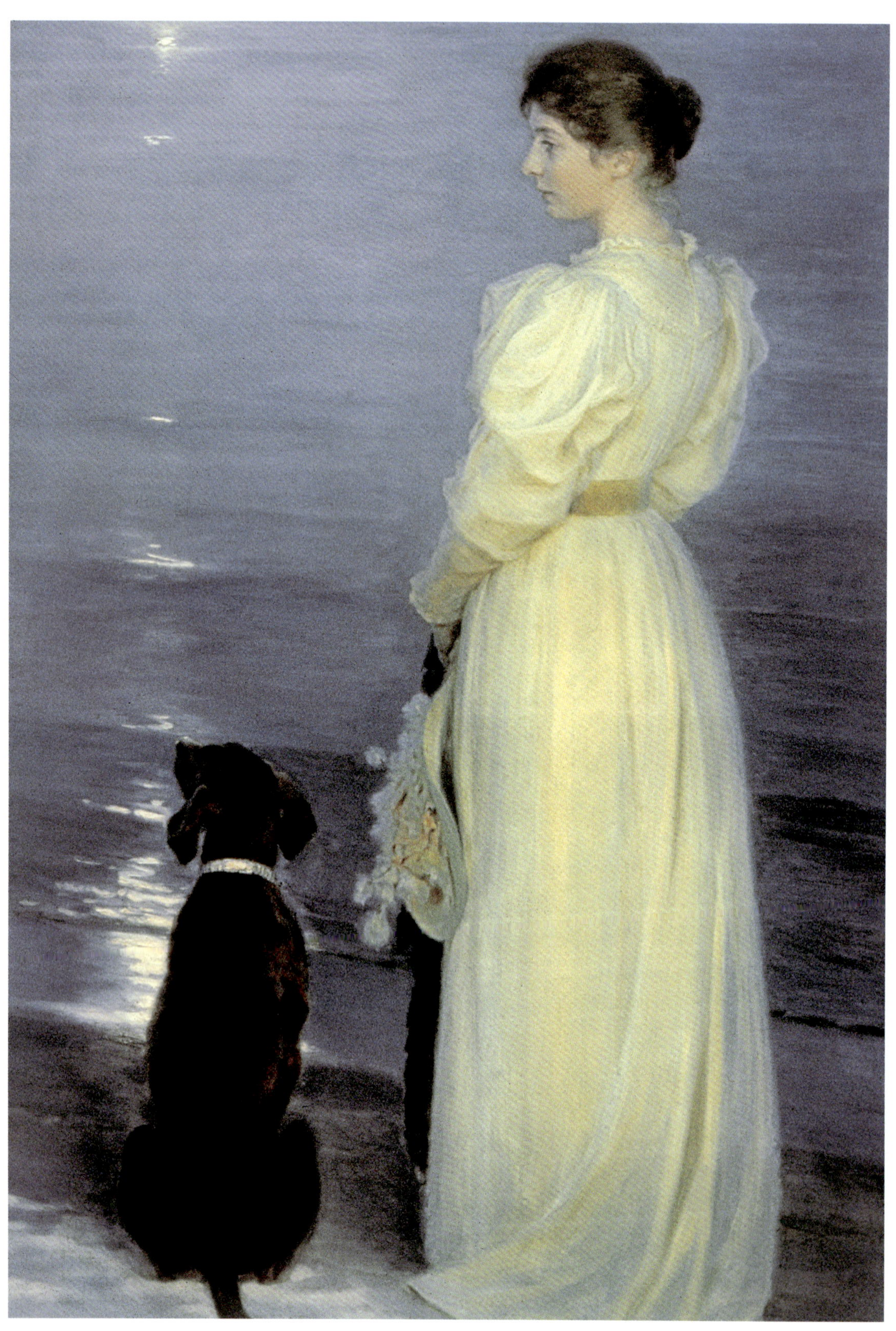

Peder Severin Krøyer (1851–1909)

Summer Evening at Skagen, the
Artist's Wife with a Dog on the Beach

Soir d'été à Skagen. La femme
de l'artiste et son chien

Sommerabend in Skagen. Die
Frau des Künstlers mit Hund

Noche de verano en Skagen. La
mujer del artista con perro

Sera d'estate a Skagen, moglie
dell'artista con un cane sulla spiaggia

Zomeravond in Skagen. De vrouw
van de kunstenaar met hond

1892, Oil on canvas/Huile sur toile,
206 × 123 cm, Skagens Museum, Skagen

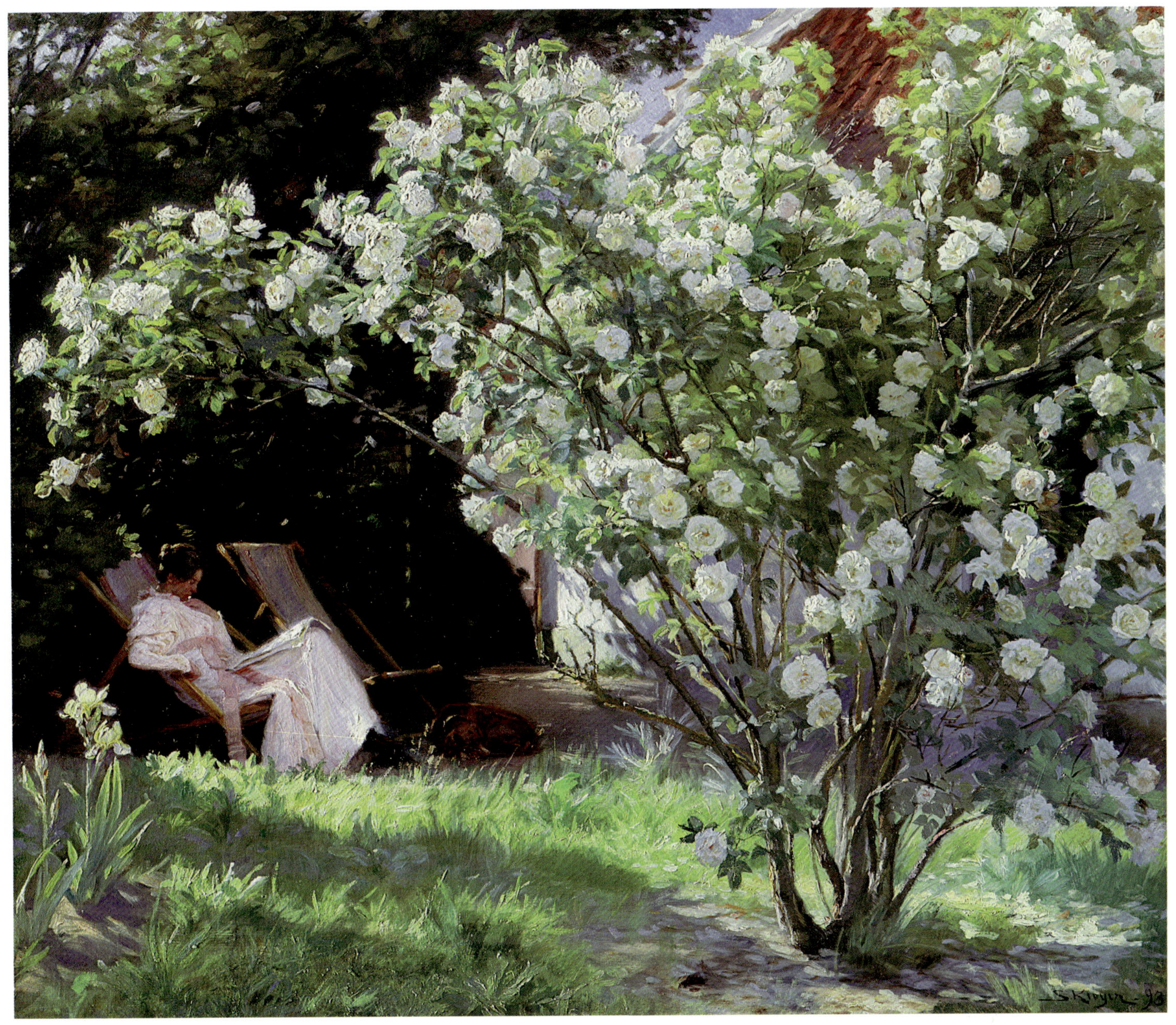

Peder Severin Krøyer (1851–1909)

Roses *or* The Artist's Wife in the Garden at Skagen

Le jardin de roses. La femme de l'artiste dans le jardin de Skagen

Im Rosengarten. Die Frau des Künstlers im Garten von Skagen

En el jardín de rosas. La mujer del artista en el jardín de Skagen

Rose *o* La moglie dell'artista nel giardino di Skagen

In de rozentuin. De vrouw van de kunstenaar in de tuin van Skagen

1883, Oil on canvas/Huile sur toile, 67,5 × 76,5 cm, Skagens Museum, Skagen

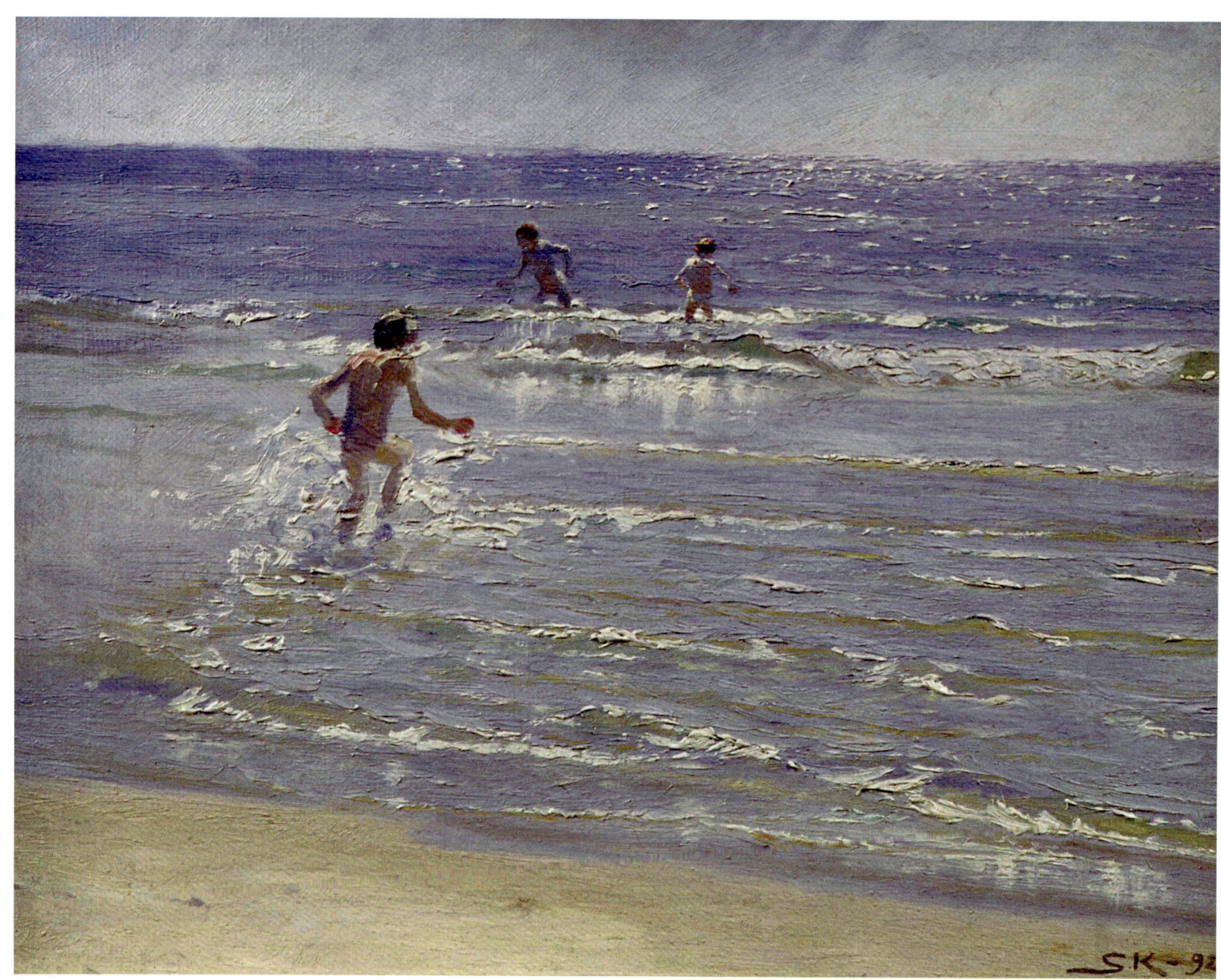

Peder Severin Krøyer (1851–1909)

Sunshine at Skagen: Boys Swimming

Soleil à Skagen : jeunes garçons se baignant

Sonnenschein in Skagen: Badende Jungen

Día soleado en Skagen: Jóvenes bañándose

Sole a Skagen: bambini che fanno il bo

Zonneschijn in Skagen: badende jongens

1892, Oil on canvas/Huile sur toile, 33 × 40,5 cm, Private collection

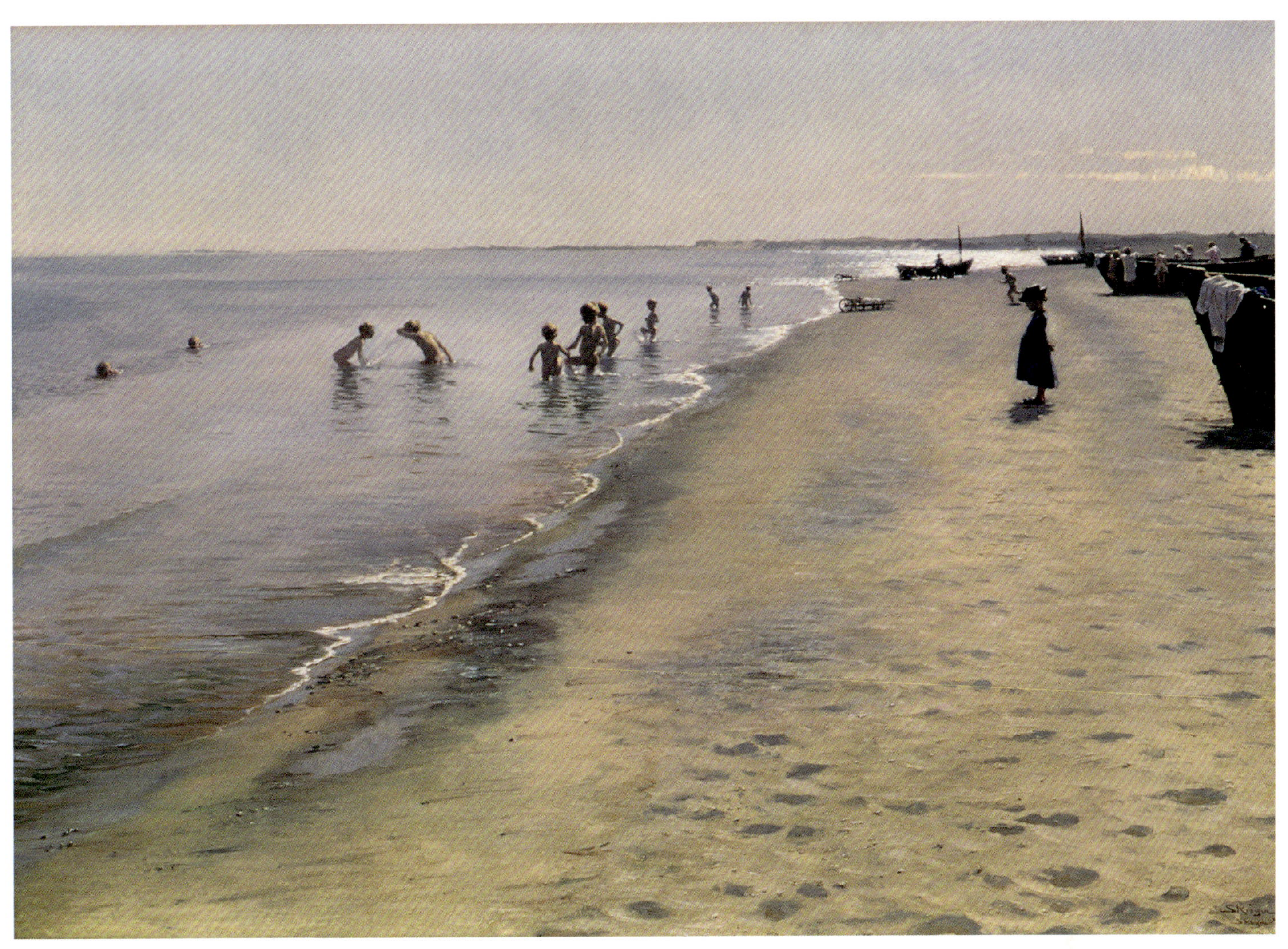

Peder Severin Krøyer (1851–1909)

Summer Day at the South Beach of Skagen

Jour d'été à la plage de Skagen

Sommertag am Südstrand von Skagen

Día de verano en la playa meridional de Skagen

Giorno d'estate sulla spiaggia a sud di Skagen

Zomerdag op het zuidstrand van Skagen

1884, Oil on canvas/Huile sur toile, 154,5 × 212 cm, Hirschsprung Collection, København

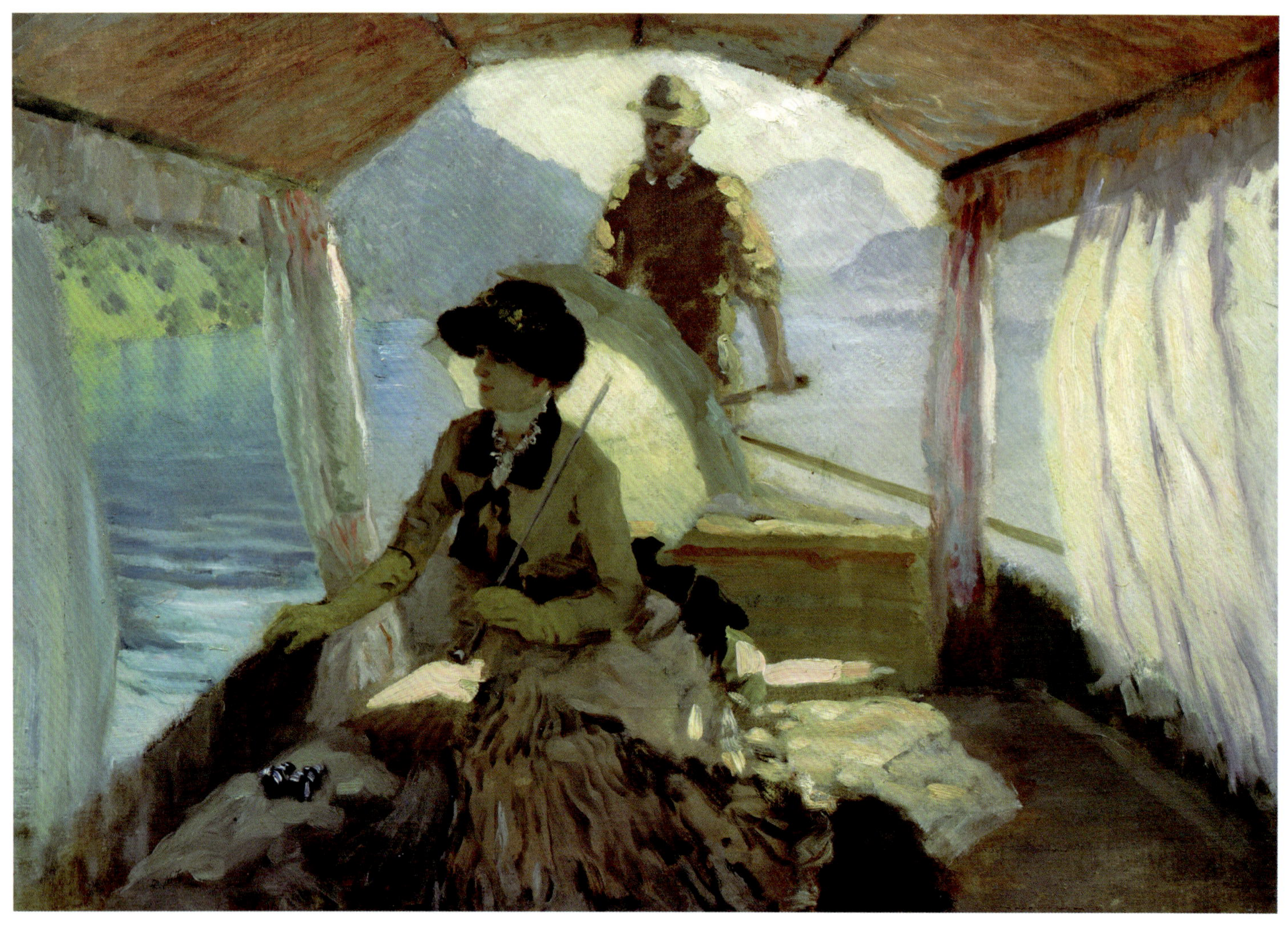

Giuseppe De Nittis (1846–84)

On the Lake of Quattro Cantoni

Sur le lac des quatre cantons

Auf dem Vierwaldstättersee

En el lago de Quattro Cantoni

Sul lago dei Quattro Cantoni

Op het Vierwoudstrekenmeer

1881, Oil on canvas/Huile sur toile, 60 × 90 cm, Dini Collection, Montecatini Terme

Giovanni Segantini (1858–99)

Afternoon in the Alps

Un après-midi dans les Alpes

Ein Nachmittag in den Alpen

Una tarde en los Alpes

Pomeriggio sulle Alpi

Een middag in de Alpen

1892, Oil on canvas/Huile sur toile, 85,5 × 79,5 cm, Ōhara Museum of Art, Kurashiki

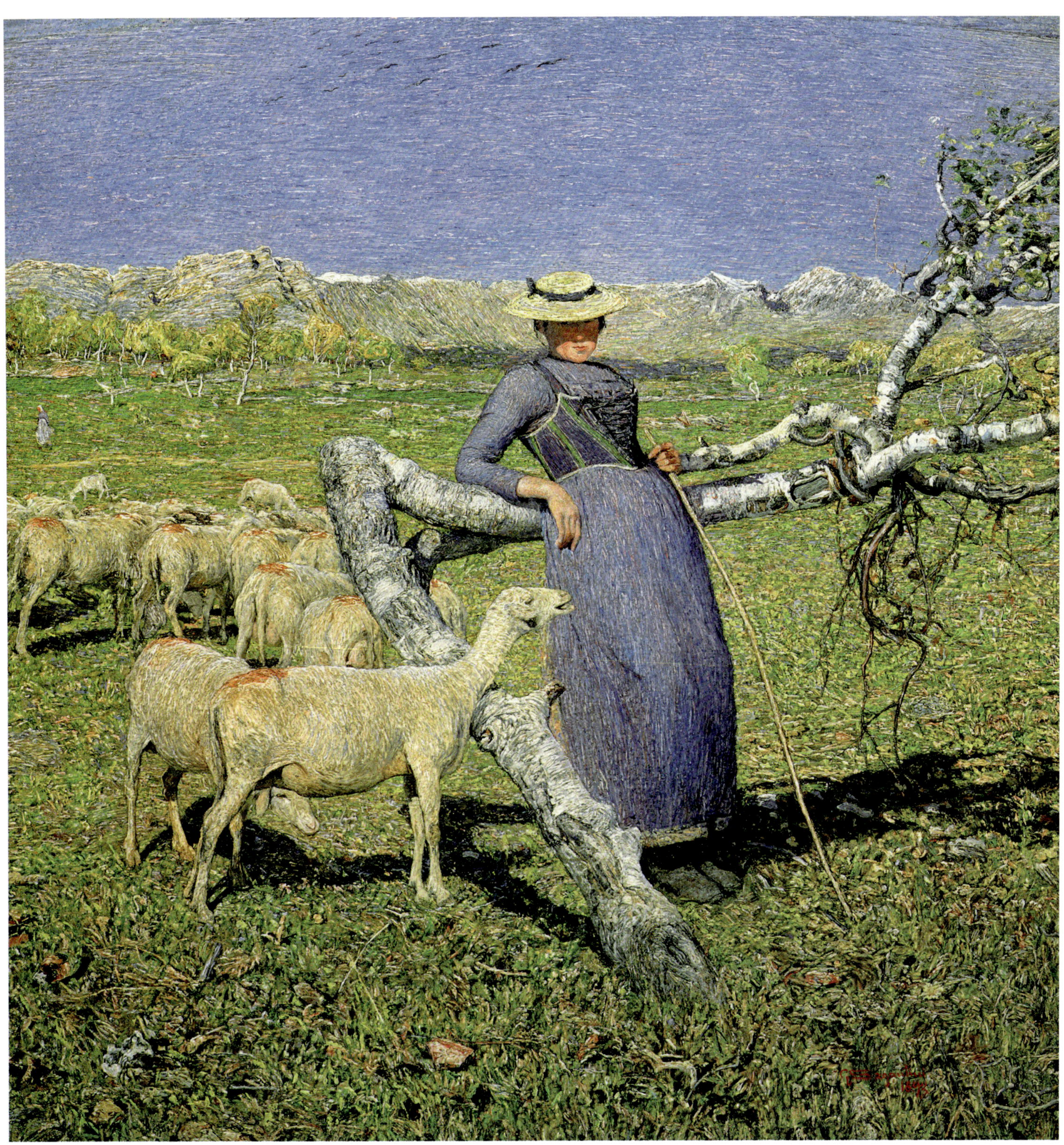

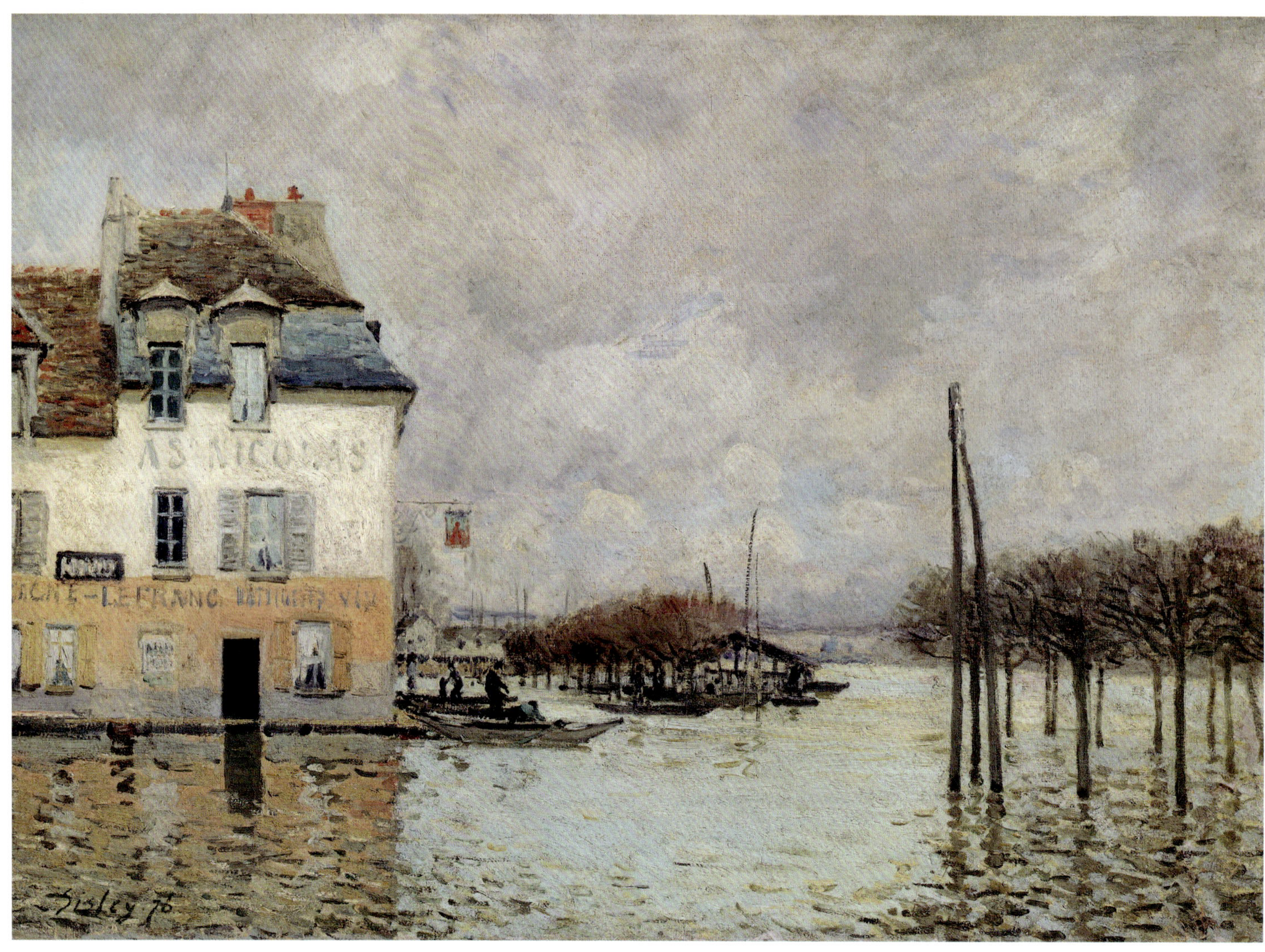

Alfred Sisley (1839–99)

The Flood at Port Marly

L'inondation à Port-Marly

Überschwemmung in Port-Marly

La inundación en Port-Marly

L'inondazione a Port-Marly

Overstroming bij Port-Marly

1876, Oil on canvas/Huile sur toile, 60 × 81 cm, Musée d'Orsay, Paris